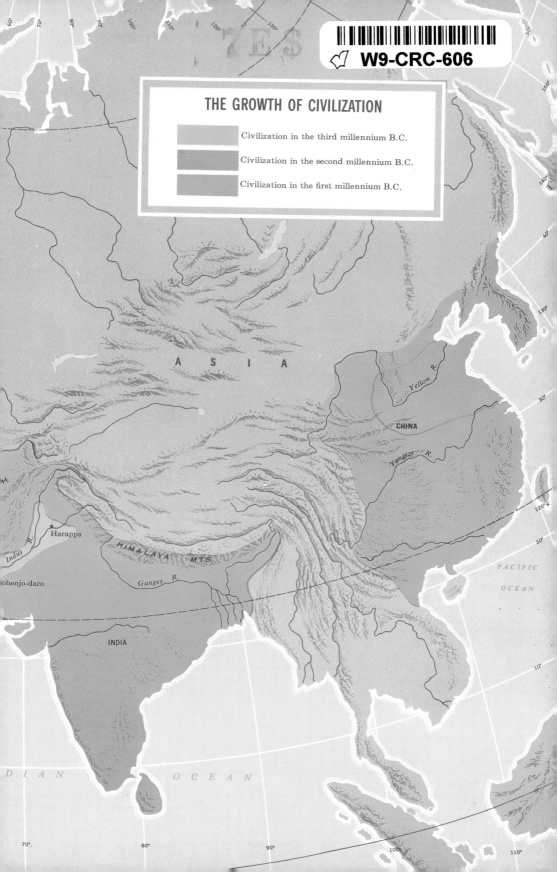

THE GROWTH OF CIVILIZATION

Civilization in the third millennium B.C.

Civilization in the second millennium B.C.

Civilization in the first millennium B.C.

W9-CRC-606

A S I A

Yellow R.

CHINA

Yangtze R.

Harappa

HIMALAYA MTS.

Indus R.

ohenjo-daro

Ganges R.

INDIA

PACIFIC

OCEAN

DIAN   OCEAN

World Civilizations

*Their History
and Their Culture*

FOURTH EDITION

Volume I

WORLD
CIVILIZATIONS

*from Ancient
to Contemporary*

EDWARD McNALL BURNS

and

PHILIP LEE RALPH

FOURTH EDITION

Volume I

New York W · W · NORTON & COMPANY · INC ·

To our *Students*

SBN 393 09828 1

Library of Congress Catalog Card No. 69-11696

Cartography by Harold K. Faye

PRINTED IN THE UNITED STATES OF AMERICA

3 4 5 6 7 8 9 0

Contents

PART THREE THE WORLD IN THE EARLY MIDDLE AGES

PART FOUR   THE WORLD IN THE LATER MIDDLE AGES

PART FIVE   THE TRANSITION FROM MEDIEVAL TO MODERN

Illustrations in Color

x

Illustrations in the Text

Maps

Preface

The time has long since passed when modern man could think of the world as consisting of Europe and the United States. Western culture is, of course, primarily a product of European origins. But it has never been that exclusively. Its original foundations were in Southwestern Asia and North Africa. These were supplemented by influences seeping in from India and eventually from China. From India and the Far East the West derived its knowledge of the zero, the compass, gunpowder, silk, cotton, and probably a large number of religious and philosophical concepts. But especially in recent times the East has increased in importance. It can no longer be thought of as a remote and slumbering world of no concern to anyone in the West except missionaries and manufacturers with surplus goods. The exhaustion of Europe by two World Wars, the revolt of the colored races against Caucasian domination, and the struggle for the world between the Communist powers and the United States have made every part of the earth of vital importance to every other. If peace is indivisible, so are prosperity, justice, and freedom; so, in fact, is civilization itself.

The purpose of this work is to present a compact survey of man's struggle for civilization from early times to the present. No major area or country of the globe has been omitted. Europe, the Commonwealth of Nations, the Middle East, Southeast Asia, Africa, India, China, Japan, and North, Central, and South America have all received appropriate emphasis. Obviously, the history of none of them could be covered in full detail. The authors believe, however, that a broad view of the world as a whole is necessary to understand the basic problems of any of its parts. This thesis acquires additional validity as the nations increase in interdependence. Perspective in history becomes more and more urgent as the momentous problems of our own generation press for solution. If there is any basic philosophical interpretation underlying the narrative, it is the conviction that most of human progress thus far has resulted from the growth of intelligence and respect for the rights of man, and that therein lies the chief hope for a better world in the future.

The First Edition of *World Civilizations* was published in 1955, the Second in 1958, and the Third in 1964. Since the publication of the earlier editions numerous discoveries and reinterpretations have resulted from historical research. To take account of these is one of the major objectives of the present edition. We are now able to see more clearly the revolutionary trends of our times. To describe and assess the significance of such developments as the decline of Western Europe, the ascendancy of the Soviet Union and the United States, the power struggle between East and West, the nationalist revolt against imperialism, the recurring international crises, and the awesome achievements in the fields of thermonuclear energy, cybernetics, and space exploration a new edition of *World Civilizations* becomes necessary. But the present edition is not a mere enlargement of its predecessors. Much new material has ben added, but substantial portions of the old have been eliminated, and rewriting has been done throughout. Notable changes include: an increased amount of political history, especially of the medieval and modern periods, and of Russia; new assessments of India, China, and Japan and the emerging nations of Africa and Southeast Asia; new chapters on the Industrial Revolutions of the nineteenth and twentieth centuries; division and reorganization of the chapter on Democracy and Nationalism in the nineteenth century; abandonment of the chapter on the Return to International Anarchy and insertion of chapters on New Power Relationships and the Revolution of Our Time. The Fourth Edition of *World Civilizations* has been entirely remapped by the noted cartographer, Harold K. Faye. Illustrations in most cases have been enlarged, with the addition of numerous new ones from archives both Western and Oriental. The color plates, which so greatly enhanced the value of the previous edition, have been retained and improved in clarity and brightness. Available for use with the new edition is a Teacher's Manual and a new Study Guide, whose distinctive feature is the inclusion of many extracts from original sources.

As its title indicates, this work is not exclusively or even primarily a political history. Political narrative is recognized as important, but it is not the whole substance of history. In the main, the facts of political history are subordinated to the development of institutions and ideas or are presented as the groundwork of cultural, social, and economic movements. The authors consider the effects of the Industrial Revolutions to be no less important than the Napoleonic Wars. They believe it is of greater value to understand the significance of Newton, Darwin, and Einstein than it is to be able to name the kings of France. In accordance with this broader conception of history, more space has been given to the teachings of John Locke and John

Stuart Mill than to the military exploits of Gustavus Adolphus or the Duke of Wellington.

In preparing this revision the authors have benefited from the assistance and counsel of many individuals whose services no words of appreciation can adequately measure. Professor Ardath W. Burks of Rutgers University has read and criticized the material on the Far East. Professor James R. Shirley of Northern Illinois University has thoroughly examined the chapters on the Middle and Far East, and also those on early Europe and the Commonwealth of Nations. All of the chapters on Europe and the United States have been critically reviewed by Professors David L. Cowen of Rutgers University and Eugen Weber of the University of California at Los Angeles. In addition, various sections of the material have been carefully criticized by able specialists in their fields. They are: Professor Gene Brucker of the University of California, Berkeley, for the early modern chapters, and Professor Lancelot L. Farrar of the University of Washington for the chapters on later modern history and the contemporary world. Professor Paul Henry Lang of Columbia University, distinguished historian of music, has rewritten the sections on music. Professor Earle Field of San Fernando Valley State College has reviewed the maps and made valuable recommendations for additions and improvements. Mrs. Lynn Masciarelli has rendered efficient service in typing and proofreading. The help of Professor Remigio U. Pane of Rutgers University with the Spanish and Italian pronunciations; of Dr. F. Gunther Eyck with the German pronunciations; of Mrs. Eric Wendelin with the Spanish and Portuguese pronunciations; and of Dr. Madeleine Charanis, Dr. Lucy Huang, and Professor Ardath W. Burks with the French, Chinese, and Japanese pronunciations, respectively, is gratefully acknowledged. Finally, the authors are indebted to their wives for their aid with the laborious tasks of typing, checking, proofreading, and indexing, and for their patience, devotion, and understanding.

EDWARD McNALL BURNS
PHILIP LEE RALPH

Picture Acknowledgments

The corporations, public agencies, and individuals listed below have generously provided photographs or other materials to illustrate *World Civilizations*. Specific contributions are indicated in the list of illustrations by the name of the donor in full or by code letters after the title of the picture furnished.

American Museum of Natural History (AMNH)
American Philosophical Society
American School of Classical Studies, Athens (Agora Excavations)
American Telephone and Telegraph Company
Anderson, Rome
Wayne Andrews
Arab Information Bureau
Arabian-American Oil Company
Arena Chapel, Padua
Australian News and Information Bureau (ANIB)
Baltimore & Ohio Railroad (B&O RR)
Bayeux Public Library
John Barrington Bayley
Belgian Government Tourist Bureau (BGTB)
Bethlehem Steel Corporation
J. David Bowen
John P. Bradford
Brazilian Government Trade Bureau
British Information Services (BIS)
British Museum (BM)
British Transport Commission
British Travel Association (BTA)
John Bryson, *Saturday Evening Post*
Canadian Pacific Railway
Chase Manhattan Bank Museum of Moneys of the World (Chase)
Chinese News Service
Stephen C. Clark
Colombia National Tourist Bureau (CNTB)
Creole Petroleum

Electronic Music Center of Columbia and Princeton Universities
Ford Motor Company
Henry Ford Museum, Dearborn
Fitzwilliam Museum, Cambridge
Foreign Operations Administration
Alison Frantz
Free Europe Press
French Embassy, Press and Information Division (FEPI)
French Government Tourist Office (FGTO)
French National Railroad (FNR)
Marcel Gautherot
Philip Gendreau, New York
Germanic Museum, Nuremberg
German Railroads
German Tourist Information Office (GTIO)
Ghana Information Services
Greek Information Office (GIO)
Henry E. Huntington Library and Art Gallery (Huntington)
Iglesia San Tomé, Toledo, Spain
Government of India Tourist Office (GITO)
Information Service of India (ISI)
International Harvester Company
Israel Government Tourist Office (IGTO)
Israel Office of Information (IOA)
Italian State Tourist Office (ISTO)
Consulate General of Japan, New York
Japan National Tourist Organization (JNTO)
Japan Tourist Association

Japan Travel Information Office (JTIO)

Jewish Museum of New York, Frank J. Darmstaedter (JMNY)

P. Kidson and U. Pariser, *Sculpture at Chartres* (Alec Tiranti, Ltd.)

Kuwait Oil Company

Robert Lehman

Lever Brothers

His Highness the Prince of Liechtenstein

Marshall MacDuffie

Mauritshuis, The Hague

Metropolitan Museum of Art, New York (MMA)

Mexican National Tourist Council

Minneapolis Institute of Art

Mitsubishi-Nippon Heavy Industries, Ltd.

Morgan Library, New York (Morgan)

Museum of Fine Arts, Boston

Museum of Modern Art, New York (Modern)

National Archives

National Gallery of Art

National Geographic Magazine

National Museum, Naples

Joseph Needham, Oxford University Press

Richard J. Neutra

Nelson Gallery—Atkins Museum

New York Academy of Medicine (NYAM)

New York Public Library, Picture Collection and Print Collection (NYPL)

Oriental Institute, University of Chicago

Pakistan Consulate General

Pan American Union (PAU)

Philadephia Museum of Art (PMA)

Phillips Memorial Gallery

Pitti Palace, Florence

Prado, Madrid

Press Information Bureau, Government of India (PIBI)

Her Majesty the Queen

Rutgers University, Department of Art (Rutgers)

Santa Maria della Grazie, Milan

Seattle World's Fair

A. A. Schechter Associates

Sistine Chapel

South African Information Service

Spanish Tourist Office (STO)

Sperry-Rand Corporation

Standard Oil Company of New Jersey

Olli Steltzer

Swiss National Tourist Office

Tennessee Valley Authority

Alec Tiranti, Ltd.

Trans World Airlines (TWA)

Uffizi Gallery, Florence (Uffizi)

United China Colleges (UCC)

United Nations

USAID

United States Army

United States Lines·Company

United States Marine Corps

United States Navy

University Prints (UP)

V. W. van Gogh

Victoria and Albert Museum

Whitney Museum of American Art

Yale University Press

FROM SPECIAL COLLECTIONS AND GIFTS IN THE METROPOLITAN MUSEUM OF ART, NEW YORK

BEQUEST OF BENJAMIN ALTMAN, 1913: Arm chair upholstered in Beauvais tapestry after design by Berain.

BEQUEST OF WILLIAM K. VANDERBILT, 1920: Secretaire: ebony with black marble top; black and gold lacquer panels; ormolu mounts, with the cipher of Marie Antoinette.

BEQUEST OF MRS. H. O. HAVEMEYER, 1929. THE H. O. HAVEMEYER COLLECTION: *Portrait of a Young Man*, Bronzino; *Boy with a Greyhound*, Veronese; *Portrait of a Gentleman*, Ingres; *Pink and Green*, Degas; *Montagne Sainte Victoire with Aqueduct*, Cézanne; *Still Life*, Cézanne.

GIFT OF HENRY PAYNE BINGHAM, 1937: *Venus and Adonis*, Peter Paul Rubens.

GIFT OF ANN PAYNE BLUMENTHAL, 1941: Arm chair *(bergère)*.

JULES S. BACHE COLLECTION: *Madonna and Child*, Luca della Robbia; *Portrait of a Young Man*, Bellini (1949); *Portrait of a Lady*, Domenico Veneziano (1949).

THE ALFRED STIEGLITZ COLLECTION, 1949: *Sea and Gulls*, John Marin.

BEQUEST OF SAMUEL A. LEWISOHN, 1951: *Ia Orana Maria*, Gauguin.

BEQUEST OF MARY WETMORE SHIVELY IN MEMORY OF HER HUSBAND, HENRY L. SHIVELY: *Portrait of Louis XV as a Child, in Royal Costume*, Hyacinthe Rigaud.

FROM SPECIAL COLLECTIONS AND GIFTS IN THE MUSEUM OF MODERN ART, NEW YORK

MRS. SIMON GUGGENHEIM FUND: *Piano Lesson*, Henri Matisse; *Three Musicians*, Pablo Picasso; *I and the Village*, Marc Chagall.

ACQUIRED THROUGH THE LILLIE P. BLISS BEQUEST: *The Starry Night*, Vincent van Gogh; *The Table*, George Braque.

MRS. JOHN D. ROCKEFELLER, JR., FUND: *Around the Fish*, Paul Klee.

World Civilizations

*Their History
and Their Culture*

FOURTH EDITION

Volume I

PART ONE

The Dawn of History

No one knows the place of origin of the human species. There is evidence, however, that it may have been south central Africa or possibly central or south central Asia. Here climatic conditions were such as to favor the evolution of a variety of human types from primate ancestors. From their place or places of origin members of the human species wandered to southeastern and eastern Asia, northern Africa, Europe, and eventually, to America. For hundreds of centuries they remained primitive, leading a life which was at first barely more advanced than that of the higher animals. About 5000 B.C. a few of them, enjoying special advantages of location and climate, developed superior cultures. These cultures, which attained knowledge of writing and considerable advancement in the arts and sciences and in social organization, began in that part of the world known as the Near Orient. This region extends from the western border of India to the Mediterranean Sea and to the farther bank of the Nile. Here flourished, at different periods between 5000 and 300 B.C., the mighty empires of the Egyptians, the Babylonians, the Assyrians, the Chaldeans, and the Persians, together with the smaller states of such peoples as the Cretans, the Sumerians, the Phoenicians, and the Hebrews. In other parts of the world the beginnings of civilization were retarded. There was nothing that could be called civilized life in China until about 2000 B.C. And, except on the island of Crete, there was no civilization in Europe until more than 1000 years later.

A Chronological Table *

	GEOLOGICAL PERIOD	CHARACTERISTIC FORMS OF LIFE	CULTURE PERIODS	AND	CHARACTERISTIC ACHIEVEMENTS
3 billion years ago	Precambrian	One-celled organisms First invertebrates: worms, algae			
510 million years ago	Paleozoic — Cambrian	Mollusks, sponges			
	Ordovician	Insects, first vertebrates			
	Silurian	Corals, sharks, seaweed Lungfish, crustaceans			
	Devonian	Earliest amphibians			
	Mississippian	Large amphibians Ferns			
	Pennsylvanian				
	Permian				
180 million years ago	Mesozoic — Triassic	Giant reptiles			
	Jurassic	Diversified reptiles, birds			
90 million years ago	Cretaceous	Marsupials, bony fishes Trees			
	Cenozoic — Tertiary — Paleocene	Early mammals, first primates			
	Eocene	Primitive apes, ancestors of monkeys			
	Oligocene	Ancestors of great apes			
	Miocene	Ancestors of man, modern mammals			
	Pliocene	Early human species, other primates	Lower Paleolithic		Spoken language, knowledge of fire, burial of dead, stone tools and weapons
1 million years ago	Quaternary — Pleistocene	Present-day animals and races of men	Upper Paleolithic		Needles, harpoons, fishhooks, dart throwers, magic, art, social organization, cooking of food
	Recent		Neolithic		Agriculture, domestication of animals, pottery, houses, navigation, institutions
7000 years ago			Civilized man		Bronze, iron, writing, technology, science, literature, philosophy, etc.

* Adapted from time scale by Geological Names Committee, 1958.

CHAPTER 1

The Earliest Beginnings

As we turn to the past itself . . . we might well begin with a pious tribute to our nameless [preliterate] ancestors, who by inconceivably arduous and ingenious effort succeeded in establishing a human race. They made the crucial discoveries and inventions, such as the tool, the seed, and the domesticated animal; their development of agriculture, the "neolithic revolution" that introduced a settled economy, was perhaps the greatest stride forward that man has ever taken. They created the marvelous instrument of language, which enabled man to discover his humanity, and eventually to disguise it. They laid the foundations of civilization: its economic, political, and social life, and its artistic, ethical, and religious traditions. Indeed, our "savage" ancestors are still very near to us, and not merely in our capacity for savagery.
—Herbert J. Muller, *The Uses of the Past*

I. THE MEANING OF HISTORY

Broadly defined, history is a record and interpretation of man's achievements, hopes and frustrations, struggles and triumphs. This conception has not always been the prevailing one. At one time history was quite generally regarded as "past politics." Its content was restricted largely to battles and treaties, to the personalities and policies of statesmen, and to the laws and decrees of rulers. But important as such data are, they do not constitute the whole substance of history. Actually, history comprises a record of all of man's accomplishments in every sphere, whether political, economic, intellectual, or social. It embraces also a chronicle of his dreams and ideals, his hopes, triumphs, and failures. Perhaps most important of all, it includes an inquiry into the causes of the chief political and economic movements, a search for the forces that impelled man toward his great undertakings, and the reasons for his successes and failures.

History defined

3

Whether history is a science, and whether it can be used as an instrument for predicting the future, are questions that do not yield conclusive answers. With regard to the first, about all we can say is that both the study and the writing of history should be made as scientific as possible. This means that the scientific attitude should be brought to bear upon the solution of all of history's problems, be they political, intellectual, moral, or religious. As the American philosopher, the late John Dewey, pointed out, the scientific attitude demands a skeptical and inquiring approach toward all issues and a refusal to form conclusive judgments until all available evidence has been amassed and examined. Obviously, this approach rules out such conceptions of history as the patriotic, the racial, or the providential. Scientific history cannot be made to serve the purposes of national greatness, race supremacy, or the doctrine of a Chosen People.

History as a
chart for the
future

The value of history as a chart for the future has tormented the minds of philosophical historians for scores of centuries. The father of scientific history, Thucydides, who lived in Athens in the fifth century B.C., asserted that events do "repeat themselves at some future time—if not exactly the same, yet very similar." The British essayist Thomas Carlyle and the American philosopher William James saw in the stimulating genius of eminent individuals the motivating force of historical progress. What would have been the future of Germany, James asked, if Bismarck had died in his cradle, or of the British Empire if Robert Clive had shot himself, as he tried to do at Madras? Great stages of civilization could be accounted for only by an exceptional concourse of brilliant individuals within a limited time. But James offered no theory as to the conditions likely to produce such a concourse.

The most elaborate hypothesis in modern times concerning inevitability in history was developed by Karl Marx in the nineteenth century. Marx taught that individuals are mere instruments of forces more powerful than they. These forces, he contended, are exclusively economic and are grounded in changes in modes of production. Thus the change from a feudal economy to a commercial and industrial economy brought into existence the capitalist epoch and the rule of the bourgeois class. In time capitalism would be superseded by socialism, and, finally, by communism. The course of history was consequently predetermined, and future changes would succeed one another in the same mechanical fashion as they had in the past.

Although the theories of Marx have attracted considerable attention, they cannot be accepted as gospel by scientific historians. The motivation of human events is too complex to be forced into a single pattern. It is impossible to predict the future in terms of a single theory or thesis. No crystal ball exists which will enable anyone to foretell with certainty that every revolution must be followed by counterrevolution, that every war begets new wars, or that progress is an inescapable law. Greed is undoubtedly a powerful motive for human action, but this does not mean that economic causation must be accepted as a universal rule. Fear is also a powerful motive, in somes cases overbalancing greed. Other psychological motives, including sex and the lust for power, likewise play a part in the determination of human actions. In short, no one explanation will suffice, and a vast amount of research will be necessary before there can be any assurance that all the possible driving forces have been discovered.

One final question remains. Is history a unilinear process, an unbroken stream of progress toward higher and nobler achievements? Or is it simply a process of change marked by a general trend of advancement but with many interruptions and setbacks? Scarcely a historian would deny that some ideas and discoveries have come down through the centuries with no change except in the direction of improvement. This would be true of much of the mathematics of the ancient Egyptians, the Babylonians, and the Greeks. But other examples illustrate the opposite. Aristarchus of Samos, in the third century B.C., propounded a heliocentric theory. It was superseded, largely for religious reasons, about 400 years later by the geocentric theory. It was not reaffirmed until the time of Copernicus in the sixteenth century A.D. Although Hellenistic physicians came close to a discovery of the circulation of the blood, knowledge of their achievement lay buried for 1500 years and had to await rediscovery in the seventeenth century by Sir William Harvey, the English physician and anatomist. As with individual accomplishments, so with whole cultures. The first three millennia of written history were strewn with the wreckage of fallen empires and extinct civilizations. Egypt, Mesopotamia, Persia, Greece, and Rome fell prey one after the other to external conquest, internal conquest, or a combination of both. Many elements of the old cultures survived, but they were frequently modified or woven into quite different patterns. As Lincoln said, we cannot escape history, and the influence which history presses upon us is more complicated than we usually suspect.

The concept of a stream of history versus a succession of cultures

2. HISTORY AND PREHISTORY

It is the custom among many historians to distinguish between historic and prehistoric periods in the evolution of human society. By the former they mean history based upon written records. By the latter they mean the record of man's achievements before the invention of writing. But this distinction is not altogether satisfactory. It suggests that human accomplishments before they were recorded in characters or symbols representing words or concepts were not important. Nothing could be farther from the truth. The foundations, at

The so-called prehistoric era

5

least, of many of the great accomplishments of modern technology, and even of social and political systems, were laid before human beings could write a word. It would seem preferable, therefore, that the whole period of man's life on earth should be regarded as historic, and that the era before the invention of writing be designated by some term such as "preliterate." The records of preliterate societies are, of course, not books and manuscripts, but tools, weapons, fossils, utensils, carvings, paintings, and fragments of jewelry and ornamentation. These, commonly known as "artifacts," are often just as valuable as the written word in providing knowledge of a people's deeds and modes of living.

Periods of
man's history

The entire span of human history can be divided roughly into two periods, the Age of Stone and the Age of Metals. The former is identical with the Preliterate Age, or the period before the invention of writing. The latter coincides with the period of history based upon written records. The Preliterate Age covered at least 95 per cent of man's existence and did not come to an end until about 5000 B.C. The Age of Metals practically coincides with the history of civilized nations. The Age of Stone is subdivided into the Paleolithic, or Old Stone Age, and the Neolithic, or New Stone Age. Each takes its name from the type of stone tools and weapons characteristically manufactured during the period. Thus during the greater part of the Paleolithic Age implements were commonly made by chipping pieces off a large stone or flint and using the core that remained as a hand ax or "fist hatchet." Toward the end of the period the chips themselves were used as knives or spearheads, and the core thrown away. The Neolithic Age witnessed the supplanting of chipped stone tools by implements made by grinding and polishing stone.

3.   THE CULTURE OF LOWER PALEOLITHIC MEN

The earliest Stone
Age men

The Paleolithic period can be dated from roughly 1,750,000 B.C. to 10,000 B.C. It is commonly divided into two stages, an earlier or Lower Paleolithic and a later or Upper Paleolithic. The Lower Paleolithic was much the longer of the two, covering about 75 per cent of the entire Old Stone Age. During this time at least four species of men inhabited the earth. The oldest was apparently a creature whose skeletal remains were found in 1960–1964 by Louis S. B. Leakey in what is now Tanzania, East Africa. Leakey named this creature *Homo habilis*, or "man having ability." Estimated to be at least 1,750,000 years old, the remains included parts of the skull, hands, legs, and feet. That *Homo habilis* was a true ancestral human being is indicated by evidence that he walked erect and that he used crude tools. It must not be supposed, of course, that these tools represented any high degree of manufacturing skill or inventive talent. For the most part, they consisted of objects taken from nature:

The Skull (left) of a Young Woman of the Species Homo habilis, believed to have lived in Tanzania, East Africa, about 1,750,000 years ago. On the right is the skull of a present-day African. Though *Homo habilis* was smaller than a pygmy, the brain casing was shaped like that of modern man.

bones of large animals, limbs from trees, and chunks of stone, perhaps broken or crudely chipped.

Two other early inhabitants of the Lower Paleolithic were Java man and Peking man. Java man, whose scientific name is *Pithecanthropus erectus,* was long thought to be the oldest of manlike creatures, but it is now generally agreed that the date of his origin was about 500,000 B.C. His skeletal remains were found on the island of Java in 1891. Originally only a skull-cap, a thigh bone, three teeth and a jaw bone were discovered; in recent years, however, other fragments have been unearthed, with the result that it is now possible to reconstruct the entire skull of Pithecanthropus. It has been established that his cranial capacity was nearly double that of a male gorilla, but only two-thirds that of modern man. Java man

The remains of Peking man or *Sinanthropus pekinensis* were found in China, about forty miles southwest of Peking between 1926 and 1930. Since the latter date, fragments of no fewer than 32 skeletons of the Sinanthropus type have been located, making possible a complete reconstruction of at least the head of this ancient species. Anthropologists generally agree that Sinanthropus and Pithecanthropus are of approximately the same antiquity, and that both probably descended from the same ancestral type. Until recently many scientists believed that the so-called Piltdown man, whose fragmentary "remains" were found in England in 1911, was a contemporary of the Java and Peking species. But in 1953 it was revealed that "Piltdown man" was a hoax. The fragments, which in- Peking man cluded a skull-cap and a jaw bone, had been skillfully altered. The jaw bone was actually that of an ape, chemically treated to make it appear aged, while the skull-cap was only about 50,000 years old.

During the last 25,000 years of the Lower Paleolithic period a fourth species of ancient man made his appearance. He was *Homo neanderthalensis*, famous as an early cave man. His skeletal fragments were first discovered in the valley of the Neander, near Düsseldorf, northwestern Germany, in 1856. Since then numerous other discoveries have been made, in some cases complete skeletons, in such widely separated regions as Belgium, Spain, Italy, Yugoslavia, Russia, and Palestine. So closely did Neanderthal man resemble modern man that he is classified as a member of the same genus, the genus *Homo*. The resemblance, however, was by no means perfect. Neanderthal men, on the average, were only about five feet, four inches in height. They had receding chins and heavy eyebrow ridges. Although their foreheads sloped back and their brain cases were low-vaulted, their average cranial capacity was slightly greater than that of modern Caucasians. What this may have signified with respect to their intelligence cannot be determined.

The knowledge we possess of the culture of Lower Paleolithic men is scanty indeed. The skills they achieved and the learning they acquired must have been pitiful in quantity even when compared with the accomplishments of modern primitive men. Yet Neanderthal man and his successors were not mere apes, forgetting in a moment the chance triumphs they had made. They undoubtedly had the capacity for speech, which enabled them to communicate with their fellows and to pass on what they had learned to succeeding generations. We are justified in assuming also that they possessed reasoning ability, however crudely it may have been developed. Practically from the beginning, therefore, they were probably tool-using creatures, employing their wits to fashion implements and weapons. Perhaps at first these would be nothing but limbs broken from trees to be used as clubs. Eventually it was discovered that stones could be chipped in such a way as to give them cutting edges. The butt was then held in the palm of the hand. Thus evolved the so-called hand ax or fist hatchet, which appears to have served the combined purposes of a cleaver, saw, scraper, and knife.

Before the end of the Lower Paleolithic period, Neanderthal man seems largely to have abandoned the use of the fist hatchet. Improved methods of chipping stone enabled him to rely primarily upon the flakes themselves. The result was the development of spearheads, borers, and much superior knives and scrapers. Indications have been found also of a degree of advancement in nonmaterial culture. In the entrances to caves where Neanderthal man lived, or at least took refuge, evidence has been discovered of flint-working floors and stone hearths where huge fires appear to have been made. These would suggest the origins of cooperative group

Neanderthal man

Lower Paleolithic culture

Improvements made by Neanderthal man

8

THE CRADLE OF CIVILIZATION
A PHYSICAL MAP

------ Probable ancient shorelines

1000 miles

TURKESTAN

Jaxartes R.

Oxus R.

Aral
Sea

Ural R.

Volga R.

Don R.

CASPIAN SEA

ELBURZ MTS.

PLATEAU OF IRAN

Indus R.

ARABIAN SEA

PERSIAN GULF

KURDISTAN HIGHLANDS

ARMENIAN HIGHLANDS

CAUCASUS MTS.

Sea of Azov

Dnieper R.

Dniester R.

Danube R.

CARPATHIAN MTS.

BALKAN MTS.

BLACK SEA

Bosporus

Sea of Marmara

Dardanelles

Halys R.

ANATOLIA OR ASIA MINOR

TAURUS MTS.

Maeander R.

Tigris

Euphrates R.

MESOPOTAMIA

SYRIAN DESERT

Jordan R.

Dead Sea

LEBANON MTS.

CYPRUS

ARABIAN DESERTS

SINAI PENINSULA

ISTHMUS OF SUEZ

Nile Delta

EGYPT

Nile R.

First Cataract

NUBIAN DESERT

RED SEA

LIBYAN DESERT

MEDITERRANEAN SEA

Aegean Sea

CRETE

PELOPONNESUS

Ionian Sea

Adriatic Sea

ALPS

APPENINES

Tiber R.

Tyrrhenian Sea

SICILY

CORSICA

SARDINIA

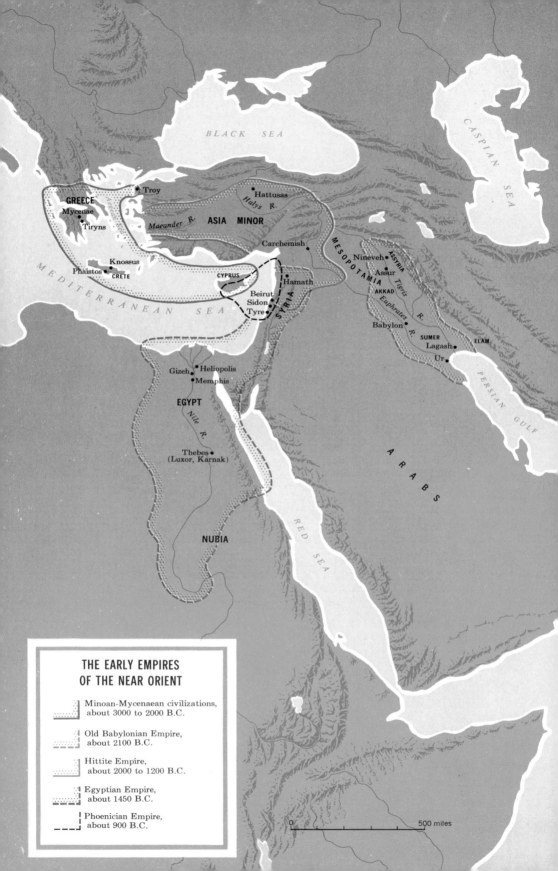

BLACK SEA

CASPIAN SEA

GREECE
Troy
Mycenae
Tiryns
Maeander R. ASIA MINOR
Hattusas
Halys R.

Carchemish
Nineveh ASSYRIA
Assur
MESOPOTAMIA
Tigris R.

Knossus
Phaïstos   CRETE
CYPRUS
Hamath   SYRIA
Beirut
Sidon
Tyre

MEDITERRANEAN SEA

AKKAD
Euphrates R.
Babylon
SUMER
Lagash   ELAM
Ur

PERSIAN GULF

Gizeh   *Heliopolis*
Memphis

EGYPT

Nile R.

A R A B S

Thebes
(Luxor, Karnak)

RED SEA

NUBIA

THE EARLY EMPIRES
OF THE NEAR ORIENT

Minoan-Mycenaean civilizations,
about 3000 to 2000 B.C.

Old Babylonian Empire,
about 2100 B.C.

Hittite Empire,
about 2000 to 1200 B.C.

Egyptian Empire,
about 1450 B.C.

Phoenician Empire,
about 900 B.C.

0   500 miles

life and possibly the crude beginnings of social institutions. More significance may be attached to Neanderthal man's practice of bestowing care upon the bodies of his dead, interring with them in shallow graves tools and other objects of value. Perhaps this practice indicates the development of a religious sense, or at least a belief in some form of survival after death.

4. UPPER PALEOLITHIC CULTURE

About 30,000 B.C. the culture of the Old Stone Age passed from the Lower Paleolithic stage to the Upper Paleolithic. The Upper Paleolithic period lasted for only about 200 centuries, or from 30,000 to 10,000 B.C. A new and superior type of human being dominated the earth in this time. Biologically these men were closely related to modern man. Their foremost predecessors, Neanderthal men, had ceased to exist as a distinct variety. What became of the Neanderthalers is not known. According to one school of opinion, they were probably exterminated by their conquerors or perished through failure of their food supply. According to another school, they lost their identity merely through interbreeding with the newcomers. One branch of them in a remote area of the world may actually have been the ancestors of the new race that now became dominant.

The Upper Paleolithic period

The name used to designate the prevailing breed of Upper Paleolithic men is Cro-Magnon, from the Cro-Magnon cave in Dordogne, France, where some of the most typical remains were discovered. Cro-Magnon men were tall, broad-shouldered, and erect, the males averaging over six feet. They had high foreheads, well-developed chins, and a cranial capacity about equal to the modern average. The heavy eyebrow ridges so typical of earlier species were absent. Whether Cro-Magnon men left any survivors is a debatable question. They do not seem to have been exterminated but appear to have been driven into mountainous regions and to have been absorbed ultimately into later races.

Cro-Magnon man

Upper Paleolithic culture was markedly superior to that which had gone before. Not only were tools and implements better made, but they existed in greater variety. They were not fashioned merely from flakes of stone and an occasional shaft of bone; other materials were used in abundance, particularly reindeer horn and ivory. Examples of the more complicated tools included the bone needle, the fishhook, the harpoon, the dart thrower, and, at the very end, the bow and arrow. That Upper Paleolithic man wore clothing is indicated by the fact that he made buttons and toggles of bone and horn and invented the needle. He did not know how to weave cloth, but animal skins sewn together proved a satisfactory substitute. It is certain that he cooked his food, for enormous hearths, evidently used for roasting flesh, have been discovered. In the vicinity of one at

Upper Paleolithic culture: tools and weapons

Center: *Reconstruction of the Skulls of Four Types of Stone Age Men:* Java, Peking, Neanderthal, Cro-Magnon.

Top left: *Early Paleolithic Tools.* From left to right, a fist hatchet, a carving tool, and a side scraper.

Bottom left: *Late Paleolithic Tools and Implements.* From left to right, a bone harpoon point, a flint knife blade or spear point, and beads or pendants of elks' teeth.

Top right: *Examples of Upper Paleolithic Engraving and Sculpture.* The two objects at the top and upper right are dart throwers. At the lower right is the famous Venus of Willendorf.

Bottom right: *Cave Drawings at Lascaux, France.* Characteristic examples of the realism of Cro-Magnon man's art.

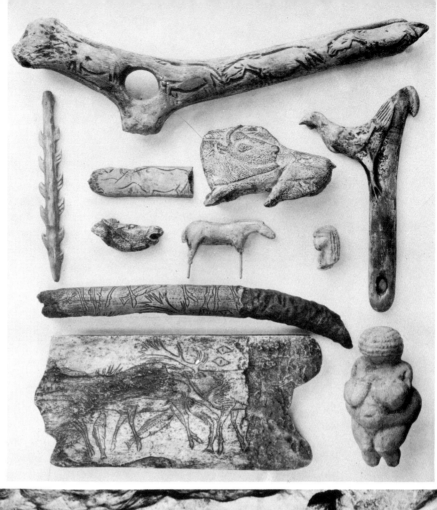

Solutré, in southern France, was a mass of charred bones, estimated to contain the remains of 100,000 large animals. Although Cro-Magnon man built no houses, except a few simple huts in regions where natural shelters did not abound, his life was not wholly nomadic. Evidences found in the caves that were his usual homes indicate that he must have used them, seasonally at least, for years at a time.

With respect to nonmaterial elements there are also indications that Upper Paleolithic culture represented a marked advancement. Group life was now more regular and more highly organized than ever before. The profusion of charred bones at Solutré and elsewhere probably indicates cooperative enterprise in the hunt and sharing of the results in great community feasts. The amazing workmanship displayed in tools and weapons and highly developed techniques in the arts could scarcely have been achieved without some division of labor. It appears certain, therefore, that Upper Paleolithic communities included professional artists and skilled craftsmen. In order to acquire such talents, certain members of the communities must have gone through long periods of training and given all their time to the practice of their specialties. In consequence they would have to be supported by the rest of the group. Thus an aristocracy would arise, and possibly the highest members of it would enjoy enough prestige to become rulers with limited authority.

Substantial proof exists that Cro-Magnon man had highly developed notions of a world of unseen powers. He bestowed more care upon the bodies of his dead than did Neanderthal man, painting the corpses, folding the arms over the heart, and depositing pendants, necklaces, and richly carved weapons and tools in the graves. He formulated an elaborate system of sympathetic magic designed to increase his supply of food. Sympathetic magic is based upon the principle that imitating a desired result will bring about that result. Applying this principle, Cro-Magnon man made paintings on the walls of his caves depicting the capture of reindeer in the hunt. At other times he fashioned clay models of the bison or mammoth and mutilated them with dart thrusts. The purpose of such representations was quite evidently to facilitate the very results portrayed and thereby to increase the hunter's success and make easier the struggle for existence. Possibly incantations or ceremonies accompanied the making of the pictures or images, and it is likely that the work of producing them was carried on while the actual hunt was in progress.

The Upper Paleolithic period witnessed some slight intellectual progress. Cro-Magnon man could count, and the first mathematical records in the history of mankind made their appearance. These consisted of various objects: a notched javelin or dart thrower, for example, or a stag tooth scored horizontally with a sharp tool and worn as a pendant. All of them were probably records of animals slain in the hunt. A bare possibility exists that Cro-Magnon man developed a primitive system of writing. Various interesting signs have been discovered which give the appearance of being characters of a written language. They were probably nothing more, however, than conventionalized symbols of natural objects. An abundance of other evidence can be found that the art of this period often showed a tendency toward conventionalization. The possibility that a knowledge of writing existed at this time must therefore be regarded as remote.

The supreme achievement of Cro-Magnon man was his art—an achievement so original and resplendent that it ought to be counted among the Seven Wonders of the World. Nothing else illustrates so well the great gulf between his culture and that of his predecessors. Upper Paleolithic art included nearly every branch that the material culture of the time made possible. Sculpture, painting, carving, and engraving were all represented. The ceramic arts and architecture were lacking; pottery had not yet been invented; and the only buildings erected were of simple design.

The art *par excellence* of Cro-Magnon man was painting. Here were exhibited the greatest number and variety of his talents—his discrimination in the use of color, his meticulous attention to detail, his capacity for the employment of scale in depicting a group, and above all, his genius for naturalism. Especially noteworthy was the painter's skill in representing movement. A large proportion of murals depict animals running, leaping, browsing, chewing the cud, or facing the hunter at bay. Ingenious devices were often employed to give the impression of motion. Chief among them was the drawing or painting of additional outlines to indicate the areas in which the legs or the head of the animal had moved. The scheme was so shrewdly executed that no appearance whatever of artificiality resulted.

Cave-man art throws a flood of light on many problems relating to primitive mentality and folkways. To a certain extent it was undoubtedly an expression of a true aesthetic sense. Cro-Magnon man did obviously take some delight in a graceful line or symmetrical pattern or brilliant color. The fact that he painted and tattooed his body and wore ornaments gives evidence of this. But his chief works of art can scarcely have been produced for the sake of creating beautiful objects. Such a possibility must be excluded for several reasons. To begin with, the best of the paintings and drawings are usually to be found on the walls and ceilings of the darkest and most inaccessible parts of the caves. The gallery of paintings at Niaux, for instance, is more than half a mile from the entrance of the cavern. No one could see the artists' creations except in the imperfect light of torches or of primitive lamps, which must have smoked and sputtered badly, for the only illuminating fluid was animal fat. Further-

Upper Paleolithic art

Painting

Significance of Upper Paleolithic art

13

more, there is evidence that Cro-Magnon man was largely indifferent toward his work of art after it was finished. He did not cherish it with the passing of the years, nor did he spend much time in admiring it. On the contrary, he was likely to use the very same surface for a new production. Numerous examples have been found of paintings or drawings superimposed upon earlier ones of the same or of different types. Evidently the important thing was not the finished work itself, but the act of making it.

Art an aid in
the struggle for
existence

For Paleolithic man, art was a serious business. The real purpose of nearly all of it was apparently not to delight the senses but to make easier the struggle for existence by increasing the supply of animals useful for food. The artist himself was not an aesthete but a magician, and his art was a form of magic designed to promote the hunter's success. In this purpose lay its chief significance and the foundation of most of its special qualities. It suggests, for example, the real reason why game animals were almost the exclusive subjects of the great murals and why plant life and inanimate objects were seldom represented. It aids us in understanding Cro-Magnon man's neglect of finished paintings and his predominant interest in the process of making them. Finally, magical purposes go far toward explaining the spectacular genius of the artist himself, for the very existence of the community was believed to depend upon the competent performance of his duties, and consequently no effort would be spared in giving him a thorough training.

Upper Paleolithic culture came to an untimely end about 10,000 B.C. Internal decay, exemplified by the decline of art, seems to have been one of the causes. A more obvious and doubtless more effective cause of the decline of the culture as a whole was partial destruction of the food supply. As the last great glacier retreated farther and farther northward, the climate of southern Europe became too warm for the reindeer, and they gradually migrated to the shores of the Baltic. The mammoth, whether for the same or for different reasons, became extinct. Representatives of the magnificent Cro-Magnon race probably followed the reindeer northward, but apparently they did not continue their cultural achievements.

5. NEOLITHIC CULTURE

The last stage of preliterate culture is known as the Neolithic period, or the New Stone Age. The name is applied because stone weapons and tools were now generally made by grinding and polishing instead of by chipping or fracturing as in the preceding periods. The bearers of Neolithic culture were new varieties of modern man who poured into Africa and southern Europe from western Asia. Since no evidence exists of their later extermination or wholesale migration, they must be regarded as the immediate ancestors of most of the peoples now living in Europe.

It is impossible to fix exact dates for the Neolithic period. The culture was not well established in Europe until about 3000 B.C., though it certainly originated earlier. There is evidence that it existed in Egypt as far back as 5000 B.C., and that it probably began at an equally early date in southwestern Asia. There is also variation in the dates of its ending. It was superseded in the Nile valley by the first literate civilization soon after the year 4000.[1] Except on the island of Crete it did not come to an end anywhere in Europe before 2000, and in northern Europe much later still. In a few regions of the world it has not terminated yet. The natives of some islands of the Pacific, the Arctic regions of North America, and the jungles of Brazil are still in the Neolithic culture stage except for a few customs acquired from explorers and missionaries.

In many respects the New Stone Age was the most significant in the history of the world thus far. The level of material progress rose to new heights. Neolithic man had a better mastery of his environ- ment than any of his predecessors. He was less likely to perish from a shift in climatic conditions or from the failure of some part of his food supply. This decided advantage was the result primarily of the development of agriculture and the domestication of animals. Whereas all of the men who had lived heretofore were mere food-gatherers, Neolithic man was a *food-producer*. Tilling the soil and keeping flocks and herds provided him with much more dependable food resources and at times yielded him a surplus. These circumstances made possible a more rapid increase of population, promoted a settled existence, and fostered the growth of institutions. Such were the elements of a great social and economic revolution whose importance it would be almost impossible to exaggerate.

The new culture also derives significance from the fact that it was the first to be distributed over the *entire* world. Although some earlier cultures, especially those of Neanderthal and Cro-Magnon men, were widely dispersed, they were confined chiefly to the accessible mainland areas of the Old World. Neolithic man penetrated into every habitable area of the earth's surface—from Arctic wastes to the jungles of the tropics. He apparently made his way from a number of centers of origin to every nook and cranny of both hemispheres. He traveled incredible distances by water as well as by land, and eventually occupied every major island of the oceans, no matter how remote. Even Hawaii, situated 4000 miles from the Asiatic mainland, proved not to be beyond his reach. Whether he launched his vessel or raft for some visible goal, and then drifted out of his course and by a lucky accident was washed ashore before he starved to death, or whether he got there by skill or intent, it is certain that he did arrive, for when the white men came the natives of the Hawaiian Islands had essentially the same pattern of culture as Neolithic men everywhere else.

The historian would have difficulty in overestimating the impor-

[1] All dates in Egyptian history prior to 2000 are approximations and may represent a margin of error of several centuries.

tance of the Neolithic migrations. The net result was that they distributed a similar pattern of culture over the entire world. The few elements of earlier cultures which had managed to survive were almost completely inundated. Their disappearance means that we now have no way of discovering more than a small part of what went on in Paleolithic man's mind—whether he believed that government is an evil or that private property is sacred or that the world was created out of nothing. The fact that we find particular notions in the primitive mind of today does not prove that they are inseparable from the blood and sinew of the species, for it is necessary to remember that all existing primitive races are the beneficiaries or the victims of a common heritage.

Importance of the
Neolithic migrations

New tools and
technical skills

The invention of boats and rafts was not the only example of Neolithic man's mechanical ingenuity. He developed the arts of knitting, of spinning, and of weaving cloth. He made the first pot-

Neolithic Dwellings. Examples shown are restorations of Swiss lake dwellings. They were commonly erected on poles or stilts for purposes of defense.

tery and knew how to produce fire artificially by friction. He built houses of wood and sun-dried mud. Toward the end of the period he discovered the possibilities of metals, and a few implements of copper and gold were added to his stock. Since nothing was yet known of the arts of smelting and refining, the use of metals was limited to the more malleable ones occasionally found in the pure state in the form of nuggets.

Importance of
agriculture and
the domestication
of animals

But the real foundation stones of the Neolithic culture were the domestication of animals and the development of agriculture. Without these it is inconceivable that the culture would have attained the complexity it did. More than anything else they were responsible for the settled mode of existence, for the growth of villages and social institutions. They stimulated the rise of a division of labor and encouraged the practice of exchange. They compelled man constantly to seek new methods of harnessing nature and thereby led to an increase in his physical equipment and his store of knowledge.

The first animal to be domesticated is generally thought to have been the dog, on the assumption that he would be continually hanging around the hunter's camp to pick up bones and scraps of meat. Eventually it would be discovered that he could be put to use in hunting, or possibly in guarding the camp. After achieving success in domesticating the dog, Neolithic man would logically turn his attention to other animals, especially to those he used for food. Before the period ended, at least five species—the cow, the dog, the goat, the sheep, and the pig—had been made to serve his needs. Not all of them in all parts of the world, however. The Neolithic tribes of the New World domesticated no animals at all, except the hairless dog in some parts of Mexico, the llama and the alpaca in the Andean highland, and the guinea pig and the turkey in a few other regions.

Origins of the domestication of animals

The exact spot where agriculture originated has never been positively determined. All we know is that wild grasses which were probably the ancestors of the cereal grains have been found in a number of places. Types of wheat grow wild in Asia Minor, in the Caucasus, and in Mesopotamia. Wild ancestors of barley have been reported from North Africa, from Persia, from Asia Minor, and from Turkestan. Though it is probable that these were the first crops of Neolithic agriculture, they were by no means the only ones. Millet, vegetables, and numerous fruits were also grown. Flax was cultivated in the Old World for its textile fiber, and in some localities the growing of the poppy for opium had already begun. In the New World maize (Indian corn) was the only cereal crop, but the American Indians cultivated numerous other products, including tobacco, beans, squashes, pumpkins, and potatoes.

The beginning of agriculture

Historically, the most important feature of Neolithic culture was probably the development of institutions. An institution may be defined as a combination of group beliefs and activities organized in a relatively permanent fashion for the purpose of fulfilling some group need. It ordinarily includes a body of customs and traditions, a code of rules and standards, and physical extensions such as buildings, punitive devices, and facilities for communication and indoctrination. Since man is a social being, some of these elements probably existed from earliest times, but institutions in their fully developed form seem to have been an achievement of the Neolithic Age.

The nature of institutions

One of the most ancient of human institutions is the family. Sociologists do not agree upon how it should be defined. Historically, however, the family has always meant a more or less permanent unit composed of parents and their offspring, which serves the purposes of care of the young, division of labor, acquisition and transmission of property, and preservation and transmission of beliefs and cus-

Definition of the family

Polygamy

The nature of
primitive religion;
rites and cere-
monies

toms. The family is not now, and never has been, exclusively biolog-ical in character. Like most institutions, it has evolved through a long period of changing conventions which have given it a variety of functions and forms.

The family during Neolithic times appears to have existed in both polygamous and monogamous forms. The term polygamy is used by sociologists to mean any type of plural marriage—either a plurality of husbands or a plurality of wives. The scientific name for the former is *polyandry*, and for the latter *polygyny*. Polyandry seems always to have been rare. At the present time it is confined to a few Eskimo communities, to the Wahuma tribes of East Africa, and to southern India and Tibet. It appears to develop under conditions of extreme poverty where a number of men must pool their resources in order to purchase or support a wife, or where female infanticide is practiced as a means of controlling population growth. The latter custom soon results in an excess of males. Polygyny arises under a variety of conditions. In some cases it results from a preponderance of females. For example, the Arctic seal-hunter's life is so hazardous that in some villages the number of men may be less than half the number of women. In a few instances polygyny has been resorted to as a means of producing a rapid increase in the population. Since one man can procreate far more offspring than one woman can bear, such peoples as the ancient Hebrews encouraged the taking of extra wives in order that the group might multiply rapidly and thereby protect itself against absorption or annihilation by hostile neighbors. Still a third factor in the origin of polygyny has been the love of display. Rulers and other rich men have maintained a plurality of wives as a form of conspicuous consumption. King Solomon kept a harem of 700 wives and 300 concubines, not necessarily because of a voracious sexual appetite, but in order to impress other monarchs with his ability to support such a large establishment. He was inter-ested also, of course, in political alliances with as many as possible of the surrounding monarchs, and marrying their daughters was a con-venient means of establishing these.

A second institution developed in more complex form by Neo-lithic man was religion. On account of its infinite variations, it is hard to define, but perhaps the following would be accepted as an accurate definition of the institution in at least its basic character: "Religion is everywhere an expression in one form or another of a sense of dependence on a power outside ourselves, a power which we may speak of as a spiritual or moral power." [2] Modern anthro-pologists emphasize the fact that early religion was not so much a matter of belief as a matter of rites. For the most part, the rites came first; the myths, dogmas, and theologies were later rationalizations. Primitive man was universally dependent upon nature—on the regu-lar succession of the seasons, on the rain falling when it should, on the growth of plants and the reproduction of animals. Unless he

18 [2] A. R. Radcliffe-Brown, *Structure and Function in Primitive Society*, p. 157.

performed sacrifices and rites these natural phenomena, according to his notion, would not occur. For this reason he developed rain-making ceremonies in which water was sprinkled on ears of corn to imitate the falling of the rain. The ceremonial dances of the American Indians often had a similar import. The members of a whole village or even a whole tribe would attire themselves in animal skins and mimic the habits and activities of some species they depended upon for food. They apparently had a vague feeling that by imitating the life pattern of the species they were helping to guarantee its continuance.

But there was also another element conspicuously present in primitive religion. This was the element of fear. Modern primitive men, at least, live in an almost constant state of alarm and dread. As an old Eskimo medicine man said to the explorer Knud Rasmussen: "We do not believe; we fear." [3] Everything strange and unfamiliar is fraught with danger. The savage fears not only sickness and death but also hunger, drought, storms, the spirits of the dead, and the animals he has killed. Every misfortune, loss, or failure is the harbinger of other misfortunes and failures unless the evil influence that caused it is appeased, paralyzed, or annihilated. To accomplish such ends, charms, incantations, and other devices of magic potency seem to be a vital necessity.

It follows that a large part of primitive man's religion consists of ceremonial precautions to ward off evil. For example, no savage will risk swimming across a dangerous river without first endeavoring by prayers or incantations to win its favor. An Eskimo who has killed a polar bear must present it with tools and weapons pleasing to it; if the bear is a female, women's knives and needle cases are given. Bestowal of these gifts is considered necessary to appease the wrath of the bear's soul and keep it from wreaking damage. In West Africa, the hunter who has killed a hippopotamus disembowels it, strips himself naked, crawls inside the carcass, and bathes his entire body with the animal's blood. Throughout the procedure he prays to the spirit of the hippo that it will bear him no ill-will for having killed it, and that it will not incite other hippopotami to attack his canoe in revenge.[4]

Still another of the great institutions to be developed by Neolithic man was the state. By way of definition, the state may be described as an organized society occupying a definite territory and possessing an authoritative government independent of external control. The essence of the state is sovereignty, or the power to make and administer laws and to preserve social order by punishing men for infractions of those laws. A state must not be confused with a nation. The latter is an ethnic concept, used to designate a people bound together by ties of language, customs, or racial origin or by common memories or a belief in a common destiny. A nation may or may not

[3] Lucien Lévy-Bruhl, *Primitives and the Supernatural*, p. 22.
[4] Lucien Lévy-Bruhl, *How Natives Think*, p. 238.

occupy a definite territory and does not possess the element of sovereignty. It may not even have an independent government, as for example, the Poles during the long period when they were under Austrian, German, and Russian rule. At the present time most nations are also states, but this condition has resulted largely from the breaking up of empires in the twentieth century.

Except in time of crisis, the state does not exist in a very large proportion of preliterate societies—a fact which probably indicates that its genesis was rather late in the Neolithic culture stage. Most primitive communities have no permanent system of courts, no police agencies, and no governments with coercive power. Custom takes the place of law, the blood-feud is the mode of administering justice, and there is very little conception of crime against the community. To primitive man, offenses are mostly what we call "torts," or private wrongs between individuals or families, in the punishment of which no public authority takes part. The acceptance of *wergeld,* or blood-money, is a common practice, and even felonies such as murder are regarded merely as offenses against the victim's family. Since the family of the victim has been deprived of a valuable member, the proper satisfaction is a money payment. If this is not offered, the family may retaliate in kind by killing the offender or a member of the offender's family.

The origin of the state was probably the consequence of a variety of factors. We are certainly justified in assuming the development of agriculture to have been one of the most important. In sections like the Nile valley, where a large population lived by cultivating intensively a limited area of fertile soil, a high degree of social organization was absolutely essential. Ancient customs would not suffice for the definition of rights and duties in such a society, with its high standard of living, its unequal distribution of wealth, and its wide scope for the clash of personal interests. New measures of social control would become necessary, which could scarcely be achieved in any other way than by setting up a government of sovereign authority and submitting to it; in other words, by establishing a state. The initial forms of public control would be few and tentative, but they would be gradually extended, until finally a state, not necessarily despotic, but with full authority, would come into being.

A number of ancient states evidently owed their origin to war activities. That is, they were founded for purposes of conquest, for defense against invasion, or to make possible the expulsion of an invader from the country. The Hebrew monarchy seems to have been a product of the first of these reasons. With the war for the conquest of Canaan none too successful, the Hebrew people besought their leader Samuel to give them a king, that they might be "like all the nations" with a powerful ruler to keep them in order and to lead them to victory in battle. One has only to observe the effects of modern warfare, both offensive and defensive, in enlarging the

Absence of the
state in many
primitive societies

A variety of
causes of the
origin of the state

Origin of the
state in military
causes

powers of government to see how similar influences might have operated to bring the state into existence in the first place.

Religion doubtless contributed to the origin of states in some areas. Medicine men, or shamans, frequently exercise a kind of sovereignty. Though they may command no physical force, their power to impose religious penalties and to strike terror into the hearts of their followers gives them a degree of coercive authority. In all probability some of them made themselves kings. It is conceivable that in other cases the state arose from the natural expansion of group life, with its resulting complexities and conflicts. As the population increased in limited areas, customary law and family administration of justice proved inadequate, and political organization became necessary as a substitute. In the domain of politics as in every other sphere concerned with social origins, no one explanation can be made to accommodate all the facts.

6.   CULTURES AND CIVILIZATIONS

The stages of man's advancement described thus far have been referred to as *cultures*. This word is commonly used to designate societies or periods which have not yet attained to a knowledge of writing and whose general level of achievement is comparatively primitive. But the term has other meanings. It is sometimes applied to intellectual and artistic accomplishments, to literature, art, music, philosophy, and science. It is employed by some historians to designate the whole complex pattern of ideas, achievements, traditions, and characteristics of a nation or empire at a particular time.

The term *civilization* also carries a variety of meanings. The German philosopher of history Oswald Spengler referred to civilizations as decadent phases of highly developed cultures. When a great people or empire was in its prime, he characterized its social and intellectual pattern as a culture. When it passed its prime and became ossified and stagnant, he described it as a "civilization." The noted British historian, Arnold J. Toynbee, also sees world history as a succession of cultural units. But he designates each of the primary ones, throughout its development, as a "civilization." He distinguishes between civilizations and "primitive societies" largely on a quantitative basis. The latter are "relatively short-lived, are restricted to relatively narrow geographical areas, and embrace relatively small numbers of human beings." [5]

The term *civilization* has still another meaning. Since each culture has peculiar features of its own, and since some cultures are more highly developed than others, we can speak quite properly of a civilization as a superior culture. We can say that a culture deserves to be called a civilization when it has reached a stage of advancement in which writing has come to be used to a considerable extent, some progress has been made in the arts and sciences, and political, social,

[5] D. C. Somervell (ed.), A. J. Toynbee's *A Study of History*, I, 35.

and economic institutions have developed sufficiently to conquer at least some of the problems of order, security, and efficiency in a complex society. This is the sense in which the term will be used throughout the remainder of this book.

7. FACTORS RESPONSIBLE FOR THE ORIGIN AND GROWTH OF CIVILIZATIONS

Origin and growth of civilizations variously explained

What causes contribute to the rise of civilizations? What factors account for their growth? Why do some civilizations reach much higher levels of development than others? Inquiry into these questions is one of the chief pursuits of social scientists. Some decide that factors of geography are the most important. Others stress economic resources, food supply, contact with older civilizations, and so on. Usually a variety of causes is acknowledged, but one is commonly singled out as deserving special emphasis.

Geographic theories: the climatic hypothesis

Probably the most popular of the theories accounting for the rise of superior cultures are those which come under the heading of geography. Prominent among them is the hypothesis of climate. The climatic theory, advocated in days past by such notables as Aristotle and Montesquieu, received its most eloquent exposition in the writings of an American geographer, Ellsworth Huntington. Huntington acknowledged the importance of other factors, but he insisted that no nation, ancient or modern, rose to the highest cultural status except under the influence of a climatic stimulus. He described the ideal climate as one in which the mean temperature seldom falls below the mental optimum of 38 degrees or rises above the physical optimum of 64 degrees. But temperature is not alone important. Moisture is also essential, and the humidity should average about 75 per cent. Finally, the weather must not be uniform: cyclonic storms, or ordinary storms resulting in weather changes from day to day, must have sufficient frequency and intensity to clear the atmosphere every once in a while and produce those sudden variations in temperature which seem to be necessary to exhilarate and revitalize man.[6]

Evidence in favor of the climatic hypothesis

Much can be said in favor of the climatic hypothesis. Certainly some parts of the earth's surface, under existing atmospheric conditions, could never cradle a superior culture. They are either too hot, too humid, too cold, or too dry. Such is the case in regions beyond the Arctic Circle, the larger desert areas, and the jungles of India, Central America, and Brazil. Evidence is available, moreover, to show that some of these places have not always suffered under climate so adverse as that now prevalent. Various inhospitable sections of Asia, Africa, and America contain unmistakable traces of more salubrious days in the past. Here and there are the ruins of towns and cities where now the supply of water seems totally inadequate.

22   [6] Ellsworth Huntington, *Civilization and Climate*, 3d ed., pp. 220-23.

Roads traverse deserts which at present are impassable. Bridges span river beds which have had no water in them for years.

The best-known evidences of the cultural importance of climatic change are those pertaining to the civilization of the Mayas. Mayan civilization flourished in Guatemala, Honduras, and on the peninsula of Yucatan in Mexico from about 400 to 1500 A.D. Numbered among its achievements were the making of paper, the invention of the zero, the perfection of a solar calendar, and the development of a system of writing partly phonetic. Great cities were built; marked progress was made in astronomy; and sculpture and architecture were advanced to high levels. At present most of the civilization is in ruins. No doubt many factors conspired to produce its untimely end, including deadly wars between tribes, but climatic change was also probably involved. The remains of most of the great cities are now surrounded by jungles, where malaria is prevalent and agriculture difficult. That the Mayan civilization or any other could have grown to maturity under conditions like these is hard to believe.

Related to the climatic hypothesis is the soil-exhaustion theory. A group of modern conservationists has hit upon this theory as the sole explanation of the decay and collapse of the great empires of the past and as a universal threat to the nations of the present and future. At best it is only a partial hypothesis, since it offers no theory of the birth or growth of civilizations. But its proponents seem to think that almost any environment not ruined by man is capable of nourishing a superior culture. The great deserts and barren areas of the earth, they maintain, are not natural but artificial, created by man through bad grazing and farming practices. Conservationists discover innumerable evidences of waste and neglect that have wrought havoc in such areas as Mesopotamia, Palestine, Greece, Italy, China, and Mexico. The majestic civilizations that once flourished in these countries were ultimately doomed by the simple fact that their soil would no longer provide sufficient food for the population. As a consequence, the more intelligent and enterprising citizens migrated elsewhere and left their inferiors to sink slowly into stagnation and apathy. But the fate that overtook the latter was not of their making alone. The whole nation had been guilty of plundering the forests, mining the soil, and pasturing flocks on the land until the grass was eaten down to the very roots. Among the tragic results were floods alternating with droughts, since there were no longer any forests to regulate the run-off of rain or snow. At the same time, much of the top soil on the close-cropped or excessively cultivated hillsides was blown away or washed into the rivers to be carried eventually down to the sea. The damage done was irreparable, since about 300 years are required to produce a single inch of top soil.

Yet another of the geographic theories is the contention that the topography of the earth's surface has been the main conditioning

The topographical
theory

element in the rise of civilizations. A famous champion of this theory was the nineteenth-century English historian Henry Thomas Buckle. Buckle divided the principal environments of man into two classes: (1) those that stimulate the imagination, and (2) those that sharpen the understanding. To illustrate the former he submitted the example of India, where the works of nature are of "startling magnitude," overawing man and impressing him with a sense of his own insignificance. The natives therefore torture themselves, invent cruel and terrifying gods, and practice a religion of hideous orgies. They are pessimists and fatalists, denying all value to life and repudiating the ability of man to understand and control his world. As an example of the second class of environments, Buckle referred to Greece, where the face of nature is more ordinary and "less threatening to man." Such an environment, he argued, promotes the elevation of man, generates an attitude of optimism, and stimulates a feeling of confidence in the powers of the human mind. He considered it no miracle, therefore, that Greece should have been able to produce one of the world's most distinguished cultures and some of the greatest critical thinkers of all time.[7]

Criticism of the
topographical
theory

The topographical theory seems to have comparatively little to confirm it. No geologist would agree that coastal indentations and the altitude of mountain ranges have altered much within the range of historic time. Greece has no fewer harbors now than in the age of Pericles, nor has Mount Olympus risen in recent years to any proportions of "startling magnitude." Yet the modern Greeks do not match their ancestors in intellectual accomplishment. If the influence of topography was at one time conducive to rational thinking and to the development of confidence and joy in achievement, why should that influence have ceased to operate? On the other hand, there is no gainsaying the fact that a long and irregular coast line is an asset in the development of trade, and therefore an important advantage in the diffusion and reception of knowledge.

The adversity
theory of Arnold
J. Toynbee

The most recent hypothesis of the origin of civilizations is Toynbee's adversity theory. According to this theory, conditions of hardship or adversity are the real causes which have brought into existence superior cultures. Such conditions constitute a *challenge* which not only stimulates men to try to overcome it but generates additional energy for new achievements. The challenge may take the form of a desert, a jungle area, rugged topography, or a grudging soil. The Hebrews and Arabs were challenged by the first, the Indians of the Andean Highland by the last. The challenge may also take the form of defeat in war or even enslavement. Thus the Carthaginians, as a result of defeat in the First Punic War, were stimulated to conquer a new empire in Spain; centuries later, Oriental captives enslaved by the Romans strengthened and propagated their religious heritage until Rome itself succumbed to it. In general it is true that the greater the challenge, the greater the achievement;

[7] H. T. Buckle, *The History of Civilization in England*, 2d ed., pp. 93–106.

nevertheless, there are limits. The challenge must not be too severe, else it will deal a crushing blow to all who attempt to meet it.

The majority of historians believe that the genesis of civilizations cannot be explained except on the basis of a complex of causes. Not any one factor, but a combination of several must be taken into account. Among these factors they place uppermost the geographic and economic elements of favorable climate, fertile soil, access to good harbors, and an abundance of mineral resources. They also accord a high place to opportunities for interchange of ideas with other peoples of a comparable level of advancement. Civilizations do not develop in isolated corners of the world. The backwardness of Australia, New Zealand, and South Africa before the coming of Europeans was probably due to this cause. These sections were favorably situated so far as climate and resources were concerned, but they were too remote to be affected by the stimulus of progress elsewhere. It is common also for historians to emphasize the concentration of population in limited areas and the invention of new skills and processes as factors in the origin of high cultures. Historians also recognize the importance of religion as an influence in the transition from primitive to civilized life. The earliest forms of social regulation were probably for religious purposes. Religion provided the oldest law codes and systems of morality and perhaps also the foundations of philosophy and science. Priests constituted the most ancient class of educated men, and there is reason to believe that it was they who invented the first systems of writing.

A number of factors must be taken into account in explaining the origin of civilizations

8. WHY THE EARLIEST CIVILIZATIONS BEGAN WHERE THEY DID

Which of the great civilizations of antiquity was the oldest is still a sharply debated question. The judgment of some scholars inclines toward the Egyptian, though a larger body of authority supports the claims of the Tigris-Euphrates valley. These two areas were geographically the most favored sections in the general region of the so-called Fertile Crescent. The Fertile Crescent is that wide belt of productive land which extends northwestward from the Persian Gulf and then down the Mediterranean coast almost to Egypt. It forms a semicircle around the northern part of the Arabian desert. Here larger numbers of artifacts of undoubted antiquity have been found than in any other sections of the Near Orient. Furthermore, progress in the arts and sciences had reached unparalleled heights in both of these areas as early as 3000 B.C., when most of the rest of the world was steeped in ignorance. If the foundations of this progress were really laid elsewhere, it seems strange that they should have disappeared, although of course there is no telling what the spade of the archaeologist may uncover in the future.

The Nile and the Tigris-Euphrates valleys probably the centers of the oldest civilizations

Of the several causes responsible for the earliest rise of civilizations in the Nile and Tigris-Euphrates valleys, geographic factors **25**

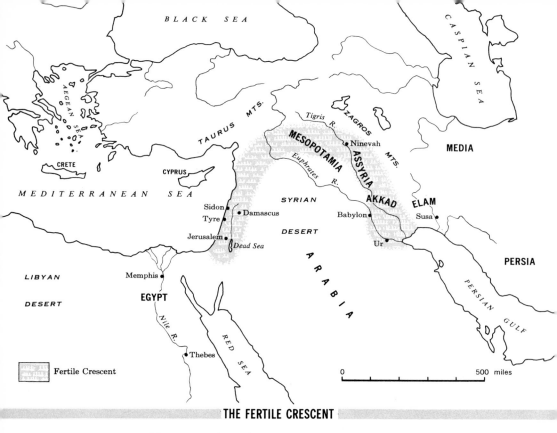

THE FERTILE CRESCENT

A limited area of
fertile soil in the
Nile valley

would seem to have been the most important. Both regions had the
notable advantage of a limited area of exceedingly fertile soil. Although it extended for a distance of 750 miles, the valley of the Nile
was not more than ten miles wide in some places, and its maximum
width was thirty-one miles. The total area was less than 10,000
square miles, or roughly the equivalent of the State of Maryland.
Through countless centuries the river had carved a vast canyon or
trench, bounded on either side by cliffs ranging in height from a
few hundred to a thousand feet. The floor of the canyon was
covered with a rich alluvial deposit, which in places reached a depth
in excess of thirty feet. The soil was of such amazing productivity
that as many as three crops per year could be raised on the same
land. This broad and fertile canyon constituted the cultivable area
of ancient Egypt. Here several million people were concentrated. In
Roman times the population of the valley approximated seven million, and probably it was not much smaller in the days of the
Pharaohs. Beyond the cliffs there was nothing but desert—the
Libyan desert on the west and the Arabian on the east.

In the Tigris-Euphrates valley similar conditions prevailed. As in
Egypt, the rivers provided excellent facilities for inland transportation and were alive with fish and waterfowl for a plentiful supply of
protein food. The distance between the Tigris and Euphrates rivers
at one point was less than twenty miles, and nowhere in the lower
valley did it exceed forty-five miles. Since the surrounding country

A similar
condition in
Mesopotamia

26

was desert, the people were kept from scattering over too great an
expanse of territory. The result, as in Egypt, was the welding of the
inhabitants into a compact society, under conditions that facilitated
a ready interchange of ideas and discoveries. As the population increased, the need for agencies of social control became ever more
urgent. Numbered among such agencies were government, schools,
legal and moral codes, and institutions for the production and distribution of wealth. At the same time conditions of living became
more complex and artificial and necessitated the keeping of records
of things accomplished and the perfection of new techniques.
Among the consequences were the invention of writing, the practice of smelting metals, the performance of mathematical operations,
and the development of astronomy and the rudiments of physics.
With these achievements the first great ordeal of civilization was
passed.

Climatic influences also played their part in both regions. The atmosphere of Egypt is dry and invigorating. Even the hottest days
produce none of the oppressive discomfort which is often experienced during the summer seasons in more northern countries. The
mean temperature in winter varies from 56 degrees in the Delta to
66 degrees in the valley above. The summer mean is 83 degrees and
an occasional maximum of 122 is reached, but the nights are always
cool and the humidity is extremely low. Except in the Delta, rainfall
occurs in negligible quantities, but the deficiency of moisture is
counteracted by the annual inundations of the Nile from July to
October. Also very significant from the historical standpoint is the
total absence of malaria in Upper Egypt, while even in the coastal
region it is practically unknown. The direction of the prevailing
winds is likewise a favorable factor of more than trivial importance.
For more than three-quarters of the year the wind comes from the
north, blowing in opposition to the force of the Nile current. The
effect of this is to simplify immensely the problem of transportation. Upstream traffic, with the propulsion of the wind to counteract the force of the river, presents no greater difficulty than down-
stream traffic. This factor in ancient times must have been of
enormous advantage in promoting communication among a numerous people, some of whom were separated by hundreds of miles.

Climatic advan-
tages in Egypt

Climatic conditions in Mesopotamia do not seem to have been
quite so favorable as in Egypt. The summer heat is more relentless;
the humidity is somewhat higher; and tropical diseases take their
toll. Nevertheless, the torrid winds from the Indian Ocean, while
enervating to human beings, blow over the valley at just the right
season to bring the fruit of the date palm to a full ripeness. More
than anything else the excellent yield of dates, the dietary staple of
the Near Orient, encouraged the settlement of large numbers of
people in the valley of the two rivers. Finally, the melting of the
snows in the mountains of the north produced an annual flooding of
the Babylonian plain similar to that in Egypt. The effect was to en-

Climatic influences
in Mesopotamia

27

rich the soil with moisture and to cover it over with a layer of mud of unusual fertility. At the same time, it should be noted that water conditions in Mesopotamia were less dependable than in Egypt. Floods were sometimes catastrophic, a factor which left its mark on the development of culture.

Most significant of all of the geographic influences, however, was the fact that the scanty rainfall in both regions provided a spur to initiative and inventive skill. In spite of the yearly floods of the rivers there was insufficient moisture left in the soil to produce abundant harvests. A few weeks after the waters had receded, the earth was baked to a stony hardness. Irrigation was accordingly necessary if full advantage was to be taken of the richness of the soil. As a result, in both Egypt and Mesopotamia elaborate systems of dams and irrigation canals were constructed as long ago as five thousand years. The mathematical skill, engineering ability, and social cooperation necessary for the development of these projects were available for other uses and so fostered the achievement of civilization.

The importance
of scanty rainfall
as a spur to
initiative

The question remains to be answered, which of the two civilizations, the Egyptian or the Mesopotamian, was the older? This question thus far has defied a satisfactory answer. It is possible to present various facts which seem to suggest the priority of Egypt. Most important of all, the dwellers in the Nile valley enjoyed geographic advantages which were denied to the natives of Mesopotamia: a less enervating atmosphere, a climate comparatively free from disease, and the availability of metals and good building stone. Egypt, moreover, was well protected from invasion and from intermixture with more backward peoples. On the east and west were trackless deserts, on the north was a harborless coast line, and on the south the rocky barriers of a series of cataracts prevented the inroads of African savages. Only at the two northern corners could the valley be penetrated easily. By contrast, Mesopotamia was relatively unprotected. Not one of its boundaries afforded any appreciable degree of security. It stood as a constant temptation to the hungry hordes of nomads in the surrounding mountains and deserts. As a consequence, the progress of cultural evolution was subject to frequent interruptions by the invasions of pillaging tribes.

Until recently most historians appeared to take it for granted that the Egyptian civilization was the older. They based their assumption upon the conclusions of two of the world's most renowned Egyptologists, James H. Breasted and Alexandre Moret. Between the two world wars of the twentieth century, however, facts were unearthed which seemed to prove a substantial Mesopotamian influence in the Nile valley as early as 3500 B.C. This influence was exemplified by the use of cylinder seals, methods of building construction, art motifs, and elements of a system of writing of undoubted Mesopotamian origin. That such achievements could have radiated into Egypt from the Tigris-Euphrates valley at so early a date indi-

Uncertainty as
to which civiliza-
tion was older

cated beyond doubt that the Mesopotamian civilization was one of vast antiquity. It did not necessarily prove, though, that it was older than the Egyptian. For the achievements mentioned were not taken over and copied slavishly. Instead, the Egyptians modified them radically to suit their own culture pattern. On the basis of this evidence, it would seem that the only conclusion which can be safely drawn is that both civilizations were very old, and that to a large extent they developed concurrently.

SELECTED READINGS

· *Items so designated are available in paperbound editions.*

ANTHROPOLOGICAL AND ARCHAEOLOGICAL WORKS

· Boas, Franz, *The Mind of Primitive Man*, New York, 1927 (Free Press, 1965).

Breasted, James H., *The Dawn of Conscience*, New York, 1934. An excellent treatise on the origin of religious and ethical concepts.

· ———, *History of Egypt*, New York, 1912 (Bantam). Still one of the best.

· Ceram, C. W., *Gods, Graves and Scholars*, New York, 1951. Popular but scholarly.

· Childe, V. G., *Man Makes Himself*, London, 1936 (Mentor, 1952).

· ———, *New Light on the Most Ancient East*, New York, 1934 (Evergreen).

Dawson, Christopher, *The Age of the Gods*, New York, 1937.

Herskovits, M. J., *Man and His Works*, New York, 1948. One of the best introductions to anthropology.

Lévy-Bruhl, Lucien, *How Natives Think*, London, 1926.

———, *Primitives and the Supernatural*, New York, 1935. A superlative study of primitive "Logic."

· Linton, Ralph, *The Tree of Culture*, New York, 1955 (Vintage, abr.).

MacCurdy, G. G., *Human Origins*, New York, 1924, 2 vols.

Magoffin, R. V. D., and Davis, E. C., *The Romance of Archaeology*, New York, 1929.

· Malinowski, Bronislaw, *Crime and Custom in Savage Society*, New York, 1951 (Littlefield, 1959). The most provocative and valuable study on the subject.

Osborn, H. F., *Men of the Old Stone Age*, New York, 1915.

· Radcliffe-Brown, A. R., *Structure and Function in Primitive Society*, Glencoe, Ill., 1952 (Free Press, 1952). Stimulating and informative.

· Radin, Paul, *Primitive Religion*, New York, 1937 (Dover, 1957).

Renard, Georges, *Life and Work in Prehistoric Times*, New York, 1929.

INTERPRETATIONS OF HISTORY

Butterfield, Herbert, *History and Human Relations*, New York, 1952.

· Clough, Shepard B., *The Rise and Fall of Civilization*, New York, 1951 (Columbia University Press, 1961).

Kahler, Erich, *The Meaning of History*, New York, 1964.

· Muller, H. J., *The Uses of the Past*, New York, 1952 (Galaxy).

· Ralph, Philip L., *The Story of Our Civilization*, New York, 1954.

· Somervell, D. C., ed., A. J. Toynbee, *A Study of History*, New York, 1947-57, 2 vols. (Galaxy, 6 vols.). An excellent abridgement of a monumental work.

Spengler, Oswald, *The Decline of the West*, 1-vol. ed., New York, 1934. The gist of his philosophy is contained in the Introduction.

Ancient Civilizations of the East and West

POLITICAL	CULTURAL
4000 B.C.	
Pre-dynastic period in Egypt, *ca.* 4000–3100	Solar calendar in Egypt, *ca.* 4000
Sumerian supremacy in Mesopotamia, *ca.* 4000–2000	Egyptian hieroglyphic writing, *ca.* 3500
	Development of irrigation, mathematics, rudimentary astronomy in Egypt and Mesopotamia, *ca.* 3500–2500
Old Kingdom in Egypt, *ca.* 3100–2200	Cuneiform writing, *ca.* 3200
	Invention of principle of alphabet in Egypt, *ca.* 3000
3000 B.C. Minoan-Mycenaean civilization, *ca.* 3000–1000	Construction of great pyramids in Egypt, *ca.* 2700
	Philosophy in Egypt, *ca.* 2500
Middle Kingdom in Egypt, 2052–1786	
2000 B.C. Aryan invasions of India, 2000–1500	
Hittite empire, 2000–1200	
Old Babylonian kingdom, 1950–1650	Code of Hammurabi, *ca.* 1790
Hyksos conquer Egypt, 1786–1575	
Kassites conquer Babylonians, *ca.* 1650	Egyptian temple architecture, 1580–1090
1500 B.C. The Empire in Egypt, 1575–1087	Development of alphabet by Phoenicians, *ca.* 1500
Shang Dynasty in China, *ca.* 1523–1027	Invention of decimal system and discovery of principal of zero in India, 1500–1000
Hebrew conquest of Canaan, *ca.* 1300–900	Realistic sculpture of Assyrians, 1300–600
Chou Dynasty in China, 1027–249	Composition of the *Vedas*, 1200–800
1000 B.C. United Hebrew Monarchy, 1025–935	
Secession of Ten Tribes of Israel, 935	
Kingdom of Israel, 935–722	
Kingdom of Judah, 935–586	
Feudalism in China, 800–250	The *Upanishads*, 800–600
Assyrian empire, 750–612	Division of day into hours and minutes, *ca.* 600
Assyrian conquest of Egypt, 670	Calculation of length of year, *ca.* 600
Chaldean empire, 612–539	Deuteronomic Code, *ca.* 600
Babylonian captivity, 586–539	Confucius, 551?–479?
Persian empire, 559–330	Lao-tzu, *ca.* 550
Persian conquest of Egypt, 525	
500 B.C. Persian Empire under Darius, 522–486	Book of Job, *ca.* 500
Invasion of India by Alexander the Great, 327–326	Mo Ti, 468?–382?
Reign of Emperor Asoka in India, *ca.* 273–232	Mencius, 373?–288?

Dates are B.C. unless given as A.D.

ECONOMIC	RELIGIOUS	
	Creation and Flood epics in Mesopotamia, *ca.* 4000	**4000 B.C.**
Development of serfdom in Mesopotamia and in Egypt, *ca.* 3500	Egyptian sun worship, *ca.* 3500	
	Ethical religion in Egypt, *ca.* 3000	**3000 B.C.**
	Egyptian belief in personal immortality, *ca.* 2500	
Large-scale industry in Egypt and Crete, *ca.* 2000		**2000 B.C.**
	Demon worship and witchcraft in Babylonia, *ca.* 1900	
Slavery in Egypt, *ca.* 1580		
Introduction of use of iron by Hittites, *ca.* 1500		**1500 B.C.**
	Religious revolution of Ikhnaton, 1375	
World trade of Phoenicians, *ca.* 1000–500	Hebrew worship of Yahweh, *ca.* 1000	**1000 B.C.**
Rise of caste system in India, 1000–500		
	Ten Commandments, *ca.* 700	
Slavery in Assyria, *ca.* 750	Prophetic Revolution, 800–600	
	Hebrew doctrine of universal monotheism, *ca.* 600	
Invention of coinage by Lydians, *ca.* 600	Astral religion of Chaldeans, 600–500	
World trade of Chaldeans, 600–500	Divination and astrology, 600–500	
	Zoroastrianism, *ca.* 600–300	
	Founding of Jainism in India, 599–527	
	Babylonian Captivity of Jews, 586–539	
Royal Road of Persians, *ca.* 500	Gautama Buddha, *ca.* 563–483	**500 B.C.**
Use of iron in China, *ca.* 500	Mithraism, *ca.* 300 B.C. 275 A.D.	
Development of coinage in China, *ca.* 400	Gnosticism, *ca.* 100 B.C.–100 A.D.	
	Rise of Christianity, *ca.* 25 A.D.	

CHAPTER 2

The Egyptian Civilization

How great is that which thou has done, O lord of gods. Thy plans and thy counsels are those which come to pass throughout. Thou sentest me forth in valor, thy strength was with me. No land stood before me, at the mention of thee. I overthrew those who invaded my boundary, prostrated in their place. . . . It was ordained because of thy victory-bringing commands, it was given because of thy kingdom-bestowing power.
—*Utterance of King Ramses III before his father, Amon-Re, ruler of the gods, from The Great Inscription in the Second Court relief in Medinet Habu temple*

The Neolithic culture stage came to an end in some parts of the world soon after 5000 B.C. It seems to have disappeared first of all in the Nile valley, and perhaps just as early in the area watered by the Tigris and Euphrates. Progress toward a higher cultural level appears to have been especially rapid in Egypt; not only that, but the achievements of the Egyptians laid the foundation for a great deal of the work of other peoples. It is therefore appropriate that we begin our study of the historic cultures with the rise of civilization on the banks of the Nile.

The rise of civilization in Egypt

I. THE PRE-DYNASTIC PERIOD

Since there was no enduring unified state in the valley of the Nile until about 3200 B.C., the centuries from 4000 to 3100 are referred to as the pre-dynastic period.[1] In the early part of this period the country seems to have consisted of a number of "nomes," or city-states, each of them independent, although evidently cooperating with others for economic ends. Shortly after the beginning of the fourth millennium a fusion of states took place to form two large

Meaning of the pre-dynastic period

[1] Some authorities give the year 3400 as the approximate date for the beginning of the First Dynasty. Although recent research seems to favor about 3100, it should be remembered that all dates prior to 2000 are largely a matter of conjecture.

kingdoms, one in the north and one in the south. How the consolidations were effected no one knows, but possibly they were accomplished through voluntary agreement or peaceful acquiescence in the rule of some capable prince. There is little evidence of military conquest. These kingdoms endured until the end of the pre-dynastic period, although they seem to have been united for a brief interval soon after their establishment.

The racial complexion of pre-dynastic Egypt was essentially the same as in later epochs. The inhabitants belonged to the Mediterranean branch of the Caucasian race; but they were not a pure strain, and there is nothing to indicate that racial factors as such were of importance in the development of their culture. They were a short, dark, long-headed people, with straight, black hair, deep-set eyes, and slightly aquiline noses. Some of them showed traces of Negroid and Libyan intermixture and possibly of the blood of Semites and other western Asiatic peoples. Their language contained evidences of Semitic elements, which would likewise indicate close relations with some of the natives of Asia.

The racial
character of the
Egyptians

The pre-dynastic period was by no means insignificant in the cultural history of Egypt. Outstanding progress was made in the arts and crafts and even in some of the sciences. Tools, weapons, and ornaments were expertly fashioned from flint, copper, and gold. New processes of finishing, glazing, and decorating pottery were discovered, with the result that the Egyptians of this period were able to make vessels of as high utility and artistic excellence as any produced by their later descendants. Other important achievements included the development of an efficient system of irrigation, the reclamation of swamp lands, and the weaving of a superior quality of linen cloth.

Material progress
in pre-dynastic
Egypt

But these were not all of their accomplishments. There is evidence that the pre-dynastic Egyptians evolved a system of laws based upon custom, which were held in such high repute that they were later considered binding even upon the Pharaoh himself. A system of writing appears also to have come into use. Although no actual specimen of such writing has ever been found, the examples that have survived from the First Dynasty partake of so complex a nature that they must have originated much earlier. Finally, the Egyptians of this period invented the first solar calendar in the history of man. It seems to have been based upon the annual reappearance of Sirius, the "Dog Star," and it provided for twelve months of thirty days each, with five feast days added at the end of the year. According to the computations of modern Egyptologists, this calendar was put into effect about the year 4200 B.C. The existence of a reasonably accurate calendar at this time argues that a considerable development of mathematics, and possibly the other sciences, had already been attained.

Intellectual
progress

2. POLITICAL HISTORY UNDER THE PHARAOHS

About 3100 B.C. the kingdoms of Northern and Southern Egypt were combined into a single political unit, apparently for the second time, although the earlier union was of brief duration. The tradi- tional founder of the new state was Menes, who therefore became known as the founder of the First Dynasty. Five other dynasties followed in regular order until 2200 B.C. During the first two dynasties the capital was maintained at Thinis in Upper Egypt. The Third Dynasty transferred the seat of government to Memphis on the southern edge of the Delta, in order to secure the advantage of a more central location of administrative functions. Here it remained for approximately five centuries. The period from about 2800 to 2300 B.C. is accordingly called the Memphite period, and the entire age of the first six dynasties is known as the period of the Old Kingdom.

The government of the Old Kingdom did not actually approach the degree of personal absolutism that is commonly believed to have existed. It was nearer a theocracy than an autocracy. The absolutism of the king was exercised not in his own behalf but as the vicar of the god. It was the god as the personification of justice and social order who actually ruled, according to the prevailing conception; the monarch was his agent. It is true, of course, that the king was himself considered divine, the son of the sun god Re. He was held in such high respect that he could not be mentioned by name, but had to be referred to as "Pharaoh," from the Egyptian "per-o" meaning "great house" or "royal house." He was forbidden to marry anyone outside of his immediate family, lest the divine blood be contaminated by an inferior strain. It is to be noted, however, that in all his official actions his authority was limited by the ancient law, which was believed to embody the divine will. He was not above the law, but subject to it. To compare him, therefore, with the divine-right monarchs of more modern times is to misunderstand his function.

No separation of church and state existed in the Old Kingdom. The Pharaoh's chief subordinates were the priests, and he was himself the chief priest. But he had other agents also: a vizier or prime minister, a royal treasurer, a chief architect, a superintendent of public works, a chief justice, and forty-two nomarchs. The last were the governors of the nomes or local districts into which the country was divided. Originally they were appointed by the Pharaoh and were supposed to execute his will, but gradually they made their positions hereditary and usurped for themselves more and more prerogatives of sovereignty. Their usurpations were probably not difficult, for the Kingdom was large, and centralized control was not easily maintained.

The position of Pharaoh was hereditary, but the privilege of suc-

cession to the office involved responsibilities. Usually the crown
prince served an apprenticeship under his father as superintendent
of public works or vizier. He thus came to the throne as an enlightened and educated statesman, familiar with the needs of the country
and schooled in the great public enterprises of mining, construction
of public works, and irrigation. It was well that he was thus prepared, for as king he was obliged by custom to devote a great deal
of his time to inspection and management of the various projects designed to promote the national interest. The divinity that doth
hedge a king did not exempt the Pharoah from arduous service for
the public welfare.

What has been said already about the importance of Egyptian law
suggests that judicial procedure of fairly high quality must have
been followed. Such was the case. Although the Old Kingdom had
no well-defined class of professional judges, the administrative officials who served at times in a judicial capacity were learned in the
law and boasted of their even-handed justice in deciding cases. Altogether six courts, to which different administrative officials were
assigned from time to time as judges, composed the judicial branch
of the government. Over them all was the chief justice, who sometimes held the position of vizier as well. Appeals could also be taken
to the Pharaoh himself under certain circumstances. Apparently no
class of cases was excluded from the regular jurisdiction of the
courts. Records show that even cases of treason in the king's household were tried with the same scrupulous regard for legal procedure
that was exhibited in the trials of petty offenders. The Pharoahs of
the Old Kingdom had not yet learned the infamous distinction between political "crimes" and ordinary crimes which has been drawn
by the rulers of some modern states.

The government of the Old Kingdom was founded upon a policy
of peace and nonaggression. In this respect it was almost unique
among ancient states. The Pharaoh had no standing army, nor was
there anything that could be called a national militia. Each nome had
its local militia, but it was commanded by the civil officials, and
when called into active service it generally devoted its energies to
labor on the public works. In case of a threat of invasion the various
local units were assembled at the call of the Pharaoh and placed under the command of one of his civil subordinates. At no other time
did the head of the government have a military force at his disposal.
The Egyptians of the Old Kingdom were content for the most part
to work out their own destinies and to let other nations alone. The
reasons for this attitude are to be found in the protected position of
their country, in their possession of land of inexhaustible fertility,
and in the fact that their state was a product of cooperative need
instead of being grounded in exploitation.

After a solid millennium of peace and relative prosperity the Old
36 Kingdom came to an end about 2200 B.C. Several causes appear to

have been responsible: the usurpation of power by the nomarchs; POLITICAL HISTORY
the persistence of particularism, or "states' rights" sentiment; the
growth of individualism; and the financial burdens imposed upon
the people by Pharaohs with grandiose schemes for national development. The period which followed is called the Feudal Age. Save End of the Old Kingdom
for intervals of order and progress it was marked by anarchy,
aggrandizement of the power of the nobles, social revolution of the
masses, and invasion by Negroid and Asian tribes. It did not end
until the rise of the Eleventh Dynasty about 2050 B.C.—an event
which ushered in the next great stage in Egyptian history, which is
known as the Middle Kingdom.

The government of the Middle Kingdom was notably weaker
than that of the Old Kingdom. Dynasties of Pharaohs continued a
nominal rule, but extensive authority gravitated into the hands of The Middle Kingdom (2052–1786 B.C.)
the nomarchs and nobles of lesser rank. The glory of these men was
to govern as benevolent despots, performing in their local bailiwicks
the functions rightfully belonging to the head of the state. In time
they, too, were assailed by the masses, with the result that after 2000
B.C. the Pharaohs of the Twelfth Dynasty were able to regain a
measure of their former power. The people themselves were rewarded by appointments to government positions and by grants of
land and vested rights in particular occupations. The whole population, regardless of birth or rank, appears to have been accorded privileges hitherto reserved for the few. For this reason the government
of the Twelfth Dynasty is sometimes referred to as the first democratic kingdom in history. The period of its rule was a golden age of
social justice and intellectual achievement, although the forms of
theocracy still survived.

With the end of the Twelfth Dynasty, Egypt entered another era
of internal chaos and foreign invasion which lasted for more than
two centuries, or from 1786 to 1575 B.C. The contemporary records The invasion of the Hyksos
are scanty, but they seem to show that the internal disorder was the
result of a counterrevolt of the nobles. The Pharaohs were again reduced to impotence, and much of the social progress of the preceding age was destroyed. About 1750 the land was invaded by the
Hyksos, or the "Shepherd Kings," a mixed horde originating in
western Asia. They extended a nominal rule over the whole country, although their effective sovereignty was probably confined to
the Delta. Their military prowess is commonly ascribed to the fact
that they possessed horses and war chariots, but their victory was
certainly made easier by the dissension among the Egyptians themselves. Their rule had profound effects upon Egyptian history. Not
only did they familiarize the Egyptians with new methods of warfare; but by providing them with a common grievance in the face of
foreign tyranny they also enabled them to forget their differences
and unite in a common cause. Thus the path was cleared for the
restoration of strong government over the whole country.

Expulsion of the
Hyksos and
founding of the
Empire

Near the end of the seventeenth century the rulers of Upper Egypt launched a revolt against the Hyksos, a movement which was eventually joined by most of the natives of the valley. By 1575 all of the conquerors who had not been killed or enslaved had been driven from the country. The hero of this victory, Ahmose I, founder of the Eighteenth Dynasty, now made himself despot of Egypt. The regime he established was much more highly consolidated than any that had hitherto existed. In the great resurgence of nationalism which had accompanied the struggle against the Hyksos, local patriotism was annihilated, and with it the power of the nobles. Most of the nomarchs had opposed the rise of Ahmose; his final triumph made their position untenable and left them with no alternative but to surrender their claims to sovereignty.

The period which followed the accession of Ahmose is called the period of the Empire. It lasted from 1575 to 1087 B.C., during which time the country was ruled by three dynasties of Pharaohs in succession, the Eighteenth, Nineteenth, and Twentieth. No longer was the prevailing state policy pacific and isolationist; a spirit of aggressive imperialism rapidly pervaded the nation. The causes of this change are not far to seek. The military ardor generated by the successful war against the Hyksos whetted an appetite for further victories. A vast military machine had been created to expel the invader, which proved to be too valuable an adjunct to the Pharaoh's power to be discarded immediately. Besides, there were fears, either real or imaginary, of new invasions from western Asia.

The first steps in the direction of the new policy were taken by the immediate successors of Ahmose in making extensive raids into Palestine and claiming sovereignty over Syria. The lust for empire reached its zenith some years later during the reign of Thutmose III, who came to the throne in 1490 B.C. With one of the most formidable armies of ancient times he speedily annihilated all opposition in Syria and eventually made himself master of a vast domain extending from the Euphrates to the farther cataracts of the Nile. Phoenicians, Canaanites, Hittites, and Assyrians acknowledged his suzerainty or paid him tribute. But he never succeeded in welding the conquered peoples into loyal subjects, and his death was the signal for widespread revolt in Syria. His successors suppressed the uprising and managed to hold the empire together for some time, but ultimate disaster could not be averted. More territory had been annexed than could be managed successfully. The influx of wealth into Egypt weakened the national fiber by fostering corruption and luxury, and the constant revolts of the vanquished eventually sapped the strength of the state beyond all hope of recovery. By the twelfth century most of the conquered provinces had been permanently lost.

The government of the Empire resembled that of the Old Kingdom, except for the fact that it was more absolute. Military power rather than national unity was now the basis of the Pharaoh's rule. A professional army was always available with which to overawe his subjects. His eldest son, who in the Old Kingdom had served an apprenticeship as vizier, was now the highest ranking officer in the standing army. Scarcely any vestige of local authority remained. The nation was divided into more than fifty administrative units, many of them purely arbitrary, and over each was appointed a "count" or governor as the direct representative of the monarch's rule. Most of the former nobles now became courtiers or members of the royal bureaucracy under the complete domination of the king. The Pharaoh was not yet a divine-right monarch, but the actual extent of his power had begun to approach that of more modern despots.

The last of the great Pharaohs was Ramses III, who ruled from 1182 to 1151 B.C. He was succeeded by a long line of nonentities who inherited his name but not his ability. By the middle of the twelfth century Egypt had fallen prey to numerous ills of barbarian invasion and social decadence. Libyans and Nubians were swarming over the country and gradually debasing cultural standards. About the same time the Egyptians themselves appear to have lost their creative talent; their intellects seem to have been led astray by the seductions of magic and superstition; and the inevitable result was domination of the national life by a crude religious formalism. To win immortality by magic devices was now the commanding interest of men of every class. The process of decline was hastened also by the growing power of the priests, who finally usurped the royal prerogatives and dictated the Pharaoh's decrees.

From the middle of the tenth century to nearly the end of the eighth a dynasty of Libyan barbarians occupied the throne of the Pharaohs. The Libyans were followed by a line of Ethiopians or Nubians, who came in from the desert regions west of the Upper Nile. In 670 Egypt was conquered by the Assyrians, who succeeded in maintaining their supremacy for only eight years. After the collapse of Assyrian rule in 662 the Egyptians regained their independence, and a brilliant renaissance of culture ensued. It was doomed to an untimely end, however, for in 525 B.C. the country was conquered by the Persians. The ancient civilization was never again revived.

3. EGYPTIAN RELIGION

Religion played a dominant role in the life of the ancient Egyptians. The Greek description of the Egyptians as "the most religious of men" is something of an exaggeration, and yet there is no denying that belief in the supernatural was as important to the culture of the Nile valley as to any other civilization, past or present. Religion left its impress upon almost every department of Egyptian life. The

Funerary Papyrus. The scene shows the heart of a princess of the XXIst Dynasty being weighed in a balance before the god Osiris. On the other side of the balance are the symbols for life and truth.

art was an expression of religious symbolism. The literature and philosophy were suffused with religious teachings. The government of the Old Kingdom was to a large extent a theocracy, and even the military Pharaohs of the Empire professed to rule in the name of the god. Economic energy and material resources in considerable amounts were squandered in providing elaborate tombs and in maintaining a costly ecclesiastical system.

The early religious evolution The religion of the ancient Egyptians evolved through various stages from simple polytheism to philosophic monotheism. In the beginning each city or district appears to have had its local deities, who were guardian gods of the locality or personifications of nature powers. The unification of the country under the Old Kingdom resulted not only in a consolidation of territory but in a fusion of divinities as well. All of the guardian deities were merged into the great sun god Re or Ra. In later times, with the establishment of a Theban dynasty in control of the government, this deity was commonly called Amon or Ammon-Re from the name of the chief god of Thebes. The gods who personified the vegetative powers of nature were fused into a deity called Osiris, who was also the god of the Nile. Throughout Egyptian history these two great powers who ruled the universe, Re and Osiris, vied with each other for supremacy. Other deities, as we shall see, were recognized also, but they occupied a distinctly subordinate place.

During the period of the Old Kingdom the solar faith, embodied in the worship of Re, was the dominant system of belief. It served as

40

was essentially a god of the dead; he bestowed no rewards upon men in this life. As a consequence of his worship the minds of the Egyptian masses were oriented more and more toward the afterlife. Too much emphasis came to be placed upon winning salvation in the world to come, and not enough upon cooperation with Re to promote the reign of righteousness in this world. The solar faith did not die out during the time of the Middle Kingdom, but it was clearly reduced to second place.

Egyptian ideas of the hereafter attained their full development in the later history of the Middle Kingdom. For this reason elaborate preparations had to be made to prevent the extinction of one's earthly remains. Not only were bodies mummified but wealthy men left munificent endowments to provide their mummies with food and other essentials. As the religion advanced toward maturity, however, a less naïve conception of the afterlife was adopted. The dead were now believed to appear before Osiris to be judged according to their deeds on earth.

All of the departed who met the tests included in this system of judgment entered a celestial realm of physical delights and simple pleasures. Here in marshes of lilies and lotus-flowers they would hunt wild geese and quail with never-ending success. Or they might build houses in the midst of orchards with luscious fruits of unfailing yield. They would find lily-lakes on which to sail, pools of sparkling water in which to bathe, and shady groves inhabited by singing birds and every manner of gentle creature. The unfortunate victims whose hearts revealed their vicious lives were condemned to perpetual hunger and thirst in a place of darkness, forever cut off from the glorious light of Re.

The perfection of the Egyptian religion

The Egyptian religion attained its highest perfection about the end of the Middle Kingdom and the beginning of the Empire. By this time the solar faith and the cult of Osiris had been merged in such a way as to preserve the best features of both. The province of Re as the god of the living, as the champion of good in this world, was accorded almost equal importance with the functions of Osiris as the giver of personal immortality and the judge of the dead. The religion was now quite clearly an ethical one. Men repeatedly avowed their desire to do justice because such conduct was pleasing to the great sun god.

Priestcraft and superstition

Soon after the establishment of the Empire the religion which has just been described underwent a serious debasement. Its ethical significance was largely destroyed, and superstition and magic gained the ascendancy. The chief cause seems to have been that the long and bitter war for the expulsion of the Hyksos fostered the growth of irrational attitudes and correspondingly depreciated the intellect. The result was a marked increase in the power of the priests, who preyed upon the fears of the masses to promote their own advantage. Greedy for gain, they inaugurated the practice of selling

42

Egyptian Pottery Jar, with Painted Decoration, *ca.* 3600 B.C. It was filled with food or water and placed in the tomb to provide for the needs of the body in the afterlife.

An Egyptian Official and His Son. Painted limestone, *ca.* 2500 B.C.

Painted limestone figures, *ca.* 1300 B.C.

Tomb model of an Egyptian fishing boat, *ca.* 2000 B.C.

Wall painting of an Egyptian house, *ca.* 1400 B.C.

Farm Hand Plowing. Egyptian tomb figures, *ca.* 1900 B.C.

Gold and Inlay Pendant of Princess Sit Hat-Hor Yunet. Egyptian, Twelfth Dynasty.

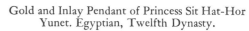

Jeweled Headdress of Gold, Carnelian, and Glass. Egyptian, 1475 B.C.

Thutmose III as Amon, 1450 B.C. The Pharaoh wears the crown and the beard of the god, and carries a scimitar and the symbol of "life."

A scribe writing on a papyrus r Egyptian, ca. 1415 B.C.

Silversmiths Working on a Stand and a Jar. Egyptian, ca. 1450 B.C.

Girl Musicians Playing a Harp, Lute, Pair of Oboes, and Lyre. Egyptian, ca. 1410 B.C.

Scarab or Beetle-Shaped Charm of a Pharaoh, ca. 1395 B.C. The beetle was sacred in ancient Egypt.

Shawabty ("to answer") Figures, ca. 1400 B.C. These were put in the tomb to do any degrading work the rich man might be called upon to do in the next world. Rich men were buried with hundreds of such figures.

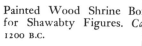

Painted Wood Shrine Bo for Shawabty Figures. Ca 1200 B.C.

All pictures courtesy MMA.

See color plates at pages 40, 41, 73

an official religion whose chief function w the state and to the people collectively. T. representative of this faith on earth; throug. god was maintained. The belief prevailed als Pharaoh's body and keeping it in an everlast. tribute to the eternal existence of the nation. Bu guardian deity. He was in addition the god of riȝ and truth and the upholder of the moral order o. offered no spiritual blessings or even material rewa. dividuals, nor did he concern himself in any other ʌ nary human welfare. The solar faith was not a re masses as such, except in so far as their welfare coincic of the state.

The cult of Osiris, as we have already observed, bega. ence as a nature religion. The god personified the growth c tion and the life-giving powers of the Nile. The career of O. wrapped about with an elaborate legend. In the remote past, a ing to belief, he had been a benevolent ruler, who taught his ɬ agriculture and other practical arts and gave them laws. After a he was treacherously slain by his wicked brother Set, and his bʌ cut into pieces. His wife Isis, who was also his sister, went in sear\ of the pieces, put them together, and miraculously restored his bod} to life. The risen god regained his kingdom and continued his benefi- cent rule for a time, but eventually descended to the nether world to serve as judge of the dead. Horus, his posthumous son, finally grew to manhood and avenged his father's death by killing Set.

Originally this legend seems to have been little more than a nature myth. The death and resurrection of Osiris symbolized the recession of the Nile in the autumn and the coming of the flood in the spring. But in time the Osiris legend began to take on a deeper significance. The human qualities of the deities concerned—the paternal solici- tude of Osiris for his subjects, the faithful devotion of his wife and son—appealed to the emotions of the average Egyptian, who was now able to see his own tribulations and triumphs mirrored in the lives of the gods. More important still, the death and resurrection of Osiris came to be regarded as conveying a promise of personal im- mortality for man. As the god had triumphed over death and the grave, so might also the individual who followed him faithfully in- herit everlasting life. Finally, the victory of Horus over Set ap- peared to foreshadow the ultimate ascendancy of good over evil.

With the growing perception of these implications, the cult of Osiris gradually became the more popular branch of the Egyptian religion. The worship of the sun god Re required such lofty powers of abstraction that it made little appeal to the average man. Espe- cially during the period of the Middle Kingdom, when individual- ism rose to its greatest heights, the popular cult received more than its share of attention. The result was not altogether fortunate. Osiris

Egyptian ideas the hereafter

Rewards punishm

Signific the Osir

The popularity of the cult of Osiris

41

magical charms, which were supposed to have the effect of preventing the heart of the deceased from betraying his real character. They also sold formulas which, inscribed on rolls of papyrus and placed in the tomb, were alleged to be effective in facilitating the passage of the dead to the celestial realm. The aggregate of these formulas constituted what is referred to as the Book of the Dead. Contrary to the general impression, it was not an Egyptian Bible, but merely a collection of mortuary inscriptions. Some of them proclaimed the moral purity of the deceased; others threatened the gods with disaster unless the persons whose names they bore were granted eternal reward. All of them were purchased in the belief that they guaranteed an entrance into the kingdom of Re. Good deeds and a clear conscience now seemed to be considered outmoded.

See color plates at page 73

This degradation of the religion at the hands of the priests into a system of magical practices finally resulted in a great reformation or religious revolution. The leader of this movement was the Pharaoh Amenhotep IV, who began his reign about 1375 B.C. After some fruitless attempts to correct the most flagrant abuses, he resolved to crush the system entirely. He drove the priests from the temples, hacked the names of the traditional deities from the public monuments, and commanded his people to worship a new god whom he called "Aton," an ancient designation for the physical sun. He changed his own name from Amenhotep ("Amen rests") to Ikhnaton, which meant "Aton is satisfied." Ikhnaton is the name by which he is commonly known in history.

The religious revolution of Ikhnaton

More important than these physical changes was the new set of doctrines enunciated by the reforming Pharaoh. According to eminent authorities, he taught first of all a religion of universal monotheism; Aton, he declared, was the only god in existence, the god not merely of Egypt but of the whole universe.[2] He restored the ethical quality of the national religion at its best by insisting that Aton was the author of the moral order of the world and the rewarder of men for integrity and purity of heart. He envisaged the new god as an eternal creator and sustainer of all that is of benefit to man, and as a heavenly father who watches with benevolent care over all his creatures. Conceptions like these of the unity, righteousness, and benevolence of God were not attained again until the time of the Hebrew prophets some 600 years later.

Ikhnaton's doctrines

The revolution of Ikhnaton was not an enduring success. Because of its challenge to ancient myths and magical practices it was not popular with the masses. Moreover, the Pharaohs who followed Ikhnaton were not inspired by the same devoted idealism. Such was particularly the case of the famous Tutenkhamen, who allowed the corrupt and mercenary priests to regain their power. The result was

The results of Ikhnaton's revolution

[2] J. H. Breasted, *A History of Egypt*, p. 376; see also Alexandre Moret, *From Tribe to Empire*, pp. 298–300.

a revival and a gradual extension of the same old superstitions that had prevailed before Ikhnaton's reign. For the great masses of the nation the ethical significance of the religion was permanently lost, and they were thrown back once more to ignorance and priestly greed. Among the educated classes, however, the influence of Ikhnaton's teachings lingered for some time. Although the god Aton was no longer recognized, the qualities he represented continued to be held in high esteem. What happened was that the attributes of Aton were now transferred by the educated minority to Ammon-Re. The traditional solar deity was acclaimed as the only god and the embodiment of righteousness, justice, and truth. He was worshiped, moreover, as a merciful and loving being "who heareth prayers, who giveth the hand to the poor, who saveth the weary."[3] It should be noted also that to this religion of ethical monotheism was added an element of personal salvation through repentance. The religious philosophers of the time developed the new idea that the god would refrain from punishing the penitent sinner who humbly implored forgiveness.

Adherence by the intelligent few to these noble ideas was not enough to save the religion from complete degeneracy and ruin. The spread of superstition, the popularity of magic, and the paralyzing grip of a degenerate priesthood were far too deadly in their effects to be overcome by exalted doctrines. In the end the whole system of belief and worship was engulfed by formalism and ignorance and by fetishism (worship of magical objects), animal worship, necromancy (black magic: foretelling the future by communing with the dead), and other magical crudities. The commercialism of the priests was more rampant than ever, and the chief function of the organized religion had come to be the sale of formulas and charms which would stifle the conscience and trick the gods into granting eternal salvation. The tragedy was compounded by the fact that as the religion decayed it exerted a baneful effect upon the rest of the culture. Philosophy, art, and government were so closely linked with religion that all of them went down together.

The return of decay

4. EGYPTIAN INTELLECTUAL ACHIEVEMENTS

I. PHILOSOPHY The philosophy of ancient Egypt was chiefly ethical and political, although traces of broader philosophic conceptions are occasionally to be found. The idea that the universe is controlled by mind or intelligence, for example, is a notion that appeared from time to time in the writings of priests and sages. Other philosophic ideas of the ancient Egyptians included the conception of an eternal universe, the notion of constantly recurring cycles of events, and the doctrine of natural cause and effect. Few, if any, of Egyptian writers could be classified as "pure" philosophers. They

The general character of Egyptian philosophy

44   [3] J. H. Breasted, *The Dawn of Conscience*, p. 316.

were concerned primarily with religion and with questions of individual conduct and social justice.

The earliest examples of ethical philosophy are contained in the *Maxims* of Ptahhotep, who served as vizier under one of the Pharaohs of the Fifth Dynasty about 2500 B.C. The work consists of some forty paragraphs of sage advice left by the vizier for the instruction of his son. About half of them are aphorisms of practical wisdom intended for the guidance of the young man in the pursuit of wordly success. Others, however, inculcate morality of a very high order. The son is enjoined to be gracious, tolerant, kindly, and cheerful, but above all to be righteous and just, even to the sacrifice of his own advantage, for "the power of righteousness is that it endures." The author also counsels the avoidance of greed, sensuality, and pride, and urges moderation and restraint.[4] Elementary though these maxims are, they are nevertheless highly significant, for they are the first expressions of moral idealism in all the world's literature.

During the Middle Kingdom ethical philosophy displayed a more sophisticated trend. Indeed, its most prominent characteristics were attitudes of pessimism and disillusionment. One reason was that the ancient faith in the religion of Re had broken down. Men no longer believed that preserving the material remains of the Pharaoh would insure the immortality of the nation. Another was that the collapse of the united kingdom and the prevalence of social disorder and foreign invasion produced a feeling of insecurity and hopelessness. Above all, the growth of intellectual maturity made the older conceptions of life and the world appear naïve and groundless. The consequence was a tendency toward the opposite extreme of believing in nothing.

A characteristic example of the new philosophic trend was the *Song of the Harp-Player*, which one of the Pharaohs of the Eleventh Dynasty had engraved on the wall of his tomb-chapel about 2050 B.C. It expresses a philosophy of complete skepticism regarding an existence in the afterworld: "None cometh from thence that he may tell us how they fare." The gods are not recognized, except that Re is conceived as a blind, impersonal force. No importance is attached to the traditional rewards of virtue and effort; fame, riches, and power are empty delusions. Death is the common fate of Pharaoh and servant alike, and no one knows the day or the hour of its coming. The logical course for man to pursue is therefore to follow desire, to seek his pleasure while he may. But self-indulgence is not enough. One should also strive to gain a good name, by giving "bread to him who hath no field," and by other benevolent works.[5]

With the accession of the Eleventh Dynasty about 2050 B.C.,

[4] *Ibid.*, pp. 129–39.
[5] *Ibid.*, pp. 163–67.

Egypt returned to a semblance of order and prosperity. It was natural that the political philosophy of the time should reflect the welcome change. The most famous specimen of this philosophy is a work which has been given the title of the *Plea of the Eloquent Peasant.* Its authorship is unknown, but it was probably written at the behest of an intelligent Pharaoh who wanted to inculcate high standards of official morality in his subordinates and impress the people with the justice of his rule. It is composed in narrative form and relates the story of a peasant who has been robbed by an unscrupulous official. The victim appeals to the official's superiors, who, at the instance of the Pharaoh, encourage him to unburden himself of all his grievances and to expound his conception of administrative justice. In the course of his pleas the peasant contends that officers of state have the following duties: to act as the father of the orphan, the husband of the widow, and the brother of the forsaken; to ward off the robber and protect the wretched; to execute punishment upon whom it is due; to judge impartially and to speak no falsehood; and to promote such an order of harmony and prosperity that no one may suffer from hunger or cold or thirst. Few nobler conceptions of the functions of rulers have ever been set forth by political philosophers. We are not to suppose that the sentiments expressed were actually those of the peasant. The story is fictitious. The philosophy it contains reflects the ideals of an enlightened Pharaoh.

II. SCIENCE   The branches of science which first absorbed the attention of the Egyptians were astronomy and mathematics. Both were developed for practical ends—to compute the time of the Nile inundations, to lay out the plans for pyramids and temples, and to solve the intricate problems of irrigation and public control of economic functions. The Egyptians were not pure scientists; they had little interest in the nature of the physical universe as such—a fact which probably accounts for their failure to advance very far in the science of astronomy. They perfected a solar calendar, as we have already learned, mapped the heavens, identified the principal fixed stars, and achieved some success in determining accurately the positions of stellar bodies. Nearly all of these accomplishments were made in the pre-dynastic period and in the Old Kingdom. In later times the interest in astronomy waned.

The science of mathematics was more highly developed. The Egyptians laid the foundations for at least two of the common mathematical subjects—arithmetic and geometry. They devised the arithmetical operations of addition, subtraction, and division, although they never discovered how to multiply except through a series of additions. They invented the decimal system, but they had no symbol for zero. Fractions caused them some difficulty: all those with a numerator greater than one had to be broken down into a series, each with *one* as the numerator, before they could be used in

The *Plea of the Eloquent Peasant*

The character of Egyptian science; astronomy

Achievements in mathematics

46

mathematical calculations. The only exception was the fraction two-thirds, which the scribes had learned to use as it stood. The Egyptians also achieved a surprising degree of skill in mensuration, computing with accuracy the areas of triangles, rectangles, and hexagons. The ratio of the circumference of a circle to its diameter they calculated to be 3.16. They learned how to compute the volume of the pyramid and the cylinder, and even the volume of the hemisphere.

The third branch of science in which the Egyptians did some remarkable work was medicine, although progress was slow until the age of the Middle Kingdom. Early medical practice was conservative and profusely corrupted by superstition, but a document dating from about 1700 B.C. reveals a fairly adequate conception of scientific diagnosis and treatment. Egyptian physicians were frequently specialists: some were oculists; others were dentists, surgeons, specialists in diseases of the stomach, and so on. In the course of their work they made many discoveries of lasting value. They recognized the importance of the heart and had some appreciation of the significance of the pulse. They acquired a degree of skill in the treatment of fractures and performed simple operations. Unlike some peoples of later date they ascribed disease to natural causes. They discovered the value of cathartics, noted the curative properties of numerous drugs, and compiled the first *materia medica,* or catalogue of medicines. Many of their remedies, both scientific and magical, were carried into Europe by the Greeks and are still employed by the peasantry of isolated regions.

Medicine

In other scientific fields the Egyptians contributed little. Although they achieved feats which rival modern engineering, they possessed but the scantiest knowledge of physics. They knew the principle of the inclined plane, but they were ignorant of the pulley. To their credit also must be assigned considerable progress in metallurgy, the invention of the sundial, and the making of paper and glass. With all their deficiencies as pure scientists, they equaled or surpassed in actual accomplishment most of the other peoples of the ancient Near Orient.

Other scientific accomplishments

III. WRITING AND LITERATURE   The Egyptians developed their first form of writing during the pre-dynastic period. This system, known as the *hieroglyphic,* from the Greek words meaning sacred carving, was originally composed of pictographic signs denoting concrete objects. Gradually certain of these signs were conventionalized and used to represent abstract concepts. Other characters were introduced to designate separate syllables which could be combined to form words. Finally, twenty-four symbols, each representing a single consonant sound of the human voice, were added early in the Old Kingdom. Thus the hieroglyphic system of writing had come to include at an early date three separate types of characters, the pictographic, syllabic, and alphabetic.

The hieroglyphic system

The ultimate step in this evolution of writing would have been the complete separation of the alphabetic from the non-alphabetic characters and the exclusive use of the former in written communication. The Egyptians were reluctant to take this step. Their traditions of conservatism impelled them to follow old habits. Although they made frequent use of the consonant signs, they did not commonly employ them as an independent system of writing. It was left for the Phoenicians to do this some 1500 years later. Nevertheless, the Egyptians must be credited with the invention of the principle of the alphabet. It was they who first perceived the value of single symbols for the individual sounds of the human voice. The Phoenicians merely copied this principle, based their own system of writing upon it, and diffused the idea among neighboring nations. In the ultimate sense it is therefore true that the Egyptian alphabet was the parent of every other that has ever been used in the Western world.

Egyptian literature was largely philosophical and religious. The former type has already been discussed. By far the best specimens of the latter were the *Memphite Drama*, the *Royal Sun Hymn* of Ikhnaton, and the hymns of personal piety which have survived from the period of the Empire. The *Memphite Drama*, written about 3000 B.C., was a theological dialogue in which various gods discoursed on the doctrines of the solar religion. The object of the work was apparently to promote the national worship of the sun god Re. Its pervading theme was the idea that Re was the arbiter of human destiny, the author of good, and the giver of life to the "peaceful" and of death to the "guilty." The *Royal Hymn* of Ikhnaton, composed by the great reforming Pharaoh of the fourteenth century B.C., was a stately ode in praise of the majesty, providence, and justice of Aton, "the sole God, beside whom there is no other." It was the supreme embodiment of the Egyptian conception of universal monotheism.

Literature of a deeper emotional quality was exemplified by the hymns of personal piety, written during the two or three hundred years that followed the death of Ikhnaton. They likewise avow a belief in one God, but they call him by the more ancient name of Amon, and celebrate his loving kindness rather than his splendor and majesty. He is acclaimed as the "Lord of sweetness who giveth breath to every one he loveth" and bestows his tender care upon his humblest creatures. He is merciful, wise, and just, and forgives those who call upon his name. "Punish me not for my many sins" is a common supplication addressed to him. The following is a typical excerpt from one of these hymns:

> Thou, O Amon, art the lord of the silent
> Who cometh at the cry of the poor.
> When I cry to thee in my affliction,
> Then thou comest and savest me.

That thou mayest give breath to him who is bowed down,
And mayest save me lying in bondage.[6]

In addition to the philosophical and religious works, there were
many writings of a lighter sort. Folk songs of the common people at
their labors, stories of travel and adventure, odes of victory in battle, and charming love lyrics that suggest the style and imagery of
the Biblical Song of Solomon are among the several types which
have come down to us. The popular literature of Egypt is especially
significant for its influence, since much of its content was copied by
later Oriental peoples, and for the light which it throws upon the
society of the common man. It portrays the average Egyptian in his
prevailing moods of cheerful resignation and joy in the simpler
pleasures. It reveals a society comparatively free from the grosser
forms of tyranny and ignorance. We are given the impression of a
standard of living that was not indescribably poor and mean, in
which the middle classes, at least, could acquire the rudiments of an
education and thereby escape from a life of drudgery and pain.

Popular literature

5. THE MEANING OF EGYPTIAN ART

No single interpretation will suffice to explain the meaning of
Egyptian art. Its purposes were varied, and the ideals it was supposed to represent changed with the shifting tendencies of political
and social history. In general, it expressed the aspirations of a collec-
tivized national life. It was not art for art's sake, nor did it serve to
convey the individual's reactions to the problems of his personal
world. Yet there were times when the conventions of a communal
society were broken down, and the supremacy was accorded to a
spontaneous individual art that sensed the beauty of the flower or
caught the radiant idealism of a youthful face. Seldom was the
Egyptian genius for faithful reproduction of nature entirely suppressed. Even the rigid formalism of the official architecture was
commonly relieved by touches of naturalism—columns in imitation
of palm trunks, lotus-blossom capitals, and occasional statues of
Pharaohs that were not conventionalized types but true individual
portraits.

*The character
of Egyptian art*

*See color plates
at page 73*

In most civilizations where the interests of society are exalted
above those of its members, architecture is at once the most typical
and the most highly developed of the arts. Egypt was no exception.
Whether in the Old Kingdom, Middle Kingdom, or Empire it was
the problems of building construction that absorbed the talent of
the artist. Although painting and sculpture were by no means primitive, they nevertheless had as their primary function the embellishment of temples. Only at times did they rise to the status of
independent arts.

Architecture

[6] *Ibid.*, p. 315.

The Pyramids of Gizeh with the Sphinx in the Foreground. The pyramid on the right is the Great Pyramid of Khufu or Cheops.

The characteristic examples of Old Kingdom architecture were the pyramids, the first of which were built at least as early as 2700 B.C. An amazing amount of labor and skill were expended in their construction. The Greek historian Herodotus estimated that 100,000 men must have been employed for twenty years to complete the single pyramid of Khufu at Gizeh. Its total height exceeds 480 feet, and the more than two million limestone blocks it contains are fitted together with a precision which few modern masons could duplicate. Each of the blocks weighs about two and a half tons. They were evidently hewn out of rock cliffs with drills and wedges and then dragged up earthen ramps by gangs of men and pried into place.

The significance of the pyramids is not easy to comprehend. They may have been intended for the economic purpose of providing employment opportunities. Such a theory would assume that the population had increased to overcrowding, and that the resources of agriculture, mining, industry, and commerce were no longer adequate to provide a livelihood for all the people. But whatever the validity of this theory, it is hardly a complete explanation. The pyramids also had a political and religious significance. Their construction was an act of faith, the expression of an ambition to endow the state with permanence and stability. As indestructible tombs of the rulers they were believed to guarantee immortality to the people, for the Pharaoh was the embodiment of the national life. It is possible also that they were intended to serve as symbols of sun worship. As the tallest structures in Egypt they would catch the first light of the rising sun and reflect it to the valley below.

During the Middle Kingdom and the Empire the temple displaced the pyramid as the leading architectural form. No longer was preservation of the material remains of the Pharaoh considered so important, nor was there quite the same credulous faith in the identification of the ruler with the nation. On the other hand, there was the same interest in structures of massive proportions which would express the national strength and the belief in the eternity of the culture. But these structures were not tombs. The most noted examples of them were the great temples at Karnak and Luxor, built during the period of the Empire. Many of their gigantic, richly carved columns still stand as silent witnesses of a splendid architectural talent.

Egyptian temples were characterized first of all by massive size. The temple at Karnak, with a length of about 1300 feet, covered the largest area of any religious edifice ever built. Its central hall alone could contain almost any of the Gothic cathedrals of Europe. But even its enormous bulk was not enough to satisfy the passion for grandeur. Artificial devices were employed to make the building seem larger than it really was. As an example, the height of the ceiling was progressively diminished from the entrance toward the rear to create the illusion of a long perspective and therefore of a vast expanse of floor. The columns used in the temples had stupendous proportions. The largest of them were seventy feet high, with diameters in excess of twenty feet. It has been estimated that the capitals which surmounted them could furnish standing room for a hundred men.

As already mentioned, Egyptian sculpture and painting served primarily as adjuncts to architecture. The former was heavily laden with conventions that restricted its style and meaning. Statues of

Detail of the Temple of Karnak. Most of this building has collapsed or been carried away, but the huge pylons and statues give an idea of the massiveness of Egyptian temples.

Pharaohs were commonly of colossal size. Those produced during the Empire ranged in height from seventy-five to ninety feet. Some of them were colored to resemble life, and the eyes were frequently inlaid with rock crystal. The figures were nearly always rigid, with the arms folded across the chest or fixed to the sides of the body and with the eyes staring straight to the front. Countenances were generally represented as impassive, utterly devoid of emotional expression. Anatomical distortion was frequently practiced: the natural length of the thighs might be increased, the squareness of the shoulders accentuated, or all of the fingers of the hand made equal in length. A familiar example of non-naturalistic sculpture was the Sphinx. This represented the head of a Pharaoh on the body of a lion. The purpose was probably to symbolize the notion that the Pharaoh possessed the lion's qualities of strength and courage. The figures of sculpture in relief were even less in conformity with nature. The head was presented in profile, with the eye fullface; the torso was shown in the frontal position, while the legs were rendered in profile. Such were the general tendencies, but it should be noted that they were not universal. Occasionally the artist succeeded in a partial defiance of conventions, as is evidenced by the production of some highly individual likenesses of the later Pharaohs. The most notable example was a beautiful limestone head of Ikhnaton, found some years ago at Amarna, which clearly portrayed the quality of dreamy mysticism inherent in the soul of the great reformer.

The meaning of Egyptian sculpture is not hard to perceive. The colossal size of the statues of Pharaohs was doubtless intended to symbolize their power and the power of the state they represented. It is significant that the size of these statues increased as the empire expanded and the government became more absolute. The conventions of rigidity and impassiveness, which dominated not only the statues of rulers but even the sculptures of less formal description such as the figure of *The Seated Scribe*, were meant to express the timelessness and stability of the national life. Here was a nation which, according to the ideal, was not to be torn loose from its moorings by the uncertain mutations of fortune but was to remain fixed and imperturbable. The portraits of its chief men consequently must betray no anxiety, fear, or triumph, but an unvarying calmness throughout the ages. In similar fashion, the anatomical distortion can probably be interpreted as a deliberate attempt to express some national ideal. There is certainly no reason to believe that it was practiced through ignorance of the laws of proportion or inability to copy the natural form. Very likely it was intended as a denial of mortality. The eternal existence of the people might easily be thought to depend upon investing their leaders with attributes which would serve to protest their death as ordinary human beings. The most eloquent device for this purpose was representation of the

Colossus of Ramses II (XIXth Dynasty). Though almost modern in its sharp, cubist lines, this statue is typically Egyptian in the imperturbable expression of the face and the conventionalized treatment of shoulders, arms, and legs.

body of a Pharaoh with the head of a god, but the other examples of non-naturalistic portrayal probably had a similar object.

Though most of Egyptian painting has perished, that which survives is largely free from political and religious conventions. Certainly it was not dominated by them to the extent that architecture and sculpture were. The reason is perhaps to be found in the fact that painting developed late and did not have time to become weighted down with a mass of traditions. Religion did exert its influence, but in a positive manner. The best paintings were those created during the reign of Ikhnaton and immediately after. The gospel of the reforming king, with its reverence for nature as the handiwork of God, fostered a revival of realism in art which was particularly evident in painting. As a result, the murals of this period exhibit a decided talent for representation of the striking phenomena of the world of experience. They have particular merit as examples of the portrayal of movement. They caught the instant action of the wild bull leaping in the swamp, the headlong flight of the frightened stag, and the effortless swimming of ducks in the pond. Even the paintings in the great temple of Luxor made a similar appeal to the

Painting

See color plates at pages 40, 41, 73

53

senses; the blue ceiling studded with stars and the flowers and trees emblazoned on the columns and walls bore witness to the artist's appreciation of the beauty of his natural environment.

6. SOCIAL AND ECONOMIC LIFE

The social organization of Egypt was distinguished by a surprising degree of fluidity. No inflexible caste system ever developed. All men were equal in the sight of the law. Although degrees of economic inequality naturally existed, no man's status was unalterably fixed, unless he was a member of the royal family. Even serfs appear to have been capable of rising above their humble condition. Freemen quite regularly made the transition from one social order to another. Such a structure of society differed in marked degree from the stratified social regimes in other parts of the Orient—in India and Mesopotamia, for example.

During the greater part of the history of Egypt the population was divided into five classes: the royal family; the priests; the nobles; the middle class of scribes, merchants, artisans, and farmers; and the serfs. During the Empire a sixth class, the professional soldiers, was added, ranking immediately below the nobles. Thousands of slaves were captured in this period also, and these formed for a time a seventh class. Despised by freemen and serfs alike, they were forced to labor in the government quarries and on the temple estates. Gradually, however, they were enrolled in the army and even in the personal service of the Pharaoh. With these developments they ceased to constitute a separate class. The position of the various ranks of society shifted from time to time. In the Old Kingdom the nobles and priests among all of the Pharaoh's subjects held

The absence of a caste system

The principal classes

Fishing and Fowling: Wall Painting Thebes, XVIIIth Dynasty. Most of the women appear to belong to the prosperous classes, while the simple garb and insignificant size of the men indicates that they are probably slaves.

the supremacy. During the Middle Kingdom the classes of commoners came into their own. Scribes, merchants, artisans, and serfs rebelled against the nobles and wrested concessions from the government. Particularly impressive is the dominant role played by the
merchants and industrialists in this period. The establishment of the
Empire, accompanied as it was by the extension of government
functions, resulted in the ascendancy of a new nobility, made up
primarily of bureaucrats. The priests also waxed in power with the
growth of magic and superstition.

The gulf that separated the standards of living of the upper and
lower classes of Egypt was perhaps even wider than it is today in
Europe and America. The wealthy nobles lived in splendid villas The gulf between
that opened into fragrant gardens and shady groves. Their food had rich and poor

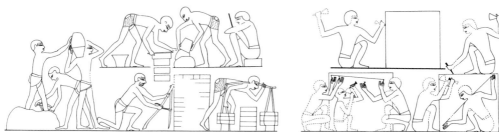

Left: *Making Sun-dried Bricks.* Nile mud (generally mixed with chaff or
straw) is being worked with a hoe, carried away in buckets and dumped in a
pile. Lying on the ground in a row are three bricks, from the last of which
a wooden mold, used in shaping them, is being lifted. An overseer with a
stick is seated close by. The finished bricks are carried off by means of a yoke
across the shoulders. From a wall-painting at Thebes about 1500 B.C.
Right: *Stonecutters Dressing Blocks.* Men with mallets and chisels are dressing
down blocks to true surfaces. Below, two of them test the accuracy of the
dressed surface. After two edges of the block are determined, a cord is
stretched between two pegs to help gauge how much remains to be chiseled
away.

all the richness and variety of sundry kinds of meat, poultry, cakes,
fruit, wine, beer, and sweets. They ate from vessels of alabaster,
gold, and silver, and adorned their persons with expensive fabrics
and costly jewels. By contrast, the life of the poor was wretched indeed. The laborers in the towns inhabited congested slums composed of mud-brick hovels with roofs of thatch. Their only furnishings were stools and boxes and a few crude pottery jars. The peasants on the great estates enjoyed a less crowded but no more
abundant life.

The basic social unit among the Egyptians was the monogamous
family. No man, not even the Pharaoh, could have more than one
lawful wife. Concubinage, however, was a socially reputable institu- The Egyptian
tion. Women occupied an unusually enviable status. Wives were not family
secluded, and there is no record of any divorce. Women could own
and inherit property and engage in business. Almost alone among **55**

Oriental peoples the Egyptians permitted women to succeed to the throne. Another extraordinary social practice was close inbreeding. The ruler as son of the great sun god was required to marry his sister or some other female of his immediate family lest the divine blood be contaminated. There is evidence that many of his subjects followed the identical custom. As yet, historians have been unable to discover any positive traces of racial degeneration produced by this practice, probably for the reason that the Egyptian stock was genetically sound to begin with.

The educational system of this ancient people was about what one would expect in a highly integrated society. Attached to the treasury were a number of public schools equipped for the training of

The educational system

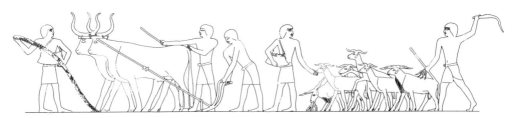

Sowing Seed and Working It into the Soil. From a bag which he wears over his left shoulder, the sower casts seed under the feet of cattle yoked to a plow. The plow is here used to harrow the soil. While one laborer guides the cows with a stick, another guides the plow straight and keeps the plowshare in the ground by bearing down on the handles. Sheep are then driven across the field to trample in the seed. From wall paintings at Sheikh Saïd, about 2700 B.C.

the thousands of scribes whose services were necessary in the keeping of records and accounts and in the administration of government functions. Many of them were also employed in a private capacity by the owners of the landed estates and by the leaders of the business world. Admission to these schools was open to any promising youth regardless of class. Apparently instruction was provided free of charge by the government because of the vital need for trained men. None but thoroughly utilitarian subjects had any place in the curriculum; the purpose was not education in the broader sense, but practical training. In spite of their limitations, these schools did provide for the poor but talented youth an avenue of escape from a life of hopeless drudgery.

The Egyptian economic system rested primarily upon an agrarian basis. Agriculture was diversified and highly developed, and the soil yielded excellent crops of wheat, barley, millet, vegetables, fruits, flax, and cotton. Theoretically the land was the property of the king, but in the earlier periods he granted most of it to his subjects, so that in actual practice it was largely in the possession of individuals. Commerce did not amount to much before 2000 B.C., but after

Agriculture, trade, and industry

that date it grew rapidly to a position of first-rate importance. A flourishing trade was carried on with the island of Crete, with Phoenicia, Palestine, and Syria. The chief articles of export consisted of wheat, linen fabrics, and fine pottery. Imports were confined largely to gold, silver, ivory, and lumber. Of no less significance than commerce was manufacturing as a branch of economic life. As early as 3000 B.C. large numbers of people were already engaged in industrial pursuits, mostly in separate crafts. In later times factories were established, employing twenty or more persons under one roof, and with some degree of division of labor. The leading industries were quarrying, shipbuilding, and the manufacture of pottery, glass, and textiles.

From an early date the Egyptians made progress in the perfection of instruments of business. They knew the elements of accounting and bookkeeping. Their merchants issued orders and receipts for goods. They invented deeds for property, written contracts, and wills. While they had no system of coinage, they had nevertheless attained a money economy. Rings of copper or gold of definite weight circulated as media of exchange. This Egyptian ring-money is apparently the oldest currency in the history of civilizations. Probably it was not used except for larger transactions. The simple dealings of the peasants and poorer townsfolk doubtless continued on a basis of barter.

The development of instruments of business

The Egyptian economic system was always collectivistic. From the very beginning the energies of the people had been drawn into socialized channels. The interests of the individual and the interests of society were conceived as identical. The productive activities of the entire nation revolved around the huge state enterprises, and the government remained by far the largest employer of labor. It should be noted, though, that during the Old and Middle Kingdoms this collectivism was not all-inclusive; a considerable sphere was left for private initiative. Merchants conducted their own businesses; many of the craftsmen had their own shops; and as time went on, larger and larger numbers of peasants gained the status of independent farmers. The government continued to operate the quarries and mines, to build pyramids and temples, and to farm the royal estates.

Economic collectivism

The extreme development of state control came with the founding of the Empire. The growth of a military absolutism and the increasing frequency of wars of conquest augmented the need for revenue and for unlimited production of goods. To fulfill this need the government extended its control over every department of economic life. The entire agricultural land again became the property of the Pharaoh, in fact as well as in theory. Although large sections of it were granted to favorites of the king, most of it was worked by royal serfs and slaves. The free middle class of earlier days now largely disappeared. The services of craftsmen were conscripted for the erection of magnificent temples and for the manufacture of im-

The extreme development of state control under the Empire

plements of war, while foreign trade became a state monopoly. As the Empire staggered toward its downfall, the government absorbed more and more of the economic activities of the people.

Except during the reign of Ikhnaton, a corrupt alliance existed between the Pharaohs of the Empire and the priests. Greedy for power and plunder, the members of the ecclesiastical hierarchy supported the kings in their ambitions for despotic rule. As a reward they were granted exemption from taxation and a generous share of the national wealth. War captives were turned over to them in such numbers that they actually held two per cent of the population of the country as temple slaves. In addition, they received from their generous patrons one-seventh of the arable land, hundreds of thousands of cattle, and nearly a hundred ships. They employed a great host of artisans in the manufacture of amulets and funerary equipment, which they sold at tremendous profit to the worshipers. Without question these priestly enterprises meant a serious drain on the national resources and thereby contributed to economic and social decay. Too large a proportion of the wealth of Egypt was being squandered on sterile projects of the church and the state, on other-worldly preparations, and on the conquest of an empire.

Defects in the economic system

7. THE EGYPTIAN ACHIEVEMENT AND ITS IMPORTANCE TO US

Few civilizations of ancient times surpassed the Egyptian in importance to the modern world. Even the influence of the Hebrews was not much greater. From the land of the Pharaohs came the germ and the stimulus for numerous intellectual achievements of later centuries. Important elements of philosophy, mathematics, science, and literature had their beginnings there. The Egyptians also developed one of the oldest systems of jurisprudence and political theory. They perfected the achievements of irrigation, engineering, and the making of pottery, glass, and paper. They were one of the first peoples to have any clear conception of art for other than utilitarian purposes, and they originated architectural principles that were destined for extensive use in subsequent history. Notable among these were the column, the colonnade, the lintel, the obelisk, and the clerestory, a low wall with windows looking out upon the roof of the main part of the building.

Egyptian contributions: (1) intellectual and artistic

More significant still were the Egyptian contributions in the fields of religion and individual and social ethics. Aside from the Persians, the dwellers on the banks of the Nile were the only people of the ancient world to build a national religion around the doctrine of personal immortality. Egyptian priests and sages likewise were the first to preach universal monotheism, the providence of God, forgiveness of sins, and rewards and punishments after death. Finally, Egyptian ethical theory was the source from which various nations

(2) religious and ethical

derived standards of personal and social morality; for it embraced not only the ordinary prohibitions of lying, theft, and murder, but included also the exalted ideals of justice, benevolence, and the equal rights of all men.

SELECTED READINGS

· *Items so designated are available in paperbound editions.*

· Alfred, Cyril, *The Egyptians*, New York, 1963 (Praeger).

Breasted, James H., *The Dawn of Conscience*, New York, 1934. An excellent account of the development of religious and ethical concepts.

———, *History of Egypt*, New York, 1912. Still one of the best histories of ancient Egypt.

· Cottrell, Leonard, *Life under the Pharaohs*, New York, 1960 (Tempo, 1964).

· Desroches-Noblecourt, Christiane, *Egyptian Wall Paintings*, New York, 1962 (Mentor).

· Edwards, I. E. S., *The Pyramids of Egypt*, Baltimore, 1962 (Penguin).

· Emery, W. B., *Archaic Egypt*, Baltimore, 1961 (Penguin).

· Frankfort, Henri, *et al.*, *Before Philosophy*, Baltimore, 1949 (Penguin). A splendid account of early man's thinking.

Glanville, S. R. K., *The Legacy of Ancient Egypt*, Oxford, 1957.

· Kramer, S. N., *Mythologies of the Ancient World*, New York, 1961 (Anchor).

· Lloyd, Seton, *The Art of the Ancient Near East*, New York, 1962 (Praeger).

Moret, Alexandre, *The Nile and Egyptian Civilization*, New York, 1928. Interesting in its contrast with Breasted.

· Moscati, Sabatino, *The Face of the Ancient Orient*, New York, 1962 (Anchor).

Shorter, A. W., *Everyday Life in Ancient Egypt*, London, 1932. One of the few works of its kind, therefore valuable.

· Smith, W. S., *Art and Architecture of Ancient Egypt*, Baltimore, 1958 (Penguin).

· Steindorff, G., and Steele, K. C., *When Egypt Ruled the East*, Chicago, 1942 (Phoenix). A useful supplement to Breasted.

· Wilson, J. A., *The Burden of Egypt*, Chicago, 1951. An excellent interpretation. Also available in paperback under the title, *The Culture of Ancient Egypt* (Phoenix).

SOURCE MATERIALS

Breasted, J. H., *Ancient Records of Egypt*, Chicago, 1929, 5 vols.

· ———, *Development of Religion and Thought in Ancient Egypt*, Gloucester, Mass., 1959 (Torchbook).

Budge, E. A. W., *Osiris and the Egyptian Resurrection*, New York, 1911, 2 vols.

· Pritchard, J. B., ed., *Ancient Near Eastern Texts*, Princeton, 1950 (Princeton University Press).

CHAPTER 3

The Mesopotamian Civilization

If a son strike his father, they shall cut off his fingers.

If a man destroy the eye of another man, they shall destroy his eye.

If one break a man's bone, they shall break his bone.

If one destroy the eye of a freeman or break the bone of a freeman, he shall pay one mina of silver.

If one destroy the eye of a man's slave or break a bone of a man's slave he shall pay one-half his price.
——*The Code of Hammurabi*, lines 195–199.

The other of the most ancient civilizations was that which began in the Tigris-Euphrates valley at least as early as 4000 B.C. This civilization was formerly called the Babylonian or Babylonian-Assyrian civilization. It is now known, however, that the civilization was not founded by either the Babylonians or the Assyrians but by an earlier people called the Sumerians. It seems better, therefore, to use the name Mesopotamian to cover the whole civilization, even though Mesopotamia is sometimes applied only to the northern portion of the land between the two rivers. The Mesopotamian civilization was unlike the Egyptian in many respects. Its political history was marked by sharper interruptions. Its ethnic composition was less homogeneous, and its social and economic structure gave wider scope to individual initiative.

The differences in ideals and in religious and social attitudes were perhaps more fundamental. The Egyptian culture was predominantly ethical, the Mesopotamian legalistic. The Egyptian outlook on life, except during the Middle Kingdom, was generally one of cheerful resignation, comparatively free from the cruder superstitions. By contrast, the Mesopotamian view was gloomy, pessimistic, and enthralled by morbid fears. Where the native of Egypt believed in immortality and dedicated a large part of his energy to preparation for the life to come, his Mesopotamian contemporary lived in the present and cherished few hopes regarding his fate beyond the grave. Finally, the civilization of the Nile valley embodied concepts of monotheism, a religion of love, and of social equalitarianism; that of the Tigris-Euphrates was more selfish and practical. Its religion seldom evolved beyond the stage of primitive polytheism, and its arts bore few of the natural and personal qualities of the Egyptian.

On the other hand, there were similarities too striking to be ignored. Both civilizations made progress in ethical theory and in concepts of social justice. Both had their evils of slavery and imperialism, of oppressive kings and greedy priests. Both had common problems of irrigation and land boundaries; and, as a result, both made notable progress in the sciences, especially in mathematics. Finally, rivalry among small states led eventually to consolidation and to the growth of mighty empires, especially in the case of Mesopotamia.

1. FROM THE SUMERIAN TO THE PERSIAN CONQUEST

The Sumerians

The pioneers in the development of the Mesopotamian civilization were the people known as Sumerians, who settled in the lower Tigris-Euphrates valley between 5000 and 4000 B.C. Their precise origin is unknown, but they seem to have come from the plateau of central Asia. They spoke a language unrelated to any now known, although their culture bore a certain resemblance to the earliest civilization of India. With little or no difficulty they subjugated the natives already in the lower valley, a mysterious people who were just emerging from the Neolithic stage.

Sumerian political history

About 2400 B.C. the Sumerians were conquered by Sargon I, the ruler of a nation of Semites who had established themselves in a section of the valley known as Akkad. This conquest was the prelude to the founding of the first great Semitic empire in western Asia, for soon afterward Sargon conquered the Elamites and all of northern Syria to the Mediterranean Sea. But like so many states that have had their roots in conquest, this empire was short-lived. Sargon's death was the signal for the first of a series of Sumerian revolts. Although these revolts were suppressed, they weakened the state and paved the way for its overthrow by the Guti, a fierce barbarian people from the north. Finally, about 2150 B.C., the Sumerians, under the leadership of the city of Ur, rebelled successfully against the rule of the Guti and established their power over all of Sumer and Akkad.

The rise and fall of the Old Babylonians

The new Sumerian empire did not survive long. It was annexed by the Elamites in the twenty-first century and about 1950 B.C. was conquered by a Semitic people known as the Amorites, who had come in from the fringes of the Arabian desert. Since they made the village of Babylon the capital of their empire they are commonly called the Babylonians, or the Old Babylonians, to distinguish them

from the Neo-Babylonians or Chaldeans who occupied the valley much later. The rise of the Old Babylonians inaugurated the second important stage of the Tigris-Euphrates civilization. Although most of the Sumerian culture survived, Sumerian dominance was now at an end. The Babylonians established an autocratic state and during the reign of their most famous king, Hammurabi, extended their dominion north to Assyria. But after his time their empire gradually declined until it was finally overthrown by the Kassites about 1650 B.C.

With the downfall of Old Babylonia a period of retrogression set in which lasted for 600 years. The Kassites were barbarians with no interest in the cultural achievements of their predecessors. Their lone contribution was the introduction of the horse into the Tigris-Euphrates valley. The old culture would have died out entirely had it not been for its partial adoption by another Semitic people who, as early as 3000 B.C., had founded a tiny kingdom on the plateau of Assur some 500 miles up the Tigris River. These people came to be called the Assyrians, and their ultimate rise to power marked the beginning of the third stage in the development of the Mesopotamian civilization. They began to expand about 1300 B.C. and soon afterward made themselves masters of the whole northern valley. In the tenth century they overturned what was left of Kassite power in Babylonia. Their empire reached its height in the eighth and seventh centuries under Sargon II (722–705 B.C.), Sennacherib (705–681), and Assurbanipal (668–626). It had now come to include nearly all of the civilized world of that time. One after another, Syria, Phoenicia, the Kingdom of Israel, and Egypt had fallen victims to Assyrian military prowess. Only the little Kingdom of Judah was able to withstand the hosts of Nineveh, probably because of an outbreak of pestilence in the ranks of Sennacherib's army.[1] *The Kassites and the Assyrians*

Brilliant though the successes of the Assyrians were, they did not endure. So rapidly were new territories annexed that the empire soon reached an unmanageable size. The Assyrians' genius for government was far inferior to their appetite for conquest. Subjugated nations chafed under the cruel despotism that had been forced upon them and, as the empire gave signs of cracking from within, determined to regain their freedom. The death blow was delivered by the Kaldi or Chaldeans, a nation of Semites who had settled southeast of the valley of the two rivers. Under the leadership of Nabopolassar, who had served the Assyrian emperors in the capacity of a provincial governor, they organized a revolt and finally captured Nineveh in 612 B.C. *The downfall of the Assyrians and the rise of the Chaldeans*

Nabopolassar was succeeded by his son Nebuchadnezzar, who ruled until 562 B.C. During the reign of the latter the Chaldeans rose to the mastery of a new cosmopolitan empire in the Near Orient. The last vestiges of Assyrian authority were annihilated in all of the *The Chaldean empire*

[1] Hebrew prophets declared that an angel of the Lord visited the camp of the Assyrians by night and slew 185,000 of them. II Kings 19:35.

more valuable sections of the Fertile Crescent. Even the Kingdom of Judah, which had successfully defied the Assyrian "wolves," fell an easy victim to the relentless energy of Nebuchadnezzar. The temple at Jerusalem was looted and burned, King Zedekiah was blinded, and he and several thousands of his countrymen were carried off into captivity in Babylon.

But the empire of the Chaldeans did not long survive the death of its greatest ruler. During the reigns of his successors the nation turned to indulgence in antiquarian interests—to the worship of the achievements of the Old Babylonians, whom they ignorantly revered as their ancestors. Jealous contention arose between the kings and the priests; and the Medes, a tributary nation on the eastern border, began to give trouble. But the major reason for the downfall of the Chaldean empire was the insatiable greed of its founder. It was lust for power and glory that led him to repeat the blunders of the Assyrian monarchs before him in conquering an unwieldy empire and in humiliating proud peoples. The handwriting on the wall which Belshazzar is supposed to have seen at his famous feast should have been intended for Nebuchadnezzar.[2]

In 539 B.C. the empire of the Chaldeans fell, after an existence of less than a century. It was overthrown by Cyrus the Persian, as he himself declared, "without a battle and without fighting." The easy victory appears to have been made possible by assistance from the Jews and by a conspiracy of the priests of Babylon to deliver the city to Cyrus as an act of vengeance against the Chaldean king, whose policies they did not like. Members of other influential classes appear also to have looked upon the Persians as deliverers.

Although the Persian state incorporated all of the territories that had once been embraced by the Mesopotamian empires, it included many other provinces besides. It was the vehicle, moreover, of a new and different culture. The downfall of Chaldea must therefore be taken as marking the end of Mesopotamian political history.

2. SUMERIAN ORIGINS OF THE CIVILIZATION

More than to any other people, the Mesopotamian civilization owed its character to the Sumerians. Much of what used to be ascribed to the Babylonians and Assyrians is now known to have been developed by the nation that preceded them. The system of writing was of Sumerian origin; likewise the religion, the laws, and a great deal of the science and commercial practice. Only in the evolution of government and military tactics and in the development of the arts was the originating talent of the later conquerors particularly manifest.

Through the greater part of their history the Sumerians lived in a loose confederation of city-states, united only for military purposes.

[2] Compare the Old Testament account in Daniel 5:24-31.

At the head of each was a *patesi,* who combined the functions of chief priest, commander of the army, and superintendent of the irrigation system. Occasionally one of the more ambitious of these rulers would extend his power over a number of cities and assume the title of king. Not until about 2000 B.C., however, were all of the Sumerian people united under a single authority of the same nationality as themselves.

The Sumerian economic pattern was relatively simple and permitted a wider scope for individual enterprise than was generally allowed in Egypt. The land was never the exclusive property of the king either in theory or in practice. Neither was trade or industry a monopoly of the government. The temples, however, seem to have fulfilled many of the functions of a collectivist state. They owned a

The Ancient Sumerian City of Ur as seen from the air.

large portion of the land and operated business enterprises. Because the priests alone had the technical knowledge to calculate the seasons and lay out canals, they controlled the irrigation system. The masses of the people had little they could call their own. Many of them were serfs, but even those who were technically free were little better off, forced as they were to pay high rents and to labor on public works. Slavery in the strict sense of the word was not an important institution. Most of those referred to as slaves were really serfs, who had mortgaged their persons in payment of debt. They do not appear to have been an especially degraded class. They could own property, work for wages when their master did not need them, and even marry free women. Doubtless the great majority of them were of Sumerian stock, a fact which helps to explain their rather liberal treatment.

Agriculture was the chief economic pursuit of most of the citizens, and the Sumerians were excellent farmers. By virtue of their **65**

Diorama of a Part of Ur about 2000 B.C. A modern archaeologist's conception. Walls are omitted to show interiors at left.

knowledge of irrigation they produced amazing crops of cereal grains and subtropical fruits. Since most of the land was divided into large estates held by the rulers, the priests, and the army officers, the average rural citizen was either a tenant farmer or a serf. Commerce was the second most important source of the nation's wealth. A flourishing trade was established with all of the surrounding countries, revolving around the exchange of metals and timber from the north and west for agricultural products and manufactured goods from the lower valley. Nearly all of the familiar adjuncts of business were highly developed; bills, receipts, notes, and letters of credit were regularly used. Custom required that deals be confirmed by written agreements, signed by witnesses. Merchants employed salesmen who traveled to distant regions and sold goods on commission. In all major transactions bars or ingots of gold and silver served as money, the standard unit of exchange being the silver shekel, approximately equal in weight to a modern 50-cent piece but with a much greater purchasing power.

The most distinctive achievement of the Sumerians was their system of law. It was the product of a gradual evolution of local usage, but it was finally incorporated into a comprehensive code after the middle of the third millennium. Only a few fragments of this law have survived in their original form, but the famous code of Hammurabi, the Babylonian king, is now recognized to have been little more than a revision of the code of the Sumerians. Ultimately this code became the basis of the laws of nearly all of the Semites—Babylonians, Assyrians, Chaldeans, and Hebrews.

The following may be regarded as the essential features of the Sumerian law:

(1) The *lex talionis*, or law of retaliation in kind—"an eye for an eye, a tooth for a tooth, a limb for a limb," etc.

(2) Semiprivate administration of justice. It was incumbent upon the victim himself or his family to bring the offender to justice. The court served principally as an umpire in the dispute between the plaintiff and defendant, not as an agency of the state to maintain public security, although constables attached to the court might assist in the execution of the sentence.

(3) Inequality before the law. The code divided the population into three classes: patricians or aristocrats; burghers or commoners; serfs and slaves. Penalties were graded according to the rank of the victim, but also in some cases according to the rank of the offender. The killing or maiming of a patrician was a much more serious offense than a similar crime committed against a burgher or a slave. On the other hand, when a patrician was the offender he was punished *more severely* than a man of inferior status would be for the same crime. The origin of this curious rule was probably to be found in considerations of military discipline. Since the patricians were army officers and therefore the chief defenders of the state, they could not be permitted to give vent to their passions or to indulge in riotous conduct.

(4) Inadequate distinction between accidental and intentional homicide. A person responsible for killing another accidentally did not escape penalty, as he would under modern law, but had to pay a fine to the family of the victim, apparently on the theory that children were the property of their fathers and wives the property of their husbands.

Quite as much as their law, the religion of the Sumerians illuminates their social attitudes and the character of their culture. They did not succeed in developing a very exalted religion; yet it occupied an important place in their lives. To begin with, it was polytheistic and anthropomorphic. They believed in a number of gods and goddesses, each a distinct personality with human attributes. Shamash, the sun god; Enlil, the lord of the rain and wind; and Ishtar, the goddess of the female principle in nature, were only a few of them. Although the Sumerians had a special deity of the plague in the person of the god Nergal, their religion was really monistic in the sense that they regarded all of their deities as capable of both good and evil. Shamash, for example, as the god of the sun gave warmth and light for the benefit of man; but he might also send his burning rays to bake the soil and to wither the tender plants before they had time to yield their fruits. Religious dualism, involving a belief in entirely separate divinities of good and evil, did not appear in the Mesopotamian civilization until much later.

The character of Sumerian religion

The Sumerian religion was a religion for this world exclusively; it offered no hope for a blissful, eternal afterlife. The afterlife was a mere temporary existence in a dreary, shadowy place which later came to be called Sheol. Here the ghosts of the dead lingered for a time, perhaps a generation or so, and then disappeared. No one

A religion for this world, not for the next

Male Votive Figure, Sumer.
This statue of white gypsum,
colored with bitumen, shows
the conventionalized treatment
of hair and beard and the huge,
staring eyes common to Mesopotamian art. Observe also the
immense thumbs and the fingers
of equal length.

could look forward to resurrection in another world and a joyous
eternal existence as a recompense for the evils of this life; the victory of the grave was complete. In accordance with these beliefs the
Sumerians bestowed only limited care upon the bodies of their
dead. No mummification was practiced, and no elaborate tombs
were built. Corpses were commonly interred beneath the floor of
the house without a coffin and with comparatively few articles for
the use of the ghost.

Spiritual content had no place of conspicuous importance in this
religion. As we have seen, the gods were not spiritual beings but

A religion
neither ethical
nor spiritual

creatures cast in the human mold, with most of the weaknesses and
passions of mortal men. Nor were the purposes of the religion any
more spiritual. It provided no blessings in the form of solace, uplift
of the soul, or oneness with God. If it benefited man at all, it did so
chiefly in the form of material gain—abundant harvests and prosperity in business. At the same time, the religion did, at least, have an
ethical content. All the major deities in the Sumerian pantheon were
extolled in hymns as lovers of truth, goodness, and justice. The goddess Nanshe, for example, was said "to comfort the orphan, to make
disappear the widow, to set up a place of destruction for the
mighty." Yet the same deities who personified these noble ideals
created such evils as falsehood and strife, and endowed every human

Fragments of Jewelry Found at Ur in Two Graves of Ladies-in-Waiting to the Queen. The materials used are gold, carnelian, and lapis lazuli. Dating from 3500–2800 B.C., it is the oldest jewelry in the world.

being with a sinful nature. "Never," it was said, "has a sinless child been born to its mother." [3]

A dominant idea in the Sumerian religion was the notion that man was created in order that he might serve the gods—not merely by worshipping them, but also by giving them food. This notion was revealed in the famous Creation and Flood epics, which provided the framework for the much later Hebrew stories in the Old Testament. The Creation epic related the magic triumph of the god Marduk over the jealous and cowardly gods who had created him, the formation of the world out of the body of one of his slain rivals, and finally, in order that the gods might be fed, the making of man out of clay and dragon's blood. The whole account was crude and revolting, with nothing in it to appeal to a spiritual or moral sense. Almost as barbarous was the Sumerian version of the Flood. Grown jealous of man, the gods decided to destroy the whole race of mortals by drowning. One of their number, however, betrayed the secret to a favorite inhabitant of the earth, instructing him to build an ark for the salvation of himself and his kind. The flood raged for seven days, until the whole earth was covered with water. Even the gods "crouched like a dog on the wall." Finally the tumult was stilled and the waters subsided. The favored man came forth from the ark and offered grateful sacrifice. As a reward he was given "life like a god" and translated to "the place where the sun rises."

In the field of intellectual endeavor the Sumerians achieved no small distinction. They produced a system of writing which was destined to be used for a thousand years after the downfall of their nation. This was the celebrated *cuneiform* writing, consisting of wedge-shaped characters imprinted on clay tablets with a square-tipped reed. At first a pictographic system, it was gradually transformed into an aggregate of syllabic and phonetic signs, some 350 in number. No alphabet was ever developed out of it. The Sumerians wrote nothing that could be called philosophy, but they did make

The Creation and Flood epics

Intellectual achievements

[3] S. N. Kramer, *History Begins at Sumer,* pp. 106–107.

some notable beginnings in science. In mathematics, for example, they surpassed the Egyptians in every field except geometry. They discovered the processes of multiplication and division and even the extraction of square and cube root. Their systems of numeration and of weights and measures were duodecimal, with the number sixty as the most common unit. They invented the water clock and the lunar calendar, the latter an inaccurate division of the year into months based upon cycles of the moon. In order to bring it into harmony with the solar year, an extra month had to be added from time to time. Astronomy was little more than astrology, and medicine was a curious compound of herbalism and magic. The reper-

The Great Ziggurat, or flat-topped temple, at Ur.

tory of the physician consisted primarily of charms to exorcise the evil spirits which were believed to be the cause of the disease.

The supreme literary achievement of the Sumerians was the *Gilgamesh Epic*, which in continuous form dates from about 2000, though portions of it are much older. It relates the activities of Gilgamesh, a legendary king of insatiable appetites who tyrannizes the people of Erech. Its themes are common to literature throughout the ages—the quest for fame, the need for friendship, the longings and satisfactions of love, the fear of death, and the desire for immortality.

As artists, the Sumerians excelled in metalwork, gem carving, and sculpture. They produced some remarkable specimens of naturalistic art in their weapons, vessels, jewelry, and animal representations, which revealed alike a technical skill and a gift of imagination. Evidently religious conventions had not yet imposed any paralyzing in-

Sumerian
literature

fluence, and consequently the artist was still free to follow his own impulses. Architecture, on the other hand, was distinctly inferior, probably because of the limitations enforced by the scarcity of good building materials. Since there was no stone in the valley, the architect had to depend upon sun-dried brick. The characteristic Sumerian edifice, extensively copied by their Semitic successors, was the *ziggurat*, a terraced tower set on a platform and surmounted by a shrine. Its construction was massive, its lines were monotonous, and little architectural ingenuity was exhibited in it. The royal tombs and private houses showed more originality. It was in them that the Sumerian inventions of the arch, the vault, and the dome were regularly employed, and the column was used occasionally.

3. OLD BABYLONIAN "CONTRIBUTIONS"

Although the Old Babylonians were an alien nation, they had lived long enough in close contact with the Sumerians to be influenced profoundly by them. They had no culture of their own worthy of the name when they came into the valley, and in general they simply appropriated what the Sumerians had already developed. With so excellent a foundation to build upon, they should have made remarkable progress; but such was not the case. When they ended their history, the state of civilization in the Tigris-Euphrates valley was little more advanced than when they began.

First among the significant changes which the Old Babylonians made in their cultural inheritance may be mentioned the political and legal. As military conquerors holding in subjection numerous vanquished nations, they found it necessary to establish a consolidated state. Vestiges of the old system of local autonomy were swept away, and the power of the king of Babylon was made supreme. Kings became gods, or at least claimed divine origin. A system of royal taxation was adopted as well as compulsory military service. The system of law was also changed to conform to the new condition of centralized despotism. The list of crimes against the state was enlarged, and the king's officers assumed a more active role in apprehending and punishing offenders, although it was still impossible for any criminal to be pardoned without the consent of the victim or the victim's family. The severity of penalties was decidedly increased, particularly for crimes involving any suggestion of treason or sedition. Such apparently trivial offenses as "gadding about" and "disorderly conduct of a tavern" were made punishable by death, probably on the assumption that they would be likely to foster disloyal activities. Whereas under the Sumerian law the harboring of fugitive slaves was punishable merely by a fine, the Babylonian law made it a capital crime. According to the Sumerian code, the slave who disputed his master's rights over him was to be sold; the Code of Hammurabi prescribed that he should have his ear cut off. Adultery was also made a capital offense, whereas under the Sumerian law it did not even necessarily result in divorce. In a few particulars the new system of law revealed some improvement. Wives and children sold for debt could not be held in bondage for longer than four years, and a female slave who had borne her master a child could not be sold at all.

The Old Babylonian laws also reflect a more extensive development of business than that which existed in the preceding culture. That a large middle class traded for profit and enjoyed a privileged position in society is evidenced by the fact that the commercial provisions of Hammurabi's code were based upon the principle of "Let the buyer beware." The Babylonian rulers did not believe in a regime of free competition, however. Trade, banking, and industry were subject to elaborate regulation by the state. There were laws regarding partnership, storage, and agency; laws respecting deeds, wills, and the taking of interest on money; and a host of others. For a deal to be negotiated without a written contract or without witnesses was punishable by death. Agriculture, which was still the occupation of a majority of the citizens, did not escape regulation. The code provided penalties for failure to cultivate a field and for neglect of dikes and canals. Both government ownership and private tenure of land were permitted; but, regardless of the status of the owner, the tenant farmer was required to pay two-thirds of all he produced as rent.

Religion at the hands of the Old Babylonians underwent numerous changes both superficial and profound. Deities that had been venerated by the Sumerians were now neglected and new ones exalted in their stead. Marduk, originally the local god of the town of Babylon, was elevated to the highest position in the pantheon. Ishtar remained the chief goddess. Tammuz, her brother and lover, who had been of no special significance in the Sumerian religion, now became the third most important divinity. His death in the autumn and resurrection in the spring symbolized the death and rebirth of vegetation. But the death and resurrection of the god had more than a symbolic meaning; vaguely at least they were conceived as the real causes of the nature processes themselves, and the god's rites were a form of magic. They carried no spiritual significance, however, conveying no promise of the resurrection of man from the dead or of personal immortality. The Old Babylonians were no more otherwordly in their outlook than the Sumerians. The religions of both peoples were fundamentally materialistic.

Equally noteworthy was an increase in superstition. Astrology, divination, and other forms of magic took on added significance. A morbid consciousness of sin gradually displaced the essentially amoral attitude of the Sumerians. In addition, an increased emphasis was placed upon the worship of demons. Nergal, the god of the plague, came to be envisaged as a hideous monster seeking every

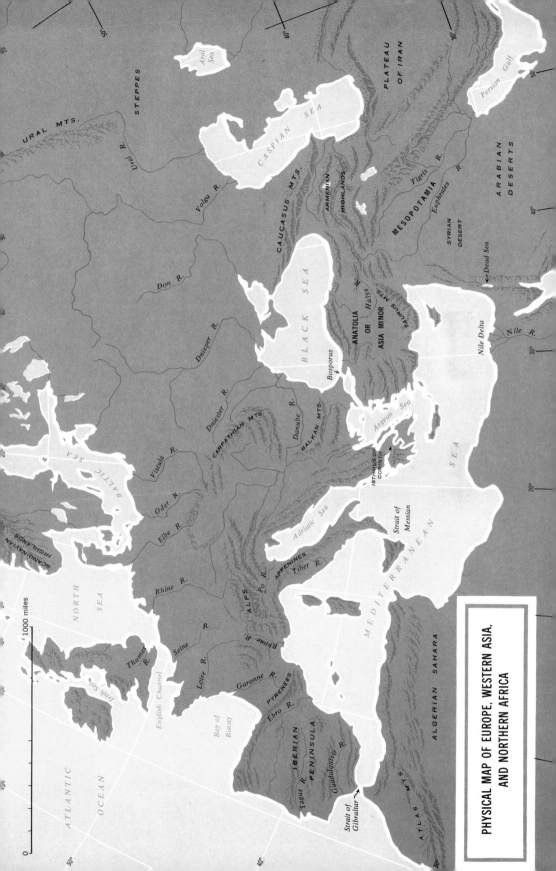

PHYSICAL MAP OF EUROPE, WESTERN ASIA, AND NORTHERN AFRICA

Head of Ramses II, 1324–1258 B.C.

Part of the Egyptian "Book of the Dead." A collection of magic formulas to enable the deceased to gain admission to the realm of Osiris and to enjoy its eternal benefits.

Stele or Grave Marker. It shows the deceased being presented to the Sun god on his throne. She is holding her heart in her hand.

A hieroglyphic character for the idea "Millions of Years," 500–330 B.C.

Bronze Bull, Symbol of Strength. Arabian, VI cent. B.C.

A carved sandstone capital, ca. 370 B.C., representing a bundle of papyrus reeds.

Panel of Glazed Brick, Babylon, Sixth Century B.C. An ornamental relief on a background of earth brown. The lion is in blue, white, and yellow glazes.

chance to strike down his victims. Hordes of other demons and malevolent spirits lurked in the darkness and rode through the air bringing terror and destruction to all in their path. Against them there was no defense except sacrifices and magic charms. If the Old Babylonians did not invent witchcraft, they were at least the first "civilized" people to magnify it to serious proportions. Their laws invoked the death penalty against it, and there is evidence that the power of witches was widely feared. Whether the growth of demonology and witchcraft was a result of the increasing unhealthfulness of the climate of the Tigris-Euphrates valley, or of the needs of a centralized, conquering state to inspire fear in its subjects is a question which cannot be answered; but it is probable that the latter is the chief explanation.

There seems to be little doubt that intellectually and artistically the Mesopotamian civilization suffered a partial decline during the period of Babylonian rule. This was not the first instance of cultural retrogression in history, but it was one of the most pronounced. Nothing of great importance was added to the scientific discoveries of the Sumerians, except for advancement in mathematics; they discovered, for example, the solution of quadratic equations. Literature showed some improvement over the earlier writings. The *Gilgamesh Epic*, for instance, was embellished and enlarged. Although most of the legends themselves were of Sumerian origin, it was Babylonian poets who wove them into powerful descriptive style. A kind of prototype of the Book of Job, the so-called *Babylonian Job*, was also written in this period. It relates the story of a pious sufferer who is afflicted he knows not why, and it contains some mature reflections on the helplessness of man and the impenetrable mysteries of the universe. As an example of Oriental philosophy it is not without merit. The graphic arts, on the other hand, definitely deteri-

The decline of intellect and the arts

orated. The Babylonians lacked the creative interest and talent to surpass the fresh and ingenious carving and engraving of the Sumerians. Moreover, sculpture fell under the domination of religious and political conventions, with the result that originality was stifled.

4. THE METAMORPHOSIS UNDER ASSYRIA

The evolution of Assyrian supremacy

Of all the peoples of the Mesopotamian area after the time of the Sumerians, the Assyrians went through the most completely independent evolution. For several centuries they had lived a comparatively isolated existence on top of their small plateau in the upper valley of the Tigris. Eventually they came under the influence of the Babylonians, but not until after the course of their own history had been partially fixed. As a consequence, the period of Assyrian supremacy (from about 1300 B.C. to 612 B.C.) had more nearly a peculiar character than any other era of Mesopotamian history.

A nation of warriors

The Assyrians were preeminently a nation of warriors; not because they were racially different from any of the other Semites, but because of the special conditions of their own environment. The limited resources of their original home and the constant danger of attack from hostile nations around them forced the development of warlike habits and imperial ambitions. It is therefore not strange that their greed for territory should have known no limits. The more they conquered, the more they felt they had to conquer, in order to protect what they had already gained. Every success excited ambition and riveted the chains of militarism more firmly than ever. Disaster was inevitable.

Features of Assyrian militarism

The exigencies of war determined the whole character of the Assyrian system. The state was a great military machine. The army commanders were at once the richest and the most powerful class in the country. Not only did they share in the plunder of war, but they were frequently granted huge estates as rewards for victory. At least one of them, Sargon II, dared to usurp the throne. The military establishment itself represented the last word in preparedness. The standing army greatly exceeded in size that of any other nation of the Near Orient. New and improved armaments and techniques of fighting gave to the Assyrian soldiers unparalleled advantages. Iron swords, heavy bows, long lances, battering rams, fortresses on wheels, and metal breastplates, shields, and helmets were only a few examples of their superior equipment.

Terrorism

But swords and spears and engines of war were not their only instruments of combat. As much as anything else the Assyrians depended upon frightfulness as a means of overcoming their enemies. Upon soldiers captured in battle, and sometimes upon noncombatants as well, they inflicted unspeakable cruelties—skinning them alive, impaling them on stakes, cutting off ears, noses, and sex organs, and then exhibiting the mutilated victims in cages for the benefit of cities that had not yet surrendered. Accounts of these cruelties are not taken from atrocity stories circulated by their enemies; they come from the records of the Assyrians themselves. Their chroniclers boasted of them as evidences of valor, and the people believed in them as guaranties of security and power. It is clear why the Assyrians were the most hated of all the nations of antiquity.

Seldom has the decline of an empire been so swift and so complete as was that of Assyria. In spite of her magnificent armaments and her wholesale destruction of her foes, Assyria's period of imperial splendor lasted little more than a century. Nation after nation conspired against her and finally accomplished her downfall. Her enemies took frightful vengeance. The whole land was so thoroughly sacked and the people so completely enslaved or exterminated that it has been difficult to trace any subsequent Assyrian influence upon history. The power and security which military strength was supposed to provide proved a mockery in the end. If Assyria had been utterly defenseless, her fate could hardly have been worse.

The tragedy of Assyrian militarism

With so complete an absorption in military pursuits, it was inevitable that the Assyrians should have neglected in some measure the arts of peace. Perhaps their major achievement was their system of administration. The empire comprised a mixture of self-governing cities and subject rural areas. In many cases the former had charters which allowed them a considerable measure of independence under councils of elders. The rural districts were controlled by local lords who exploited the peasants virtually as serfs. On the fringes of the empire were numerous "satellites" ruled by military governors under the close supervision of agents and spies from the Assyrian capital. Industry and commerce appear to have declined under the regime of the Assyrians; for such pursuits were generally scorned as beneath the dignity of a soldierly people. As compared with the thousands of business tablets left by the Old Babylonians, only a few hundred have ever been found at Nineveh. The minimum of manufacturing and trade which had to be carried on was left quite largely to the Arameans, a people closely related to the Phoenicians and the Hebrews. The Assyrians themselves preferred to derive their living from agriculture. The land system included both public and private holdings. The temples held the largest share of the landed wealth. Although the estates of the crown were likewise extensive, they were constantly being diminished by grants to army officers.

Assyrian political and economic achievements

Neither the economic nor the social order was sound. The frequent military campaigns depleted the energies and resources of the nation. In the course of time the army officers became a pampered aristocracy, delegating their duties to their subordinates and devoting themselves to luxurious pleasures. The stabilizing influence of a

Defects in the economic system

prosperous and intelligent middle class was precluded by the rule that only foreigners and slaves could engage in commercial activities. Yet more serious was the treatment accorded to the lower classes, the serfs and the slaves. The former comprised the bulk of the rural population. Some of them cultivated definite portions of their master's estates and retained a part of what they produced for themselves. Others were "empty" men, without even a plot to cultivate and dependent on the need for seasonal labor to provide for their means of subsistence. All were extremely poor and were subject to the additional hardships of labor on public works and compulsory military service. The slaves, who were chiefly an urban working class, were of two different types: the domestic slaves, who performed household duties and sometimes engaged in business for their masters; and the war captives. The former were not numerous and were allowed a great deal of freedom, even to the extent of owning property. The latter suffered much greater miseries. Bound by heavy shackles, they were compelled to labor to the point of exhaustion in building roads, canals, and palaces.

Whether the Assyrians adopted the law of the Old Babylonians has never been settled. Undoubtedly they were influenced by it, but several of the features of Hammurabi's code are entirely absent. Notable among these are the *lex talionis* and the system of gradation of penalties according to the rank of the victim and the offender. Whereas the Babylonians prescribed the most drastic punishments for crimes suggestive of treason or sedition, the Assyrians reserved theirs for such offenses as abortion and unnatural vice, probably for the military reason of preventing a decline in the birth rate. Another contrast is the more complete subjection of Assyrian women. Wives were treated as chattels of their husbands, the right of divorce was placed entirely in the hands of the male, a plurality of wives was permitted, and all married women were forbidden to appear in pub-

Assyrian Relief Sculptures: A Winged Being and the Armsbearer of the King. Alabaster slab from the palace of Ashurnasir-apal, 9th century, B.C.

lic with their faces unveiled. Here, according to Professor Olmstead, was the beginning of the Oriental seclusion of women.[4]

That a military nation like the Assyrians should not have taken first rank in intellectual achievement is easily understandable. The atmosphere of a military campaign is not favorable to reflection or disinterested research. Yet the demands of successful campaigning may lead to a certain accumulation of knowledge, for practical problems have to be solved. Under such circumstances the Assyrians accomplished some measure of scientific progress. They appear to have divided the circle into 360 degrees and to have estimated locations on the surface of the earth in something resembling latitude and longitude. They recognized and named five planets and achieved some success in predicting eclipses. Since the health of armies is important, medicine received considerable attention. More than 500 drugs, both vegetable and mineral, were catalogued and their uses indicated. Symptoms of various diseases were described and were generally interpreted as due to natural causes, although incantations and the prescription of disgusting compounds to drive out demons were still commonly employed as methods of treatment.

Scientific
achievements

In the domain of art the Assyrians surpassed the Old Babylonians and at least equaled the work of the Sumerians, although in different form. Sculpture was the art most highly developed, particularly in the low reliefs. These portrayed dramatic incidents of war and the hunt with the utmost fidelity to nature and a vivid description of movement. The Assyrians delighted in depicting the cool bravery of the hunter in the face of terrific danger, the ferocity of lions at bay, and the death agonies of wounded beasts. Unfortunately this art was limited almost entirely to the two themes of war and sport. Its purpose was to glorify the exploits of the ruling class. Architecture ranked second to sculpture from the standpoint of artistic excellence. Assyrian palaces and temples were built of stone, obtained from the mountainous areas of the north, instead of the mud brick of former times. Their principal features were the arch and the dome. The column was also used but never very successfully. The chief demerit of this architecture was its hugeness, which the Asyrians appeared to regard as synonymous with beauty.

The excellence
of Assyrian art

Assyrian culture reached its height in the seventh century during the reign of Assurbanipal. A man of considerable refinement, he was almost the only ruler of the nation to devote any attention to the patronage of learning and the arts. He ordered his scribes to collect all the copies of Babylonian writings that could be found on every conceivable subject and bring them to the royal library at Nineveh. Where necessary he authorized revisions to be made in order to bring the ancient learning into harmony with more recent knowledge. Under Assurbanipal's patronage the royal library came to contain more than 22,000 tablets. Many of them were magic formulas,

Assurbanipal,
patron of culture

[4] A. T. E. Olmstead, *History of Assyria*, p. 553.

Assyrian Winged Bull. Now in Oriental Institute, University of Chicago. Its precise significance is unknown, but it may have been intended to symbolize the Assyrian militarists' worship of strength and speed.

but included in the lot were thousands of letters, business documents, and military chronicles. The king himself was the author of an autobiography and of numerous letters that displayed some literary talent. But the most important of the original compositions of the Assyrians were their narratives of military campaigns, which, in their highly embellished and deliberately exaggerated form, represent one of the earliest attempts at patriotic historical writing.

5. THE CHALDEAN RENASCENCE

The Mesopotamian civilization entered its final stage with the overthrow of Assyria and the establishment of Chaldean supremacy. This stage is often called the Neo-Babylonian, because Nebuchadnezzar and his followers restored the capital at Babylon and attempted to revive the culture of Hammurabi's time. As might have been expected, their attempt was not wholly successful. The Assyrian metamorphosis had altered that culture in various profound and ineffaceable ways. Besides, the Chaldeans themselves had a history of their own which they could not entirely escape. Nevertheless, they did manage to revive certain of the old institutions and ideals. They restored the ancient law and literature, the essentials of the Old Babylonian form of government, and the economic system of their supposed ancestors with its dominance of industry and trade. Farther than this they were unable to go.

It was in religion that the failure of the Chaldean renascence was most conspicuous. Although Marduk was restored to his traditional

The Chaldean or final stage in Mesopotamian civilization

place at the head of the pantheon, the system of belief was little more than superficially Babylonian. What the Chaldeans really did was to develop an astral religion. The gods were divested of their limited human qualities and exalted into transcendent, omnipotent beings. They were actually identified with the planets themselves. Marduk became Jupiter, Ishtar became Venus, and so on. Though still not entirely aloof from man, they certainly lost their character as beings who could be cajoled and threatened and coerced by magic. They ruled the universe almost mechanically. While their immediate intentions were sometimes discernible, their ultimate purposes were inscrutable.

Two significant results flowed from these amazing conceptions. The first was an attitude of fatalism. Since the ways of the gods were past finding out, all that man could do was to resign himself to his fate. It behooved him therefore to submit absolutely to the gods, to trust in them implicitly, in the vague hope that the results in the end would be good. Thus arose for the first time in history the conception of piety as submission—a conception which was adopted in several other religions, as we shall see in succeeding chapters. For the Chaldeans it implied no otherwordly significance; one did not resign himself to calamities in this life in order to be justified in the next. The Chaldeans had no interest in a life to come. Submission might bring certain earthly rewards, but in the main, as they conceived it, it was not a means to an end at all. It was rather the expression of an attitude of despair, of humility in the face of mysteries that could not be fathomed.

The second great result which came from the growth of an astral religion was the development of a stronger spiritual consciousness. This is revealed in the penitential hymns of unknown authors and in the prayers which were ascribed to Nebuchadnezzar and other kings as the spokesmen for the nation. In most of them the gods are addressed as exalted beings who are concerned with justice and righteous conduct on the part of men, although the distinction between ceremonial and genuine morality is not always sharply drawn. It has been asserted by one author that these hymns could have been used by the Hebrews with little modification except for the substitution of the name of Yahweh for that of the Chaldean god.[5]

With the gods promoted to so lofty a plane, it was perhaps inevitable that man should have been abased. Creatures possessed of mortal bodies could not be compared with the transcendent, passionless beings who dwelt in the stars and guided the destinies of the earth. Man was a lowly creature, sunk in iniquity and vileness, and hardly even worthy of approaching the gods. The consciousness of sin already present in the Babylonian and Assyrian religions now reached a stage of almost pathological intensity. In the hymns the

[5] Morris Jastrow, *The Civilization of Babylonia and Assyria*, p. 217.

sons of men are compared to prisoners, bound hand and foot, languishing in darkness. Their transgressions are "seven times seven." Their misery is increased by the fact that their evil nature has prompted them to sin unwittingly.[6] Never before had men been regarded as so hopelessly depraved, nor had religion been fraught with so gloomy a view of life.

Chaldean
morality

Curiously enough, the pessimism of the Chaldeans does not appear to have affected their morality very much. So far as the evidence reveals, they indulged in no rigors of asceticism. They did not mortify the flesh, nor did they even practice self-denial. Apparently they took it for granted that man could not avoid sinning, no matter how hard he tried. They seem to have been just as deeply engrossed in the material interests of life and in the pursuit of the pleasures of the senses as any of the earlier nations. Indeed, it seems that they were even more greedy and sensual. Occasional references were made in their prayers and hymns to reverence, kindness, and purity of heart as virtues, and to oppression, slander, and anger as vices, but these were intermingled with ritualistic conceptions of cleanness and uncleanness and with expressions of desire for physical satisfactions. When the Chaldeans prayed, it was not always that their gods would make them good, but more often that they would grant long years, abundant offspring, and luxurious living.

Chaldean
achievements in
astronomy

Aside from religion, the Chaldean culture differed from that of the Sumerians, Babylonians, and Assyrians chiefly in regard to scientific achievements. Without doubt the Chaldeans were the most capable scientists in all of Mesopotamian history, although their accomplishments were limited primarily to astronomy. They worked out the most elaborate system for recording the passage of time that had yet been devised, with their invention of the seven-day week and their division of the day into twelve double-hours of 120 minutes each. They kept accurate records of their observation of eclipses and other celestial occurrences for more than 350 years—until long after the downfall of their empire. The motivating force behind Chaldean astronomy was religion. The chief purpose of mapping the heavens and collecting astronomical data was to discover the future the gods had prepared for the race of men. Since the planets were gods themselves, that future could best be divined in the movements of the heavenly bodies. Astronomy was therefore primarily astrology.

Other aspects of
Chaldean culture

Sciences other than astronomy continued in a backward state. There is evidence that the Chaldeans knew the principle of the zero and laid at least some of the foundations of algebra. Medicine showed little advance beyond the stage it had reached under the Assyrians. The same was true of the remaining aspects of Chaldean culture. Art differed only in its greater magnificence. Literature, dominated by the antiquarian spirit, revealed a monotonous lack of originality. The writings of the Old Babylonians were extensively

[6] *Ibid.*, pp. 471–74.

copied and reedited, but they were supplemented by little that was new.

6. THE MESOPOTAMIAN LEGACY

Notwithstanding the uneven development of the Mesopotamian civilization, its influence has not been less than that of Egypt. From one or another of the four Mesopotamian nations we get a considerable number of our culture elements: the seven-day week; the fact that the dials on our watches and clocks contain numerals up to twelve, corresponding to the Chaldean division of the day into twelve double-hours; the belief in horoscopes; the superstition of planting crops according to the phases of the moon; the twelve signs of the zodiac; the circle of 360 degrees, the arithmetical process of multiplication; square and cube root; and the foundations of algebraic equations.

Mesopotamian influence: (1) upon the modern world

The influence exerted upon various nations of antiquity was even more significant. The Persians were profoundly affected by Chaldean culture. The Hittites, who aided the Kassites in overthrowing the Babylonians about 1650 B.C., adopted the clay tablets, the cuneiform writing, the *Gilgamesh Epic*, and much of the religion of the nation they conquered. The Babylonian religion also had its effect upon the Phoenicians, as evidenced by their worship of Astarte (Ishtar) and Tammuz. From the Sumerians or Old Babylonians the Canaanites derived a large part of their law as well as a good many of their religious beliefs. But the principal heirs of Mesopotamian culture were the Hebrews. Possibly as far back as 1800 B.C. some of their ancestors had lived for a time in the northwestern portion of the valley between the two rivers. Numerous Mesopotamian traits were also acquired indirectly through contact with the Canaanites and Phoenicians. It was probably in this manner that the Hebrews came into possession of the Creation and Flood legends, the basic elements of the Book of Job, and a system of law which had its ultimate origin in the Mesopotamian civilization. An even greater influence was exerted during the period of the Captivity, from 586 to 539 B.C. During these years the Jews were brought into direct association for the first time with a rich and powerful nation. In spite of their hatred of their captors they unconsciously adopted many of their ways. There is evidence, for example, that they acquired some of the Chaldean penchant for trade. In addition, much of the symbolism, pessimism, fatalism, and demonology of the Chaldeans passed into the religion of Judah, transforming it markedly from the character it had had in the time of the Prophets.[7]

(2) upon the Persians, Phoenicians, Canaanites, and Hebrews

Mesopotamian institutions and beliefs also exerted their influence upon the Greeks and the Romans, although for the most part indirectly. The Stoic philosophy with its doctrines of determinism and

[7] The Hebrew calendar to this day contains a month named in honor of the god Tammuz.

THE
MESOPOTAMIAN
CIVILIZATION

(3) upon the
Greeks and the
Romans

pessimism may have reflected that influence in some measure, since its originator, Zeno, was a Semite, probably a Phoenician. A better case could possibly be made for the Mesopotamian origin of such Roman practices as divination, worship of the planets as gods, and the use of the arch and the vault. Several of these elements were introduced to the Romans by the Etruscans, a people of western Asiatic origin. Others were brought in by the Romans themselves as a result of their military campaigns in Asia Minor. That there were natives of the Mesopotaman region resident in Rome, in the later centuries of the Empire's history, at least, is evidenced by the fact that the Romans used the name "Chaldeans" as synonymous with "astrologers" and sought the aid of such persons on numerous occasions in divining the future.

SELECTED READINGS

· *Items so designated are available in paperbound editions.*

Braidwood, R. J., *The Near East and the Foundations for Civilization*, Eugene, Ore., 1946.
· Chiera, Edward, *They Wrote on Clay*, Chicago, 1956 (Phoenix).
· Childe, V. G., *What Happened in History*, Baltimore, 1946 (Penguin).
· Contenau, G., *Everyday Life in Babylonia and Assyria*, New York, 1954 (Norton Library). Based on recent archaeological evidence and well illustrated.
Coulborn, Rushton, *The Origin of Civilized Societies*, Princeton, 1959.
· Frankfort, Henri, *The Birth of Civilization in the Near East*, Bloomington, Ind., 1951 (Anchor). Brief but useful.
——, *The Intellectual Adventure of Ancient Man*, Chicago, 1946. Contains evidence of the pessimism of the Mesopotamian peoples.
Jastrow, Morris, *The Civilization of Babylonia and Assyria*, Philadelphia, 1915.
· Kramer, S. N., *History Begins at Sumer*, New York, 1959 (Anchor).
· ——, *Sumerian Mythology*, New York, 1961 (Torchbook).
——, *The Sumerians, Their History, Culture, and Character*, Chicago, 1963.
· Lloyd, Seton, *Foundations in the Dust*, Baltimore, 1955 (Penguin).
Olmstead, A. T. E., *History of Assyria*, New York, 1923. The standard work. Perhaps a little too favorable.
· Woolley, C. L., *The Sumerians*, New York, 1928 (Norton Library). A pioneer work, brief and interestingly written.
· ——, *Ur of the Chaldees*, Baltimore, 1950 (Norton Library).

SOURCE MATERIALS

Barton, G. A., *The Royal Inscriptions of Sumer and Akhad*, New Haven, 1929.
Harper, R. F., ed. and tr., *Assyrian and Babylonian Literature*.
——, ed., *The Code of Hammurabi*, Chicago, 1904.
Johns, C. H. W., *Assyrian Deeds and Documents*, 4 vols.
Luckenbill, D. D., ed., *Ancient Records of Assyria and Babylonia*, Chicago, 1926, 2 vols.
Pritchard, J. B., ed., *Ancient Near Eastern Texts Relating to the Old Testament*, rev. ed., Princeton, 1955.
Rogers, R. W., ed. and tr., *Cuneiform Parallels to the Old Testament*, New York, 1926, 2 vols.
· Sandars, N. K., ed., *The Epic of Gilgamesh*, New York, 1964 (Penguin).

CHAPTER 4

The Civilization of Ancient Persia

That would we choose, Ahura-Mazdah and Righteousness the beautiful, so that we may think and speak and do whatever is the best of deeds for both worlds. For the reward for the best deed we strive, that security and fodder be preserved for the Kine, whatever we be instructed or uninstructed, whether rulers or subjects. Truly to the best of rulers is the Kingdom, for we ascribe the Kingdom to Ahura-Mazdah and to Best Righteousness. As a man or a woman knows what is right, with fervor let him execute what is right, for himself and for whomsoever he can bring to understanding.

—A. T. Olmstead, *Seven-fold Yasna*

The Chaldeans, as we have seen, were the last of the nations with a culture essentially Mesopotamian. In 539 B.C. the Persians conquered the valley of the two rivers and soon afterward the whole empire of the Chaldean kings. But the Persians established what was really a new civilization. While they adopted much from the Chaldeans, they made no effort to preserve the old culture intact, and they introduced a great many new elements from other sources. Their religion was entirely different, and their art was compounded of elements taken from nearly every people they conquered. They did not continue the Chaldean interest in science or the development of business and industry. Finally, it should be remembered that the empire of the Persians included a great many territories which had never been subject to the Chaldean kings.

Persia produces a new civilization

I. THE EMPIRE AND ITS HISTORY

Comparatively little is known of the Persians before the sixth century B.C. Up to that time they appear to have led an obscure and peaceful existence on the eastern shore of the Persian Gulf. Their homeland afforded only modest advantages. On the east it was

The Persian background

83

hemmed in by high mountains, and its coast line was destitute of harbors. The fertile valleys of the interior, however, were capable of providing a generous subsistence for a limited population. Save for the development of an elaborate religion, the people had made little progress. They had no system of writing, but they did have a spoken language closely related to Sanskrit and to the languages of ancient and modern Europe. It is for this reason alone and not because of race that they are accurately referred to as an Indo-European people. At the dawn of their history they were not an independent nation but were vassals of the Medes, a kindred people who ruled over a great empire north and east of the Tigris River.

The rise of Cyrus

In 559 B.C. a prince by the name of Cyrus became king of a southern Persian tribe. About five years later he made himself ruler of all the Persians and then developed an ambition for dominion over neighboring peoples. As Cyrus the Great he has gone down in history as one of the most sensational conquerors of all time. Within the short space of twenty years he founded a vast empire, larger than any that had previously existed. It is impossible to believe that his successes were due entirely to the force of his own personality. To begin with, he was accepted by the Medes as their king soon after he became ruler of the Persians. The reasons for this are not entirely known. According to various traditions he was the grandson or the son-in-law of the Median king. Perhaps a vague feeling of national kinship impelled Medes and Persians to unite under a common leader. At any rate, Cyrus' "conquest" of the Medes was achieved with such slight opposition that it meant little more than a change of dynasties. Cyrus profited also from the dissension within the Chaldean state, as we noted in the preceding chapter, and from the decrepit condition of other Near Eastern empires. Moreover, the geographic conditions of the Persian homeland were particularly conducive to expansion. The limited area of fertile land, the lack of other resources, and the rich bordering countries inviting conquest were factors which made it virtually inevitable that the nation would break through the confines of its original territory just as soon as the pinch of poverty began to be felt. Perhaps to an even greater extent the successes of the Persians were the result of military superiority and their tolerant policies toward their subjects. They relied primarily upon the bow instead of the lance or spear, overwhelming an enemy with arrows before he could come close to them. They won the allegiance of the conquered by allowing them to keep their own religions and by adopting many of their customs.

The conquests
of Cyrus

The first of the real conquests of Cyrus was the kingdom of Lydia, which occupied the western half of Asia Minor and was separated from the lands of the Medes only by the Halys River, in what is now northern Turkey. Perceiving the ambitions of the Persians, Croesus, the famous Lydian king, determined to wage a preventive war to preserve his own nation from conquest. He formed alliances with Egypt and Sparta and then consulted the Greek oracle at Delphi as to the advisability of an immediate attack. According to Herodotus, the oracle replied that if he would cross the Halys and assume the offensive he would destroy a great army. He did, but that army was his own. His forces were completely overwhelmed, and his prosperous little kingdom was annexed as a province of the Persian state. Seven years later, in 539 B.C., Cyrus took advantage of discontent and conspiracies in the Chaldean empire to capture the city of Babylon. His victory was an easy one, for he had the assistance of the Jews within the city and of the Chaldean priests, who were dissatisfied with the policies of their king. The conquest of the Chaldean capital made possible the rapid extension of control over the whole empire and thereby added the Fertile Crescent to the domains of Cyrus.

The great conqueror died in 529 B.C., apparently as the result of wounds received in a war with barbarian tribes. Soon afterward a succession of troubles overtook the state he had founded. Like so many other empire builders both before and since, he had devoted too much energy to conquest and not enough to internal development. He was succeeded by his son Cambyses, who conquered Egypt in 525 B.C. During the new king's absence revolt spread throughout his Asiatic possessions. Chaldeans, Elamites, and even the Medes strove to regain their independence. The chief minister of the realm, abetted by the priests, organized a movement to gain possession of the throne for a pretender who was one of their puppets. Upon learning of conditions at home, Cambyses set out from Egypt with his most dependable troops, but he was murdered on the way. The most serious of the revolts was finally crushed by Darius, a powerful noble, who killed the pretender and seized the throne for himself.

The successors of Cyrus

Darius I, or the Great, as he has been called by his admirers, ruled the empire from 522 to 486 B.C. The early years of his reign were occupied in suppressing the revolts of subject peoples and in improving the administrative organization of the state. He completed the division of the empire into satrapies, or provinces, and fixed the annual tribute due from each province. He standardized the currency and weights and measures. He repaired and completed a primitive canal from the Nile to the Red Sea. He followed the example of Cyrus in tolerating and protecting the institutions of subject peoples. Not only did he restore ancient temples and foster local cults, but he ordered his satrap of Egypt to codify the Egyptian laws in consultation with the native priests. But in some of his military exploits Darius overreached himself. In order to check the incursions of the Scythians, he crossed the Hellespont, conquered a large part of the Thracian coast, and thereby aroused the hostility of the Athenians. In addition, he increased the oppression of the Ionian Greeks on the shore of Asia Minor, who had fallen under Persian domination with the conquest of Lydia. He interfered with their trade, collected heavier tribute from them, and forced them to serve

Darius the Great

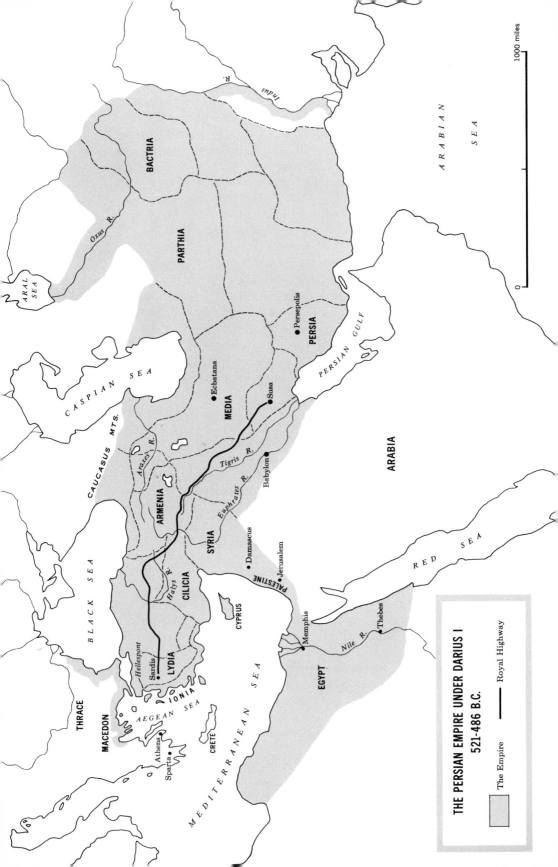

THE PERSIAN EMPIRE UNDER DARIUS I
521-486 B.C.

The Empire

Royal Highway

1000 miles

ARAL SEA

CASPIAN SEA

CAUCASUS MTS.

BLACK SEA

AEGEAN SEA

MEDITERRANEAN SEA

RED SEA

ARABIAN SEA

PERSIAN GULF

Oxus R.

Indus R.

Araxes R.

Tigris R.

Euphrates R.

Halys R.

Nile R.

Hellespont

BACTRIA

PARTHIA

MEDIA

PERSIA

ARMENIA

SYRIA

CILICIA

LYDIA

IONIA

THRACE

MACEDON

CRETE

CYPRUS

PALESTINE

EGYPT

ARABIA

Ecbatana

Susa

Persepolis

Babylon

Damascus

Jerusalem

Sardis

Athens

Sparta

Memphis

Thebes

in his armies. The immediate result was a revolt of the Ionian cities with the assistance of Athens. And when Darius attempted to punish the Athenians for their part in the rebellion, he found himself involved in a war with nearly all the states of Greece.

Darius the Great died while the war with the Greeks was still raging. The struggle was prosecuted vigorously but ineffectively by his successors, Xerxes I and Artaxerxes. By 479 B.C. the Persians had been driven from all of Greece. Though they recovered temporarily possession of the Ionian islands and continued to hold sway as a major power in Asia, their attempt to extend their dominion into Europe had come to an end. The last century and a half of the empire's existence was marked by frequent assassinations, revolts of provincial governors, and barbarian invasions, until finally, in 330 B.C., its independence was annihilated by the armies of Alexander the Great.

Although the Persian government had its defects, it was certainly superior to most of the others that had existed in the Near Orient. The Persian kings did not imitate the terrorism of the Assyrians. They levied tribute upon conquered peoples, but they generally allowed them to keep their own customs, religions, and laws. Indeed, it may be said that the chief significance of the Persian empire lay in the fact that it resulted in a synthesis of Near Eastern cultures, including those of Persia itself, Mesopotamia, Asia Minor, the Syria-Palestine coast, and Egypt.

In theory the Persian king was an absolute monarch ruling by the grace of the god of light. By divine appointment he claimed the right to rule over the whole earth. He styled himself "the king of kings." In the sculptured reliefs he appears seated on a high throne, wearing a purple robe and a tiara on his head. A stool protects his feet from contact with the ground. In practice his dignity was less imposing. He had to defer to the chief nobles of the realm and to pay some regard to the ancient laws of the Medes and Persians. The satraps, or governors of the twenty provinces, were really "subordinate kings." Their power was so great that they posed a constant threat to the security of the empire. Though carefully checked by inspectors, the "eyes and ears of the king," several of them did rebel and attempt to seize the imperial throne. The Persian kings found it expedient to appoint leaders of the subject peoples to high positions in the government. These leaders took their places in the councils of the satraps and even became officers in the army. Like the Persians who held such positions, they were rewarded with bounties and grants of land. Needless to say, not all the subject nations received equal treatment. The Medes, as the people most closely related to the Persians and the first to be conquered, were the most highly favored. The Jews ranked second, perhaps because they had assisted the Persians in the overthrow of the Chaldeans. They were permitted to return to their native land and even to convoke their own local assembly. To supplement these administrative concessions the

Persian kings built excellent roads to help hold their empire together. Most famous was the Royal Road, some 1600 miles in length.
It extended from Susa near the Persian Gulf to Ephesus on the coast
of Asia Minor. So well kept was this highway that the king's messengers, traveling day and night, could cover its entire length in less
than a week. Other roads linked the various provinces with one or
another of the four Persian capitals: Susa, Persepolis, Babylon, and
Ecbatana. Although they naturally contributed to ease of trade, the
highways were all built primarily to facilitate control over the outlying sections of the empire.

2. PERSIAN CULTURE

The culture of the Persians, in the narrower sense of intellectual
and artistic achievements, was largely derived from that of previous
civilizations. Much of it came from Mesopotamia, but a great deal of
it from Egypt, and some from Lydia and northern Palestine. Their
system of writing was originally the Babylonian cuneiform, but in
time they devised an alphabet of thirty-nine letters, based upon the
alphabet of the Arameans who traded within their borders. In science they accomplished nothing, except to adopt with some slight
modifications the solar calendar of the Egyptians and to encourage
exploration as an aid to commerce. They deserve credit also for
diffusing a knowledge of the Lydian coinage throughout many parts
of western Asia.

It was the architecture of the Persians which gave the most positive expression of the eclectic character of their culture. They
copied the raised platform and the terraced building style that had
been so common in Babylonia and Assyria. They imitated also the
winged bulls, the brilliantly colored glazed bricks, and other decorative motifs of Mesopotamian architecture. But at least two of the
leading features of Mesopotamian construction were not used by
the Persians at all—the arch and the vault. In place of them they
adopted the column and the colonnade from Egypt. Such matters as
interior arrangement and the use of palm and lotus designs at the
base of columns also point very distinctly toward Egyptian influence. On the other hand, the fluting of the columns and the volutes
or scrolls beneath the capitals were not Egyptian but Greek,
adopted not from the mainland of Greece itself but from the Ionian
cities of Asia Minor. If there was anything unique about Persian
architecture, it was the fact that it was purely secular. The great
Persian structures were not temples but palaces. They served to
glorify not gods, but the "King of Kings." The most famous were
the magnificent residences of Darius and Xerxes at Persepolis. The
latter, built in imitation of the temple at Karnak, had an enormous
central audience-hall containing a hundred columns and surrounded
by innumerable rooms which served as offices and as quarters for
the eunuchs and members of the royal harem.

PALACE AT PERSEPOLIS

Above: *The Great Palace of Darius and Xerxes at Persepolis.* Persian architecture made use of fluted columns, probably copied from the Greeks, and reliefs resembling those of the Assyrians.

Right: *Persian Sculpture.* Two reliefs from the staircase of the Great Palace at Persepolis.

3. THE ZOROASTRIAN RELIGION

By far the most enduring influence left by the ancient Persians was that of their religion. Their system of faith was of ancient origin. It was already highly developed when they began their conquests. So strong was its appeal, and so ripe were the conditions for its acceptance, that it spread through most of western Asia. Its doctrines turned other religions inside out, displacing beliefs which had been held for ages. The world outlook of nations to this day has been both uplifted and perverted by it.

Although the roots of this religion can be traced as far back as the fifteenth century B.C., its real founder was Zoroaster,[1] who appears to have lived in the early sixth century B.C. From him the religion derives its name of Zoroastrianism. He seems to have conceived it to be his mission to purify the traditional beliefs of his people—to eradicate polytheism, animal sacrifice, and magic—and to establish their worship on a more spiritual and ethical plane. That the movement he led was the natural accompaniment of the transition to a more civilized agricultural existence is revealed in his teaching of reverence for the cow and in his prescription of cultivation of the soil as a sacred duty. In spite of his reforming efforts many of the old superstitions survived and were gradually fused with the new ideals.

In many respects Zoroastrianism had a character unique among the religions of the world up to that time. First of all, it was dualistic—not monistic like the Sumerian and Babylonian religions, in which the same gods were capable of both good and evil; nor did it make any pretensions to monotheism, or belief in a single divinity, as did the late Egyptian and Hebrew religions. Two great deities ruled over the universe: one, Ahura-Mazda,[2] supremely good and incapable of any wickedness, embodied the principles of light, truth, and righteousness; the other, Ahriman, treacherous and malignant, presided over the forces of darkness and evil. The two were engaged in a desperate struggle for supremacy. Although they were about evenly matched in strength, the god of light would eventually triumph, and the world would be saved from the powers of darkness.

In the second place, Zoroastrianism was an eschatological religion. "Eschatology" is the doctrine of last or final things. It includes such ideas as the coming of a messiah, the resurrection of the dead, a last judgment, and the translation of the redeemed into a paradise eternal. According to the Zoroastrian belief the world would endure for 12,000 years. At the end of 9000 years the second coming of Zoroaster would occur as a sign and a promise of the ultimate redemption of the good. This would be followed in due course by the miraculous birth of a messiah, whose work would be the perfection of the

---

[1] "Zoroaster" is the corrupt Greek form of the Persian name Zarathustra.
[2] The name was frequently abbreviated to Mazda.

good as a preparation for the end of the world. Finally the last great day would arrive when Ahura-Mazda would overpower Ahriman and cast him down into the abyss. The dead would then be raised from their graves to be judged according to their deserts. The righteous would enter into immediate bliss, while the wicked would be sentenced to the flames of hell. Ultimately, though, all would be saved; for the Persian hell, unlike the Christian, did not last forever.

From what has been said already, the inference will readily be drawn that the Zoroastrian religion was definitely an ethical one. Although it contained suggestions of predestination, of the election of some from all eternity to be saved, in the main it rested upon the assumption that men possessed free will, that they were free to sin or not to sin, and that they would be rewarded or punished in the afterlife in accordance with their conduct on earth. The virtues commended by the religion made an imposing list. Some were obviously of economic or political origin: diligence, the keeping of contracts, obedience to rulers, the begetting of numerous offspring, and tilling the soil ("He who sows corn sows holiness"). Others had a broader significance: Ahura-Mazda commanded that men should be truthful, that they should love and help one another to the best of their power, that they should befriend the poor and practice hospitality. The essence of these broader virtues was perhaps expressed in another of the god's decrees: "Whosoever shall give meat to one of the faithful . . . he shall go to Paradise."

(3) an ethical religion

The forms of conduct forbidden were sufficiently numerous and varied to cover the whole list of the Seven Cardinal Sins of medieval Christianity and a great many more. Pride, gluttony, sloth, covetousness, wrathfulness, lust, adultery, abortion, slander, and waste were among the more typical. The taking of interest on loans to others of the same faith was described as the "worst of sins," and the accumulation of riches was strongly discountenanced. The restraints which men were to practice included also a kind of negative Golden Rule: "That nature alone is good which shall not do unto another whatever is not good for its own self." It is pertinent to add that the original Zoroastrianism condemned the ascetic way of life. Self-inflicted suffering, fasting, and even excessive grief were prohibited on the ground that they injured both mind and body and rendered human beings unfit for the duties of agriculture and the begetting of children. Temperance rather than complete abstinence was the traditional Persian ideal.[3]

The principal sins

Zoroastrianism is especially significant because it was a revealed religion—apparently the first of its type in the history of the Western world. Its followers were believed to be the exclusive possessors of truth; not because they were wiser than other men, but because they shared the secrets of the god. As members of his substance they automatically partook of his wisdom; not in its entirety, of

(4) a revealed religion

[3] The quotations in the last two paragraphs are taken from J. O. Hertzler, *The Social Thought of the Ancient Civilizations*, pp. 149–158.

course, but of certain portions of it. The truth they possessed was therefore occult. It could not be deduced by logic or discovered by investigation. Part of it was in the form of sacred writings—the *Avesta,* believed to have been sent down from heaven—but much of it consisted of an oral revelation received by Zoroaster from Mazda and transmitted to his disciples. Contrary to general opinion, revealed religions have not been very common in the Western world. The Egyptians had no bible or any other Word of God, and neither did the Mesopotamian nations. Likewise, the religions of Greece and Rome rested upon no Truth vouchsafed by the gods. Zoroastrianism, Judaism, Christianity, and Islam are the only faiths, with the possible exception of Hinduism, which have had divine revelation as one of their essential elements. Without doubt this has been a factor augmenting their strength, but it has accounted in some measure also for their dogmatism and intolerance.

4. THE MYSTICAL AND OTHERWORLDLY HERITAGE FROM PERSIA

The religion of the Persians as taught by Zoroaster did not long continue in its original state. It was corrupted, first of all, by the persistence of primitive superstitions, of magic and priestcraft. The farther the religion spread, the more of these relics of barbarism were engrafted upon it. As the years passed, additional modification resulted from the influence of alien faiths, particularly that of the Chaldeans. The outcome was the growth of a powerful synthesis in which the primitive priestliness, messianism, and dualism of the Persians were combined with the pessimism and fatalism of the Neo-Babylonians.

Out of this synthesis gradually emerged a profusion of cults, alike in their basic dogmas but according them different emphasis. The oldest of these cults was Mithraism, deriving its name from Mithras, the chief lieutenant of Mazda in the struggle against the powers of evil. At first only a minor deity in the religion of Zoroastrianism, Mithras finally won recognition in the hearts of many of the Persians as the god most deserving of worship. The reason for this change was probably the emotional appeal made by the incidents of his career. He was believed to have been born of a rock in the presence of a small group of shepherds, who brought him gifts in token of their reverence for his great mission on earth. He then proceeded to subdue all the living creatures around him, taming many of them and rendering them useful to man. The better to accomplish his purpose, he entered into a compact with the sun, obtaining warmth and light that agriculture might flourish. But the most important of his exploits was the capture of the divine bull. Seizing the animal by the horns, he struggled desperately until he had forced him into a cave, where, in obedience to a command from the sun, he slew him. From the blood and flesh of the bull came all manner of herbs, grain, and other plants valuable to man. No sooner had these things been accomplished than Ahriman produced a drought on the earth; but Mithras thrust his spear into a rock and the waters gushed forth. Next the god of evil sent a flood, but Mithras caused an ark to be built to permit the escape of one man with his flocks. Finally, his work accomplished, Mithras ate a sacramental meal with the sun and ascended into heaven. In due time he would return and bestow immortality upon all of the faithful.

The ritual of Mithraism was both elaborate and significant. It included a complicated initiation ceremony of seven stages or degrees, the last of which cemented a mystic fellowship with the god. Prolonged self-denial and laceration of the flesh were necessary accompaniments of the initiation process. Admission to full membership in the cult entitled one to participate in the sacraments, the most important of which were baptism and a sacred meal of bread, water, and possibly wine. Still other observances included lustration (ceremonial cleansing with holy water), the burning of incense, chanting sacred music, and the keeping of sacred days. Of the last, Sunday and the twenty-fifth of December were the specific examples. In imitation of the Chaldean astral religion, each day of the week was dedicated to a celestial body. Since the sun as the giver of light and the faithful ally of Mithras was the most important of these bodies, his day was naturally the most sacred. The twenty-fifth of December also possessed its solar significance: as the approximate date of the winter solstice it marked the return of the sun from his long journey south of the Equator. It was in a sense the "birthday" of the sun, since it connoted the revival of his life-giving powers for the benefit of man.

The ritual and observances of Mithraism

Exactly when the worship of Mithras became a definite cult is unknown, but it was certainly not later than the fourth century B.C. Its characteristics became firmly established during the period of social ferment which followed the collapse of Alexander's empire, and its spread at that time was exceedingly rapid. In the last century B.C. it was introduced into Rome, although it was of little importance in Italy itself until after 100 A.D. It drew its converts especially from the lower classes, from the ranks of soldiers, foreigners, and slaves. Ultimately it rose to the status of one of the most popular religions of the Empire, the chief competitor of Christianity and of old Roman paganism itself. After 275, however, its strength rapidly waned. How much influence this astonishing cult exerted is impossible to say. Its superficial resemblance to Christianity is certainly not hard to perceive, but this does not mean, of course, that the two were identical, or that one was an offshoot of the other. Nevertheless, it is probably true that Christianity as the younger of the two rivals borrowed a good many of its externals from Mithraism, at the same time preserving its own philosophy essentially untouched.

The spread and influence of Mithraism

One of the principal successors of Mithraism in transmitting the legacy from Persia was Manicheism, founded by Mani, a high-born

Manicheism

priest of Ecbatana, about 250 A.D. Like Zoroaster he conceived it to be his mission to reform the prevailing religion, but he received scant sympathy in his own country and had to be content with missionary ventures in India and western China. About 276 A.D. he was condemned and crucified by his Persian opponents. Following his death his teachings were carried by his disciples into practically every country of western Asia and finally into Italy about 330 A.D. Large numbers of western Manicheans, the great Augustine among them, eventually became Christians.

The strict
dualism of the
Manicheans

Of all the Zoroastrian teachings, the one that made the deepest impression upon the mind of Mani was dualism. It was therefore natural that it should have become the central doctrine of the new faith. But Mani gave to this doctrine a broader interpretation than it had ever received in the earlier religion. He conceived not merely of two deities engaged in a relentless struggle for supremacy, but of a whole universe divided into two kingdoms, each the antithesis of the other. The first was the kingdom of spirit ruled over by a God eternally good. The second was the kingdom of matter under the dominion of Satan. Only "spiritual" substances such as fire, light, and the souls of men were created by God. Darkness, sin, desire, and all things bodily and material owed their origin to Satan. Human nature itself was evil, for the first parents of the race had received their physical bodies from the prince of darkness.

The moral im-
plications of
dualism

The moral implications of this rigorous dualism were readily apparent. Since everything connected with sensation or desire was the work of Satan, man should strive to free himself as completely as possible from enslavement to his physical nature. He should refrain from all forms of sensual enjoyment, the eating of meat, the drinking of wine, the gratification of sexual desire. Even marriage was prohibited, for this would result in the begetting of more physical bodies to people the kingdom of Satan. In addition, man should subdue the flesh by prolonged fasting and infliction of pain. Recognizing that this program of austerities would be too difficult for ordinary mortals, Mani divided the race of mankind into the "perfect" and the "secular." Only the former would be obliged to adhere to the full program as the ideal of what all should hope to attain. The latter were merely required to eschew idolatry, avarice, fornication, falsehood, and the eating of meat. To aid the children of men in their struggle against the powers of darkness, God had sent prophets and redeemers from time to time to comfort and inspire them. Noah, Abraham, Zoroaster, Jesus, and Paul were numbered among these divine emissaries; but the last and greatest of them was Mani.

The influence of Manicheism is very difficult to estimate, but it was undoubtedly considerable. People of all classes in the Roman Empire, including some members of the Christian clergy, embraced its doctrines. In its Christianized form it became one of the principal sects of the early Church,[4] and it exerted some influence upon the

[4] See pp. 364–65.

development of the Albigensian heresy as late as the twelfth and
thirteenth centuries. It inspired extravagant Christian speculations
upon the dualism between God and the devil and between spirit and
matter. Not only did it contribute to the asceticism of Christianity,
but it strengthened also the doctrines of original sin and the total
depravity of man, as taught by some theologians. Finally, it was a
sovereign source of the famous duality of ethical standards set up by
St. Augustine and other Church Fathers: (1) a standard of perfection for the few (the monks and nuns), who would withdraw from
the world and lead saintly lives as an example for the rest; and (2) a
socially possible standard for the ordinary Christians.

The third most important cult which developed as an element in
the Persian heritage was Gnosticism (from the Greek *gnosis*, meaning knowledge). The name of its founder is unknown, and likewise
the date of its origin, but it was certainly in existence as early as the
first century A.D. It reached the height of its popularity in the latter
half of the second century. Although it gained some followers in
Italy, its influence was confined primarily to the Near East.

The feature which most sharply distinguished this cult from the
others was mysticism. The Gnostics denied that the truths of religion could be discovered by reason or could even be made intelligi-
ble. They regarded themselves as the exclusive possessors of a secret
spiritual knowledge revealed to them directly by God. This knowledge was alone important as a guide to faith and conduct. In like
manner, their religious observances were highly esoteric, that is,
fraught with hidden meaning known only to the initiated. Sacraments in great profusion, innumerable baptisms, mystic rites, and
the use of holy formulas and sacred numbers constituted the leading
examples.

The combined influence of these several Persian religions was
enormous. Most of them were launched at a time when political and
social conditions were particularly conducive to their spread. The
breakup of Alexander's empire about 300 B.C. inaugurated a peculiar
period in the history of the ancient world. International barriers
were broken down; there was an extensive migration and intermingling of peoples; and the collapse of the old social order gave
rise to profound disillusionment and a vague yearning for individual
salvation. Men's attentions were centered as never before since the
downfall of Egypt upon compensations in a life to come. Under
such circumstances religions of the kind described were bound to
flourish like the green bay tree. Otherwordly, mystical, and messianic, they offered the very escape that men were seeking from a
world of anxiety and confusion.

Although not exclusively religious, the heritage left by the Persians contained few elements of a secular nature. Their form of government was adopted by the later Roman monarchs, not in its
purely political aspect, but in its character of a divine-right despot-

The influence of Manicheism

Gnosticism

The mysticism of the Gnostics

The combined influence of the several off-shoots of Zoroastrianism

ism. When such emperors as Diocletian and Constantine I invoked divine authority as a basis for their absolutism and required their subjects to prostrate themselves in their presence, they were really submerging the state in the religion as the Persians had done from the time of Darius. At the same time the Romans were impressed by the Persian idea of a world empire. Darius and his successors conceived of themselves as the rulers of the whole civilized world, with a mission to reduce it to unity and, under Ahura-Mazda, to govern it justly. For this reason they generally conducted their wars with a minimum of savagery and treated conquered peoples humanely. Their ideal was a kind of prototype of the *Pax Romana*. Traces of Persian influence upon certain Hellenistic philosophies are also discernible; but here again it was essentially religious, for it was confined almost entirely to the mystical theories of the Neo-Platonists and their philosophical allies.

SELECTED READINGS

· *Items so designated are available in paperbound editions.*

Burn, A. R., *Persia and the Greeks,* New York, 1962.
Cambridge Ancient History, Vol. IV.
· Cumont, Franz, *The Mysteries of Mithra,* Chicago, 1903 (Dover). A thorough analysis, interestingly presented.
Dhalla, M. N., *History of Zoroastrianism,* New York, 1938. A scholarly and balanced account.
Duchesne-Guillemin, Jacques, *The Western Response to Zoroaster,* New York, 1958.
· Frye, R. N., *The Heritage of Persia,* New York, 1962 (Mentor).
· Ghirshman, Roman, *Iran,* Baltimore, 1954 (Penguin).
Huart, C. I., *Ancient Persian and Iranian Civilization,* New York, 1927. A standard work, but limited in coverage.
· Olmstead, A. T. E., *History of the Persian Empire (Achaemenid Period),* Chicago, 1948 (Phoenix). Detailed and complete but somewhat uncritical.
Oppenheim, A. L., *Ancient Mesopotamia: Portrait of a Dead Civilization,* Chicago, 1964.
Pavry, J. D. C., *The Zoroastrian Doctrine of a Future Life,* New York, 1929.
Rogers, R. W. A., *A History of Ancient Persia from Its Earliest Beginnings to the Death of Alexander,* New York, 1929. Good for political history.
Zaehner, R. C., *The Dawn and Twilight of Zoroastrianism,* New York, 1961.

SOURCE MATERIALS

Darmesteter, James, tr., "The Zend-Avesta," *Sacred Books of the East,* Vol. III.
· Duchesne-Guillemin, Jacques, *Hymns of Zarathustra,* Boston, 1963 (Beacon).
· Herodotus, *The Persian Wars,* Baltimore, 1954 (Penguin).
Hertzler, J. O., *The Social Thought of the Ancient Civilizations,* New York, 1961, pp. 149–68.

CHAPTER 5

The Hebrew Civilization

I am the Lord thy God, which brought thee out of the land of
Egypt from the house of bondage.
Thou shalt have none other Gods before me.
Thou shalt not make thee any graven image, or any likeness of
any thing that is in heaven above, or that is in the earth beneath,
or that is in the waters beneath the earth:
Thou shalt not bow down thyself unto them, nor serve them: for
I the Lord thy God am a jealous God, visiting the iniquity of the
fathers upon the children unto the third and fourth generation of
them that hate me . . .

—*Deuteronomy* v. 6–9

Of all the peoples of the ancient Orient, none, with the possible exception of the Egyptians, has been of greater importance to the
modern world than the Hebrews. It was the Hebrews, of course, **Importance of**
who provided much of the background of the Christian religion— **the Hebrew**
its Commandments, its stories of the Creation and the Flood, its con- **civilization**
cept of God as lawgiver and judge, and more than two-thirds of its
Bible. Hebrew conceptions of morality and political theory have
also profoundly influenced modern nations, especially those in
which the Calvinist faith has been strong. On the other hand, it is
necessary to remember that the Hebrews themselves did not develop their culture in a vacuum. No more than any other people
were they able to escape the influence of nations around them. Hebrew religion, as a consequence, contained numerous elements
which were quite clearly derived from Egyptian and Mesopotamian
sources. Despite all the efforts of prophets to purge the Hebraic
faith of foreign corruptions, many of them still remained, and
others were added later. As we shall soon discover, Hebrew law was
based largely upon Old Babylonian origins, though of course with
modifications. Hebrew philosophy was partly Egyptian and partly
Greek. Long before the Book of Job was ever written, there was an
Old Babylonian drama of similar character. No one can deny, of **97**

course, that the Hebrews were capable of original achievement; at the same time, we cannot overlook the fact that they were influenced greatly by the older civilizations around them.

1. HEBREW ORIGINS AND RELATIONS WITH OTHER PEOPLES

Origin of the
Hebrews and their
name

The origin of the Hebrew people is still a puzzling problem. Certainly they were not a separate race, nor did they have any physical characteristics sufficient to distinguish them clearly from other nations around them. The origin of their name is uncertain. According to some scholars, it was derived from Habiru, a name invented by their enemies and meaning the equivalent of "alien," "transient," or "nomad." [1] According to other accounts, it is related to the Egyptian name Apiru. But most authorities agree that Habiru and Apiru are exact equivalents. The original Hebrew form of the two was Ibri.

Hebrew
migrations

Most scholars agree that the original home of the Hebrews was the Arabian Desert. The first definite appearance of the founders of the nation of Israel, however, was in northwestern Mesopotamia. Apparently as early as 1800 B.C. a group of Hebrews under the leadership of Abraham had settled there. Later Abraham's grandson Jacob led a migration westward and began the occupation of Palestine. It was from Jacob, subsequently called Israel, that the Israelites derived their name. Sometime after 1600 B.C. certain tribes of Israelites, together with other Hebrews, went down into Egypt to escape the consequences of famine. They appear to have settled in the vicinity of the Delta and to have been enslaved by the Pharaoh's government. Around 1300–1250 B.C. their descendants found a new leader in the indomitable Moses, who freed them from bondage, led them to the Sinai Peninsula, and persuaded them to become worshipers of Yahweh, a god whose name is sometimes written erroneously as Jehovah. Hitherto Yahweh had been the deity of Hebrew shepherd folk in the general locality of Sinai. Making use of a Yahwist cult as a nucleus, Moses welded the various tribes of his followers into a confederation, sometimes called the Yahweh Amphictyony. It was this confederation which played the dominant role in the conquest of Palestine, or the Land of Canaan.

The Promised
Land

With its scanty rainfall and rugged topography, Palestine as a haven for the Children of Israel left much to be desired. For the most part it was a barren and inhospitable place. But compared with the arid wastes of Arabia it was a veritable paradise, and it is not surprising that the leaders should have pictured it as a "land flowing with milk and honey." Most of it was already occupied by the Canaanites, another people of Semitic speech who had lived there for centuries. Through contact with the Babylonians, Hittites, and Egyptians they had built up a culture which was no longer primi-

98   [1] T. J. Meek, *Hebrew Origins*, pp. 7–11.

tive. They practiced agriculture and carried on trade. They knew the use of iron and the art of writing, and they had adapted the laws of Hammurabi's code to the needs of their simpler existence. Their religion, which was also derived in large part from Babylonia, was cruel and sensual, including human sacrifice and temple prostitution.

The Hebrew conquest of the land of Canaan was a slow and difficult process. Seldom did the tribes unite in a combined attack, and even when they did, the enemy cities were well enough fortified to resist capture. After several generations of sporadic fighting the Hebrews had succeeded in taking only the limestone hills and a few of the less fertile valleys. In the intervals between wars they mingled freely with the Canaanites and adopted no small amount of their culture. Before they had a chance to complete the conquest, they found themselves confronted by a new and more formidable enemy, the Philistines, who had come into Palestine from Asia Minor and from the islands of the Aegean Sea. Stronger than either the Hebrews or Canaanites, the new invaders rapidly overran the country and forced the Hebrews to surrender much of the territory they had already gained. It is from the Philistines that Palestine derives its name.

2. THE RECORD OF POLITICAL HOPES AND FRUSTRATIONS

The crisis produced by the Philistine conquests served not to discourage the Hebrews but to unite them and to intensify their ardor for battle. Moreover, it led directly to the founding of the Hebrew monarchy about 1025 B.C. Up to this time the nation had been ruled by "judges," who possessed little more than the authority of religious leaders. But now with a greater need for organization and discipline, the people demanded a king to rule them and to go out before them and fight their battles. The man selected as the first incumbent of the office was Saul, "a choice young man and a goodly," a member of the tribe of Benjamin.

In spite of his popularity at the start, the reign of King Saul was not a happy one, either for the nation or for the ruler himself. Only a few suggestions of the reasons are given in the Old Testament account. Evidently Saul incurred the displeasure of Samuel, the last of the great judges, who had expected to remain the power behind the throne. Before long there appeared on the scene the ambitious David, who, with the encouragement of Samuel, carried on skillful maneuvers to draw popular support from the king. Waging his own military campaigns, he achieved one bloody triumph after another. By contrast, the armies of Saul met disastrous reverses. Finally the king himself, being critically wounded, requested his armor-bearer to kill him. When the latter would not, he drew his own sword, fell upon it, and died.

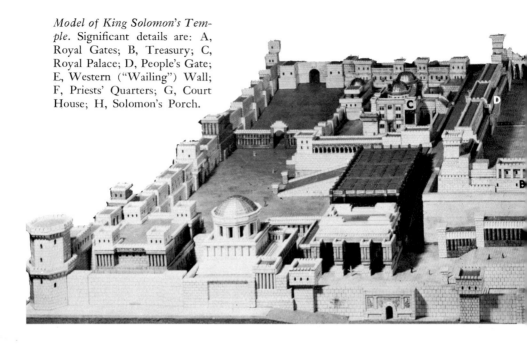

Model of King Solomon's Temple. Significant details are: A, Royal Gates; B, Treasury; C, Royal Palace; D, People's Gate; E, Western ("Wailing") Wall; F, Priests' Quarters; G, Court House; H, Solomon's Porch.

David now became king and ruled for forty years. His reign was one of the most glorious periods in Hebrew history. He smote the

The mighty David

Philistines hip and thigh and reduced their territory to a narrow strip of coast in the south. He united the Twelve Tribes into a consolidated state under an absolute monarch, and he began the construction of a magnificent capital at Jerusalem. But strong government, military glory, and material splendor were not unmixed blessings for the people. Their inevitable accompaniments were high taxation and conscription. As a consequence, before David died, rumblings of discontent were plainly to be heard in certain parts of his kingdom.

David was succeeded by his son Solomon, the last of the kings of the united monarchy. As a result of the nationalist aspirations of

Solomon aspires to Oriental magnificence

later times, Solomon has been pictured in Hebrew lore as one of the wisest, justest, and most enlightened rulers in all history. The facts of his career furnish little support for such a belief. About all that can be said in his favor is that he was a shrewd diplomat and an active patron of trade. Most of his policies were oppressive, although of course not deliberately so. Ambitious to copy the luxury and magnificence of other Oriental despots, he established a harem of 700 wives and 300 concubines and completed the construction of sumptuous palaces, stables for 4000 horses, and a costly temple in Jerusalem. Since Palestine was poor in resources, most of the materials for the building projects had to be imported. Gold, silver, bronze, and cedar were brought in in such quantities that the revenues from taxation and from the tolls levied upon trade were insufficient to pay for them. To make up the deficit Solomon ceded

100

twenty towns and resorted to the corvée, or the system of con-
scripting labor. Every three months 30,000 Hebrews were drafted
and sent into Phoenicia to work in the forests and mines of King
Hiram of Tyre, from whom the most expensive materials had been
purchased.

Solomon's extravagance and oppression produced acute discontent among his subjects. His death in 935 B.C. was the signal for open
revolt. The ten northern tribes, refusing to submit to his son
Rehoboam, seceded and set up their own kingdom. Sectional differences played their part also in the disruption of the nation. The
northern Hebrews were sophisticated and accustomed to urban living. They benefited from their location at the crossroads of Near
Eastern trade. While this factor increased their prosperity, it also
caused them to be steeped in foreign influences. By contrast, the
two southern tribes were composed very largely of pastoral and
agricultural folk, loyal to the religion of their fathers, and hating the
ways of the foreigner. Perhaps these differences alone would have
been sufficient in time to break the nation asunder.

The secession of the Ten Tribes

After the secession the ten northern tribes came to be known as
the Kingdom of Israel,[2] while the two southern tribes were called
henceforth the Kingdom of Judah. For more than two centuries the
two little states maintained their separate existences. But in 722 B.C.
the Kingdom of Israel was conquered by the Assyrians. Its inhabitants were scattered throughout the vast empire of their conquerors
and were eventually absorbed by the more numerous population
around them. They have ever since been referred to as the Lost Ten

The fate of Israel and Judah

[2] Or the Kingdom of Samaria, from the name of its capital city.

101

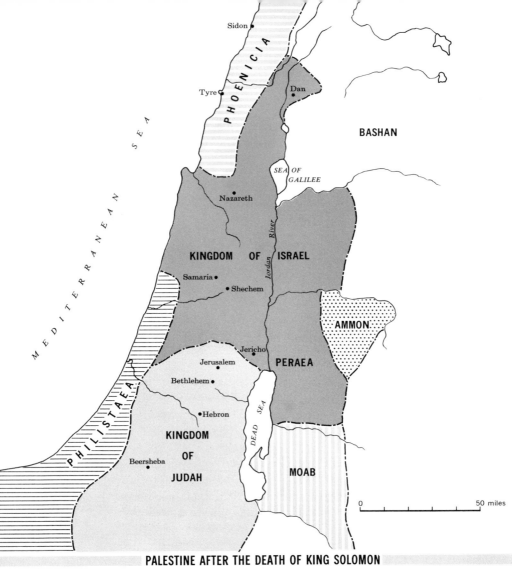

Sidon •

PHOENICIA

Tyre •   • Dan

BASHAN

SEA OF
GALILEE

• Nazareth

Jordan River

KINGDOM   OF   ISRAEL

Samaria •
    • Shechem

MEDITERRANEAN SEA

AMMON

Jericho •

Jerusalem •   PERAEA

Bethlehem •

PHILISTAEA

• Hebron

DEAD SEA

KINGDOM

Beersheba •   OF

JUDAH   MOAB

0   50 miles

PALESTINE AFTER THE DEATH OF KING SOLOMON

Tribes of Israel. The Kingdom of Judah managed to survive for more than a hundred years longer, successfully defying the Assyrian menace. But in 586 B.C., as we have already learned, it was over-thrown by the Chaldeans under Nebuchadnezzar. Jerusalem was plundered and burned, and its leading citizens were carried off into captivity in Babylon. When Cyrus the Persian conquered the Chaldeans, he freed the Jews and permitted them to return to their native land. Few were willing to go, and considerable time elapsed before it was possible to rebuild the temple. From 539 to 332 B.C. Palestine was a vassal state of Persia. In 332 B.C. it was conquered by Alexander and after his death was placed under the rule of the Ptolemies of Egypt. In 63 B.C. it became a Roman protectorate. Its po-litical history as a Jewish commonwealth was ended in 70 A.D. after a desperate revolt which the Romans punished by destroying Jerusa-

102

lem and annexing the country as a province. The inhabitants were
gradually diffused through other parts of the Empire.

The destruction of Jerusalem and annexation of the country by
the Romans were the principal factors in the so-called *Diaspora*, or
dispersion of the Jews from Palestine. Even earlier large numbers of   The *Diaspora*
them had fled into various parts of the Greco-Roman world on account of difficulties in their homeland. In their new environment
they rapidly succumbed to foreign influences, a fact which was of
tremendous importance in promoting a fusion of Greek and Oriental ideas. It was a Hellenized Jew, St. Paul, who was mainly responsible for remolding Christianity in accordance with Greek philosophical doctrines.

3. THE HEBREW RELIGIOUS EVOLUTION

Few peoples in history have gone through a religious evolution
comparable to that of the Hebrews. Its cycle of development ranged
all the way from the crudest superstitions to the loftiest spiritual and   Reasons for the
ethical conceptions. Part of the explanation is doubtless to be found   varied evolution
in the peculiar geographic position occupied by the Hebrew people.   of Hebrew
Located as they were after their conquest of Canaan on the high-   religion
road between Egypt and the major civilizations of Asia, they were
bound to be affected by an extraordinary variety of influences.

At least five different stages can be distinguished in the growth of
the Hebrew religion. The first we can call the pre-Mosaic stage,
from the earliest beginnings of the people to approximately 1100   The pre-Mosaic
B.C. This stage was characterized at first by animism, the worship of   stage
spirits that dwelt in trees, mountains, sacred wells and springs, and
even in stones of peculiar shape. Diverse forms of magic were practiced also at this time—necromancy, imitative magic, scapegoat sacrifices, and so on. Numerous relics of these early beliefs and practices are preserved in the Old Testament. For example, the reference in Deuteronomy 33:16 to the Lord as "Him that dwelt in the
bush." See also II Kings 6:5–7, in which the story is related of how
Elisha made an axehead float by throwing a piece of wood into the
water. According to the principle of imitative magic, the floating of
the wood on the water brought the axehead to the surface.

Gradually animism gave way to anthropomorphic gods. How this
transition occurred cannot be determined. Perhaps it was related to
the fact that Hebrew society had become patriarchal, that is, the fa-   Anthropomorphic
ther exercised absolute authority over the family and descent was   gods
traced through the male line. The gods may have been thought to
occupy a similar position in the clan or tribe. Apparently few of the
new deities were as yet given names; each was usually referred to
merely by the generic name of "El," that is, "God." They were
guardian deities of particular places and probably of separate tribes.
No *national* worship of Yahweh was known at this time.   **103**

The second stage, which lasted from the twelfth century B.C. to the ninth, is frequently designated the stage of national monolatry. The term may be defined as the exclusive worship of one god but without any denial that other gods exist. Due chiefly to the influence of Moses, the Hebrews gradually adopted as their national deity during this period a god whose name appears to have been written "Jhwh" or "Yhwh." How it was pronounced no one knows, but scholars generally agree that it was probably uttered as if spelled "Yahweh." The meaning is also a mystery. When Moses inquired of Yahweh what he should tell the people when they demanded to know what god had sent him, Yahweh replied: "I AM THAT I AM: and he said, Thus shalt thou say unto the children of Israel, I AM hath sent me unto you." [3] Neither at this time nor in any other period of ancient history did the Hebrews refer to their god as "Jehovah." The latter name was the result of a blunder committed by Christian Hebraists of the thirteenth century A.D.[4]

During the time of Moses and for two or three centuries thereafter Yahweh was a somewhat peculiar deity. He was conceived almost exclusively in anthropomorphic terms. He possessed a physical body and the emotional qualities of men. He was capricious, on occasions, and somewhat irascible—as capable of evil and wrathful judgments as he was of good. His decrees were often quite arbitrary, and he would punish the man who sinned unwittingly just about as readily as him whose guilt was real.[5] Omnipotence was scarcely an attribute that Yahweh could claim, for his power was limited to the territory occupied by the Hebrews themselves. When Naaman the Syrian decided to become a follower of Yahweh, he could solve the problem of territorial dominion only by taking two mules' burden of good Palestinian earth with him.[6] But in spite of these limitations the Hebrews revered their God as their only guide and deliverer, the protector of widows and orphans, and the swift avenger of the nation's wrongs.

The religion of this stage was neither primarily ethical nor profoundly spiritual. Yahweh was revered as a supreme lawgiver and as the stern upholder of the moral order of the universe. According to Biblical account, he issued the Ten Commandments to Moses on top of Mount Sinai. Old Testament scholars, however, do not generally accept this tradition. They admit that a primitive Decalogue may have existed in Mosaic times, but they doubt that the Ten Commandments in the form in which they are preserved in the Book of Exodus go back any farther than the seventh century. In any event,

[3] Exodus 3:13–14.
[4] Adolphe Lods, *Israel from Its Beginnings to the Middle of the Eighth Century*, p. 321.
[5] By way of illustration, he struck Uzza dead merely because that unfortunate individual placed his hand upon the Ark of the Covenant to steady it while it was being transported to Jerusalem. I Chronicles 13:9–10.
[6] II Kings 5:17.

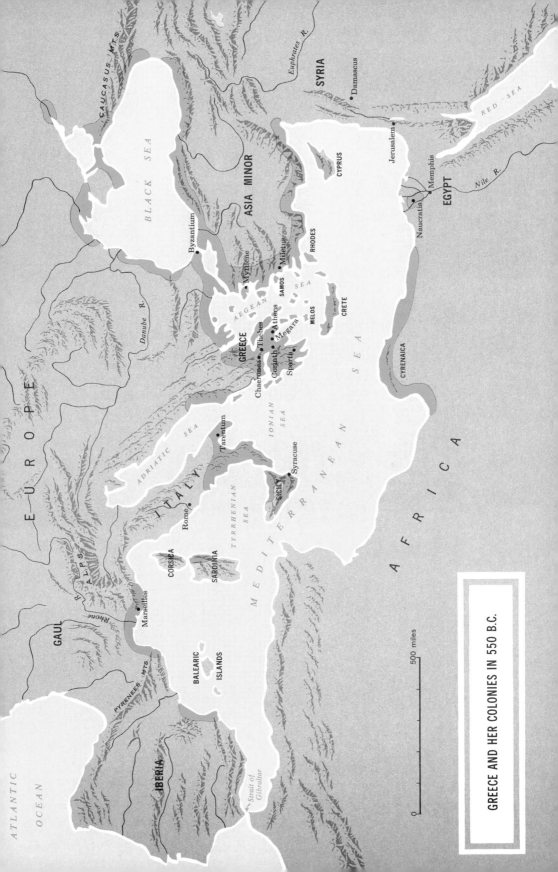

GREECE AND HER COLONIES IN 550 B.C.

EUROPE

ATLANTIC OCEAN

GAUL

IBERIA

Rhone R.

ALPS

PYRENEES MTS.

Strait of Gibraltar

Marseilles

BALEARIC ISLANDS

CORSICA

SARDINIA

Rome

ITALY

TYRRHENIAN SEA

Tarentum

ADRIATIC SEA

SICILY

Syracuse

MEDITERRANEAN SEA

IONIAN SEA

Danube R.

CAUCASUS MTS.

BLACK SEA

Byzantium

ASIA MINOR

GREECE

Chaeronea

Thebes

Corinth

Megara

Sparta

Athens

Mytilene

AEGEAN SEA

SAMOS

Miletus

MELOS

RHODES

CRETE

Euphrates R.

SYRIA

Damascus

Jerusalem

CYPRUS

RED SEA

Memphis

Naucratis

EGYPT

Nile R.

CYRENAICA

AFRICA

500 miles

0

Geometric Horse, VIII cent. B.C. Greek art of this early period was angular, formal, and conventionalized.

Geometric Jar, VIII cent. B.C. Another example of the stylized decorative patterns of early Greek art.

Sphinx, *ca.* 540–530 B. Though doubtless of Orient derivation, Greek sphinxes ha a softer and more human a pect than the Oriental.

Statue of an Amazon, one of the fabled tribe of women warriors, V cent. B.C. (Roman copy)

Departure of a Warrior. Gravestone, *ca.* 530 B.C., a period when naturalism was the dominant note of Greek art.

Athena, *ca.* 460 B.C. T young, graceful patro goddess of Athens is abo to send forth an owl as sign of victory.

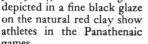

Jar, 500–490 B.C. The figures depicted in a fine black glaze on the natural red clay show athletes in the Panathenaic games.

Chorus of Satyrs, *ca.* 420 B.C. The background is black with the figures in red clay. The satyrs, dressed in fleecy white, with flowing tails, are the chorus of a play.

Toilet Box, 465–460 B.C., showi the Judgment of Paris, an early i cident in the Trojan War.

it is clear that Moses' God was interested just about as much in sacrifice and in ritualistic observances as he was in good conduct or in purity of heart. Moreover, the religion was not vitally concerned with spiritual matters. It offered naught but material rewards in this life and none at all in a life to come. Finally, the belief in monolatry was corrupted by certain elements of fetishism, magic, and even grosser superstitions that lingered from more primitive times or that were gradually acquired from neighboring peoples. These varied all the way from serpent worship to bloody sacrifices and licentious fertility orgies.

By the ninth century the Hebrew faith was badly in need of reform from within. Superstition and idolatry had steadily increased with the passing of the years until the worship of Yahweh was scarcely distinguishable from the worship of the Phoenician and Canaanite Ba'als. First to sense the need for drastic changes were the leaders of ascetic sects such as the Nazirites and Rechabites, who denounced the foreign corruptions and clamored for a return to what they thought was the simple piety of their fathers. To emphasize their hatred of everything foreign, they condemned the refinements of civilized life and urged that the people dwell in tents. Their work was followed by that of the vehement preacher Elijah, who dragged the priests of the Ba'al cults from their altars and slew them with his own hands. Notwithstanding his crusade against the foreign cults,

Remains of an Ancient Synagogue at Capernaum. Capernaum was supposed to have been the scene of many of the miracles attributed to Jesus. Here also he called out Peter, Andrew, and Matthew to be his disciples.

Elijah did not deny the existence of their gods; but he insisted that Yahweh was a god of righteousness and the only deity whom the Hebrews should worship.

The really important work of religious reform, however, was accomplished by the great prophets—Amos, Hosea, Isaiah,[7] and Micah. And their achievements represented the third stage in the development of the Hebrew religion, the stage of the prophetic revolution, which occupied the eighth and seventh centuries B.C. The great prophets were men of much broader vision than Elijah or the leaders of the ascetic sects. Their outlook was progressive; they did not demand a return to some age of simplicity in the past but taught that the religion should be infused with a new philosophy and a new conception of the ends it was supposed to serve. Three basic doctrines made up the substance of their teachings: (1) rudimentary monotheism—Yahweh is the Lord of the universe; He even makes use of nations other than the Hebrews to accomplish his purposes; the gods of other peoples are false gods and should not be worshiped for any reason; (2) Yahweh is a god of righteousness exclusively; He is not really omnipotent, but His power is limited by justice and goodness; the evil in the world comes from man not from God; (3) the purposes of religion are chiefly ethical; Yahweh cares nothing for ritual and sacrifice, but that men should "seek justice, relieve the oppressed, judge the fatherless, plead for the widow." Or as Micah expressed it: "What doth the Lord require of thee, but to do justly, and to love mercy, and to walk humbly with thy God?" [8]

These doctrines contained a definite repudiation of nearly everything that the older religion had stood for. Such, however, was apparently not the intention of the prophets. They conceived it rather as their mission to restore the religion to its ancient purity. The crudities within it they regarded as foreign corruptions. But like many such leaders, they builded better than they knew. Their actual accomplishments went so far beyond their original objectives that they amounted to a religious revolution. To a considerable extent this revolution also had its social and political aspects. Wealth had become concentrated in the hands of a few. Thousands of small farmers had lost their freedom and had passed under subjection to rich proprietors. If we can believe the testimony of Amos, bribery was so rife in the law courts that the plaintiff in a suit for debt had merely to give the judge a pair of shoes and the defendant would be handed over as a slave.[9] Overshadowing all was the threat of

[7] Many Old Testament authorities consider the Book of Isaiah the work of two authors. They ascribe the first part to Isaiah, and the second part, beginning with Chapter 40, to Deutero-Isaiah, or the Second Isaiah. The Second Isaiah is more emphatic than the first in denying the existence of the gods of other peoples. It dates from the period of the Exile.

[8] Micah 6:8.

[9] Amos 2:6. This, of course, was poetic propaganda and may have been slightly exaggerated.

Assyrian domination. To enable the nation to cope with that threat, the prophets believed that social abuses should be stamped out and the people united under a religion purged of its alien corruptions.

The results of this revolution must not be misinterpreted. It did eradicate some of the most flagrant forms of oppression, and it rooted out permanently most of the barbarities that had crept into the religion from foreign sources. But the Hebrew faith did not yet bear much resemblance to modern orthodox Judaism. It contained little of a spiritual character and hardly a trace of the mystical. Instead of being otherwordly, it was oriented toward this life. Its purposes were social and ethical—to promote a just and harmonious society and to abate man's inhumanity to man—not to confer individual salvation in an afterlife. As yet there was no belief in heaven and hell or in Satan as a powerful opponent of God. The shades of the dead went down into Sheol to linger there for a time in the dust and gloom and then disappear.

The religion not yet otherworldly or mystical

Nevertheless, the ideals of the prophetic revolution probably represented the highest perfection of the Hebrew religion. After that time it shifted its emphases, responding again to outside influences. The first of these influences made themselves felt during the period of the Babylonian Captivity from 586 to 539 B.C., which constitutes a fourth stage in the evolution of the religion. As a result of association with the Neo-Babylonians, the Jews adopted ideas of pessimism, fatalism, and the transcendence of God. No longer did they conceive of Yahweh as intimately concerned with the social problems of His people, but as an omnipotent, unapproachable being whose essential characteristic was holiness. His thoughts were not men's thoughts nor His ways the ways of mortals. Man's chief duty was to submit absolutely to His inscrutable will.[10] The forms of the religion were also profoundly changed. In a desperate attempt to preserve the identity of the Jews as a nation, their leaders adopted or revived customs and observances which, they believed, would serve to distinguish them as a peculiar people. The institution of the Sabbath, the forms of synagogal worship, the practice of circumcision, and elaborate distinctions between clean and unclean foods were now given places of fundamental importance. While it is true that most of these observances were of pre-Exilic origin, they had not been regarded as religious essentials for many years. The prophets, moreover, had emphatically denied their importance. The growth of extensive regulations for the conduct of ritual inevitably increased the power of the priests, with the result that Judaism was gradually transformed into an ecclesiastical religion.

The stage of the Exile or Babylonian Captivity

The final significant stage in Hebrew religious evolution was the post-Exilic stage or the period of Persian influence. This period may

---

[10] These ideas are to be found in the Book of Ezekiel and in the writings of Deutero-Isaiah (Isaiah 40–55) which date from the period of the Captivity; also in the Book of Job, written a century or more later.

be considered to have covered the years from 539 to about 300 B.C. Perhaps enough has been said already to indicate the character of the influence from Persia. It will be recalled from the preceding chapter that Zoroastrianism was a dualistic, messianic, otherwordly, and esoteric religion. In the period following the Exile these ideas gained wide acceptance among the Jews. They adopted a belief in Satan as the Great Adversary and the author of evil. They developed an eschatology, including such notions as the coming of a spiritual savior, the resurrection of the dead, and a last judgment. They turned their attention to salvation in an afterworld as more important than enjoyment of this life. Lastly, they embraced the conception of a revealed religion. The Book of Ezekiel, for example, was asserted to have been prepared by God in heaven and given to the man whose name it bears with instruction to "eat" it.[11] In time the idea grew that many other books had been dictated directly by Yahweh to certain of His followers. With the adoption of beliefs such as these the Hebrew faith had evolved far from the strict monotheism and the simple ethical religion of the days of the prophets.

4. HEBREW CULTURE

In certain respects the Hebrew genius was inferior to that of some other great nations of antiquity. In the first place, it revealed no talent for science. Not a single important discovery in any scientific field has ever been traced to the ancient Hebrews. Nor were they particularly adept in appropriating the knowledge of others. They could not build a bridge or a tunnel except of the crudest sort. Whether it was from lack of interest in these things or whether it was because of too deep an absorption in religious affairs is not clear. In the second place, they seem to have been almost entirely devoid of artistic skill. Their only examples of the glyptic arts were engraved seals similar to those made by the Sumerians and Hittites and used for the purpose of affixing signatures. They had no architecture, sculpture, or painting worthy of mention. The famous temple at Jerusalem was not a Hebrew building at all but a product of Phoenician skill, for Solomon imported artisans from Tyre to finish the more complicated tasks.

It was rather in law, literature, and philosophy that the Hebrew genius was most perfectly expressed. Although all of these subjects were closely allied with religion, they did have their secular aspects. The finest example of Jewish law was the Deuteronomic Code, which forms the core of the Book of Deuteronomy. Despite claims of its great antiquity, it was probably an outgrowth of the prophetic revolution. It was based in part upon an older Code of the Covenant,

[11] Ezekiel 3:1–4.

which was derived in considerable measure from the laws of the Canaanites and the Old Babylonians.[12] In general, its provisions were more enlightened than those of Hammurabi's code. One of them enjoined liberality to the poor and to the stranger. Another commanded that the Hebrew slave who had served six years should be freed, and insisted that he must not be sent away empty. A third provided that judges and other officers should be chosen by the people and forbade them to accept gifts or to show partiality in any form. A fourth condemned witchcraft, divination, and necromancy. A fifth denounced the punishment of children for the guilt of their fathers and affirmed the principle of individual responsibility for sin. A sixth prohibited the taking of interest on any kind of loan made by one Jew to another. A seventh required that at the end of every seven years there should be a "release" of debts. "Every creditor that lendeth aught unto his neighbour shall release it; he shall not exact it of his neighbour, or of his brother . . . save when there shall be no poor among you." [13]

The Shekel of Ancient Israel. Depicted are the two sides of the silver shekel of 141-137 B.C. This coin weighs 220 grains; a United States silver dollar weighs 412.5 grains. The Chaldeans and Phoenicians also had coins called shekels.

As one would expect from the circumstances out of which it grew, a cardinal purpose of the Deuteronomic Code was to infuse into Jewish society a more democratic and equalitarian character. Its authors were not interested in abstract principles. For example, they did not condemn slavery as wrong in itself; they sought merely to prevent the permanent enslavement of Jews. Nevertheless, it is undeniably true that this code did provide for more political and social democracy than the laws of any other Oriental nation except Egypt. Even the king himself was forbidden to accumulate great wealth or to indulge in ostentatious luxury. No military despotism of the Assyrian or Babylonian type was to be tolerated. The king was not above the law but very definitely subject to it; he was re-

Democratic and equalitarian ideals

---

[12] C. F. Kent, *The Message of Israel's Lawgivers*, p. 24.
[13] Deuteronomy 15:1-4.

quired to have constantly with him a copy of the code and to "read therein all the days of his life . . . that his heart be not lifted up above his brethren, and that he turn not aside from the commandment." [14] Moreover, his power and that of his officers was strictly limited. The administration of justice was left almost entirely in the hands of the people. In cases of disputed guilt the elders of the city would decide, but the punishment provided in the code would be inflicted by the family of the victim or by the community at large. The conscription of labor for foreign service was also prohibited, and exemption from military duty was required to be granted to the man who had built a new house, planted a new vineyard, or married a new wife, and even to the man who was "fearful and faint-hearted . . . lest his brethren's heart faint as well as his heart." [15]

Hebrew literature

The literature of the Hebrews was by far the best that the ancient Orient ever produced. Nearly all of it now extant is preserved in the Old Testament and in the books of the so-called Apocrypha. Except for a few fragments like the Song of Deborah in Judges 5, it is not really so ancient as is commonly supposed. Scholars now recognize that the Old Testament was built up mainly through a series of collections and revisions (redactions) in which the old and new fragments were merged and generally assigned to an ancient author, Moses, for example. But the oldest of these redactions was not prepared any earlier than 850 B.C. The majority of the books of the Old Testament were of even more recent origin, with the exception, of course, of certain of the chronicles. As one would logically expect, the philosophical books were of late authorship. Although the bulk of the Psalms were ascribed to King David, a good many of them actually refer to events of the Captivity. It seems certain that the collection as a whole was the work of several centuries. Most recent of all were the books of Ecclesiastes, Esther, and Daniel, composed no earlier than the third century B.C. Likewise, the Apocrypha, or books of doubtful religious authority, did not see the light of day until Hebrew civilization was almost extinct. Some, like Maccabees I and II, relate events of the second century B.C. Others including the Wisdom of Solomon and the Book of Enoch were written under the influence of Greco-Oriental philosophy.

Amos' indictment
of social abuses

Not all of the writings of the Hebrews had high literary merit. A considerable number were dull, repetitious chronicles. Nevertheless, most of them, whether in the form of battle song, prophecy, love lyric, or drama, were rich in rhythm, concrete images, and emotional vigor. Few passages in any language can surpass the scornful indictment of social abuses voiced by the prophet Amos:

[14] Deuteronomy 17:18–20.
[15] Deuteronomy 20:5–8. It is necessary to remember, however, that there was a strong utopian element in this code. We cannot be sure that all its provisions were actually accepted by the government. Nevertheless, it did express ideals that were superior to those of most other ancient peoples.

Hear this, O ye that swallow up the needy, even to make the
poor of the land to fail,
Saying, when will the new moon be gone, that we may sell
corn?
And the sabbath that we may set forth wheat,
Making the ephah small, and the shekel great,
And falsifying the balances by deceit?
That we may buy the poor for silver, and the needy for a pair
of shoes;
Yea, and sell the refuse of the wheat?

The most beautiful of Hebrew love lyrics was the Song of Songs, or the Song of Solomon. Its theme was quite probably derived from an old Canaanite hymn of spring, celebrating the passionate affec- *The Song of* tion of the Shulamith or fertility goddess for her lover, but it had *Songs* long since lost its original meaning. The following verses are typical of its sensuous beauty:

I am the rose of Sharon
and the lily of the valleys.
As the lily among thorns,
so is my love among the daughters.

.   .   .   .

My beloved is white and ruddy,
the chiefest among ten thousand.
His head is as the most fine gold;
his locks are bushy and black as a raven:
His eyes are as the eyes of doves by the rivers of waters,
washed with milk and fitly set.
His cheeks are as a bed of spices, as sweet flowers;
his lips like lilies, dropping sweet smelling myrrh.

.   .   .   .

How beautiful are thy feet with shoes, O prince's daughter!
The joints of thy thighs are like jewels,
the work of the hands of a cunning workman.

Few authorities would deny that the supreme achievement of the Hebrew literary genius was the Book of Job. In form the work is a drama of the tragic struggle between man and fate. Its central theme *The Book of* is the problem of evil: how it can be that the righteous suffer while *Job* the eyes of the wicked stand out with fatness. The story was an old one, adapted very probably from the Babylonian writing of similar content, but the Hebrews introduced into it a much deeper realization of philosophical possibilities. The main character, Job, a man of unimpeachable virtue, is suddenly overtaken by a series of disasters: **111**

he is despoiled of his property, his children are killed, and his body
is afflicted with a painful disease. His attitude at first is one of stoic
resignation; the evil must be accepted along with the good. But as
his sufferings increase he is plunged into despair. He curses the day
of his birth and delivers an apostrophe to death, where "the wicked
cease from troubling and the weary be at rest."

Then follows a lengthy debate between Job and his friends over
the meaning of evil. The latter take the traditional Hebraic view
that all suffering is a punishment for sin, and that those who repent
are forgiven and strengthened in character. But Job is not satisfied
with any of their arguments. Torn between hope and despair, he
strives to review the problem from every angle. He even considers
the possibility that death may not be the end, that there may be
some adjustment of the balance hereafter. But the mood of despair
returns, and he decides that God is an omnipotent demon, destroying without mercy wherever His caprice or anger directs. Finally,
in his anguish he appeals to the Almighty to reveal Himself and
make known His ways to man. God answers him out of the whirlwind with a magnificent exposition of the tremendous works of
nature. Convinced of his own insignificance and of the unutterable
majesty of God, Job despises himself and repents in dust and ashes.
In the end no solution is given of the problem of individual suffering. No promise is made of recompense in a life hereafter, nor does
God make any effort to refute the hopeless pessimism of Job. Man
must take comfort in the philosophic reflection that the universe is
greater than himself, and that God in the pursuit of His sublime
purposes cannot really be limited by human standards of equity and
goodness.

As philosophers the Hebrews surpassed every other people before
the Greeks, including the Egyptians. Although they were not brilliant metaphysicians and constructed no great theories of the universe, they did concern themselves with most of the problems relating to the life and destiny of man. Their thought was essentially
personal rather than abstract. Probably the earliest of their writings
of a distinctly philosophical character were the Old Testament
Book of Proverbs and the Apocryphal Book of Ecclesiasticus. In
their final form both were of late composition, but much of the material they contain was doubtless quite ancient. Not all of it was
original, for a considerable portion had been taken from Egyptian
sources, especially from the writings of Amenemope, who lived
about 1000 B.C. The philosophy of Proverbs and Ecclesiasticus is not
very profound and may be considered as representing the mental
adolescence of the Hebrew nation. It is almost entirely ethical, but
its appeal is primarily to prudential considerations, not to the will of
God or to any absolute standards of right and wrong. It has as its
essential teaching: be temperate, diligent, wise, and honest, and you
will surely be rewarded with prosperity, long life, and a good name

among men. Only in such isolated passages as the following is any recognition given to higher motives of sympathy or respect for the rights of others: "Whoso mocketh the poor reproacheth his Maker; and he that is glad at calamities shall not be unpunished." [16]

A much more profound and critical philosophy is contained in Ecclesiastes, an Old Testament book, not to be confused with the Apocryphal Ecclesiasticus mentioned above. The author of Ecclesiastes is unknown. In some way it came to be attributed to Solomon, but he certainly did not write it, for it includes doctrines and forms of expression unknown to the Hebrews for hundreds of years after his death. Modern critics date it no earlier than the third century B.C. The basic ideas of its philosophy may be summarized as follows:

Ecclesiastes

(1) Mechanism. The universe is a machine that rolls on forever without evidence of any purpose or goal. There is nothing new under the sun, no progress, merely endless repetition of the past. Sunrise and sunset, birth and death are but separate phases of constantly recurring cycles.

(2) Fatalism. Man is a victim of the whims of fate. There is no necessary relation between effort and success: "The race is not to the swift, nor the battle to the strong, neither yet bread to the wise . . . but time and chance happeneth to them all."

(3) Skepticism. Knowledge of ultimate things is impossible. There is no evidence of any soul or any life after death. Men and beasts are alike: "all are of the dust, and all turn to dust again."

(4) Pessimism. All is vanity and vexation of spirit. Fame, riches, extravagant pleasure are snares and delusions in the end. Although wisdom is better than folly, even it is not a sure key to happiness, for an increase in knowledge brings a keener awareness of suffering. Only a good name and joy in the work of one's hands are much to be prized.

(5) Moderation. Extremes of asceticism and extremes of indulgence are both to be avoided. "Be not righteous over much . . . be not over much wicked: why shouldest thou die before thy time?" [17]

5. THE MAGNITUDE OF THE HEBREW INFLUENCE

The influence of the Hebrews, like that of most other Oriental peoples, has been chiefly religious and ethical. While it is true that the Old Testament has served as a source of inspiration for much of the literature and art of the Renaissance and early modern civilizations, this has resulted largely because the Bible was already familiar material as a part of the religious heritage. The same explanation can be applied to the use of the Old Testament as a source of law and

The nature of the Hebrew influence

[16] Proverbs 17:5.
[17] For a more complete analysis of the philosophy of Ecclesiastes see Morris Jastrow, *A Gentle Cynic*.

Hebrew
foundations of
Christianity:
the beliefs of
the Pharisees

political theory by the Calvinists in the sixteenth century, and by many other Christians both before and since.

But these facts do not mean that the Hebrew influence has been slight. On the contrary, the history of nearly every Western civilization during the past two thousand years would have been radically different without the heritage from Israel. For it must be remembered that Hebrew beliefs were among the principal foundations of Christianity. The relationship between the two religions is frequently misunderstood. The movement inaugurated by Jesus of Nazareth is commonly represented as a revolt against Judaism; but such was only partly the case. On the eve of the Christian era the Jewish nation had come to be divided into three main sects: a majority sect of Pharisees, and two minority sects of Sadducees and Essenes. The Pharisees represented the middle classes and some of the better educated common folk. They believed in the resurrection, in rewards and punishments after death, and in the coming of a political messiah. Intensely nationalistic, they advocated participation in government and faithful observance of the ancient ritual. They regarded all parts of the law as of virtually equal importance, whether they applied to matters of ceremony or to obligations of social ethics.

The Sadducees
and the Essenes

Representing altogether different strata of society, the minority sects disagreed with the Pharisees on both religious and political issues. The Sadducees, including the priests and the wealthier classes, were most famous for their denial of the resurrection and of rewards and punishments in an afterlife. Although temporarily, at least, they favored the acceptance of Roman rule, their attitude toward the ancient law was even more inflexible than that of the Pharisees. The sect of Essenes, the smallest of them all, was possibly the most influential. Its members, who were drawn from the lower classes, practiced asceticism and preached otherworldliness as means of protest against the wealth and power of priests and rulers. They ate and drank only enough to keep themselves alive, held all their goods in common, and looked upon marriage as a necessary evil. Far from being fanatical patriots, they regarded government with indifference and refused to take oaths under any conditions. They emphasized the spiritual aspects of religion rather than the ceremonial, and stressed particularly the immortality of the soul, the coming of a religious messiah, and the early destruction of the world. Their most noted member appears to have been John the Baptist, though he later repudiated the sect on the ground that it was preparing only its own followers and not the nation as a whole for the coming of the messiah.

The Dead Sea
scrolls

Until recently scholars were dependent for their knowledge of the Essenes almost entirely upon secondary sources. But in 1947 an Arab shepherd unwittingly opened the way to one of the most spectacular discoveries of documentary evidence in world history.

The Dead Sea Scrolls. Now on display in an underground vault at the Hebrew University in Jerusalem. The oldest extant examples of Hebrew religious literature, they furnish us with evidence of the activities of the Essenes, and mystical and other worldly sects, about the beginning of the Christian era.

Searching for a lost sheep on the western shore of the Dead Sea, he threw a stone that entered a hole in the rocks and made such a peculiar noise that he ran away in fright. He returned, however, with a friend to investigate and discovered a cave in which were stored about fifty cylindrical earthen jars stuffed with writings on leather scrolls. Studied by scholars, the scrolls revealed the existence of a monastic community which flourished from about 130 B.C. to 67 A.D. Its members lived a life of humility and self-denial, holding their goods in common, and devoting their time to prayer and sacraments and to studying and copying Biblical texts. They looked forward confidently to the coming of a messiah, the overthrow of evil, and the establishment of God's kingdom on earth. That they belonged to the same general movement that fostered the growth of the Essenes seems almost beyond question.

All branches of Judaism except the Sadducees strongly influenced the development of Christianity. Indeed, many Christians regard their religion as the completion and fulfillment of the religion of the Jews. From Jewish sources Christianity obtained its cosmogony, or

Hebrew influence upon Christianity

115

theory of the origin of the universe; the Ten Commandments; and a large portion of its theology. Jesus himself, although he condemned the Pharisees for their legalism and hypocrisy, did not repudiate all of their tenets. Like them he revered the prophets, believed in rewards and punishments after death, and considered the Jewish people the chosen of God. Instead of abolishing the ancient law, as he is popularly supposed to have done, he demanded its fulfillment, insisting, however, that it should not be made the essential part of religion. To what extent the beliefs and practices of the Christian religion were molded by the more radical Judaism of the Essenes and kindred sects is a question whose answer must await further research. Perhaps the fundamental influence was slight. Nonetheless, we know that many early Christians practiced asceticism, regarded government with indifference, held all their goods in common, and believed in the imminent end of the world. These parallels do not mean, of course, that Christianity was a mere adaptation of beliefs and practices emanating from Judaism. On account of various factors there was much in it that was unique; but that is a subject which can be discussed more conveniently in another connection.[18]

Ethical and political influence of the Hebrews

The ethical and political influence of the Hebrews has also been substantial. Their moral conceptions have been a leading factor in the development of the negative approach toward ethics which has prevailed for so long in Western countries. For the early Hebrews, "righteousness" consisted primarily in the observance of taboos. Although a positive morality of charity and social justice made rapid headway during the time of the prophets, this in turn was partly obscured by the revival of priestly influence in the period that followed. As a result, the Torah or Pentateuch (the first five books of the Old Testament), which embraced the code of personal behavior for the Jew, came to be crammed with ritualistic prohibitions. With respect to political influence, the record is more impressive. Hebrew ideals of limited government, the sovereignty of law, and regard for the dignity and worth of the individual have been among the major formative influences which have shaped the growth of modern democracy. It is now almost universally recognized that the traditions of Judaism contributed equally with the influence of Christianity and Stoic philosophy in fostering recognition of the rights of man and in promoting the development of the free society.

SELECTED READINGS

· *Items so designated are available in paperbound editions.*
· Albright, W. F., *The Archaeology of Palestine*, Baltimore, 1960 (Penguin).
  Anderson, B. W., *Rediscovering the Bible*, New York, 1951.

[18] See chapter on The Civilization of Early Medieval Europe.

Baron, S. W., *A Social and Religious History of the Jews,* New York, 1937, 3 vols. Complete and scholarly.

Bertholet, Alfred, *A History of Hebrew Civilization,* London, 1926.

· Chase, Mary E., *Life and Language in the Old Testament,* New York, 1955 (Norton Library).

· Davies, A. P., *The Meaning of the Dead Sea Scrolls,* New York, 1956 (Mentor).

· De Burgh, W. G., *The Legacy of the Ancient World,* 3d ed., New York, 1960 (Penguin). A good survey of the influence of Hebrew thought.

Finegan, Jack, *Light from the Ancient Past,* Princeton, 1946.

Fritsch, C. T., *The Qumrān Community,* New York, 1956. Relates the importance of the Dead Sea Scrolls.

· Frye, R. N., *The Heritage of Persia,* Cleveland, 1963 (Mentor).

· Kenyon, K. M., *Archaeology in the Holy Land,* New York, 1960 (Praeger).

Klausner, Joseph, *The Messianic Idea in Israel,* New York, 1955.

Lods, Adolphe, *Israel from Its Beginnings to the Middle of the Eighth Century,* New York, 1932. Excellent on religious, intellectual, and social history.

————, *The Prophets and the Rise of Judaism,* New York, 1951.

· Meek, T. J., *Hebrew Origins,* rev., New York, 1951 (Torchbook).

Oesterley, W. O. E., and Robinson, T. H., *Hebrew Religion, Its Origin and Development,* New York, 1932. One of the best interpretations.

Olmstead, A. T. E., *History of Palestine and Syria,* New York, 1931.

· Orlinsky, H. M., *Ancient Israel,* Ithaca, 1956 (Cornell). Brief but good.

· Roth, Cecil, *The Dead Sea Scrolls,* New York, 1965 (Norton Library). Author contends that the scrolls were not produced by the Essenes but by the Zealots, a warlike sect deeply involved in the rebellion against Rome in 66 A.D.

Smith, J. M. P., *The Moral Life of the Hebrews,* Chicago, 1923.

————, *The Origin and History of Hebrew Law,* Chicago, 1931.

Vaux, Roland de, *Ancient Israel: Its Life and Institutions,* New York, 1962. Especially valuable for archaeological data.

SOURCE MATERIALS

The Apocrypha, Ancient Hebrew writings of doubtful authorship. Not recognized as scriptural by Hebrew and Protestant theologians.

· Gaster, T. H., trans., *The Dead Sea Scriptures in English Translation.* New York, 1964 (Anchor).

The Old Testament, especially the following books and portions of books: Deuteronomy 5, 12–21; Ecclesiastes; Amos; I Samuel 8–31; II Samuel; I Kings 1–12; Job; Proverbs; Isaiah 1–12, 40–66; Micah; Psalms.

Pritchard, J. B., ed., *Ancient Near Eastern Texts Relating to the Old Testament,* rev. ed., Princeton, 1955.

CHAPTER 6

The Hittite, Minoan-Mycenaean, and Lesser Cultures

But for them among these gods will be bled for annual food:
to the god Karnua one steer and one sheep;
to the goddess Kupapa one steer and one sheep;
to the divinity Sarku one sheep;
and a Kutupalis sheep to the male divinities.
—Hittite sacrifice formula, translated
from a hieroglyph by
H. T. Bossert

A few other ancient cultures of the Near Orient require more than passing attention. Chief among them are the Hittite, Minoan-Mycenaean, Phoenician, and Lydian cultures. The Hittites are important primarily as intermediaries between East and West. They were one of the main connecting links between the civilizations of Egypt, the Tigris-Euphrates valley, and the region of the Aegean Sea. It appears certain also that they were the original discoverers of iron. The Minoan-Mycenaean civilization is significant for its remarkable achievements in the arts and for its quality of freedom and courage for experimentation. Though many of its achievements perished, there is evidence that the Greeks owed to these Aegean peoples a considerable debt. The Greek religion, for example, contained numerous Minoan-Mycenaean elements. Of the same origin were probably the devotion of the Greeks to athletics, their system of weights and measures, their knowledge of navigation, and perhaps also a great many of their artistic traditions. As for the Phoenicians, no one could overlook the importance of their distribution of a knowledge of the alphabet and a primitive commercial law to the surrounding civilized world. The Lydians have gone down in history as the originators of the first system of coinage.

Importance of these cultures

119

I. THE HITTITES AND THE PHRYGIANS

Until about a century ago little was known of the Hittites except their name. They were commonly assumed to have played no role of any significance in the drama of history. The slighting references to them in the Bible give the impression that they were little more than a half-barbarian tribe. But in 1870 some curiously inscribed stones were found at Hamath in Syria. This was the beginning of an extensive inquiry which has continued with a few interruptions to the present day. It was not long until scores of other monuments and clay tablets were discovered over most of Asia Minor and through the Near East as far as the Tigris-Euphrates valley. In 1907 some evidences of an ancient city were unearthed near the village of Boghaz-Keui in the province of Anatolia. Further excavation eventually revealed the ruins of a great fortified capital which was known as Hattusas or Hittite City. Within its walls were discovered more than 20,000 documents and fragments, most of them apparently laws and decrees.

On the basis of these finds and other evidences gradually accumulated, it was soon made clear that the Hittites were once the rulers of a mighty empire covering most of Asia Minor and extending to the upper reaches of the Euphrates. Part of the time it included Syria as well and even portions of Phoenicia and Palestine. The Hittites reached the zenith of their power during the years from 2000 to 1200 B.C. In the last century of this period they waged a long and exhausting war with Egypt, which had much to do with the downfall of both empires. Neither was able to regain its strength. After 1200 B.C. Carchemish on the Euphrates River became for a time the leading Hittite city, but as a commercial center rather than as the capital of a great empire. The days of imperial glory were over. Finally, after 717 B.C., all the remaining Hittite territories were conquered and absorbed by the Assyrians, Lydians, and Phrygians.

The mystery of
the race and
language of the
Hittites

Where the Hittites came from and what were their relationships to other peoples are problems which still defy a perfect solution. As depicted by the Egyptians, some of them appear to have been of a Mongoloid type. All had enormous hooked noses, receding foreheads, and slanting eyes. Most modern scholars trace their place of origin to Turkestan and consider them related to the Greeks. Their language was Indo-European. Its secret was unlocked during World War I by the Czech scholar Bedrich Hrozny. Since then thousands of clay tablets making up the laws and official records of the emperors have been deciphered. They reveal a civilization resembling more closely the Old Babylonian than any other.

Hardly enough evidence has yet been collected to make possible an accurate appraisal of Hittite civilization. Some modern historians refer to it as if it were on a level with the Mesopotamian or even with the Egyptian civilization. Such may have been the case from the material standpoint, for the Hittites undoubtedly had an extensive knowledge of agriculture and a highly developed economic life in general. They mined great quantities of silver, copper, and lead, which they sold to surrounding nations. They discovered the mining and use of iron and made that material available for the rest of the civilized world. Trade was also one of their principal economic pursuits. In fact, they seem to have depended almost as much upon commercial penetration as upon war for the expansion of their empire.

On the other hand, there is nothing as yet to indicate any marked superiority in intellectual attainments, although of course no one can tell what future research may reveal. The thousands of tablets so far recovered appear to be business, legal, and religious documents primarily. The literature of the Hittites consisted chiefly of mythology, including adaptations of the *Gilgamesh Epic* and of creation and flood legends from the Old Babylonians. They had nothing that could be described as philosophy, nor is there any evidence of scientific originality outside of the metallurgical arts. They evidently possessed some talent for the perfection of writing, for in addition to a modified cuneiform adapted from Mesopotamia they also developed a hieroglyphic system which was partly phonetic in character.

The intellectual level of Hittite culture

One of the most significant achievements of the Hittites was their system of law. Although reflecting Babylonian influence, it was in considerable measure unique. Approximately two hundred separate paragraphs or decrees, covering a great variety of subjects, have been translated. They reflect a society comparatively urbane and sophisticated but subject to minute governmental control. The title to all land was vested in the king or in the governments of the cities. Grants were made to individuals only in return for military service and under the strict requirement that the land be cultivated. If anyone failed to perform these obligations, his holdings reverted to the state. Prices were fixed in the laws themselves for an enormous number of commodities—not only for articles of luxury and the products of industry, but even for food and clothing. All wages and fees for services were likewise minutely prescribed, with the pay of women fixed at less than half the rate for men.

Hittite law

On the whole, the Hittite law was more humane than that of the Old Babylonians. Death was the punishment for only eight offenses —such as witchcraft, sex relations with animals, and theft of property from the palace. Even premeditated murder was punishable only by a fine. Mutilation was not specified as a penalty at all except for arson or theft when committed by a slave. The contrast with the cruelties of Assyrian law was much more striking. Not a single example is to be found in the Hittite decrees of such fiendish punishments as flaying, castration, and impalement, which the rulers at Nineveh seemed to think necessary for maintaining their authority.

Humane character of Hittite law

Hittite Sculpture. Perhaps the most highly conventionalized sculpture of the ancient world was that of the Hittite reliefs. Noteworthy are the animal legs and tails with human torsos and heads, the Mesopotamian treatment of the hair and beard, the fingers of even length, and the huge noses. Curious also is the facing position of the king's feet.

Unfortunately the reasons for this more liberal spirit of the Hittite lawgivers remain enshrouded in mystery.

The art of the Hittites

The art of the Hittites was not of outstanding excellence. So far as we know, it included only sculpture and architecture. The former was generally crude and naïve, but at the same time it revealed a freshness and vigor all too uncommon in the work of Oriental peoples. Most of it was in the form of reliefs depicting scenes of war and mythology. Architecture was ponderous and huge. Temples and palaces were squat, unadorned structures with small, two-columned porches and great stone lions guarding the entrance.

Hittite religion

Not a great deal is known about the Hittite religion except that it had an elaborate mythology, innumerable deities, and forms of worship of Mesopotamian origin. The name of the chief male deity seems to have been Addu, a god of the storm, who was always represented with a bolt of lightning issuing from his hand. But the chief place in the pantheon was given to a mother goddess of fertility, whose name is unknown. A sun god was also worshiped, along with a host of other deities, some of whom appear to have had no particular function at all. The Hittites seem to have welcomed into the divine company practically all of the gods of the peoples they conquered and even of the nations that bought their wares. The practices of the religion included divination, sacrifice, purification ceremonies, and the offering of prayers. Nothing can be found in the records to indicate that the religion was in any sense ethical.

The chief historical importance of the Hittites probably lies in the role which they played as intermediaries between the Tigris-Euphrates valley and the westernmost portions of the Near East. Doubtless in this way certain culture elements from Mesopotamia were transmitted to the Canaanites and Hyksos and perhaps to the peoples of the Aegean islands. But the Hittite culture itself appears not to have been without direct influence. It seems to have been reflected in the social customs of the Phrygians, who flourished from about 900 to 300 B.C. Their territory occupied the west central portion of Asia Minor, extending as far east as the Halys River. In language and literature they appear to have been related to the Greeks, and they constituted an important channel for the transmission of culture elements to the Greeks and Romans. Their most widely copied institution was the cult of Cybele, the Great Mother, which spread rapidly and influenced the mystery religions of both Greece and Italy. The chief deities of the cult were Cybele, the Earth Mother, and Sabazius, the Son, who died and rose from the dead each year with the death and rebirth of vegetation. Its ceremonies were characterized by ecstatic frenzy, bloody sacrifices, and wild, orgiastic dances. The Phrygians were conquered by the Lydians about 610 B.C. but recovered their power and enjoyed a semi-independent and relatively prosperous status for another two centuries. Their early kings were all named either Gordius or Midas.

The Goddess Kybele (Cybele), or Great Mother, on a Processional Car Drawn by Lions. Although this statue was produced by the Romans in the second century A.D., the Goddess herself was of Phrygian origin. She became one of the most popular deities of the ancient world.

The tomb of one of them was discovered in 1957 by a University of Pennsylvania archaeological expedition near Ankara, the capital of modern Turkey.

2. THE MINOAN-MYCENAEAN CIVILIZATION

A long-forgotten
civilization

By a strange coincidence the discovery of the existence of the Hittite and Minoan-Mycenaean civilizations was made at just about the same time. Before 1870 scarcely anyone dreamed that great civilizations had flourished on the Aegean islands and on the shores of Asia Minor for hundreds of years prior to the rise of the Greeks. Students of the *Iliad* knew, of course, of the references to a strange people who were supposed to have dwelt in Troy, to have kidnaped the fair Helen, and to have been punished by the Greeks for this act by the siege and destruction of their city; but it was commonly supposed that these accounts were mere figments of a poetical imagination.

The discoveries
by Schliemann
and others

The first discovery of a highly developed Aegean culture center was made not by a professional archaeologist but by a retired German businessman, Heinrich Schliemann. Fascinated from early youth by the stories of the Homeric epics, he determined to dedicate his life to archaeological research as soon as he had sufficient income to enable him to do so. Luckily for him and for the world he accumulated a fortune in Russian petroleum and then retired from business to spend both time and money in the pursuit of his boyhood dreams. In 1870 he began excavating at Troy. Within a few years he had uncovered portions of nine different cities, each built upon the ruins of its predecessor. The second of these cities he identified as the Troy of the *Iliad*, although it has been proved since that Troy was the seventh city. After fulfilling his first great ambition, he started excavations on the mainland of Greece and eventually uncovered two other Aegean cities, Mycenae and Tiryns. The work of Schliemann was soon followed by that of other investigators, notably the Englishman Sir Arthur Evans, who discovered Knossos, the resplendent capital of the Minoan kings of Crete. Up to the present time more than half of the ancient Aegean sites have been carefully searched, and a wealth of knowledge has been accumulated about various aspects of the culture.

The favorable
natural environ-
ment of Crete

The Minoan-Mycenaean civilization appears to have originated on the island of Crete, from which it spread to the mainland of Greece and to Asia Minor. In few other cases in history does the geographic interpretation of culture origins fit so neatly. Crete has a benign and equable climate, neither so hot as to make men lazy nor so cold as to require a life of unceasing struggle. While the soil is fertile, it is not of unlimited area; consequently, as the population increased, men were impelled to sharpen their wits and to contrive new means of

earning a living. Some emigrated; others took to the sea; but a larger number remained at home and developed articles for export. The latter included, especially, wine and olive oil, pottery, gems and seals, knives and daggers, and objects of skilled craftsmanship. The chief imports were foodstuffs and metals. As a result of such trade, the country became an industrial and commercial nation with prosperous cities and extensive contacts with the surrounding civilized world. Added to these factors of a favorable environment were the beauties of nature, which abounded almost everywhere, stimulating the development of a marvelous art.

The Minoan civilization was one of the earliest in the history of the world. As far back as 3000 B.C. the natives of Crete had made the transition from the Neolithic stage to the age of metals and probably to the age of writing. The first peak of advancement was attained under the leadership of the cities of Knossos and Phaistos about 1800 B.C. Recently evidence has been found of the existence of another great city, Kato Zakros, on the east coast of Crete. Here was a huge palace of 250 rooms, with a swimming pool, parquet floors, and thousands of decorated vases. About 1450 B.C. this palace was destroyed by volcanic eruptions followed by violent earthquakes. Other cities probably suffered a similar fate, although Knossos and Phaistos were rebuilt. A new dynasty came to the throne of Crete. A new system of writing was adopted, and a new cycle of civilization began which carried Minoan culture to its greatest heights.

The Minoan civilization one of the oldest in the world

After about fifty years of uncertainty the Minoan-Mycenaean civilization rose to new heights of brilliance and strength. Troy and the cities of Crete were rebuilt, and other great centers were established at Mycenae and Tiryns. Soon afterward Cretan hegemony was extended over the remaining portions of the Aegean world. But the new age of power and splendor was not destined for long duration. The island's resources were substantially depleted, and commerce with Egypt had diminished. In the sixteenth century B.C. a group of barbarian Greeks subsequently known as Achaeans expanded from their original home in the northern Peloponnesus and eventually conquered Mycenae. Gradually absorbing the material culture of the vanquished, they became rich and powerful sea lords. About 1400 B.C. they overwhelmed the city of Knossos, and soon the whole island of Crete passed under their sway. Although they were no longer a primitive people, they seem never to have appreciated the finer aspects of Cretan culture. As a result this period of Mycenaean supremacy was marked by a decline in art and probably in intellect as well. In the thirteenth century the Mycenaeans waged their successful war with the Trojans, but less than 200 years later they themselves fell the victims of barbarian invasion. The new hordes that came in were also Greeks, but they belonged to the group known as Dorians (originally from somewhere on the Balkan peninsula). Their culture was relatively

The glory and the downfall of the Minoan-Mycenaean civilization

primitive, except for the fact that they had iron weapons. For centuries they had lived on the mainland of Greece, gradually penetrating farther southward. About 1250 B.C. they began their conquest of
the Mycenaean cities. Two hundred years later the Minoan-
Mycenaean civilization had passed into the limbo of history.

The racial character of the Minoan people has been determined
with substantial accuracy. Archaeological data from Crete have
been found in sufficient profusion to leave little doubt that its ancient inhabitants were a composite nation. Their ancestors appear
to have come from Syria and Anatolia and were closely related to
the Hittites and to the earliest invaders of India. At the same time
there is evidence—from the fact that their artists depicted them
with long heads, short, slender bodies, and dark, wavy hair—that
they bore a relationship to the Egyptians. Although they occupied
Greek territory, they were not Greeks at all in the historic meaning
of that name. The true Greeks, as we shall presently see, were of
altogether different ethnic origin.

The Minoan civilization was probably one of the freest and most
progressive in all the Near Orient. The ruler was known by the title
of Minos, which was roughly the equivalent of Pharaoh (hence the
name *Minoan*). That it was a title of divinity is shown by the fact
that it was occasionally used as if it referred to a god. But the Minos
was no bristling war lord like the Assyrian and Persian kings. His
professional army was small; he had no great fortified cities; nor is
there any indication of his use of conscription. He did have a large
and efficient navy, but this was for defense against external attack
and for the protection of trade, not to overawe the citizens at home.

On the other hand, there was some regimentation of industry;
whether benevolent or not is unknown. The king was the chief
capitalist and entrepreneur in the country. The factories in connection with his palace turned out great quantities of fine pottery, textiles, and metal goods. Some of their products were intended to supply the needs of the court, but many were sold at home and abroad
for profit. Although private enterprise was not prohibited, the owners of smaller establishments were naturally at some disadvantage in
competing with the king. Nevertheless, numerous privately owned
factories did flourish, especially in cities other than the capital, and
agriculture and trade were also in private hands. Gournia, for example, had its foundries for the manufacture of bronze, Therasia its
olive-oil refineries, and Phaistos its potteries. It must be understood
that these establishments, both royal and private, were factories in
nearly every modern sense of the word. While they did not use
power-driven machinery, they were engaged in large-scale production, and there was division of labor and centralized control and
supervision of workers. The hundreds of women employed in the
royal textile factory worked under the supervision of the queen.

These Aegean people of nearly all classes appear to have led happy

Scenes from the Bull Ring, Cretan Painting, about 1500 B.C. Evident are the Cretans' devotion to sport and the skill and agility of their athletes. The body and horns of the bull, however, are exaggerated as are the slenderness of the athletes and their full-face eyes in profile heads.

and fairly prosperous lives. If slavery existed at all, it certainly occupied an unimportant place. The dwellings in the poorest quarters of great industrial towns such as Gournia were substantially built and commodious, often with as many as six or eight rooms, but we do not know how many families resided in them. If we can judge from the number of inscriptions found in the homes of the common people, literacy was well-nigh universal. Women enjoyed complete equality with men. Regardless of class there was no public activity from which they were debarred, and no occupation which they could not enter. Crete had its female bull fighters and even female pugilists. Ladies of the upper strata devoted much time to fashion. Dressed in their tight-fitting bodices and bell-shaped skirts with flounces which would not have been much out of style in nineteenth-century Europe, they vied with each other for attention in the theaters and at public entertainments of numerous kinds.

The natives of the Aegean area delighted in games and sports of every description. Chess, dancing, running matches, and boxing rivaled each other in their attraction for the people. The Cretans were the first to build stone theaters where processions and music entertained large audiences. But the most popular of all the diversions, as a spectacle at least, was the rodeo or bull-leaping exhibition. This sport was not so cruel as modern bullfighting, since there was no picador to torture the bull or matador to kill him. As soon as the animal was sufficiently infuriated to charge head down, an athlete would seize him by the horns, leap upon his back, turn a few somersaults, and then jump to the ground. No doubt these exhibitions were somewhat lacking in the tragic beauty which Ernest Hemingway saw in the Spanish bullfight, but they were just as spectacular.

The religion of the subjects of Minos was a medley of strange characteristics. First of all it was matriarchal. The chief deity was

127

not a god but a goddess, who was the ruler of the entire universe—the sea and the sky as well as the earth. All existing things were emanations from her. But it was especially as the embodiment of fecundity, and therefore as the source of all life, that she attained her chief significance. In this capacity she was often represented as a madonna with bared breasts, carrying the holy child or tenderly watching over him. The serpent and the dove were her constant companions, possibly as active symbols of her generative power or of her qualities of wisdom and mercy. Originally no male deity appears to have been worshiped, but later a god was associated with the goddess as her son and lover. Although, like the divine sons in several other religions, he apparently died and rose from the dead, he was never regarded by the Cretans as of particular importance.

The mother
goddess

In the second place, the Minoan religion was thoroughly monistic. The mother goddess was the source of evil as well as of good, but not in any morbid or terrifying sense. Though she brought the storm and spread destruction in her path, these served for the replenishment of nature. Death itself was interpreted as the condition prerequisite for life. Whether the religion had any ethical purposes is unknown. Its followers undoubtedly looked forward to a happy survival in another world, although not necessarily as a reward for good deeds done on earth. The dead were buried with solicitous care and provided with nearly every accessory that would enhance their comfort and pleasure. Food and drink, toilet articles, lamps, razors, mirrors, and games were the principal articles furnished for the deceased of all classes and ages. In addition, the hunter was given his spear, the sailor a miniature of his favorite boat, children their toys, and rich men their servants in effigy. No signs of any belief in a place of future punishment have ever been found.

Symbols
and sacrifices

Other rather curious features included the worship of animals and birds (the bull, the snake, and the dove); the worship of sacred trees; the veneration of sacred objects which were probably reproductive symbols (the double-axe, the pillar, and the cross); and the employment of priestesses instead of priests to administer the rites of the cult. By far the most important act of worship was sacrifice. At the great religious festivals hundreds of animals and large quantities of grain and fruit were brought as grateful offerings to the goddess and her son. It is doubtful, however, that these sacrifices represented in any sense an atonement for sin. They were intended rather to provide sustenance for the deities and to bring man into sacramental fellowship with them. The common Oriental idea of the scapegoat sacrifice, or the shedding of blood for the remission of sins, would appear to have been foreign to the Cretan temperament.

For many years after the discovery of the Minoan-Mycenaean civilization its system of writing remained a complete enigma. At

length, however, Sir Arthur Evans succeeded in showing that these

Central Staircase of the Palace of Minos.

Aegean people produced not only one system of writing but three—a hieroglyphic script and two linear scripts, which were used in successive periods. In 1953 an English scholar, Michael Ventris, announced that he had discovered a method which would enable him to decipher the second of these scripts, Linear Script B. This script, used during the Mycenaean stage, was actually a form of Greek. Linear Script A continues to belong to the realm of mystery.[1] No literary texts of the Minoan-Mycenaean civilization have yet been unearthed. It is impossible therefore to tell whether any literature or philosophy had been written. The problem of scientific achievements is easier of solution, since we have material remains for our guidance. Archaeological discoveries on the island of Crete indicate that the ancient inhabitants were gifted inventors and engineers. They built excellent roads of concrete about eleven feet wide. Nearly all the basic principles of modern sanitary engineering were known to the designers of the palace of Knossos, with the result that the royal family of Crete in the seventeenth century B.C. enjoyed comforts and conveniences that were not available to the wealthiest rulers of Western countries in the seventeenth century A.D.

Minoan-Mycenaean writing and scientific achievements

If there was any one achievement of these Aegean people that appears more than others to emphasize the vitality and freedom of their culture, it was their art. With the exception of the Greek, no other art of the ancient world was quite its equal. Its distinguishing features were delicacy, spontaneity, and naturalism. It served not to glorify the ambitions of an arrogant ruling class or to inculcate the

Minoan-Mycenaean art

[1] Although his findings are widely disputed, one scholar, Cyrus H. Gordon, maintains that Linear Script A derives from a Semitic Script.

doctrines of a religion, but to express the delight of the ordinary man in the world of beauty around him. As a result, it was remarkably free from the retarding influence of ancient tradition. It was unique, moreover, in the universality of its application, for it extended not merely to paintings and statues but even to the humblest objects of ordinary use.

Of the major arts, architecture was the least developed. The great palaces were not remarkably beautiful buildings but rambling structures designed primarily for capaciousness and comfort. As more and more functions were absorbed by the state, the palaces were en-

Architecture

Throne Room in the Palace of Minos. The throne and bench are original; the fresco has been restored in accordance with fragments found on the site which are now in the Candia Museum on the island of Crete. A remarkable grace characterizes the lilies and the body and head of the mythical animal.

larged to accommodate them. New quarters were annexed to those already built or piled on top of them without regard for order or symmetry. The interiors, however, were decorated with beautiful paintings and furnishings. The architecture of Crete may be said to have resembled the modern international style in its subordination of form to utility and in its emphasis upon a pleasing and livable interior as more important than external beauty.

Painting

Painting was the art supreme of the Aegean world. Nearly all of it consisted of murals done in fresco, although painted reliefs were occasionally to be found. The murals in the palaces of Crete were by all odds the best that have survived from ancient times. They re-

130

vealed almost perfectly the remarkable gifts of the Minoan artist—
his instinct for the dramatic, his sense of rhythm, his feeling for
nature in her most characteristic moods. He loved to depict the
furious gallop of the frightened deer, the stealthy tread of the cat
stalking its prey in the weeds, or the graceful bending of the lily on
its slender stem.

Sculpture and the ceramic and gem-carving arts were also developed to a high stage of perfection. The sculpture of the Cretans
differed from that of any other people in the ancient Near Orient. It
never relied upon size as a device to convey the idea of power. The
Cretans produced no colossi like those of Egypt or reliefs like those
of Babylonia depicting a king of gigantic proportions smiting his
puny enemies. Instead, they preferred sculpture in miniature.
Nearly all of the statues of human beings or of deities that the
archaeologists have found are smaller than life-size. Neither was the
plastic art of Crete essentially propagandistic. Its dominant purpose,
as in the case of painting, was to express the individual's delight in
the color and drama of his environment. Likewise, the delicately
painted pottery, thin as eggshell, the skillfully engraved and inlaid
daggers and knives, and the gems and seals of infinitely varied design
revealed an almost incredible mastery of materials and respect for
the form and beauty of nature.

The point must be emphasized that the Minoan achievements in
the arts, government, and social life were not equaled in the
Mycenaean stage. Compared with the Cretans, the Mycenaeans were
barbarians who failed to appreciate the subtle refinements of
Minoan culture. Their governments were more overbearing and absorbed to a greater extent the energies and achievements of the people. Their arts were more formal and less lifelike. But inasmuch as
the Mycenaeans were Greeks, further consideration of their culture
belongs more properly in the chapter that follows.

Much has been written about the significance of the Minoan-
Mycenaean civilization and its relation to the surrounding cultures.
By some historians it is regarded as a mere offshoot of the civilization of Egypt. A number of facts can be adduced to support this
view. Both civilizations were ethnically similar. Their governments
were alike in their theocratic character. Both societies contained elements of matriarchy and economic collectivism. But that is about as
far as the comparison can be carried. The differences were just as
marked. The Aegean people built no great pyramids or magnificent
temples. Only in painting did their art resemble that of Egypt very
closely. The systems of writing of the two civilizations appear to
have been of entirely independent origin, as is evidenced by the fact
that a knowledge of Egyptian helps very little in deciphering
Cretan. Whereas the Egyptian religion was an elaborate ethical system based upon the worship of a sun god of righteousness and justice, the religion of the Aegean venerated a goddess of nature with
no evidence of a concept of ethical purpose. Finally, the two peo-

ples differed in their basic philosophies of life. The Egyptians believed in the sacrifice of personal interests to the glory and eternity of the state and looked to rewards in an after-existence as a just compensation for good deeds on earth. The people of the Aegean were individualists, intent upon living their own lives of pleasurable activity and concerned with the hereafter merely as an extension of their pleasant and satisfying earthly careers.

The influence of the Minoan-Mycenaean civilization is not easy to estimate. The Philistines, who came from some part of the Aegean world, introduced certain aspects of the culture into Palestine and Syria. There is reason to believe that various elements of Phoenician art and the Samson legends of the Old Testament were really acquired from the Philistines. It is probable also that the religious and aesthetic traditions of the Cretans and perhaps something of their spirit of freedom influenced the Greeks. But a considerable part of the Minoan-Mycenaean civilization was lost or destroyed following the downfall of Knossos. The conquerors were barbarians who were unable to appreciate much of the culture of the people they conquered and consequently allowed it to perish.

Despite its limited influence the Minoan-Mycenaean civilization, especially in its Minoan form, is not without importance for the student of history; for it was one of the few in ancient times which assured to most of its citizens a reasonable share of happiness and prosperity, free from the tyranny of a despotic state and a crafty priesthood. The apparent absence of slavery, brutal punishments, forced labor, and conscription, together with the substantial equality of classes and the dignified status accorded to women, all point to a social regime in striking contrast with those of the Asiatic empires. If additional evidence of this contrast is needed, it can be found in the art of the various nations. The Cretan sculptor or painter gloried not in portraying the slaughter of armies or the sacking of cities but in picturing flowery landscapes, joyous festivals, thrilling exhibitions of athletic prowess, and similar scenes of a free and peaceful existence. Last of all, the Minoan-Mycenaean civilization is significant for its worldly and progressive outlook. This is exemplified in the devotion of the people to comfort and opulence, in their love of amusement, in their individualism, zest for life, and courage for experimentation.

3.   THE LYDIANS AND THE PHOENICIANS

When the Hittite empire fell in the eighth century B.C., its successor in its main areas of power was the kingdom of Lydia. The Lydians established their rule in what is now the territory of the Turkish Republic in Anatolia. They quickly secured control of the Greek cities on the coast of Asia Minor and of the entire plateau west of the Halys River. But their power was short-lived. In 550 B.C. their fabulous king, Croesus, fancied he saw a good opportunity to

add to his domain the territory of the Medes east of the Halys. The
Median king had just been deposed by Cyrus the Persian. Thinking
this meant an easy triumph for his own armies, Croesus set out to
capture the territory beyond the river. After an indecisive battle
with Cyrus, he returned to his own capital (Sardis) for reinforce-
ments. Here Cyrus caught him unprepared in a surprise attack and
captured and burned the city. The Lydians never recovered from
the blow, and soon afterward all of their territory, including the
Greek cities on the coast, passed under the dominion of Cyrus the
Great.

The Lydians were a people of Indo-European speech, who were
probably a mixture of native peoples of Asia Minor with migrant
stocks from eastern Europe. Benefiting from the advantages of
favorable location and abundance of resources, they enjoyed one of
the highest standards of living of ancient times. They were famous
for the splendor of their armored chariots and the quantities of gold
and articles of luxury possessed by the citizens. The wealth of their
kings was legendary, as attested by the simile "rich as Croesus." The
chief sources of this prosperity were gold from the streams, wool
from the thousands of sheep on the hills, and the profits of the extensive commerce which passed overland from the Tigris-Euphrates
valley to the Aegean Sea. But with all their wealth and opportunities
for leisure, they succeeded in making only one original contribution
to civilization. This was the coinage of money from electrum or
"white gold," a natural mixture of gold and silver found in the sands
of one of their rivers. Hitherto all systems of money had consisted
of weighed rings or bars of metal. The new coins, of varying sizes,
were stamped with a definite value more or less arbitrarily given by
the ruler who issued them.

In contrast with the Lydians, who gained their ascendancy as a
result of the downfall of the Hittites, were the Phoenicians, who
benefited from the break-up of Aegean supremacy. But the Phoenicians were neither conquerors nor the builders of an empire. They
exerted their influence through the arts of peace, especially through
commerce. During most of their history their political system was a
loose confederation of city-states, which frequently bought their security by paying tribute to foreign powers. The territory they
occupied was the narrow strip between the Lebanon Mountains and
the Mediterranean Sea and the islands off the coast. With good harbors and a central location, it was admirably situated for trade. The
great centers of commerce included Tyre, Sidon, and Beirut. Under
the leadership of the first, Phoenicia reached the zenith of her cultural brilliance, from the tenth to the eighth century B.C. During the
sixth century she passed under the domination of the Chaldeans and
then of the Persians. In 332 B.C. Tyre was destroyed by Alexander
the Great after a siege of seven months.

The Phoenicians were a people of Semitic language, closely related to the Canaanites. They displayed very little creative genius,

but were remarkable adapters of the achievements of others. They produced no original art worthy of the name, and they made but slight contributions to literature. Their religion, like that of the Canaanites, was characterized by human sacrifice to the god Moloch and by licentious fertility rites. They excelled, however, in specialized manufactures, in geography and navigation. They founded colonies at Carthage and Utica in North Africa, at Palermo on the island of Sicily, on the Balearic Islands, and at Cadiz and Malaga in Spain. They were renowned throughout the ancient world for their glass and metal industries and for their purple dye obtained from a mollusk in the adjacent seas. They developed the art of navigation to such a stage that they could sail by the stars at night. To less venturesome peoples, the North Star was known for some time as the Phoenicians' star. A company of Phoenicians is believed to have circumnavigated Africa. Phoenician ships and sailors were recruited by all the great powers. The most lasting achievement of the Phoenicians, however, was the completion and diffusion of an alphabet based upon principles discovered by the Egyptians. The Phoenician contribution was the adoption of a system of signs representing the sounds of the human voice, and the elimination of all pictographic and syllabic characters. The Egyptians, as we have seen, had accomplished the first of these steps but not the second.

4. LESSONS FROM THE HISTORY OF THE NEAR ORIENT EMPIRES

Like most other periods in world history, the period of the empires we have studied thus far was an era of contention and strife. Nearly all of the great empires, and the majority of the smaller states as well, devoted their energies most of the time to policies of expansion and aggression. The only notable exceptions were the Minoan and Egyptian, but even the Egyptians, in the later period of their history, yielded to no one in their addiction to imperialism. The causes were largely geographic in nature. Each nation grew accustomed to the pursuit of its own interests in some fertile river valley or on some easily defended plateau. Isolation bred fear of foreigners and an incapacity to think of one's own people as members of a common humanity. The feelings of insecurity that resulted seemed to justify aggressive foreign policies, the waging of preventive wars, and the annexation of neighboring states to serve as buffers against a hostile world. Of course, greed played a part also, especially when conquest came to be regarded as equivalent to opportunity for plunder.

It seems possible to trace nearly all of the woes of the Near Orient nations to wars of aggression and imperialist greed. Arnold J. Toynbee has shown this in devastating fashion in the case of the Assyrians. He contends that it was no less true of such later peoples as the Spartans, the Carthaginians, the Macedonians, and the Ottoman Turks. Each made militarism and conquest its gods and wrought such destruction upon itself that when it made its last heroic stand against its enemies, it was a mere "corpse in armor." Not death by foreign conquest but national suicide was the fate which befell it.[2] The way of the warrior brought race intolerance, a love of ease and luxury, crime and racketeering, and crushing burdens of taxation. Expansion of empire promoted a fictitious prosperity, at least for the upper classes, and aroused enough envy among poorer nations to make them willing conspirators against a rich neighbor who could easily be portrayed as an oppressor. The current stirrings of revolt in underdeveloped nations, which Adlai Stevenson called the "revolution of rising expectations," had its parallels far back in ancient history.

SELECTED READINGS

· *Items so designated are available in paperbound editions.*

Akurgal, Ekren, *Art of the Hittites,* New York, 1962.
· Blegen, C. W., *Troy,* London and New York, 1963 (Cambridge University Press).
Burn, A. R., *Minoans, Philistines and Greeks,* New York, 1930.
Ceram, C. W., *The Secret of the Hittites,* New York, 1956. The best of recent works.
· Chadwick, John, *The Decipherment of Linear B,* New York, 1958 (Vintage).
· Gordon, Cyrus H., *The Ancient Near East,* New York, 1965 (Norton Library).
· ———, *The Common Background of Greek and Hebrew Civilizations,* New York, 1965 (Norton Library).
· Gurney, O. R., *The Hittites,* Baltimore, 1962 (Penguin).
· Harden, Donald, *The Phoenicians,* New York, 1962 (Praeger).
· Hutchinson, R. W., *Prehistoric Crete,* Baltimore, 1962 (Penguin).
· Lloyd, Seton, *Early Anatolia,* Baltimore, 1956 (Penguin).
· Nilsson, M. P., *The Mycenaean Origin of Greek Mythology,* New York, 1963 (Norton Library).
Palmer, L. R., *Mycenaeans and Minoans,* New York, 1962. Must be read with care. Author is not entirely impartial.
· Pendlebury, J. D. S., *The Archaeology of Crete,* New York, 1965 (Norton Library).
Wace, A. J. B., *Mycenae,* Princeton, 1949.
Willetts, R. F., *Aristocratic Society in Ancient Crete,* London, 1955.

SOURCE MATERIALS

Evans, Sir Arthur, *Scripta Minoa; the Written Documents of Minoan Crete.*
Hertzler, J. O., *The Social Thought of the Ancient Civilizations,* New York, 1961, pp. 135–44.
Ventris, M., and Chadwick, J., *Documents in Mycenaean Greek,* Cambridge, 1956.

[2] D. C. Somervell (ed.), A. J. Toynbee's *A Study of History,* I, 338–43.

CHAPTER 7

Ancient Indian Civilization

Hinduism does not distinguish ideas of God as true and false, adopting one particular idea as the standard for the whole human race. It accepts the obvious fact that mankind seeks its goal of God at various levels and in various directions, and feels sympathy with every stage of the search.

S. Radhakrishnan, *The Hindu View of Life*

The subcontinent of India has an area slightly more than half that of the United States and is inhabited by almost three times as many people. Not only is India a vast and densely populated region but in addition it includes many different levels of culture, different religions, languages, and economic conditions, and its history is extremely complex. Five or six separate families of languages are represented among its people. The population contains admixtures of all of the three great races of mankind—black, yellow, and white —in various combinations and proportions. One of the most ancient peoples, a Negrito strain related to the Pygmies of Africa, has almost disappeared from India but is still found in the Andaman Islands to the east. In striking contrast to this type are the fair-skinned Mediterraneans of the north and northwest, descendants of the Indo-Aryans who invaded the country some 3500 years ago. The most widespread group in southern India is that known as Dravidian, but because the term is applied to all whose language belongs to the Dravidian family it no longer denotes a single ethnic stock. Another type, perhaps more ancient than the Dravidians, is called Australoid, because of its relationship with primitive peoples extending over parts of southeastern Asia and as far east as Australia. The Mongolian element is confined chiefly to the border region of the north and northeast. Alpine types are found along the western coast, sometimes with a slight Nordic admixture (evidenced by gray or blue eyes). Thus the common practice of referring to the natives of

The peoples of India

137

ANCIENT INDIA ca. 500 B.C.

India as "colored" or "brown-skinned" is misleading. Their skins are indeed of various shades, but since early times white stocks have been conspicuously present, especially in northern India. Even today some of the most typical examples of the tall variety of the Mediterranean white race can be seen in the Punjab and the north-west frontier. Yet they exist in close proximity to people who reveal Alpine, Australoid, Mongoloid, or Negrito features. Over the course of centuries, and in spite of the inexorable segregation of the caste system in historic times, India has been a human melting pot.

Geographically India falls into two main divisions. The southern **138** triangle or peninsular portion, known as the Deccan, lies entirely

within the tropics. The northern or continental half, also triangular
in shape, is in the same latitudes as Mexico and the southern United
States and has temperatures ranging from tropical heat to the intense
cold of the northern mountain peaks. The northern Deccan is
semi-mountainous and heavily forested, and shelters some of the
primitive hill tribes whose ancestors were crowded into the wilderness by the pressure of expansion from more civilized communities.
The greater part of the peninsula, however, is a gently sloping
plateau, traversed by rivers, and containing rich agricultural lands.
The northern half of India, called Hindustan, is bounded on the
north by the lofty Himalayan range and is separated from the
Deccan by the low-lying Vindhya Mountains. Most of Hindustan is
a level plain comprising an area about as large as France, Germany,
and Italy combined, drained by the great river systems of the Indus
and the Ganges. The rivers of Hindustan take their rise in the Himalayas or beyond and are fed by snows and glaciers. The Indus and
the Brahmaputra each originate in Tibet and flow in opposite directions around the mountain ranges until they turn south into India,
bringing with them virgin soil from the highlands which is deposited on the plain. The gently flowing Ganges, less subject to floods
than the Indus, is the most beneficent of all. Referred to as "Mother
Ganges," it has long been the sacred river of the Hindus. It is no
wonder that its central valley, where every inch of soil is productive
and no stone even the size of a pebble can be found, is one of the

Tea Plantation in Darjeeling. Tea is one of modern India's most important
crops, but its cultivation was not begun until the nineteenth century, under
the British. Darjeeling, a leading center of tea production, is a beautifully
located hill station on the slopes of the Himalayas in northeastern India.   **139**

most densely populated spots in the world. The mouths of the Ganges (in Bengal) are surrounded by forbidding jungle, and a desert separates the lower Indus valley from the Ganges and its tributaries; but the Indo-Gangetic region as a whole is lavishly endowed by nature. Here the most influential centers of Indian civilization have been located.

All India enjoys the advantage of the monsoon rains, and the greater part of the country is suitable for cultivation. Moreover, there is no impenetrable barrier between Hindustan and the Deccan and there has always been communication between the two sections. In spite of its size and contrasting terrain, India is a natural geographic unit. That its peoples have been united politically only during relatively brief periods of their history is attributable to many factors, including disturbances from without, but it cannot be ascribed to geographic necessity.

I.   THE VEDIC AGE IN INDIA

Remains of Neolithic and of early metal-age cultures have been discovered both in Hindustan and the Deccan. The first highly advanced civilization began its history as early as 3000 B.C. and reached its peak between 2500 and 2000 B.C. It covered an area in the Indus valley at least as large as Italy and possibly much larger. It was essentially an urban civilization, with a cosmopolitan society, bustling enterprises, and extensive trade with the outside world. Two metropolitan centers have thus far been uncovered—Mohenjo-Daro, about 300 miles from the seacoast, and Harappa, about 400 miles farther up the river. Both were durably constructed of brick and laid out in accordance with ambitious and intelligent planning. Private houses were solidly built of brick and equipped with bathrooms which drained into sewer pipes running underneath the principal streets and discharging into the river. Evidences of intellectual achievement are scanty, although proofs are available that standards of measurement and a system of writing had been developed. The latter, which has not yet been deciphered, was evidently syllabic and designed to be read in alternate lines from right to left and left to right. Several of the arts reflected a high degree of skill, especially the fabrication of small objects for personal adornment. Some examples of sculpture, also, indicate a talent for grace and naturalness. The religion of this early civilization centered upon the worship of fertility deities, notably a mother goddess. The principal rite was animal sacrifice.

Archaeological evidence supports the conclusion that the Indus valley civilization was one of the earliest in the world and that it was comparable in level of achievement to those of contemporary Egypt and Mesopotamia. Whether it was indigenous to India or was introduced by settlers from the west is still a matter of speculation. It

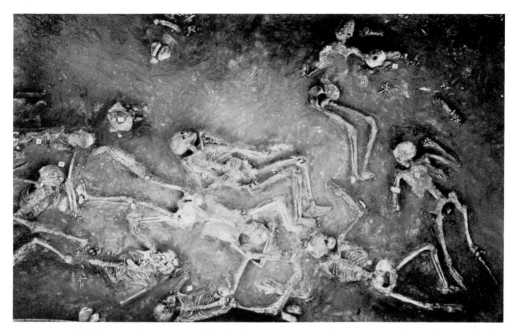

Skeletons at Mohenjo-Daro. Although the downfall of this culture is a mystery, barbarian conquest was an important factor.

Bull Seal. Impression of stone seal from Mohenjo-Daro, 2500 B.C., probably used as a signature. The animal figure (of a Brahmani bull or zebu) is assumed to have had religious significance.

long maintained intercourse with other civilized regions, especially Mesopotamia, where Indus-type stone seals and other objects belonging to the period about 2350 B.C. have been discovered. For reasons unknown the Indus valley civilization disappeared from the scene of history about 1500 B.C. It may have succumbed to barbarian conquest, although possibly a plague or flood or some other natural disaster hastened the process. Whatever the causes, the civilization went down to so complete an oblivion that no one was aware of its existence until evidences were unearthed by archaeologists about forty years ago. Shortly before the downfall of the Indus valley cities, India was invaded by seminomadic tribes who were destined to be the founders of a more enduring civilization. These

Downfall of the Indus civilization: the Aryan invasions

141

were the so-called Aryans,[1] or Indo-Aryans, who came in by way of Afghanistan through the passes of the Hindu Kush Mountains. For many centuries the Aryan influence was confined to northern India, and here it developed the distinctive Hindu pattern of society, culture, and religion. Though the Aryan (Indo-European) languages never became dominant in the south, they are the most widely spoken group of languages in India today.

Scantiness of the
early records

For some 1000 years following the Indo-Aryan invasions the political history of India is largely unknown. There is no reason to assume a wholesale displacement of population. As the invading tribes extended their sway over northern India they intermingled with the inhabitants of the conquered regions. The process of assimilation between conquerors and conquered affected the culture of the invaders to a degree that cannot be clearly determined but which undoubtedly was profound, especially in the development of religion and social structure. The absence of reliable historical records for such a long period of time, among people who achieved a variegated, colorful, and highly intellectual civilization, is extraordinary. The scarcity of historical information is not entirely accidental, although it is partly accounted for by the fact that the Indo-Aryans had no system of writing until about 1000 years after their settlement in India. A more potent cause was the character of their

[1] "Aryan" was the name by which these invaders identified themselves. The theory of a distinctive Aryan race, expounded from time to time by various propagandists, has been exploded. In current usage the term "Aryan" is properly applied only to a family of related languages (the Indo-European group).

Dancing Girl. Bronze statuette of a girl dancer, from Mohenjo-Daro, a striking example of the art of the ancient Indus civilization. Bracelets and bangles have retained their popularity among the women of India to the present day.

Dyers' troughs or drains, uncovered at Mohenjo-Daro.

civilization itself and especially of their philosophy, which stressed the importance of timeless qualities and the relative insignificance of temporal events and conditions. When they looked back to the past, they were inclined to give free scope to their imagination and to reckon in terms of vast eras and aeons, symmetrical but fantastic, extending to millions or even billions of years. The failure to produce factual chronicles does not mean that no changes or exciting events occurred. On the contrary, the available evidence suggests the normal amount of conflict, turmoil, and upheaval. But it is almost impossible to separate fact from fable, and in so far as the political history can be reconstructed it is largely repetitive and devoid of impressive achievement.

The sources of information for early Indo-Aryan civilization are almost exclusively in literary tradition. The oldest literary monument is the collection of religious poems and hymns called the *Vedas.* No one knows when they were composed. The oldest portions may have originated as early as 3000 B.C., and they were passed on orally without any written aids whatsoever until several centuries after the collection was complete. The *Vedas* reflect the culture of

Vedas and epics

Unicorn Seal. The "unicorn" (perhaps actually the profile of an ox) is the animal most frequently depicted on the Indus civilization seals. The object under the animal's head may represent a brazier or incense holder. The inscription has not been deciphered. This specimen was found in the Deccan, some 600 miles from the Indus Valley.

143

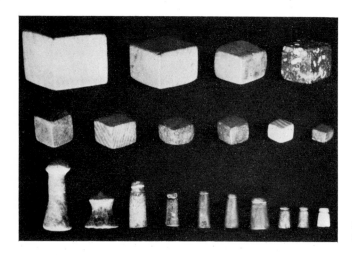

Weights. Stone blocks used by merchants of the Indus civilization as standard units of weight.

the primitive Aryan communities in the upper Indus valley and the "Middle Land" between the two rivers, or roughly the period from 2000 to 800 B.C., which is accordingly called the Vedic age. The latter portion of the *Vedas,* however, shows that profound changes had taken place during these centuries. The second major literary landmark consists of two long epic poems, the *Ramayana* and the *Mahabharata.* Like the *Vedas,* and in spite of their tremendous bulk, the epics were preserved by memory and oral repetition for many generations, but they reflect a different set of conditions, customs, and beliefs from those most typical of the *Vedas.* The epics reveal that by the close of the Vedic age Indo-Aryan culture had been transformed into a complex and stratified social and religious system. It had become Hinduism.

In the early Vedic period the Indo-Aryan tribes had a simple, largely pastoral economy. They cultivated barley and probably other grains, using a wooden plow drawn by bullocks. They ate the flesh of sheep, goats, and oxen, usually at the time of sacrificing these animals to the gods, but their favorite foods were dairy products—milk, cream, and ghee (melted butter). Cattle were the most prized possessions and served as a medium of exchange. Apparently they were not yet worshiped nor was their slaughter forbidden. Domesticated animals also included the horse, used to pull the war chariot and also for chariot racing, of which sport the Aryans were very fond. All the common handicrafts, including metal work, were practiced. Music, both vocal and instrumental—with flutes, drums, cymbals, and stringed lutes or harps—was a popular source of entertainment, as was dancing. Gambling with dice was a national pastime and seems to have come close to being a national obsession.

In its typical features this early Indian society was vigorous and uninhibited, its members delighting in song and dance, in feasting, carousing, and feats of strength. Warfare was frequent, and many stories have been preserved of the incredible powers of strong-

Economic life in the Vedic period

armed heroes. The social unit was the patriarchal family, which does not necessarily imply that the father exercised tyrannical power over his dependents. His functions were religious as well as economic. The wife assisted her husband in sacrifices at the domestic hearth, and women apparently enjoyed almost equal freedom with men. Polygamy was permissible, but such later Hindu institutions as the immolation of a widow upon her husband's funeral pyre (suttee) and child marriage were completely unknown.

As might be expected, political and legal institutions were rudimentary among the primitive Aryans. Each tribe had its king (raja), whose chief function was to lead his warriors in battle. Associated with the king in ruling was an assembly. Its composition and duties are not at all clear, but its existence suggests a limitation upon the royal authority. Some of the tribes were organized as aristocratic republics rather than hereditary monarchies, with government resting with the heads of the clans or an elected raja. In the early days the raja's powers could hardly have been awe-inspiring in any case. He had no populous cities from which to extract riches, only country villages; and the villages managed their own internal affairs, paying part of their produce to the raja for "protection." The handling of crime and punishment followed patterns similar to those of many other primitive societies. The injured party or his family was expected to take the initiative in prosecuting an offender. Compensation for injuries was usually a payment in money or commodities to the plaintiff or, in the case of murder, to the victim's family. Theft was the most frequent complaint, especially cattle stealing, even though this crime was looked upon as highly reprehensible. An insolvent debtor—usually one who had gambled too recklessly—might be enslaved to his creditor.

The most significant achievement of the Vedic age was the composition of the poetry and prose which give the period its name. Ultimately there were four *Vedas*, each containing a large collection of prayers, chants, or hymns, supplemented by prose commentary. The literal meaning of *Veda* is "knowledge" or "wisdom," and the entire collection was believed to have been imparted to ancient seers by the gods rather than invented by men. The *Vedas* constitute the canonical books of the Indo-Aryan—and of the later Hindu—religion; they were considered divinely inspired and uniquely sacred, as were the Hebrew and Christian Scriptures by the members of those faiths. However, because the early Aryans were illiterate, their sacred books were said to have been "heard" rather than "revealed." The *Vedas* cover an amazing variety and range of subjects. Some portions are litanies intended to be chanted by priests during a sacrifice. Others are catalogues of spells and charms, including alleged remedies for fever and snake bite, love formulas, and recipes for exterminating one's enemies. Still others incorporate customs and folklore or display a profound insight into philosophical or religious truth. Although much of the content of the *Vedas* is repetitive and monotonous, in vividness and imagination the best verses deserve to rank with the *Iliad* of Homer.

The religion of the early Aryans as illustrated in the *Vedas* was a comprehensive polytheism, with little ethical significance. Their gods—*deva*, or "shining ones"—were the forces of nature or personifications of these forces. No images or temples were erected, and worship consisted chiefly in performing sacrifices to the gods. Grain and milk were sacrificed, animal flesh was burned upon the altars (the worshipers themselves eating the flesh), but the choicest offering was *soma*, an alcoholic beverage fermented from the juice of a mountain plant. The gods were looked upon in much the same way as the Olympian deities were regarded by the Greeks. They were conceived as splendid and powerful creatures, with human attributes but immortal as long as they drank the *soma* juice, and, on the whole, benevolent. It was assumed that they would reward men out of gratitude for the homage and gifts presented to them. Gradually, however, the insidious notion took root that if the holy rites were conducted with unfailing accuracy they would compel the god to obedience, whether he was willing or not. It is easy to see how such an interpretation would enhance the prestige and authority of the priests who controlled the wonder-working formulas.

The roster of gods was a large one and tended to increase. While several deities can be identified with those of other Indo-European peoples, they did not have as clear-cut personalities as the Greek or Norse gods. The Indian mind ran toward specialization and abstraction, tending to invent a new god or a new variant of an old god for every conceivable occasion. Dyaus, lord of the bright sky, was equivalent to the Greek Zeus (though less important). Varuna represented the sky or heaven in its capacity to encompass all things and hold the universe together. He was called Asura, a term which suggests close kinship with the supreme Persian deity, Ahura-Mazda. At least five different divinities were identified with the sun. One of them, Mitra, shared a common origin with the Persian Mithras, but this deity did not assume the prominence in India that Mithras attained in Persia and the West. Surya was the sun's golden disk, Pushan embodied its power to assist vegetation and animal growth, and Vishnu personified the swift-moving orb that traverses the sky in three strides.

The most popular deity of all in Vedic times was Indra, whose original significance is uncertain. He was alleged to have benefited mankind by slaying a malignant serpent, the demon of drought, thus releasing the pent-up waters to refresh the earth. Also, it was said, he discovered the light, made a path for the sun, and created lightning. He was chiefly honored as a mighty warrior and god of battle, the slayer of demons and the "black-skinned" enemies of the Aryans. Indra was supposed to be particularly fond of *soma*, which fired his blood for combat, and he was reputed to be able to drink three lakes of this potent fluid at one draft while devouring the flesh of 300 buffaloes. *Soma*, the sacred liquor, was also deified, as was the sacrificial fire, Agni. Agni was conceived both as a god and as the mouth of the gods or as the servant who carried their savory food offerings up to the heavens for them.

Although religion in the Vedic age was hardly spiritual, it contained traces of such a quality. Some hymns to Varuna are remarkable for their devoutness and ethical content. Varuna is described as the great regulator of the universe, who keeps the rivers in their courses and the sun and planets in their proper orbits. He is also pictured as the upholder of rules and ordinances for both gods and men, capable of binding sinners with fetters. To him were addressed prayers for forgiveness of sin. Offenses likely to incur divine wrath included not only infractions of religious taboos but also violations of the moral code, such as adultery, witchcraft, gambling, and drunkenness. However, despite intimations of a belief in life after death, by far the greater emphasis was placed upon the enjoyment of life here and now.

Associated with each of the *Vedas* is a prose manual called a *Brahmana* because it was for the instruction and assistance of the Brahmans (priests) who officiated at the sacrifices. While the Vedic hymns are generally unaffected and artless, the *Brahmanas* betray a shrewd calculation on the part of the custodians of the sacred traditions and also illustrate the tendency of such traditions to degenerate into empty mechanical formulas. A modern Indian scholar describes the *Brahmanas* as "an arid desert of puerile speculations on ritual ceremonies," and even as "filthy and repulsive," with a morality "no higher than that of primitive medicine-men." [2] The greed and arrogance of the Brahmans is illustrated by such assertions as that judgment should always be awarded to a Brahman in every dispute with a layman and that murder is not actually murder unless the victim is a Brahman.

In view of the decadent tendencies evident in the *Brahmanas* it is all the more notable that the concluding portion of Vedic literature is of an elevated philosophical character, giving proof both of intel- lectual maturity and of ethical and spiritual insight. Evidently, side by side with the naïve popular cults and with the mechanical rituals of priestcraft had grown up a tradition of skepticism and bold speculation, which attempted to delve beneath the surface of sense experience and formulate answers to eternally recurring questions. This concluding portion, called *Vedanta* ("end of the *Vedas*"), comprises the famous *Upanishads*, of which there are some 200. The *Upanishads* (the word means a "sitting down near" or session with a teacher) are treatises or rambling discourses in prose and poetry,

[2] B. K. Ghosh, in *The History and Culture of the Indian People*, Vol. II, *The Vedic Age*, pp. 225, 418.

dealing with the nature of being, man, and the universe. Their content varies in subject matter and in quality of thought, ranging from the trivial and absurd to the sublime. Scholars and philosophers from the Occident as well as from the Orient have long been attracted by the subtle probing, the sweeping imagination, and the idealistic concepts evident in the *Upanishads*, the best of which are equal to the finest products of Greek philosophical genius. Although part of the *Vedas*, the *Upanishads* largely ignore the popular mythology of the Vedic hymns and also constitute a challenge to the presumptuousness of the Brahmans and their version of religion as consisting in adherence to ritual and ceremony.

**Philosophy of
the *Upanishads***

While the *Upanishads* do not fall into a single pattern of thought, their most essential philosophical teachings are fairly consistent. The key concepts, which may be described as idealistic, monistic, and pantheistic, are: (1) the supreme reality of the World Soul or Absolute Being; (2) the unreality of the material world; (3) transmigration, or the rebirth of individual souls; and (4) the attainment of serenity through escape from the cycle of recurring births by union with Absolute Being. Evil and suffering are explained on the ground that they are incidental to matter and material creatures. But matter is held to be an illusion (*maya*); the only true reality is the soul or spirit. If the soul could manage to disentangle itself from matter (which actually is only an appearance anyway), it would be free from discord and suffering. Not only does life in the flesh entail sorrow and pain, but, according to this philosophy, death fails to provide relief because the soul will be born again into another body. In developing the theory of an endless chain of births, the philosophers of the *Upanishads* insisted that the process was not purely accidental and uncontrollable. They taught that a person's conduct in life determined the type of body and condition which he would experience in his next incarnation. He might go down in the scale—even to the animal or insect level—or he might go up—to the state of a noble, king, or saint. This is the *karma* doctrine, which holds that actions, thoughts, and motives bear fruit. It resembles the Christian teaching, "Whatsoever a man soweth, that shall he also reap"—except that the retribution or reward for actions is held over to another earthly existence. However, if it is assumed that all physical existence is unsatisfactory and illusory, obviously there is not much to be gained from moving a few rungs up the ladder of human wretchedness. Hence the *Upanishads* taught that preferable even to the faithful performance of *dharma* (moral uprightness and the conscientious discharge of one's duties) was a deliberate break with the habits and engagements which lead to the renewal of births. Separation from the chain of births could be achieved only by following a standard of conduct higher than that of righteousness in the ordinary sense of the term. Evil action would produce evil fruit or **148** *karma,* and righteous action would produce good *karma;* but still more desirable was conduct which, being "neither black nor white," could lead to the extinction of *karma* altogether. In other words, only when a person acts with complete disinterestedness, detaching himself entirely from the idea of reward for his merit, do the fetters which bind him to the world of sense begin to loosen and ultimately dissolve. When this happens, the liberated soul attains blessedness or *nirvana*, which does not mean either annihilation or entrance into a heaven, but a union with *Brahma*, the undefinable Universal Soul or eternal Absolute Being.

The philosophy of the *Upanishads* is pessimistic regarding the world and man's present state, because it depreciates everything material and holds that the natural physical life is a burden. However, it is optimistic as to ultimate ends and as to the possibility of human emancipation. It teaches that there is in every man an indestructible fragment of reality. The basic precept is that *atman* (the individual soul) is actually a part of *Brahma* (the Universal Soul or rational principle which pervades the universe); and that although the soul has been separated from its source it can be reunited with it—not through a miracle but through the individual's own efforts. Moreover, the state of *nirvana*, while a remote goal for the majority, is declared to be attainable during the mortal existence of a sufficiently dedicated person.

2. THE EPIC AGE: THE EMERGENCE OF HINDUISM

Long before the *Vedas* were completed, the two Indian epics were in process of development. The epics were not cast into their final form until sometime between 400 B.C. and 200 A.D., but they refer to events of a much earlier date, and the Epic age overlaps with the Vedic. The epics were composed in Sanskrit, a dialect which is derived from but not identical with that of the *Vedas*, and which came to be regarded as the "classical" form of the Indo-Aryan speech, somewhat as Latin is regarded as classical by the Indo-European peoples of Europe. Furthermore, in spite of the lack of precise dividing dates, it is clear that the epics represent a later stage of social and cultural evolution than do the *Vedas*.

The Indian epics are comparable to the epic poems of the ancient Greeks in that they celebrate the deeds of legendary national heroes, but they are much more encyclopedic and diffuse than the Homeric poems. The *Mahabharata*, the longer of the two Indian epics, is more than seven times the length of the *Iliad* and *Odyssey* combined. While the epics treat of bloody conflicts and amazing exploits, they also incorporate quantities of religious lore, and through the centuries they, rather than the *Vedas*, have served as a Bible for the common people. This is partly because the Brahmans imposed

Ravana, Rama, and Lakshmana. An Indian painting of the eighteenth century depicting an incident from the *Ramayana.* Rama, the epic hero, and his brother Lakshmana are fighting against Ravana, the demon king of Ceylon, who carried off Rama's faithful wife Sita.

restrictions upon the study of the sacred Vedic texts, whereas anyone could listen to a recitation of the epics.

The *Ramayana* has as its central theme the story of Prince Rama, who, with his beautiful wife Sita, was exiled through the jealous intrigue of a wicked stepmother. It relates how Sita was carried off to Ceylon by the demon king of that country and finally recovered by Rama with the help of a monkey general. The narrative is highly artificial as well as fantastic, and easily lends itself to allegorical interpretation. The poem indicates some familiarity with both southern India and Ceylon and provides evidence that Aryan influence, if not extensive conquests, had penetrated into the Deccan. The story was reworked many times in later Indian literature and embellished with symbolism. Rama and Sita came to be idealized as the perfect types of manly courage and feminine purity and devotion, respectively, and Rama was traditionally regarded as an incarnation of the god Vishnu. It is possible that the poem may be, in part, an allegory of the progress of agriculture, in which Rama represents the plow and Sita the furrow. (In the epic, after returning to her husband's kingdom she is swallowed up by the earth.)

The *Mahabharata* is just as enigmatic as the *Ramayana,* though livelier in its story and richer in the variety and scope of its subject matter. "If it is not in the *Mahabharata,* it is not in India," has become a proverb. A narrative core, which gives the poem its name, is the account of a great battle between two related but feuding fami-

The Ramayana

The Mahabharata

lies, the Pandavas and the Kauravas, of Bharata descent. The "Great
Bharata War" probably commemorates a historic battle fought near
the modern city of Delhi about 1400 B.C., but the epic version is a
tissue of myth and fable. Some scholars believe that the Pandavas
(who on the whole are the heroes of the story) were not really
kinsmen of the Kauravas but a different tribe altogether, perhaps of
Mongolian race. The five Pandava brothers are described as having
one wife in common, an obvious reference to the institution of
polyandry, which was foreign to the Aryan communities but which
is still practiced by the Tibetans. As a chronicle of battle the poetic
version is gory enough but full of odd contradictions. Acts of ruthlessness and chicanery are recorded along with examples of exaggerated chivalry and scrupulousness. The god Krishna (supposedly
one of the incarnations of Vishnu) takes part in the encounter with
rare impartiality—serving as charioteer for one of the Pandava
princes but sending his own forces to fight on the other side. The
battle is described as raging furiously for eighteen days, by which
time practically all the antagonists on both sides have been killed.
Finally the five royal Pandava brothers, victorious but the sole survivors of their line, renounce the world and, with their wife and
dog, set off for the Himalayas in search of Paradise. Some of the
contradictions and inconsistencies in the account can be explained
by the fact that the poem was several centuries in the making. Ethical sensibilities and the warriors' code of conduct changed considerably during this period until rough-and-ready practices which
were once considered normal came to be looked upon with disapproval.

Interpolated in the story of the great war is a philosophical dialogue which contrasts startlingly with the rapid pace and bloody
tone of the main narrative. This passage, which like the rest of the
Mahabharata is of unknown authorship, is called the *Bhagavad-Gita*
or "the Lord's Song." In form, it is a discourse between the warrior
Arjuna and his charioteer Krishna (who represents the god
Vishnu), precipitated by Arjuna's reluctance to begin the slaughter
of his relatives when the lines of battle are drawn up. In substance, it
is a dramatic and colorful exposition of some of the most fertile
ideas of the *Upanishads*, with greater emotional impact because it
speaks not in abstractions but in terms of love for a personal god. At
the outset of the dialogue Arjuna expresses his aversion to combat,
saying flatly that he will not engage in it: "Better I deem it . . . to
face them weaponless, and bare my breast to shaft and spear, than
answer blow with blow." Krishna assures him that he must fight,
not because there is any virtue in it but because as a member of the
warrior caste fighting is his duty (*dharma*). Similarly, Arjuna is reminded that both death and birth are only incidents and that the
soul is indestructible: "Life is not slain." Soon, however, the conversation proceeds to a penetrating discussion of the value of different

The *Bhagavad-
Gita*

types of action, suggestive of Christian arguments over the respective merits of "faith" and "works." Krishna outlines four levels of conduct or four paths to virtue. At the lowest level are good works, prescribed by reason. Better than works of diligence is knowledge: "The right act is less than the right-thinking mind." Still higher is worship or pure devotion, meditation which is above the bonds of sense and "troubled no longer by the priestly lore." But on the very highest level is placed the renunciation of self. The ideal worshiper, while not neglecting his duty, will play his part "with unyoked soul," "with spirit unattached." He acts "unmoved by passion and unbound by deeds, setting result aside"—that is, with no thought of reward either material or spiritual. Although in the dialogue the warrior is enjoined to fulfill his warlike function—with complete indifference to victory or defeat—the *Bhagavad-Gita* verses have been interpreted by some Hindus, including Mahatma Gandhi, as a text for pacifism.

Aside from their narrative and philosophical interest, the epics reveal that during the 1000 or 1500 years since the settlement of the Indo-Aryans in India extensive changes had taken place among the people, especially in religion and the organization of society. The carefree, boisterous optimism of the early Vedic period was giving way to attitudes of pessimism, discouragement, and resignation; society, instead of being flexible and largely uninhibited, was tending toward a rigid stratification of functions and privileges. The causes of such marked change are not entirely clear. But whatever the reasons, before the close of the Epic age Indian society had assumed many of the characteristics which have distinguished it down to modern times. Together they make up the culture complex which is Hinduism.

Popular religion had changed from a simple polytheism to an intricate network of beliefs and rituals with a tremendous hierarchy of gods. The catalogue and ranking of deities and the forms of worship varied from one locality to another and among different strata of the population. With a few exceptions, the more prominent of the early Aryan deities faded into the background as new gods were added to the pantheon with the absorption of local pre-Aryan cults. Eventually the number of divine and semidivine beings accorded recognition ran into the thousands, or possibly millions. Thus, while philosophy was tending toward monotheism, the popular faiths were moving in the opposite direction. Three gods, however, came to be considered as paramount, although without agreement as to their qualities and import. Vishnu, the old solar deity, believed to have had many incarnations, was worshiped under several names. He was still conceived as a benevolent and cheerful god, "the Preserver," representing the creative or formative principle in the universe. Because he was supposed to disapprove of bloodshed, Vishnu received no animal sacrifice but was offered garlands of flowers. Quite different was Shiva, "the Destroyer," (perhaps identical with one of the Indus valley deities), who, in spite of his frightening aspects, has proved to be a more widely favored object of worship than Vishnu. Typically Shiva was pictured as five-faced and four-armed. He was regarded as beneficent in some aspects because destructive force—symbolized by the dance of Shiva—is a necessary agency in the evolution of the world and living forms, but his power could be prostrating. While some devotees of Shiva were ascetics and mystics, among other groups his worship called for bloody sacrifice, and was also associated with a fertility cult employing orgiastic rites. The third and least influential of the major deities was Brahma, a personification of the Absolute Being or World Soul of the philosophers. Representing an abstract principle, Brahma did not seize upon the popular imagination as did Vishnu and Shiva. He was visualized as a tiny figure who could sit on a lotus leaf. This god, however, has stimulated mystic contemplation. The avowed end of the famous *yoga* discipline is to attain a union of the soul with Brahma.

In many respects Hinduism differs from the pattern of religion familiar to Western peoples. It has no creed, no set of dogmas, no single congregation of the faithful, no established church. It assumes that divine truth wears many faces and that the paths to salvation are myriad. Hinduism is actually a social and religious complex, presenting a wide range of variations from region to region and from one social level to another, but given coherence by the authority accorded to the Brahmans or priests. Throughout India the Brahmans established themselves as ministrants of the rites and recipients of reverence and material compensation. They did not enforce any orthodox creed or crusade against heretics, but they insisted successfully that only they could mediate between gods and men. The chief points of emphasis in Hinduism as a social discipline came to be: (1) respect for and support of the Brahmans; (2) noninjury to animal life, especially cattle (although there are many exceptions to this rule); (3) the inferior status of women; and (4) acceptance of the regulations of caste.

Chief features of Hinduism

The chief distinguishing characteristic of Hindu religious and social life is the institution of caste, the most rigorous and refined instrument of segregation ever invented. Caste is much more complex than the typical division of a nation into social or economic classes, even when these classes are hereditary. Aside from heredity, membership in a caste is not based upon any single principle nor does it follow a logical pattern. The best definition of caste is a simple one: "A group of families internally united by peculiar rules for the observance of ceremonial purity, especially in the matters of diet and marriage." Typically, a person must marry within his or her caste and should not accept food from a member of a lower caste. Caste is the antithesis of democracy. It is a vast hierarchy,

The institution of caste

exalting the Brahmans at the top and degrading the "untouchables" or outcastes at the bottom of the social pyramid.

The development of the caste system

According to orthodox Hindu tradition, caste has always existed; it is part of the order of nature. The word used to denote it (*jat*) literally means "species." Historical evidence, however, shows that caste developed gradually over a long period of time. Caste was unknown to the Indo-Aryan society of the early Vedic age, but by the time of the epics it was already regarded as an ancient institution. Thus the system has probably been operating in India for the past 3000 years, and its origins are lost in obscurity. Its starting point, undoubtedly, was the racial pride of the Aryan conquerors, who were determined to prevent contamination by intermarriage with the supposedly inferior "black-skinned" peoples whom they were fighting and reducing to subjection. In this case the distinction was based on color (*varna*); but as time went on various other criteria entered into the drawing of caste lines, including occupations, religious deviation, migrations from one section of India to another, and later invasions by non-Hindu peoples who could not be expelled but who might be prevented from destroying the Hindu system by assigning them a place within it. While the origins of caste are obscure and its causes multiple, the development and final acceptance of the institution was probably influenced by the exertions of the Brahmans in their struggle for a position of dominance over all other groups, a struggle in which they did not scruple to use religious weapons to discomfit their competitors. The keenest rivalry was between the Brahmans and the warrior nobles (including rajas). The nobles had the advantage of being recognized wielders of authority backed by force; but the Brahmans had the advantage of education, mastery of the sacred *Vedas*, and wonder-working powers in the eyes of the people. Socially the Brahmans and nobles were on a par. There are records of Brahman kings and of kings or nobles who became skilled in the *Vedas*. But eventually the Brahmans won recognition for their claim to the highest rank of all, and the nobles were forced to accept classification as the second caste (*kshatriya*). As the price of their pre-eminence, the Brahmans were expected to devote themselves more unreservedly to their religious and educational functions, adopting a modest and mildly ascetic manner of life and leaving political dominion to the *kshatriyas*. However, as tutors and advisers to kings, the Brahmans managed to retain considerable political influence.

The major castes

Once the principle of caste was accepted by the leading groups in society, it was not difficult to impose it upon the others. Originating in northern India, the institution was extended among the Dravidians and other peoples of the Deccan as Aryan influence permeated that region. Many occupational groups or guilds became castes, but division does not always follow vocational lines. Brahmans may, without incurring disapproval, engage in a variety of occupations, including comparatively humble ones. At the same time, members of the higher castes avoid tasks which are considered defiling, such as the disposal of corpses, butchering animals, or preparing hides. It is impossible to enumerate precisely the castes of India because the number is enormous and fluctuates from time to time. Theoretically, there are four great castes with subdivisions: *brahmans* (priests), *kshatriyas* (warriors), *vaisyas* (farmers, herdsmen, and artisans), and *sudras* (laborers, servants, and slaves). Actually, except for the first, these categories have little significance. Probably they once represented the general classes of Aryan society before caste had taken hold, but they are much too broad to define caste as it has existed in historic times. The effective divisions are more minute. There are some 1800 subdivisions of Brahmans alone, and the total number of castes and subcastes in India has been reckoned at more than 3000.

Undeniably caste has had a stultifying effect upon Indian society. The rules of caste observance are arbitrary, tedious, and time-con-

Dravidian Temple of Nataraja at Chidambaram. The gorgeously sculptured spire is a gem of Dravidian art; the temple is believed to be the oldest in South India.

suming, especially in the everyday matters of social intercourse and eating. The fear of pollution becomes an obsession. Not only are there varying degrees of uncleanness in food (depending on the ingredients and the method of cooking as well as who has prepared it), but absolute prohibitions on certain foods restrict the diet unduly, impairing the health of the population. Whether or not a consequence of caste, the position of women in the patriarchal society of India became degraded as the caste system solidified. A man might in some cases marry beneath his caste; for a woman to do so was considered shameful. Caste duty for a woman lay in absolute obedience to her father and then to her husband. The deplorable custom of child marriage was introduced, defended with the argument that it saved a girl from the monstrous crime of falling in love with any other man than her future husband. Although child marriages made it inevitable that there would be a large number of widows, a widow was shamed by the belief that some sin of hers had caused her husband's death. She was forbidden to remarry and could best redeem her reputation by committing suicide in flames on her husband's pyre. The most inhumane feature of caste was the treatment accorded the lowest groups in the scale, especially the "Untouchables," who were considered to be outside the border of even the lowest caste, and therefore hardly human beings at all. In southern India the greatest humiliation of the "Untouchables" took place. Their shadow, it was thought, would pollute a well. They were required to live in segregated quarters and to warn people of their approach by uttering cries.

The fact that the caste system has endured in India for tens of centuries and is still operative (though with important changes) is a testimony to the toughness of social institutions, once they have become established. At the same time it should be pointed out that the role of caste in India was not wholly negative. On the positive side it gave the Indian people a sense of identity when confronted with alien cultures or conquerors. It also offered the individual a feeling of security within his group and fostered various forms of mutual assistance. In spite of inter-caste rivalries, the separate castes learned to cooperate with one another, notably in the constitution and administration of local village councils. Eventually caste came to be looked upon as a normal and necessary arrangement, especially as it was hedged about by religious sanctions. Particularly effectual were the twin beliefs: *karma* and the transmigration or rebirth of souls. These concepts, which were given an idealistic intepretation by the philosophers of the *Upanishads,* served in the popular imagination to explain and justify caste. If a person was born into a high caste he was thought to be receiving his reward for meritorious behavior in a previous existence. He had produced good *karma,* which carried him upward on the ladder. Similarly, a member of the despised castes was supposed to have incurred his lot because of misdeeds in a previous incarnation. Unfair as the distinctions of caste seemed to be, they were accepted as a just and precise recognition of the individual's deserts. The person who suffered abuse was told to blame only himself and to strive for perfection within the prescribed limits of his present caste in order that his condition would be improved the next time his soul returned to earth. Since it was possible to go either up or down in the succession of births, patience, diligence, and conformity became supreme virtues. Devotion to duty and the certainty of retribution—*dharma* and *karma*—were the cement which held the caste structure together.

3. REFORM MOVEMENTS: THE RISE OF BUDDHISM

In the sixth century B.C. the stratification of society and the hardening of religious ritual provoked a simmering discontent that found an outlet in several protest movements, led by members of the nobility. Because these protests were directed against the extravagant claims of the Brahmans, they assumed at the outset a heretical or even antireligious form. Most of them proved to be only temporary, but two resulted in philosophical and religious schools of enduring influence—Jainism and Buddhism. There were many parallels between these two movements. They originated in the same section of India, north of the Ganges in eastern Hindustan, and the leader of each was a member of the noble or *kshatriya* caste. Each repudiated the authority of priests and *Vedas*, rejecting all the paraphernalia of religion and replacing it by a system of philosophy. At the same time each was ethical and reformist, attempting to provide moral and personal satisfaction to its adherents. Each drew heavily upon the background of Hindu philosophic tradition and formulated goals which, though original in form, were not alien to the spirit of this tradition. And, ironically, each finally turned into a religion, Jainism taking its place within Hinduism, and Buddhism becoming a separate faith. Although Buddhism carried within itself many elements of Hindu thought, it ultimately obtained its widest following in Asian lands outside India and practically disappeared in the country of its birth. However, Buddhism flourished in India for 1000 years after the life of its founder; it helped to liberalize Hinduism and to keep it from becoming an agency of unlimited exploitation in the hands of the Brahmans. Buddhism also contributed heavily to Indian architecture and sculpture, and the Buddhist sacred texts were the first works committed to writing in India.

The revolt against Brahmanism

Jainism is associated with a figure known as Mahavira ("Great Hero"), who, although probably not its founder, gave it a distinctive form. Mahavira expounded a complex metaphysics which embraced the notion that not only living creatures but almost every object possesses a soul. Employing the familiar concepts of trans-

Jainism

157

Jain Temples on Girnar Mountain. These exhibit the lavish sculpture characteristic of Indian architecture.

migration and *karma,* he held that the soul when attached to matter is in bondage and that it will never be content until freed from and entirely independent of the physical body. The purport of his message was to point out the way to the soul's liberation. Insisting that prayers and worship were of no avail, he prescribed a course of mental and moral discipline, the highest stage of which was withdrawal into a state of meditation with complete denial of the claims of the flesh. The exalting of extreme asceticism remained one of the chief characteristics of Jainism, and particular honor was reserved for the zealot who was able to carry self-denial to the point of starving himself to death, as a number of Jain saints are reputed to have done. Another cardinal emphasis among the Jains (derived from their animistic belief in a multiplicity of souls) is the doctrine of *ahimsa,* or the necessity of refraining from injury to any living creature. This doctrine has led to commendable efforts to prevent cruelty to animals, although it has sometimes been carried to extremes in attempting to protect even pests and vermin. Surrounded by the atmosphere of Hinduism, the Jains relinquished their early antireligious tenets, instituting prayers to various deities, including the deified Mahavira. The Jain sect, which numbers slightly more than a million members, is monastic in organization. The monks are

bound by five vows, while the laity, who are considered part of the order although not of the same degree of holiness as the monks, may subscribe to "small vows." Through plying the trade of moneylending the Jains became a wealthy order, in spite of their rigorous asceticism.

Much more significant than Jainism was the contemporary movement destined to be known as Buddhism because its founder, Gautama, was accorded the title of Buddha, "the Enlightened One." Gautama (*ca.* 563–483 B.C.) was the son of the head of a small state located on the slopes of the Himalayas in what is now Nepal. This tribal state, like many others of that time, elected its ruler; hence Gautama, although of noble blood, was not a hereditary prince as later tradition claimed. Little is known about the events of his life, but legends have supplied innumerable details, most of them miraculous. There is factual evidence to support the conclusion that he was one of those rare personalities who deliberately relinquished a safe and comfortable existence in order to devote himself to the quest of higher values and the service of his fellow men. Tradition has it that at the age of twenty-nine he left his sumptuous abode in the middle of the night after a fond glance at his young wife and infant son, cut off his hair, and sent back his jewels and fine clothes to his father. Then came years of wandering and disappointment in which he found no answer to the problem that vexed him—the cause and cure of human suffering. After studying philosophy with the Brahmans he concluded that this was a vain pursuit. Next, it is said, he spent six years practicing an extreme asceticism, until his body had almost wasted away. This course he also abandoned as leading only to despair. The climax of his life came when, discouraged and weary, he sat down under a large Bo tree to meditate. Suddenly he had an overwhelming experience, a revelation or a flash of insight in which he seemed to penetrate the mystery of evil and suffering. Henceforth he was free from doubts, but, instead of retiring to enjoy his state of Enlightenment, he determined to teach others how they might also secure it. For the next forty years until his death at the age of eighty, he wandered through the Ganges valley, relying upon charity for his livelihood and instructing the disciples who gathered about him.

The substance of Gautama Buddha's teachings has been better preserved than the facts of his life. Some scholars consider him the most intellectual of all the founders of the world's great religions. He had no intention of establishing a religion, and his ideas, although conditioned by his Hindu religious background, were not sectarian. His doctrines embodied a philosophy or metaphysics, a psychology, and an ethics, of which the last is most important. The basis of his philosophy was materialism. In direct opposition to the absolute idealism of the *Upanishads* (and in contrast to Mahavira's teaching), he held that nothing exists except matter and denied the actuality of the soul. Because matter is in a state of flux, constantly changing its form, he said that all things are impermanent. Hence, there is no Absolute Being or fixed universal principle other than the law of change—growth and decay. Buddha's psychological principles followed logically from his materialist metaphysics. If there is no soul, no permanent entity, there can be no distinct individual personality or being. Not only the soul but the *self* is an illusion, he affirmed. What seems to be an individual personality is only a bundle of attributes (such as sense experience and consciousness) held together temporarily as the spokes of a wheel are fastened around the hub.

Gautama's doctrine of selflessness

Gautama's negative and deflating intellectual doctrines were intended to be encouraging rather than discouraging, as shown in the development of his system of ethics. The source of human anguish is, as he saw it, the individual's attempt to attain the unattainable. Desire or craving is the root of all evil. It can never be satisfied because the desired objects and emotional states are transitory; but the abandonment of desire can bring satisfaction and peace (the state of *nirvana*). The most persistent and futile craving, underlying a multitude of vain desires, is the ego impulse—the struggle to enhance and perpetuate the self. Since, according to Gautama, the self is only an illusion, the egoist is doomed to chase a will-o'-the-wisp. Thus it follows that selflessness is more realistic as well as more satisfying than selfishness. Oddly enough, Gautama, while denying the existence of the soul, retained the doctrine of *karma*, insisting that a person's actions would affect the condition of another person yet unborn—just as an expiring lamp can light the flame of another lamp. The ultimate goal which he projected was, like that of the Vedic philosophers, the complete extinction of *karma* through the cultivation of selflessness, so that the cycle of births, travail, and tragedy would be no more.

Gautama's ethical teachings

In his ethical teachings Gautama's emphasis was positive rather than negative. He proclaimed the ideal of universal love, to be exemplified by service and helpfulness. Rather than a saintly hermit, he was apparently a gifted teacher, with a stock of homely illustrations and parables. He gave sensible advice in regard to domestic and marital relations, occupations, business matters, and so on. As a rule of personal conduct he advocated "the Middle Path," by which he meant the avoidance of extremes—renouncing both indulgence and injurious asceticism, rejecting prayers and ritual and also the idea of escape into a heaven of bliss. Gautama repeatedly declared that dogmas are much less important than behavior and inner attitudes. And he was firmly opposed to forcing ideas upon anyone, believing that discussion and the power of example are the only valid means of establishing truth. Although he was an ethical rather than a social reformer and made no direct attack upon the caste system, caste distinctions were dissolved among his own group of disciples. He admonished his followers to develop their faculties to the full and to exert themselves for the benefit of others. His last words are said to have been, "Work out your emancipation with diligence."

The Buddhist movement in Gautama's lifetime had few of the characteristics of a religion. In the course of a century or two, however, it developed its own rites, mystic symbols, and other supernatural elements. The Buddhists in India gradually became an order of monks and nuns. Candidates for admission to the order were required to undergo a long period of training. After completing the training, the novitiate shaved his head, put on the yellow robes, and took the monastic vows of poverty and chastity. In contrast to Christian monks, he did not take a vow of obedience, because membership was considered a matter of free choice. The monks customarily remained in a monastery during the three months of the rainy season, which Gautama had devoted to instructing his disciples; for the rest of the year they lived as wandering mendicants, dependent upon the alms which they received in their beggars' bowls as they passed from village to village. Lay men or women who accepted the Buddhist teachings and contributed to the support of the monks were considered adherents of the faith and entitled to its benefits.

Buddhism after Gautama

Various sects of Buddhism arose as the movement spread. The two principal schools, representing a cleavage which apparently began soon after Gautama's death, are the *Hinayana* ("Lesser Vehicle") and the *Mahayana* ("Great Vehicle"). The term *Hinayana* was at first applied reproachfully, because the members of this group were bent upon their own self-perfection, claiming that it was possible for the diligent individual to attain *nirvana* in three lifetimes. The *Mahayana* school was characterized by the doctrine of the buddha-elect—a person who had won Enlightenment but chose deliberately to remain in the world of sorrow in order to work for the liberation of all mankind. In spite of its noble beginning, however, the *Mahayana* tradition became more corrupted than the *Hinayana* as time went on. The *Hinayana* school of Buddhism is represented in its purest form in Ceylon, where it was established as early as the third century B.C., and it is also the prevailing religion of Burma and Thailand. In these countries, Gautama is still theoretically regarded as a man, but in actual practice he is worshiped as a deity, and offerings of flowers or incense are made to his image. The intellectual vigor and the moral challenge of Gautama's teachings have been greatly obscured, and elements of primitive religions have retained their hold on the people. However, the Buddha's emphasis upon kindliness, patience, and the avoidance of injury to living creatures is still prominent. *Mahayana* Buddhism was eventually developed in many different forms in Nepal, Tibet, and eastern Asia. It came to include the worship not only of Buddha but of his several supposed reincarnations, and it also transformed the concept of *nirvana* into a conventional paradise of bliss.

Buddhist sects

ANCIENT
INDIAN
CIVILIZATION

Intellectual
achievements in
ancient India

During the period so far discussed, covering more than 1000 years, the physical and external aspects of Indian civilization were still elementary. Writing was unknown until the eighth, or perhaps the seventh, century B.C., and even then it was used only for business purposes. The people lived in villages or small towns rather than cities, architecture was very simple, and political units were small. There was none of the magnificence which characterized ancient Egypt, Mesopotamia, or the extinct Indus valley civilization. To a remarkable degree the achievements of the ancient Indians were in the fields of the imagination and intellect, expressed in song and poetry, in the epics, and in philosophical and religious speculation. Their intellectual achievements included also considerable scientific progress. Medicine was highly developed as early as the Vedic age. Not only were many specific remedies listed, but dissection was practiced and delicate operations were performed. The knowledge of human anatomy was extensive, and a beginning had been made in the study of embryology. Medical science and the surgeon's vocation were held in high respect, until the caste system introduced a fear of pollution through bodily contact with unclean persons. Many fanciful elements, however, were intermingled with medical lore. An appreciable knowledge of astronomy was acquired in spite of its perversion into astrology. The suggestion that the earth revolves on its axis and that the sun only appears to rise and set was put forward in the *Vedas*, apparently without being taken very seriously. The most brilliant scientific attainments were those in mathematics. The ancient Indians were able to handle extremely large numbers in their calculations and knew how to extract square and cube roots. Besides using the decimal system they invented the all-important principle of the zero, which was eventually adopted by the rest of the world. In geometry their progress was not equal to that of the Greeks, but they surpassed the Greeks in the development of algebra.

Conquest of the
Indus valley by
Alexander the
Great

During the fourth and third centuries B.C., partly in response to stimulation from without, political developments in India led temporarily in the direction of greater efficiency and unification. As a result of the conquests of the Persian king, Darius I, about 500 B.C., the Indus valley had become a province (satrapy) of the Persian empire, furnishing mercenary soldiers and an annual tribute in gold. After Alexander the Great, the famous Macedonian conqueror, overthrew the Persian empire, he conducted his troops eastward through the passes of the Hindu Kush Mountains into the upper Indus valley (327–326 B.C.). He spent less than two years in India but traversed most of the Punjab, fought and negotiated with local rajas, and installed Macedonian officials in the region. Although Alexander's invasion provides the first verifiable date in Indian history, it made so little impression upon the Hindus that their contemporary records do not even mention his name. However, the invasion promoted cultural exchange between the Hindus and the Greek-speaking world, and, more immediately, it paved the way for the erection of a powerful state in India.

In the revolts and confusion that followed the death of Alexander in 323 B.C., an Indian adventurer named Chandragupta Maurya seized the opportunity to found a dynasty. Chandragupta had profited from observing Greek military tactics and led in the movement to expel the Macedonian officials from India. Then he turned his army against the Magadha kingdom, which was the strongest state in Hindustan at this time. He defeated and killed the Magadhan king and established himself as ruler in the capital city of Pataliputra (now Patna) on the Ganges. When Seleucus (Alexander's successor in Syria and Persia) tried to recover the lost Indian territory, Chandragupta defeated him soundly and forced him to cede Baluchistan and part of Afghanistan. Chandragupta extended his power over most of northern India and founded the first empire in Indian history. Although his dynasty, known as the Maurya, lasted less than a century and a half, its record is a distinguished one.

Chandragupta was a much more imposing figure than the rajas of the Vedic age. His government was efficient but very harsh. Social and economic activities were carefully regulated, an elaborate tax system had been devised, and the death penalty was meted out freely, sometimes through the administering of poison. The king kept a large standing army, with divisions of infantry, cavalry, chariots, and elephants. In spite of his far-reaching authority, and his maintenance of secret police or spies, he seems to have lived in dread of assassination and took the precaution to change his sleeping quarters every night. On the credit side was his construction and improvement of public irrigation works and the building of roads. The Royal Road, from the capital to the western frontier, was 1200 miles long.

The greatest member of the Maurya Dynasty, and one of the most remarkable rulers in the annals of any civilization, was Chandragupta's grandson, King Asoka, the royal patron of Buddhism, whose beneficent reign lasted some forty years (*ca.* 273–232 B.C.). Merely as a conqueror Asoka could lay claim to fame, because he held under Mauryan rule not only Hindustan and the region northwest of the Indus but most of the Deccan as well, thus bringing the greater part of India into one administration. His conquests, however, were the aspect of his reign that he considered least important. In fact, he fought only one major war—by which he was enabled to gain control of the Deccan—and he felt remorseful ever after for the bloodshed which accompanied this campaign. Attracted to the Buddhist teachings, he at first became a lay adherent and later took the formal vows and joined the order but without relinquishing his position as king. He attempted, rather, to exemplify the precepts of Buddhism in his personal life and to apply them to the administration of the empire. Thus, without being a theocrat or divine-right ruler, he provides an almost unique example of the injection of religious idealism into statecraft.

It is impossible to know how completely Asoka's benign purposes were carried out. He was particularly active in establishing rest houses for travelers, in having trees planted, wells dug, and watering places built along the roads for the refreshment of man and beast, and in improving facilities for the treatment of the sick. He sent commissioners throughout the kingdom to inquire into the needs of the people, teach them religion, and report on their spiritual progress. In deference to the Buddhist injunction against taking life, Asoka gave up hunting (replacing this sport by "pious tours" or pilgrimages) and gradually reduced the meat consumption in the royal household until—according to his announcement—only a vegetable diet was permitted. He reformed the harsh system of punishments which his grandfather had used, but he did not entirely abolish the death penalty. There is no evidence of any trend toward democracy in Asoka's government. He adhered to the tradition of autocratic rule, but exercised it with conscience and benevolence. Although he was earnest in his support of Buddhism, Asoka opposed fanaticism. He made religious toleration a state policy and urged that the Brahmans of all the Hindu sects be treated with respect. He stated that he cared less about what his subjects believed than he did about their actions and attitudes. To commemorate his authority he

Asokan Bull Capital. From Rampurva, Bihar (northeastern India), third century B.C. Emperor Asoka erected huge stone pillars and utilized some already standing as impressive memorials to his own authority and to the law of Buddha. The bell-shaped capital shows the influence of contemporary Persian architecture.

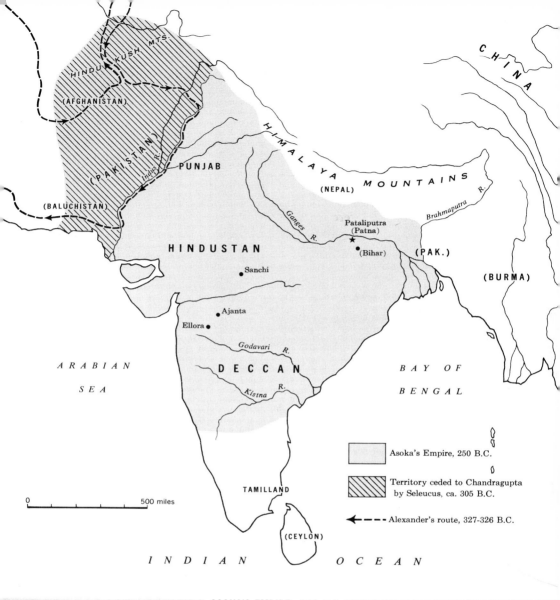

ASOKA'S EMPIRE • 250 B.C.

had erected in various parts of his empire gigantic sandstone pillars, each cut from a single block of stone and standing forty or fifty feet high. The capitals of animal figures and the beautifully polished surface of these columns—some of which are still preserved—testify to the engineering and artistic skill of the royal workmen.

Asoka's patronage during his long reign contributed markedly to the growth of the Buddhist religion. He sent missionaries of the faith to Ceylon, Burma, Kashmir, Nepal, and apparently even west to Macedonia, Syria, and Egypt. The king's own son was the missionary to Ceylon. Buddhist monks held a general council in 250 B.C. at Asoka's capital, Pataliputra, where they agreed upon the basic

Asoka's patronage of Buddhism

165

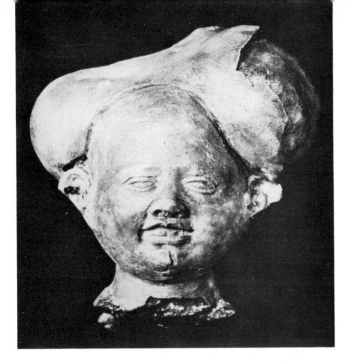

Laughing Boy. Terracotta head of a laughing boy, from Pataliputra (Patna). An example of the realistic sculpture of the Maurya period.

texts that should be regarded as authentic. This "Council of Patna" established the canonical books of Buddhism, especially for the *Hinayana* school. The Buddhist scriptures are the oldest written literature of India—that is, they were the first to be committed to writing. However, although the texts were settled upon in 250 B.C., they were still memorized and transmitted only by word of mouth. Except for the excerpts in Asoka's rock carvings, the texts were not actually written out in full until about 80 B.C. in Ceylon.

Asoka's extraordinary administrative system did not long survive him. His successors seem to have been mediocrities who lacked both **End of the Maurya** his reforming zeal and his organizing ability. In 184 B.C. the last **Dynasty** Maurya ruler was assassinated by the army commander, an ambitious Brahman who seated his own family on the throne. The efficiency of Asoka's government was not duplicated until about 500 years after the end of his dynasty.

SELECTED READINGS

· *Items so designated are available in paperbound editions.*

· Basham, A. L., *The Wonder that Was India: A Survey of the Culture of the Indian Sub-Continent Before the Coming of the Muslims,* New York, 1955 (Evergreen) Illustrated.

· Brown, D. M., *The White Umbrella: Indian Political Thought from Manu to Gandhi,* Berkeley, 1953 (California). A brief sketch.

Brown, W. N., *The United States and India and Pakistan,* rev. ed., Cambridge, Mass., 1963. An excellent general introduction to Indian history.

Cambridge History of India, Vol. I.

Cambridge History of India, Supplementary Volume: Wheeler, Mortimer, *The Indus Civilization.*

Conze, Edward, *Buddhist Thought in India,* London, 1962.

· Dasgupta, S. N., *Indian Idealism,* London, 1933 (Cambridge).

Eliot, Charles, *Hinduism and Buddhism: An Historical Sketch,* 3 vols., New York, 1954. A standard work.

Garratt, G. T., ed., *The Legacy of India,* Oxford, 1937. A valuable collection of essays on various aspects of Indian culture.

Ghoshal, U. N., *A History of Indian Political Ideas: The Ancient Period and the Period of Transition to the Middle Ages,* 3rd ed., New York, 1959. Reflects wide reading in Western political theory as well as thorough study of the Indian sources.

Ghurye, G. S., *Caste and Race in India,* London, 1932. Scientific in spirit; readable and informative.

Hutton, J. S., *Caste in India,* Cambridge, 1946.

Kabir, Humayun, *The Indian Heritage,* New York, 1955. An interesting and informative summary of ancient Hindu thought.

Kramrisch, Stella, *The Art of India: Traditions of Indian Sculpture, Painting, and Architecture,* New York, 1954. Admirable collection of photographs, with brief introduction.

Lee, S. E., *A History of Far Eastern Art,* New York, 1965.

Majumdar, R. C., ed., *The History and Culture of the Indian People,* London, 1951; Vol. I; 2nd ed., Bombay, 1953, Vol. II. An advanced work by Indian scholars.

Moreland, W. H., and Chatterjee, A. C., *A Short History of India,* 4th ed., London, 1957.

Morgan, K. W., ed., *The Path of the Buddha,* New York, 1956.

———, *The Religion of the Hindus,* New York, 1953. A sympathetic study.

Panikkar, K. M., *A Survey of Indian History,* London, 1947. Includes material on cultural and intellectual history.

· Piggott, Stuart, *Prehistoric India,* Baltimore, 1950. (Penguin)

· Prabhavananda, Swami, and Manchester, F., *The Upanishads, Breath of the Eternal,* New York, 1957 (Mentor).

· Radhakrishnan, Sarvepalli, *The Hindu View of Life,* New York, 1939 (Macmillan). A popular essay by a distinguished contemporary Indian philosopher and statesman (former President of India).

· Rawlinson, H. G., *India, a Short Cultural History,* rev. ed., New York, 1952 (Praeger). An excellent interpretive study.

Rowland, Benjamin, *The Art and Architecture of India: Buddhist, Hindu, Jain,* Baltimore, 1953. Informative and discriminating.

Smith, F. H., *The Buddhist Way of Life,* London, 1951.

Smith, V. A., *Asoka,* Oxford, 1920.

Spear, Percival, *India: A Modern History,* Ann Arbor, 1961.

———, ed., *The Oxford History of India,* 3rd ed., New York, 1958. A thorough revision of a standard older history; has up-to-date bibliographies.

Vogel, J. P., *Buddhist Art in India, Ceylon and Java,* Oxford, 1936.

Wheeler, Mortimer, *Early India and Pakistan to Ashoka,* New York, 1959. A brief authoritative account by a leading archaeologist.

SOURCE MATERIALS

Arnold, Edwin, tr., "The Bhagavad-Gita or Song Celestial," *Harvard Classics, Sacred Writings,* Vol. II.

· de Bary, W. T., ed., *Sources of Indian Tradition,* "Brahmanism"; "Jainism and Buddhism"; "Hinduism." (Columbia).

ANCIENT INDIAN CIVILIZATION

· Edgerton, Franklin, tr., *The Bhagavad Gita,* (Torchbooks). Translation and interpretation.

Goddard, Dwight, ed., *A Buddhist Bible.*

· Hamilton, C. H., ed., *Buddhism, a Religion of Infinite Compassion* (Library of Liberal Arts).

Lin Yutang, ed., *The Wisdom of China and India,* Hymns from the *Rigveda,* Selections from the *Upanishads.*

Mueller, Max, tr., "The Upanishads," *Sacred Books of the East,* Vol. I.

· Narayan, R. K., *Gods, Demons and Others* (Compass). Fine translation of ancient Indian stories.

The *Ramayana* and the *Mahabharata,* Everyman's Library edition.

Sastri, S. R., tr., *The Bhagavadgita.* An accurate translation with explanatory and critical comment.

CHAPTER 8

Ancient Chinese Civilization

There have been many kings, emperors, and great men in history who enjoyed fame and honor while they lived and came to nothing at their death, while Confucius, who was but a common scholar clad in a plain gown, became the acknowledged Master of scholars for over ten generations. All people in China who discuss the six arts, from the emperors, kings, and princes down, regard the Master as the final authority. He may be called the Supreme Sage.
—*Historical Records* of Ssu-ma Ch'ien (145-*ca*. 85 B.C.)

The beginning of a high civilization in China did not occur until about a thousand years after the flowering of the Indus-valley civilization in India. However, when once established the Far Eastern culture continued—not without changes and interruptions but with its essential features intact—into the twentieth century of our own era. The civilization of China, although it took form much later than that of Egypt, Mesopotamia, or the Indus valley, is one of the oldest in existence. The reasons for the long survival are partly geographic and partly historical. During most of her history China did not have aggressive organized states on her borders. More important, perhaps, the pacifist influence of her great philosophers and ethical teachers kept her imperialism within bounds. The Chinese people considered other peoples as inferiors but still members of one great family and seldom provoked either the enmity or the envy of surrounding countries. They did their share of conquering, but the lands they annexed were almost exclusively undeveloped territories. They rarely attempted to impose their will upon conquered peoples by force, but considered it their mission to assimilate them and make them the beneficiaries of their superior ethical system.

Reasons for long survival of Chinese civilization

169

I. THE FORMATIVE STAGE

In our study of preliterate cultures we have learned already that China was the home of one of the earliest human species, the so-called Peking man. His skeletal remains were found between 1926 and 1930 in a cave about forty miles southwest of Peking (Peiping). Anthropologists estimate that his species lived at least 500,000 years ago, and that he was probably a contemporary of Java man, one of the oldest human types. Peking man's culture was, of course, extremely primitive, but there is evidence that he used crude stone tools, had a knowledge of fire, and buried his dead. Whether the members of his species were the ancestors of the historic Chinese people is a debated question. An eminent German anthropologist, Franz Weidenreich, maintains that the descent was direct. He bases his conclusion upon peculiarities in the skulls, jaws, and incisor teeth of the ancient specimens which have their counterparts among modern Mongolian peoples.

Although the discovery of Peking man proves the existence of human beings with an Old Stone Age culture in China at least 500,000 years ago, there are many gaps in the record subsequent to that time. Evidence is still scanty for the Late or Upper Paleolithic period (as it is reckoned in Europe), when the advance of the Arctic ice sheet brought a bitter climate to northern China. There is no doubt as to human habitation of northern China during the Neolithic period, when the climate became warmer again and was perhaps less dry than at present so that conditions were favorable for agriculture. Remains have been found of two types of Neolithic culture in this region, each representing a rather late stage. One was located close to the Yellow River in modern Honan province. On the basis of its painted pottery of excellent workmanship it has been identified as of Central Asiatic origin. It may quite possibly have been an offshoot of the Neolithic culture which flourished among the vase painters of southern Turkestan.

The other type of Late Neolithic culture had its center farther east, in the Shantung peninsula, and is distinguished by two varieties of unpainted pottery—one white in color, the other very thin and with a glossy black surface. The black-pottery culture, as it has come to be called, has no counterpart in Europe or western Asia and is believed to have originated in the Far East, possibly on some island of the Pacific. It spread westward, however, into the region occupied by the painted-pottery folk, and tended to displace their way of life, as is indicated by changes in the technique of pottery manufacture. The most noteworthy fact concerning the black-pottery Neolithic people is that they seem to have contributed the basic pattern for Chinese society and culture, in an elementary form, of course. This would mean that the most influential Far Eastern civilization was indigenous from the outset and not an importation from some distant region where institutions and techniques had already been matured. Archaeology tends to confirm the tradition of the Chinese people that their ancestors were not immigrants from another land but had always lived on "the good earth" of the eastern river valleys.

By about 1500 B.C. the east central portion of the Yellow River valley was occupied by people of Mongolian stock who had passed beyond the Neolithic into the Bronze Age, had learned how to build fortified cities, and possessed the essential attributes of civilization, including writing. The era of this Bronze Age people corresponds to the period of the Shang Dynasty in Chinese history. It was long believed by scholars that the Shang Dynasty was almost purely legendary. Excavations of the 1930's, however, have proved that it was very real and have recovered many impressive examples of its workmanship. Dates have not yet been precisely established, but the civilization was flourishing by 1400 B.C. A study of the objects which have been unearthed and especially the all-important deciphering of inscriptions have made it possible to construct a fairly complete picture of this formative period of Chinese history.

Racially the Shang people present no significant contrast to the earlier Neolithic inhabitants of the Yellow River valley nor to the Chinese of later times. Their culture, too, was a continuation and improvement of that of the Neolithic farming communities which had produced the black pottery. Presumably the dynasty was inaugurated by the conquest of a military chieftain, with no extensive displacement of population. The Shang kingdom occupied only a small part of China. The area under effective control may have been no more than 40,000 square miles, or about the size of the state of Ohio. The Shang people carried on trade with other communities—also agricultural but more primitive than their own—in the Yangtze valley to the south, and they had to defend themselves against barbarian and nomadic tribes from the north and west. The principal royal residence and seat of government was the city which they called by the name of Shang, situated at the northern tip of Honan province, about 80 miles north of the Yellow River (the site of modern Anyang).

Agriculture was the chief source of livelihood of the Shang people, although their tools for cultivating the soil were still quite primitive. Grains were the principal crops, especially wheat and millet. Rice was also used, but this may have been imported from the Yangtze region. It is possible that a system of irrigation had been developed. Hunting and herding contributed to the food supply. Many animals had been domesticated, including not only the dog, pig, goat, sheep, ox, horse, and chicken but also the water buffalo, monkey, and probably the elephant. Dog flesh as well as pork was a popular item of diet. But in spite of the importance of animal husbandry, Shang society was by no means nomadic; and if it had ever passed through such a stage the evidence has disappeared, even from folk traditions and literature. Though developing in close proximity to the wandering herdsmen of Mongolia, the Chinese were primarily a nation of farmers.

The houses the Shang people constructed show an intelligent adaptation to the environment. The soil of northeastern China is composed largely of loess, fine particles of loam and dust borne by northwest winds from the central plateaus and deposited in the river valley and along the northeastern coast. This soil, which from its color has given rise to such geographical names as Yellow River and Yellow Sea, packs into a hard mass, solid enough to make durable walls. The Neolithic inhabitants of the region commonly lived in pits hollowed out of the loess. In Shang times rural villagers apparently also occupied pit dwellings, but the city residents built more comfortable houses above ground. For a foundation the firmly packed earth served admirably. Upon the rectangular foundation was erected a gabled-roof structure, with wooden poles holding up the central ridge of the roof and shorter posts supporting each of the two sides at the eaves. Thatching was used for the roof and packed earth for the outside walls of the house. This type of dwelling, which by coincidence is closer in design to the European style of home than to the tents of Mongolia or the mud-brick houses of Egypt and Mesopotamia, has been employed by the Chinese throughout their history.

The specimens of Shang craftsmanship that archaeologists have recovered reveal a high degree of skill and versatility. In spite of familiarity with metal, Shang artisans still made many objects of stone—knives, axes, and even dishes—as well as of bone, shell, and horn. Bone implements inlaid with turquoise and exquisitely carved pieces of ivory were produced in abundance. Cowrie shells were used for jewelry and probably also served as money. Several types of pottery were manufactured. The black variety seems to have been discontinued, but a fine white pottery made of porcelain clay, chiefly for ceremonial purposes, was undoubtedly a variation of the Neolithic prototype. The bow and arrow was the most formidable weapon for the hunt or for combat. Bamboo arrows were feathered and tipped with bronze or bone points. The bow was of the composite or reflex type, formed of two separate arcs of wood held together with horn, and said to be almost twice as powerful as the famous English long bow. Two-horse chariots, of elaborate workmanship and with spoked wheels, were probably the exclusive property of the aristocracy. Armor was made of leather, sometimes reinforced with wooden slats. Evidently the people were fond of music. For musical instruments they employed drums, stones emitting a bell-like tone when struck, and a small pipe of hollow bone with five finger-holes—more like an ocarina than a flute.

The artistry of the Shang people is illustrated most strikingly by their sculpture and engraving. The examples of sculpture thus far

discovered are generally of small dimensions. A marble ox head,
however, greater than life-size and fitted with a pin as if it had been
fastened to a body, suggests that some large statuary was produced.
Shang metal work was truly remarkable, especially the superb
bronze castings of intricate design. Bronze articles included weapons

Bronze Tripod Cup. Shang Dynasty
(1523–1027 B.C.). Used in sacrificial
ceremonies.

and chariot and harness fittings, but most impressive were the ob- Art of the Shang
jects intended for religious and ceremonial functions—tripods, liba- people
tion bowls, drinking cups, and grotesquely figured masks. The technique employed in their making was superlative. A leading American specialist in early Chinese culture asserts that it was more
flawless than the technique employed for bronze sculpture at the
height of the Italian Renaissance.

As has already been mentioned, this early civilization possessed a
system of writing. The writing brush and an ink made of soot had
been invented. Writing materials included silk cloth and wood, and Earliest system of
it is quite possible that books were compiled with pages which were writing in China
narrow strips of bamboo joined together by a thong. Fortunately, a
great many specimens of writing have been preserved inscribed on
pieces of animal bone, horn, and tortoise shells. Practically all these
were produced by the Shang people for one purpose only, which
was to obtain the counsel of deities or ancestral spirits concerning
future events or a proposed course of action. They represented a
process of divination by the king and priests; hence they are re- **173**

Above: *Bronze Ritual Vessel*. Shang Dynasty.

Below: *Bronze Ritual Vessel with Removable Top.* Shang Dynasty.

ferred to as "oracle bones." The ancient procedure apparently was as follows. After a question had been directed to the spirits, a flat piece of split cattle bone or a tortoise shell was heated until it cracked; then the shape of the crack was studied to ascertain the answer from the spirit world. The majority of the oracle bones contain no writing; but for some unknown reason, in about 10 per cent of the cases the question was engraved upon the object after the divination rite had been performed. Although the inscriptions are brief, a careful study of them has thrown light upon many aspects of Shang society and activities.

Evolution of
Shang writing

The Shang writing was not primitive but in an advanced pictographic stage. While the Shang symbols are the earliest examples found in the Far East, they presuppose a long period of evolution from more rudimentary forms. Each character represented an entire word, as it does in the classical Chinese. In some cases, only the shape of the sign has changed. For example, the Shang character for *sun* was round—obviously a picture of the sun—while now it is square. Practically all the principles which the Chinese literary language employs in the process of character formation were already in use. The Shang characters were not only pictographs but sometimes ideographs, in which the meaning was conveyed by combining different symbols or concepts (the sun and moon joined together represent *bright* or *brightness;* the sun rising behind a tree stands for *east*). The phonetic principle was also applied. A character having one meaning might be used to indicate a word of different meaning but pronounced the same way. To avoid confusion, the

174

phonetic symbol was combined with a conceptual symbol in the same character. Not surprisingly, fewer characters were employed in Shang times than later, although it is probable that the list compiled from the oracle bones is only partial. About 2500 characters have been distinguished in the Shang records; the written language eventually came to include more than twenty times that number.

Little definite information is available as to the political and social institutions of the Shang period. Governmental power was vested hereditarily in a royal family, but on the death of the king the crown passed to his younger brother in preference to the king's own sons. In addition to military activities, the king probably supervised public works and was important as the chief religious functionary. He was assisted by an educated class of priests, who served as astrologers, performed the divination rites, and supervised the calendar. Because the calendar was a lunar one, it frequently had to be adjusted to bring it into harmony with the solar year. There is some evidence from the oracle bones that the Shang priests had made considerable achievements in mathematics and astronomy. As early as the fourteenth century B.C. they recorded eclipses and perhaps had already conceived the decimal system.

Political and social institutions of the Shang period

The family was the basic social institution. The king, or a great aristocrat, might have several wives, but monogamy seems to have been the more usual practice even in the royal family, as it almost certainly was among the people generally. The position of women, at least within the upper classes, was good. Slavery existed and there were gradations in the ranks of society, but there is no evidence of a feudal system during this period.

The family

Ample testimony exists for the religious practices of the Shang people. They worshiped many natural objects and forces—the earth, rivers, the winds, even the directions (East, West, and South). To these gods they performed sacrifices, not out of doors but in temples. Burnt offerings of animal flesh were common, and a kind of wine or beer made from millet was also considered acceptable. Although the Shang were in some ways highly civilized, there is gruesome evidence that they practiced human sacrifice on a large scale. Apparently the victims were usually captives who had been taken in battle, and sometimes raiding expeditions were sent out for the express purpose of securing a batch of foreign tribesmen to be offered in sacrifice. The principal deity seems to have been a god concerned primarily with rainfall, the crops, and war. His name, Shang Ti, has persisted into later times. There is no evidence that Shang religion was essentially spiritual or ethical; it was directed toward the procuring of human prosperity, as among the Sumerians and Babylonians. The king was not a divinity like the Egyptian pharaoh, but he became an object of worship after his death, and sacrifices were performed to the departed spirits of both kings and queens. The royal tombs were sumptuous affairs. A large pit was excavated, provided

Religion of the Shang period

with stairways, and a wooden tomb chamber was constructed at the bottom. The royal corpse was surrounded with magnificent furnishings, including figured bronzes and pottery, marble statuary, and richly adorned implements and jewels. After the funeral ceremonies the entire excavation was filled with firmly tamped earth.

It is noteworthy that the typical Chinese institution of ancestor worship was already in existence, at least in the circle of the court. Ancestral spirits were believed to possess the power of helping or hurting their descendants, and yet they depended upon their living representatives for nourishment in the form of food offerings. It was also customary, even among people of humble circumstance, to bury valuable objects with the deceased. Divination by means of the oracle bones—the practice which bequeathed so many valuable inscriptions—was a by-product of the cult of ancestor worship and the belief in the potency of departed spirits.

The Shang society represents the earliest genuine civilization of Eastern Asia for which historical records are available. In addition, it laid the foundation and provided materials for the distinctive Chinese culture pattern, as illustrated by methods of agriculture, handicrafts, artistic and architectural forms, emphasis upon the family as the basic social unit, religious concepts, and a system of writing. About 1027 B.C. the city of Shang was taken and the dynasty overthrown by semibarbarous invaders from the west. However, these barbarians assimilated, continued, and finally surpassed the culture of the Shang people whom they had conquered, and gave their own name (Chou) to the longest dynasty of China's history.

2. THE CHOU DYNASTY, THE CLASSICAL AGE OF CHINA (*ca.* 1027–249 B.C.)

While the civilization of the Vedic Age in India was still in its early stages, in the Yellow River valley of China the Shang Dynasty was succeeded by the Chou. However, the seizure of power by the Chou warriors did not bring such a pronounced change in the character of society and culture as did the Indo-Aryan invasion of India. The Chou people, located to the west of the Shang frontier, had had considerable contact with the Shang state previous to their conquest of it. Women from the Shang royal family had been given as wives to some of the Chou rulers—probably in the vain hope that marriage alliances would lessen the danger of attack from that quarter. Although the Chou people of the eleventh century B.C. were hardly more than barbarians, they were not distinct in race from the Shang, and their leaders had sufficient appreciation of Shang culture to wish to continue it. Even when the capital city was taken and the government overthrown, a Shang prince was allowed to continue to administer lands in the center of the state, with the "assistance" of younger sons of the Chou royal house. After this

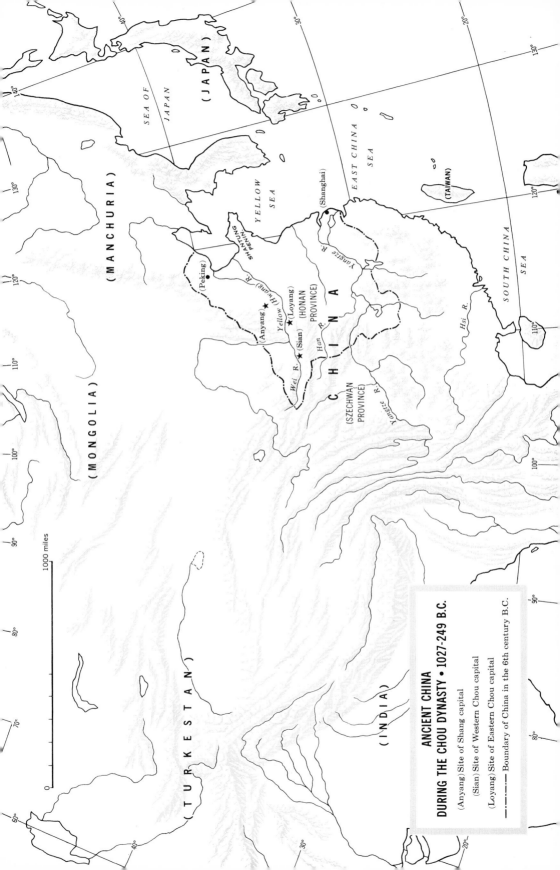

**ANCIENT CHINA
DURING THE CHOU DYNASTY • 1027-249 B.C.**

(Anyang) Site of Shang capital

(Sian) Site of Western Chou capital

(Loyang) Site of Eastern Chou capital

—·—·— Boundary of China in the 6th century B.C.

1000 miles

(TURKESTAN)

(INDIA)

(MONGOLIA)

(MANCHURIA)

(JAPAN)

SEA OF JAPAN

YELLOW SEA

SHANTUNG PENIN.

(Peking)

(Anyang)

Yellow R. (Hwang)

(Sian)

Wei R.

(Loyang)

(HONAN PROVINCE)

Han R.

CHINA

(SZECHWAN PROVINCE)

Yangtze R.

Hsi R.

(Shanghai)

Yangtze R.

EAST CHINA SEA

(TAIWAN)

SOUTH CHINA SEA

prince became involved in an unsuccessful rebellion of the recently conquered people, he was executed, and a large number of Shang subjects were removed from the scene of the rebellion to a region south of the Yellow River. But even then the Shang royal line was not entirely extinguished—probably as much from fear of provoking the powerful Shang ancestral spirits as from a desire to placate the conquered subjects.

Efforts of the
Chou rulers to
establish
legitimacy

The new dynasty exerted zealous efforts to convince the people that it was a legitimate succession rather than a usurpation. Its spokesmen advanced the claim that the last Shang ruler had been incompetent and debauched, and that the divine powers had used the Chou as an instrument for his removal. The "Mandate of Heaven," they alleged, had been transferred from the Shang house to the Chou. There is no evidence that the Shang king was guilty of the faults ascribed to him, but the charge, even if a fabrication, shows the desire of the conquerors to fit their authority into accepted conventions rather than to break with the past. And the concept of governmental power as a commission from Heaven rather than an absolute and inalienable right—although possibly invented by the Chou for propaganda purposes—was to become a persistent element in Chinese political history.

The Chou form of government was a monarchy, although not identical with that of the Shang. The throne was hereditary by primogeniture, as in most European monarchies, whereas under the Shang it had passed from older brother to younger brother. The early Chou rulers maintained their capital near modern Sian (Shensi province) in the Wei valley, where their power had already been established. In addition to the Shang territory they added other conquests, especially southward in the middle Yangtze valley. The king exercised direct rule over the region surrounding his capital but administered the outlying areas indirectly, through appointed officials who were given almost complete jurisdiction within their own districts. The Chou administrative system was roughly similar to that which developed in Europe in the age of feudalism some 2000 years later. The district governors, originally members of the royal family or generals of proved competence, were the king's vassals, but they were also great territorial lords, exercising wide military and judicial powers, and they gradually transformed their position from that of appointive official to hereditary ruler. Chou feudalism—like the later European variety—contained elements of danger for the central government, although for two or three centuries the Chou court was strong enough to remove overly ambitious officials and keep its own authority paramount.

By the eighth century B.C. the vigor of the ruling house had declined to the point where it was no longer able to protect the western frontier effectively against the attacks of barbarians. The fortunes of the dynasty seemed to reach their lowest point in 771 B.C.,

Bronze Ceremonial Vessel. Chou Dynasty (1027–249 B.C.).

when a worthless king almost duplicated the villainies that had been unjustifiably attributed to the last of the Shang rulers. King Yu, particularly through his extravagant efforts to amuse his favorite concubine, angered the nobles beyond endurance. When he lit the beacon fires to summon aid in the face of a combined attack by barbarian tribes and one of the outraged nobles, his men refused to answer the summons. King Yu was killed and his palace looted. The dynasty might have been ended then and there, but the nobles of the realm found it expedient to install the king's son as nominal head, keeping in their own hands the actual authority over their respective dominions. This event marks the close of the "Western Chou" period. The royal seat of government was now moved about 100 miles farther east into safer territory (near the modern city of Honan), and the ensuing period (771–*ca.* 250 B.C.) is known accordingly as the "Eastern Chou."

Decline of the "Western Chou" Dynasty

During the 500 years of the Eastern Chou Dynasty, China suffered from political disunity and internal strife. The king actually ruled over a domain much smaller than that of some of the great hereditary princes. For the kingdom as a whole his powers, while theoretically supreme (he was officially styled "Son of Heaven"), were limited to religious and ceremonial functions and to adjudicating disputes concerning precedence and the rights of succession in the various states. In spite of these conditions, however, it is not quite accurate to describe the Eastern Chou era as an age of feudalism. It is true that hereditary nobles enjoyed social prominence, wealth, and power, and acquired different degrees of rank, roughly

Conditions under the "Eastern Chou" Dynasty

179

equivalent to the European titles of duke, marquis, count, viscount, and baron. They became lords and vassals, held fiefs for which they owed military service, and were supported by the labor of the peasants on their lands. These warrior aristocrats not only raised armies and collected revenues from their dominions but also administered justice. Custom supplied the greater part of law, but severe penalties, including fines, mutilation, and death, were inflicted upon offenders. Nevertheless, a number of factors prevented the complete ascendancy of a feudal regime. In the first place, a large proportion of the nobility failed to acquire estates of their own and remained jealous of the great territorial lords. The lesser aristocracy, generally well educated and frequently unemployed, constituted a sort of middle class that could not fit comfortably into a feudalized society. More important still, towns were growing and trade increasing throughout the Chou period, and the merchants (including part of the aristocracy) attained economic importance. Moreover, rulers of the larger states successfully pushed forward a program of centralization within their own dominions. They introduced regular systems of taxation, based upon agriculture. To offset the entrenched position of the nobles they developed their own administrative bureaucracies and staffed them with trained officials, recruited largely from the ranks of the lesser aristocracy. In spite of the disorganized condition of China as a whole, the period provided valuable experience in the art of government which could eventually be drawn upon in the task of reuniting the country.

Although China was divided during the Eastern Chou period into many principalities with shifting boundaries and frequent wars, a
Expansion of the frontiers
few of the larger states held the balance of power, especially four which were located on the outer frontiers to the north, west, and south. Usually one state at a time was recognized as paramount and its ruler, designated as "First Noble," took the lead in organizing the defense of the kingdom as a whole and even in collecting the revenues. The boundaries of Chinese civilization were extended by the aggressive initiative of the rulers of the frontier states. The Shantung peninsula, the seacoast as far south as modern Shanghai and Hangchow, and the rich Yangtze valley were all brought under Chinese jurisdiction. Thus the total area was much larger than the old Shang kingdom and included more than half of the eighteen provinces which have constituted the state of China during the greater portion of its history. The southern part of Manchuria was also occupied, and walls of earth—the first stages of the famous Great Wall of China—were constructed both south and north of the Yellow River for protection against the nomads of Mongolia.

Beginning about the middle of the fifth century B.C., internal conditions became extremely chaotic, inaugurating a bloody period known as that of "the Warring States." The relatively restrained
competition which the feudal principalities had carried on with one

another gave way to a struggle for supremacy in which proprieties and recognized codes were disregarded. The rulers of several of the states even assumed the title of "king" (*wang*), previously reserved for the prince of Chou. In the fourth and third centuries B.C. the state of Ch'in, seated in the Wei valley on the western frontier, gained ascendancy over the others. Not only were the Ch'in rulers aggressive, but within their own dominions they had developed the most effectively centralized government in China. After annexing the fertile plain lying south of the Wei valley (in modern Szechwan province), they constructed a splendid irrigation system which has lasted until the present day. Probably the Ch'in people had also mingled with and absorbed some of the barbarian tribesmen, but they were no less Chinese in culture than their rivals. In spite of alliances formed against them by other feudal princes, the Ch'in forces, employing ruthlessness, massacre, and treachery, annexed one region after another. Finally, in 256 B.C., they seized the tiny remaining portion of the royal domain and ended the Chou Dynasty. Within thirty-five years the Ch'in prince had brought all the Chinese territories under his control and, to indicate the extent of his triumph, assumed the imposing title of "First Emperor" (Shih Huang Ti). Although the Ch'in Dynasty hardly outlasted its founder, it did China the valuable service of abolishing the remnants of feudalism. The highly centralized government which the Ch'in emperor established did not prove to be permanent, but the feudal system never reappeared.

Large Bronze Bell. This bell with bosses or nipples, decorative panels, and inscriptions, is typical of the "Middle Chou" style (ninth century B.C.). It was hung from the ring at the base of the shaft and was sounded by striking with a wooden mallet. The bell has a scooped mouth instead of being even at the bottom. (In the picture it is resting on a cushion.)

During the 800 or 900 years of the Chou Dynasty, in spite of internal conflicts, cultural progress was almost continuous. The period is regarded as the classical age of Chinese civilization, and its contributions were fundamental to the whole subsequent history of the Far East. As has already been indicated, the culture of the Chou was based upon foundations that had been laid by their predecessors.

Ceremonial Bronze Basin. Chou Dynasty. The inscription on this bronze piece, known as the *San P'an*, records the settlement of a territorial dispute between the feudal states of San and Nieh in Western Shensi Province.

Cultural progress under the Chou

Handicraft techniques improved under the Chou and the smelting of iron was introduced, although iron did not entirely displace bronze. While the great majority of the population lived in rural villages, there were some large towns and the merchant class assumed importance. Trade was by no means exclusively local. With the introduction of the donkey, and especially the camel (probably not before the third century B.C.), it became possible to develop caravan trade routes across Central Asia for the transportation of grain, salt, silk, and other commodities. Coined copper money came into use before the close of the fifth century B.C. The manufacture of silk, already an old industry, was increased, and the fibers of several domestic plants were also employed in making textiles.

Economic life

From time immemorial the all-important Chinese enterprise has been farming. It was extended under the Chou by reclamation measures—the building of irrigation canals and reservoirs and the draining of swamps—and also by acquisition of the moist and fertile rice-producing lands of the Yangtze valley. Probably the methods of cultivation which were developed during the Shang and Chou periods were essentially the same as they have remained ever since.

The persistence of unvarying techniques over a long period of 3000 years is attributable not to the inability of the Chinese to progress but to the fact that these techniques were admirably adapted to the terrain and to the objectives of Chinese society. While they were primitive in some ways, they embodied a great deal of experience and foresight. China has been said to possess a "vegetable civilization," because its people, while not socially or intellectually stagnant, adapted themselves so completely to the potentialities of their environment. The typical Chinese farming village—with fields of various sizes, often tiny but all carefully tended—appears almost as if it were part of the natural landscape instead of being an effort on man's part to manipulate nature for his own benefit. Although China is a large country, the relative scarcity of arable land made it difficult for food production to keep pace with an expanding population. Much of the country is hilly or mountainous, and the north and west portions are subject to drought which cannot be entirely overcome by irrigation. Consequently, attention was lavished upon every suitable plot that could be found. The bulk of labor was done by hand, with simple tools but in such a way as to produce the greatest possible yield. Wastes which had fertilizing value were collected and returned to the soil, as were ashes and even powdered sun-dried bricks when no longer serviceable for building purposes. Crops were rotated to avoid soil exhaustion, and hillsides were terraced to conserve moisture and prevent erosion.

The motivating principle was to secure the maximum of foodstuffs for human consumption. Therefore, grains, vegetables, and root crops were favored over orchards or decorative gardens, although these, of course, were found on the estates of the wealthy. Another result was the relative scarcity of animals, except in the north where a cool climate made wool production desirable. Although draft animals had been known from early times and the ox-drawn plow was introduced about the sixth century B.C., their use was restricted because of the cheapness and—on small plots—greater efficiency of human labor. Besides, hayfields or grazing lands to provide animal fodder represented a curtailment of the area devoted to producing foodstuffs for human beings. The Chinese have subsisted largely on a vegetable diet, not because they had religious scruples against eating flesh as did the Hindus, but for practical reasons of economy. Instead of raising crops to feed cattle and then eating the cattle, they preferred to consume the crops directly themselves. For meats they chose animals that could be reared inexpensively—chickens, ducks, and especially pigs, which were also useful scavengers, and fish, with which even temporary ponds could be profitably stocked. Chinese methods of agriculture thus were intensive rather than extensive. As compared with modern Western countries, particularly the United States and Canada, the yield was low in proportion to the number of men employed and the hours of

Chinese methods
of agriculture

183

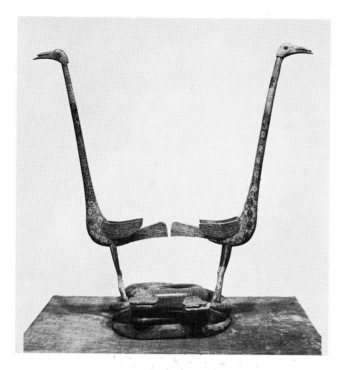

Drum Stand of Lacquered Wood. Late Chou Dynasty.

labor, but high in terms of acreage. While Chinese farming demanded exacting and arduous toil on the part of the cultivators, it made possible the growth of a large population.

Society during the Chou period had a decidedly aristocratic character. There was a tremendous gulf between the great landowners and the peasants who comprised the vast majority of the people. But while class lines were rigidly drawn, Chinese society was never stratified by a caste system like that of India. There were only two clearly distinguished classes, the commoners or serfs and the nobles; and as civilization became more complex the nobility included contrasting interests and conditions rather than remaining a solidly united order. Because the numbers of the aristocracy tended to increase, many of them consequently possessed little or no landed property. They were forced to seek administrative employment with a powerful noble, to engage in trade, or even to undertake menial occupations, thereby undermining the fiction of the inherent superiority of the hereditary aristocracy. Unfortunately, very little is known about the condition of the lower classes. Evidently before the close of the Chou period a considerable number of peasants had become landowners. Others, however, were actually slaves, and most of the commoners were serfs, attached to the soil without having legal title to it and compelled to give the lord a large share of the produce.

While the family is always a basic social institution, it has been so **184** to an almost unique degree in China. Here the family was a tightly

Class divisions of
an aristocratic
society

organized unit, bent upon preserving the welfare of its members against any outside agency, official or unofficial, and was probably the only safeguard of any consequence against the unlimited exploitation of the lower classes. Typically the Chinese family was large because it embraced several generations. When a son married he customarily brought his bride home to live under the paternal roof or in a closely neighboring house. Theoretically the family also included the departed ancestral spirits, thus extending vertically into time as well as horizontally among contemporary relatives. Authority was vested in the father (or grandfather), and the utmost emphasis was placed upon respect for elders, so that even grown men were bound by their parents' wishes. Such a custom led to extreme conservatism and sometimes inflicted hardships upon youth, but it had the advantage of developing qualities of patience, loyalty, and consideration for the helpless aged.

Women became definitely subordinate to men in the patriarchal family and in Chinese society at large, although their position was not utterly intolerable. Allegedly, in early Chou times the young men and maidens of the peasant class were allowed to choose their mates freely after a Spring Festival characterized by complete license. However that may be, among the aristocracy neither men nor women had freedom of choice in marriage unless they defied convention and parental authority. Marriages were arranged by the parents of the respective parties, usually with the assistance of a matchmaker or go-between. After the bride was brought to her husband's home she was considered as on probation for a three-month period, after which if she had proved satisfactory she was allowed to participate in the ancestral sacrifice and became an accepted member of the family. In regard to the laxity of conduct permitted and the right of divorce, the woman was also at a disadvantage. Only the husband could have recourse to divorce, and he could obtain it on any one of a number of grounds, including that his wife talked too much. Actually, however, divorces were rare, especially among people of humble circumstance. Undoubtedly the practices of polygamy and concubinage, permitting a man to have more than one consort, added to the hardships and humiliation of women. But these practices were confined to the wealthy classes and were by no means universal among them. In spite of the inferior position of woman in Chinese society, she had definite rights and privileges and on the whole was much better off than in the caste-ridden society of India. It is strange that, in a predominantly agrarian economy such as China's, labor in the fields was not regarded as woman's normal work, although among poor families she often had to assist. The wife's own family did not renounce all interest in her when she left their home for her husband's and might interfere in case she was abused. Children were taught to love and venerate both parents, and as a woman grew older she shared in the

Subordination of women

honors accorded to age. The domineering position which a grand-mother or mother-in-law sometimes assumed became proverbial.

The Chinese family was not only an economic and sociological unit but a religious and political one as well. Some scholars maintain that during the Chou period the servile peasants were not permitted the dignity of having surnames, and that they had no share in the cult of ancestor worship. However, that condition could not endure in view of the tremendous emphasis placed upon family relationships among the dominant classes, in public administration, and in the literature of the age. Throughout the greater part of Chinese history, religion for the ordinary person consisted largely in caring for his family graves and making prayers and offerings to the spirits of his ancestors. As a political unit the family enforced discipline and considered misconduct on the part of one of its members as a collective disgrace. Very commonly the inflicting of punishment for minor offenses was left to the head of a family rather than to a public official. The strong solidarity and sense of collective responsibility of the family had disadvantages as well as advantages. Because the family was answerable for the behavior of its members, one of them might be punished for the misconduct of another if the true offender was not apprehended by the authorities, or a whole family might be wiped out for a crime committed by one person. On the whole, however, the family gave the individual a greater feeling of security and support than has been typical in most societies.

Religion was fundamentally the same as it had been in Shang times. Many deities were worshiped, ranging from local spirits and nature gods with limited powers to such majestic divinities as Earth and Heaven. The practice of human sacrifice gradually disappeared and came to be strongly condemned, but animals, agricultural produce, and liquor were offered upon the altars. Evidence of a "chariot sacrifice" was uncovered by archaeologists north of the Yellow River when they excavated a deep pit about 30 feet square. In this instance seventy-two horses harnessed to twelve chariots, and eight dogs with bells fastened to their necks, had apparently been placed in the pit and buried alive. While worship did not necessarily include prayer, prayers were sometimes written out and burned with the sacrificial offering. A prominent deity from Chou times on was the one called T'ien, translated as "Heaven." Although of separate origin, this divinity was similar to and became practically identical with the earlier Shang Ti. T'ien was not conceived of primarily as a personal god but as representing the supreme spiritual powers collectively, the universal moral law, or an underlying impersonal cosmic force. It was by the "Mandate of Heaven" (*T'ien-ming*) that the king was supposed to rule, and he was referred to as "Son of Heaven," without, however, implying that he was divine. The worship of the earth as an agricultural deity came to be supplemented by the veneration of a specific locality with which the for-

tunes of the worshipers were associated. Every village had its sacred THE CHOU
mound of earth; the lord of large territories had a mound to repre- DYNASTY, THE
sent his domain; and the mound of the king was believed to have CLASSICAL AGE
significance for the whole land of China. The most important rituals
took place either at these mounds or in ancestral temples.

Among the Chinese at this time, as among the Hindus, there was
no clear-cut religious system, no fixed creed, and no church. In contrast to Hindu society, however, the Chinese priests did not become   Extraordinary
a sacrosanct class in a position to dominate other groups. The   characteristics of
priests, like those of the ancient Greeks, were merely assistants in   Chinese religion
the ritual. The indispensable religious functionaries were the heads
of families, including, of course, the king, whose ancestral spirits
were particularly formidable, and who propitiated the great deities
of the rivers, earth, and sky. For most of the people religion was
either a family affair, consisting of social functions invested with
sentiment and emphasizing filial piety, or a matter of state, maintained by the proper authorities to ensure the general welfare. Sacrifices to the greatest gods were ordinarily performed only by the
highest officials, to lesser deities by lower officials, and so on down
to the ordinary folk who sacrificed to their own ancestors in the
form of wooden tablets. They believed that the spirits of these ancestors could bring prosperity to the family and that dire consequences would follow any neglect of the rites. Aside from traditional ceremonies, everyday life was complicated by a medley of
folklore and superstition hardly classifiable as religion but exerting a
potent influence. This included the belief in witchcraft, in good
and evil omens, in divination and spirit messages conveyed through
mediums, and in the necessity of avoiding offense to numerous
malignant beings. "Hungry ghosts," whose sacrifices had been neglected or cut off through the extinction of a family, were considered especially dangerous. In spite of the strong faith that the soul
outlived the body, the notion of rewards and punishments in an
afterlife was almost entirely lacking. The worst fate that could happen to a disembodied spirit, it was thought, was for it to be deprived
of the nourishment supplied by sacrificial offerings.

By far the most significant contributions of the Chou period were
in the fields of literature and philosophy. The Shang system of writing, already highly advanced, was continued with slight modifica-   Written records of
tions. Evidently the Chinese now considered written records as in-   the Chou period
dispensable to the conduct of both public and private affairs. They
sometimes recorded important transactions in lengthy inscriptions
on bronze vessels, but they more frequently wrote with the brush
upon wood or cloth of silk. Books composed of thin strips of
bamboo were produced in abundance. Although only a minority of
the population was literate, it must have been a large minority and
included the feudal nobility as well as the merchants. In contrast to
the Feudal Age of Western Europe when writing was confined **187**

almost entirely to the clergy, the Chou aristocrats were versed in literature and kept full records of their properties, their dependents, and sometimes of their personal activities. Not only the king but the head of every feudal state maintained archives to preserve the luster of family traditions and to aid in settling disputes with rival princes. The Chinese, even in ancient times, were at the opposite pole from the Hindus in their attitude toward the importance of chronology and the recording of factual events (although this does not mean that Chinese documents were entirely accurate or free from fanciful elements). A young nobleman or prince, in the process of his education, was reminded by his tutors that later generations would study the annals of his administration and that he should, accordingly, choose his actions with care. Princes were regularly given instruction in history "to stimulate them to good conduct and warn them against evil"—apparently with no better results than have attended most modern efforts in this direction.

Of the tremendous output of Chou literature, only a few authentic portions have survived (aside from the imperishable bronze inscriptions). Some of them, however, are from a date earlier than 600 B.C. Probably the most ancient work is the *Book of Changes*. It contains a collection of hexagrams formed of straight and broken lines arranged in different combinations, with accompanying text. The figures, like the earlier Shang oracle bones, were used for divination. Thus the book was originally hardly more than a sorcerer's manual, but it came to be venerated as a work of mystic and occult wisdom.[1] Very different is the *Document Classic* (less accurately called "*Book of History*"), which is a collection of official documents, proclamations, and speeches purporting to be from the early Chou period. The *Book of Etiquette*, dealing with ceremonial behavior, formal occasions, and preparation for adult responsibilities, was intended to assist in the education of the lesser aristocracy. Most interesting of all is the *Book of Poetry*, an anthology of about 300 poems covering a wide range of subjects and moods. Some of the poems are religious, in the nature of prayers or hymns to accompany the rites of sacrifice; others celebrate the exploits of heroes; still others are lyrical in quality, voicing the laments of a discharged official, a soldier's homesickness, delight in the beauties of nature, and the frustration or rapture of young lovers. Neither in quantity nor in profundity do these odes approach the *Vedas* of India, but they are graceful in expression and show vividly the practical down-to-earth temperament of the Chinese and their lively interest in and optimistic attitude toward the business of living—at least among the aristocracy. While the poems on the whole are neither philosophical nor spiritual, a few suggest the reforming fervor of the Hebrew prophets.

Literature of the
Chou period

[1] For a contrary view see H. Wilhelm, *Change; Eight Lectures on the I Ching*, trans. C. F. Baynes, New York, 1960. Wilhelm interprets the classic as an affirmation of man's ability to control his own destiny.

In view of the extent and the variety of writing during the Chou period, the literary collections which have survived are rather disappointing. But this deficiency is amply compensated for by achievements in the realm of philosophy, which reached a brilliant climax between the sixth and third centuries B.C. For some unexplained reason—perhaps by mere coincidence—philosophical activity of a high order was carried on at about the same time in three widely separated regions of the ancient world. While the Greeks were inquiring into the nature of the physical universe, and Indian thinkers were pondering the relationship of the soul to Absolute Being, Chinese sages were attempting to discover the basis of human society and the underlying principles of good government. The Chinese thinkers were not much interested in either physical science or metaphysics; the philosophy they propounded was social, political, and ethical. Exhortatory and reformist in tone, it undoubtedly reflected the influence of the recurrent strife and political disorders of a period when feudal ideas and institutions were becoming increasingly irrelevant but had not yet been clearly repudiated. Against the background of upheaval which marked the late Chou era, philosophers sought to formulate principles for the stabilizing of society and the betterment of the individual. The leaders in this intellectual activity were largely from the lesser aristocracy, men of energy and ambition who could not find employment suitable to their talents and who were distressed by the turbulent state of public affairs. They were a scholarly group, fond of disputation, but also maintaining an interest in the practice of government and sometimes holding administrative posts or coaching pupils who aspired to such posts. It was a time of lively interchange of ideas, and a great variety of opinions was put forward. Out of this intellectual ferment and debate—one of the most productive in the annals of human thought —four main philosophic schools emerged, the most important being the Confucianist and the Taoist.

Confucius (*ca.* 551–479 B.C.), who has proved to be one of the most influential men in all history, was largely a failure from the standpoint of what he hoped to accomplish. He spent his life advocating reforms that were not adopted; yet he left an indelible stamp upon the thought and political institutions of China and other lands that came under Chinese influence. He was a native of the state of Lu (in modern Shantung province) and was reputed to have been the child of an aged father, a gentleman soldier named K'ung (Confucius is the Latinized form of the name K'ung Fu-tzu, or "Master K'ung"). Probably his family was of the lesser aristocracy, respectable but poor. In any event, he showed a sincere interest in the common people and did not choose his disciples on the basis of birth or rank. When he was only about twenty-one he began to teach informally a group of young friends who were attracted by his alert mind and by his precocious knowledge of traditional forms and usages. Although his reputation spread rapidly, little is known concerning the incidents of his career. Possibly as a mature man he held office for a short time under the Duke of Lu. For more than ten years, until old age overtook him, he wandered from state to state, refusing to be employed as a time-serving flatterer but continually hoping that some ruler would give him a chance to apply his ideals and thus set in motion a tide of reform that might sweep the entire country. Although revered by his small band of disciples, some of whom became officeholders, Confucius received no offer of appointment that he could accept in good conscience. Finally he returned to his native country where he died, discouraged, at the age of seventy-two.

Frustrated as a statesman, Confucius made his real contribution as a teacher. The memoranda of his conversations with his disciples (the *Analects*)—which are considered on the whole authentic, even though not written down in the master's lifetime—convey the impression of a lively and untrammeled mind which challenged those with whom it came in contact. Like his contemporary Gautama Buddha, and like his near-contemporary Socrates, Confucius earnestly believed that knowledge was the key to happiness and successful conduct. He also believed that almost anyone was capable of acquiring knowledge, but only through unrelenting effort. He insisted that his student-disciples should think for themselves, saying that if he had demonstrated one corner of a subject it was up to them to work out the other three corners, and constantly pricking their complacency. He recognized the difficulties in the thorough assimilation of ideas and was never satisfied with quick agreement. While no ascetic, he frowned on indulgence and urged his associates to strive continually for improvement. Though he had moments of petulance and harshness, the nobility of his character is unmistakable, and he refused to let his disappointments make him cynical. His regret, he said, was not that he was misunderstood but that he did not understand others sufficiently.

The doctrines of Confucius centered upon the good life and the good community. He respected religious ceremonies as part of established custom, but he refused to speculate on religious or supernatural questions, saying, in substance: "We do not know life; how can we understand death? We do not fully understand our obligations to the living; what can we know of our obligations to the dead?" He was optimistic regarding the material world and regarding human nature, which he thought was essentially good; but he believed that the individual's worth would not be realized unless he was properly guided in the development of his faculties. For this reason he stressed propriety and the observance of ceremonial forms—which he thought were helpful in the acquisition of self-discipline—although he was really more concerned with sincerity and intelligence than with appearances. Impressed as he was by the evils of feudal contention, Confucius advocated the restoration of central authority in the kingdom, combined, however, with a logical distribution of power. He visualized the ideal state as a benevolent paternalism, with the ruler not only commanding but also setting an example of conduct for the people to follow. He did not endorse a totalitarian system, nor mere passivity on the part of the people. He intended the ruler to be guided in his administration by the judgment of his officials, chosen on the basis of merit from the class of scholars. The health of the entire state would depend upon the welfare of each village, and harmony would be achieved by the combined efforts of the common people from below and of the officials from above.

Confucius' teachings therefore embodied a political philosophy, which regarded the state as a natural institution but modifiable by man, and devoted to promoting the general well-being and the fullest growth of individual personalities. The state existed for man, not man for the state. On the ethical side he emphasized fellow feeling or reciprocity, the cultivation of sympathy and cooperation, which must begin in the family and then extend by degrees into the larger areas of association. He stressed the importance of the five cardinal human relationships which were already traditional among the Chinese: (1) ruler and subject, (2) father and son, (3) elder brother and younger brother, (4) husband and wife, and (5) friend and friend. These could be expanded indefinitely and were not bounded even by Chinese lines. The logic of this train of thought was summarized in the famous saying, "All men are brothers." But Confucius argued that a person must be a worthy member of his own community before he could think in terms of world citizenship. Laying no claim to originality, Confucius urged a return to an ideal order which he attributed to the ancients but which actually had never existed. Unknowingly, he was supplying guiding principles which could be utilized in the future.

Aside from its founder, the ablest exponent of the Confucianist school was Mencius (Meng-tzu), who lived about a century later (*ca.* 373–288 B.C.) Like his master, Mencius affirmed the inherent goodness of human nature and the necessity of exemplary leadership to develop it. He looked upon government primarily as a moral enterprise, and he was more emphatic than Confucius in insisting that the material condition of the people should be improved. He wanted the government to take the initiative in lessening inequalities and in raising the living standards of the common folk. Perhaps because political confusion had increased since Confucius' day, he was outspoken in criticizing contemporary rulers. He taught that only a benevolent government, resting upon the tacit consent of the people, can possess the "Mandate of Heaven," and he defended the people's right to depose a corrupt or despotic sovereign. Hsün-tzu (*ca.* 300–237 B.C.) is usually classified as a Confucianist,

The political and ethical philosophy of Confucius

Mencius and Hsün-tzu

although his precepts diverged radically from those of Mencius. While both Confucius and Mencius had started with the assumption that man has a natural propensity for good, Hsün-tzu regarded human nature as basically evil. However, like the earlier Confucianists he believed that man can be improved by proper education and rigorous discipline. He laid great stress upon observance of ritual, formal training in the classics, and a strictly hierarchical ordering of society. In spite of his gloomy view of the natural man, he was far from a complete pessimist. He recommended vigorous action by the state to institute reforms and, like Mencius, favored the regulation of economic activities.

Lao-tzu and
Taoism

The Taoist philosophical school was in many ways the opposite of the Confucianist. Its traditional founder was Lao-tzu ("Old Sage"), a shadowy figure of the sixth century B.C. Little is known about the facts of his life, and some scholars doubt that he was an actual historical person. According to tradition he served as an official at the Chou capital in charge of the archives until, becoming weary of the world, he set out for the western mountains in quest of peace and, at the request of a guard at the mountain pass, set down his words of wisdom in a little book before he disappeared. But the real authorship of the *Tao Teh Ching* (Classic of Nature and Virtue), from which the principles of Taoism are derived, is undetermined, and it may not have been written earlier than the third century B.C. The book is not only brief but enigmatical, paradoxical, and perhaps ironical. With its terse and cryptic style it seems almost like an intentional antidote to the Confucian glorification of scholarship, exhortation, and patient explanation. On the whole the Taoist book exalts nature (sometimes in the sense of impersonal cosmic force, "the Boundless" or Absolute) and deprecates human efforts. Its spirit is romantic, mystical, anti-intellectual. It not only lauds the perfection of nature but idealizes the primitive, suggesting that people would be better off without the arts of civilization, living in blissful ignorance and keeping records by means of knotted cords rather than writing. Wealth creates avarice and laws produce criminals, it asserts. It is useless to try to improve society by preachment, ritual, or elaborate regulations; the more virtue is talked about the less it is practiced. "Those who teach don't know anything; those who know don't teach." A person learns more by staying home than by traveling; the wise man sits and meditates instead of bustling about trying to reform the world.

Taoist political and
ethical philosophy

As a political philosophy, Taoism advocates laissez faire. Unlike Confucius, Lao-tzu believed that governmental interference was the source of iniquity and that, if people were left to follow their intuition, they would live in harmony with nature and with one another. Nevertheless, Lao-tzu's ideal was not pure anarchism. Like Confucius he assumed the necessity of a wise and benevolent (although largely passive) ruler, and agreed that the only legitimate purpose of government was to promote human happiness. Perhaps his thought also reflects a rural protest against both the self-important aristocracy and the artificial society of the rapidly growing towns. In Lao-tzu's teachings there are strains of pacifism and the doctrine of non-retaliation for injury ("The virtuous man is for patching up; the vicious man is for fixing guilt"); of the efficacy of love in human relations ("Heaven arms with love those it would not see destroyed"); and of equalitarianism ("It is the way of Heaven to take away from those that have too much and give to those that have not enough"). The Taoist school produced several able thinkers in late Chou times and played a part in the shaping of Chinese philosophical traditions. However, in contrast to Confucianism, the Taoist doctrines were eventually transformed into a religious system, with a priesthood, temples, ritual, and emotional elements. But the Taoism which became one of the prominent religions of China had little connection with the principles expounded in the *Tao Teh Ching*.

A third school of political and ethical philosophy was associated with Mo Ti (or Mo-tzu), whose career is placed in the middle of the fifth century B.C. A man of decided originality, Mo Ti may have been of peasant stock; his sympathies lay with the downtrodden, and he regarded luxury and extravagance with aversion. The distinguishing feature of his thought is that he combined the doctrine of utilitarianism—insisting that everything should be judged by its usefulness—with a sweeping idealism that drew inspiration from religious faith. He condemned elaborate ceremonies dear to Confucianists, including the traditional three-year period of mourning, on the ground that they entailed needless expense. Sports, amusements, and even music met his disapproval because they were unproductive, absorbing energies which might be employed in useful labor. The pressing need, as he saw it, was to increase the supply of food and basic commodities to improve the health, longevity, and numbers of the population; and such a program called for hard work on the part of both common people and officials. His strong denunciation of offensive warfare was also rooted in utilitarianism.

Mo Ti

Mo Ti's ethics were by far the boldest of any of the Chinese philosophers. In place of the Confucian system of an expanding series of loyalties beginning with the family and radiating outward, he proclaimed the universal and impartial love of all mankind and declared that there can be no satisfactory community until the distinction between "self" and "other" is completely transcended. Applying his utilitarian yardstick, he reasoned that, by cultivating sympathy and mutual helpfulness with everyone, the individual was ensuring his own welfare as well as contributing to the security of others. But while his doctrine of universal and impartial affection linked altruism to self-interest, it called for a rare degree of discipline and high-mindedness, and its similarity to the ethics of Chris-

Altruism and utilitarianism

193

tianity has often been remarked. Mo Ti believed that the state, like other human institutions, was created by divine ordinance and that it was the duty of the ruler to carry out the will of Heaven, which he interpreted to mean promoting the common welfare. Although the Mohist school, as it is called, was prominent for a while and attracted many adherents, it practically disappeared after the downfall of the Chou Dynasty—partly because of the enmity of the Confucianists—and the teachings of the utilitarian philosopher were almost entirely forgotten until modern times.

The Legalist school

A fourth philosophical school, known as the "Legalist," stood far removed both from the bold idealism of Mo Ti and the optimistic humanism of Confucius. Formulated during the hectic period which witnessed the final collapse of the Chou Dynasty and the triumph of the Ch'in, it reflects Hsün-tzu's harsh view of human nature and his emphasis upon coercive discipline. At the same time the Legalists were indebted to Taoism in their contempt for scholarship, the intelligentsia, and conventional ethics; and in their preference for a simple agrarian society over a mobile, sophisticated, and economically diversified one. But, unlike the Taoists, they did not exalt nature or any supernatural agency, and they completely rejected laissez faire. Rather than mystics they were hardheaded realists, or even cynics. Asserting that man is by nature hopelessly selfish and incorrigible, they prescribed complete and unquestioning submission to the ruler. People's behavior, they argued, could be controlled only by carefully defined rewards and punishments, by a code of laws which was fundamentally punitive and which derived not from custom or natural instinct but from the will of the sovereign. Of all the schools of Chinese political thought, the Legalist was the most uncompromisingly authoritarian. Although its principles were systematically applied only during the short-lived Ch'in Dynasty, they exerted a continuing influence upon later dynasties also—tempered somewhat by the opposing Confucian tradition—and they find perhaps more than an echo in the present Chinese totalitarian regime.

Significance of the
Chou period

Although the later centuries of the Chou Dynasty were marked by strife and unrest and encumbered by the remnants of decaying feudal institutions, the material basis for a productive society had been laid and intellectual progress had reached a high point. An abundant and many-sided literature was in existence. Philosophers had come to grips in mature fashion with fundamental problems of individual and group behavior. Scholarship was an honorable profession, and scholars were considered indispensable to the business of government. There was a growing tradition—not yet very effective—that government entailed moral responsibilities as well as privileges, that those who exercised authority did so on sufferance and only so long as they conformed to the "Decree of Heaven." Moreover, the Chinese had come to think of themselves as composing a unique society, not merely a political affiliation but the "Middle

Kingdom"—the heart of civilization as contrasted with outlying "barbarian" areas. They had already mingled with and partially absorbed many non-Chinese tribes, and it is significant that the distinction between their civilization and the "barbarian" regions was not based upon race or nationality. The attitude of superiority which they adopted sometimes made them arrogant, but it gave them a toughness in resisting the shock of invasion and other adversities.

SELECTED READINGS

· *Items so designated are available in paperbound editions.*

Bishop, C. W., *Origin of the Far Eastern Civilizations*, Washington, 1942.

Ch'en, K. K. S., *Buddhism in China; a Historical Survey*, Princeton, 1964. A solid and lucid study.

· Creel, H. G., *The Birth of China*, New York, 1937 (Ungar). A fascinating account of archaeological exploration of Shang civilization, and an excellent introduction to the basic culture pattern of ancient China.

· ———, *Chinese Thought from Confucius to Mao Tse-tung*, Chicago, 1953 (Mentor).

· ———, *Confucius and the Chinese Way*, New York, 1960 (Torchbooks). Among eminent Sinologists, Creel is outstanding in his ability to communicate ideas to the general reader.

· Fitzgerald, C. P., *China, a Short Cultural History*, rev. ed., New York, 1954 (Praeger). Frequently unconventional in viewpoint; commendable for space devoted to social phenomena.

· Fung Yu-lan, (Derk Bodde, ed.), *A Short History of Chinese Philosophy*, New York, 1948 (Macmillan).

· Goodrich, L. C., *A Short History of the Chinese People*, 3rd ed., New York, 1959 (Torchbooks). Brief but informative; fulfills the promise of its title.

King, F. H., *Farmers of Forty Centuries, or Permanent Agriculture in China, Korea and Japan*, Emmaus, Penn., 1948. A classic description of the East Asian agrarian economy.

Latourette, K. S., *The Chinese, Their History and Culture*, 4th ed., 2 vols. in one, 1964. A solid contribution, comprehensive in scope, with extensive bibliographies.

Lee, S. E., *A History of Far Eastern Art*, New York, 1965.

Li Chi, *The Beginnings of Chinese Civilization: Three Lectures Illustrated with Finds at Anyang*, Seattle, 1957.

Needham, Joseph, *Science and Civilization in China*, New York, 1954, Vol. I; 1956, Vol. II; 1959, Vol. III. A far-ranging study; challenges long-accepted notions.

Reischauer, E. O., and Fairbank, J. K., *A History of East Asian Civilization*, Vol. I: *The Great Tradition*, Boston, 1960. A scholarly, insightful, and readable survey of the history and culture of China and Japan from earliest times to the nineteenth century; illustrated.

Watson, Burton, *Early Chinese Literature*, New York, 1962. Discusses and analyzes important works of philosophy, history, and poetry from the Chou to the Han Dynasty.

SOURCE MATERIALS

· de Bary, W. T., ed., *Sources of Chinese Tradition*, "The Classical Period" (Columbia).

Chai Ch'u, and Chai, Winberg, *A Treasury of Chinese Literature*.

Chan Wing-tsit, ed. and tr., *A Source Book in Chinese Philosophy*. Traces the history of Chinese philosophy from Confucianism to Communism.

Lin Yutang, ed., *The Wisdom of China and India*, "Laotse, the Book of Tao."

Mei, Y. P., tr., *The Ethical and Political Works of Motse*.

Soothill, W. E., tr., *The Analects of Confucius*.

Waley, Arthur, ed. and tr., *The Book of Songs; The Way and Its Power* (Evergreen); *Three Ways of Thought in Ancient China* (Anchor).

PART TWO

The World in the
Classical Era

After 600 B.C. the chief centers of civilization in the ancient world were
no longer confined to North Africa and Asia. By that time new cultures
were already growing to maturity in Greece and Italy. Both had started
their evolution considerably earlier, but the civilization of Greece did
not begin to ripen until about 600 B.C., while the Romans showed little
promise of original achievement before 500. About 300 B.C. Greek civilization, properly speaking, came to an end and was superseded by a
new culture representing a fusion of elements derived from Greece and
from the Near Orient. This was the Hellenistic civilization, which lasted
until about the beginning of the Christian era and included not only the
Greek peninsula but Egypt and most of Asia west of the Indus River.
The outstanding characteristic that served to distinguish these three
civilizations from their predecessors was secularism. No longer did religion absorb the interests of man to the extent that it did in ancient
Egypt or in the nations of Mesopotamia. The state was now above the
church, or perhaps we should say it included the church, and the authority of the priests to determine the direction of cultural evolution was
greatly reduced. Somewhat similar developments were taking place in
the Far East. In India, Hinduism and the dominance of the Brahman
caste were challenged by the ethical and non-theological system of
Guatama Buddha. Buddhism also spread to China and Japan and became
a major stimulus of cultural vitality in all three countries.

A Chronological Table *Dates are B.C. unless given as A.D.*

POLITICS	ARTS AND LETTERS

800 B.C.

Mycenaean stage, *ca.* 1500–1100
Dark Ages of Greek history, 1100–800
Beginning of city-states in Greece, *ca.* 800
Rome founded, *ca.* 750
Feudalism in China, *ca.* 800–250
Age of the Tyrants in Greece, 650–500
Reforms of Solon, 594–560
Reforms of Cleisthenes, 508–502

Vedas in India, 1200–800

Iliad and *Odyssey*, *ca.* 800
Upanishads, 800–600

Doric architecture, 650–500
Aeschylus, 525–456

500 B.C.

Overthrow of monarchy in Rome and establishment of republic, *ca.* 500
Patrician-plebeian struggle in Rome, 500–287
Greco-Persian War, 493–479
Delian League, 479–404
Perfection of Athenian democracy, 461–429
Law of the Twelve Tables (Rome), *ca.* 450
Peloponnesian War, 431–404

Phidias, 500?–432?
Ionic architecture, *ca.* 500–400

Sophocles, 496–406
Herodotus, 484–425
Euripides, 480–406
Thucydides, 471?–400?
Parthenon, *ca.* 460

400 B.C.

Decline of democracy in Greece, 400
Theban supremacy in Greece, 371–362
Macedonian conquest of Greece, 338–337
Conquests of Alexander the Great, 336–323
Division of Alexander's empire, 323

Aristophanes, 448?–380?
Corinthian architecture, *ca.* 400–300
Praxiteles, 370?–310?

300 B.C.

Classical age of Hindu culture, *ca.* 300–800 A.D.

Hortensian Law (Rome), 287
Punic Wars, 264–146

Reign of Emperor Asoka in India, *ca.* 273–232
Ch'in Dynasty in China, 221–207
Building of Great Wall in China, *ca.* 220
Han Dynasty in China, 206 B.C.–220 A.D.

200 B.C.

100 B.C.

Revolt of the Gracchi, 133–121

Beginning of Japanese state, *ca.* 100

Vergil, 70–19
Horace, 65–8

Dictatorship of Julius Caesar, 46–44
Principate of Augustus Caesar, 27 B.C.–14 A.D.

Tacitus, 55?–117? A.D.
Colosseum, *ca.* 80 A.D.

100 A.D.

Barbarian invasions of Rome, *ca.* 100–476 A.D.
Completion of Roman law by the great jurists, *ca.* 200 A.D.

300 A.D.

Diocletian, 284–305 A.D.
Constantine I, 306–337 A.D.

Beginning of temple architecture in India, 400 A.D.

476 A.D.

Theodosius I, 379–395 A.D.
Deposition of last of Roman emperors, 476 A.D.
Taika Reform Edict, creating imperial government in Japan based on Chinese model, 645 A.D.

Adoption of Chinese system of writing in Japan, *ca.* 405 A.D.

PHILOSOPHY AND SCIENCE	ECONOMICS	RELIGION	
	Rise of caste system in India, 1000–500	Development of worldly, non-ethical religion of the Greeks, 1200–800	800 B.C.
	Economic Revolution and colonization in Greece, 750–600		
	Rise of middle class in Greece, 750–600		
Thales of Miletus, 640?–546			
Pythagoras, 582?–507?		Gautama Buddha, ca. 563–483	500 B.C.
Confucius, 551?–479?			
Lao-tzu, ca. 550	Use of iron in China, ca. 500	Orphic and Eleusinian mystery cults, 500–100	
Protagoras, 490?–420?			
Socrates, 469–399			
Hippocrates, 460–377?			
Democritus, 470?–362?			
Sophists, ca. 450–400			
Plato, 427–347	Development of coinage in China, ca. 400		400 B.C.
Aristotle, 384–322			
Epicurus, 342–270			
Zeno (the Stoic), 320?–250?	Growth of advertising and insurance, 300 B.C.–100 A.D.		
Euclid, 323?–285			
Aristarchus, 310–230	Hellenistic world trade, 300 B.C.–100 A.D.		300 B.C.
	International money economy, 300 B.C.–100 A.D.		
	Growth of serfdom in Hellenistic empires, 300 B.C.–100 A.D.		
Archimedes, 287?–212	Growth of metropolitan cities, 300 B.C.–100 A.D.		
Eratosthenes, 276?–195?	Growth of slavery in Rome, 250–100	Oriental mystery cults in Rome, 250–50	
	Rise of middle class in Rome, 250–100		
Herophilus, 220?–150?	Decline of small farmer in Rome, 250–100		
Polybius, 205?–118	Depressions and unemployment in Hellenistic world, 200 B.C.–100 A.D		200 B.C.
Skeptics, 200–100	Decline of slavery in Hellenistic world 200 B.C.–100 A.D.	Development of mysticism and otherworldliness, 200	
Introduction of Stoicism into Rome, ca. 140			
Cicero, 106–43			100 B.C.
Lucretius, 98–55			
Seneca, 34 B.C.–65 A.D.	Decline of slavery in Rome, 27 B.C.–476 A.D.	Spread of Mithraism in Rome, 27 B.C.–270 A.D.	
		First persecution of Christians in Rome, ca. 65 A.D.	
Marcus Aurelius, 121–180 A.D.	Manufacture of paper in China, ca. 100 A.D.	Rapid development of Buddhism in China, 200–500 A.D.	100 A.D.
Galen, 130–200? A.D.			
Neo-Platonism, 250–600 A.D.	Growth of serfdom and extralegal feudalism in Rome, 300–500 A.D.	Beginning of toleration of Christians in Rome, 311 A.D.	300 A.D.
		Christianity made official religion of Roman Empire, 380 A.D.	
	Manufacture of glass and invention of gunpowder and magnetic compass in China, ca. 500 A.D.	Spread of Buddhism to Japan, ca. 552 A.D.	476 A.D.

CHAPTER 9

The Hellenic Civilization

There Lawfulness dwells and her sisters,
Safe foundation of cities,
Justice and Peace, who was bred with her,
Dispensers of wealth to men
Golden daughters of wise-counselling Right.
—Pindar, on the city of Corinth, *Olympian Ode XIII*

Now, what is characteristic of any nature is that which is best
for it and gives most joy. Such to man is the life according to reason, since it is this that makes him man.
—Aristotle, *Nichomachean Ethics*

Among all the peoples of the ancient world, the one whose culture most clearly exemplified the spirit of Western man was the Hellenic or Greek. No other of these nations had so strong a devotion to liberty, at least for itself, or so firm a belief in the nobility of human achievement. The Greeks glorified man as the most important creature in the universe and refused to submit to the dictation of priests or despots or even to humble themselves before their gods. Their attitude was essentially secular and rationalistic; they exalted the spirit of free inquiry and made knowledge supreme over faith. It was largely for these reasons that they advanced their culture to the highest stage which the ancient world was destined to reach. But the Greeks did not begin without foundations. It is necessary to remember that the groundwork for many of their achievements had already been laid by certain of the Oriental peoples. The rudiments of their philosophy and science had been prepared by the Egyptians. The Greek alphabet was derived from Phoenicia. And probably to a larger extent than we shall ever realize the Hellenic appreciation of beauty and freedom was a product of Minoan-Mycenaean influence.

The character of Hellenic civilization

I. EARLY STAGES

The early history of Greece is divided into two basic periods, the Mycenaean from about 1500 to 1100 B.C. and the Dark Ages from **203** about 1100 to 800 B.C. We have learned that in the sixteenth century a Greek people known subsequently as Achaeans burst the confines of their original home and expanded southward. In time they conquered Mycenae and made it their principal stronghold. They were henceforth called in Greek history Mycenaeans, although they had other important centers at Athens, Thebes, Pylos, and elsewhere. In 1400 B.C. they conquered Knossos. The Mycenaeans were a semibarbarous people whose social and political systems resembled those of the Orient. The great lords or kings who ruled in the fortified strongholds seemed to wield a monopoly over production, trade, and artistic activity. The chief function of their subjects was to work and strive for the king's enrichment. These officials resided in magnificent palaces surrounded by objects of gold, bronze, and ivory, skillfully fashioned by talented workmen. To obtain these riches traders and colonizers roamed the whole world of the Aegean and penetrated as far as Italy and Central Europe.

The arts of the Mycenaeans never equaled the delicacy and grace of the painting and sculpture of the Minoans. Much of it was copied boldly from the Orient, and for the most part it remained stilted and lifeless. They did, nevertheless, produce some excellent pottery and exquisitely inlaid daggers. Their massive palaces and tombs indicate that they understood stresses and how to counteract them. As we learned in the preceding chapter, the Mycenaeans had a system of writing, which has been definitely established as an early form of Greek. But they seem to have used it almost exclusively for keeping the fiscal records of their all-encompassing governments. No trace of anything resembling literature, history, or philosophy has thus far been found.

The fall of the Mycenaean civilization was a major catastrophe for the Greek world. It ushered in a period now called by historians the Dark Ages, which lasted from about 1100 to 800 B.C. Written records disappeared, except where accidentally preserved, and culture reverted to simpler forms than had been known for centuries. Whether the collapse came as a result of foreign invasion or of internal revolt against oppression has not been determined. Perhaps it was a combination of both. According to tradition, about 1200 B.C. the cities were attacked by an invading horde of more primitive Greeks known as Dorians. They were illiterate, and though they possessed weapons of iron, their knowledge of the arts and crafts was no more than rudimentary. They burned the palace at Mycenae and sacked a number of the others. Some historians maintain that the destruction of despotic Mycenae was a necessary prelude to the emergence of the freer and more enlightened Hellenic outlook.

The Greeks did not constitute a single race. When they began their migrations, they appear to have been a mixture of Alpine and Nordic stocks. Later they mingled with the Mediterranean natives who were already established in the southern portions and on the island of Crete. It is therefore absurd to attempt to explain the genius of the Greeks on the basis of purity of race, for no one knows which of the principal admixtures finally came to predominate. About all that one can accurately say is that the Hellenes were a mixed people who spoke a language of Indo-European relationship.

The culture of many of the Greeks had always been rudimentary. That of the Mycenaeans rapidly deteriorated following the destruction of Mycenae. We can therefore conclude that cultural achievement in most of Greece remained at a low ebb throughout the period from 1100 to 800 B.C. Toward the end some decorated pottery and skillfully designed metal objects began to appear on the islands of the Aegean Sea, but essentially the period was a long night. Aside from the development of writing at the very end, intellectual accomplishment was limited to folk songs, ballads, and short epics sung and embellished by bards as they wandered from one village to another. A large part of this material was finally woven into a great epic cycle by one or more poets in the ninth century B.C. Though not all the poems of this cycle have come down to us, the two most important, the *Iliad* and the *Odyssey*, the so-called Homeric epics, provide us with a rich store of information about many of the customs and institutions of the Dark Ages.

The political institutions of the Dark Ages were exceedingly primitive. Each little community of villages was independent of external control, but political authority was so tenuous that it would not be too much to say that the state scarcely existed at all. The *basileus* or ruler was not much more than a tribal leader. He could not make or enforce laws or administer justice. He received no remuneration of any kind, and had to cultivate his farm for a living the same as any other citizen. Practically his only functions were military and priestly. He commanded the army in time of war and offered sacrifices to keep the gods on the good side of the community. Although each little community had its council of nobles and assembly of warriors, neither of these bodies had any definite membership or status as an organ of government. The duties of the former were to advise and assist the ruler and prevent him from usurping despotic powers. The functions of the latter were to ratify declarations of war and assent to the conclusion of peace. Almost without exception custom took the place of law, and the administration of justice was private. Even willful murder was punishable only by the family of the victim. While it is true that disputes were sometimes submitted to the ruler for settlement, he acted in such cases merely as an arbitrator, not as a judge. As a matter of fact, the political consciousness of the Greeks of this time was so poorly developed that they had no conception of government as an indispensable agency for the preservation of social order. When Odysseus, ruler of Ithaca, was absent for twenty years, no regent was appointed in his place, and no session of the council or assembly was held. No one seemed to think that the complete suspension of government, even for so long a time, was a matter of critical importance.

The rudimentary
pattern of social
and economic life

The pattern of social and economic life was amazingly simple. Though the general tone of the society portrayed in the epics is aristocratic, there was actually no rigid stratification of classes. Manual labor was not looked upon as degrading, and there were apparently no idle rich. That there were dependent laborers of some kind who worked on the lands of the nobles and served them as faithful warriors seems clear from the Homeric epics, but they appear to have been serfs rather than slaves. The slaves were chiefly women, employed as servants, wool processors, or concubines. Many were war captives, but they do not appear to have been badly treated. Agriculture and herding were the basic occupations of free men. Except for a few skilled crafts like those of wagonmaker, swordsmith, goldsmith, and potter, there was no specialization of labor. For the most part every household made its own tools, wove its own clothing, and raised its own food. So far were the Greeks of this time from being a trading people that they had no word in their language for "merchant," and barter was the only method of exchange that was practiced.

To the Greeks of the Dark Ages religion meant chiefly a system for: (1) explaining the physical world in such a way as to remove its awesome mysteries and give man a feeling of intimate relationship with it; (2) accounting for the tempestuous passions that seized man's nature and made him lose that self-control which the Greeks considered essential for success as a warrior; and (3) obtaining such tangible benefits as good fortune, long life, skill in craftsmanship, and abundant harvests. The Greeks did not expect that their religion would save them from sin or endow them with spiritual blessings. As they conceived it, piety was neither a matter of conduct nor of faith. Their religion, accordingly, had no commandments, dogmas, or sacraments. Every man was at liberty to believe what he pleased and to conduct his own life as he chose without fear of the wrath of the gods.

As is commonly known, the deities of the early Greek religion were merely human beings writ large. It was really necessary that this should be so if the Greek was to feel at home in the world over which they ruled. Remote, omnipotent beings like the gods of most Oriental religions would have inspired fear rather than a sense of security. What the Greek wanted was not necessarily gods of great power, but deities he could bargain with on equal terms. Consequently he endowed his gods with attributes similar to his own—with human bodies and human weaknesses and wants. He imagined the great company of divinities as frequently quarreling with one another, needing food and sleep, mingling freely with men, and even procreating children occasionally by mortal women. They differed from men only in the fact that they subsisted on ambrosia and nectar, which made them immortal. They dwelt not in the sky or in the stars but on the summit of Mount Olympus, a peak in northern Greece with an altitude of about 10,000 feet.

The religion was thoroughly polytheistic, and no one deity was elevated very high above any of the others. Zeus, the sky god and wielder of the thunderbolt, who was sometimes referred to as the father of the gods and of men, frequently received less attention than did Poseidon, the sea god, Aphrodite, goddess of love, or Athena, variously considered goddess of wisdom and war and patroness of handicrafts. Since the Greeks had no Satan, their religion cannot be described as dualistic. Nearly all of the deities were capable of malevolence as well as good, for they sometimes deceived men and caused them to commit wrongs. The nearest approach to a god of evil was Hades, who presided over the nether world. Although he is referred to in the Homeric poems as "implacable and unyielding" and the most hateful of gods to mortals, he was never assumed to have played an active role in affairs on earth. He was not considered as the source of pestilence, earthquake, or famine. He did not tempt men or work to defeat the benevolent designs of other gods. In short, he was really not regarded as anything more than the guardian of the realm of the dead.

Nature of the gods and goddesses

The Greeks of the Dark Ages were almost completely indifferent to what happened to them after death. They did assume, however, that the shades or ghosts of men survived for a time after the death of their bodies. All, with a few exceptions, went to the same abode —to the murky realm of Hades situated beneath the earth. This was neither a paradise nor a hell: no one was rewarded for his good deeds, and no one was punished for his sins. Each of the shades appeared to continue the same kind of life its human embodiment had lived on earth. The Homeric poems make casual mention of two other realms, the Elysian Plain and the realm of Tartarus, which seem at first glance to contradict the idea of no rewards and punishments in the hereafter. But the few individuals who enjoyed the ease and comfort of the Elysian Plain had done nothing to deserve such blessings; they were simply persons whom the gods had chosen to favor. The realm of Tartarus was not really an abode of the dead but a place of imprisonment for rebellious deities.

Indifference to a life hereafter

Worship in early Greek religion consisted primarily of sacrifice. The offerings were made, however, not as an atonement for sin, but chiefly in order to please the gods and induce them to grant favors. In other words, religious practice was external and mechanical and not far removed from magic. Reverence, humility, and purity of heart were not essentials in it. The worshiper had only to carry out his part of the bargain by making the proper sacrifice, and the gods would fulfill theirs. For a religion such as this no elaborate institu-

The external and mechanical character of worship

tions were required. Even a professional priesthood was unnecessary. Since there were no mysteries and no sacraments, one man could perform the simple rites about as well as another. The Greek temple was not a church or place of religious assemblage, and no ceremonies were performed within it. Instead it was a shrine which the god might visit occasionally and use as a temporary house.

Conceptions of
virtue and evil

As intimated already, the morality of the Greeks in the Dark Ages had only the vaguest connection with their religion. While it is true that the gods were generally disposed to support the right, they did not consider it their duty to combat evil and make righteousness prevail. In meting out rewards to men, they appear to have been influenced more by their own whims and by gratitude for sacrifices offered than by any consideration for moral character. The only crime they punished was perjury, and that none too consistently. Nearly all the virtues extolled in the epics were those which would make the individual a better soldier—bravery, self-control, patriotism, wisdom (in the sense of cunning), love of one's friends, and hatred of one's enemies. There was no conception of sin in the Christian sense of wrongful acts to be repented of or atoned for.

The basic Greek
ideals

At the end of the Dark Ages the Greek was already well started along the road of social ideals that he was destined to follow in later centuries. He was an optimist, convinced that life was worth living for its own sake, and he could see no reason for looking forward to death as a glad release. He was an egoist, striving for the fulfillment of self. As a consequence, he rejected mortification of the flesh and all forms of denial which would imply the frustration of life. He could see no merit in humility or in turning the other cheek. He was a humanist, who worshiped the finite and the natural rather than the otherworldly or sublime. For this reason he refused to invest his gods with awe-inspiring qualities, or to invent any conception of man as a depraved and sinful creature. Finally, he was devoted to liberty in an even more extreme form than most of his descendants in the classical period were willing to accept.

2. THE EVOLUTION OF THE CITY-STATES

The origin and
nature of the
city-states

About 800 B.C. the village communities which had been founded mainly upon tribal or clan organization, began to give way to larger political units. As the need for defense increased, an acropolis or citadel was built on a high location, and a city grew up around it as the seat of government for a whole community. Thus emerged the city-state, the most famous unit of political society developed by the Greeks. Examples were to be found in almost every section of the Hellenic world. Athens, Thebes, and Megara on the mainland; Sparta and Corinth on the Peloponnesus; Miletus on the shore of Asia Minor; and Mitylene and Samos on the islands of the Aegean

Sea were among the best known. They varied enormously in both area and population. Sparta with more than 3000 square miles and Athens with 1060 had by far the greatest extent; the others averaged less than a hundred. At the peak of their power Athens and Sparta, each with a population of about 400,000, had approximately three times the numerical strength of most of their neighboring states.

More important is the fact that the Greek city-states varied widely in cultural evolution. From 800 to 500 B.C., commonly called the Archaic period, the Peloponnesian cities of Corinth and Argos were leaders in the development of literature and the arts. In the seventh century Sparta outshone many of her rivals. Preeminent above all were the Ionian cities on the coast of Asia Minor and the islands of the Aegean Sea. Foremost among them was Miletus, where, as we shall see, a brilliant flowering of philosophy and science occurred as early as the sixth century. Athens lagged behind until at least 100 years later.

Variations among the city-states

With a few exceptions the Greek city-states went through a similar political evolution. They began their histories as monarchies. During the eighth century they were changed into oligarchies. About a hundred years later, on the average, the oligarchies were overthrown by dictators, or "tyrants," as the Greeks called them, meaning usurpers who ruled without legal right whether oppressively or not. Finally, in the sixth and fifth centuries, democracies were set up, or in some cases "timocracies," that is, governments based upon a property qualification for the exercise of political rights, or in which love of honor and glory was the ruling principle.

The evolution of the city-states

On the whole, it is not difficult to determine the causes of this political evolution. The first change came about as a result of the concentration of landed wealth. As the owners of great estates waxed in economic power, they determined to wrest political authority from the ruler, now commonly called king, and vest it in the council, which they generally controlled. In the end they abolished the kingship entirely. Then followed a period of sweeping economic changes and political turmoil.

The causes of the political cycle; the growth of colonization

These developments affected not only Greece itself but many other parts of the Mediterranean world. For they were accompanied and followed by a vast overseas expansion. The chief causes were an increasing scarcity of agricultural land, internal strife, and a general temper of restlessness and discontent. The Greeks rapidly learned of numerous areas, thinly populated, with climate and soil similar to those of the homelands. The parent states most active in the expansion movement were Corinth, Chalcis, and Miletus. Their citizens founded colonies along the Aegean shores and even in Italy and Sicily. Of the latter the best known were Tarentum and Syracuse. They also established trading centers on the coast of Egypt and as far east as Babylon. The results of this expansionist movement can only be described as momentous. Commerce and industry grew to

The results of Greek expansion

be leading pursuits, the urban population increased, and wealth assumed new forms. The rising middle class now joined with dispossessed farmers in an attack upon the landholding oligarchy. The natural fruit of the bitter class conflicts that ensued was dictatorship. By encouraging extravagant hopes and promising relief from chaos, ambitious demagogues attracted enough popular support to enable them to ride into power in defiance of constitutions and laws. Ultimately, however, dissatisfaction with tyrannical rule and the increasing economic power and political consciousness of the common citizens led to the establishment of democracies or liberal oligarchies.

The similar
development of
the city-states

Unfortunately space does not permit an analysis of the political history of each of the Greek city-states. Except in the more backward sections of Thessaly and the Peloponnesus, it is safe to conclude that the internal development of all of them paralleled the account given above, although minor variations due to local conditions doubtless occurred. The two most important of the Hellenic states, Sparta and Athens, deserve more detailed study.

3. THE ARMED CAMP OF SPARTA

The peculiar
development of
Sparta

The history of Sparta [1] was the great exception to the political evolution of the city-states. Despite the fact that her citizens sprang from the same origins as most of the other Greeks, she failed to make any progress in the direction of democratic rule. Instead, her government gradually degenerated into a form more closely resembling a modern élite dictatorship. Culturally, also, the nation stagnated after the seventh century. The causes were due partly to isolation. Hemmed in by mountains on the northeast and west and lacking good harbors, the Spartan people had little opportunity to profit from the advances made in the outside world. Besides, no middle class arose to aid the masses in the struggle for freedom.

The Spartan
desire for
conquest

The major explanation is to be found, however, in militarism. The Spartans had come into the eastern Peloponnesus as an invading army. At first they attempted to amalgamate with the Mycenaeans they found there. But conflicts arose, and the Spartans resorted to conquest. Though by the end of the ninth century they had gained dominion over all of Laconia, they were not satisfied. West of the Taygetus Mountains lay the fertile plain of Messenia. The Spartans determined to conquer it. The venture was successful, and the Messenian territory was annexed to Laconia. About 640 B.C. the Messenians enlisted the aid of Argos and launched a revolt. The war that followed was desperately fought, Laconia itself was invaded,

[1] Sparta was the leading city of a district called Laconia or Lacedaemonia; sometimes the *state* was referred to by one or the other of these names. The people, also, were frequently called Laconians or Lacedaemonians.

and apparently it was only the death of the Argive commander and the patriotic pleas of the fire-eating poet Tyrtaeus that saved the day for the Spartans. This time the victors took no chances. They confiscated the lands of the Messenians, murdered or expelled their leaders, and forced the masses into serfdom. The Spartans' appetite for conquest was not unlimited, however. Following the Messenian wars they devoted themselves to keeping what they had already gained.

There was scarcely a feature of the life of the Spartans that was not the result of their wars with the Messenians. In subduing and despoiling their enemies they unwittingly enslaved themselves; for they lived through the remaining centuries of their history in deadly fear of insurrections. It was this fear which explains their conservatism, their stubborn resistance to change, lest any innovation result in a fatal weakening of the system. Their provincialism can also be attributed to the same cause. Frightened by the prospect that dangerous ideas might be brought into their country, they discouraged travel and prohibited trade with the outside world. The necessity of maintaining the absolute supremacy of the citizen class over an enormous population of serfs required an iron discipline and a strict subordination of the individual; hence the Spartan collectivism, which extended into every branch of the social and economic life. Finally, much of the cultural backwardness of Sparta grew out of the atmosphere of coarseness and hate which inevitably resulted from the bitter struggle to conquer the Messenians and hold them under stern repression.

The Spartan constitution, which tradition ascribed to an ancient lawgiver, Lycurgus, provided for a government preserving the forms of the old system of the Dark Ages. Instead of one king, however, there were two, representing separate families of exalted rank. The Spartan sovereigns enjoyed but few powers and those chiefly of a military and priestly character. A second and more authoritative branch of the government was the council, composed of the two kings and twenty-eight nobles sixty years of age and over. This body supervised the work of administration, prepared measures for submission to the assembly, and served as the highest court for criminal trials. The third organ of government, the assembly, approved or rejected the proposals of the council and elected all public officials except the kings. But the highest authority under the Spartan constitution was vested in a board of five men known as the ephorate. The ephors virtually were the government. They presided over the council and the assembly, controlled the educational system and the distribution of property, censored the lives of the citizens, and exercised a veto power over all legislation. They had power also to determine the fate of newborn infants, to conduct prosecutions before the council, and even to depose the kings if the religious omens appeared unfavorable. The Spartan government was thus very decidedly an oligarchy. In spite of the fact that the ephors were chosen for one-year terms by the assembly, they were indefinitely reeligible, and their authority was so vast that there was hardly any ramification of the system they could not control. Moreover, it should be borne in mind that the assembly itself was not a democratic body. Not even the whole citizen class, which was a small minority of the total population, was entitled to membership in it, but only those males of full political status who had incomes sufficient to qualify them for enrollment in the heavy infantry.

The population of Sparta was divided into three main classes. The ruling element was made up of the Spartiates, or descendants of the original conquerors. Though never exceeding one-twentieth of the total population, the Spartiates alone had political privileges. Next in order of rank were the perioeci, or "dwellers around." The origin of this class is uncertain, but it was probably composed of peoples that had at one time been allies of the Spartans or had submitted voluntarily to Spartan domination. In return for service as a buffer population between the ruling class and the serfs, the perioeci were allowed to carry on trade and to engage in manufacturing. At the bottom of the scale were the helots, or serfs, bound to the soil and despised and persecuted by their masters.

Among these classes only the perioeci enjoyed any appreciable measure of comfort and freedom. While it is true that the economic condition of the helots cannot be described in terms of absolute misery, since they were permitted to keep for themselves a good share of what they produced on the estates of their masters, they were personally subjected to such shameful treatment that they were constantly wretched and rebellious. On occasions they were compelled to give exhibitions of drunkenness and lascivious dances as an example to the Spartan youth of the effects of such practices. At the beginning of each year, if we can believe the testimony of Aristotle, the ephors declared war upon the helots, presumably for the purpose of giving a gloss of legality to the murder of any by the secret police upon suspicion of disloyalty.

Those who were born into the Spartiate class were doomed to a respectable slavery for the major part of their lives. Forced to submit to the severest discipline and to sacrifice individual interests, they were little more than cogs in a vast machine. Their education was limited almost entirely to military training, supplemented by exposure and merciless floggings to harden them for the duties of war. Between the ages of twenty and sixty they gave all their time to service to the state. Although marriage was practically compulsory, no family life was permitted. Husbands carried off their wives on the wedding night by a show of force. But they did not live with them. Instead, they were supposed to contrive means of escaping at night to visit them secretly. According to Plutarch, it thus some-

The class system
in Sparta

Perioeci and
helots

Discipline for
the benefit of
the state

212

times happened that men "had children by their wives before ever they saw their faces by daylight." [2] No jealousy between marital partners was allowed. The production of vigorous offspring was all-important. Whether they were born within the limits of strict monogamy was a secondary consideration. In any case, children were the property not of their parents but of the state. It may be doubted that the Spartiates resented these hardships and deprivations. Pride in their status as the ruling class probably compensated in their minds for harsh discipline and denial of privileges.

The economic organization of Sparta was designed almost solely for the ends of military efficiency and the supremacy of the citizen class. The best land was owned by the state and was originally divided into equal plots which were assigned to the Spartiate class as inalienable estates. Later these holdings as well as the inferior lands were permitted to be sold and exchanged, with the result that some of the citizens became richer than others. The helots, who did all the work of cultivating the soil, also belonged to the state and were assigned to their masters along with the land. Their masters were forbidden to emancipate them or to sell them outside of the country. The labor of the helots provided for the support of the whole citizen class, whose members were not allowed to be associated with any economic enterprise other than agriculture. Trade and industry were reserved exclusively for the perioeci.

Economic regulations

The Spartan economic system is frequently described by modern historians as communistic. It is true that some of the means of production (the helots and the land) were collectively owned, in theory at least, and that the Spartiate males contributed from their incomes to provide for a common mess in the clubs to which they belonged. But with these rather doubtful exceptions the system was as far removed from communism as it was from anarchy. Essentials of the communist ideal include the doctrines that all the instruments of production shall be owned by the community, that no one shall live by exploiting the labor of others, and that all shall work for the benefit of the community and share the wealth in proportion to need. In Sparta commerce and industry were in private hands; the helots were forced to contribute a portion of what they produced to provide for the subsistence of their masters; and political privileges were restricted to an hereditary aristocracy, most of whose members performed no socially useful labor whatever. With its militarism, its secret police, its minority rule, and its closed economy, the Spartan system would seem to have resembled fascism more nearly than true communism. But even with respect to fascism the resemblance was not complete. The Spartan system was not revolutionary, as fascism usually is in the beginning, but was always rather strongly conservative.

Description of the Spartan system

[2] Plutarch, "Lycurgus," *Lives of Illustrious Men,* I, 81.

4.   THE ATHENIAN TRIUMPH AND TRAGEDY

Athens began her history under conditions quite different from those which prevailed in Sparta. The district of Attica had not been the scene of an armed invasion or of bitter conflict between opposing peoples. As a result, no military caste imposed its rule upon a vanquished nation. Furthermore, the wealth of Attica consisted of mineral deposits and splendid harbors in addition to agricultural resources. Athens, consequently, never remained a predominantly agrarian state but rapidly developed a prosperous trade and a culture essentially urban.

Until the middle of the eighth century B.C. Athens, like the other Greek states, had a monarchical form of government. During the century that followed, the council of nobles, or Council of the Areopagus, as it came to be called, gradually divested the king of his powers. The transition to rule by the few was both the cause and the result of an increasing concentration of wealth. The introduction of vine and olive culture about this time led to the growth of agriculture as a great capitalistic enterprise. Since vineyards and olive orchards require considerable time to become profitable, only those farmers with abundant resources were able to survive in the business. Their poorer and less thrifty neighbors sank rapidly into debt, especially since grain was now coming to be imported at ruinous prices. The small farmer had no alternative but to mortgage his land, and then his family and himself, in the vain hope that some day a way of escape would be found. Ultimately many of his class became serfs when the mortgages could not be paid.

Bitter cries of distress now arose and threats of revolution were heard. The middle classes in the towns espoused the cause of the peasant in demanding liberalization of the government. Finally, in 594 B.C., all parties agreed upon the appointment of Solon as a magistrate with absolute power to carry out reforms. The measures Solon enacted provided for both political and economic adjustments. The former included: (1) the establishment of a new council, the Council of Four Hundred, and the admission of the middle classes to membership in it; (2) the enfranchisement of the lower classes by making them eligible for service in the assembly; and (3) the organization of a supreme court, open to all citizens and elected by universal manhood suffrage, with power to hear appeals from the decisions of the magistrates. The economic reforms benefited the poor farmers by canceling existing mortgages, prohibiting enslavement for debt in the future, and limiting the amount of land any one individual could own. Nor did Solon neglect the middle classes. He introduced a new system of coinage designed to give Athens an advantage in foreign trade, imposed heavy penalties for idleness, ordered every man to teach his son a trade, and offered full privileges of citizenship to alien craftsmen who would become permanent residents of the country.

Significant though these reforms were, they did not allay the discontent. The nobles were disgruntled because some of their privileges had been taken away. The middle and lower classes were dissatisfied because they were still excluded from the offices of magistracy, and because the Council of the Areopagus was left with its powers intact. Worse still was the fact that Solon, like many rulers in all times, attempted to divert the people from their domestic troubles by persuading them to embark upon military adventures abroad. An old quarrel with Megara was revived, and Athens committed her fate to the uncertainties of war. The chaos and disillusionment that followed paved the way in 560 B.C. for the triumph of Peisistratus, the first of the Athenian tyrants. Although he proved to be a benevolent despot, he nevertheless destroyed many of the liberties the people had previously gained, and Hippias, one of his two sons who succeeded him, was a ruthless and spiteful oppressor.

The rise of dictatorship

In 510 B.C. Hippias was overthrown by a group of nobles with aid from Sparta. Factional conflict raged anew until Cleisthenes, an intelligent aristocrat, enlisted the support of the masses to eliminate his rivals from the scene. Having promised concessions to the people as a reward for their help, he proceeded to reform the government in so sweeping a fashion that he has since been known as the father of Athenian democracy. He greatly enlarged the citizen population by granting full rights to all free men who resided in the country at that time. He established a new Council of Five Hundred and made it the chief organ of government with power to prepare measures for submission to the assembly and with supreme control over executive and administrative functions. Members of this body were to be chosen by lot from lists of candidates submitted by the demes or townships. Any male citizen over thirty years of age was eligible. Cleisthenes also expanded the authority of the assembly, giving it power to debate and pass or reject the measures submitted by the Council, to declare war, to appropriate money, and to audit the accounts of retiring magistrates. Lastly, Cleisthenes is believed to have instituted the device of ostracism, whereby any citizen who might be dangerous to the state could be sent into honorable exile for a ten-year period. The device was quite obviously intended to eliminate men who were suspected of cherishing dictatorial ambitions. Too often its effect was to eliminate exceptional men and to allow mediocrity to flourish.

The reforms of Cleisthenes

The Athenian democracy attained its full perfection in the Age of Pericles (461–429 B.C.). It was during this period that the assembly acquired the authority to initiate legislation in addition to its power to ratify or reject proposals of the council. It was during this time also that the famous Board of Ten Generals rose to a position

The perfection of Athenian democracy

roughly comparable to that of the British cabinet. The Generals were chosen by the assembly for one-year terms and were eligible for reelection indefinitely. Pericles held the position of Chief Strategus or President of the Board of Generals for more than thirty years. The Generals were not simply commanders of the army but the chief legislative and executive officials in the state, gradually assuming most of the prerogatives Cleisthenes had given to the Council of Five Hundred. Though wielding enormous power, they could not become tyrants, for their policies were subject to review by the assembly, and they could easily be recalled at the end of their one-year terms or indicted for malfeasance at any time. Finally, it was in the Age of Pericles that the Athenian system of courts was developed to completion. No longer was there merely a supreme court to hear appeals from the decisions of magistrates, but an array of popular courts with authority to try all kinds of cases. At the beginning of each year a list of 6000 citizens was chosen by lot from the various sections of the country. From this list separate juries, varying in size from 201 to 1001, were made up for particular trials. Each of these juries constituted a court with power to decide by majority vote every question involved in the case. Although one of the magistrates presided, he had none of the prerogatives of a judge; the jury itself was the judge, and from its decision there was no appeal. It would be difficult to imagine a system more thoroughly democratic.

The Athenian democracy differed from the modern form in various ways. First of all, it did not extend to the whole population, but only to the citizen class. While it is true that in the time of Cleisthenes (508–502 B.C.) the citizens probably included a majority of the inhabitants because of his enfranchisement of resident aliens, in the Age of Pericles they were distinctly a minority. It may be well to observe, however, that within its limits Athenian democracy was more thoroughly applied than is the modern form. The choice by lot of nearly all magistrates except the Ten Generals, the restriction of all terms of public officials to one year, and the uncompromising adherence to the principle of majority rule even in judicial trials were examples of a serene confidence in the political capacity of the average man which few modern nations would be willing to accept. The democracy of Athens differed from the contemporary ideal also in the fact that it was direct, not representative. Contrary to the traditional view, the Athenians understood the principle of representation, but they never applied it except in a limited way in the selection of members of the Council of Five Hundred. They were not interested in being governed by men of reputation and ability; what vitally concerned them was the assurance to every citizen of an actual voice in the control of all public affairs. In a word, their ideal was not efficiency in government but democracy.

In the century of her greatest expansion and creativity, Athens fought two major wars. The first, the war with Persia, was an out-growth of the expansion of that empire into the eastern Mediter-ranean area. The Athenians resented the conquest of their Ionian kinsmen in Asia Minor and aided them in their struggle for freedom. The Persians retaliated by sending a powerful army and fleet to at-tack the Greeks. Although all Greece was in danger of conquest, Athens bore the chief burden of repelling the invader. The war, which began in 493 B.C. and lasted with interludes of peace for about fourteen years, is commonly regarded as one of the most sig-nificant in the history of the world. The decisive victory of the Greeks put an end to the menace of Persian conquest and forestalled at least for a time the submergence of Hellenic ideals of freedom in Near Eastern despotism. The war also had the effect of strengthen-ing democracy in Athens and making that state the leading power in Greece.

The other of the great struggles, the Peloponnesian War with Sparta, had results of a quite different character. Instead of being another milestone in the Athenian march to power, it ended in trag-edy. The causes of this war are of particular interest to the student of the downfall of civilizations. First and most important was the growth of Athenian imperialism. In the last year of the war with Persia, Athens had joined with a number of other Greek states in the formation of an offensive and defensive alliance known as the Delian League. When peace was concluded the league was not dis-solved, for many of the Greeks feared that the Persians might come back. As time went on, Athens gradually transformed the league into a naval empire for the advancement of her own interests. She used some of the funds in the common treasury for her own pur-poses. She tried to reduce all the other members to a condition of vassalage, and when one of them rebelled, she overwhelmed it by force, seized its navy, and imposed tribute upon it as if it were a conquered state. Such high-handed methods aroused the suspicions of the Spartans, who feared that an Athenian hegemony would soon be extended over all of Greece.

A second major cause was to be found in the social and cultural differences between Athens and Sparta. Athens was democratic, progressive, urban, imperialistic, and intellectually and artistically advanced. Sparta was aristocratic, conservative, agrarian, provincial, and culturally backward. Where such sharply contrasting systems exist side by side, conflicts are almost bound to occur. The attitude of the Athenians and Spartans had been hostile for some time. The former looked upon the latter as uncouth barbarians. The Spartans accused the Athenians of attempting to gain control over the north-ern Peloponnesian states and of encouraging the helots to rebel. Economic factors also played a large part in bringing the conflict to a head. Athens was ambitious to dominate the Corinthian Gulf, the principal avenue of trade with Sicily and southern Italy. This made

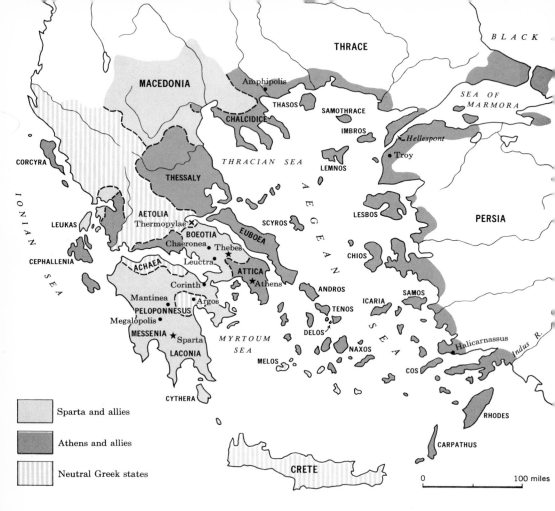

GREECE AT THE END OF THE AGE OF PERICLES

her the deadly enemy of Corinth, the chief ally of Sparta.

The war, which broke out in 431 B.C. and lasted until 404, was a record of frightful calamities for Athens. Her trade was destroyed, her democracy overthrown, and her population decimated by a terrible pestilence. Quite as bad was the moral degradation which followed in the wake of the military reverses. Treason, corruption, and brutality were among the hastening ills of the last few years of the conflict. On one occasion the Athenians even slaughtered the whole male population of the state of Melos, and enslaved the women and children, for no other crime than refusing to abandon neutrality. Ultimately, deserted by all her allies except Samos and with her food supply cut off, Athens was left with no alternative but to surrender or starve. The terms imposed upon her were drastic enough: destruction of her fortifications, surrender of all foreign possessions and practically her entire navy, and submission to Sparta as a subject

The defeat of Athens

state. Though Athens recovered her leadership for a time in the fourth century, her period of glory was approaching its end.

5. POLITICAL DEBACLE—THE LAST DAYS

Not only did the Peloponnesian War put an end, temporarily, to the supremacy of Athens; it annihilated freedom throughout the Greek world and sealed the doom of the Hellenic political genius. Following the war Sparta asserted her power over all of Hellas. Oligarchies supported by Spartan troops replaced democracies wherever they existed. Confiscation of property and assassination were the methods regularly employed to combat opposition. Although in Athens the tyrants were overthrown after a time and free government restored, Sparta was able to dominate the remainder of Greece for more than thirty years. In 371 B.C., however, Epaminondas of Thebes defeated the Spartan army at Leuctra and thereby inaugurated a period of Theban supremacy. Unfortunately Thebes showed little more wisdom and tolerance in governing than Sparta, and nine years later a combination was formed to free the Greek cities from their new oppressor. Failing to break up the alliance, the Thebans gave battle on the field of Mantinea. Both sides claimed the victory, but Epaminondas was slain, and the power of his empire soon afterward collapsed.

Continuing conflict among the city-states

The long succession of wars had now brought the Greek states to the point of exhaustion. Though the glory of their culture was yet undimmed, politically they were prostrate and helpless. Their fate was soon decided for them by the rise of Philip of Macedon. Except for a thin veneer of Hellenic culture, the Macedonians were barbarians; but Philip, before becoming their king, had learned how to lead an army while a hostage at Thebes. Perceiving the weakness of the states to the south, he determined to conquer them. A series of early successes led to the decisive victory at Chaeronea in 338 B.C. and soon afterward to dominion over all of Greece except Sparta. Two years later Philip was murdered as the sequel to a family brawl.

The Macedonian conquest

Rule over Hellas now passed into the hands of his son Alexander, a youth of twenty years. After putting to death all possible aspirants to the throne and quelling some feeble revolts of the Greeks, Alexander conceived the grandiose scheme of conquering Persia. One victory followed another until in the short space of twelve years the whole ancient Near Orient from the Indus River to the Nile had been annexed to Greece as the personal domain of one man. Alexander did not live to enjoy it long. In 323 B.C. he fell ill of Babylonian swamp fever and died at the age of thirty-two.

Alexander the Great

It is difficult to gauge the significance of Alexander's career. Historians have differed widely in their interpretations. Some have seen him as one of the supreme galvanizing forces in history. Others

219

Marble Stele with Law against Tyranny, 338 B.C. The sculptured relief shows a woman (Democracy) crowning an aged man (the People of Athens). The law provides that if anyone establishes a dictatorship in Athens, a person who kills him shall be held guiltless.

The significance of Alexander's career

would limit his genius to military strategy and organization and deny that he made a single major contribution of benefit to humanity.[3] There can be no doubt that he was a master of the art of war (he never lost a battle), and that he was intelligent and endowed with charm and physical courage. Unquestionably, also, he was a man of vibrant energy and overpowering ambitions. Just what these ambitions were is not certain. Evidence eludes us that he aspired to conquer the world or to advance the Hellenic ideals of freedom and justice. It seems doubtful that he had much interest in lofty ideals or in using military force to extend them. As the British historian A. R. Burn has said: "His abiding ideal was the glory of Alexander." [4] Nevertheless, he did introduce Macedonian standards of administrative efficiency into the government of the Near East. Aside from this, the primary significance of the great conqueror seems to lie in the fact that he carried the Hellenic drive into Asia farther and faster than would otherwise have occurred. He undoubtedly caused the Greek influence to be more widely felt. At the same time he appears to have placed too great a strain upon Hellenism with the result of encouraging a sweeping tide of Oriental influences into the West. Within a short period Hellenic and Oriental cultures interpenetrated to such an extent as to produce a new civilization. This was the Hellenistic civilization to be discussed

[3] Compare W. W. Tarn, *Alexander the Great*, and A. R. Burn, *Alexander the Great and the Hellenistic World*.

[4] *Alexander the Great and the Hellenistic World*, p. 23.

6. HELLENIC THOUGHT AND CULTURE

I. PHILOSOPHY   From what has been said in preceding chapters
it should be clear that the popular notion that all philosophy originated with the Greeks is fallacious. Centuries earlier the Egyptians
had given much thought to the nature of the universe and to the
social and ethical problems of man. The achievement of the Greeks
was rather the development of philosophy in a more inclusive meaning than it had ever possessed before. They attempted to find answers to every conceivable question about the nature of the universe, the problem of truth, and the meaning and purpose of life.
The magnitude of their accomplishment is attested by the fact that
philosophy ever since has been largely a debate over the validity of
their several conclusions.

The antecedents of Greek philosophy

Greek philosophy had its origins in the sixth century B.C. in the
work of the so-called Milesian school, whose members were natives
of the great commercial city of Miletus on the shore of Asia Minor.
Their philosophy was fundamentally scientific and materialistic.
The problem which chiefly engaged their attention was to discover
the nature of the physical world. They believed that all things could
be reduced to some primary substance or original matter which was
the source of worlds, stars, animals, plants, and men, and to which
all would ultimately return. Thales, the founder of the school, perceiving that all things contained moisture, taught that the primary
substance is water. Anaximander insisted that it could not be any
particular thing such as water or fire but some substance "un-
gendered and imperishable" which "contains and directs all things."
He called this substance the Infinte or the Boundless. A third member of the school, Anaximenes, declared that the original material of
the universe is air. Apparently he chose air as the germinal substance
because it made possible a quantitative interpretation of the universe. In other words, he maintained that the essential difference between things consists merely in the *amount* of the basic substance
they contain. Air when rarefied becomes fire; when condensed it
turns successively to wind, vapor, water, earth, and stone.

The philosophy of the Milesian school

Although seemingly naïve in its conclusions the philosophy of the
Milesian school was of real significance. It broke through the
mythological beliefs of the Greeks about the origin of the world
and substituted a purely rational explanation. It revived and
expanded the Egyptian ideas of the eternity of the universe and the
indestructibility of matter. It suggested very clearly, especially in
the teachings of Anaximander, the concept of evolution in the sense
of rhythmic change, of continuing creation and decay.

Significance of the teachings of the Milesian school

Before the end of the sixth century Greek philosophy developed a
metaphysical turn; it ceased to be occupied solely with problems of

221

the physical world and shifted its attention to abstruse questions about the nature of being, the meaning of truth, and the position of the divine in the scheme of things. First to exemplify the new tend-

ency were the Pythagoreans, who interpreted philosophy largely in terms of religion. Little is known about them except that their leader, Pythagoras, migrated from the island of Samos to southern Italy and founded a religious community at Croton. He and his followers apparently taught that the speculative life is the highest good, but that in order to pursue it, man must purify himself from the evil desires of the flesh. They held that the essence of things is not a material substance but an abstract principle, number. Their chief significance lies in the sharp distinctions they drew between spirit and matter, harmony and discord, good and evil. Perhaps it is not inaccurate to regard them as the real founders of dualism in Greek thought.

A consequence of the work of the Pythagoreans was to intensify the debate over the nature of the universe. Some of their contempo-

Renewal of the
debate over the
nature of the
universe

raries, notably Parmenides, argued that stability or permanence is the real nature of things; change and diversity are simply illusions of the senses. Directly opposed to this conception was the position taken by Heracleitus, who argued that permanence is an illusion, that change alone is real. The universe, he maintained, is in a condition of constant flux; therefore "it is impossible to step twice into the same stream." Creation and destruction, life and death, are but the obverse and reverse sides of the same picture. In affirming such views Heracleitus was really contending that the things we see and hear and feel are all that there is to reality. Evolution or constant change is the law of the universe. The tree or the stone that is here today is gone tomorrow; no underlying substance exists immutable through all eternity.

The eventual answer to the question of the underlying character of the universe was provided by the atomists. The philosopher

Solution of the
problem by the
atomists

chiefly responsible for the development of the atomic theory was Democritus, who lived in Abdera on the Thracian coast in the second half of the fifth century. As their name implies, the atomists held that the ultimate constituents of the universe are atoms, infinite in number, indestructible, and indivisible. Although these differ in size and shape, they are exactly alike in composition. Because of the motion inherent in them, they are eternally uniting, separating, and reuniting in different arrangements. Every individual object or organism in the universe is thus the product of a fortuitous concourse of atoms. The only difference between a man and a tree is the difference in the number and arrangement of their atoms. Here was a philosophy which represented the final fruition of the materialistic tendencies of early Greek thought. Democritus denied the immortality of the soul and the existence of any spiritual world. Strange as

it may appear to the minds of some people, he was a moral idealist, affirming that "Good means not merely not to do wrong, but rather not to desire to do wrong." [5]

About the middle of the fifth century B.C. an intellectual revolution began in Greece. The rise of the common man, the growth of individualism, and the demand for the solution of practical problems produced a reaction against the old ways of thinking. As a result philosophers abandoned the study of the physical universe and turned to consideration of subjects more intimately related to man himself. The first exponents of the new intellectual trend were the Sophists. Originally the term meant "those who are wise," but later it came to be used in the derogatory sense of men who employ specious reasoning. Since most of our knowledge of the Sophists was derived, until comparatively recently, from Plato, one of their severest critics, they were commonly considered to have been the enemies of all that was best in Hellenic culture. Modern research has exposed the fallacy of so extreme a conclusion, even though some members of the group lacked a sense of social responsibility and were quite unscrupulous in "making the worse appear the better cause." It is said that a few of them charged the equivalent of $10,000 to educate a single individual.

The intellectual revolution begun by the Sophists

The greatest of the Sophists was undoubtedly Protagoras, a native of Abdera who did most of his teaching in Athens. His famous dictum, "Man is the measure of all things," comprehends the essence of the Sophist philosophy. By this he meant that goodness, truth, justice, and beauty are relative to the needs and interests of man himself. There are no absolute truths or eternal standards of right and justice. Since sense perception is the exclusive source of knowledge, there can be only particular truths valid for a given time and place. Morality likewise varies from one people to another. The Spartans encourage adultery in certain cases on the part of wives as well as husbands; the Athenians seclude their women and refuse even to allow them a normal social life. Which of these standards is right? Neither is right in any absolute sense, for there are no absolute canons of right and wrong eternally decreed in the heavens to fit all cases; yet both are right in the relative sense that the judgment of man alone determines what is good.

The doctrines of Protagoras

Some of the later Sophists went far beyond the teachings of their great master. Gorgias perverted the skepticism of Protagoras into the doctrine that the human mind can never know anything except its own subjective impressions. "Nothing exists," he declared; "if anything did exist it could not be known; if a man should chance to apprehend it, it would still be a secret; he would be unable to communicate it to his fellows." [6] The individualism which was necessarily implicit in the teachings of Protagoras was twisted by Thrasymachus into the doctrine that all laws and customs are merely ex-

The extremist doctrines of the later Sophists

[5] Quoted by Frank Thilly, *History of Philosophy*, p. 40.
[6] Quoted by A. A. Trever, *History of Ancient Civilization*, I, 348.

pressions of the will of the strongest and shrewdest for their own
advantage, and that therefore the wise man is the "perfectly unjust
man" who is above the law and concerned with the gratification of
his own desires.

Yet there was much that was admirable in the teachings of all the
Sophists, even of those who were the most extreme. Without exception they condemned slavery and the racial exclusiveness of the
Greeks. They were champions of liberty, the rights of the common
man, and the practical and progressive point of view. They perceived the folly of war and ridiculed the silly chauvinism of many
of the Athenians. Perhaps their most important work was the extension of philosophy to include not only physics and metaphysics, but
ethics and politics as well. As Cicero expressed it, they "brought
philosophy down from heaven to the dwellings of men."

It was inevitable that the relativism, skepticism, and individualism
of the Sophists should have aroused strenuous opposition. In the
judgment of the more conservative Greeks these doctrines appeared
to lead straight to atheism and anarchy. If there is no final truth, and
if goodness and justice are merely relative to the whims of the individual, then neither religion, morality, the state, nor society itself
can long be maintained. The result of this conviction was the
growth of a new philosophic movement grounded upon the theory
that truth is real and that absolute standards do exist. The leaders of
this movement were perhaps the three most famous individuals in
the history of thought—Socrates, Plato, and Aristotle.

Socrates was born in Athens in 469 B.C. of humble parentage; his
father was a sculptor, his mother a midwife. How he obtained an
education no one knows, but he was certainly familiar with the
teachings of earlier Greek thinkers, presumably from extensive
reading. The impression that he was a mere gabbler in the market
place is quite unfounded. He became a philosopher on his own account chiefly to combat the doctrines of the Sophists, and he soon
gathered around him a circle of admirers, which included the two
young aristocrats, Plato and Alcibiades. In 399 B.C. he was condemned to death on a charge of "corrupting the youth and introducing new gods." The real reason for the unjust sentence was the
tragic outcome for Athens of the Peloponnesian War. Overwhelmed by resentment and despair, the people turned against Socrates because of his associations with aristocrats, including the
traitor Alcibiades, and because of his criticism of popular belief.
There is evidence that he disparaged democracy and contended that
no government was worthy of the name except intellectual aristocracy.

For the reason that Socrates wrote nothing himself, historians
have been faced with a problem in determining the scope of his
teachings. He is generally regarded as primarily a teacher of ethics
with no interest in abstract philosophy or any desire to found a new

school of thought. Certain admissions made by Plato, however, indicate that a large part of the famous doctrine of Ideas was really of Socratic origin. At any rate we can be reasonably sure that Socrates believed in a stable and universally valid knowledge, which man could possess if he would only pursue the right method. This method would consist in the exchange and analysis of opinions, in the setting up and testing of provisional definitions, until finally an essence of truth recognizable by all could be distilled from them. Socrates argued that in similar fashion man could discover enduring principles of right and justice independent of the selfish desires of human beings. He believed, moreover, that the discovery of such rational principles of conduct would prove an infallible guide to virtuous living, for he denied that anyone who truly knows the good can ever choose the evil.

By far the most distinguished of Socrates' pupils was Plato, who was born in Athens in 427 B.C., the son of noble parents. His real name was Aristocles, "Plato" being a nickname supposedly given to him by one of his teachers because of his broad frame. When he was twenty years old he joined the Socratic circle, remaining a member until the tragic death of his teacher. He seems to have drawn inspiration from other sources also, notably from the teachings of Parmenides and the Pythagoreans. Unlike his great master he was a prolific writer, though some of the works attributed to him are of doubtful authorship. The most noted of his writings are such dialogues as the *Apology*, the *Protagoras*, the *Phaedrus*, the *Timaeus*, and the *Republic*. He was engaged in the completion of another great work, the *Laws*, when death overtook him in his eighty-first year.

Plato's objectives in developing his philosophy were similar to those of Socrates although somewhat broader: (1) to combat the theory of reality as a disordered flux and to substitute an interpretation of the universe as essentially spiritual and purposeful; (2) to refute the Sophist doctrines of relativism and skepticism; and (3) to provide a secure foundation for ethics. In order to realize these objectives he developed his celebrated doctrine of Ideas. He admitted that relativity and constant change are characteristics of the world of physical things, of the world we perceive with our senses. But he denied that this world is the complete universe. There is a higher, spiritual realm composed of eternal forms or Ideas which only the mind can conceive. These are not, however, mere abstractions invented by the mind of man, but spiritual things. Each is the archetype or pattern of some particular class of objects or relation between objects on earth. Thus there are Ideas of man, tree, shape, size, color, proportion, beauty, and justice. Highest of them all is the Idea of the Good, which is the active cause and guiding purpose of the whole universe. The things we perceive with our senses are merely imperfect copies of the supreme realities, Ideas. It should be

Plato

Plato's philosophy of Ideas

225

noted that this doctrine of Ideas is clearly expounded only in Plato's earlier dialogues. In those of his middle and late career it is not emphasized.

Plato's ethical and religious philosophy was closely related to his doctrine of Ideas. Like Socrates he believed that true virtue has its basis in knowledge. But the knowledge derived from the senses is limited and variable; hence true virtue must consist in rational apprehension of the eternal Ideas of goodness and justice. By relegating the physical to an inferior place, he gave to his ethics a mildly ascetic tinge. He regarded the body as a hindrance to the mind and taught that only the rational part of man's nature is noble and good. In contrast with some of his later followers, he did not demand that appetites and emotions should be denied altogether, but urged that they should be strictly subordinated to the reason. Plato never made his conception of God entirely clear. Sometimes he referred to the Idea of the Good as if it were a divine power of subordinate rank, at other times as if it were the supreme creator and ruler of the universe. Probably the latter is what he really meant. At any rate it is certain that he conceived of the universe as spiritual in nature and governed by intelligent purpose. He rejected both materialism and mechanism. As for the soul, he regarded it not only as immortal but as preexisting through all eternity.

As a political philosopher Plato was motivated by the ideal of constructing a state which would be free from turbulence and self-seeking on the part of individuals and classes. Neither democracy nor liberty but harmony and efficiency were the ends he desired to achieve. Accordingly, he proposed in his *Republic* a famous plan for society which would have divided the population into three principal classes corresponding to the functions of the soul. The lowest class, representing the appetitive function, would include the farmers, artisans, and merchants. The second class, representing the spirited element or will, would consist of the soldiers. The highest class, representing the function of reason, would be composed of the intellectual aristocracy. Each of these classes would perform those tasks for which it was best fitted. The function of the lowest class would be the production and distribution of goods for the benefit of the whole community; that of the soldiers, defense; the aristocracy, by reason of special aptitude for philosophy, would enjoy a monopoly of political power. The division of the people into these several ranks would not be made on the basis of birth or wealth, but through a sifting process that would take into account the ability of each individual to profit from education. Thus the farmers, artisans, and merchants would be those who had shown the least intellectual capacity, whereas the philosopher-kings would be those who had shown the greatest.

The last of the great champions of the Socratic tradition was

Aristotle, a native of Stagira, born in 384 B.C. At the age of seventeen he entered Plato's Academy,[7] continuing as student and teacher there for twenty years. In 343 he was invited by King Philip of Macedon to serve as tutor to the young Alexander. Perhaps history affords few more conspicuous examples of wasted talent, except for the fact that the young prince acquired an enthusiasm for science and for some other elements of Hellenic culture. Seven years later Aristotle returned to Athens, where he conducted a school of his own, known as the Lyceum, until his death in 322 B.C. Aristotle wrote even more voluminously than Plato and on a greater variety of subjects. His principal works include treatises on logic, metaphysics, rhetoric, ethics, natural sciences, and politics. A considerable number of the writings credited to him have never been found.

Though Aristotle was as much interested as Plato and Socrates in absolute knowledge and eternal standards, his philosophy differed from theirs in several outstanding respects. To begin with, he had a higher regard for the concrete and the practical. In contrast with Plato, the aesthete, and Socrates, who declared he could learn nothing from trees and stones, Aristotle was a scientist with a compelling interest in biology, medicine, and astronomy. Moreover, he was less inclined than his predecessors to a spiritual outlook. And lastly, he did not share their strong aristocratic sympathies.

Aristotle agreed with Plato that universals, Ideas (or forms as he called them), are real, and that knowledge derived from the senses is limited and inaccurate. But he refused to go along with his master in ascribing an independent existence to universals and in reducing material things to pale reflections of their spiritual patterns. On the contrary, he asserted that form and matter are of equal importance; both are eternal, and neither can exist inseparable from the other. It is the union of the two which gives to the universe its essential character. Forms are the causes of all things; they are the purposive forces that shape the world of matter into the infinitely varied objects and organisms around us. All evolution, both cosmic and organic, results from the interaction of form and matter upon each other. Thus the presence of the form *man* in the human embryo molds and directs the development of the latter until it ultimately evolves as a human being. Aristotle's philosophy may be regarded as halfway between the spiritualism and transcendentalism of Plato, on the one hand, and the mechanistic materialism of the atomists on the other. His conception of the universe was *teleological*—that is, governed by purpose; but he refused to regard the spiritual as completely overshadowing its material embodiment.

That Aristotle should have conceived of God primarily as a First Cause is no more than we should expect from the dominance of the scientific attitude in his philosophy. Unlike Plato's Idea of the Good, Aristotle's God did not fulfill an ethical purpose. His charac-

[7] So called from the grove of Academus, where Plato and his disciples met to discuss philosophic problems.

227

ter was that of a Prime Mover, the original source of the purposive motion contained in the forms. In no sense was he a personal God, for his nature was pure intelligence, devoid of all feelings, will, or desire. Aristotle seems to have left no place in his religious scheme for individual immortality: all the functions of the soul, except the creative reason which is not individual at all, are dependent upon the body and perish with it.

Aristotle's ethical
philosophy of the
golden mean

Aristotle's ethical philosophy was less ascetic than Plato's. He did not regard the body as the prison of the soul, nor did he believe that physical appetites are necessarily evil in themselves. He taught that the highest good for man consists in self-realization, that is, in the exercise of that part of man's nature which most truly distinguishes him as a human being. Self-realization would therefore be identical with the life of reason. But the life of reason is dependent upon the proper combination of physical and mental conditions. The body must be kept in good health and the emotions under adequate control. The solution is to be found in the *golden mean*, in preserving a balance between excessive indulgence on the one hand and ascetic denial on the other. This was simply a reaffirmation of the characteristic Hellenic ideal of *sophrosyne* ("nothing too much").

The golden mean
applied to
politics

Although Aristotle included in his *Politics* much descriptive and analytical material on the structure and functions of government, he dealt primarily with the broader aspects of political theory. He considered the state as the supreme institution for the promotion of the good life among men, and he was therefore vitally interested in its origin and development and in the best forms it could be made to assume. Declaring that man is by nature a political animal, he denied that the state is an artificial product of the ambitions of the few or of the desires of the many. On the contrary, he asserted that it is rooted in the instincts of man himself, and that civilized life outside of its limits is impossible. He considered the best state to be neither a monarchy, an aristocracy, nor a democracy, but a *polity*—which he defined as a commonwealth intermediate between oligarchy and democracy. Essentially it would be a state under the control of the middle class, but Aristotle intended to make sure that the members of that class would be fairly numerous, for he advocated measures to prevent the concentration of wealth. He defended the institution of private property, but he opposed the heaping up of riches beyond what is necessary for intelligent living. He recommended that the government should provide the poor with money to buy small farms or to "make a beginning in trade and husbandry" and thus promote their prosperity and self-respect.[8]

II. SCIENCE Contrary to a popular belief, the period of Hellenic civilization, strictly speaking, was not a great age of science. The

Hellenic science

vast majority of the scientific achievements commonly thought of as Greek were made during the Hellenistic period, when the culture

228   [8] *Politics*, Maurice Francis Egan, ed., pp. 158–59.

was no longer predominantly Hellenic but a mixture of Hellenic and Oriental.[9] The interests of the Greeks in the Periclean age and in the century that followed were chiefly speculative and artistic; they were not deeply concerned with material comforts or with mastery of the physical universe. Consequently, with the exception of some important developments in mathematics, biology, and medicine, scientific progress was relatively slight.

The founder of Greek mathematics was apparently Thales of Miletus, who is supposed to have originated several theorems which were later included in the geometry of Euclid. Perhaps more significant was the work of the Pythagoreans, who developed an elaborate theory of numbers, classifying them into various categories, such as odd, even, prime, composite, even-times-even, perfect, and so forth. They are also supposed to have discovered the theory of proportion and to have proved for the first time that the sum of the three angles of any triangle is equal to two right angles. But the most famous of their achievements was the discovery of the theorem attributed to Pythagoras himself: the square of the hypotenuse of any right-angled triangle is equal to the sum of the squares on the other two sides. The Greek who first developed geometry as a science is now considered to have been Hippocrates of Chios, not to be confused with the physician, Hippocrates of Cos.[10]

The first of the Greeks to manifest an interest in biology was the philosopher Anaximander, who developed a crude theory of organic evolution based upon the principle of survival through progressive adaptations to the environment. The earliest ancestral animals, he asserted, lived in the sea, which originally covered the whole face of the earth. As the waters receded, some organisms were able to adjust themselves to their new environment and became land animals. The final product of this evolutionary process was man himself. The real founder of the science of biology, however, was Aristotle. Devoting many years of his life to painstaking study of the structure, habits, and growth of animals, he revealed many facts which were not destined to be discovered anew until the seventeenth century or later. The metamorphoses of various insects, the reproductive habits of the eel, the embryological development of the dog-fish—these are only samples of the amazing extent of his knowledge. Unfortunately he committed some errors. He denied the sexuality of plants, and although he subscribed to the general theory of evolution, he believed in the spontaneous generation of certain species of worms and insects.

Greek medicine also had its origin with the philosophers. The pioneers were Empedocles, exponent of the theory of the four elements (earth, air, fire, and water), and Alcmeon, a member of the Pythagorean school. The former discovered that blood flows to and

[9] See the chapter on The Hellenistic Civilization.
[10] George Sarton, *An Introduction to the History of Science*, I, 92.

Greek Surgical Instruments. A bas-relief from the temple of Asklepio in Athens. The open case in the middle contains operating knives. On the two sides are retractors and cupping glasses for bleeding the patient.

from the heart, and that the pores of the skin supplement the work of the respiratory passages in breathing. Alcmeon originated the practice of dissecting animal bodies, discovered the optic nerve and the Eustachian tubes, and learned that the brain is the center of the nervous system. More important still was the work of Hippocrates of Cos in the fifth and fourth centuries. By general consensus he is still regarded as the father of medicine. He dinned into the ears of his pupils the doctrine that "Every disease has a natural cause, and without natural causes, nothing ever happens." In addition, by his methods of careful study and comparison of symptoms he laid the foundations for clinical medicine. He discovered the phenomenon of crisis in disease and improved the practice of surgery. Though he had a wide knowledge of drugs, his chief reliances in treatment were diet and rest. The main fact to his discredit was his development of the theory of the four humors—the notion that illness is due to excessive amounts of yellow bile, black bile, blood, and phlegm in the system. The practice of bleeding the patient was the regrettable outgrowth of this theory.

III. LITERATURE Generally the most common medium of literary expression in the formative age of a people is the epic of heroic deeds. It is a form well adapted to the pioneering days of battle and lusty adventure when men have not yet had time to be awed by the mystery of things. The most famous of the Greek epics, the *Iliad* and the *Odyssey*, were put into written form just at the end of the Dark Ages. The first, which deals with the Trojan War, has its theme in the wrath of Achilles; the second describes the wanderings and return of Odysseus. Both have supreme literary merit in their carefully woven plots, in the realism of their character portrayals, and in their mastery of the full range of emotional intensity. They exerted an almost incalculable influence upon later writers. Their

The epic
of heroic deeds

230

style and language inspired the fervid emotional poetry of the sixth
century, and they were an unfailing source of plots and themes for
the great tragedians of the Golden Age of the fifth and fourth centuries.

The three centuries which followed the Dark Ages were distinguished, as we have already seen, by tremendous social changes. The *Development* rural pattern of life gave way to an urban society of steadily increasing complexity. The founding of colonies and the growth of commerce provided new interests and new habits of living. Individuals hitherto submerged rose to a consciousness of their power and importance. It was inevitable that these changes should be reflected in new forms of literature, especially of a more personal type. The first to be developed was the elegy, which was probably intended to be declaimed rather than sung to the accompaniment of music. Elegies varied in theme from individual reactions toward love to the idealism of patriots and reformers. Generally, however, they were devoted to melancholy reflection on the disillusionments of life or to bitter lament over loss of prestige. Outstanding among the authors of elegiac verse was Solon the legislator.

Development of the elegy

In the sixth century and the early part of the fifth, the elegy was gradually displaced by the lyric, which derives its name from the fact that it was sung to the music of the lyre. The new type of *Lyric poetry* poetry was particularly well adapted to the expression of passionate feelings, the violent loves and hates engendered by the strife of classes. It was employed for other purposes also. Both Alcaeus and Sappho used it to describe the poignant beauty of love, the delicate grace of spring, and the starlit splendor of a summer night. Meanwhile other poets developed the choral lyric, intended to express the feelings of the community rather than the sentiments of any one individual. Greatest of all the writers of this group was Pindar of Thebes, who wrote during the first half of the fifth century. The lyrics of Pindar took the form of odes celebrating the victories of athletes and the glories of Hellenic civilization. They are significant also for their religious and moral conceptions. Pindar had accepted the idea that Zeus is a god of righteousness, and that he will punish the wicked with the "direst doom" and reward the good with a life "that knows no tears."

The supreme literary achievement of the Greeks was the tragic drama. Like so many of their other great works, it had its roots in religion. At the festivals dedicated to the worship of Dionysus, the *The origins of* god of spring and of wine, a chorus of men dressed as satyrs, or goat-men, sang and danced around an altar, enacting the various parts of a dithyramb or choral lyric that related the story of the god's career. In time a leader came to be separated from the chorus to recite the main parts of the story. The true drama was born about the beginning of the fifth century when Aeschylus introduced a second "actor" and relegated the chorus to the background. The name

The origins of tragic drama

"tragedy," which came to be applied to this drama, was probably derived from the Greek word *tragos* meaning "goat."

Greek tragedy stands out in marked contrast to the tragedies of Shakespeare, Eugene O'Neill, or Arthur Miller. There was, first of all, little action presented on the stage; the main business of the actors was to recite the incidents of a plot which was already familiar to the audience, for the story was drawn from popular legends. Secondly, Greek tragedy devoted little attention to the study of complicated individual personality. There was no unfoldment of personal character as shaped by the vicissitudes of a long career. Those involved in the plot were scarcely individuals at all, but types. On the stage they wore masks to disguise any characteristics which might serve to distinguish them too sharply from the rest of humanity. In addition, Greek tragedies differed from the modern variety in having as their theme the conflict between man and the universe, not the clash of individual personalities, or the conflict of man with himself. The tragic fate that befell the main characters in these plays was external to man himself. It was brought on by the fact that someone had committed a crime against society, or against the gods, thereby offending the moral scheme of the universe. Punishment must follow in order to balance the scale of justice. Finally, the purpose of Greek tragedies was not merely to depict suffering and to interpret human actions, but to portray "the ideal conduct of the ideal Hellene in a painful situation," and to purify the emotions of the audience by representing the triumph of justice.

As already indicated, the founder of Greek tragedy was Aeschylus (525–456 B.C.). Though he is supposed to have written about eighty plays, only seven have survived in complete form, among them *The Persians, Seven against Thebes, Prometheus Bound*, and a trilogy known as *Oresteia*. Guilt and punishment is the recurrent theme of nearly all of them. The second of the dramatists, Sophocles (496–406), is often considered to have been the greatest. His style was more polished and his philosophy more profound than that of his predecessor. He was the author of over a hundred plays, eighteen of which won first or second prize. More than any other writer in Greek history, he personified the Hellenic ideal of "nothing too much." His attitude was distinguished by love of harmony and peace, intelligent respect for democracy, and profound sympathy for human weakness. The most famous of his plays now extant are *Oedipus Rex, Antigone*, and *Electra*.

The work of the last of the tragedians, Euripides (480–406), reflects a far different spirit. He was a skeptic, an individualist, a humanist, who took delight in ridiculing the ancient myths and the "sacred cows" of his time. An embittered pessimist who suffered from the barbs of his conservative critics, he loved to humble the proud in his plays and to exalt the lowly. He was the first to give the ordinary man, even the beggar and the peasant, a place in the drama.

Greek tragedy compared with modern tragedy

Aeschylus and Sophocles

Euripides

232

Euripides is also noted for his sympathy for the slave, for his condemnation of war, and for his protests against the exclusion of women from social and intellectual life. Because of his humanism, his tendency to portray men as they actually were (or even a little worse), and his introduction of the love *motif* into drama, he is often considered a modernist. It must be remembered, however, that in other respects his plays were perfectly consistent with the Hellenic model. They did not exhibit the evolution of individual character or the conflict of egos to any more notable extent than did the works of Sophocles or Aeschylus. Nevertheless, he has been called the most tragic of the Greek dramatists because he dealt with situations having analogues in real life. Among the best-known tragedies of Euripides are *Alcestis*, *Medea*, and *The Trojan Women*.

Hellenic comedy was definitely inferior to tragedy. In common with tragedy it appears to have grown out of the Dionysiac festivals, but it did not attain full development until late in the fifth century B.C. Its only outstanding representative was Aristophanes (448?–380?), a somewhat coarse and belligerent aristocrat who lived in Athens. Most of his plays were written to satirize the political and intellectual ideals of the radical democracy of his time. In *The Knights* he pilloried the incompetent and greedy politicians for their reckless adventures in imperialism. In *The Frogs* he lampooned

Hellenic comedy

Greek Theater in Epidauros. The construction, to take advantage of the slope of the hill, and the arrangement of the stage are of particular interest. Greek dramas were invariably presented in the open air.

Euripides for the innovations the latter had made in the drama. *The
Clouds* he reserved for ridicule of the Sophists, ignorantly or mali-
ciously classifying Socrates as one of them. While he was undoubtedly a clever poet with a mastery of subtle humor and imaginative
skill, his ideas were founded largely upon prejudice. He is deserving
of much credit, however, for his sharp criticisms of the stupid policies of the war-hawks of Athens during the struggle with Sparta.
Though written as a farce, his *Lysistrata* cleverly pointed a way—
however infeasible—to the termination of any war.

The Greek
historians:
Herodotus

No account of Greek literature would be complete without some
mention of the two great historians of the Golden Age. Herodotus,
the "father of history" (484–425), was a native of Halicarnassus in
Asia Minor. He traveled extensively through the Persian empire,
Egypt, Greece, and Italy, collecting a multitude of interesting data
about various peoples. His famous account of the great war between
the Greeks and the Persians included so much background that the
work seems almost a history of the world. He regarded that war as
an epic struggle between East and West, with Zeus giving victory to
the Greeks against a mighty host of barbarians.

Thucydides

If Herodotus deserves to be called the father of history, much
more does his younger contemporary, Thucydides, deserve to be
considered the founder of scientific history. Influenced by the skepticism and practicality of the Sophists, Thucydides chose to work
on the basis of carefully sifted evidence, rejecting opinion, legends,
and hearsay. The subject of his *History* was the war between Sparta
and Athens, which he described scientifically and dispassionately,
emphasizing the complexity of causes which led to the fateful clash.
His aim was to present an accurate record which could be studied
with profit by statesmen and generals of all time, and it must be said
that he was in full measure successful. If there were any defects in
his historical method, they consisted in overemphasizing political
factors to the neglect of the social and economic and in failing to
consider the importance of emotions in history. He also had a prejudice against the democratic factions in Athens after the death of
Pericles.

7. THE MEANING OF GREEK ART

The importance of
Greek art

Art even more than literature probably reflected the true character of Hellenic civilization. The Greek was essentially a materialist
who conceived of his world in physical terms. Plato and the followers of the mystic religions were, of course, exceptions, but few
other Greeks had much interest in a universe of spiritual realities. It
would be natural therefore to find that the material emblems of
architecture and sculpture should exemplify best the ideals the
234 Greek held before him.

Marble Statue of the Apollo Type. Probably end of Seventh Century B.C. At this time Greek sculpture was still under Egyptian influence, as can be seen in the headdress, the imperturbable face, and the arms and feet of this statue.

What did Greek art express? Above all, it symbolized humanism —the glorification of man as the most important creature in the universe. Though much of the sculpture depicted gods, this did not detract in the slightest from its humanistic quality. The Greek deities existed for the benefit of man; in glorifying them he thus glorified himself. Both architecture and sculpture embodied the ideals of balance, harmony, order, and moderation. Anarchy and excess were abhorrent to the mind of the Greek, but so was absolute repression. Consequently, his art exhibited qualities of simplicity and dignified restraint—free from decorative extravagance, on the one hand, and from restrictive conventions on the other. Moreover, Greek art was an expression of the national life. Its purpose was not merely aesthetic but political: to symbolize the pride of the people in their city and to enhance their consciousness of unity. The Parthenon at Athens, for example, was the temple of Athena, the protecting goddess who presided over the corporate life of the state. In providing her with a beautiful shrine which she might frequently visit, the Athenians were giving evidence of their love for their city and their hope for its continuing welfare.

The art of the Hellenes differed from that of nearly every people since their time in an interesting variety of ways. Like most of the tragedies of Aeschylus and Sophocles, it was universal. It included

The ideals embodied in Greek art

See color plates at pages 105, 264

235

Greek art
compared with
that of later
peoples

Periods in the
evolution of
Greek art

Architecture

few portraits of personalities either in sculpture or in painting.[11] The human beings depicted were generally types, not individuals. Again, Greek art differed from that of most later peoples in its ethical purpose. It was not art for the sake of mere decoration or for the expression of the artist's individual philosophy, but a medium for the ennoblement of man. This does not mean that it was didactic in the sense that its merit was determined by the moral lesson it taught, but rather that it was supposed to exemplify qualities of living essentially artistic in themselves. The Athenian, at least, drew no sharp distinction between the ethical and aesthetic spheres; the beautiful and the good were really identical. True morality, therefore, consisted in rational living, in the avoidance of grossness, disgusting excesses, and other forms of conduct aesthetically offensive. Finally, Greek art may be contrasted with most later forms in the fact that it was not "naturalistic." Although the utmost attention was given to the depiction of beautiful bodies, this had nothing to do with fidelity to nature. The Greek was not interested in interpreting nature for its own sake, but in expressing *human* ideals.

The history of Greek art divides itself naturally into three great periods. The first, which can be called the archaic period, covered the seventh and sixth centuries. During the greater part of this age sculpture was dominated by Egyptian influence, as can be seen in the frontality and rigidity of the statues, with their square shoulders and one foot slightly advanced. Toward the end, however, these conventions were thrown aside. The chief architectural styles also had their origin in this period, and several crude temples were built. The second period, which occupied the fifth century, witnessed the full perfection of both architecture and sculpture. The art of this time was completely idealistic. During the fourth century, the last period of Hellenic art, architecture lost some of its balance and simplicity and sculpture assumed new characteristics. It came to reflect more clearly the reactions of the individual artist, to incorporate traces of realism, and to lose some of its quality as an expression of civic pride.

For all its artistic excellence, Greek temple architecture was one of the simplest of structural forms. Its essential elements were really only five in number: (1) the cella or nucleus of the building, which was a rectangular chamber to house the statue of the god; (2) the columns, which formed the porch and surrounded the cella; (3) the entablature or lintel, which rested upon the columns and supported the roof; (4) the gabled roof itself; and (5) the pediment or triangular section under the gable of the roof. Two different architectural styles were developed, representing modifications of certain of these elements. The more popular was the Doric, which made use of a

[11] Most of the portraits in sculpture commonly considered Greek really belong to the Hellenistic Age, although a few were produced at the end of the fourth century B.C.

rather heavy, sharply fluted column surmounted by a plain capital. The other, the Ionic, had more slender and more graceful columns with flat flutings, a triple base, and a scroll or volute capital. The so-called Corinthian style, which was chiefly Hellenistic, differed from the Ionic primarily in being more ornate. The three styles differed also in their treatment of the entablature or lintel. In the Ionic style it was left almost plain. In the Doric and Corinthian styles it bore sculptured reliefs. The Parthenon, the best example of Greek architecture, was essentially a Doric building, but it reflected some of the grace and subtlety of Ionic influence.

According to the prevailing opinion among his contemporaries, Greek sculpture attained its acme of development in the work of Phidias (500?–432?). His masterpieces were the statue of Athena in the Parthenon and the statue of Zeus in the Temple of Olympian Zeus. In addition, he designed and supervised the execution of the Parthenon reliefs. The main qualities of his work are grandeur of conception, patriotism, proportion, dignity, and restraint. Nearly all of his figures are idealized representations of deities and mythological creatures in human form. The second most important fifth-century sculptor was Myron, noted for his statue of the discus thrower and for his glorification of other athletic types. The names of three great sculptors in the fourth century have come down to us. The most gifted of them was Praxiteles, renowned for his portrayal of humanized deities with slender, graceful bodies and countenances of philosophic repose. The best known of his works is the statue of Hermes with the infant Dionysus. His older contemporary, Scopas, gained distinction as an emotional sculptor. One of his most successful creations was the statue of a religious ecstatic, a worshiper of Dionysus, in a condition of mystic frenzy. At the end of the century Lysippus introduced even stronger qualities of realism and individualism into sculpture. He was the first great master of the realistic portrait as a study of personal character.

Details of the Three Famous Orders of Greek Architecture. A, Doric; B, Ionic; C, Corinthian.

ARCHITECTURE OF GREECE

Top, left: *The Parthenon*. The largest and most famous of Athenian temples, the Parthenon is considered the classic example of Doric architecture. Its columns were made more graceful by tapering them in a slight curve toward the top. Its friezes and pediments were decorated with lifelike sculptures of prancing horses, fighting giants, and benign and confident deities.

Bottom left: *Reconstruction of the Interior of the Parthenon*. The statue was a resplendent gold and ivory figure of Athena, guardian goddess of the city state. Like most of the rest of Parthenon sculpture, it was the work of Phidias.

Top: *The Parthenon, Detail.* Frieze depicting the Pan-Athenaic Procession to the shrine Athena.

Bottom right: *The Porch of the Maidens of the So-called Erechtheum*, a Temple of Athena on the Acropolis. The corner statue is a substitute for the original carried to London by Lord Elgin in 1801–1803.

8.   ATHENIAN LIFE IN THE GOLDEN AGE

Citizens, metics,
and slaves

The population of Athens in the fifth and fourth centuries was divided into three distinct groups: the citizens, the metics, and the slaves. The citizens, who numbered at the most about 160,000, included only those born of citizen parents, except for the few who were occasionally enfranchised by special law. The metics, who probably did not exceed a total of 100,000, were resident aliens, chiefly non-Athenian Greeks, although some were Phoenicians and Jews. Save for the fact that they had no political privileges and generally were not permitted to own land, the metics had equal opportunities with citizens. They could engage in any occupation they

The Discobolus, *or Discus Thrower, of Myron.* This statue reflects the glorification of the human body characteristic of Athens in the Golden Age. The proportions of the figure, the development and co-ordination of the muscles, and the repose and confidence of the face are perfect. The *Discobolus* is now in the Vatican Museum.

Hermes with the Infant Dionysus, by Praxiteles, Fourth Century B.C. The god Hermes is represented as a slender, graceful youth, reflecting the humanism of Greek religion. The countenance suggests an attitude of repose and philosophic contentment. Original in the Olympia Museum, Greece.

desired and participate in any social or intellectual activities. Contrary to a popular tradition, the slaves in Athens were never a majority of the population. Their maximum number does not seem to have exceeded 140,000. Urban slaves, at least, were very well treated and were sometimes rewarded for faithful service by being set free. They could work for wages and own property, and some of them held responsible positions as minor public officials and as managers of banks. The treatment of slaves who worked in the mines, however, was often cruel.

Life in Athens stands out in rather sharp contrast to that in most other civilizations. One of its leading features was the amazing degree of social and economic equality which prevailed among all the inhabitants. Although there were many who were poor, there were few who were very rich. Nearly everyone, whether citizen, metic, or slave, ate the same kind of food, wore the same kind of clothing, and participated in the same kind of amusement. This substantial equality was enforced in part by the system of *liturgies*, which were services to the state rendered by wealthy men, chiefly in the form of contributions to support the drama, equip the navy, or provide for the poor.

The amazing degree of social and economic equality

A second outstanding characteristic of Athenian life was its poverty in comforts and luxuries. Part of this was due to the low income of the mass of the people. Teachers, sculptors, masons, carpenters, and common laborers all received the same standard wage of one drachma (about 30 cents) per day. Part of it may have been due also to the mild climate, which made possible a life of simplicity. But whatever the cause, the fact remains that, in comparison with modern standards, the Athenians endured an exceedingly impoverished existence. They knew nothing of such common commodities as watches, soap, newspapers, cotton cloth, sugar, tea, or coffee. Their beds had no springs, their houses had no drains, and their food consisted chiefly of barley cakes, onions, and fish, washed down with diluted wine. From the standpoint of clothing they were no better off. A rectangular piece of cloth wrapped around the body and fastened with pins at the shoulders and with a rope around the waist served as the main garment. A larger piece was draped around the body as an extra garment for outdoor wear. No one wore either stockings or socks, and few had any footgear except sandals.

The poverty of Athenian life

But lack of comforts and luxuries was a matter of little consequence to the Athenian citizen. He was totally unable to regard these as the most important things in life. His aim was to live as interestingly and contentedly as possible without spending all his days in grinding toil for the sake of a little more comfort for his family. Nor was he interested in piling up riches as a source of power or prestige. What each citizen really wanted was a small farm or business that would provide him with a reasonable income and at the

Indifference toward material comforts and wealth

241

same time allow him an abundance of leisure for politics, for gossip in the market place, and for intellectual or artistic activities if he had the talent to enjoy them.

It is frequently supposed that the Athenian was too lazy or too snobbish to work hard for luxury and security. But this was not quite the case. True, there were some occupations in which he would not engage because he considered them degrading or destructive of moral freedom. He would not break his back digging silver or copper out of a mine; such work was fit only for slaves of the lowest intellectual level. On the other hand, there is plenty of evidence to show that the great majority of Athenian citizens did not look with disdain upon manual labor. Most of them worked on their farms or in their shops as independent craftsmen. Hundreds of others earned their living as hired laborers employed either by the state or by their fellow Athenians. Cases are on record of citizens, metics, and slaves working side by side, all for the same wage, in the construction of public buildings; and in at least one instance the foreman of a crew was a slave.[12]

In spite of expansion of trade and increase in population, the economic organization of Athenian society remained comparatively simple. Agriculture and commerce were by far the most important enterprises. Even in Pericles' day the majority of the citizens still lived in the country. Industry was not highly developed. Very few examples of large-scale production are on record, and those chiefly in the manufacture of pottery and implements of war. The largest establishment that ever existed was apparently a shield factory owned by a metic and employing 120 slaves. No other was more than half as large. The enterprises which absorbed the most labor were the mines, but they were owned by the state and were leased in sections to petty contractors to be worked by slaves. The bulk of industry was carried on in small shops owned by individual craftsmen who produced their wares directly to the order of the consumer.

Religion underwent some notable changes in the Golden Age. The primitive polytheism and anthropomorphism of the Homeric myths were largely supplanted, among intellectuals at least, by a belief in one God as the creator and sustainer of the moral law. Such a doctrine was taught by many of the philosophers, by the poet Pindar, and by the dramatists Aeschylus and Sophocles. Other significant consequences flowed from the mystery cults. These new forms of religion first became popular in the sixth century because of the craving for an emotional faith to make up for the disappointments of life. The more important of them was the Orphic cult, which revolved around the myth of the death and resurrection of Dionysus. The other, the Eleusinian cult, had as its central theme the abduction of Persephone by Hades, god of the nether world,

[12] A. E. Zimmern, *The Greek Commonwealth*, p. 258.

and her ultimate redemption by Demeter, the great Earth Mother. Both of these cults had as their original purpose the promotion of the lifegiving powers of nature, but in time they came to be fraught with a much deeper significance. They expressed to their followers the ideas of vicarious atonement, salvation in an afterlife, and ecstatic union with the divine. Although entirely inconsistent with the spirit of the ancient religion, they made a powerful appeal to certain classes and were largely responsible for the spread of the belief in personal immortality. The more thoughtful Greeks, however, seem to have persisted in their adherence to the worldly, optimistic, and mechanical faith of their ancestors and to have shown little concern about a conviction of sin or a desire for salvation in a life to come.

It remains to consider briefly the position of the family in Athens in the fifth and fourth centuries. Though marriage was still an important institution for the procreation of children who would become citizens of the state, there is reason to believe that family life had declined. Men of the more prosperous classes, at least, now spent the greater part of their time away from their families. Wives were relegated to an inferior position and required to remain secluded in their homes. Their place as social and intellectual companions for their husbands was taken by alien women, the famous *hetaerae*, many of whom were highly cultured natives of the Ionian cities. Marriage itself assumed the character of a political and economic arrangement devoid of romantic elements. Men married wives so as to ensure that at least some of their children would be legitimate and in order to obtain property in the form of a dowry. It was important also, of course, to have someone to care for the household. But husbands did not consider their wives as their equals and did not appear in public with them or encourage their participation in any form of social or intellectual activity.

The family in Athens in the Golden Age

9. THE GREEK ACHIEVEMENT AND ITS SIGNIFICANCE FOR US

No historian would deny that the achievement of the Greeks was one of the most remarkable in the history of the world. With no great expanse of fertile soil or abundance of mineral resources, they succeeded in developing a higher and more varied civilization than any of the most richly favored nations of the Near Orient. With only a limited cultural inheritance from the past to build upon as a foundation, they produced intellectual and artistic achievements which have served ever since as the chief inspiration to man in his quest for wisdom and beauty. It seems reasonable to conclude also that they achieved a more normal and more rational mode of living than most other peoples who strutted and fretted their hour upon this planet. The absence of violent revolution, except in the earlier

The magnitude of the Greek achievement

period, and during the Peloponnesian War, the infrequency of brutal crimes, and the contentment with simple amusements and modest wealth all point to a comparatively happy and satisfied existence. Moreover, the sane moral attitude of the Greek helped to keep him almost entirely free from the nervous instability and emotional conflicts which wreak so much havoc in modern society. Suicide, for example, was exceedingly rare in Greece.[13]

It is necessary to be on our guard, however, against uncritical judgments which are sometimes expressed in reference to the achievement of the Greeks. We must not assume that all of the natives of Hellas were as cultured, wise, and free as the citizens of Athens and of the Ionian states across the Aegean. The Spartans, the Arcadians, the Thessalians, and probably the majority of the Boeotians remained untutored and benighted from the beginning to the end of their history. Furthermore, the Athenian civilization itself was not without its defects. It permitted some exploitation of the weak, especially of the ignorant slaves who toiled in the mines. It was based upon a principle of racial exclusiveness which reckoned every man a foreigner whose parents were not both Athenians, and consequently denied political rights to the majority of the inhabitants of the country. Its statecraft was not sufficiently enlightened to avoid the pitfalls of imperialism and even of aggressive war. Finally, the attitude of its citizens was not always tolerant and just. Socrates was put to death for his opinions, and two other philosophers, Anaxagoras and Protagoras, were forced to leave the country. The former was condemned to death by the assembly, and the books of the latter were ordered to be burned. It must be conceded, however, that the record of the Athenians for tolerance was better than that of most other nations, both ancient and modern. There was probably more freedom of expression in Athens during the war with Sparta than there was in the United States during World War I.

Nor is it true that the Hellenic influence has really been as great as is commonly supposed. No intelligent student could accept the sentimental verdict of Shelley: "We are all Greeks; our laws, our literature, our religion, our arts have their roots in Greece." Our laws do not really have their roots in Greece but chiefly in Hellenistic and Roman sources. Much of our poetry is undoubtedly Greek in inspiration, but such is not the case with most of our prose literature. Our religion is no more than partly Greek; except as it was influenced by Plato, Aristotle, and the Romans, it reflects primarily the spirit of the Orient. Even our arts take their form and meaning from Rome almost as much as from Greece. Actually, modern civilization has been the result of the convergence of several influences coming from a variety of sources. The influence from Greece has been partly overshadowed by heritages from the Near Orient and

Undesirable features of Greek life

Hellenic influence sometimes exaggerated

[13] For a discussion of this point see E. A. Westermarck, *The Origin and Development of Moral Ideas*, pp. 247 ff.

The Acropolis Today. Occupying the commanding position is the Parthenon. To the left is the Erechtheum with its Porch of the Maidens facing the Parthenon.

from the Romans and the Germans. Philosophy appears to have been the only important segment of Greek civilization that has been incorporated into modern culture virtually intact.

In spite of all this, the Hellenic adventure was of profound significance for the history of the world. For the Greeks were the founders of nearly all those ideals we commonly think of as peculiar to the West. The civilizations of the ancient Near Orient, with the exception, to a certain extent, of the Hebrew and Egyptian, were dominated by absolutism, supernaturalism, ecclesiasticism, the denial of both body and mind, and the subjection of the individual to the group. Their political regime was the reign of force as expressed in an absolute monarch supported by a powerful priesthood. Their religion in many cases was the worship of omnipotent gods who demanded that man should humble and despise himself for the purpose of their greater glory. Culture in these mighty empires served mainly as an instrument to magnify the power of the state and to enhance the prestige of rulers and priests.

By contrast, the civilization of Greece, notably in its Athenian form, was founded upon ideals of freedom, optimism, secularism, rationalism, the glorification of both body and mind, and a high regard for the dignity and worth of the individual man. Insofar as the individual was subjected at all, his subjection was to the rule of the majority. This, of course, was not always good, especially in times of crisis, when the majority might be swayed by prejudice. Religion was worldly and practical, serving the interests of human beings.

245

Worship of the gods was a means for the ennoblement of man. As opposed to the ecclesiasticism of the Orient, the Greeks had no organized priesthood at all. They kept their priests in the background and refused under any circumstances to allow them to define dogma or to govern the realm of intellect. In addition, they excluded them from control over the sphere of morality. The culture of the Greeks was the first to be based upon the primacy of intellect—upon the supremacy of the spirit of free inquiry. There was no subject they feared to investigate, or any question they regarded as excluded from the province of reason. To an extent never before realized, mind was supreme over faith, logic and science over superstition.[14]

The supreme tragedy of the Greeks was, of course, their failure to solve the problem of political conflict. To a large degree, this conflict was the product of social and cultural dissimilarities. Because of different geographic and economic conditions the Greek city-states developed at an uneven pace. Some went forward rapidly to high levels of cultural superiority, while others lagged behind and made little or no intellectual progress. The consequences were discord and suspicion, which gave rise eventually to hatred and fear. Though some of the more advanced thinkers made efforts to propagate the notion that the Hellenes were one people who should reserve their contempt for non-Hellenes, or "barbarians," the conception never became part of a national ethos. Athenians hated Spartans, and *vice versa*, just as vehemently as they hated Lydians or Persians. Not even the danger of Asian conquest was sufficient to dispel the distrust and antagonism of Greeks for one another. The war that finally broke out between Athenians and Spartans sealed the doom of Hellenic civilization just as effectively as could ever have resulted from foreign conquest. For a time it appeared as if a new world, largely devoid of ethnic distinctions, might emerge from the ruins of the Greek city-states as a result of the conquests of Alexander the Great. Alexander dreamed of such a world, in which there would be neither Athenian nor Spartan, Greek nor Egyptian, but unfortunately neither he nor his generals knew any means of achieving it except to impose it by force. The parallels between the last phases of Hellenic history and the developments in our own time are at least interesting, if not conclusive.

The tragedy of Hellenic history

SELECTED READINGS

· *Items so designated are available in paperbound editions.*

· Agard, Walter, *What Democracy Meant to the Greeks*, Chapel Hill, 1942 (University of Wisconsin).

[14] For further discussion of the contrast between Hellas and the Orient see the admirable study by Edith Hamilton, *The Greek Way*.

- Andrewes, Antony, *The Greek Tyrants*, New York, 1963 (Torchbook).
- Barker, Ernest, *Greek Political Theory: Plato and His Predecessors*, New York, 1919, 2 vols. (Barnes & Noble). One of the best of the commentaries.
- Boardman, John, *Greek Art*, New York, 1964 (Praeger).
- ———, *The Greeks Overseas*, Baltimore, 1964 (Penguin).
- Burn, A. R., *Pericles and Athens*, New York, 1949 (Collier).
- Clagett, Marshall, *Greek Science in Antiquity*, New York, 1963 (Collier).
- Dickinson, G. L., *The Greek View of Life*, New York, 1927 (Ann Arbor, Collier). An excellent interpretation.
- Dodds, E. R., *The Greeks and the Irrational*, Berkeley, 1963 (Univ. of California).
- Ehrenberg, Victor, *The Greek State*, New York, 1960 (Norton Library).
- Farrington, Benjamin, *Greek Science*, Baltimore, 1961 (Penguin).
- Forsdyke, John, *Greece Before Homer*, New York, 1964 (Norton Library).
- Freeman, Kathleen, *The Greek City-States*, New York, 1963 (Norton Library).
- Glotz, Gustave, *Ancient Greece at Work*, London, 1927 (Norton Library).
- Hamilton, Edith, *The Greek Way*, New York, 1930 (Norton Library). Thoughtful and stimulating.
- Kitto, H. D. F., *The Greeks*, Baltimore, 1957 (Penguin). Probably the best one-volume survey in English.
- Larsen, J. A. O., *Representative Government in Greek and Roman History*, Berkeley, 1955 (University of California).
- MacKendrick, Paul, *The Greek Stones Speak*, New York, 1962 (Mentor).
- Marrou, H. I., *A History of Education in Antiquity*, New York, 1964 (Mentor).
- Mitchell, H., *Sparta*, New York, 1952 (Cambridge).
- Nilsson, M. P., *A History of Greek Religion*, New York, 1964 (Norton Library). Interesting and authoritative.
  Richter, G. M. A., *Greek Art*, New York, 1963.
  Ridder, A. H. P. de, and Deonna, Waldemar, *Art in Greece*, New York, 1927. An excellent one-volume account.
- Rose, H. J., *A Handbook of Greek Literature*, New York, 1960 (Dutton).
- ———, *A Handbook of Greek Mythology*, New York, 1959 (Dutton).
- Snell, Bruno, *The Discovery of the Mind*, New York, 1960 (Torchbook).
  Starr, C. G., *The Origins of Greek Civilization*, New York, 1961.
- Webster, T. B. L., *From Mycenae to Homer*, New York, 1964 (Norton Library).
- Zimmern, A. E., *The Greek Commonwealth*, New York, 1911 (Galaxy). Good, though perhaps a bit too laudatory of the Athenians.

SOURCE MATERIALS

Most Greek authors have been translated in the appropriate volumes of the Loeb Classical Library, Harvard University Press.

In addition the following may be helpful:

- Barnstone, Willis (trans.), *Greek Lyric Poetry*, New York, 1962 (Bantam).
- Kagan, Donald, *Sources in Greek Political Thought*, Glencoe, Ill., 1965 (Free Press).
- Kirk, G. S., and Raven, J. E., *The Presocratic Philosophers*, Cambridge, 1957 (Cambridge University Press).

CHAPTER 10

The Hellenistic Civilization

Beauty and virtue and the like are to be honored, if they give
pleasure, but if they do not give pleasure, we must bid them
farewell.
——Epicurus, "On the End of Life"

I agree that Alexander was carried away so far as to copy oriental
luxury. I hold that no mighty deeds, not even conquering the
whole world, is of any good unless the man has learned mastery
of himself.
—Arrian, *Anabasis of Alexander*

The death of Alexander the Great in 323 B.C. constituted a water-
shed in the development of world history. Hellenic civilization as it
had existed in its prime now came to an end. Of course, the old institutions and ways of life did not suddenly disappear, but Alexander's career had cut so deeply into the old order that it was inconceivable that it could be restored intact. The fusion of cultures and
intermingling of peoples resulting from Alexander's conquests accomplished the overthrow of many of the ideals of the Greeks in
their Golden Age of the fifth and fourth centuries. Gradually a new
pattern of civilization emerged, based upon a mixture of Greek and
Oriental elements. To this new civilization, which lasted until about
the beginning of the Christian era, the name Hellenistic is the one
most commonly applied.

A new stage in world history

Though the break between the Hellenic and Hellenistic eras was
as sharp as that between any two other civilizations, it would be a
mistake to deny all continuity. The language of the new cultured
classes was predominantly Greek, and even the hordes of people
whose heritage was non-Greek considered it desirable to have some
Hellenic culture. Hellenic achievements in science provided a foundation for the great scientific revolution of the Hellenistic Age.
Greek emphasis upon logic was likewise carried over into Hellenistic philosophy, though the objectives of the latter were in many
cases quite different. In the spheres of the political, social, and eco-

Comparison of the Hellenistic Age with the Golden Age of Greece

nomic the resemblances were few indeed. The classical ideal of democracy was now superseded by despotism perhaps as rigorous as any that Egypt or Persia had ever produced. The Greek city-state survived in some parts of Greece itself, but elsewhere it was replaced by the big monarchy, and in the minds of some leaders by notions of a world state. The Hellenic devotion to simplicity and the golden mean gave way to extravagance in the arts and to a love of luxury and riotous excess. Golden Age intensity of living was superseded by a craving for novelty and breadth of experience. In the economic realm the Athenian system of small-scale production was supplanted largely by the growth of big business and vigorous competition for profits. In view of these changes it seems valid to conclude that the Hellenistic Age was sufficiently distinct from the Golden Age of Greece to justify its being considered the era of a new civilization.

I. POLITICAL HISTORY AND INSTITUTIONS

The Hellenistic
states

When Alexander died in 323 B.C., he left no legitimate heir to succeed him. His nearest male relative was a feeble-minded half-brother. Tradition relates that when his friends requested him on his deathbed to designate a successor, he replied vaguely, "To the best man." After his death his highest-ranking generals proceeded to divide the empire among them. Some of the younger commanders contested this arrangement, and a series of wars followed which culminated in the decisive battle of Ipsus in 301 B.C. The result of this battle was a new division among the victors. Seleucus took possession of Persia, Mesopotamia, and Syria; Lysimachus assumed control over Asia Minor and Thrace; Cassander established himself in Madeconia; and Ptolemy added Phoenicia and Palestine to his original domain of Egypt. Twenty years later these four states were reduced to three when Seleucus defeated and killed Lysimachus in battle and appropriated his kingdom. In the meantime most of the Greek states had revolted against the attempts of the Macedonian king to extend his power over them. By banding together in defensive leagues several of them succeeded in maintaining their independence for nearly a century. Finally, between 146 and 30 B.C. nearly all of the Hellenistic territory passed under Roman rule.

Divine monarchy
the dominant
form of govern-
ment

The dominant form of government in the Hellenistic Age was the despotism of kings who represented themselves as at least semi-divine. Alexander himself was recognized as a son of God in Egypt and was worshipped as a god in Greece. His most powerful successors, the Seleucid kings in western Asia and the Ptolemies in Egypt, made systematic attempts to deify themselves. A Seleucid monarch, Antiochus IV, adopted the title "Epiphanes" or "God Manifest." The later members of the dynasty of the Ptolemies signed their decrees "Theos" (God) and revived the practice of sis-

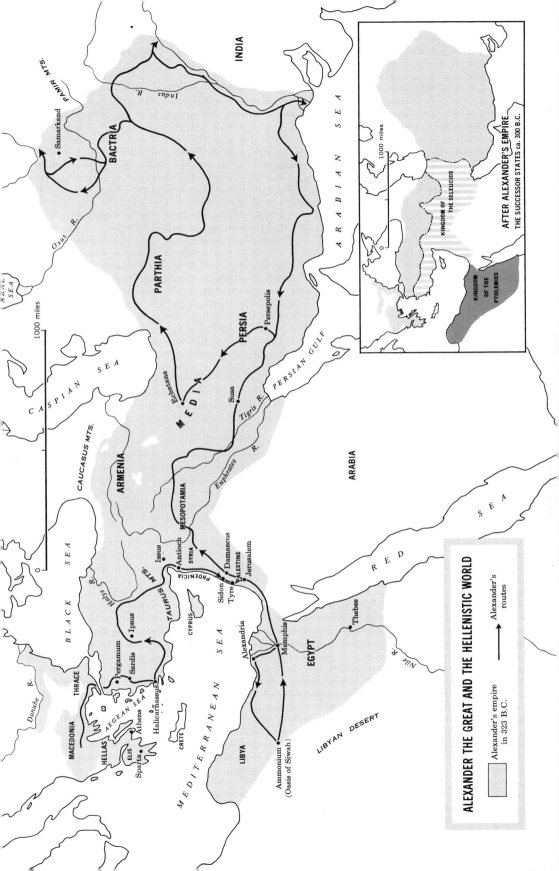

ALEXANDER THE GREAT AND THE HELLENISTIC WORLD

Alexander's empire in 323 B.C.

→ Alexander's routes

AFTER ALEXANDER'S EMPIRE.
THE SUCCESSOR STATES ca. 300 B.C.

KINGDOM OF THE SELEUCIDS

KINGDOM OF THE PTOLEMIES

1000 miles

ARAL SEA

PAMIR MTS.

• Samarkand

BACTRIA

Oxus R.

Indus R.

INDIA

PARTHIA

CASPIAN SEA

ARMENIA

CAUCASUS MTS.

MEDIA

PERSIA

Ecbatana •

• Susa

Tigris R.

• Persepolis

Euphrates R.

PERSIAN GULF

ARABIAN SEA

MESOPOTAMIA

Issus •

Antioch •

SYRIA

Damascus •

PHOENICIA

Sidon •

Tyre •

PALESTINE

Jerusalem •

ARABIA

RED SEA

TAURUS MTS.

Halys R.

BLACK SEA

Danube R.

THRACE

MACEDONIA

• Pergamum

• Sardis

• Ipsus

CYPRUS

AEGEAN SEA

HELLAS

ELIS

• Athens

Sparta •

Halicarnassus

CRETE

MEDITERRANEAN SEA

Alexandria •

• Memphis

EGYPT

• Thebes

Nile R.

LIBYA

Ammonium • (Oasis of Siwah)

LIBYAN DESERT

1000 miles

THE HELLENISTIC CIVILIZATION

ter marriage which had been followed by the Pharaohs as a means of preserving the divine blood of the royal family from contamination. Only in the kingdom of Macedonia was despotism tempered by a modicum of respect for the liberties of the citizens.

The Achaean and Aetolian Leagues

Two other political institutions developed as by-products of Hellenistic civilization: the Achaean and Aetolian Leagues. We have already seen that most of the Greek states rebelled against Macedonian rule following the division of Alexander's empire. The better to preserve their independence, several of these states formed alliances among themselves, which were gradually expanded to become confederate leagues. The states of the Peloponnesus, with the exception of Sparta and Elis, were united in the Achaean League; the Aetolian federation included nearly all of central Greece with the exception of Athens. The organization of these leagues was essentially the same in both cases. Each had a federal council composed of representatives of the member cities with power to enact laws on subjects of general concern. An assembly which all of the citizens in the federated states could attend decided questions of war and peace and elected officials. Executive and military authority was vested in the hands of a general, elected for one year and eligible for reelection only in alternate years. Although these leagues are frequently described as federal states, they were scarcely more than confederacies. The central authority, like the government of the American States under the Articles of Confederation, was dependent upon the local governments for contributions of revenue and troops. Furthermore, the powers delegated to the central government were limited primarily to matters of war and peace, coinage, and weights and measures. The chief significance of these Leagues is to be found in the fact that they embodied the principle of representative government and constituted the nearest approach ever made in Greece to voluntary national union.

2. SIGNIFICANT ECONOMIC AND SOCIAL DEVELOPMENTS

The economic revolution and its causes

The history of the Hellenistic civilization was marked by economic developments second only in magnitude to the Commercial and Industrial Revolutions of the modern era. Several important causes can be distinguished: (1) the opening up of a vast area of trade from the Indus River to the Nile as a result of the Alexandrian conquests; (2) the rise in prices as a consequence of the release of the enormous Persian hoard of gold and silver into the channels of circulation, resulting in an increase in investment and speculation; and (3) the promotion of trade and industry by governments as a means of augmenting the revenues of the state. The net result of these factors was the growth of a system of large-scale production, trade, and finance, with the state as the principal capitalist and entrepreneur.

252

Agriculture was as profoundly affected by the new developments as any other branch of the economic life. The most striking phenomena were the concentration of holdings of land and the degradation of the agricultural population. One of the first things the successors of Alexander did was to confiscate the estates of the chief landowners and add them to the royal domain. The lands thus acquired were either granted to the favorites of the king or leased to tenants under an arrangement calculated to ensure an abundant income for the crown. The tenants were generally forbidden to leave the lands they cultivated until after the harvest and were not allowed to dispose of their grain until after the king had had a chance to sell the share he received as rent at the highest price the market would bring. When some of the tenants went on srike or attempted to run away, they were all bound to the soil as hereditary serfs. Many of the small independent farmers also became serfs when they got into debt as a result of inability to compete with large-scale production.

In an effort to make all of the resources of the state contribute to the profit of the government, the rulers of Egypt and the Seleucid empire promoted and regulated industry and trade. The Ptolemies established factories and shops in nearly every village and town to be owned and operated by the government for its own financial benefit. In addition, they assumed control over all of the enterprises that were privately owned, fixing the prices the owners could charge and manipulating markets to the advantage of the crown. A similar plan of regimentation for industry, although not on quite so ambitious a scale, was enforced by the Seleucid rulers of western Asia. Trade was left by both of these governments very largely in private hands, but it was heavily taxed and regulated in such a way as to make sure that an ample share of the profits went to the king. Every facility was provided by the government for the encouragement of new trading ventures. Harbors were improved, warships were sent out to police the seas, and roads and canals were built. Moreover, the Ptolemies employed famous geographers to discover new routes to distant lands and thereby gain access to valuable markets. As a result of such methods Egypt developed a flourishing commerce in the widest variety of products. Into the port of Alexandria came spices from Arabia, copper from Cyprus, gold from Abyssinia and India, tin from Britain, elephants and ivory from Nubia, silver from the northern Aegean and Spain, fine carpets from Asia Minor, and even silk from China. Profits for the government and for some of the merchants were often as high as 20 or 30 per cent.

Further evidence of the significant economic development of the Hellenistic Age is to be found in the growth of finance. An international money economy, based upon gold and silver coins, now became general throughout the Near East. Banks, usually owned by the government, developed as the chief institutions of credit for

The concentration of land ownership

State regimentation of industry and trade

The growth of finance

business ventures of every description. Because of the abundance of capital, interest rates gradually declined from 12 per cent in the third century to 7 per cent in the second. Speculation, cornering of markets, intense competition, the growth of large business houses, and the development of insurance and advertising were other significant phenomena of this remarkable age.

According to the available evidence, the Hellenistic Age, during the first two centuries at least, was a period of prosperity. Although serious crises frequently followed the collapse of speculative booms, they appear to have been of short duration. But the prosperity that existed seems to have been limited chiefly to the rulers, the upper classes, and the merchants. It certainly did not extend to the peasants or even to the workers in the towns. The daily wages of both skilled and unskilled workers in Athens in the third century had dropped to less than half of what they had been in the Age of Pericles. The cost of living, on the other hand, had risen considerably. To make matters worse, unemployment in the large cities was so serious a problem that the government had to provide free grain for many of the inhabitants. Slavery declined in the Hellenistic world, partly because of the influence of the Stoic philosophy, but mainly for the reason that wages were now so low that it was cheaper to hire a free laborer than to purchase and maintain a slave.

An interesting result of social and economic conditions in the Hellenistic Age was the growth of metropolitan cities. Despite the fact that a majority of the people still lived in the country, there

The disparity between rich and poor

The growth of metropolitan cities

Hellenistic Coins. Obverse and reverse sides of the silver tetradrachma of Macedon, 336–323 B.C. Objects of common use from this period often show as much beauty of design as formal works of art.

was an increasing tendency for men to become dissatisfied with the dullness of rural living and to flock into the cities, where life, if not easier, was at least more exciting. But the chief reasons are to be found in the expansion of industry and commerce, in the enlargement of governmental functions, and in the desire of former independent farmers to escape the hardships of serfdom. Cities multiplied and grew in the Hellenistic empires almost as rapidly as in nineteenth- and twentieth-century America. Antioch in Syria quadrupled its population during a single century. Seleucia on the Tigris grew from nothing to a metropolis of several hundred thousand in less than two centuries. The largest and most famous of all the Hellenistic cities was Alexandria in Egypt, with over 500,000 inhabitants and possibly as many as 1,000,000. No other city in ancient times, not even Rome, surpassed it in size or in magnificence. Its streets were well paved and laid out in regular order. It had splendid public buildings and parks, a museum, and a library of 750,000 volumes. It was the most brilliant center of Hellenistic cultural achievement, especially in the field of scientific research. The masses of its people, however, were a disorganized mob without any share in the brilliant and luxurious life around them, although it was paid for in part out of the fruits of their labor.

3. HELLENISTIC CULTURE: PHILOSOPHY, LITERATURE, AND ART

Hellenistic philosophy exhibited two trends that ran almost parallel throughout the civilization. The major trend, exemplified by Stoicism and Epicureanism, showed a fundamental regard for reason as the key to the solution of man's problems. This trend was a manifestation of Greek influence, though philosophy and science, as combined in Aristotle, had now come to a parting of the ways. The minor trend, exemplified by the Skeptics, Cynics, and various Oriental cults, tended to reject reason, to deny the possibility of attaining truth, and in some cases to turn toward mysticism and a reliance upon faith. Despite the differences in their teachings, the philosophers of the Hellenistic Age were generally agreed upon one thing: the necessity of finding some way of salvation for man from the hardships and evils of his existence.

Trends in philosophy

Epicureanism and Stoicism both originated about 300 B.C. The founders were, respectively, Epicurus (342–270) and Zeno (fl. after 300), who were residents of Athens; the former was born on the island of Samos, and the latter was a native of Cyprus, probably of Phoenician descent. Epicureanism and Stoicism had several features in common. Both were individualistic, concerned not with the welfare of society primarily, but with the good of the individual. Both were materialistic, denying categorically the existence of any spiritual substances; even divine beings and the soul

Epicureanism and Stoicism

255

were declared to be formed of matter. In Stoicism and Epicureanism alike there were definite elements of universalism, since both implied that men are the same the world over and recognized no distinctions between Greeks and "barbarians." Lastly, the two philosophies were similar in their doctrines that concepts and abstractions are nothing but names, that only particular things are real, and that all knowledge has its basis in sense perception.

The Stoics' pursuit of tranquillity of mind through fatalism

But in many ways the two systems were quite different. Zeno and his principal disciples taught that the cosmos is an ordered whole in which all contradictions are resolved for ultimate good. Evil is, therefore, relative; the particular misfortunes which befall human beings are but necessary incidents to the final perfection of the universe. Everything that happens is rigidly determined in accordance with rational purpose. Man is not master of his fate; his destiny is a link in an unbroken chain. He is free only in the sense that he can accept his fate or rebel against it. But whether he accepts or rebels, he cannot overcome it. The supreme duty of man is to submit to the order of the universe in the knowledge that that order is good; in other words, to resign himself as graciously as possible to his fate. Through such an act of resignation he will attain to the highest happiness, which consists in tranquillity of mind. The individual who is most truly happy is therefore the man who by the assertion of his rational nature has accomplished a perfect adjustment of his life to the cosmic purpose and has purged his soul of all bitterness and whining protest against evil turns of fortune.

The ethical and social teachings of the Stoics

The Stoics developed an ethical and social theory that accorded well with their general philosophy described above. Believing that the highest good consists in serenity of mind, they naturally emphasized duty and self-discipline as cardinal virtues. Recognizing the prevalence of particular evil, they taught that men should be tolerant and forgiving in their attitudes toward one another. Unlike their contemporaries, the Cynics, they did not recommend that man should withdraw from society but urged participation in public affairs as a duty for the citizen of rational mind. They condemned slavery and war, but it was far from their purpose to preach any crusade against these evils. They were disposed to think that the results that would flow from violent measures of social change would be worse than the diseases they were supposed to cure. Besides, what difference did it make if the body were in bondage so long as the mind was free? Despite its negative character, the Stoic philosophy was the noblest product of the Hellenistic Age. Its equalitarianism, pacifism, and humanitarianism were important factors in mitigating the harshness not only of that time but of later centuries as well.

Whereas the Stoics went back to Heracleitus for much of their conception of the universe, the Epicureans derived their metaphysics chiefly from Democritus. Epicurus taught that the basic ingredients of all things are minute, indivisible atoms, and that change and growth are the results of the combination and separation of these particles. Nevertheless, while accepting the materialism of the atomists, Epicurus rejected their absolute mechanism. He denied that an automatic, mechanical motion of the atoms can be the cause of all things in the universe. Though he taught that the atoms move downward in perpendicular lines because of their weight, he insisted upon endowing them with a spontaneous ability to swerve from the perpendicular and thereby to combine with one another. The chief reason for this peculiar modification of the atomic theory was to make possible a belief in human freedom. If the atoms were capable only of mechanical motion, then man, who is made up of atoms, would be reduced to the status of an automaton, and fatalism would be the law of the universe. In this repudiation of the mechanistic interpretation of life, Epicurus was probably closer to the Hellenic spirit than either Democritus or the Stoics.

Epicurus and non-mechanistic atomism

The ethical philosophy of the Epicureans was based upon the doctrine that the highest good for man is pleasure. But they did not include all forms of indulgence in the category of genuine pleasure. The so-called pleasures of the debauched man should be avoided, since every excess of carnality must be balanced by its portion of pain. On the other hand, a moderate satisfaction of bodily appetites is permissible and may be regarded as a good in itself. Better than this is mental pleasure, sober contemplation of the reasons for the choice of some things and the avoidance of others, and mature reflection upon satisfactions previously enjoyed. The highest of all pleasures, however, consists in serenity of soul, in the complete absence of both mental and physical pain. This end can be best achieved through the elimination of fear, especially fear of the supernatural, since that is the sovereign source of mental pain. Man must recognize from the study of philosophy that the soul is material and therefore cannot survive the body, that the universe operates of itself, and that the gods do not intervene in human affairs. The gods live remote from the world and are too intent upon their own happiness to bother about what takes place on earth. Since they do not reward or punish men either in this life or in a life to come, there is no reason why they should be feared. The Epicureans thus came by a different route to the same general conclusion as the Stoics—the supreme good is tranquillity of mind.

The Epicurean pursuit of tranquillity of mind through overcoming fear of the supernatural

The ethics of the Epicureans as well as their political theory rested squarely upon a utilitarian basis. In contrast with the Stoics, they did not insist upon virtue as an end in itself but taught that the only reason why man should be good is to increase his own happiness. In like manner, they denied that there is any such thing as absolute justice; laws and institutions are just only in so far as they contribute to the welfare of the individual. Certain rules have been found necessary in every complex society for the maintenance of

The ethical and political theories of the Epicureans

security and order. Men obey these rules solely because it is to their advantage to do so. Thus the origin and existence of the state are rooted directly in self-interest. Generally speaking, Epicurus held no high regard for either political or social life. He considered the state as a mere convenience and taught that the wise man should take no active part in public life. Unlike the Cynics, he did not propose that man should abandon civilization and return to nature; yet his conception of the happiest life was essentially passive and defeatist. The wise man will recognize that he cannot eradicate the evils in the world no matter how strenuous and intelligent his efforts; he will therefore withdraw to "cultivate his garden," study philosophy, and enjoy the fellowship of a few congenial friends.

The defeatist
philosophy of the
Skeptics

A more radically defeatist philosophy was that propounded by the Skeptics. Although Skepticism was founded by Pyrrho, a contemporary of Zeno and Epicurus, it did not reach the zenith of its popularity until about a century later under the influence of Carneades (214–129 B.C.). The chief source of inspiration of the Skeptics was the Sophist teaching that all knowledge is derived from sense perception and therefore must be limited and relative. From this they deduced the conclusion that we cannot prove anything. Since the impressions of our senses deceive us, no truth can be certain. All we can say is that things *appear* to be such and such; we do not know what they really *are*. We have no definite knowledge of the supernatural, of the meaning of life, or even of right and wrong. It follows that the sensible course to pursue is suspension of judgment; this alone can lead to happiness. If man will abandon the fruitless quest for absolute truth and cease worrying about good and evil, he will attain that equanimity of mind which is the highest satisfaction that life affords. Carneades, however, taught that this did not necessarily mean inaction. Though we cannot discover ultimate truth, there is, he maintained, "probable" evidence resulting from "the persuasiveness of sensations," which provides a reliable guide for decision and action in all ordinary cases. The Skeptics were even less concerned than the Epicureans with political and social problems. Their ideal was the typically Hellenistic one of escape for the individual from a world he could neither understand nor reform.

The nonrational trend in Hellenistic thought reached its farthest extreme in the philosophies of Philo Judaeus and the Neo-Pythagoreans in the last century B.C. and the first century A.D. The proponents of the two systems were in general agreement as to their basic teachings, especially in their predominantly religious viewpoint. They believed in a transcendent God so far removed from the world as to be utterly unknowable to mortal minds. They conceived the universe as being sharply divided between spirit and matter. They considered everything physical and material as evil; man's soul is imprisoned in his body, from which an escape can be effected only through rigorous denial and mortification of the flesh. Their

The new religious
philosophies

attitude was mystical and nonintellectual: truth comes neither from science nor from reason but from revelation. Philo maintained that the books of the Old Testament were of absolute divine authority and contained all truth; the ultimate aim in life is to accomplish a mystic union with God, to lose one's self in the divine. Both Philo and the Neo-Pythagoreans influenced the development of Christian theology—Philo, in particular, with his dualism of matter and spirit and his doctrine of the Logos, or highest intermediary between God and the universe.

Hellenistic literature is significant mainly for the light it throws upon the character of the civilization. Most of the writings showed little originality or depth of thought. But they poured forth from the hands of the copyists in a profusion that is almost incredible when we consider that the art of printing by movable type was unknown. The names of at least 1100 authors have been discovered already, and more are being added from year to year. Much of what they wrote was trash, comparable to some of the cheap novels of our own day. Nevertheless, there were several works of more than mediocre quality and a few which met the highest standards ever set by the Greeks.

The leading types of Hellenistic poetry were the drama, the pastoral, and the mime. Drama was almost exclusively comedy, represented mainly by the plays of Menander. His plays were entirely different from the comedy of Aristophanes. They were distinguished by naturalism rather than by satire, by preoccupation with the seamy side of life rather than with political or intellectual issues. Their dominant theme was romantic love, with its pains and pleasures, its intrigues and seductions, and its culmination in happy marriage. The greatest author of pastorals and mimes was Theocritus of Syracuse, who wrote in the first half of the third century B.C. His pastorals, as the name implies, celebrate the charm of life in the country and idealize the simple pleasures of rustic folk. The mimes, on the other hand, portray in colorful dialogue the squabbles, ambitions, and varied activities of the bourgeoisie in the great metropolitan cities.

The field of prose literature was dominated by the historians, the biographers, and the authors of utopias. By far the ablest of the writers of history was Polybius of Megalopolis, who lived during the second century B.C. From the standpoint of his scientific approach and his zeal for truth, he probably deserves to be ranked second only to Thucydides among all the historians in ancient times; but he excelled Thucydides in his grasp of the importance of social and economic forces. Although most of the biographies were of a light and gossipy character, their tremendous popularity bears eloquent testimony to the literary tastes of the time. Even more significant was the popularity of the utopias, or descriptive accounts of ideal states. Virtually all of them depicted a life of social and eco-

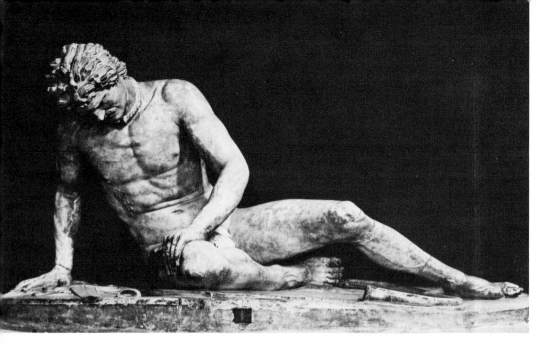

The Dying Gaul. A good example of Hellenistic realism in sculpture, which often reflected a preoccupation with the morbid and sensational. Every detail of the warrior's agony is dramatically portrayed. Now in the Capitoline Museum, Rome.

nomic equality, free from greed, oppression, and strife, on an imaginary island or in some distant, unfamiliar region. Generally in these paradises money was considered to be unknown, trade was prohibited, all property was held in common, and all men were required to work with their hands in producing the necessaries of life. We are probably justified in assuming that the profusion of this utopian literature was a direct result of the evils and injustices of Hellenistic society and a consciousness of the need for reform.

Hellenistic art

Hellenistic art did not preserve all of the characteristic qualities of the art of the Greeks. In place of the humanism, balance, and restraint which had distinguished the architecture and sculpture of the Golden Age, qualities of exaggerated realism, sensationalism, and voluptuousness now became dominant. The simple and dignified Doric and Ionic temples gave way to luxurious palaces, costly mansions, and elaborate public buildings and monuments symbolical of power and wealth. A typical example was the great lighthouse of Alexandria, which rose to a height of nearly 400 feet, with three diminishing stories and eight columns to support the light at the top. Sculpture likewise exhibited tendencies in the direction of extravagance and sentimentality. Many of the statues and figures in relief were huge and some of them almost grotesque. Violent emotionalism and exaggerated realism were features common to the majority. Among the examples of this type of sculpture may be mentioned the *Laocoön* and the frieze of the Great Altar of Zeus at Pergamum

See color plate at page 264

with its giant gods, ferocious animals, and hybrid monsters mingled in desperate combat to symbolize the struggle of Greeks with Gauls. But by no means all of Hellenistic sculpture was overwrought and grotesque. Some of it was distinguished by a calmness and poise and compassion for human suffering reminiscent of the best work of the great fourth-century artists. Statues which exemplify these superior qualities include the *Aphrodite of Melos* (*Venus de Milo*) and the *Winged Victory of Samothrace*.

4. THE FIRST GREAT AGE OF SCIENCE

The most brilliant age in the history of science prior to the seventeenth century A.D. was the period of the Hellenistic civilization. Indeed, many of the achievements of the modern age would scarcely have been possible without the discoveries of the scientists of Alexandria, Syracuse, Pergamum, and other great cities of the Hellenistic world. The reasons for the phenomenal development of science in the centuries after the downfall of Alexander's empire are not far to seek. Alexander himself had given some financial encouragement to the progress of research. More important was the stimulus provided for intellectual inquiry by the fusion of Chaldean and Egyptian science with the learning of the Greeks. Possibly a third factor was the new interest in luxury and comfort and the demand for practical

The Winged Victory of Samothrace. In this figure and in the *Venus de Milo*, Hellenistic sculptors preserved some of the calmness and devotion to grace and proportion characteristic of Hellenic art in the Golden Age. Now in the Louvre.

knowledge which would enable man to solve the problems of a disordered and unsatisfying existence.

The sciences which received major attention in the Hellenistic Age were astronomy, mathematics, geography, medicine, and physics. Chemistry, aside from metallurgy, was practically unknown. Except for the work of Theophrastus, who was the first to recognize the sexuality of plants, biology was also largely neglected. Neither chemistry nor biology bore any definite relationship to trade or to the forms of industry then in existence, and apparently they were not regarded as having much practical value.

The most renowned of the earlier astronomers of this time was Aristarchus of Samos (310–230 B.C.), who is sometimes called the "Hellenistic Copernicus." His chief title to fame comes from his deduction that the earth and the other planets revolve around the sun. Unfortunately this deduction was not accepted by his successors. It conflicted with the teachings of Aristotle and with the anthropocentric ideas of the Greeks. Besides, it was not in harmony with the beliefs of the Jews and other Orientals who made up so large a percentage of the Hellenistic population. The only other astronomer of much importance in the Hellenistic Age was Hipparchus, who did his most valuable work in Alexandria in the latter half of the second century B.C. His chief contributions were the invention of the astrolabe, the approximately correct calculation of the diameter of the moon and its distance from the earth, and the discovery of the precession of the equinoxes. His fame was eventually overshadowed, however, by the reputation of Ptolemy of Alexandria, the last of the Hellenistic astronomers. Although Ptolemy made few original discoveries, he systematized the work of others. His principal writing, the *Almagest*, based upon the geocentric theory, was handed down to medieval Europe as the classic summary of ancient astronomy.

Closely allied with astronomy were two other sciences, mathematics and geography. The Hellenistic mathematician of greatest renown was, of course, Euclid (*ca.* 323–*ca.* 285 B.C.), erroneously considered the founder of geometry. Until the middle of the nineteenth century his *Elements of Geometry* remained the accepted basis for the study of that branch of mathematics. Much of the material in this work was not original but was a synthesis of the discoveries of others. The most original of the Hellenistic mathematicians was probably Hipparchus, who laid the foundations of both plane and spherical trigonometry. Hellenistic geography owed most of its development to Eratosthenes (*ca.* 276–*ca.* 195 B.C.), astronomer, poet, philologist, and librarian of Alexandria. By means of sun dials placed some hundreds of miles apart, he calculated the circumference of the earth with an error of less than 200 miles. He produced the most accurate map that had yet been devised, with the surface of the earth divided into degrees of latitude and longitude. He propounded the theory that all of the oceans are really one, and he was the first to suggest the possibility of reaching India by sailing west. One of his successors divided the earth into the five climatic zones which are still recognized, and explained the ebb and flow of the tides as due to the influence of the moon.

Perhaps none of the Hellenistic advances in science surpassed in importance the progress in medicine. Especially significant was the work of Herophilus of Chalcedon, who conducted his researches in Alexandria about the beginning of the second century. Without question he was the greatest anatomist of antiquity and, according to Galen, the first to practice human dissection. Among his most important achievements were a detailed description of the brain, with an attempt to distinguish between the functions of its various parts; the discovery of the significance of the pulse and its use in diagnosing illness; and the discovery that the arteries contain blood alone, not a mixture of blood and air as Aristotle had taught, and that their function is to carry blood from the heart to all parts of the body. The value of this last discovery in laying the basis for a knowledge of the circulation of the blood can hardly be overestimated.

The ablest of the colleagues of Herophilus was Erasistratus, who flourished in Alexandria about the middle of the third century. He is considered the founder of physiology as a separate science. Not only did he practice dissection, but he is believed to have gained a great deal of his knowledge of bodily functions from vivisection. He discovered the valves of the heart, distinguished between motor and sensory nerves, and taught that the ultimate branches of the arteries and veins are connected. He was the first to reject absolutely the humoral theory of disease and to condemn excessive blood-letting as a method of cure. Unfortunately this theory was revived by Galen, the great encyclopedist of medicine who lived in the Roman Empire in the second century A.D.

Prior to the third century B.C. physics had been a branch of philosophy. It was made a separate experimental science by Archimedes of Syracuse (ca. 287–212 B.C.). Archimedes discovered the law of floating bodies, or specific gravity, and formulated with scientific exactness the principles of the lever, the pulley, and the screw. Among his memorable inventions were the compound pulley, the tubular screw for pumping water, the screw propeller for ships, and the burning lens. Although he has been called the "technical Yankee of antiquity," there is evidence that he set no high value upon his ingenious mechanical contraptions and preferred to devote his time to pure scientific research.

Certain other individuals in the Hellenistic Age were quite willing to give all their attention to applied science. Preeminent among them was Hero or Heron of Alexandria, who lived in the last century B.C. The record of inventions credited to him almost passes belief. The list includes a fire engine, a siphon, a jet engine, a hydraulic organ, a slot machine, a catapult operated by compressed air, a

263

thermoscope, and even a steam engine. How many of these inventions were really his own is impossible to say, but there appears to be no question that such contrivances were actually in existence in his time or soon thereafter. Nevertheless, the total progress in applied science was comparatively slight, probably for the reason that human labor continued to be so abundant and cheap that it was not worthwhile to substitute the work of machines.

5. RELIGION IN THE HELLENISTIC AGE

The new trend in
religion

If there was one aspect of the Hellenistic civilization which served more than others to accent the contrast with Hellenic culture, it was the new trend in religion. The civic religion of the Greeks as it was in the age of the city-states had now almost entirely disappeared. For the majority of the intellectuals its place was taken by the philosophies of Stoicism, Epicureanism, and Skepticism. Some who were less philosophically inclined turned to the worship of Fortune or became followers of dogmatic atheism.

The popularity of
mystic religions

Among the masses a tendency to embrace emotional religions was even more clearly manifest. The Orphic and Eleusinian mystery cults attracted more votaries than ever before. The worship of the Egyptian mother-goddess Isis threatened for a time to become dominant throughout the Near Orient. The astral religion of the Chaldeans likewise spread rapidly, with the result that its chief product, astrology, was received with fanatical enthusiasm throughout the Hellenistic world. But the most powerful influence of all came from the offshoots of Zoroastrianism, especially from Mithraism and Gnosticism. While all of the cults of Oriental origin resembled each other in their promises of salvation in a life to come, Mithraism and Gnosticism had a more ethically significant mythology, a deeper contempt for this world, and a more clearly defined doctrine of redemption through a personal savior. These were the ideas which satisfied the emotional cravings of the common people, convinced as they were of the worthlessness of this life and ready to be lured by extravagant promises of better things in a world to come. If we can judge by conditions in our own time, some of the doctrines of these cults must have exerted their influence upon members of the upper classes also. Even the most casual observer of modern society knows that pessimism, mysticism, and otherworldliness are not confined to the downtrodden. In some cases the keenest disgust with this life and the deepest mystical yearnings are to be found among those whose pockets bulge with plenty.

The influence of
the Jews

A factor by no means unimportant in the religious developments of the Hellenistic Age was the dispersion of the Jews. As a result of Alexander's conquest of Palestine in 332 B.C. and the Roman conquest about three centuries later, thousands of Jews migrated to

264 various sections of the Mediterranean world. It has been estimated

Bronze Mirror Case, V cent. B.C. Greek articles of everyday use were commonly finished with the same delicacy and precision as major works of art.

Diadoumenos, after Polykleitos, V cent. B.C. An idealized statue of a Greek athlete tying the "diadem," or band of victory, around his head.

Bracelet Pendant, IV–III cent. B.C. This tiny figure of the god Pan is a masterpiece of detail and expression.

Woman Arranging Her Hair, 400–300 B.C. Sculptors of antiquity took pride in these statuettes of ordinary people in ordinary activities, which were usually made of terra cotta painted soft blue, pink, or yellow.

Head of an Athlete, *ca.* 440–420 B.C. The sculptor aimed to express manly beauty in perfect harmony with physical and intellectual excellence.

Comic Actor, 200–100 B.C. Hellenistic realism often included portrayal of ugly and even deformed individuals.

Sleeping Eros, 250–150 B.C. Along with a penchant for realism, Hellenistic sculptors were fond of portraying serenity or repose.

Statuette of Hermarchos, III cent. B.C. An example of the realism of Hellenistic sculpture.

All pictures courtesy MMA.

Unidentified Man, I cent. B.C. The Romans excelled in portraits of sharp individuality.

Augustus, Reigned 31 B.C.–14 A.D. This portrait suggests the contradictory nature of the genius who gave Rome peace after years of strife.

Constantine, Reigned 306–337 A.D. The head is from a statue sixteen feet in height. Such coloss marked the decline of Roman sculpture.

Wall Painting, I cent. B.C. From a villa near Pompeii.

Mosaic, I cent. A.D. A floor design composed of small pieces of colored marble fitted together to form a picture.

Wall Painting of a Satyr Mask, I cent. B.C. The belief in satyrs, thought to inhabit forests and pastures, was taken over from the Greeks.

Mummy Portrait, II cent. A.D. A Roman woman buried in Egypt.

Architectural Wall Painting from a Pompeiian Villa, I cent. B.C. suggesting the Greek origin o Roman forms of architecture.

that 1,000,000 of them lived in Egypt in the first century A.D. and 200,000 in Asia Minor. They mingled freely with other peoples, adopting the Greek language and no small amount of the Hellenic culture which still survived from earlier days. At the same time they played a major part in the diffusion of Oriental beliefs. Their religion had already taken on a spiritual and messianic character as a result of Persian influence. Their leading philosopher of this time, Philo Judaeus of Alexandria, developed a body of doctrine representing the farthest extreme which mysticism had yet attained. Many of the Hellenistic Jews eventually became converts to Christianity and were largely instrumental in the spread of that religion outside of Palestine. A notable example, of course, was Saul of Tarsus, known in Christian history as the Apostle Paul.

6.   A FORETASTE OF MODERNITY?

With the possible exception of the Roman, no great culture of ancient times appears to suggest the spirit of the modern age quite so emphatically as does the Hellenistic civilization. Here as in the world of the twentieth century were to be found a considerable variety of forms of government, the growth of militarism, a decline of respect for democracy, and a trend in the direction of authoritarian rule. Many of the characteristic economic and social developments of the Hellenistic Age are equally suggestive of contemporary experience: the growth of big business, the expansion of trade,

Hellenistic civilization compared with that of the modern age

Statue of an Old Market Woman. In the Hellenistic Age the idealism and restraint of Hellenic art were succeeded by a tendency to portray the humble aspects of life and to express compassion for human suffering. Original in the Metropolitan Museum of Art, New York.

the zeal for exploration and discovery, the interest in mechanical inventions, the devotion to comfort and the craze for material prosperity, the growth of metropolitan cities with congested slums, and the widening gulf between rich and poor. In the realms of intellect and art the Hellenistic civilization also bore a distinctly modern flavor. This was exemplified by the exaggerated emphasis upon science, the narrow specialization of learning, the penchant for realism and naturalism, the vast production of mediocre literature, and the popularity of mysticism side by side with extreme skepticism and dogmatic unbelief.

Because of these resemblances there has been a tendency among certain writers to regard our own civilization as decadent. But this is based partly upon the false assumption that the Hellenistic culture was merely a degenerate phase of Greek civilization. Instead, it was a new social and cultural organism born of a fusion of Greek and Oriental elements. Moreover, the differences between the Hellenistic civilization and that of the contemporary world are perhaps just as important as the resemblances. The Hellenistic political outlook was essentially cosmopolitan; nothing comparable to the national patriotism of modern times really prevailed. Despite the remarkable expansion of trade in the Hellenistic Age, no industrial revolution ever took place, for reasons which have already been noted. Finally, Hellenistic science was somewhat more limited than that of the present day. Modern pure science is to a very large extent a species of philosophy—an adventure of the mind in the realm of the unknown. Notwithstanding frequent assertions to the contrary, much of it is gloriously impractical and will probably remain so.

SELECTED READINGS

· *Items so designated are available in paperbound editions.*

· Burn, A. R., *Alexander the Great and the Hellenistic World*, New York, 1962 (Collier).

· Bury, J. B., and others, *The Hellenistic Age*, New York, 1923.

Cary, Max, *The Legacy of Alexander: A History of the Greek World from 323 to 146 B.C.*, New York, 1932.

· Clagett, Marshall, *Greek Science in Antiquity*, New York, 1963 (Collier).

Festugière, A. J., *Epicurus and His Gods*, Cambridge, Mass., 1956.

· Finley, M. I., *The Ancient Greeks: An Introduction to Their Life and Thought*, New York, 1963 (Compass).

· Grant, F. C., *Hellenistic Religions*, New York, 1963 (Library of Liberal Arts).

Hadas, Moses, *Hellenistic Culture*, New York, 1959.

· Hamilton, Edith, *The Echo of Greece*, New York, 1964 (Norton Library).

· Larsen, J. A. O., *Representative Government in Greek and Roman History*, Berkeley, 1955 (University of California).

Robinson, C. A., Jr., *Alexander the Great*, New York, 1947.

Rostovtzev, M. I., *Social and Economic History of the Hellenistic World*, Oxford, 1941, 3 vols. Detailed but well written.

Starr, C. G., *A History of the Ancient World*, New York, 1964.
· Tarn, W. W., *Alexander the Great*, Boston, 1956 (Beacon).
· ———, *Hellenistic Civilization*, New York, 1952 (Meridian).
  Vermeule, Emily, *Greece in the Bronze Age*, Chicago, 1964.
· Wilcken, Ulrich, *Alexander the Great*, New York, 1967 (Norton Library).

SOURCE MATERIALS

Greek source materials for the Hellenistic period are available in the appropriate volumes of the Loeb Classical Library, Harvard University Press.

CHAPTER 11

Roman Civilization

Like Hercules, citizens, they said just now
He had sought the laurel at the cost of death:
Returning from Spain, seeking his household gods,
    Caesar has conquered.

After sacrifice to the just gods, let his
wife come forth, happy for her matchless husband,
And the sister of our famous leader, and,
    Wearing the bands of

Suppliants, mothers of young men and maidens
Who are now safe . . .
          —Horace, *Odes*, III,xiv

Long before the glory of Greece had begun to fade, another civilization, derived in large measure from that of the Greeks, had started its growth on the banks of the Tiber in Italy. In fact, by the time the Greeks had entered their Golden Age, Rome was already a dominant power on the Italian peninsula. For more than six centuries thereafter her might increased, and she still maintained her supremacy over the civilized world when the glory of Greece was no more than a memory. *The rise of Rome*

But the Romans never equaled the Greeks in intellectual or artistic accomplishments. The reasons may have been partly geographic. Except for some excellent marble and small quantities of copper, gold, and iron, Italy has no mineral resources. Her extensive coast line is broken by only two good harbors, Tarentum and Naples. On the other hand, the amount of her fertile land is much larger than that of Greece. As a consequence, the Romans were practically destined to remain a predominantly agrarian people through the greater part of their history. They never enjoyed the intellectual stimulus which comes from extensive trading with other nations. In addition, the topography of Italy is such that the peninsula was more easily accessible to invasion than was Greece. The Alps opposed no effec- *Why Roman civilization was generally inferior to that of the Greeks* tual barrier to the influx of peoples from central Europe, and the low-lying coast in many places invited conquest by sea. As a result, domination of the country by force was more common than peaceful intermingling of immigrants with original settlers. The Romans became absorbed in military pursuits almost from the moment of their settlement on Italian soil, for they were forced to defend their own conquests against other invaders.

1. FROM THE BEGINNING TO THE OVERTHROW OF THE MONARCHY

Archaeological evidence indicates that Italy was inhabited at least as far back as the Upper Paleolithic Age. At this time the territory was occupied by a people closely related to the Cro-Magnon race of southern France. In the Neolithic period people of Mediterranean stock entered the land, some coming in from northern Africa and others from Spain and Gaul. The beginning of the Bronze Age witnessed several new invasions. From the lake country north of the Alps came the first of the immigrants of the Indo-European language group. They were herdsmen and farmers, who brought the horse and the wheeled cart into Italy. Their culture was based upon the use of bronze, although after 1000 B.C. they appear to have acquired a knowledge of iron. These Indo-European invaders seem to have been the ancestors of most of the so-called Italic peoples, including the Romans. Racially they were probably related to the Hellenic invaders of Greece.

Probably during the eighth century B.C. two other nations of immigrants occupied different portions of the Italian peninsula: the Etruscans and the Greeks. Where the Etruscans came from is a question which has never been satisfactorily answered. Most authorities believe that they were natives of some part of the Near Orient, probably Asia Minor. Although their writing has never been completely deciphered, enough materials survive to indicate the nature of their culture. They had an alphabet based upon the Greek, a high degree of skill in the metallurgical arts, a flourishing trade with the East, and a religion based upon the worship of gods in human form. They bequeathed to the Romans a knowledge of the arch and the vault, the practice of divination, and the cruel amusement of gladiatorial combats. The Etruscans established a great empire in the sixth century that included Latium, the Po valley, and Campania. The Greeks located mainly along the southern and southwestern shores of Italy and on the island of Sicily. Their most important settlements were Tarentum, Syracuse, and Naples, each of which was an entirely independent city-state. From the Greeks the Romans derived their alphabet, a number of their religious concepts, and much of their art and mythology.

The actual founders of Rome were Italic peoples who lived in the

ETRUSCAN ART
AND ARTIFACTS

Top left *Busts of Jove.* Etruscan art is often considered independent, but influences from Greece and the Near East are clearly discernible.

Top right *Bronze Cauldron on Iron Tripod.* Found in Regalini-Galassi tomb, Cerveteri.

Votive Chariot. Chariot racing, was much the vogue among the Etruscans.

Etruscan Art. Typical scene on sarcophagus shows preparations for funeral. Etruscans often depicted social events, sports, funeral banquets, and processions, either in painting or relief, on their tombs.

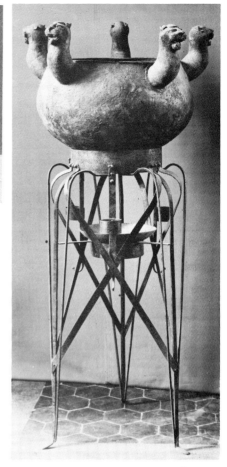

district of Latium south of the Tiber River. Though the exact year of the founding of the city is unknown, recent archaeological research places the event quite near the traditional date of 753 B.C. Latium included a number of towns, but Rome, by reason of its strategic location, soon came to exercise an effective suzerainty over several of the most important of them. One conquest followed another until, by the end of the sixth century B.C., the territory dominated by the Roman state was probably coextensive with the whole Latin plain from the slopes of the Apennines to the Mediterranean Sea.

The political evolution of Rome in this early period resembled in some ways the governmental development of the Greek communities in the formative stage of their history. But it was far from being the same. The Romans appear from the first to have had a much stronger interest in authority and stability than in liberty or democracy. Their state was essentially an application of the idea of the patriarchal family to the whole community, with the king exercising a jurisdiction over his subjects comparable to that of the head of the family over the members of his household. But just as the authority of the father was limited by custom and by the requirement that he respect the wishes of his adult sons, the sovereignty of the king was limited by the ancient constitution, which he was powerless to change without the consent of the chief men of the realm. His prerogatives were not primarily legislative but executive and judicial. He punished men for infractions of order, usually by infliction of the death penalty or by flogging. He judged all civil and criminal cases, but he had no authority to pardon without the consent of the assembly. Although his accession to office had to be confirmed by the people, he could not be deposed, and there was no one who could really challenge the exercise of his regal powers.

In addition to the kingship the Roman government of this time included an assembly and a Senate. The former was composed of all the male citizens of military age. As one of the chief sources of sovereign power, according to the theory, this body had an absolute veto on any proposal for a change in the law which the king might make. Besides, it determined whether pardons should be granted and whether aggressive war should be declared. But it was essentially a ratifying body with no right to initiate legislation or recommend changes of policy. Its members could not even speak except when invited to do so by the king. The Senate, or council of elders, comprised in its membership the heads of the various clans which formed the community. Even more than the common citizens, the rulers of the clans embodied the sovereign power of the state. The king was only one of their number to whom they had delegated the active exercise of their authority. When the royal office became vacant, the powers of the king immediately reverted to the Senate until the succession of a new monarch had been confirmed by the

The government
of Rome under
the monarchy;
the powers of the
king

people. In ordinary times the chief function of the Senate was to examine proposals of the king which had been ratified by the assembly and to veto them if they violated rights established by ancient custom. It was thus almost impossible for fundamental changes to be made in the law even when the majority of the citizens were ready to sanction them. This extremely conservative attitude of the ruling classes persisted until the end of Roman history.

Toward the end of the sixth century B.C. senatorial jealousy of the kings increased to such a point that the monarchy was overthrown and an oligarchic republic set up. While the real nature of this revolution was doubtless a movement of the aristocracy to gain supreme power for itself, factors of nationalism may also have played some part in it. Tradition relates that the last of the Roman kings was an Etruscan, whose family, the Tarquins, had usurped the royal office some years before. The Romans of later centuries described in lurid fashion the wicked deeds of these rulers and implied that the overthrow of the monarchy was due primarily to a revolt against alien oppressors. In any event the Etruscan empire was already in a state of decay. Its collapse made easier the establishment of Roman dominance in Italy.

The overthrow of the monarchy

2. THE EARLY REPUBLIC

The history of the Roman Republic for more than two centuries after its establishment was one of almost constant warfare. The causes which led to the series of conflicts are not easy to untangle. It is possible that the overthrow of the Tarquins resulted in acts of reprisal by their kinsmen in neighboring countries. It is conceivable also that other nations on the borders took advantage of the confusion accompanying the revolution to slice off portions of Roman territory. But doubtless the compelling reason was desire for more land. The Romans were already a proud and aggressive people with a rapidly growing population. As the number of the inhabitants increased, the need for outlets into new territory became ever more urgent. Their final conquests included the Greek cities in the southernmost portion of Italy. Not only did these add to the Roman domain, but they also brought the Romans into fruitful contact with Greek culture. The Romans were then frequently confronted with revolts of peoples previously conquered: the Aequi, the Volsci, and several of the Latin nations. The suppression of these revolts awakened the suspicions of surrounding states and sharpened the appetite of the victors for further triumphs. New wars followed each other in what seemed an unending succession, until by 265 B.C. Rome had conquered the entire Italian peninsula, with the exception of the Po valley.

The origins of Roman imperialism

This long series of military conflicts had profound social and economic effects upon the subsequent history of Rome. It affected adversely the interests of the poorer citizens and furthered the concentration of land in the possession of wealthy proprietors. Long service in the army forced the ordinary farmers to neglect the cultivation of the soil, with the result that they fell into debt and frequently lost their farms. Many took refuge in the city, until they were settled later as tenants on great estates in the conquered territories. The wars had the effect also of confirming the agrarian character of the Roman nation. The repeated acquisition of new lands made it possible to absorb the entire population into agricultural pursuits. As a consequence there was no need for the development of industry and commerce as means of earning a livelihood. Lastly, as in the case of Sparta, the Roman wars of conquest enslaved the nation to the military ideal.

During this same period of the early Republic, Rome underwent some significant political changes. These were not products so much of the revolution of the sixth century as of the developments of later years. The revolution which overthrew the monarchy was about as conservative as it is possible for a revolution to be. Its chief effect was to substitute two elected consuls for the king and to exalt the position of the Senate by vesting it with control over the public funds and with a veto on all actions of the assembly. The consuls themselves were usually senators and acted as the agents of their class. They did not rule jointly, but each was supposed to possess the full executive and judicial authority which had previously been wielded by the king. If a conflict arose between them, the Senate might be called upon to decide; or, in time of grave emergency, a dictator might be appointed for a term not greater than six months. In other respects the government remained the same as in the days of the monarchy.

Not long after the establishment of the Republic a struggle began by the common citizens for a larger share of political power. Before the end of the monarchy the Roman population had come to be divided into two great classes—the patricians and the plebeians. The former were the aristocracy, wealthy landowners, who were apparently the descendants of the old clan leaders. They monopolized the seats in the Senate and the offices of magistracy. The plebeians were the common people—small farmers, craftsmen, and tradesmen. Many were clients or dependents of the patricians, obliged to fight for them, to render them political support, and to cultivate their estates in return for protection. The grievances of the plebeians were numerous. Compelled to pay heavy taxes and forced to serve in the army in time of war, they were nevertheless excluded from all part in the government except membership in the assembly. Moreover, they felt themselves the victims of discriminatory decisions in judicial trials. They did not even know what legal rights they were supposed to enjoy, for the laws were unwritten, and no

one but the consuls had the power to interpret them. In suits for debt the creditor was frequently allowed to sell the debtor into slavery. It was in order to obtain a redress of these grievances that the plebeians rebelled soon after the beginning of the fifth century B.C.

The plebeians gained their first victory about 470 B.C., when they forced the patricians to agree to the election of a number of tribunes with power to protect the citizens by means of a veto over unlawful acts of the magistrates. This victory was followed by a successful demand for codification of the laws about 450 B.C. The result was the publication of the famous Law of the Twelve Tables, so called because it was written on tablets of wood. Although the Twelve Tables came to be revered by the Romans of later times as a kind of charter of the people's liberties, they were really nothing of the sort. For the most part they merely perpetuated ancient custom without even abolishing enslavement for debt. They did, however, enable the people to know where they stood in relation to the law, and they permitted an appeal to the assembly against a magistrate's sentence of capital punishment. About a generation later the plebeians won eligibility to positions as lesser magistrates, and about 366 B.C. the first plebeian consul was elected. Since ancient custom provided that, upon completing their term of office, consuls should automatically enter the Senate, the patrician monopoly of seats in that body was broken. The final plebeian victory came in 287 B.C. with the passage of the Hortensian Law (named for the dictator Quintus Hortensius), which provided that measures enacted by the assembly should become binding upon the state whether the Senate approved them or not.

The victories of the plebeians

The significance of these changes must not be misinterpreted. They did not constitute a revolution to gain more liberty for the individual but merely to curb the power of the magistrates and to win for the common man a larger share in government. The state as a whole remained as despotic as ever, for its authority over the citizens was not even challenged. As Theodor Mommsen says, the Romans from the time of the Tarquins to that of the Gracchi "never really abandoned the principle that the people were not to govern but to be governed." [1] Because of this attitude the grant of full legislative powers to the assembly seems to have meant little more than a formality; the Senate continued to rule as before. Nor did the admission of plebeians to membership in the Senate have any effect in liberalizing that body. So high was its prestige and so deep was the veneration of the Roman for authority, that the new members were soon swallowed up in the conservatism of the old. Moreover, the fact that the magistrates received no salaries prevented most of the poorer citizens from seeking public office.

Significance of the Plebeian victories

Intellectually and socially the Romans appear to have made but slow advancement as yet. The times were still harsh and crude.

[1] *The History of Rome*, I. 313.

Though writing had been adopted as early as the sixth century, little use was made of it except for the copying of laws, treaties, and funerary inscriptions and orations. Inasmuch as education was limited to instruction imparted by the father in manly sports, practical arts, and soldierly virtues, probably the great majority of the people were still illiterate. War and agriculture continued as the chief occupations for the bulk of the citizens. A few craftsmen were to be found in the cities, and a minor development of trade had occurred, evidenced by the founding of a maritime colony at Ostia on the coast in the fourth century. But the comparative insignificance of Roman commerce at this time is pretty clearly revealed by the fact that the country had no standard system of coinage until 269 B.C.

The period of the early Republic was the period when the Roman religion assumed the character it was destined to retain through the greater part of the nation's history. In several ways this religion resembled the religion of the Greeks, partly for the reason that the Etruscan religion was deeply indebted to the Greek, and the Romans, in turn, were influenced by the Etruscans. Both the Greek and Roman religions were worldly and practical with neither spiritual nor ethical content. The relation of man to the gods was external and mechanical, partaking of the nature of a bargain or contract between two parties for their mutual advantage. The deities in both religions performed similar functions: Jupiter corresponded roughly to Zeus as god of the sky, Minerva to Athena as goddess of wisdom and patroness of craftsmen, Venus to Aphrodite as goddess of love, Neptune to Poseidon as god of the sea, and so on. The Roman religion no more than the Greek had any dogmas or sacraments or belief in rewards and punishments in an afterlife.

The religion of
the Romans com-
pared with that
of the Greeks

But there were significant differences also. The Roman religion was distinctly more political and less humanistic in purpose. It served not to glorify man or to make him feel at home in his world but to protect the state from its enemies and to augment its power and prosperity. The gods were less anthropomorphic; indeed, it was only as a result of Greek and Etruscan influences that they were made personal deities at all, having previously been worshiped as *numina* or animistic spirits. The Romans never conceived of their deities as quarreling among themselves or mingling with human beings after the fashion of the Homeric divinities. Finally, the Roman religion contained a much stronger element of priestliness than the Greek. The priests, or pontiffs as they were called, formed an organized class, a branch of the government itself. They not only supervised the offering of sacrifices, but they were guardians of an elaborate body of sacred traditions and laws which they alone could interpret. It must be understood, however, that these pontiffs were not priests in the sense of intermediaries between the individual Roman and his gods; they heard no confessions, forgave no sins, and administered no sacraments.

The morality of the Romans in this as in later periods had almost no connection with religion. The Roman did not ask his gods to make him good, but to bestow upon the community and upon his family material blessings. Morality was a matter of patriotism and of respect for authority and tradition. The chief virtues were bravery, honor, self-discipline, reverence for the gods and for one's ancestors, and duty to country and family. Loyalty to the state took precedence over everything else. For the good of the state the citizen must be ready to sacrifice not only his own life but, if necessary, the lives of his family and friends. The courage of certain consuls who dutifully put their sons to death for breaches of military discipline was a subject of profound admiration. Few peoples in European history with the exception of the Spartans and perhaps the modern Germans have ever taken the problems of national interest so seriously or subordinated the individual so completely to the good of the state.

Morality in the early Republic

3. THE FATEFUL WARS WITH CARTHAGE

By 265 B.C., as we have already learned, Rome had conquered and annexed the whole of Italy, except for the Po valley. Proud and confident of her strength, she was almost certain to strike out into new fields of empire. The prosperous island of Sicily was not yet within her grasp, nor could she regard with indifference the situation in other parts of the Mediterranean world. She was now prone to interpret almost any change in the *status quo* as a threat to her own power and security. It was for such reasons that Rome after 264 B.C. became involved in a series of wars with other great nations which decidedly altered the course of her history.

The beginning of imperialism on a major scale

The first and most important of these wars was the struggle with Carthage, a great maritime empire that stretched along the northern coast of Africa from Numidia to the Strait of Gibraltar. Carthage had originally been founded about 800 B.C. as a Phoenician colony. In the sixth century it severed its ties with the homeland and gradually developed into a rich and powerful nation. The prosperity of its upper classes was founded upon commerce and upon exploitation of the silver and tin resources of Spain and Britain and the tropical products of north central Africa. Conditions within the country were far from ideal. The Carthaginians appear to have had no conception of free and orderly government. Shameless bribery and cynical oppression of the masses were methods regularly employed by the plutocracy to maintain its dominant position. The form of government itself can best be described as an oligarchy. At the head of the system were two magistrates, or *suffetes*, who exercised powers approximating those of the Roman consuls. The real governors, however, were thirty merchant princes who constituted an inner council of the Senate. By methods constitutional and other-

Carthage

wise these men controlled elections and dominated every other branch of the government. The remaining 270 members of the Senate appear to have been summoned to meet only on special occasions. In spite of these political deficiencies and a gloomy and cruel religion, Carthage had a civilization superior in luxury and scientific attainment to that of Rome when the struggle between the two countries began.

The initial clash with Carthage began in 264 B.C.[2] The primary cause was Roman jealousy over Carthaginian expansion in Sicily. Carthage already controlled the western portion of the island and was threatening the Greek cities of Syracuse and Messana on the eastern coast. If these cities should be captured, all chances of Roman occupation of Sicily would be cut off. Faced with this danger, Rome declared war upon Carthage with the hope of forcing her back into her African domain. Twenty-three years of fighting finally brought victory to the Roman generals. Carthage was compelled to surrender her possessions in Sicily and to pay an indemnity of 3200 talents, or about 2½ million dollars at present silver prices.

Causes of the First Punic War

But the Romans were unable to stand the strain of this triumph. They had had to put forth such heroic efforts to win that when victory was finally secured it made them more arrogant and greedy than ever. As a result, the struggle with Carthage was renewed on two different occasions thereafter. In 218 B.C. the Romans interpreted the Carthaginian attempt to rebuild an empire in Spain as a threat to their interests and responded with a declaration of war. This struggle raged through a period of sixteen years. Italy was ravaged by the armies of Hannibal, the famous Carthaginian commander, whose tactics have been copied by military experts to the present day. Rome escaped defeat by the narrowest of margins. Only the durability of her system of alliances in Italy saved the day. As long as these alliances held, Hannibal dared not besiege the city of Rome itself for fear of being attacked from the rear. In the end Carthage was more completely humbled than before. She was compelled to abandon all her possessions except the capital city and its surrounding territory in Africa, and to pay an indemnity of 10,000 talents.

The Second Punic War

Roman vindictiveness and avarice reached their zenith about the middle of the second century B.C. By this time Carthage had recovered a modicum of her former prosperity—enough to excite the envy and fear of her conquerors. Nothing would now satisfy the senatorial magnates but the complete destruction of Carthage and the expropriation of her land. In 149 B.C. the Senate dispatched an ultimatum demanding that the Carthaginians abandon their city and settle at least ten miles from the coast. Since this demand was tanta-

The Third Punic War and the destruction of Carthage

---

[2] The wars with Carthage are known as the Punic Wars. The Romans called the Carthaginians *Poeni*, i.e., Phoenicians, whence is derived the adjective "Punic."

mount to a death sentence for a nation dependent upon commerce, it was refused—as the Romans probably hoped it would be. The result was the Third Punic War, which was fought between 149 and 146 B.C. Seldom has the world witnessed a more desperate and more barbarous struggle. The final assault upon the city was carried into the houses of the natives themselves, and a frightful butchery took place. When the resistance of the Carthaginians was finally broken, the few citizens who were left to surrender were sold into slavery, and their once magnificent city was razed to the ground. The land was organized into a Roman province with the best areas parceled out as senatorial estates.

The wars with Carthage had momentous effects upon Rome. First, they brought her into conflict with eastern Mediterranean powers and thereby paved the way for world dominion. During the Second Punic War, Philip V of Macedon had entered into an alliance with Carthage and had plotted with the king of Syria to divide Egypt between them. In order to punish Philip and to forestall the execution of his plans, Rome sent an army into the East. The result was the conquest of Greece and Asia Minor and the establishment of a protectorate over Egypt. Thus before the end of the second century B.C. virtually the entire Mediterranean area had been brought under Roman dominion. The conquest of the Hellenistic East led to the introduction of semi-Oriental ideas and customs into Rome. Despite formidable resistance, these ideas and customs exerted considerable influence in changing some aspects of social and cultural life.

Results of the wars with Carthage: (1) conquest of the Hellenistic East

By far the most important effect of the Punic Wars was a great social and economic revolution that swept over Rome in the third and second centuries B.C. The incidents of this revolution may be enumerated as follows: (1) a marked increase in slavery due to the capture and sale of prisoners of war; (2) the decline of the small farmer as a result of the establishment of the plantation system in conquered areas and the influx of cheap grain from the provinces; (3) the growth of a helpless city mob composed of impoverished farmers and workers displaced by slave labor; (4) the appearance of a middle class comprising merchants, moneylenders, and "publicans" or men who held government contracts to operate mines, build roads, or collect taxes; and (5) an increase in luxury and vulgar display, particularly among the *parvenus* who fattened on the profits of war.

(2) a social and economic revolution

As a consequence of this social and economic revolution, Rome was changed from a republic of yeoman farmers into a nation with a complex society and new habits of luxury and indulgence. Though property had never been evenly distributed, the gulf which separated rich and poor now yawned more widely than before. The old-fashioned ideals of discipline and devotion to the service of the state were sadly weakened, and men began to make pleasure and

The transformation of Roman Society

279

wealth their gods. A few members of the senatorial aristocracy exerted efforts to check the evil tendencies and to restore the homely virtues of the past. The eminent leader of this movement was Cato the Elder, who inveighed against the new rich for their soft living and strove to set an example to his countrymen by performing hard labor on his farm and dwelling in a house with a dirt floor and no plaster on the walls. But his efforts had little effect, perhaps because of his own inconsistencies. He fought everything new, the good as well as the evil. He staunchly defended slavery and condemned the humane philosophy of Stoicism. The rich continued to indulge their expensive tastes and to rival each other in vulgar consumption of wealth. At the same time public morality decayed. Tax gatherers plundered the provinces and used their illicit gains to purchase the votes of the poor. The anarchic masses in the city came to expect that politicians would feed them and provide for their amusement with ever more brutal shows. The total effect was so serious that some authorities date the beginning of Rome's decline from this period.[3]

4. THE STORM AND STRESS OF THE LATE REPUBLIC

The new period of turbulence

The period from the end of the Punic Wars in 146 B.C. to about 30 B.C. was one of the most turbulent in the history of Rome. It was between these years that the nation reaped the full harvest of the seeds of violence sown during the wars of conquest. Bitter class conflicts, assassinations, desperate struggles between rival dictators, wars, and insurrections were the all too common occurrences of this time. Even the slaves contributed their part to the general disorder: first, in 104 B.C. when they ravaged Sicily; and again in 73 B.C. when 70,000 of them under the leadership of Spartacus held the consuls at bay for more than a year. Spartacus was finally slain in battle and 6000 of his followers were captured and crucified.

The revolt of the Gracchi: the land program of Tiberius

The first stage in the conflict between classes of citizens began with the revolt of the Gracchi. The Gracchi were leaders of the liberal, pro-Hellenic elements in Rome and had the support of the middle classes and a number of influential senators as well. Though of aristocratic lineage themselves, they earnestly strove for a program of reforms to alleviate the country's ills. They considered these to be a result of the decline of the free peasantry, and proposed the simple remedy of dividing state lands among the landless. The first of the brothers to take up the cause of reform was Tiberius. Elected tribune in 133 B.C., he proposed a law that restricted the current renters or holders of state lands to a maximum of 620 acres. The excess was to be confiscated by the government and given to the poor in small plots. Conservative aristocrats bitterly

[3] See D. C. Somervell (ed.), A. J. Toynbee's *A Study of History*, I, 258.

opposed this proposal and brought about its veto by Tiberius' colleague in the tribunate, Octavius. Tiberius removed Octavius from office, and when his own term expired, determined to stand for re-election. Both of these moves were unconstitutional and gave the conservative senators an excuse for violence. Armed with clubs and legs of chairs, they went on a rampage during the elections and murdered Tiberius and 300 of his followers.

Nine years later Gaius Gracchus, the younger brother of Tiberius, renewed the struggle for reform. Though Tiberius' land law had finally been enacted by the Senate, Gaius believed that the crusade must go further. Elected tribune in 123 B.C., and reelected in 122, he procured the enactment of various laws for the benefit of the less privileged. The first provided for stabilizing the price of grain in Rome. For this purpose great public granaries were built along the Tiber River. A second law proposed to extend the franchise to Roman allies, giving them the rights of Latin citizens. Still a third gave the middle class the right to make up the juries that tried governors accused of exploiting the provinces. (It is not without significance that most of the governors were members of the middle class.) These and similar measures provoked so much anger and contention among the classes that civil war broke out. Gaius was proclaimed an enemy of the state, and the Senate authorized the consuls to take all necessary steps for the defense of the Republic. In the ensuing conflict Gaius and 3000 of his followers were killed.

The Gracchan revolt had a broad significance. It demonstrated, first of all, that the Roman Republic had outgrown its constitution. The assembly had gained, over the years, *de facto* powers almost equal to those of the Senate. Instead of working out a peaceful accommodation to these changes, both sides resorted to violence. By so doing they set a precedent for the unbridled use of force by any politician ambitious for supreme power and thereby paved the way for the destruction of the Republic. The Romans had shown a remarkable capacity for organizing an empire and for adapting the Greek idea of a city-state to a large territory, but the narrow conservatism of their upper classes was a fatal hindrance to the health of the state. They appeared to regard all change as evil. They failed to understand the reasons for internal discord and seemed to think that repression was its only remedy.

Despite the violence of the Gracchan affair, the decay of constitutional government was not necessarily inevitable. The Romans might yet have succeeded in working out a compromise solution to their problems if only they could have kept out of war. But this they were unable to do, for the creation of so vast an empire meant frequent conflicts with bordering nations. In 111 B.C. a great struggle began with Jugurtha, the king of Numidia in northern Africa. This was followed by campaigns to punish the invading Gauls and by a war against Mithradates of Pontus, who was taking advantage

Head of Julius Caesar. Illustrates individuality of Roman portrait sculpture. In the British Museum.

of Roman misrule in the East to extend his dominion over Asia Minor. The heroes of these wars invariably returned to Italy to become leaders of one or the other of the great political factions.

The first of the conquering heroes to make capital out of his military reputation was Marius, who was elevated to the consulship by the masses in 107 B.C. and reelected six times thereafter. Unfortunately Marius was no statesman and accomplished nothing for his followers beyond demonstrating the ease with which a military leader with an army at his back could override opposition. Following the death of Marius in 86 B.C. the aristocrats took a turn at government by force. Their champion was Sulla, victor in the war with Mithradates. Appointed dictator in 82 B.C. for an unlimited term, Sulla proceeded to exterminate his opponents and to restore to the Senate its original powers. Even the senatorial veto over acts of the assembly was revived, and the authority of the tribunes was sharply curtailed. After three years of rule Sulla decided to exchange the pomp of power for the pleasures of the senses and retired to a life of luxury and ease on his Campanian estate.

It was not to be expected that the "reforms" of Sulla would stand unchallenged after he had relinquished his office, for the effect of his decrees was to give control to a bigoted and selfish aristocracy. Several new leaders now emerged to espouse the cause of the people. The most famous of them were Pompey (106–48 B.C.) and Julius Caesar (100–44 B.C.). For a time they pooled their energies and resources in a plot to gain control of the government, but later they became rivals and sought to outdo each other in bids for popular support. Pompey won fame as the conqueror of Syria and Palestine, while Caesar devoted his talents to a series of brilliant forays

The rise of military dictatorships: Marius and Sulla

The struggle between Pompey and Caesar

282

against the Gauls, adding to the Roman state the territory of modern Belgium and France. In 52 B.C., after a series of mob disorders in Rome, the Senate turned to Pompey and caused his election as sole consul. Caesar was eventually branded an enemy of the state, and Pompey conspired with the senatorial faction to deprive him of political power. The result was a deadly war between the two men. In 49 B.C. Caesar began a march on Rome. Pompey fled to the East in the hope of gathering a large enough army to regain control of Italy. In 48 B.C. the forces of the two rivals met at Pharsalus in Thessaly. Pompey was defeated and soon afterward was murdered by agents of the king of Egypt.

After dallying for a season at the court of Cleopatra in Egypt, Caesar returned to Rome. There was now no one who dared to challenge his power. With the aid of his veterans he cowed the Senate into granting his every desire. In 46 B.C. he became dictator for ten years, and two years later for life. In addition, he assumed nearly every other magisterial title that would augment his power. He was consul, censor, and supreme pontiff. He obtained from the Senate full authority to make war and peace and to control the revenues of the state. For all practical purposes he was above the law, and the other agents of the government were merely his servants. It seems unquestionable that he had little respect for the constitution, and there were rumors that he intended to make himself king. At any rate, it was on such a charge that he was assassinated in 44 B.C. by a group of conspirators, under the leadership of Brutus and Cassius, representing the old aristocracy.[4]

Caesar's triumph and downfall

Through the centuries ever since, students of history have been blinded by hero worship in estimating Caesar's political career. It is undoubtedly erroneous to acclaim him as the savior of his country or to praise him as the greatest statesman of all time. For he treated the Republic with contempt and made the problem of governing more difficult for those who came after him. What Rome needed at this time was not the rule of force, however efficiently it might be exercised, but an enlightened attempt to correct the inequities of her political and economic regime. Though it is true that Caesar carried out numerous reforms, not all of them were really fundamental. With the aid of a Greek astronomer he revised the official calendar so as to bring it into harmony with the Egyptian solar calendar of 365 days, with an extra day added every fourth year. He investigated extravagance in the distribution of public grain and reduced the number of recipients by more than 50 per cent. He made plans for codification of the law and increased the penalty for criminal offenses. By conferring citizenship upon thousands of Spaniards and Gauls he took an important step toward eliminating the distinc-

Caesar's achievements

[4] During the last few months of his life Caesar became more ill-tempered and domineering than ever. Perhaps this change was due to the fact that he was really a sick man, his old affliction of epilepsy having returned. W. E. Heitland, *The Roman Republic*, III, 355.

tion between Italians and provincials. He settled a great many of his veterans and a considerable proportion of the urban poor on unused lands not only in Italy but throughout the empire, and he ordered the proprietors of large estates to employ at least one free citizen to every two slaves. It seems fair to say that his greatest fault lay in his exercise of dictatorial power. By ignoring the Senate entirely he destroyed the main foundation on which the Republic rested.

5. ROME BECOMES SOPHISTICATED

During the last two centuries of republican history Rome came under the influence of Hellenistic civilization. The result was a modest flowering of intellectual activity and a further impetus to social change beyond what the Punic Wars had produced. The fact must be noted, however, that several of the components of the Hellenistic pattern of culture were never adopted by the Romans at all. The science of the Hellenistic Age, for example, was largely ignored, and the same was true of some of its art.

Rome under the
influence of
Hellenistic civili-
zation

One of the most notable effects of Hellenistic influence was the adoption of Epicureanism and Stoicism by numerous Romans of the upper classes. The most renowned of the Roman exponents of the Epicurean philosophy was Lucretius (98–55 B.C.), author of a didactic poem entitled *On the Nature of Things*. In writing this work Lucretius was animated by the desire to explain the universe in such a way as to liberate man from all fear of the supernatural, which he regarded as the chief obstacle to peace of soul. Worlds and all things in them, he taught, are the results of fortuitous combinations of atoms. Though he admitted the existence of the gods, he conceived of them as living in eternal peace, neither creating nor governing the universe. Everything is a product of a mechanical evolution, including man himself and his habits, institutions, and beliefs. Since mind is indissolubly linked with matter, death means utter extinction; consequently, no part of the human personality can survive to be rewarded or punished in an afterlife. Lucretius' conception of the good life was perhaps even more negative than that of Epicurus: what man needs, he asserted, is not enjoyment but "peace and a pure heart."

Roman
Epicureanism:
Lucretius

Stoicism was introduced into Rome by Panaetius of Rhodes about 140 B.C. Although it soon came to include among its converts numerous influential leaders of public life, its most distinguished representative was Cicero (106–43 B.C.), the famous orator and statesman. Although Cicero adopted doctrines from a number of philosophers, including both Plato and Aristotle, the fact remains that he derived more of his ideas from the Stoics than from any other source. Certainly his chief ethical writings, *On Duty* and the *Tusculan Disputations*, reflect substantially the doctrines of Zeno and his school. The basis of Cicero's ethical philosophy was the

The Stoic
philosophy of
Cicero

premise that virtue is sufficient for happiness, and that tranquillity of mind is the highest good. He conceived of the ideal man as one who has been guided by reason to an indifference toward sorrow and pain. In political philosophy Cicero went considerably beyond the earlier Stoics. He was one of the first to deny that the state is superior to the individual and taught that government had its origin in a compact among men for their mutual protection. In his *Republic* he set forth the idea of a higher law of eternal justice which is superior to the statutes and decrees of governments. This law is not made by man but is a product of the natural order of things and is discoverable by reason. It is the source of those rights to which all men are entitled as human beings and which governments must not assail. As we shall see presently, this doctrine influenced considerably the development of the Roman law by the great jurists of the second and third centuries A.D. By reason of his contributions to political thought, and by virtue of his urbanity and tolerance, Cicero deserves to be ranked as one of the greatest men Rome ever produced. He typified the genius of the nation at its best. It was his misfortune that, as a defender of the old Republic, he came to be associated in the public mind with the leaders of the aristocracy who had assassinated Julius Caesar. In 43 B.C. he was proscribed by Mark Antony, Caesar's friend, and hunted down and killed.

Hellenistic influence was in large measure responsible for Roman literary progress in the last two centuries of the Republic. It now became the fashion among the upper classes to learn the Greek language and to strive to reproduce in Latin some of the more popular forms of Hellenistic literature. The most noteworthy results were the comedies of Plautus (*ca.* 254–184 B.C.) and Terence (185–159 B.C.), written in imitation of the New Comedy of Menander; the passionate lyrics of Catullus (84–54 B.C.); the histories of Sallust (86–34 B.C.), which, in spite of their Caesarist bias, are among the most scientific ever produced in Rome; and the letters, essays, and orations of Cicero, which are generally regarded as the finest examples of Latin prose.

Several of the early Roman writers showed promise at times of equaling the originality and artistry of the Greeks in the classical age. Plautus, for instance, occasionally displayed a freshness of approach, a perception of philosophic implications, and a capacity for social satire. Of humble origin himself, he delighted in ridiculing the mores and institutions which the respectable classes esteemed so highly. He allowed his genius to be thwarted, however, by too slavish a dependence upon the stock characters and themes of Hellenistic comedy. After his time Latin drama degenerated into lifeless formalism. The other of the most original writers of this period was Catullus, one of the greatest lyric poets of all time. He is best known for his passionate love poems written to describe his tortured feelings while infatuated with the dissolute wife of a promi-

Roman literary progress

Plautus and Catullus

285

nent politician. For years he was unable to free himself from his ardor, and was maddened by jealousy of his rivals. But not all of his poetry dealt with the expression of personal emotion. Apparently he was an ardent republican, and in the latter part of his life he wrote coarse lampoons attacking Pompey and Caesar for their demagogic ambitions.

The conquest of the Hellenistic world accelerated the process of social change which the Punic Wars had begun. The effects were most clearly evident in the growth of luxury, in a widened cleavage between classes, and in a further increase in slavery. The Italian people, numbering about 2,000,000 at the end of the Republic, had come to be divided into four main castes: the aristocracy, the equestrians, the common citizens, and the slaves.[5] The aristocracy included the senatorial class with a total membership of 300 citizens and their families. The majority of them inherited their status, although occasionally a plebeian would gain admission to the Senate through serving a term as consul or quaestor. Most of the aristocrats gained their living as office holders and as owners of great landed estates. The equestrian order was made up of government contractors, bankers, and the wealthier merchants. Originally this class had been composed of those citizens with incomes sufficient to enable them to serve in the cavalry at their own expense, but the term *equites* had now come to be applied to all outside of the senatorial class who possessed property in substantial amount. The equestrians were the chief offenders in the indulgence of vulgar tastes and in the exploitation of the poor and the provincials. As bankers they regularly charged interest rates of 12 per cent and three or four times

[5] In addition, of course, there were numerous aliens, who really did not constitute a separate class. Many were on about the same level as the common citizens. Others were slaves.

Atrium of an Upper-class House in Pompeii, seen from the Interior. Around the atrium or central court were grouped suites of living rooms. The marble columns and decorated walls still give an idea of the luxury and refinement enjoyed by the privileged minority.

that much when they could get it. By far the largest number of the citizens were mere commoners or plebeians. Some of these were independent farmers, a few were industrial workers, but the majority were members of the city mob. When Julius Caesar became dictator, 320,000 citizens were actually being supported by the state.

The Roman slaves were scarcely considered people at all but instruments of production like cattle or horses to be worked for the profit of their masters. Notwithstanding the fact that some of them were refined and intelligent foreigners, they had none of the privileges granted to slaves in Athens. The policy of many of their owners was to get as much work out of them as possible during the years of their prime and then to turn them loose to be fed by the state when they became old and useless. Of course, there were exceptions, especially as a result of the civilizing effects of Stoicism. Cicero, for example, reported himself very fond of his slaves. It is, nevertheless, a sad commentary on Roman civilization that nearly all of the productive labor in the country was done by slaves. They produced practically all of the nation's food supply, for the amount contributed by the few surviving independent farmers was quite insignificant. At least 80 per cent of the workers employed in factories and shops were slaves or former slaves. But many of the members of the servile population were engaged in nonproductive activities. A lucrative form of investment for the business classes was ownership of slaves trained as gladiators, who could be rented to the government or to aspiring politicians for the amusement of the people. The growth of luxury also required the employment of thousands of slaves in domestic service. The man of great wealth must have his doorkeepers, his litter-bearers, his couriers (for the government of the Republic had no postal service), his valets, and his pedagogues or tutors for his children. In some great mansions there were special servants with no other duties than to rub the master down after his bath or to care for his sandals.

The status of the slaves

The religious beliefs of the Romans were altered in various ways in the last two centuries of the Republic—again mainly because of the extension of Roman power over most of the Hellenistic states. There was, first of all, a tendency of the upper classes to abandon the traditional religion for the philosophies of Stoicism and Epicureanism. But many of the common people also found worship of the ancient gods no longer satisfying. It was too formal and mechanical and demanded too much in the way of duty and self-sacrifice to meet the needs of the masses, whose lives were now empty and meaningless. Furthermore, Italy had attracted a stream of immigrants from the East, most of whom had a religious background totally different from that of the Romans. The result was the rapid spread of Oriental mystery cults, which satisfied the craving for a more emotional religion and offered the reward of a blessed immortality to the wretched and downtrodden of earth. From Egypt came

Changes in religion

287

the cult of Isis and Osiris (or Sarapis, as the god was now more commonly called), while from Phrygia was introduced the worship of the Great Mother, with her eunuch priests and wild, symbolic orgies. So strong was the appeal of these cults that the decrees of the Senate against them proved almost impossible to enforce. In the last century B.C. the Persian cult of Mithraism, which came to surpass all the others in popularity, gained a foothold in Italy.

6. THE PRINCIPATE OR EARLY EMPIRE (27 B.C.–284 A.D.)

The triumph of Octavian or Augustus Caesar

Shortly before his death in 44 B.C., Julius Caesar had adopted as his sole heir his grandnephew Octavian (63 B.C.–14 A.D.), then a young man of eighteen quietly pursuing his studies in Illyria across the Adriatic Sea. Upon learning of his uncle's death, Octavian hastened to Rome to take over control of the government. He soon found that he must share his ambition with two of Caesar's power- ful friends, Mark Antony and Lepidus. The following year the three men formed an alliance for the purpose of crushing the power of the aristocratic clique responsible for Caesar's murder. The meth- ods employed were not to the new leaders' credit. Prominent mem- bers of the aristocracy were hunted down and slain and their property confiscated. The most noted of the victims was Cicero, brutally slain by Mark Antony's soldiers though he had taken no part in the conspiracy against Caesar's life. The real murderers, Brutus and Cassius, escaped and organized an army of 80,000 republicans, but were finally defeated by Octavian and his colleagues in 42 B.C. About eight years later a quarrel developed among the members of the alliance themselves, inspired primarily by Antony's jealousy of Octavian. The ultimate outcome in 31 B.C. was the triumphant emergence of Caesar's heir as the most powerful man in the Roman state.

The revival of constitutional government

The victory of Octavian ushered in a new period in Roman his- tory, the most glorious and the most prosperous that the nation ex- perienced. Although problems of peace and order were still far from being completely solved, the deadly civil strife was ended, and the people now had their first decent opportunity to show what their talents could achieve. Unlike his great uncle, Octavian seems to have entertained no monarchical ambitions. He was determined, at any rate, to preserve the forms if not the substance of constitu- tional government. He accepted the titles of Augustus and Impera- tor conferred upon him by the Senate and the army.[6] He held the authority of proconsul and tribune permanently; but he refused to make himself dictator or even consul for life, despite the pleas of the populace that he do so. In his view the Senate and the people were

---

[6] The title Augustus signified "consecrated" and implied the idea that its bearer was specially favored by the gods. Imperator meant "victorious general."

the supreme sovereigns, as they had been under the early Republic. The title by which he preferred to have his authority designated was Princeps, or First Citizen of the State. For this reason the period of his rule and that of his successors is properly called the Principate, or early Empire, to distinguish it from the period of the Republic (sixth century B.C. to 27 B.C.) and from the period of the late Empire (284 A.D. to 476 A.D.)

Octavian, or Augustus as he was now more commonly called, ruled over Italy and the provinces for forty-four years (31 B.C.–14 A.D.). At the beginning of the period he governed by military power and by common consent, but in 27 B.C. the Senate bestowed upon him the series of offices and titles described above. His work as a statesman at least equaled in importance that of his more famous predecessor. Among the reforms of Augustus were the establishment of a new coinage system, the creation of a centralized system of courts under his own supervision, and the bestowal of a large measure of local self-government upon cities and provinces. For the nation as a whole he laid the foundations for an elaborate postal service. He insisted upon experience and intelligence as qualifications for appointment to administrative office. By virtue of his proconsular authority he assumed direct control over the provincial governors and punished them severely for graft and extortion. He abolished the old system of farming out the collection of taxes in the provinces, which had led to such flagrant abuses, and appointed his own personal representatives as collectors at regular salaries. But he did not stop with political reforms. He procured the enactment of laws designed to check the more glaring social and moral evils of the time. By his own example of temperate living he sought to discourage luxurious habits and to set the precedent for a return to the ancient virtues. *The reforms of Augustus*

After the death of Augustus in 14 A.D. Rome had few enlightened and capable rulers. Several of his successors were brutal tyrants who squandered the resources of the state and kept the country in an uproar by their deeds of bloody violence. As early as 68 A.D. the army began to take a hand in the selection of the Princeps, with the result that on several occasions thereafter the head of the government was little more than a military dictator. Between 235 and 284 A.D. sheer anarchy prevailed: of the twenty-six men who were elevated to power in that time only one escaped violent death. As a matter of fact, in the 270 years which followed the demise of Augustus, Rome had scarcely more than four or five rulers of whom much good could be said. The list would include Nerva (96–98 A.D.), Trajan (98–117), Antoninus Pius (138–161), Marcus Aurelius (161–180), and possibly Vespasian (70–79) and Hadrian (117–138). *The successors of Augustus*

These rulers and their great predecessor, Augustus, succeeded in maintaining, for about two centuries, the celebrated *Pax Romana*. On three occasions Augustus himself ceremonially closed the doors *The Pax Romana*

See color map
at page 297

of the temple of Janus to symbolize the reign of absolute peace in the Empire. Yet the *Pax Romana* was primarily a peace of subjugation. Augustus added more territory to the empire than did any other Roman ruler. His stepsons, Tiberius and Drusus, pushed the frontiers into central and eastern Europe, conquering the territories known today as Switzerland, Austria, and Bulgaria. They attempted the subjugation of the territory occupied by modern Germany, but met with only minimal success. The *Pax Romana* rested upon an efficient navy and a vast imperial army. Though comparatively small, the navy performed its functions so well that the Romans maintained their control over the Mediterranean Sea for 200 years without fighting a battle. The army, numbering about 300,000 men, was much less successful. It was badly defeated in Germany and eventually lost nearly all of the territory it had conquered there. To prevent revolts, more than twenty of its twenty-eight legions were pinned down in Spain, Syria, and Egypt and on the Rhine and the Danube. Feeding and supplying these hordes of armed men put a constant strain on the resources of the state. Even a sales tax had to be adopted to supplement the usual sources of revenue.

Reasons for the
political troubles
in Rome

How can this comparative failure of the political genius of the Romans in the very best period of their history be accounted for? The assertion is frequently made that it was due to the absence of any definite rule of hereditary succession to the office of Princeps. But this answer rests upon a misconception of the nature of the Roman constitution at this time. The government Augustus established was not intended to be a monarchy. Although the Princeps was virtually an autocrat, the authority he possessed was supposed to be derived exclusively from the Senate and the people of Rome; he could have no inherent right to rule by virtue of royal descent. The explanation must therefore be sought in other factors. The Romans were now reaping the whirlwind which had been sown in the civil strife of the late Republic. They had grown accustomed to violence as the way out when problems did not admit of an easy solution. Furthermore, the long wars of conquest and the suppression of barbarian revolts had cheapened human life in the estimation of the people themselves and had fostered the growth of crime. As a consequence it was practically inevitable that men of vicious character should push their way into the highest political office.

7. CULTURE AND LIFE IN THE PERIOD OF THE PRINCIPATE

Cultural progress
under the
Principate

From the standpoint of variety of intellectual and artistic interests the period of the Principate outshone all other ages in the history of Rome. Most of the progress took place, however, in the years from 27 B.C. to 200 A.D. It was between these years that Roman philosophy attained its characteristic form. This period witnessed also the feeble awakening of an interest in science, the growth of a distinctive art, and the production of the best literary works. After 200 A.D. economic and political decay stifled all further cultural growth.

Stoicism was now the prevailing philosophy of the Romans. Much of the influence of Epicureanism lingered and found occasional expression in the writings of the poets, but as a system it had ceased to be popular. The reasons for the triumph of Stoicism are not hard to discover. With its emphasis upon duty, self-discipline, and subjection to the natural order of things, it accorded well with the ancient virtues of the Romans and with their habits of conservatism. Moreover, its insistence upon civic obligations and its doctrine of cosmopolitanism appealed to the Roman political-mindedness and pride in world empire. Epicureanism, on the other hand, was a little too negative and individualistic to agree with the social consciousness of Roman tradition. It seemed not only to repudiate the idea of any purpose in the universe, but even to deny the value of human effort. Since the Romans were men of action rather than speculative thinkers, the Epicurean ideal of the solitary philosopher immersed in the problem of his own salvation could have no permanent attraction for them. It is necessary to observe, however, that the Stoicism developed in the days of the Principate was somewhat different from that of Zeno and his school. The old physical theories borrowed from Heracleitus were now discarded, and in their place was substituted a broader interest in politics and ethics. There was a tendency also for Roman Stoicism to assume a more distinctly religious flavor than that which had characterized the original philosophy.

Three eminent apostles of Stoicism lived and taught in Rome in the two centuries that followed the rule of Augustus: Seneca (4 B.C.–65 A.D.), millionaire adviser for a time to Nero; Epictetus, the slave (60?–120 A.D.); and the Emperor Marcus Aurelius (121–180 A.D.). All of them agreed that inner serenity is the ultimate goal to be sought, that true happiness can be found only in surrender to the benevolent order of the universe. They preached the ideal of virtue for virtue's sake, deplored the sinfulness of man's nature, and urged obedience to conscience as the voice of duty. Seneca and Epictetus adulterated their philosophy with such deep mystical yearnings as to make it almost a religion. They worshiped the cosmos as divine, governed by an all-powerful Providence who ordains all that happens for ultimate good. The last of the Roman Stoics, Marcus Aurelius, was more fatalistic and less hopeful. Although he did not reject the conception of an ordered and rational universe, he shared neither the faith nor the dogmatism of the earlier Stoics. He was confident of no blessed immortality to balance the sufferings of one's earthly career. Living in a melancholy time, he was inclined to think of man as a creature buffeted by evil fortune for which no distant perfection of the whole could fully atone. He urged, nevertheless, that men should continue to live nobly, that they should neither abandon

Marcus Aurelius. This mounted figure of the great emperor-philosopher is one of the few equestrian statues surviving from the ancient world. It was originally entirely gilded. Now on the Piazza del Campidoglio, Rome.

themselves to gross indulgence nor break down in angry protest, but that they should derive what contentment they could from dignified resignation to suffering and tranquil submission to death.

The literary achievements of the Romans bore a definite relation to their philosophy. This was especially true of the works of the most distinguished writers of the Augustan Age. Horace (65–8 B.C.), for example, in his famous *Odes* drew copiously from the teachings of both Epicureans and Stoics. He confined his attention, however, to their doctrines of a way of life, for like most of the Romans he had little curiosity about the nature of the world. He developed a philosophy which combined the Epicurean justification of pleasure with the Stoic bravery in the face of trouble. While he never reduced pleasure to the mere absence of pain, he was sophisticated enough to know that the highest enjoyment is possible only through the exercise of rational control. Perhaps the following lines express about as well as any others the essence of his view of life:

Roman literature:
Horace

> Be brave in trouble; meet distress
> With dauntless front; but when the gale
> Too prosperous blows, be wise no less
> And shorten sail.[7]

Vergil (70–19 B.C.) likewise reflects a measure of the philosophical temper of his age. Though his *Eclogues* convey something of the Epicurean ideal of quiet pleasure, Vergil was much more of a Stoic. His utopian vision of an age of peace and abundance, his brooding sense of the tragedy of human fate, and his idealization of a life in harmony with nature indicate an intellectual heritage similar to that

Vergil, Ovid, and
Livy

[7] S. Conington (trans.), *Odes*, II, 10.

of Seneca and Epictetus. Vergil's most noted work, the *Aeneid*, like several of the *Odes* of Horace, was a purposeful glorification of Roman imperialism. The *Aeneid* in fact was an epic of empire recounting the toils and triumphs of the founding of the state, its glorious traditions, and its magnificent destiny. The only other major writers of the Augustan Age were Ovid (43 B.C.?–17 A.D.) and Livy (59 B.C.–17 A.D.). The former, the greatest of Roman elegiac poets, was the chief representative of the cynical and individualist tendencies of his day. His writings, although brilliant and witty, often reflected the dissolute tastes of the time, and their popularity gives evidence of the failure of the efforts of Augustus to regenerate Roman society. The chief title of Livy to fame rests upon his skill as a prose stylist. As a historian he was woefully deficient. His main work, a history of Rome, is replete with dramatic and picturesque

The Baths of Caracalla, Rome. The gigantic scale is typical of Late Empire buildings. Elaborate and luxurious public baths like these were often presented to the people by the emperor or rich citizens. Shown is the *calidarium*, one of several types of chambers, for hot tub baths.

narrative, designed to appeal to the patriotic emotions rather than to present the impartial truth.

The literature of the period which followed the death of Augustus also exemplified conflicting social and intellectual tendencies. The novels of Petronius and Apuleius and the epigrams of Martial are specimens of individualist writing generally descriptive of the meaner aspects of life. The attitude of the authors is unmoral; their purpose is not to instruct or uplift but chiefly to tell an entertaining story or turn a witty phrase. An entirely different viewpoint is presented in the works of the other most important writers of this age: Juvenal, the satirist (60?–140 A.D.), and Tacitus, the historian (55?–117? A.D.). Juvenal wrote under the influence of the Stoics but with little intelligence and narrow vision. Laboring under the delusion that the troubles of the nation were due to moral degeneracy, he lashed the vices of his countrymen with the fury of an evangelist. A somewhat similar attitude characterized the writing

Petronius, Apuleius, Martial, Juvenal, and Tacitus

ARCHITECTURE OF ROME AND HER PROVINCES

Top outside: *A Street in Ostia, the Ancient Seaport of Rome.* The round arches and masonry columns form the balcony of a rich man's house.

Top inside: *The Arch of Titus.*

Bottom left: *The Pantheon, in Rome.* Built by the Emperor Hadrian and dedicated to the deities of the seven planets.

Top right: *Roman Aqueduct at Segovia, Spain.* Aqueducts conveyed water from the mountains to the larger cities.

Bottom: *The Maison Carrée at Nîmes, France.* The most perfect example of Roman temple extant. Reflecting possibly Etruscan influence, it was built on a high base, or *podium*, with great steps leading to the entrance. It dates from the beginning of the Christian era.

of his younger contemporary, Tacitus. The best-known of Roman historians, Tacitus described the events of his age not entirely with a view to scientific analysis but largely for the purpose of moral indictment. In his *Annals* and *Histories* he painted a lurid picture of political chaos and social corruption. His description of the customs of the ancient Germans in his *Germania* served to heighten the contrast between the manly virtues of an unspoiled race and the effeminate vices of the decadent Romans. Whatever his failings as a historian, he was a master of ironic wit and brilliant aphorism. Referring to the boasted *Pax Romana*, he makes a barbarian chieftain say: "They create a wilderness and call it peace." [8]

The period of the Principate was the period when Roman art first assumed its distinctive character as an expression of the national life. Before this time what passed for an art of Rome was really an importation from the Hellenistic East. Conquering armies brought back to Italy wagonloads of statues, reliefs, and marble columns as part of the plunder from Greece and Asia Minor. These became the property of wealthy publicans and bankers and were used to embellish their sumptuous mansions. As the demand increased, hundreds of copies were made, with the result that Rome came to have by the end of the Republic a profusion of objects of art which had no more cultural significance than the Rembrandts or Botticellis in the home of some modern broker. The aura of national glory which surrounded the early Principate stimulated the growth of an art more nearly indigenous. Augustus himself boasted that he found Rome a city of brick and left it a city of marble. Nevertheless, much of the old Hellenistic influence remained until the talent of the Romans themselves was exhausted.

The arts most truly expressive of the Roman character were architecture and sculpture. Both were monumental, designed to symbolize power and grandeur rather than freedom of mind or contentment with life. Architecture contained as its leading elements the round arch, the vault, and the dome, although at times the Corinthian column was employed, especially in the construction of temples. The materials most commonly used were brick, squared stone blocks, and concrete, the last generally concealed with a marble facing. As a further adornment of public buildings, sculptured entablatures and façades, built up of tiers of colonnades or arcades, were frequently added. Copied from Hellenistic sources and bearing little relation to the rest of the structure, many of these decorative devices were showy and unseemly. Roman architecture was devoted primarily to utilitarian purposes. The foremost examples were government buildings, amphitheaters, baths, race courses, and private houses. Nearly all were of massive proportions and solid construction. Among the largest and most noted were the Pantheon, with its dome having a diameter of 142 feet, and the Colosseum, which

Achievements in art

See color plates at page 265

Architecture and sculpture

[8] Tacitus, *Agricola*, p. 30.

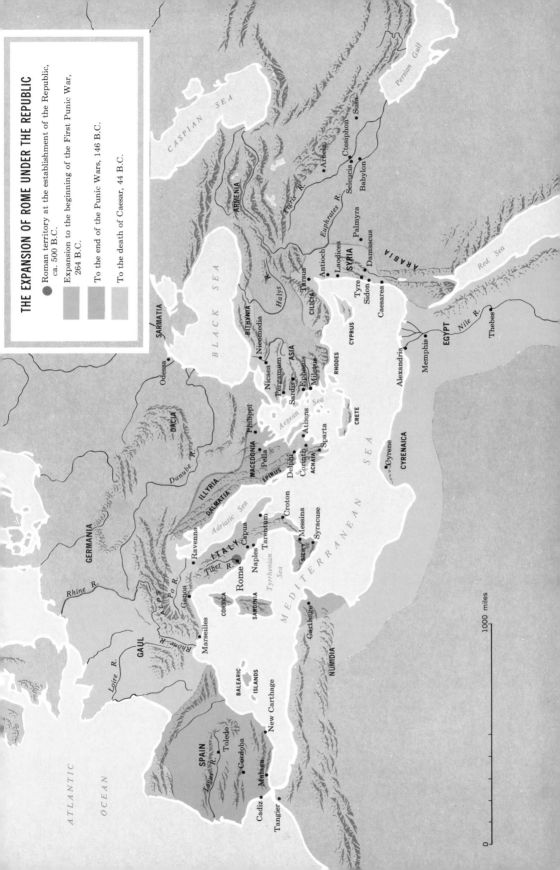

THE EXPANSION OF ROME UNDER THE REPUBLIC

- Roman territory at the establishment of the Republic, ca. 500 B.C.

  Expansion to the beginning of the First Punic War, 264 B.C.

  To the end of the Punic Wars, 146 B.C.

  To the death of Caesar, 44 B.C.

ATLANTIC OCEAN

CASPIAN SEA

Persian Gulf

SARMATIA

ARMENIA

Tigris R.

Euphrates R.

Ctesiphon
Seleucia
Babylon
Susa
Arbela

GERMANIA

DACIA

Halys

BITHYNIA

Nicomedia

Nicaea

Pergamum

ASIA

Sardis
Ephesus
Miletus

RHODES

SYRIA

Antioch
Laodicea
Tarsus
CILICIA

Palmyra
Damascus

Tyre
Sidon
Caesarea

ARABIA

Red Sea

CYPRUS

Danube R.

Rhine R.

GAUL

Loire R.

Rhône R.

ILLYRIA

DALMATIA

Adriatic Sea

Odessa

BLACK SEA

Philippi

MACEDONIA

Pella

EPIRUS

Delphi
Corinth
Athens
Sparta
ACHAIA

Aegean Sea

CRETE

Cyrene
CYRENAICA

MEDITERRANEAN SEA

Alexandria
Memphis
EGYPT

Nile R.

Thebes

ALPS

Ravenna
Genoa
Po R.

ITALY

Tiber R.
Rome
Capua
Naples
Tarentum
Croton

Marseilles

CORSICA

SARDINIA

Tyrrhenian Sea

SICILY
Messina
Syracuse

Carthage

NUMIDIA

BALEARIC ISLANDS

New Carthage

SPAIN

Tagus R.

Toledo
Cordoba
Malaga
Cadiz
Tangier

1000 miles

THE ROMAN EMPIRE AT ITS GREATEST EXTENT
98 - 117 A.D.

CASPIAN SEA

Persian Gulf

Cyrus R.

ARMENIA

Araxes R.

Tigris R.

Euphrates R.

MESOPOTAMIA

CAPPADOCIA

GALATIA

Antioch

SYRIA

Red Sea

BITHYNIA

Nile R.

ASIA

Ephesus

EGYPT

Alexandria

BLACK SEA

THRACE

MACEDONIA

DACIA

Athens

CYRENAICA

MEDITERRANEAN SEA

ILLYRIA

DALMATIA

PANNONIA

Danube R.

Syracuse

Elbe R.

CONQUESTS TO ELBE
(ABANDONED 17 A.D.)

GERMANIA

LIMES
GERMANICUS

RAETIA

APPENINES

Tiber R.

Rome

TRIPOLIS

ALPS

AFRICA

GAUL

NUMIDIA

HADRIAN'S WALL

BALTIC SEA

NORTH SEA

HIBERNIA
(IRELAND)

NORTH BRITAIN
(ANNEXED 84 A.D.)

BRITAIN

English Channel

Bay of
Biscay

MAURETANIA

SPAIN

ATLANTIC

OCEAN

Strait of
Gibraltar

1000 miles

0

could accommodate 65,000 spectators at the gladiatorial combats. Roman sculpture included as its main forms triumphal arches and columns, narrative reliefs, altars, and portrait busts and statues. Its distinguishing characteristics were individuality and naturalism. Even more than architecture it served to express the vanity and love of power of the Roman aristocracy, although some of it was marked by unusual qualities of harmony and grace.[9]

As scientists the Romans accomplished comparatively little in this period or in any other. Scarcely an original discovery of fundamental importance was made by a man of Latin nationality. This fact seems strange when we consider that the Romans had the advantage of Hellenistic science as a foundation upon which to build. But they neglected their opportunity almost completely. Why should this have been so? It was due, first of all, to the circumstance that the Romans were absorbed in problems of government and military conquest. Forced to specialize in law, politics, and military strategy, they had very little time for investigation of nature. A reason of more vital importance was the fact that the Romans were too practical-minded. They had none of that divine fire which impels man to lose himself in the quest for unlimited knowledge. They had no vigorous intellectual curiosity about the world in which they lived. In short, they were not philosophers. Contrary to the popular notion, practical-mindedness is not of itself sufficient to carry scientific progress very far. Modern science would probably have died of undernourishment long ago if it had had to depend solely upon the work of inventors and technologists.

Mainly because of this lack of talent for pure science, the achievements of the Romans were limited almost entirely to engineering and the organization of public services. They built marvelous roads, bridges, and aqueducts. They provided the city of Rome with a water supply of 300,000,000 gallons daily. They established the first hospitals in the Western world and the first system of state medicine for the benefit of the poor. But their own writers on scientific subjects were hopelessly devoid of critical intelligence. The most renowned and the most typical of them was Pliny the Elder (23-79 A.D.), who completed about 77 A.D. a voluminous encyclopedia of "science" which he called *Natural History*. This work was admittedly a compilation supposed to have been based upon the writings of nearly 500 different authors. The subjects discussed varied from cosmology to economics. Despite the wealth of material it contains, the work is of limited value. Pliny was totally unable to distinguish between fact and fable. In his estimation, the weirdest tales of wonders and portents were to be accepted as of equal value with the most solidly established facts. He described the marvels of a primitive people whose feet all turned backward, of a country where

[9] A great many of the best examples of both architecture and sculpture were produced not by Romans at all but by Greeks resident in Italy.

females conceived at the age of five and died at the age of eight, and of a tiny Mediterranean fish which could cause ships to stand still merely by clinging to them. The other best-known author of an encyclopedia of science was Seneca (4 B.C.?–65 A.D.), the Stoic philosopher, who took his own life at Nero's command in 65 A.D. Seneca was less credulous than Pliny but no more original. Besides, he maintained that the purpose of all scientific study should be to divulge the moral secrets of nature. If there was any Latin who could be considered an original scientist, the title would have to be given to Celsus, who flourished during the reign of Tiberius. Celsus wrote a comprehensive treatise on medicine, including an excellent manual of surgery, but there is a strong suspicion that the entire work was compiled, if not actually translated, from the Greek. Among the operations he described were tonsillectomy, operations for cataracts and goiter, and plastic surgery.

No account of the scientific aspects of Roman civilization would be complete without some mention of the work of Hellenistic scientists who lived in Italy or in the provinces during the period of the Principate. Nearly all of them were physicians. The most distinguished, although apparently not the most original, was Galen of Pergamum, who was active in Rome at various times during the latter half of the second century. While his fame rests primarily upon his medical encyclopedia, systematizing the learning of others, he is deserving of more credit for his own experiments which brought him close to a discovery of the circulation of the blood. He not only taught but proved that the arteries carry blood, and that severance of even a small one is sufficient to drain away all of the blood of the body in little more than half an hour. But Galen was not the only Hellenistic physician who made important contributions in this time. At least two others are entitled to more recognition than is commonly given to them: Soranus of Ephesus, the greatest gynecologist of antiquity and inventor of the speculum, and Rufus of Ephesus, who wrote the first accurate description of the liver and of the rhythm of the pulse, and was the first to recommend boiling of suspicious water before drinking it.

Roman society exhibited the same general tendencies under the Principate as in the last days of the Republic. A few significant differences, however, can be noted. Owing in part to the influence of the Stoic philosophy and in part to the abundance of free labor, slavery began to decline. Despite the efforts of Augustus to limit the manumission of slaves, the number of freedmen steadily increased. They crowded into every field of employment, including the civil service. Many succeeded in becoming proprietors of small shops, and some even became rich. Not entirely unconnected with these developments was the growth of the institution of clientage. Members of the citizen class who had lost their property or who had been driven out of business by the competition of enterprising

The Colosseum. The Colosseum was built by the Roman emperors as a place of entertainment and public exhibition. It was the scene of gladiatorial combats and of the throwing of Christians to the lions.

freedmen now frequently became "clients" or dependents of wealthy aristocrats. In return for pittances of food and money these "shabby genteel" served the great magnates by applauding their speeches and fawning before them when they appeared in public. Custom made it practically obligatory for every man of great wealth to maintain a retinue of these miserable flatterers.

Although the evidence has frequently been exaggerated, the period of the Principate was apparently marked by moral decay. According to the records there were 32,000 prostitutes in Rome during the reign of Trajan, and, if we can judge from the testimony of some of the most noted writers, homosexuality was exceedingly common and even fashionable. While political corruption had been subjected to more stringent control, crimes of violence appear to have increased. But the most serious moral indictment which can be brought against the age would seem to have been a further growth of the passion for cruelty. The great games and spectacles became bloodier and more disgusting than ever. The Romans could no longer obtain a sufficient thrill from mere exhibitions of athletic

Signs of moral decay

299

prowess; pugilists were now required to have their hands wrapped with thongs of leather loaded with iron or lead. The most popular amusement of all was watching the gladiatorial combats in the Colosseum or in other amphitheaters capable of accommodating thousands of spectators. Fights between gladiators were nothing new, but they were now presented on a much more elaborate scale. Not only the ignorant rabble attended them, but wealthy aristocrats also, and frequently the head of the government himself. The gladiators fought to the accompaniment of savage cries and curses from the audience. When one went down with a disabling wound, it was the privilege of the crowd to decide whether his life should be spared or whether the weapon of his opponent should be plunged into his heart. One contest after another was staged in the course of a single exhibition. Should the arena become too sodden with blood, it was covered over with a fresh layer of sand, and the revolting performance went on. Most of the gladiators were condemned criminals or slaves, but some were volunteers even from the respectable classes. The Princeps Commodus, the worthless son of Marcus Aurelius, entered the arena several times for the sake of the plaudits of the mob.

The spread of
Mithraism and
Christianity

Notwithstanding its low moral tone, the age of the Principate was characterized by an even deeper interest in salvationist religions than that which had prevailed under the Republic. Mithraism now gained adherents by the thousands, absorbing most of the followers of the cults of the Great Mother and of Isis and Sarapis. About 40 A.D. the first Christians appeared in Rome. The new sect grew rapidly and eventually succeeded in displacing Mithraism as the most popular of the mystery cults. For some time the Roman government was no more hostile toward Christianity than it was toward the other mystery religions. While it is a fact that some members of the sect were put to death by Nero in response to the demand for a scapegoat for the disastrous fire of 64 A.D., there was no systematic persecution of Christians as such until the reign of Decius nearly 200 years later. Even then the persecution was inspired by political and social considerations more than by religious motives. Because of their otherworldliness and their refusal to take the customary oaths in the courts or participate in the civic religion, the Christians were regarded as disloyal citizens and dangerous characters. Moreover, their ideals of meekness and nonresistance, their preaching against the rich, and their practice of holding what appeared to be secret meetings made the Romans suspect them as enemies of the established order. In the end, persecution defeated its own purpose. It intensified the zeal of those who survived, with the result that the new faith spread more rapidly than ever.

The establishment of stable government by Augustus ushered in a period of prosperity for Italy which lasted for more than two centuries. Trade was now extended to all parts of the known world, even to Arabia, India, and China. Manufacturing reached more than insignificant proportions, especially in the production of pottery, textiles, and articles of metal and glass. As a result of the development of rotation of crops and the technique of soil fertilization, agriculture flourished as never before. In spite of all this, the economic order was far from healthy. The prosperity was not evenly distributed but was confined primarily to the upper classes. Since the stigma attached to manual labor persisted as strong as ever, production was bound to decline as the supply of slaves diminished. Perhaps worse was the fact that Italy had a decidedly unfavorable balance of trade. The meager industrial development was by no means sufficient to provide enough articles of export to meet the demand for luxuries imported from the provinces and from the outside world. As a consequence, Italy was gradually drained of her supply of precious metals. By the third century signs of economic collapse were already abundant.

Economic prosperity during the first two centuries

8. ROMAN LAW

There is general agreement that the most important legacy which the Romans left to succeeding cultures was their system of law. This system was the result of a gradual evolution which may be considered to have begun with the publication of the Twelve Tables about 450 B.C. In the later centuries of the Republic the law of the Twelve Tables was modified and practically superseded by the growth of new precedents and principles. These emanated from different sources: from changes in custom, from the teachings of the Stoics, from the decisions of judges, but expecially from the edicts of the praetors. The Roman praetors were magistrates who had authority to define and interpret the law in a particular suit and issue instructions to the jury for the decision of the case. The jury merely decided questions of fact; all issues of law were settled by the praetor, and generally his interpretations became precedents for the decision of similar cases in the future. Thus a system of judicial practice was built up in somewhat the same fashion as the English common law.

The early development of Roman law

It was under the Principate, however, that the Roman law attained its highest stage of development. This later progress was the result in part of the extension of the law over a wider field of jurisdiction, over the lives and properties of aliens in strange environments as well as over the citizens of Italy. But the major reason was the fact that Augustus and his successors gave to certain eminent jurists the right to deliver opinions, or *responsa* as they were called, on the legal issues of cases under trial in the courts. The most prominent of the men thus designated from time to time were Gaius, Ulpian, Papinian, and Paulus. Although most of them held high judicial office, they had gained their reputations primarily as law-

Roman law under the Principate; the great jurists

yers and writers on legal subjects. The responses of these jurists came to embody a science and philosophy of law and were accepted as the basis of Roman jurisprudence. It was typical of the Roman respect for authority that the ideas of these men should have been adopted so readily even when they upset, as they occasionally did, time-honored beliefs.

The Roman law as it was developed under the influence of the jurists comprised three great branches or divisions: the *jus civile*, the *jus gentium*, and the *jus naturale*. The *jus civile*, or civil law, was essentially the law of Rome and her citizens. As such it existed in both written and unwritten forms. It included the statutes of the Senate, the decrees of the Princeps, the edicts of the praetors, and also certain ancient customs operating with the force of law. The *jus gentium*, or law of peoples, was the law that was held to be common to all men regardless of nationality. It was the law which authorized the institutions of slavery and private ownership of property and defined the principles of purchase and sale, partnership, and contract. It was not superior to the civil law but supplemented it as especially applicable to the alien inhabitants of the empire.

The three
divisions of
Roman law

The most interesting and in many ways the most important branch of the Roman law was the *jus naturale*, or natural law. This was not a product of judicial practice, but of philosophy. The Stoics had developed the idea of a rational order of nature which is the embodiment of justice and right. They had affirmed that all men are by nature equal, and that they are entitled to certain basic rights which governments have no authority to transgress. The father of the law of nature as a legal principle, however, was not one of the Hellenistic Stoics, but Cicero. "True law," he declared, "is right reason consonant with nature, diffused among all men, constant, eternal. To make enactments infringing this law, religion forbids, neither may it be repealed even in part, nor have we power through Senate or people to free ourselves from it." [10] This law is prior to the state itself, and any ruler who defies it automatically becomes a tyrant. With the exception of Gaius, who identified the *jus naturale* with the *jus gentium*, all of the great jurists subscribed to conceptions of the law of nature very similar to those of the philosophers. Although the jurists did not regard this law as an automatic limitation upon the *jus civile*, they thought of it nevertheless as a great ideal to which the statutes and decrees of men ought to conform. This development of the concept of abstract justice as a legal principle was one of the noblest achievements of the Roman civilization.

The *jus naturale*

9. THE LATE EMPIRE (284–476 A.D.)

The last period of Roman history, from 284 to 476 A.D., is properly called the period of the late Empire. With the accession of

[10] *The Republic*, III, 22.

Diocletian in 284, the government of Rome finally became an undisguised autocracy. It is true, of course, that constitutional government had been little more than a fiction for some time, but now all pretense of maintaining the Republic was thrown aside. Both in theory and in practice the change was complete. No longer was the doctrine advanced that the ruler was the mere agent of the Senate and the people; he was now held to be absolutely sovereign on the assumption that the people had surrendered all power to him. Diocletian adopted the regalia and ceremony of an Oriental despot. In place of the simple military garb of the Princeps he substituted a purple robe of silk interwoven with gold. He required all his subjects who were admitted to an audience with him to prostrate themselves before him. Needless to say, the Senate was now completely excluded from participation in the government. It was not formally abolished, but it was reduced to the status of a municipal council and a social club for the plutocracy. The chief reason for these political changes is undoubtedly to be found in the economic decline of the third century. The people had lost confidence in themselves, as they frequently do under such circumstances, and were ready to sacrifice all of their rights for the faint hope of security.

Diocletian's successors continued his system of absolutism. The most famous of them were Constantine I (306–337), Julian (361–363), and Theodosius I (379–395). Constantine is best known for his establishment of a new capital, called Constantinople, on the site of ancient Byzantium, and for his policy of religious toleration toward Christians. Contrary to a common belief, he did not make Christianity the official religion of the Empire; his various edicts issued in 313 simply gave Christianity equal status with the pagan cults, thereby terminating the policy of persecution. Later in his reign he bestowed upon the Christian clergy special privileges and caused his sons to be brought up in the new faith, but he continued to maintain the imperial cult. Although he was acclaimed by historians of the Church as Constantine the Great, his practice of favoring Christianity was dictated primarily by political motives. A generation after Constantine's death the Emperor Julian attempted to stimulate a pagan reaction. He was a devoted admirer of Hellenic culture and thought of Christianity as an alien and enemy religion. His attempt to accomplish a pagan revival ended in failure, partly because Christianity was too firmly entrenched, and partly because his reign was too short. The last of the noted pagan emperors, he has been branded by Christian historians as Julian the Apostate. The other most prominent of the rulers of Rome in its dying stage was Theodosius I, who, in spite of his butchery of thousands of innocent citizens on imaginary charges of conspiracy, is also known as "the Great." The chief importance of his reign comes from his decree of 380 commanding all of his subjects to become orthodox Christians. A few years later he classified participation in any of the pagan cults as an act of treason.

From the standpoint of cultural achievement the period of the Empire is of little significance. With the establishment of a despotic state and the degradation of intellect by mystical and otherworldly religions, creative talent was destroyed. The few literary works produced were characterized by an overemphasis upon form and a neglect of content. A barren and artificial rhetoric took the place of the study of the classics in the schools, and science died out completely. Aside from the teachings of the Christian Fathers, which will be discussed later, the prevailing philosophy of the age was Neo-Platonism. This philosophy, purporting to be a continuation of the system of Plato, was really an outgrowth of the doctrines of the Neo-Pythagoreans and of Philo Judaeus.[11] The first of its basic teachings was emanationism: everything that exists proceeds from God in a continuing stream of emanations. The initial stage in the process is the emanation of the world-soul. From this come the di-

vine Ideas or spiritual patterns, and then the souls of particular things. The final emanation is matter. But matter has no form or quality of its own; it is simply the privation of spirit, the residue which is left after the spiritual rays from God have burned themselves out. It follows that matter is to be despised as the symbol of evil and darkness. The second major doctrine was mysticism. The soul of man was originally a part of God, but it has become separated from him through its union with matter. The highest goal of life should be mystic reunion with the divine, which can be accomplished through contemplation and through emancipation of the soul from bondage to matter. Man should be ashamed of the fact that he possesses a physical body and should seek to subjugate it in every way possible. Asceticism was therefore the third main teaching of this philosophy.

The real founder of Neo-Platonism was Plotinus, who was born in Egypt about 204 A.D. In the later years of his life he taught in

Rome and won many followers among the upper classes. His principal successors diluted the philosophy with more and more bizarre superstitions. In spite of its anti-intellectual viewpoint and its utter indifference to the state, Neo-Platonism became so popular in Rome in the third and fourth centuries A.D. that it almost completely supplanted Stoicism. No fact could have expressed more eloquently the extent of the social and intellectual decline that the Roman nation had experienced.

10. DECAY AND DECLINE

In 476 A.D. the last of the emperors in the West, the insignificant Romulus Augustulus, was deposed, and a barbarian chieftain assumed the title of King of Rome. Though this event is commonly

[11] See pp. 258–59.

taken to have marked the end of Roman history, it was really only the final incident in a long process of disintegration. The fall of Rome did not occur with dramatic suddenness, but extended over a period of approximately two centuries. A large part of the civilization was already dead before the Empire collapsed. Indeed, for all practical purposes the pagan culture of Rome from the middle of the third century on could be considered as belonging to a dark age.

More has been written on the fall of Rome than on the death of any other civilization. The theories offered to account for the tragedy have been many and various. Moralist historians have found the explanation in the evidences of lechery unearthed at Pompeii or revealed in the satires of Juvenal and Martial. They overlook the fact, however, that nearly all of this evidence comes from the early Principate, and that in the centuries preceding the collapse of the Empire, morality became more austere through the influence of ascetic religions. Historians of a sociological bent have attributed the downfall to a declining birth rate. But there is little to indicate that Rome could have been saved by greater numbers. The Athenian civilization reached the height of its glory during the very centuries when growth of population was most strictly limited.

Alleged causes of the decline

If there was one primary factor which operated more than others to accomplish the downfall of Roman civilization, it was probably imperialism. Nearly all of the troubles that beset the country were traceable in some measure to the conquest of a great empire. It was this which was largely responsible for the creation of the city mob, for the growth of slavery, for the strife between classes and the widespread political corruption. It was also imperialism that was partly responsible for the barbarian invasions, for the exhaustion of the resources of the state to maintain a huge military machine, and for the influx of alien ideas which the Romans could not readily assimilate. The idea that Rome became a civilized nation as a result of her conquests is undoubtedly a fallacy. Instead, her repeated victories caused her ruling population to become greedy and domineering. It is true that she appropriated much of the Hellenistic culture after her conquest of the Near East; but the really valuable elements of this culture would eventually have been acquired anyway through the normal expansion of trade, while the evil consequences of domination of vast areas by force would have been avoided.

Actual causes: (1) imperialism

Another important cause, closely related to imperialism, deserves analysis: namely, the revolution in economic and social conditions that swept over Italy in the third and fourth centuries A.D. This revolution, which differed radically from the one that had occupied the third and second centuries B.C., had the following features: (1) the disappearance of money from circulation and the return to a natural economy; (2) the decline of industry and commerce; (3) the growth of serfdom and the rise of an extralegal feudalism; (4) the extension of government control over a large portion of the

(2) revolution in economic and social conditions

economic sphere; and (5) the transition from a regime of individual initiative to a regime of hereditary status. The primary cause of this revolution seems to have been the unfavorable balance of trade that Italy suffered in her commerce with the provinces. In order to check the withdrawal of precious metals from the country, the government, instead of encouraging manufactures for export, resorted to the hazardous expedient of debasing the coinage. Nero began the practice, and his successors continued it until the proportion of baser metal in the Roman coins had increased to 98.5 per cent. The inevitable result was disappearance of money from circulation. Commerce could no longer be carried on, salaries had to be paid in food and clothing, and taxes collected in produce. The scarcity of money in turn led to a decline in production, until the government intervened with a series of decrees binding peasants to the soil and compelling every townsman to follow the occupation of his father. The great landlords, now that they had control over a body of serfs, entrenched themselves on their estates, defied the central government, and ruled as feudal magnates. So close were the peasants to the margin of starvation that some of them sold their newborn children in order to escape from the burden of supporting them.

Other causes

No one can present an exhaustive list of causes of Rome's decline. Among others of at least minor significance were the following: (1) the unjust policy of taxation, which rested most heavily on the business and farming classes and resulted in the discouragement of productive enterprise; (2) the social stigma attached to work, resulting in the deliberate choice by thousands of the debasing relationship of clientage in preference to useful labor; (3) exhaustion of the soil, resulting in part from unscientific farming and in part from the attempt of too many people to make a living from the land; and (4) the disastrous plagues of Asiatic origin which broke out in 166 and 252 A.D., resulting in depopulating whole sections of Italy and thereby opening the way for barbarian incursions. To the last of these causes should be appended the fact that as lands along the low-lying coast were withdrawn from cultivation because of the competition of grain from the provinces, malaria spread. The effect of this disease in undermining the vigor of the Italian population is impossible to estimate, but it must have been considerable.

11. THE ROMAN HERITAGE

Comparison of
Rome with the
modern world

It is tempting to believe that the modern world owes a vast debt to the Romans: first of all, because Rome is nearer to us in time than any of the other civilizations of antiquity; and secondly, because Rome seems to bear such a close kinship to the modern temper. The resemblances between Roman history and the history of Great Britain or the United States in the nineteenth and twentieth centuries have often been noted. The Roman economic evolution progressed

The Forum, the Civic Center of Ancient Rome. In addition to public squares, the Forum included triumphal arches, magnificent temples, and government buildings. In the foreground is the Temple of Saturn. Behind it is the Temple of Antoninus and Faustina. The three columns at the extreme right are what is left of the Temple of Castor and Pollux, and in the farthest background is the arch of Titus.

all the way from a simple agrarianism to a complex urban system with problems of unemployment, monopoly, gross disparities of wealth, and financial crises. The Roman Empire, in common with the British and the American, was founded upon conquest and upon visions of Manifest Destiny. It must not be forgotten, however, that the spirit of Rome was the spirit of classical man, and that, consequently, the similarities between the Roman and modern civilizations are not so important as they seem. As we have noted already, the Romans disdained industrial activities, and they were incredibly naïve in matters of science. Neither did they have any idea of the modern national state; the provinces were mere appendages, not integral parts of a body politic. It was largely for this reason that the Romans never developed an adequate system of representative government. Finally, the Roman conception of religion was vastly different from our own. Their system of worship, like that of the Greeks, was external and mechanical, not inward or spiritual in any

sense. What Christians consider the highest ideal of piety—an emotional attitude of love for the divine—the Romans regarded as gross
superstition.

The influence
of Roman civili-
zation

Nevertheless, the civilization of Rome was not without a definite
influence upon later cultures. The form, if not the spirit, of Roman
architecture was preserved in the ecclesiastical architecture of the
Middle Ages and survives to this day in the design of most of our
government buildings. The sculpture of the Augustan Age also
lives on in the equestrian statues, the memorial arches and columns,
and in the portraits in stone of statesmen and generals that adorn
our boulevards and parks. Although subjected to new interpretations, the law of the great jurists became an important part of
the Code of Justinian and was thus handed down to the later
Middle Ages. Modern lawyers and especially American judges frequently cite maxims originally invented by Gaius or Ulpian. Further, the legal systems of nearly all Continental European countries
today incorporate much of the Roman law. This law was one of the
grandest of the Romans' achievements and reflected their genius for
governing a vast and diverse empire. It should not be forgotten
either that Roman literary achievements furnished much of the inspiration for the revival of learning that spread over Europe in the
twelfth century and reached its zenith in the Renaissance. Nor
should the debt of the Western world to Rome for the transmission
of Greek culture be overlooked. Perhaps not so well known is the
fact that the organization of the Catholic Church, to say nothing of
part of its ritual, was adapted from the structure of the Roman state
and the complex of the Roman religion. For example, the Pope still
bears the title of Supreme Pontiff (*Pontifex Maximus*), which was
used to designate the authority of the emperor as head of the civic
religion. But the most important element in the Roman influence has
probably been the idea of the absolute authority of the state. In the
judgment of nearly all Romans, with the exception of philosophers
such as Cicero and Seneca, the state was legally omnipotent. However much the Roman may have detested tyranny, it was really only
personal tyranny that he feared; the despotism of the Senate as the
organ of popular sovereignty was perfectly proper. This conception
survives to our own day in the popular conviction that the state can
do no wrong, and especially in the doctrines of absolutist political
philosophers that the individual has no rights except those which the
state confers upon him.

The Roman
conception of a
world empire

One other political conception, emanating from the Romans, has
had lasting significance. This is the conception of a world empire
established and maintained by a single people by virtue of its martial
prowess and its superior civilization. The Romans brought to a temporary end the regime of local independence that had prevailed during most of previous history except during the brief rule of the
Hellenistic empires. Under the *Pax Romana* none of the smaller

states was really master of its own fate. All were mere appendages of Rome, in theory if not in actuality. They had not chosen this fate for themselves but had been obliged to accept it because of the overwhelming power of their mighty neighbor. As a consequence, the Mediterranean Sea, which washed the shores of most of what was then the civilized Western world, had become a Roman lake. This same *Pax Romana* provided much of the inspiration for the *Pax Britannica* of the nineteenth century. Controlling a population amounting to one-fourth of the world's total and maintaining a navy equal in strength to the combined navies of any two other powers, Great Britain molded the destinies of most of the Western world. In this way she succeeded in preventing major wars and in acquiring cultural and economic supremacy. At the end of the nineteenth century many Americans also fell under the spell of the *Pax Romana*. Politicians and propagandists such as Albert J. Beveridge, William Allen White, and Theodore Roosevelt proclaimed it the mission of the American people to become the "master organizers" of the world, to enforce peace, and to advance the cause of human welfare. They insisted that their country had been given a divine appointment as "trustee of the civilization of the world." [12]

SELECTED READINGS

· *Items so designated are available in paperbound editions.*

POLITICAL HISTORY

· Adcock, F. E., *Roman Political Ideas and Practice*, Ann Arbor, 1964 (University of Michigan).

Bloch, Raymond, *The Origins of Rome*, New York, 1960.

Boak, A. E. R., *A History of Rome to 565 A.D.*, New York, 1929. Clear and concise.

· Cowell, F. R., *Cicero and the Roman Republic*, New York, 1948 (Penguin). A good account of the fall of the Republic.

· Haywood, R. M., *The Myth of Rome's Fall*, New York, 1962 (Apollo).

· Katz, Solomon, *The Decline of Rome*, Ithaca, 1955 (Cornell).

· Mommsen, Theodor, *The History of Rome*, Chicago, 1957 (Meridian, Wisdom Library). A reprint of a great masterpiece.

· Scullard, H. S., *From the Gracchi to Nero*, New York, 1959 (Barnes & Noble).

· Starr, C. G., *The Emergence of Rome*, Ithaca, 1953 (Cornell).

· Syme, Ronald, *The Roman Revolution*, New York, 1939 (Oxford, 1960).

· Warmington, B. H., *Carthage*, Baltimore, 1965 (Penguin).

CULTURAL AND SOCIAL HISTORY

Arnold, E. V., *Roman Stoicism*, New York, 1911.

Bailey, Cyril, ed., *The Legacy of Rome*, New York, 1924.

[12] For an extended discussion of this subject see E. M. Burns, *The American Idea of Mission*, pp. 206–10.

- Carceopino, Jerome, *Daily Life in Ancient Rome*, New Haven, 1960 (Yale University Press).
- Clagett, Marshall, *Greek Science in Antiquity*, New York, 1963 (Collier). Includes developments in late antiquity.
- Dill, Samuel, *Roman Society from Nero to Marcus Aurelius*, New York, 1905 (Meridian). Old but still highly regarded.
- Duff, J. W., *A Literary History of Rome in the Golden Age*, New York, 1964 (Barnes & Noble).
- ———, *A Literary History of Rome in the Silver Age*, New York, 1960 (Barnes & Noble, 1964).
- Fowler, W. W., *Social Life at Rome in the Age of Cicero*, New York, 1915 (St. Martin's Library).
  ———, *The Religious Experience of the Roman People*, London, 1911.
  Frank, Tenney, *Economic History of Rome*, Baltimore, 1927. Perhaps the best economic history.
- Hamilton, Edith, *The Roman Way*, New York, 1932 (Norton Library).
- Laistner, M. L. W., *The Greater Roman Historians*, Berkeley, 1947 (University of California, 1963).
- Lot, Ferdinand, *The End of the Ancient World*, New York, 1931 (Torchbook).
- Mattingly, Harold, *Christianity in the Roman Empire*, New York, 1967 (Norton Library).
- ———, *The Man in the Roman Street*, New York, 1947 (Norton Library).
  Rostovtzev, M. I., *Social and Economic History of the Roman Empire*, New York, 1957, 2 vols. Has become almost a classic.
- Starr, C. G., *Civilization and the Caesars*, New York, 1954 (Norton Library).
  Westermann, W. L., *The Slave Systems of Greek and Roman Antiquity*, Philadelphia, 1955.
- Wheeler, Mortimer, *The Art of Rome*, New York, 1964 (Praeger).

SOURCE MATERIALS

Translations of Roman authors are available in the appropriate volumes of the Loeb Classical Library.
See also:
Lewis, Naphtali, and Reinhold, M., *Roman Civilization*, New York, 1955, 2 vols.

CHAPTER 12

The Far East in Transition
(*ca.* 200 B.C.-900 A.D.)

> If brave and ambitious men have sincere understanding and aware-
> ness; if they fear and heed the warnings of disaster and use tran-
> scendent vision and profound judgment; if they . . . rid them-
> selves of the blind notion that the mandate of Heaven can be
> pursued like a deer in chase and realize that the sacred vessel of
> rule must be given from on high; . . . then will fortune and bless-
> ing flow to their sons and grandsons, and the rewards of Heaven
> will be with them to the end of their days.
> —Pan Piao, *History of the Former Han Dynasty*

During the period when the Greco-Roman classical civilization was being extended throughout the Mediterranean world by means of the Roman Empire, a high stage of cultural development had been reached in both India and China. The disturbances that character- *Contrasts of East and West* ized the downfall of the Roman Empire in the West had their paral- lels in Asia too. However, the invasions and political upheavals in the Far East did not produce the same drastic changes as those in the West. The structure of society continued without serious modifica- tion in India and China, and the cultures of these two countries at- tained a brilliant peak while Europe was experiencing its Dark Ages. In India a combination of commerical prosperity—which encour- aged the growth of large cities—and the religious enthusiasm accompanying the spread of Buddhism stimulated an outpouring of artistic talent. During this period Indian influence extended far be- yond the borders of the country. Buddhism was planted in Central Asia and from there carried to China, Korea, and Japan. Indian colonization led to the introduction of both Buddhism and Hindu- ism, together with their art and literature, in Southeast Asia and the Malay Archipelago (which is still called Indonesia). China, while **311** importing a major religion from India, showed much greater success in achieving political unification and an effective administrative system. So great was the prestige of imperial China that its culture was studied and eagerly assimilated by the Japanese in the sixth and succeeding centuries A.D. At the same time the West received some impact from the civilizations of Asia by way of the Hellenistic and imperial Roman commercial centers and, later, through the initiative of the Arabs.

I.   THE FLOWERING OF HINDU CIVILIZATION

The Maurya Dynasty, under the energetic and devout King Asoka, had projected a common rule over the greater part of India. Upon the overthrow of this dynasty early in the second century B.C., the empire quickly fell apart, leaving India in a condition of political discord. For the next several hundred years the most powerful kingdoms were centered not in the Indo-Gangetic plain but in the Deccan, where a succession of dynasties contended with one another, and some of them emerged as major states with extensive territories and resources. It is clear that by this time the arts of civilization were well advanced in southern India, even though the most distinctive historic influences—Vedic literature and philosophy, the traditional religious and social concepts of Hinduism, and the creative force of Buddhism—had originated in the north. Moreover, the invasions which began to trouble northern India did not penetrate into the Deccan. The states of the Deccan carried on commercial intercourse with neighboring and even distant areas but were not seriously threatened with hostile assaults from foreign powers. On the contrary, their merchants and missionaries were ensuring the cultural ascendancy of India over Southeast Asia.

After a period of domination by nomadic tribes from Turkestan, the political initiative in India was recovered by a native house which established a highly effective rule and was even more remarkable for its advancement of culture. The Gupta Dynasty, as it was called, governed most of northern India during the fourth and fifth centuries A.D. The dynasty's founder, Chandragupta I, was probably not descended from the Chandragupta who had instituted the Maurya Dynasty after the death of Alexander the Great, but the Guptas ruled from the same capital—Pataliputra (Patna) on the Ganges—and also revived some of the principles of the renowned King Asoka. The climax of the Gupta period came in the reign of Vikramaditya ("Sun of Power"), 375–413 A.D., which inaugurated a golden age not unworthy of comparison with Athens' Golden Age in the days of Pericles. Valuable information on conditions in northern India at this time has been preserved in the brief account written by a Chinese pilgrim, Fa Hsien, who spent six years in the realm of Vikramaditya. Buddhism had already spread into China, and the monk Fa Hsien undertook his hazardous journey to acquire sacred texts and first-hand knowledge of the religion in the land of its birth. His comments, however, were not restricted to religious matters, and because he was an intelligent and civilized foreigner, his observations may be taken as objective and generally reliable. The travels of Fa Hsien in themselves represent no mean undertaking. He made his way on foot across Sinkiang and the mountain passes, taking six years to reach India (399–405 A.D.). Here he taught himself the Sanskrit language, procured texts, drawings, and relics at the Gupta capital, and then returned to his native land by sea, spending two years in Ceylon en route and also visiting Java on the voyage. Altogether, during the fifteen years of his pilgrimage he traversed a distance of some 8000 miles.

According to Fa Hsien's testimony, Buddhism was flourishing in India, especially in the Gupta empire, but all the Hindu cults were tolerated and the rivalry among the different religions was not embittered by persecution. Evidently the impact of Buddhism and the traditions of Asoka had stimulated the growth of humane sentiments, given practical expression in public hospitals, rest houses, and other charitable institutions receiving state support. Fa Hsien asserted that the Indians scrupulously refrained from the use of liquor and were vegetarians to such an extent that they slaughtered no living creatures—undoubtedly a pious exaggeration. Apparently, also, the caste system had not become utterly rigid, probably because Buddhism was still vigorous and also because segregation was impracticable in the cosmopolitan society of the thriving commercial centers. Fa Hsien, who had no reason to bestow unmerited praise (he does not even mention the name of the great king Vikramaditya), described the government as just and beneficent. The roads, he indicated, were well kept up, brigandage was rare, taxes were relatively light, and capital punishment was unknown. He testified to a generally high level of prosperity, social contentment, and intellectual vitality at a time when the nations of Western Europe were sinking into a state of semibarbarism.

Unfortunately, another invasion of India destroyed the Gupta power and brought a period of confusion lasting for more than a century. Almost simultaneously with the formal demise of the Roman Empire in the West, a group of nomads called "White Huns" defeated the Gupta forces and made themselves masters of northern India (480 A.D.). By the early sixth century the White Huns had staked out an empire extending from Bengal in the east into Afghanistan and Central Asia. However, it was much more barbaric than its predecessors, and disrupted the splendid administrative system of the Guptas. The Huns in India were gradually absorbed by the native population, but on the northwestern borders a promising artistic movement was blighted before the Hunnish power disintegrated in accordance with the usual cycle of hastily

Culture and society under the Guptas

The overthrow of Gupta rule by Hun invaders

313

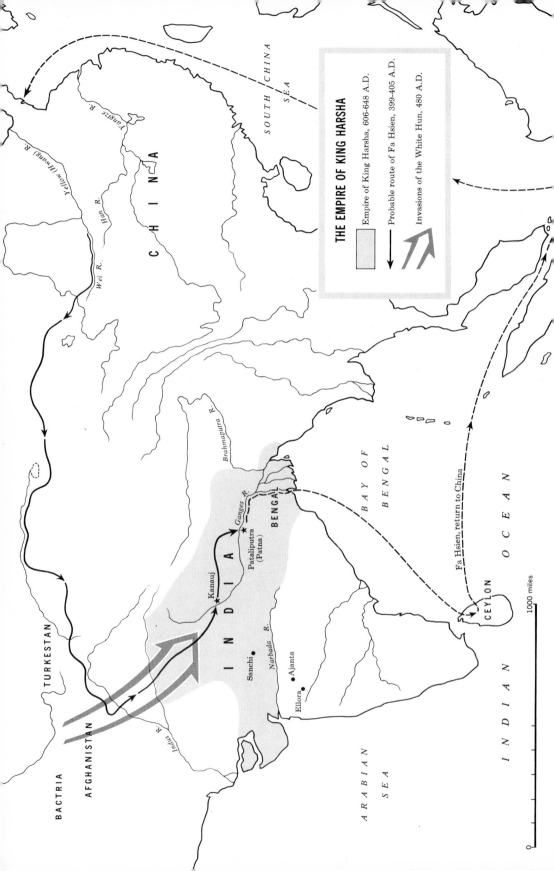

THE EMPIRE OF KING HARSHA

Empire of King Harsha, 606-648 A.D.

Probable route of Fa Hsien, 399-405 A.D.

Invasions of the White Hun, 480 A.D.

SOUTH CHINA SEA

C H I N A

Yellow (Hwang) R.

Yangtze R.

Wei R.

Han R.

TURKESTAN

BACTRIA

AFGHANISTAN

Indus R.

Narbada R.

Brahmaputra R.

Ganges R.

I N D I A

BENGAL

Kanauj

Pataliputra (Patna)

Sanchi

Ellora

Ajanta

BAY OF BENGAL

Fa Hsien, return to China

CEYLON

I N D I A N   O C E A N

A R A B I A N   S E A

1000 miles

constructed nomadic states. After the Hunnish menace receded, an able government was re-established by one of the most famous rulers in Indian history, King Harsha (606–648 A.D.).

Although Harsha's state was not literally a continuation of the Gupta, it was so similar in important features that the term "Gupta" is often used to designate the civilization of northern India from the fourth to the seventh century, a period of cultural maturity despite the devastating interlude of the Hunnish invasion. King Harsha was a mighty conqueror who, with a huge army efficiently organized in divisions of infantry, cavalry, and elephants, reunited most of northern India. He was also a capable administrator, an intelligent and prudent statesman, and a generous patron of art, literature, and religion. His capital, Kanauj, extending four miles along the river in the central Ganges valley, was a splendid city, adorned with hundreds of temples and imposing public buildings, and enlivened with festive pageantry. As in the reign of Vikramaditya, the account of a Chinese Buddhist pilgrim throws revealing light upon Harsha's administration.

According to the narrative of this pilgrim (Hsün-tsang or Yuan Chwang) and other contemporary records, Harsha's administration was in the Gupta tradition but slightly less gentle. The state revenue was derived chiefly from taxes on the royal domains, which amounted to one-sixth of the produce of the villages and could hardly be regarded as oppressive. Harsha allotted only one-fourth of his income to administrative expenses, devoting the remainder to the rewarding of public servants, to charity, and to the promotion of education, religion, and the arts. In contrast to the mild punishments employed by the earlier Gupta regime, King Harsha inflicted such severe penalties as mutilation and death through starvation. Nevertheless, crimes of violence seem to have become more numerous. Religious toleration was still the official policy. Although Harsha is supposed to have been converted to the *Mahayana* school of Buddhism, he continued to worship the Sun and Shiva, and no attempt was made to enforce a religious orthodoxy. Despite this policy, the Brahmans were beginning to recover their ascendancy, and it was only a question of time before Buddhism, with its universalist and caste-dissolving tendencies, would be crowded out or absorbed by the cults so deeply rooted in Indian local tradition, literature, and social institutions. During the upheaval which followed the death of Harsha, this trend became more pronounced.

During the first seven or eight centuries of the Christian era, in spite of invasions and disunity, political vigor and artistic and intellectual creativity in India reached their height. This period, in which Hindu civilization attained its full maturity, ranks as a major era in the history of the world's cultures. What the Periclean Age and the Augustan Age were for the classical civilizations of the West the reigns of Vikramaditya and Harsha were for India and, to a considerable extent, for other portions of Southern Asia. Undoubtedly the development of industry and commerce helps explain the generally prosperous state of Indian society and the cultural advances. At this time, and later also, India was the center of an intercontinental market, and her merchants took the initiative in navigation on the high seas. During the first two centuries A.D. there was extensive intercourse between India and the Near East, especially with the city of Alexandria. Many products were also being exported from India to the Roman West, including jewels, ivory, tortoise shells, pepper, cinnamon and other spices, fine muslin cloth, and silks of both Indian and Chinese manufacture. In exchange the Indians imported linen, glass, copper, wines, and other items, but the trade balance was so decidedly in India's favor that the Roman emperors became alarmed at the drainage of gold to the East and tried to curtail the use of silk for wearing apparel. Some of this trade was overland, but Indian merchants had from early days sailed across the Arabian Sea and up the Red Sea to Egypt. Not until the first century A.D. did Western traders discover the monsoon winds which enabled them to sail east to the Indian coast during the summer and then return when the wind direction changed in October. Traffic between the Near Eastern ports and southern India was probably even greater than with northern India. Pearls and beryls from the Deccan were especially prized, and Roman coins, testifying to a once flourishing trade, have been discovered along both the southwestern and southeastern coasts of the Indian peninsula. Apparently no obstacles were placed by the Indian rulers in the way of foreign intercourse or even against settlement by foreign traders, some of whom took up permanent residence in India. Southern India acquired small colonies of Romans, Jews, Nestorian Christians from Syria and Persia (a Syriac-speaking Christian church still exists in southwestern India), and Arabs.

Influence upon
the West

Through commercial contacts India probably exerted more influence upon the West than has been generally recognized, although much of it came somewhat later and with the Arabs as intermediaries. The Indian numerals ("Arabic"), which were not adopted by Europeans until the late Middle Ages, were perhaps known in Alexandria as early as the second century A.D. In the eighth and ninth centuries important scientific and medical treatises were translated from Sanskrit into Arabic. In addition, it is quite possible that familiarity with Indian philosophy and religion contributed a stimulus to the growth of Christian monasticism. The earliest Christian hermit-ascetics appeared in Egypt, where there was considerable knowledge of Brahmanism and Buddhism, both of which religions stressed the concepts of renunciation and mystic exaltation.

The manifold intellectual activity of this period of Indian history reflected the interests of a cosmopolitan society, the patronage of wealthy rulers, and—most strongly of all—the incentives of religious faith. High levels of scholarship were maintained both by the Brahmans and by Buddhist monks, and large libraries came into being. Particularly noteworthy were the educational foundations, for which the chief credit should be given to the Buddhists. The role of the Buddhist monks in education was comparable to that of the Christian monks of the West during the early Middle Ages, but the scope of their studies was broader because the general level of knowledge was far higher in India than in the West at this time. Some Buddhist monasteries were internationally famous centers of learning, unmatched in Europe until the rise of such universities as Paris, Montpellier, and Oxford in the late Middle Ages. One of the

Buddhist patronage of education

Ruins at Nalanda. The remains of the ancient university town, early seat of Buddhist learning.

greatest Buddhist universities, at Nalanda in the Ganges valley (in modern Bihar), was functioning as early as the fourth or fifth century A.D. Endowed by the Gupta rulers with a substantial income, it maintained residence halls for students—with free tuition, board, lodging, and medical care for poor boys who were able to pass the entrance examinations—and had a library that occupied three buildings. Pilgrims visiting the university in the seventh century reported that 5000 students were in attendance, including some from Tibet, China, and Korea. Although Nalanda was a Buddhist foundation and provided instruction in eighteen different schools of Buddhism, its faculty also offered courses in Hindu philosophy, grammar, medicine, mathematics, and in both Vedic and contemporary literature.

While the literary output was prolific and uninhibited, it betrayed a veneration for past in that Sanskrit—the ancient language of the Epic Age—became the universally accepted literary vehicle, in the Deccan as well as in Hindustan. Even the Buddhists felt constrained to translate their sacred texts from *Pali* (the dialect of King Asoka's day) into Sanskrit, and it was the Sanskrit versions

Literature: romantic narratives, fables, and drama

317

which were carried by missionaries into Central Asia, China, Korea, and ultimately Japan. Literature of the Gupta Age, in both prose and poetry, ranged from scientific treatises and biographies to tales for popular entertainment. The latter included long romantic narratives suggestive of—and perhaps the prototype of—the *Arabian Nights;* and also "Beast Fables" comparable to those attributed to Aesop. The most impressive literary medium was the drama, which, as in Europe somewhat later, evolved out of a popular type of religious instruction and entertainment. The Sanskrit drama, in its perfected form, combined song, dance, and gesture with narrative and dialogue, and thus resembled the Western opera or cantata more than the typical stage play. The plots, often diffuse, were usually concerned with romantic love, drew heavily upon legendary themes from the epics, and resorted to miracles whenever necessary to resolve a difficulty in the story. Although they employed pathos, the dramas were never tragedies, always ending happily. They also utilized the peculiarly artificial device of having the principal characters speak in classical Sanskrit while women and lesser figures used the less elegant dialect of ordinary conversation. Although the Sanskrit drama never provided the suspense or realism characteristic of the modern Western theater, it did attain undeniable beauty, both in descriptions of nature and in lyrical passages expressing human emotions of tenderness and anguish.

The most superb expression of the Indian creative faculties during these centuries was in art, especially architecture and sculpture, although some excellent paintings were also produced. By the Gupta era, architecture was nearing a point of perfection, as evidenced by imposing stone structures in all sections of India. As in so many other fields, the Buddhists pioneered in the development of artistic forms. The evolution of the Buddhist monasteries and temples set the pattern for practically the whole of Hindu architecture (and sculpture also). During the early centuries when *Hinayana* Buddhism was dominant, neither temples nor images of Gautama were made. Hence the first typical Buddhist monument was the *stupa,* a simple burial mound in the shape of a dome or hemisphere crowned with an umbrella—the Indian symbol of sovereignty. Inside the brick- or rock-faced mound was buried a sacred relic, usually some object associated with Gautama or with a revered Buddhist saint. The most famous *stupa* is the large one at Sanchi in the very center of India, still in an excellent state of preservation, although it was begun in Asoka's reign and substantially completed during the first century B.C. More impressive than the stone-faced mound (which has a diameter at the base of 120 feet) are the four carved gateways surrounding the *stupa*. These massive fences of stone are supported by pillars 35 feet high and, in spite of their huge proportions, are adorned with intricate carvings, both pictorial and symbolic, with a profusion of delicately formed human and animal figures. After the

The Great Stupa at Sanchi. Begun by Asoka and completed under the Andhra Dynasty (72–25 B.C.), it was originally a burial mound containing relics of the Buddha. The fully developed stupa, designed with mathematical precision, became an architectural symbol of the cosmos. The tiered mast on top of the structure represents the earth's axis penetrating the dome of heaven.

stupa, the next step in the evolution of religious architecture was the assembly hall, where monks and lay disciples gathered to honor the memory of Gautama, the "Master of the Law." These halls were commonly tunneled out of solid rock in a mountain or the side of a cliff. Their general plan was similar to that of the Roman basilica and early Christian church in that it emphasized a central passageway or nave separated from aisles on either side by round columns. Paralleling the evolution of the temple was the development of the Buddhist monastery. Like the assembly hall or temple, the monastery was often carved out of a single mass of rock, with successive stories of cells or cubicles so arranged that the structure as a whole appeared to be a terraced pyramid. Devotees of the Hindu cults soon began to construct temples in imitation of the Buddhist and eventually even more elaborate.

Although some free-standing temples were erected as early as the first century A.D., for several centuries the Indians seemed to prefer the more arduous method of hewing their edifices out of the solid rock of caves and cliffs. More than 1200 rock-cut temples and monasteries were executed in various sections of India, the larger proportion being along the western coast. The two most remarkable groups of cliff excavations are located at Ajanta and Ellora, about 70 miles apart, in the northern part of what later became Hyderabad. The Ajanta caves were Buddhist sanctuaries, some of them dating from the second century B.C. and some from as late as the fifth century A.D. They include both assembly halls and monasteries, com-

Rock-cut temples and monasteries

319

Entrance to the Ajanta Caves. The Gupta period (fourth to seventh centuries A.D.) constitutes the Golden Age of Indian art—in sculpture, architecture, and painting—as well as the climax of classical Sanskrit literature.

plete with stone beds, tables, water cisterns, and niches for oil reading lamps. The even more splendid caves at Ellora represent about 900 years of architectural and sculptural enterprise, extending from the fourth to the thirteenth century. The Buddhists were the first to utilize the site, but some of the caves were the work of Jains and the largest number were constructed as Hindu temples, of tremendous size and lavish design.

Temples composed of separate stone blocks, in contrast to the cave type, began to be more common in Gupta times and were typical of the most active period of Hindu temple building, between the sixth and the thirteenth centuries. The essential architectural features of these free-standing Hindu temples are (1) a base consisting of a square or rectangular chamber to house the image of the god, and (2) a lofty tower which rises from the roof of the chamber and dominates the entire edifice. The shape of the tower distinguishes the two main styles of Hindu temples. The "Dravidian" style, found only in the tropics, is identified by a terraced steeple divided into stories like a step pyramid and decidedly reminiscent of the early Buddhist rock-cut monasteries. The "Indo-Aryan" style, prevalent in northern India, has a curvilinear tower with vertical ribs which may possibly be derived from the Buddhist *stupa*.

Sculpture usually develops in close conjunction with architecture, and this was especially true in India, where so many sacred halls and chambers were literally carved out of stone. Decorative engravings, including figures in relief, were typically an integral part of the

Free-standing
temples

320

Eastern Gateway of the Great Stupa at Sanchi. The relief carvings, depicting incidents from the life of the Buddha, are remarkable for their fine detail, vitality, and naturalism.

Yakshi or "Tree Spirit." A female figure derived from an early fertility cult but here symbolizing the transition from the sensuous world of illusion to the world of the spirit.

THE GOLDEN AGE OF INDIAN ART

Limestone Medallion from a Great Stupa at Amaravati, Southeastern India (second century A.D.). This court scene depicts Gautama's life before his renunciation of the world. Many of the Amaravati carvings were burned to make lime in the nineteenth century. This one is in the Government Museum at Madras.

building itself. Chiseled decorations were very successfully applied to the gateways and pillars surrounding some of the early Buddhist *stupas*. The figures on the gates of the great *stupa* at Sanchi (first century B.C.) are particularly fine examples. Although they were intended to commemorate events of sacred tradition and embody pious symbolism, they are invested with vigor, freshness, and spontaneity, suggesting an uninhibited delight in the natural world rather than a brooding melancholy. Meanwhile a significant school of sculpture was arising in northwestern India and beyond the borders in Afghanistan and Bactria. The initial stimulus undoubtedly was Greek or Hellenistic, but Persian and other influences played a part, and the school developed its own original characteristics with Buddhist concepts predominant. It was in this region that the figure of Gautama was delineated for the first time, and relief sculptures depicted the legendary incidents of his life from infancy to Enlightenment. The large statues of the Buddha clearly revealed Greek influence at the beginning: the head resembled an Apollo or Zeus and the garment was draped like a toga rather than a monk's robe. However, there was a gradual approach toward the conventional form—in cross-legged posture and an attitude of benign repose—which eventually came to represent the Buddha all over the Far East. This Greco-Buddhist school of sculpture continued to flourish in the border regions of Central Asia, acquiring a more and more hearty realism, until it was snuffed out by the Hun invasions in the early sixth century.

During the Gupta Age, Indian sculpture largely emancipated itself from foreign influences and assumed characteristics peculiarly expressive of Indian ideals. The treatment of the human form was handled with a subtle delicacy, conveying a sense both of rhythmic movement and tranquillity. Garments on the figures were shown as almost transparent or suggested only in faint outline so that the effect is that of nudity, although chaste rather than voluptuous. The harmonious proportions and graceful curves of the limbs were derived from a study of plant forms as well as from human anatomy. Thus Gupta art, particularly as exemplified in the statues of Buddha, was idealistic and spiritual rather than realistic.

The richest creations of the Hindu artistic genius are to be found in the relief sculpture and fresco paintings executed in the rock-cut temples upon which so much energy was expended during the period corresponding to the Classical and Medieval ages of the West. The Buddhist caves at Ajanta contain the most important surviving collection of wall paintings. After almost 2000 years they are still magnificent in both form and color even though they were executed upon a none-too-durable plaster. While religious in inspiration, they are nevertheless spontaneous and unrestrained, skillfully combining the naturalism of the early Buddhist *stupa* carvings with a poetic mysticism. The paintings proclaim an unabashed delight in physical

Relief Sculpture in the Hindu Cave temple at Ellora, Hyderabad (eighth century A.D.). The central figures are the god Shiva and his consort Parvati.

beauty and seem to suggest the conviction that the physical and spiritual aspects of experience can be brought into perfect accord, just as some of the art of the Italian Renaissance attempted to fuse the pagan ideal of joyous living with the Christian ideal of renunciation. In the Hindu temples, which increased in number from the seventh century on as Buddhism began to decline, decoration was usually in sculpture rather than painting. The relief sculptures in the Hindu cave-temples at Ellora have never been surpassed in India and rank among the supreme masterpieces of the world's art. In these carvings not only the gods but a galaxy of figures and dramatic episodes out of India's historic and legendary past seem to come alive. Many scenes are boldly realistic, but the Hindu tendency toward abstraction is also evident in the practice of depicting gods with several pairs of arms or several faces to signify their separate attributes. The themes portrayed range from voluptuous ecstasy and heroic struggle to attitudes of piety and mystic contemplation. A somewhat different effect, that of a soaring idealism, is attained in a gigantic bust of the god Shiva in an eighth-century temple at Elephanta (an island in Bombay harbor). The three faces of this statue are believed to represent the three-fold aspects of divine being—as creator, preserver, and destroyer. While the facial expressions vary appropriately, there is a captivating harmony rather than grotesque contrast among them. The whole figure evokes a feeling of masterful strength and profound serenity. The Buddhist and Hindu art of these creative centuries indicates that at least the upper and middle classes of Indian society were not yet bowed down by fatalism or by the incubus of the caste system; nor were they living in dread of a foreign conqueror.

While the Indian communities were bringing their civilization to a point of refinement, they were also implanting it among various other peoples of Southeastern Asia. Indian navigators and merchants **323**

The spread of
Indian culture

were active in the eastern waters of the Indian Ocean as well as in the Arabian Sea to the west and apparently led the world in maritime enterprise during this period. Some of the Indian states maintained navies and had a Board of Shipping as a governmental department. They not only promoted commerce but chartered companies of merchants, giving them trade monopolies in certain areas and authority to establish colonies. During the early centuries A.D. Indian colonies were planted in the Malay Peninsula, Annam (eastern Indochina), Java, Sumatra, and many other islands of the Malay Archipelago. Between the fifth and tenth centuries an empire ruled by a Buddhist dynasty and possessing formidable naval strength was based on the island of Sumatra. It also controlled western Java, extended into the Malay Peninsula, sent colonists to Borneo and from thence to the Philippine Islands. It dominated the Strait of Malacca and effectively policed the waters of this area against piracy. Although weakened by a long struggle with one of the Hindu mainland states, the empire (known as the Srivijaya) remained intact until the fourteenth century. Indian influence was extensive in the peninsula of Indochina—in the Cham state on the southeastern coast (later absorbed into the Annamese empire), in the Cambodian kingdoms of the lower Mekong valley, and among the Thais (Siamese) to the northwest.

Southeast Asia
as an outpost of
Indian culture

The political vicissitudes of these various Eastern states were too complex to be enumerated here, but the entire region long remained an outpost of Indian culture. Sanskrit literature was introduced, along with Buddhism and the leading cults of Hinduism. Art and architecture, originating in Indian prototypes, were assiduously cultivated and attained considerable individuality. During the eighth and ninth centuries the Srivijaya empire in Sumatra and Java was perhaps the foremost center of Buddhist art. A colossal *stupa* in central Java, dating from the late eighth century, is considered by some

Angkor Wat from the West. This temple, built during the twelfth century to honor the Hindu god Vishnu, is the largest of the Angkor temples in Cambodia.

the greatest Buddhist monument in the world. Actually, although crowned with a *stupa*, this structure is a whole mountaintop carved into nine stone terraces, with staircases, covered gateways, balustrades, and four galleries containing 1500 sculptured panels. In the ninth century, building on an ambitious scale was in progress in the Cambodian empire established by the Khmers, a native people who wielded dominion over a large part of Indochina between the ninth and the fourteenth centuries, and who responded energetically to the stimulus of Indian cultural contacts. Their capital city, Angkor (recovered from the jungle by French archaeologists in the twentieth century), was of almost incredible magnificence in its heyday. Among several huge temples the most imposing was that of Angkor Wat, about a mile south of the capital, built during the twelfth century and said to be the largest work of its kind in the world, surpassing in mass even Luxor and Karnak of ancient Egypt. Angkor Wat was dedicated to the Hindu god Vishnu and was also designed as a tomb for the emperor, who was deified after his death and identified in some way with Vishnu. The storied carvings, however, honored various Hindu deities, warned sinners of the numerous hells awaiting the wicked, celebrated the king's earthly conquests, and depicted scenes from the classic Sanskrit epics of India. While Hindu influence was ascendant in Cambodia, Buddhism was also a potent force there. Khmer statues of Buddha are distinguished by the "smile of Angkor"—a countenance expressing the height of benevolence and the supreme peace associated with the attainment of an inner state of enlightenment or *nirvana*.

During the Middle Ages the whole region surrounding the Bay of Bengal, while comprising separate political units, was dominated by Indian culture, imparted through commerical contacts and manifest in the fields of religion, literature, and art. The creative activity in this "Greater India" was not inferior to that of the motherland. In some ways it was even bolder, more vigorous and experimental, and it continued to flourish after the onslaught of fanatical Moslem conquerors from Afghanistan had brought a decay in India. However, a decline finally overtook the Buddhist and Hindu civilizations of Southeast Asia as the result of exhausting struggles among the competing states, pressure from China to the north, and—more decisive—the impact of Arab and other Moslem adventurers who traded, proselytized, and conquered successfully in this area during the fourteenth, fifteenth, and sixteenth centuries.

"Greater India"

2. THE TERRITORIAL, POLITICAL, AND CULTURAL GROWTH OF CHINA

The Ch'in Dynasty, inaugurated after the overthrow of the Chou, lasted only fourteen years (221–207 B.C.), but it was one of the most important in Chinese history because it carried out a drastic reorganization of the government with permanent effects upon the character of the state. The founder of the dynasty, who assumed the title of "First Emperor" (Shih Huang Ti), was a man of iron will and administrative genius. He did away with the rival kingdoms, divided the country into provinces, and instituted an elaborate bureaucracy directly responsible to himself. The centralized administration and effective military organization that had been carefully cultivated in the state of Ch'in was now applied to all of China, thus effecting a momentous break with the past. The feudal institutions of 500 years' standing were almost completely extinguished and the government was brought into direct contact with the people. Determined to eliminate any competition for authority, the emperor's chief minister forbade the philosophic schools to continue their discussions and commanded their writings to be destroyed. His order for the burning of the books was a sweeping one, carrying the death penalty for disobedience, although copies of the forbidden works were locked up in the imperial library. Some Taoist writings were exempted from the proscription because the emperor was attracted by their reputed magic-working formulas. He was particularly anxious to root out the Confucianist and Mohist teachings because they emphasized moral restraints upon the ruler and his dependence upon the advice of learned counselors.

Every aspect of Shih Huang Ti's reign reveals tremendous force of personality and a ruthless determination. He carried out con-

The Great Wall of China at Nankow Pass. The Wall was erected about 221–207 B.C. for defense against Northern invaders.

Ancient Irrigation Canal. Still in use, this is part of one of the oldest and most elaborate irrigation systems in the world.

quests in all directions. In the south he not only annexed regions but built canals, one of which linked the Yangtze to the West River (of which Canton is the principal port). While raising large armies by conscription he disarmed the bulk of the Chinese people as a precautionary measure. With forced labor he executed an ambitious building program that included a network of military roads radiating from his capital. His most impressive engineering project was to complete and join together the series of fortifications in the north, by which he created the Great Wall of China, reaching from the seacoast some 1400 miles inland. At his capital (near Sian, the site of the old Western Chou capital) he had constructed a sumptuous palace measuring 2500 by 500 feet and capable of accommodating 10,000 people. In addition to such undertakings he and his ministers found time to standardize weights, measures, and even the axle length of carts, and—still more important—to unify the style of writing in China, with the result that communication among the various sections was made easy in spite of the diversity of spoken dialects. In his administrative policies the First Emperor probably borrowed some features from the Persian monarchs and from the Indian ruler Chandragupta Maurya. That he made a great impression not only upon the Chinese but upon foreign powers is illustrated by the fact that his country came to be known in other lands as "China"—after the name of his dynasty. This indomitable monarch's chief weakness was his addiction to superstitious fancies. He undertook several journeys in search of the elixir of immortality and died on one of these expeditions. Three years later his dynasty ended in a round of court conspiracies and assassinations, and his great palace was burned to the ground.

The Ch'in emperor had aimed at a social as well as political reconstruction, and although this was a more difficult undertaking it succeeded in part. On the whole his policy was to encourage and promote agriculture above commerce, assisting the farmers and holding the merchant class in check. Officially he abolished serfdom, decreeing that the peasants should be owners of the lands they **327** worked. It is doubtful, however, that their lot was actually much better than before. Not only were there great differences between the small and the large proprietors, but the poor peasants became burdened with debts contracted with the merchants and moneylenders, the very group the government had intended to restrain. The Ch'in ruler exacted heavy taxes of various sorts, including a poll tax, and conscripted men for military and labor service with a callous disregard for human suffering. Thus, while the state was concerning itself more directly and actively than ever before with the welfare of the whole community, it reduced the dignity and freedom of the individual to a minimum. Large numbers of the population were forcibly moved from one region to another and many were made slaves of the state. People's actions and, as far as possible, their thoughts also were controlled by the government. The Ch'in rule carried into practice the Legalist doctrines of coercion, punishment, and fear, and bore a striking resemblance to the European totalitarian regimes of the twentieth century.

The overthrow of the Ch'in Dynasty was followed soon afterward by the establishment of the Han, founded by a military adventurer who had risen from the ranks. In the course of Chinese history many dynasties came and went—some very brief and some with only a local jurisdiction—but most of them tended to follow a similar course and met with a similar fate. From time to time a new ruling house was inaugurated by force or usurpation, sometimes by an alien or by a leader of lowly birth (the founder of the Han Dynasty was said to have come from a poor peasant family). If he could vindicate his authority and maintain order, he was looked upon as a legitimate ruler entitled to all the imperial dignities, regardless of the previous status of his family. To be accepted, however, the dynasty had to promote general prosperity as well as defend the country and suppress internal strife. The typical dynastic cycle of China illustrates not only the rise and fall of successive ruling families but also the close relationship between the condition of society and the durability of a political regime. Usually during the early years of a dynasty vigorous and efficient rule was accompanied by internal peace, prosperity, and an increase in population. When the imperial court and its officers became venal and corrupt, neglected administrative problems, and demanded exorbitant taxes, domestic upheaval ensued, frequently joined to the threat of attack from without. If the dynasty failed to resolve the crisis, it went down in bloodshed, and a new firm hand seized control, cleared away the debris, and began the process all over again under a new dynastic name. The rise and fall of the Han Dynasty (206 B.C.–220 A.D.) illustrates the general pattern which was typical of China's successive political episodes. At the same time the Han Dynasty marks one of the most splendid periods in Chinese history, characterized by cultural progress and by the development of a form of government so satisfactory that its essential features remained unchanged—except for temporary interruptions—until the present century.

The Han government was a centralized bureaucracy but conducted with some regard for local differences and with deference to ancient traditions. Certain aspects of feudalism were reintroduced as the first Han emperor granted estates in the form of fiefs to his relatives and other prominent figures. However, the danger of feudal principalities becoming powerful and independent, as had happened in Chou times, was circumvented by a decree requiring the estates of nobles to be divided among the heirs instead of passing intact to the eldest son. Chinese society was still far from being equalitarian, but its aristocratic structure had been severely jolted. The imperial administration cut across class lines, and there was little danger that it would ever again be constituted on feudal principles. The power of the old Chou states was broken beyond recovery. Obviously, the Han rulers were profiting from and continuing the work begun by the hated house of Ch'in, although they softened the harshest features of the Ch'in regime. Whereas the Ch'in emperor had antagonized the class of scholars, the Han ruler sought their favor and support and instructed his officials to recommend to the public service young men of ability irrespective of birth. The Confucianists profited most from the government's policy of toleration toward the philosophical schools. Some of their books had escaped the flames, and the scholars had long memories. Under the patronage of the emperor, Confucianist teachings were reinterpreted, with more emphasis upon the supremacy of the central authority than Confucius had probably intended. Thus, instead of serving as a stumbling block, they assisted in the creation of an efficient imperial government.

The Han government

The Han rule, while energetic, efficient, and relatively enlightened, was sufficiently severe. As under the Ch'in, ambitious public works of reclamation and canal- and road-building entailed enormous labor, much of which was performed by slaves. Taxes were high, the salt and iron industries were made state monopolies, and the currency was debased to yield a profit to the government at the expense of the people. At the same time, the emperor attempted to regulate prices, not merely for the protection of the poorer consumers but to divert the middleman's profit into the imperial coffers. The government also participated in the rapidly expanding foreign commerce of the empire.

The severity of Han rule

As under most strong dynasties, efforts were directed to expanding the territorial frontiers. The Huns after many campaigns were forced to acknowledge Han suzerainty and compelled to furnish tribute and military support. Chinese control was established over much of Central Asia, including not only the Tarim basin of Sinkiang but parts of Turkestan beyond the mountains. Southern Man-

Expansion of the empire

329

churia and northern Korea were annexed, and Chinese settlers and culture penetrated this area. The provinces south of the Yangtze were secured and also northeastern Indochina (Tonkin). Both in territorial extent and in power, China under the Han was almost equal to the contemporary Roman Empire. Nor was China isolated from other civilized areas. Her trade connections were far-reaching, especially by the caravan routes which traversed Sinkiang and Turkestan. The Chinese had also begun to venture on the high seas, although ocean traffic was conducted chiefly by Indian navigators who sailed to the South China Sea and the Gulf of Tonkin. Chinese merchants exchanged products not only with India and Ceylon, but also with Japan, Persia, Arabia, Syria, and—indirectly—with Rome. The trade balance was generally favorable to China because of the high price commanded by her leading export, silk, frequently paid for in gold or precious stones.

The Han Dynasty reached its climax in the latter half of the second century B.C., under the able leadership of an emperor who ruled for more than fifty years (Han Wu Ti, 140–87 B.C.). At the opening of the first century A.D. a usurper named Wang Mang seized the throne and attempted to carry out radical reforms. If he had succeeded in realizing his program, the character of Chinese society would have been revolutionized. Wang Mang decreed the nationalization of all land so that it could be divided into equal plots and given to the peasant cultivators. He fixed prices and anticipated the agricultural-assistance policies of modern Western nations by having the state enter directly into the commodity market, buying up surpluses and holding them to sell during periods of scarcity. He also arranged government loans at low rates of interest to help struggling farmers. Even more startling was his decision to abolish slavery, although he found it impossible to enforce this measure and substituted in its place a special tax upon slave owners. His humanitarian projects on behalf of the forgotten men of toil earned for Wang the unrelenting antagonism of merchants and wealthy property owners. Revolts broke out against him; he was assassinated and his program scrapped (23 A.D.). The Han family recovered the throne and retained it for two more centuries—a period known as the Later or Eastern Han because the capital was moved eastward to the site of Honan. The Later Han period exhibited the typical symptoms of decay at court and within the ruling house, although the administrative system remained intact and China's reputation in foreign parts was upheld by skillful diplomacy and force of arms. The dynasty crumbled as rebellions broke out and power passed into the hands of war lords, one of whom deposed the Han emperor in 220 A.D.

For almost four centuries after the ending of the Han Dynasty, China was in a condition of turbulence and upheaval. The country was divided, warfare was frequent, and it seemed that all the gains

Tribulations and downfall of the Han rulers

of the previous era were in jeopardy. Although the dates are not identical, this period of political disunity in China is comparable to the time of confusion which Europe experienced after the fall of the Roman Empire in the West. As in Europe during the Early Middle Ages, the central government was weak or nonexistent; barbarian invasions affected a wide area; and, just as Christianity became rooted among the Latin and Germanic peoples of the West, a new otherworldly religion—Buddhism—made tremendous headway in China. Aside from these parallels, however, China's period of disunion was very different from the Early Middle Ages in Europe. In China there was no appreciable decline in commerce or in city life, nor was there a serious modification of culture and institutions. The absence of a strong central authority was the only real disadvantage from which the country suffered, and this defect could be remedied by reviving the administrative machinery which had been temporarily disrupted. The Han state had been a practical and effective expression of Chinese experience, utilizing existing social and economic institutions and emphasizing ancient traditions. Consequently, even a long period of semi-anarchy could not destroy China's civilization. This period, dismal as it was, gave evidence of the toughness of Chinese society and culture, embodied in the patriarchal family, the village organization, and the sturdy enterprise of farmers who literally worshiped the soil on which they labored and were determined to make it support them regardless of the political controversies that raged on all sides.

As might be expected, the nomadic peoples on China's northern borders took advantage of her internal weakness to overrun the country. For about 250 years, from the fourth to the late sixth century A.D., practically all northern China including the Wei and Yellow River valleys was ruled by nomad dynasties of Hunnish, Turkish, and related stocks. It was not, however, successfully incorporated into any of the extensive but short-lived empires which arose in Central Asia and often impinged upon India as well as China. The dominance of non-Chinese rulers over the Yellow River valley—the historic center of Chinese culture—did not by any means destroy this culture. On the contrary, the rulers seemed eager to be accepted as custodians and defenders of civilization, and in the Far East civilization was synonymous with Chinese institutions. The nomads who settled south of the Great Wall assimilated the speech and customs of the older inhabitants. One of the few permanent changes in the habits of the Chinese people that can be attributed to their contact with the steppe nomads was in costume. During the fourth and fifth centuries they adopted trousers and boots similar to those worn by the northern horsemen, and this style of dress gradually supplanted the flowing tunic even in south China.

The contrast between China and Western Europe during the medieval era is accentuated by the fact that four centuries of dis-

A period of turbulence and disunity

Nomad invasions

Restoration of
power and uni-
ty under the
T'ang Dynasty
(618–907)

The height of
T'ang power

Decline of the
T'ang empire

unity in China were followed by another vigorous and highly successful dynasty, the T'ang (618–907), which re-established the
imperial administration, again pushed back the territorial frontiers,
and promoted brilliant cultural achievements. Thus, at the very time
when feudalism was taking root in Europe and a new type of civilization was in process of formation there, China was resuming the
course that had been marked out in Han times. Although it followed
so closely upon the period of invasion and division, the T'ang Dynasty in many respects marked the culmination of China's cultural
evolution.[1]

The T'ang Dynasty was at its height during the first half of the
eighth century, covered almost entirely by one distinguished reign,
when the area under Chinese control was slightly greater than the
Han dominions and greater than it has ever been since under a native Chinese monarch. Wars in Mongolia broke the power of the
Turks, who had been dominant there for about 150 years, and some
of them became allies of the T'ang emperor. Parts of Manchuria
were annexed, all Korea was tributary for a brief span, and control
was again asserted over northern Indochina.The most redoubtable
advances were in Central Asia. Chinese jurisdiction was recognized
as far west as the Caspian Sea and the borders of Afghanistan and
India, and some of the Indus valley princes accepted Chinese suzerainty. In carrying out their military exploits the T'ang rulers relied
heavily upon the assistance of the non-Chinese peoples with whom
their subjects were by this time familiar, either as friends or as foes.
Now that the Chinese dragon was in the ascendancy, Mongols,
Turks, and Huns were glad to be accepted as allies.

Imposing as was the T'ang hegemony over Central Asia, it could
not be maintained indefinitely. When the rapid expansion of Islam
and the Saracenic empire began under Arab leadership in the
seventh century, it seemed for a while that China, in spite of her
remoteness from the West, was the only power to offer effective resistance. The last Sassanid king of Persia, fleeing from the Arabs,
sought refuge at the T'ang court, and T'ang forces with the assistance of local princes checked the Moslem advance in Turkestan.
The check was only temporary, however. When the T'ang administration passed its zenith (about 750), the Arabs gained control of
Turkestan—bequeathing the religion of Islam as a permanent heritage—and for a time their influence extended as far east as the
border of China's Kansu province. The T'ang rulers also encountered trouble with Tibet, which previously had remained in isolation from the turbulent politics of Central Asia. Early in the seventh
century a kingdom was founded in the highland country by a
leader who attained sufficient prestige to be given both a Chinese

[1] Actually the brief Sui Dynasty (589–618) had already reunited China and
inaugurated the new era of progress.

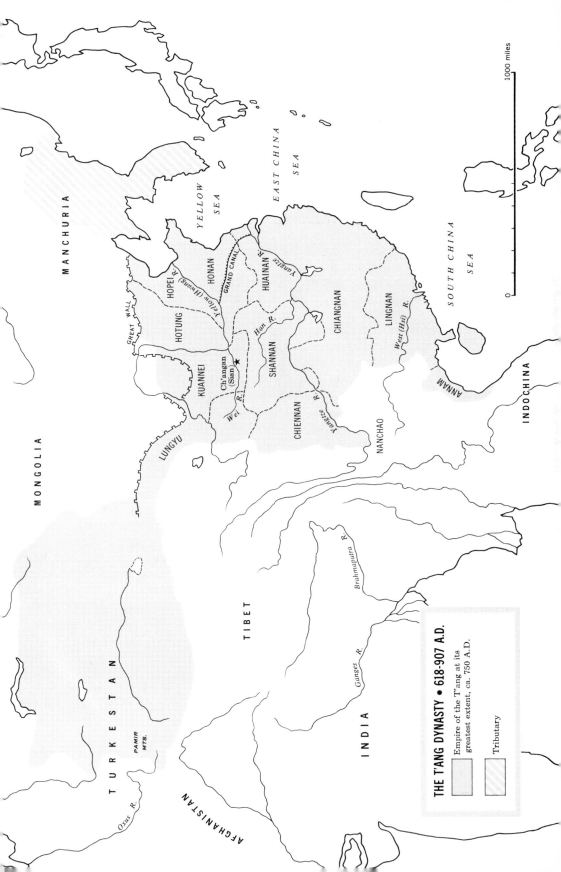

MONGOLIA

MANCHURIA

TURKESTAN

PAMIR
MTS.

Oxus R.

AFGHANISTAN

TIBET

Brahmaputra R.

Ganges R.

INDIA

GREAT WALL

LUNGYU

KUANNEI

Ch'angan (Sian)

Wei R.

CHIENNAN

SHANNAN

Han R.

Yangtze R.

HOTUNG

HOPEI

Yellow (Hwang) R.

HONAN

GRAND CANAL

HUAINAN

Yangtze R.

CHIANGNAN

NANCHAO

LINGNAN

West (Hsi) R.

ANNAM

INDOCHINA

YELLOW SEA

EAST CHINA SEA

SOUTH CHINA SEA

1000 miles

0

THE T'ANG DYNASTY • 618-907 A.D.

Empire of the T'ang at its greatest extent, ca. 750 A.D.

Tributary

and an Indian princess in marriage. The Tibetans invaded Chinese territory several times, allied themselves alternately with the Turks and with the Arabs, and interrupted trade between China and Persia by blocking the passes through the Pamir Mountains. In 798 the T'ang court succeeded in obtaining a treaty of alliance with the famous Harun-al-Raschid, caliph of Baghdad, and the Tibetan power subsided in the ninth century. Meanwhile, a division of Turks had reoccupied Mongolia, and in spite of a long struggle the Chinese were unable to hold their northern and western frontiers inviolate. By the end of the ninth century internal rebellions, together with governmental corruption and decadence in the ruling house, had led again to a state of general disorder.

The civil service

The T'ang administrative machinery, similar to the Han, was centralized under the emperor and staffed by a large bureaucracy. China proper was divided into fifteen provinces, which were subdivided into prefectures, and these again into smaller units or subprefectures, and each of the units was headed by an official appointed from the capital. The Han practice of recruiting talent for the imperial service had now developed into a rudimentary civil-service system in which written examinations were offered periodically throughout the provinces, and officeholders were chosen from among the successful candidates. Appointments were not confined solely to those who had taken the examinations, nor were all successful candidates rewarded with positions; but the system did provide opportunities for public service to young men of ability from every class of the population, in keeping with the policy advocated by Confucius a thousand years earlier.

Chinese society
under the T'ang

Since the abolition of feudalism and the establishment of peasant proprietorship by the Ch'in emperor, the character of Chinese society had not greatly changed. Many peasants were tenants rather than independent owners, and slavery had not entirely disappeared, although the precentage of slaves in the population was small. Inequalities in wealth and distinctions of rank were conspicuous. The T'ang emperors supported a titled nobility of several grades, but its prestige was based upon governmental favor rather than upon the possession of landed estates. Instead of hereditary titles carrying administrative power as in a feudal regime, the titles were bestowed upon eminent officials as a reward for their services. Ordinarily the emperor did not rule as a military despot but maintained a clear separation between the civil and military authority. It was only during periods of weakness and disorder that war lords usurped political functions. By T'ang times the Chinese had acquired a conviction that military regimes were incompatible with a normal, civilized state of affairs. By tradition society was believed to be properly composed of five classes ranked in the order of their value to the commonwealth. These were, first, scholars; second, farmers; third, artisans; fourth, merchants; and last, soldiers, lumped together with

beggars, thieves, and bandits.[2] The notable aspects of this classification are the high recognition granted to intellectual ability, the
deprecation of violence and of nonproductive occupations, and the
fact that the categories are based upon individual talents and capaci-
ties rather than upon birth. The five-class system was never fully
realized or perfectly respected, but it was an ideal which tended to
lessen the rigidity of Chinese institutions. On the more practical
side, the prominence of scholars in the administration and the system of competitive examinations helped to prevent the dominance
of aristocratic families. In addition, the circumstance that the imperial throne did not remain in any one family for more than a few
centuries provided an object lesson not to be forgotten.

Continuing the policy of encouraging agriculture, every vigorous
dynasty gave attention to irrigation works, usually maintained public granaries to provide food distribution in famine years, and some- Agriculture
times attempted to relieve the farmers from their heavy burden of
debt and taxes. Nevertheless, while China was already one of the
world's leading agricultural countries, the poorer peasants undoubtedly suffered from a miserably low standard of living as has been the
case throughout history. Furthermore, the farmer bore the chief
burden of supporting the state. Theoretically the emperor reserved
the right to redistribute holdings, but in practice he was usually
content to break the power of overly ambitious wealthy houses that
might challenge his own authority. Too often the interest of officials
in the peasants centered upon the fact that they constituted the most
lucrative and dependable source of taxation, collectible either in
produce or labor, the latter including conscription for military
service.

Curiously enough, in spite of the honored position of the farmer
and the pro-agrarian policies of the government, the merchant class
attained a prominence far superior to that of European merchants Commerce
during this period, and the steady increase of trade induced the
growth of thriving cities. During the eighth century the T'ang capital in the Wei valley (on the site of Sian, but known during this
period as Ch'ang-an), the eastern terminus of the trans-Asiatic
caravan routes, apparently had a population of close to 2 million,
while the population of China as a whole was between 40 and 50
million—about 7 per cent of the present number. Foreign commerce
was greater under the T'ang than ever before, and an increasing
proportion of it was oceanic, the leading ports of exchange being
Canton and other cities along the southeast coast, where merchants
of various nationalities from the Near and Middle East were to be
found. In addition to silk and spices, porcelain ware was becoming a
notable item in China's export trade.

[2] A famous ancient Chinese proverb is: "Good iron is not used to make a
nail; a good man is not used to make a soldier." **335**

Significant developments in religion took place during the period under consideration. By all odds the most important was the introduction of Buddhism, which brought the Chinese for the first time into contact with a complex religion with an elaborate theology, ecclesiastical organization, and emphasis upon personal salvation. For several centuries following the life of Gautama, the Buddhist faith gained such momentum in the regions surrounding India that it was bound to reach China. It was brought in over the northern trade routes as early as the first century A.D. and made rapid headway during the period of disunion that followed the collapse of the Han Dynasty. Buddhism met with a mixed reception in China, arousing both enthusiastic interest and repugnance. Mysticism, asceticism, contempt for the physical world, and the concept of transmigration of souls were quite alien to Chinese tradition; and the monastic life seemed to involve a repudiation of sacred family loyalties. On the other hand, Buddhism offered consolations not found in the native Chinese cults or philosophical disciplines. It was non-aristocratic, open to all classes, and—in contrast to the Confucian emphasis upon the inflexible will of Heaven—its *karma* doctrine affirmed that anyone could improve his chances in a future existence by diligent application. Converts were attracted by the rich symbolism of the new religion, and the voluminous scriptures which the Buddhist missionaries brought with them impressed the Chinese, who venerated scholarship. Buddhism's otherworldly orientation appealed particularly to the downtrodden and oppressed. In spite of violent opposition from some Chinese rulers, Buddhism continued to recruit adherents; congregations of women as well as of men were organized; pilgrims went to India to study and returned with copies of the Buddhist canons. By about 500 A.D. China had practically become a Buddhist country.

It might be supposed that after the restoration of a strong monarchy the interest in this imported salvationist faith would have subsided, but such was not the case. Although a few of the T'ang emperors tried to root out Buddhism (one emperor is reputed to have destroyed 40,000 temples), several of them encouraged it, and it was under the T'ang Dynasty that Chinese Buddhism reached its height as a creative influence. Many varieties of the religion had been brought into China—chiefly of the *Mahayana* school—and others were developed on Chinese soil, appealing to different temperaments and degrees of education. One of the most popular sects, called the "Pure Land" or "Lotus" school, promised an easy salvation in a Western Paradise to all who invoked the name of Amida (or Amitabha). Amida, theoretically an incarnation of Buddha, was actually visualized as a god, alleged to have been born of a lotus in the heavenly Western realm of bliss. Several of the sects, however, encouraged a zeal for scholarship and also stimulated interest in the problems of government and society. The most vigorous philosoph-

336

ical speculation under the T'ang was found in Buddhist circles. But
in spite of the great success of Buddhism its triumph was not comparable to the ascendancy of Christianity in Western Europe during
this same period. The Chinese Buddhists were not united in a common discipline, had no coercive power, and their organization did
not replace or challenge the authority of the state as did the Christian hierarchy in the West. And the fact that Buddhism was practiced in almost all parts of the country did not mean that other religions had ceased to exist. The idea of an inclusive universal church
was foreign to Chinese conceptions.

Paralleling the spread of Buddhism, Taoism, which had originated
as a philosophical school, acquired the characteristic features of an
otherworldly religion with wide popular appeal. Taoism developed
not only a priesthood but an ecclesiastical hierarchy headed by a
"Prince Celestial Master," who established pontifical headquarters in
south central China. This Taoist hierarchy was given official recognition in the eighth century and was not formally abolished until
1927. The religion, incorporating many primitive beliefs, expounded
the Way (*Tao*), which was interpreted to mean the road to individual happiness defined usually in material terms, although it offered
elements to attract intellectuals and encouraged acts of charity.
Taoism was greatly affected by Buddhism and borrowed ideas from
the foreign faith, including the concepts of *karma* and transmigration and the belief in thirty-three heavens and eighteen hells. Its
priesthood was modeled after the Buddhist monastic order, except
that the Taoists did not practice celibacy; and the later Taoist scriptures show a strong resemblance to Buddhist texts. Inevitably rivalry sprang up between the two competing religions, but neither
was able to eliminate the other and both received imperial as well as
popular support. Some Taoist apologists claimed that their master,
Lao-tzu, had actually been the Buddha or else had instructed him;
while Buddhists countered with the assertion that Lao-tzu had rendered homage to Gautama.

In spite of the popularity of Taoism and the temporary ascendancy of Buddhism, Confucianism began to be revived in the later
T'ang period and retained its hold upon the allegiance of the Chinese. Although usually described as one of the three great religions
of China, Confucianism was not and never became a religion in the
strict sense of the term. It was a body of ethical principles, of etiquette and formal ceremony, and also—as a result of the policies of
Han and T'ang emperors—a code of government, strengthened by
the practice of recruiting officials from scholars versed in the Confucian classics. Veneration for the great teacher finally became part
of the state cult and was invested with formal religious observances.
The later Han emperors had prescribed sacrifices to Confucius in
every large city, and a T'ang ruler of the seventh century ordered
temples to be built in his honor in each prefecture and subprefec-

ture. Thus the sage, together with other famous men of antiquity, revered rulers, outstanding generals, etc., was ensured perpetual homage and respect, but he was not worshiped as were the Buddhist and Taoist deities. The Chinese idea of religion, it should be remembered, was different from that of most other peoples. The typical Chinese would be a Confucianist as a matter of course; but he might also be a Taoist, a Buddhist, or a combination of both.

Economic and cultural changes

Many economic and cultural changes took place during the thousand years between the Ch'in Dynasty and the end of the T'ang. Some items were borrowed from Western lands—grapes and alfalfa among the agricultural products, astrological concepts and the seven-day week from the Manicheans. The Chinese began to use coal for fuel and for smelting iron in the fourth century A.D., far in advance of Europeans. Their astrologers had observed sunspots as early as 28 B.C.; a crude seismograph was constructed in 132 A.D. The magnetic compass, apparently developed by the Taoists around 500 A.D., was used chiefly to determine favorable locations for grave sites. The properties of gunpowder had also been discovered. At this time, however, gunpowder was employed not to blow people to bits but in the manufacture of firecrackers to frighten away evil spirits. The highly important invention of paper (made of bark, hemp, and rags) was achieved by the beginning of the second century A.D., and printing from blocks was introduced about 500 years later. By the tenth century the printing of books was common not only in China but in Korea and Japan.

The arts

A great deal of the intellectual and artistic progress of this era must be credited to the Buddhists, whose contributions were not confined to religion exclusively. Buddhism enriched Chinese music by the introduction of a liturgy of vocal chants and also with several new musical instruments, including the psaltery, guitar or mandolin and other stringed instruments, the reed organ, clarinet,

The Ancestor of all Seismographs. Invented by a Chinese mathematician and geographer in 132 A.D. it was described in a contemporary document as an "earthquake weathercock." These conjectural reconstructions show the interior of the bronze, bell-shaped instrument. (A) The pendulum carries jointed arms radiating in eight directions, each arm ending in a crank connected with a dragon head. (B) When an earth tremor causes the pendulum to swing, one of the dragon heads is raised and releases a ball which drops into the mouth of a toad below. After the swing of the pendulum, a catch mechanism immobilizes the instrument. Thus, by observing which ball has fallen, it is possible to determine the direction of the initial shock wave.

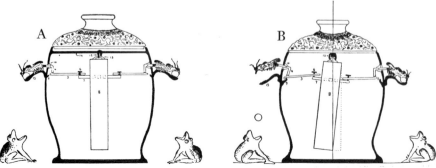

Two Carved Wood Bodhisattvas T'ang Dynasty. The Bodhisattva, or Buddha-to-be, represented a person eligible for enlightenment but who remained in the world to help others on the upward path. In Mahayana Buddhism a number of Bodhisattvas came to be worshipped as deities.

and a type of flute. It was in the visual arts, however, that the impetus of Buddhism was most notable. The Buddhists of northern India, who had absorbed artistic motifs from the Greeks and Persians, spread them into Central Asia and thence into China. During the period of disunion and the early T'ang Dynasty, Chinese sculpture reached its climax, successfully blending together Indian, Iranian, and Hellenic characteristics into a distinctive Chinese style. Superbly beautiful examples of this sculpture have survived, the best of which were produced in the late sixth and early seventh centuries. The most impressive works of architecture were Buddhist temples or sacred grottoes in northwestern China, carved out of rock caves after the Indian manner. Painting, too, reached a peak of realism and sensitivity which has rarely been surpassed. Skill in this medium was stimulated by the Chinese habit of writing with brush and ink, and pictorial figures or scenes were often combined with masterly specimens of calligraphy executed on scrolls of silk. Some paintings in fresco have been preserved from T'ang times and, like the sculpture, they show Buddhist influence. Outstanding among the minor arts was the production of pottery figurines representing human beings and animals with grace and naturalness, used chiefly as funeral presents to the departed. The manufacture of white porcelain—the beginning of the world-famous "china" ware—apparently began in the sixth or seventh century.

As early as Chou times, the Chinese civilization was highly literary, and by the T'ang period China had probably the most abundant **339**

*Porcelain Ewer or Pitcher, in the
Form of a Court Lady.*

Literature

collection of writings of any nation in the world. Philosophical activity did not equal the creative age of Confucius, Mo Ti, and Mencius, but a great variety of literary forms had come into existence, showing maturity of thought, sophistication, and aesthetic sensitivity. Writers of the T'ang period produced histories, essays, dictionaries, short stories and romances for popular entertainers, an embryonic form of the drama, and—outshining all the rest—poetry. Poetry had been developing prolifically during the centuries of disunion and civil strife. The influence of Buddhism and Taoism imparted emotional intensity and a quality of mysticism conducive to lyrical richness. The final result was a flowering in the eighth and ninth centuries which made the T'ang the supreme age of Chinese poetry. The verse forms were usually short, with words carefully chosen to evoke beauty of tone as well as to convey pithy thought and vivid imagery. While sometimes expressing philosophical ideas, they were frequently poignant in mood and romantic in theme, treating especially of nature, love, and friendship. A few of the best examples were tinged with a deep melancholy, expressing compassion for the miserable lot of the poor, distress over abuses in government, revulsion against the senseless brutality of war, and bewilderment at the apparent triumph of evil over good.

3.   EARLY CIVILIZATION IN JAPAN

Of the great civilizations of the Far East, Japan's was the latest to develop. In origin it was derived from and was largely an adaptation of cultures from the mainland, especially from China. However, the

340

fact that the Japanese lagged many centuries behind China and India and made their most rapid progress under the stimulus of borrowings from China does not prove that the island dwellers were lacking in ability or originality. Not only did the Japanese display remarkable ingenuity in assimilating foreign elements and in modifying them to meet their particular needs, but during some periods of history they seemed to possess more initiative than any of the other Far Eastern nations. The backwardness of Japan in early times is explained, at least in part, by the geographical circumstance of her isolation from the continent of Asia. Before oceanic commerce was well advanced, the Japanese islands could not be readily affected by political and cultural changes taking place on the mainland. These islands stand in the same relationship to Asia as do the British Isles to Europe. Just as European civilization was slowly extended from the Near Eastern centers westward to Italy and then to the northern countries, reaching Britain last of all, so Far Eastern civilization gradually radiated from the Yellow River valley to the south, west, and northeast, and necessarily reached Japan belatedly. Actually Japan is much more remote from the neighboring continent than is Britain from Continental Europe. At the narrowest point the Strait of Dover is only about 20 miles wide, while more than 100 miles separate the islands of Japan from the closest point on the Korean peninsula.

The retarded development of civilization in Japan

Japan's geographic setting is in some ways very favorable. Of the approximately 3000 islands composing the group, only about 600 are inhabited, and the bulk of the population is concentrated on the four principal islands. The entire archipelago lies within the temperate zone, and the largest island, Honshu, holding about half of the Japanese people, lies between almost exactly the same latitudes as the state of California. The Black Current drifting northward from tropical seas, moderates the severity of winter; and cyclonic storms, while sometimes destructive, bring fluctuations in temperature that are conducive to physical and mental vigor. Their proximity to the ocean made it easy for the Japanese to develop navigation and to become hardy fishermen. With its expanse of seacoast, mountains, volcanoes and snow-capped peaks, the region is scenically one of the most beautiful in the world, a factor which has undoubtedly contributed to the keen aesthetic sensibilities of the Japanese people. At the same time Japan is by no means perfectly endowed by nature and suffers from several disadvantages. Except for having fair deposits of coal, the islands are poor in mineral resources. Even more serious has been the scarcity of good agricultural land, owing to the rocky or mountainous character of much of the country. Although throughout most of their history the Japanese have been a nation of farmers, only about 16 per cent of their soil is cultivable. This sufficed when the population was small and generally stationary; it has posed a tremendous problem in modern times.

Geographic advantages and disadvantages

EARLY JAPAN

Small as is the land area of Japan (slightly less than that of California) and in spite of its relative isolation, it was inhabited even in early times by people of various stocks as the result of successive migrations from the continent. The earliest inhabitants, so far as is known, were a primitive people who possessed a Neolithic culture, crude in many respects but distinguished by pottery of striking design and skillfully fashioned weapons. They are represented today by the Ainu, a light-colored, flat-faced, and hairy people, who have largely disappeared except from Hokkaido and the Kurile Islands to the north. For the most part the Japanese nation is descended from

Mongoloid invaders who crossed over to the islands at various times during the Neolithic Age and even later, chiefly by way of Korea.

Mongoloid invaders who crossed over to the islands at various times during the Neolithic Age and even later, chiefly by way of Korea. From the time of the Ch'in Dynasty on, the settlers in Japan possessed some knowledge of Chinese culture, which had already penetrated into Korea. Bronze mirrors, carved jewels, and swords of Chinese or Mongolian type appear in graves dating from the second and first centuries B.C. By the close of the first century B.C. the Japanese had begun to use iron as well as bronze.

Quite understandably, the leading centers of cultural evolution were in the south and west of Japan—the areas closest to Korea, from which the chief migrations came—and developments in this region gradually spread to the north and east. The real nucleus of the Japanese state was the peninsula of Yamato, on the southeastern side of the great island of Honshu, to which a group of families had migrated from Kyushu (opposite Korea) perhaps as early as the first century A.D. The Japanese communities at this time were very primitive. People wore clothing made from hemp or bark, although silk was not entirely unknown. They carried on trade by barter only and had no system of writing. The chief unit of society was the clan, a group of families claiming to be related by blood. Each clan venerated some particular deity, who was supposed to be the ancestor of the group; but the worship of human ancestors had not yet become an institution. The headship of the clan was vested hereditarily in a specific family, and the clan leader served both as a warrior chieftain and as priest. In primitive Japanese society women seem to have held a position of prominence, perhaps even of superiority. The clan head was sometimes a woman, and evidence points to the conclusion that originally the family was matriarchal, with descent traced through the mother—a remarkable circumstance in view of the rigid subordination of women in later times. The transition to a partiarchal system, however, was effected at an early date. According to Chinese accounts from the third century A.D., polygamy was a common practice, especially among men of the higher classes. Various crafts and skills were organized as occupational groups in the form of guilds with hereditary membership. Each guild was attached to a clan and tended to merge with it eventually, although a few guilds whose members performed distinctive services, such as administering religious rites, retained an independent existence and honorable status. Members of the agricultural and artisans' guilds, on the other hand, were practically serfs. Society was decidedly aristocratic, rank was generally hereditary, and slavery existed, although the number of slaves was relatively small.

The early Japanese religion, while comparable to that of other primitive peoples, was in some ways unique. It was basically animistic, a type of unreflecting and almost universal nature worship, with no well-defined conception of the nature of divine being. In a general way it was polytheistic, except that the term probably suggests too definite a catalogue of gods or too precise a theology. The Japanese later gave their religion the name of *Shinto* ("the way of the Gods"), simply because they needed to distinguish it from Buddhism when this articulate and mature faith began to compete with the native cult. Although the Japanese recognized some great deities, associated with the sun, moon, earth, crops, and storms, these were not endowed with distinct personalities and were not represented by images. Objects of worship were designated as *kami*, a term meaning "superior" but which was applied to almost anything having mysterious or interesting properties, ranging from heavenly phenomena to irregularly shaped stones and such lowly objects as sand, mud, and vermin. No sharp line was drawn between the natural and the supernatural or between magic and worship. The notion of life after death was extremely shadowy, and religion was largely devoid of ethical content. It involved taboos and scrupulous concern for ceremonial cleanness, with purification rites to remove contamination, but the requirements were not based on considerations of morality or even always of health. Uncleanness, for example, was associated with childbirth, with contact with the dead, and with wounds whether inflicted honorably or not. To placate the gods, respectful gestures, prayers, and sacrifices were employed. Offerings of food and drink gradually tended to be superseded by symbolic objects—of pottery, wood, and eventually paper.

In spite of its diffuse and elementary character, the native Japanese religion was not lacking in attractive elements. It reflected an attitude of cheerfulness and a rare sympathy for and appreciation of nature. The gods were not thought of as cruel and terrifying creatures; even the god of the storm was generally conceived as benign. On the whole, the religion of the Japanese was one "of love and gratitude rather than of fear, and the purpose of their religious rites was to praise and thank as much as to placate and mollify their divinities." [3] It was enlivened also with picturesque legends and poetic phrases that suggest a spontaneous delight in the natural world.

The clan which was dominant on the plain of Yamato, and gradually acquired an ascendancy over adjacent regions, probably came from Kyushu and claimed descent from the Sun Goddess. There was nothing remarkable in such a claim because all important families traced their ancestry to gods or goddesses. However, myths associated with the Sun Goddess assumed greater significance as the Yamato clan extended its political power and attempted to secure fuller recognition of its paramountcy over the other clans, for which purpose it was helpful to foster the legend that the Yamato chief

344   [3] G. B. Sansom, *Japan, a Short Cultural History*, p. 47.

had been divinely appointed to rule over Japan (even though most
of it was still unconquered from the aborigines). According to this
legend the Sun Goddess had sent down to earth her own grandson,
Ninigino-Mikoto. Ninigi, "thrusting apart the many-piled clouds of
Heaven, clove his way with an awful way-cleaving" to land on the
western island of Kyushu, carrying with him the three symbols of
Japanese royalty—a jewel, a sword, and a mirror. The grandson of
this Ninigi, it was related, advanced along the coast of the larger
island to Yamato, where he began to rule as Jimmu, the "first emperor." National tradition dates the empire from February 11, 660
B.C. Actually, it was at least 600 or 700 years later that the Yamato
state was established, and then it was anything but imperial. The
saga of the Sun Goddess and her descendants did not become a distinctive element in the national cult of Japan until the sixth century
A.D., and not until the modern era was it deliberately exploited on a
national scale for the purpose of instilling a fanatical and unquestioning patriotism among the people.

For many centuries the Japanese maintained contact with and
continued to receive cultural impetus from Korea, which means that
they were being influenced indirectly by the older and richer civili- Cultural in-
zation of China of the Han and later dynasties. The Japanese even fluences from
controlled a small section at the southern tip of Korea from about China via Korea
100 to 560 A.D. and intervened in Korean politics to maintain a balance of power, siding with one and then another of the three kingdoms into which Korea was divided during this time. Of fundamental importance for the later history of Japan was the introduction,
by way of Korea, of the Chinese system of writing (about 405 A.D.)
and of Buddhism (about 552 A.D.).

While the technique of writing was essential to the advance of
civilization, it was unfortunate for the Japanese that they acquired it
from China. If they had been able to devise or borrow a phonetic or Japanese writing
alphabetic system, the problem of writing their language would
have been comparatively simple. The Chinese characters—fundamentally pictographic or ideographic, with very little apparent relationship to the pronunciation of the words for which they stand
—had been developed to a state of complexity and utilized in
producing masterpieces of Chinese literature; but they were ill
suited to represent Japanese. The Japanese language is phonetically
quite different from the Chinese, and the attempt to write it with
Chinese characters was a feat as difficult as it would be to try to
write English in Chinese characters. Nevertheless, the Japanese
struggled heroically with the task and eventually developed a script
of their own, or, rather, two varieties of script. Although the original Chinese characters were abbreviated considerably and, during
the ninth and tenth centuries, given phonetic value by identification
with individual Japanese syllables, the resulting product was still
cumbersome. Hence, the process of learning to write Japanese was, **345**

and still is, a laborious undertaking. The fact that the system of writing is alien to the structure, inflection, and idiosyncrasies of the spoken language has hampered clarity of expression and partially accounts for the tendency toward ambiguity in many official Japanese documents. To compensate for these disadvantages, however, along with the Chinese-derived script a great many Chinese words were adopted bodily by the Japanese, enriching their language in vocabulary and concepts. In view of the circumstances in which writing was introduced in Japan, a person who wished to become educated was almost bound to learn the Chinese language, especially since it was the vehicle of all literature considered worthy of the name. For several centuries Japanese scholars, officials, and men of letters wrote in classical Chinese, in somewhat the same manner that educated Europeans used Latin during the Middle Ages and later.

In the middle of the sixth century Buddhism began to obtain a foothold in Japan. The first Buddhist missionary is said to have come from Korea; other evangelists of the new faith arrived not only from Korea but from China and even from India. As in the case of China, the *Mahayana* school of Buddhism, with its elaborate theology and emphasis upon the soul's redemption, was most in evidence. And, just as had happened in China, a number of different sects arose in Japan from time to time. The appearance of Buddhism in Japan produced perhaps even greater agitation than had accompanied its introduction into China a few centuries earlier. The Chinese were at least familiar with mystical concepts through Taoism, but the Japanese had had no previous experience either with this type of otherworldly religion or with any analogous philosophy. Part of the appeal of Buddhism to the Japanese lay in its novelty. The Buddhist scriptures raised questions that had apparently never occurred to the Japanese before—as to the soul, the nature of the immaterial world, rewards and punishments after death—and then proceeded to answer them with impressive eloquence. For a while, sharp controversy raged over the acceptability of the foreign faith (the first statue of the Buddha sent from Korea was thrown into a canal when an epidemic of disease broke out). However, one prominent aristocratic family in Yamato, the Soga, adopted and championed the cause of Buddhism and prevailed upon the imperial clan to favor it, so that before the close of the sixth century the success of the religion was assured. To some extent its success was attributable to political maneuvers and expediency. In patronizing the scholarly faith the Soga family sought to enhance its own prestige and, through the benefit of whatever supernatural power the religion contained, to secure an advantage in the struggle against rival families. Buddhism rapidly acquired a wide following both among the common people and the aristocracy and became so firmly entrenched that it could survive any shift in equilibrium among the

346

contending clans. Probably its popularity is largely explained by its being interpreted as a miraculous protector against disasters both in this world and the next rather than by its philosophical heritage. Nevertheless, the increasing familiarity with Buddhist doctrines stimulated intellectual activity and was conducive to the cultivation of attitudes of sympathy and humaneness.

One of the most significant aspects of the spread of Buddhism in Japan was that it proved to be a highly effective medium for disseminating Chinese culture, especially art, architecture, and literature. Temples and shrines were erected, paintings and images of the Buddha were produced, and libraries of the sacred texts were accumulated. Converts from the aristocratic class frequently went to China to study, returning with a broadened viewpoint and refined tastes. The native Japanese cult, now beginning to be called *Shinto,* was by no means extinguished, but it was influenced considerably by contact with Buddhism. There was very little antagonism between the two religions. Buddhism in Japan became tinged with national traditions, and frequently the same shrine was regarded as sacred to both faiths. The Japanese priests, whether Buddhist or Shinto, did not constitute a hierarchy with coercive powers over the people any more than did the priests in China, although the Buddhist monasteries gained in economic importance as they were endowed with lands.

During the most vigorous period of the T'ang Dynasty, the impact of Chinese civilization upon Japan reached such a climax that it marks a turning point in the evolution of Japanese institutions. It is not at all strange that the Japanese turned avidly to China for tutelage at this time. China under the early T'ang rulers was one of the most highly civilized states in the world, as well as the most powerful, and in the Far East had no close rivals for such a distinction. Throughout the seventh and eighth centuries the government in Yamato sent a succession of official embassies to the T'ang court, largely for the purpose of recruiting personnel trained in the sciences, arts, and letters. The result was a wholesale copying of Chinese techniques and ideas, affecting almost every aspect of Japanese life and society. Chinese medical practices, military tactics, and methods of road building were introduced; also styles of architecture, of household furniture, and even of dress. A system of weights and measures was adopted, and in the early eighth century coined money came into use. Many works of art had previously been imported and copied, but now Japanese painters and sculptors began to display both technical proficiency and originality. The Chinese classics, especially the Confucian writings, were studied intently, since every well-bred person was expected to be familiar with them. Along with these concrete and visible innovations came an attempt to fit the social structure into the Chinese pattern. A new·emphasis

347

EARLY JAPANESE ART

Japanese Religious Sculpture (twelfth century or earlier). Wooden figure of Bishamon, revered as one of the Four Guardian Kings of the Buddhist kingdom.

Benten Playing on a Biwa. A Japanese painting on silk, by an artist of the Heian (Fujiwara) Period, 893-1185.

was placed upon family solidarity and filial devotion, including the duty of sacrificing to ancestral spirits.[4] Japanese leaders and intellectuals seemed determined to remake their country in the image of China.

The most comprehensive project involved nothing less than reconstituting the government according to the T'ang model. It was announced by a decree known as the Taika Reform Edict, issued in 645 A.D. by the Yamato ruler at the instigation of a clique of scholar-reformers. This declaration, rather than the mythical events of 660 B.C., represents the founding of the Japanese imperial system. By the Taika Edict the ruler assumed the role not of a mere clan leader but of an emperor, with absolute power, although professedly honoring Confucian principles. All Japan was to be divided into provinces, prefectures, and subprefectures, which would be administered by a centrally appointed bureaucracy recruited from the populace. Faithful to the example of China, the reformers instituted a civil service, offering examinations to candidates for government posts, whose selection would be based not on familiarity with the problems of Japan but on proficiency in Chinese philosophy and classical literature. To give the new administration an economic foundation and to bring it to bear directly upon the people, the Reform Edict proclaimed that all the land belonged to the emperor, and that it would be divided equitably among the farmers and redistributed every six years. In return, every landholder would be required to pay taxes (in commodities, money, or labor) directly to the state.

The Taika Reform Edict

Altogether, the reform program of the seventh century was one of the most ambitious that any government has ever attempted. It sought to graft upon a still fairly primitive society an administrative system that was the product of almost a thousand years of evolution among a people with cultural maturity and deeply entrenched traditions. Similarly, it involved an effort on the part of one corner of Japan to impose its regime on the entire area, much of which had hardly advanced beyond the Neolithic stage. In adopting the scheme of a centralized paternalism, one aspect of the Chinese prototype was studiously avoided: namely, the concept that imperial authority is conditional upon the promotion of public welfare and that it may be terminated—by rebellion as a last resort—if it fails in this objective. The Yamato group tried to attach a bureaucracy of scholar-officials to a government that called for perpetual rule by one family, whose head occupied a position of inviolable sanctity. To strengthen the prestige of the emperor, greater emphasis than ever before was placed upon his reputed descent from the Sun Goddess. He was represented as the embodiment of a "lineal succession un-

Consolidation of the Japanese government

[4] Some Japanese scholars deny that the custom of ancestor worship was an importation; but in any case it was intensified by contacts with the Chinese. An unfortunate consequence was the increasing subordination of women to male authority in the patriarchal family and in society at large.

broken for ages eternal" and as divine in his own person—a significantly different concept from that of the "Mandate of Heaven," the conditional and temporary divinity that hedged the Chinese emperor. In addition to this fundamental contrast between the official Chinese and Japanese theories as to the ultimate basis and limits of political authority, there was a notable divergence in practice also. China knew many different dynasties, most of them begun through rebellion or usurpation; but when a vigorous emperor sat on the throne he usually ruled effectively and sometimes autocratically, as is attested by the records of the first few rulers of every major dynasty. In Japan, on the other hand, while the imperial family was never dethroned in spite of violent or revolutionary changes within society and in foreign relations, and while the fiction of imperial sanctity was carefully preserved, the actual power for the most part was exercised by some other family, agency, or clique, using the sacred imperial office as a front. Indirect government, sometimes removed by several stages from the nominal sovereign, has been the rule rather than the exception in Japan ever since her attempt to incorporate the Chinese political machinery.

In view of the inherent difficulties, it is not surprising that the reform program of the seventh century was not entirely successful.

Partial failure of the reform program

The new administrative system existed on paper but not as an operating reality. The imperial clan, which had previously enjoyed only a limited and largely ceremonial authority over the others, could not compel absolute obedience from remote areas, and aristocratic traditions were too strong to be broken immediately. The emperor made it a practice to appoint clan heads as officials in their own territories instead of replacing them by loyal servants sent out from the capital. Thus the local magnates acquired new titles and kept much of their former power. Examinations were provided for candidates desiring posts in the government service, but important positions were almost always reserved for members of the aristocracy, while capable men of the lower class found themselves employed as underlings and clerks. The announced policy of land equalization, which was intended to serve as the basis for a uniform tax system, was the most dismal failure of all. It had been inspired by the Chinese ideal of community interest in the land, a sentiment which condemned the appropriation of land for the exclusive benefit of any individual and taught that it should be distributed equally among the cultivators. This was only a theory in China, and in Japan it was thoroughly unrealistic. Later large proprietors managed to evade taxation and so increased the burden upon the poorer farmers that some of them ran away from their homes in sheer desperation. In this manner the amount of taxable land diminished, and the emperors themselves contributed to the process by giving away estates to courtiers or to endow Buddhist monasteries. Furthermore, the decree regarding periodic redistribution of land applied only to the

fields that had already been brought under rice cultivation, a relatively small area. As the frontier clans added to their domains either
by conquest from the aborigines or by reclaiming waste lands for
cultivation, these new territories were regarded as personal holdings
not directly subject to imperial assessment. Consequently, economic
progress lessened rather than increased the proportion of the land
under effective control by the central government. Instead of securing large funds from taxation, the court became more and more dependent for revenue upon estates that were owned outright by the
imperial family.

Although the central government failed in its political objectives,
it succeeded in promoting cultural progress to an appreciable degree. Before the seventh century there had been no fixed Japanese
capital even in Yamato, or in fact no cities at all. Impressed with the
splendor of the T'ang capital, the great city of Ch'ang-an, the Japanese determined to build one like it to serve as the imperial headquarters. Their city, begun in 710 and located near the modern
town of Nara, followed the Chinese model faithfully in its broad
streets and carefully aligned squares of equal size, although it was
unwalled and much smaller than Ch'ang-an. Even so, its plan was
too large for the population that occupied it. In 794 a more imposing capital was built at Kyoto, which has been an important city
ever since. The construction of these cities under imperial patronage, with palaces, temples, and other public buildings, provided a
stimulus to all the arts. Scholarship, bent on the production of histories, treatises, and literary criticism, also flourished at the imperial
court. If the bureaucracy had little real public responsibility, its
members could find satisfaction and enhanced social prestige in
polishing their classical Chinese, translating Buddhist sutras, painting, or composing poetry of a rather strained and artificial type.
The refinement of ceremony and etiquette also received much attention. Life in court circles tended to become effete and frivolous,
but it harbored some artistic and intellectual talent of high caliber.
Odd as it may seem, the best Japanese literature of this period was
produced by women of the nobility and of the imperial household.
Their contributions, outstanding in the tenth and eleventh centuries,
were chiefly prose, typically in the form of diaries but including
one justly famous romantic novel (*Tale of Genji*). In this instance it
was fortunate that women, even of the court, were not held to the
same educational standards as men. "While the men of the period
were pompously writing bad Chinese, their ladies consoled themselves for their lack of education by writing good Japanese, and
created, incidentally, Japan's first great prose literature." [5]

[5] E. O. Reischauer, *Japan Past and Present*, p. 35.

SELECTED READINGS

· Items so designated are available in paperbound editions.

INDIA — *See also Readings for Chapter 7*

Bowie, Theodore, ed., *The Arts of Thailand: A Handbook of Architecture, Sculpture and Painting of Thailand*, Bloomington, Ind., 1961.

Grousset, René, *The Civilizations of the East*, New York, 1931, Vol. II.

Panikkar, K. M., *India and the Indian Ocean*, New York, 1945.

Sen, Gertrude E., *The Pageant of India's History*, Vol. I, New York, 1948.

van Leur, J. C., *Indonesian Trade and Society*, New York, 1955.

CHINA — *See also Readings for Chapter 8*

Bagchi, P. C., *India and China, a Thousand Years of Cultural Relations*, rev. ed., New York, 1951.

Balazs, Etienne, *Chinese Civilization and Bureaucracy*, New Haven, 1964. An important interpretation of Chinese society.

Carter, T. F., and Goodrich, L. C., *The Invention of Printing in China and Its Spread Westward*, 2nd ed., New York, 1955.

Eberhard, W., *History of China*, Berkeley, 1950 (E. W. Dickes, tr.). Particularly full on the period of disunion.

Eliot, Charles, *Hinduism and Buddhism: An Historical Sketch*, Vol. III, New York, 1954. Buddhism in China.

· Lattimore, Owen, *The Inner Asian Frontiers of China*, 2nd ed., New York, 1951 (Beacon).

Munsterberg, Hugo, *Short History of Chinese Art*, New York, 1949.

Shryock, J. K., *The Origin and Development of the State Cult of Confucius*, New York, 1932.

Sickman, L., and Soper, A., *The Art and Architecture of China*, Baltimore, 1956. Reliable; richly illustrated.

Sullivan, Michael, *An Introduction to Chinese Art*, Berkeley, 1961.

Sun, E. Z., and De Francis, John, *Chinese Social History*, Washington, 1956. Translations of articles by modern Chinese scholars.

· Wittfogel, K. A., *Oriental Despotism: A Comparative Study of Total Power*, New Haven, 1957 (Yale). Attempts to explain the despotic character of the Chinese imperial government by the necessities of a "hydraulic society," in which flood control and efficient irrigation systems were imperative.

Wright, Arthur F., *Buddhism in Chinese History*, Stanford, 1959. Brief but good.

Zurcher, E., *The Buddhist Conquest of China: The Spread and Adaptation of Buddhism in Early Medieval China*, 2 vols., Leiden, 1959. An illuminating study of the interaction between Chinese culture and Buddhism to the early fifth century A.D.

JAPAN

Anesaki, Masaharu, *Art, Life and Nature in Japan*, Boston, 1933.

——, *History of Japanese Religion*, London, 1930.

Brower, R. H., and Miner, E., *Japanese Court Poetry*, Stanford, 1961. Covers the period from the sixth to the fourteenth centuries.

Eliot, Charles, *Japanese Buddhism*, New York, 1959. A standard text, reprinted from the 1935 edition.

· Munsterberg, Hugo, *The Arts of Japan: An Illustrated History*, Rutland, Vt., 1957 (Tuttle).

Paine, R. T., and Soper, A., *The Art and Architecture of Japan*, Baltimore,
1955. Well illustrated.

Reischauer, E. O., *Japan Past and Present*, rev. ed., New York, 1953. A very
lucid and well-organized summary of the main strands in Japanese history.

———, and Fairbank, J. K., *East Asia: The Great Tradition*, Boston, 1960.

Sansom, George B., *A History of Japan to 1334*, Stanford, 1958. An outstanding work by an eminent British scholar with a mastery of the Japanese
language and sources and a gift for interpretive historical writing.

———, *Japan: A Short Cultural History*, rev. ed., New York, 1952. Substantial; informative at a mature level; readable.

Swann, Peter C., *An Introduction to the Arts of Japan*, New York, 1958.

Trewartha, G. T., *Japan: A Physical, Cultural and Regional Geography*,
Madison, Wis., 1945.

· Warner, Langdon, *The Enduring Art of Japan*, Cambridge, Mass., 1952
(Evergreen).

Yukio, Y., *Two Thousand Years of Japanese Art*, New York, 1958.

SOURCE MATERIALS

Aston, W. G., tr., *Nihongi: Chronicles of Japan from the Earliest Times to
A.D. 697*, 2 vols.

Ayscough, Florence, *Tu Fu, the Autobiography of a Chinese Poet*.

Beal, Samuel, tr., *Buddhist Records of the Western World*, 2 vols.

Bynner, Witter, and Kiang Kanghu, trs., *The Jade Mountain, a Chinese Anthology*.

· de Bary, W. T., ed., *Sources of Chinese Tradition*, "The Imperial Age: Ch'in
and Han"; "Neo-Taoism and Buddhism," New York, 1960 (Columbia).

· ———, ed., *Sources of Indian Tradition*, "Hinduism," New York, 1958
(Columbia).

· ———, ed., *Sources of Japanese Tradition*, "Ancient Japan"; "The Heian
Period," New York, 1964 (Columbia).

Hung, William, *Tu Fu, China's Greatest Poet*

Jenyns, Soame, *T'ang Dynasty Poems*.

· Keene, Donald, ed., *Anthology of Japanese Literature, from the earliest era
to the mid-nineteenth century*, New York, 1956 (Evergreen).

Lin Yutang, ed., *The Wisdom of China and India*, New York, 1949.

Reischauer, E. O., tr., *Ennin's Diary* (a Japanese Buddhist monk in T'ang
China), New York, 1955.

Sanskrit Dramas: *Sakuntala, The Little Clay Cart*.

Van Buitenen, J. A. B., tr., *Tales of Ancient India* (from Sanskrit texts of the
medieval period), Chicago, 1959.

Waley, Arthur, tr., *Ballads and Stories from Tun-Huang, an Anthology*
(T'ang era); *The Tale of Genji; Translations from the Chinese*, New
York, 1960.

Watson, Burton, tr., *Records of the Grand Historian of China, Translated
from the Shih Chi of Ssu-ma Ch'ien*, 2 vols., New York, 1961.

PART THREE

The World in the
Early Middle Ages

During the period from 284 to 476 A.D. Roman civilization was strongly influenced by a revival of Oriental ideals of despotism, otherworldliness, pessimism, and fatalism. In the midst of economic distress and cultural decay men lost interest in earthly achievement and began to yearn for spiritual blessings in a life after death. This change in attitude was due primarily to the spread of Oriental religions, especially Christianity. When the Roman Empire finally collapsed, the victory of Orientalism was almost complete. The result was the evolution of new civilizations, compounded in part of elements taken from Greece and from Rome but with religion as a dominant factor behind most of their achievements. Altogether three new cultures finally emerged: the civilization of western Europe in the early Middle Ages, the Byzantine civilization, and the Saracenic civilization. The periods covered by the history of all three overlapped. The civilization of western Europe in the early Middle Ages extended from about 400 to 1000. Although Constantine established his capital on the site of ancient Byzantium in the fourth century A.D., Byzantine civilization did not begin its independent evolution until after 500. It survived until the capture of Constantinople by the Turks in 1453. The Saracenic civilization flourished from the seventh century to the end of the thirteenth. India and China bloomed in their fullest splendor between 600 and 900 and were by no means stagnant during the remainder of the period.

A Chronological Table

<table>
<tr><th></th><th>WESTERN EUROPE</th><th>BYZANTINE EMPIRE</th></tr>
</table>

WESTERN EUROPE

Germanic migrations and invasions,
  100 B.C.–600 A.D.
Rise of the Papacy, 50–300
Growth of the colonate, *ca.* 200–500

BYZANTINE EMPIRE

Rise of monasticism, *ca.* 300
Council of Nicaea, 325
Constantinople established as capital, 330

300

Invasions of England by Angles and Sax-
  ons, 400–600
Decline of industry and commerce, 400–
  800
Capture of Rome by Visigoths, 410
St. Augustine's *City of God*, 413–426
Merovingian dynasty in France, 481–751   Monophysite movement, 450–565
Ostrogothic rule in Italy, 493–552
Boethius' *Consolation of Philosophy*, 523
Origin of Seven Liberal Arts, *ca.* 550

500

Justinian's empire, 527–565
Revision and codification of Roman law,
  527–535
Construction of church of Santa Sophia,
  532–537
Byzantine conquest of Italy, 535–552

Lombard invasion of Italy, 568

Iconoclastic movement, 725–850

Battle of Tours, 732
Carolingian dynasty, 751–887
Development of feudalism, 800–1300
Charlemagne's empire, 800–814
Unification of England under Saxon
  Kings, 802–1066
Treaty of Verdun, 843
Holy Roman Empire, 962–
Founding of national monarchy in France,
  987

800

Separation of Eastern and Western
  churches, 1054
Battle of Manzikert, 1071

The Crusades, 1096–1204

1100

Capture of Constantinople by Crusaders
  of Fourth Crusade, 1204

Capture of Constantinople by Ottoman
  Turks, 1453

1453

THE SARACENS

INDIA AND THE FAR EAST

Rapid development of Buddhism in China, 200–500
Flowering of Hindu culture, 300–800

Adoption of Chinese system of writing in Japan, *ca.* 405

Manufacture of glass and invention of firecrackers and magnetic compass in China, *ca.* 500

Mohammed, 570?–632

Spread of Buddhism to Japan, *ca.* 552

The Hegira, 622
Capture of Mecca, 630
Conquest of Persia, Egypt, Palestine, Syria, North Africa, Spain, 632–732
Division of Islam into sects—Sunnites, Shiites, and Sufis, *ca.* 640

Porcelain manufacture in China, *ca.* 600
T'ang Dynasty in China, 618–907
Civil-service examinations in China, 618

Taika Reform Edict, creating imperial government in Japan based on Chinese model, 645

Development of steel manufacturing, textile manufacturing, leather tooling, and paper making, *ca.* 800–1400

Block printing in China, *ca.* 800

Feudalism in Japan, rise of *Samurai*, 800–1600
Sung Dynasty in China, 960–1279

Hindu-Arabic system of numerals, *ca.* 1000
Saracenic world trade, *ca.* 1000–1500

Moslem Invasions of India, 1000–1500

Cultivation of cotton, sugar, oranges, lemons, bananas, coffee, *ca.* 1100
Transmission of complete works of Aristotle to Europe, *ca.* 1150

Genghis Khan, 1162?–1217

Transmission of compass and astrolabe to Europe, *ca.* 1400

Sack of Delhi by Timur, 1398

CHAPTER 13

The Civilization of Early
Medieval Europe

Think not that I am come to destroy the law, or the prophets:
I am not come to destroy, but to fulfill.
— Jesus of Nazareth, The Sermon on the Mount, *Matthew* v.17

Although checked for the time, this pernicious susperstition
[Christianity] broke out again . . . throughout the City, in which
the atrocities and shame from all parts of the world center and
flourish. Therefore those who confessed were first seized, then on
their information a great multitude were convicted, not so much
of the crime of incendiarism, as of hatred of the human race.
— Tacitus on Nero's persecution of Christians

Sometime during the Renaissance the practice arose of dividing the
history of the world into three great epochs: ancient, medieval, and
modern. This classification has come to be accepted with almost
dogmatic finality. It ties in with the average man's belief that this
planet of ours has witnessed only two great periods of progress: the
time of the Greeks and the Romans and the age of modern invention. Between these two periods were the Middle Ages, popularly
regarded as an interlude of abysmal ignorance and superstition when
man lived enveloped in a cowl, oblivious of the wonders of knowledge, and concerned only with escape from the miseries of this
world and the torments of hell. The very word "medieval" has an
odious meaning in the average mind of today. It has come to be a
synonym for reactionary or unprogressive. Thus when a modern
reformer wishes to cast reproach upon the ideas of his conservative
opponent, all he has to do is to brand them as "medieval."

The reason for such erroneous judgments lies in the conventional
notion that the entire medieval period from the fall of Rome to the
beginning of the Renaissance was a cultural unit, that the ideals and

Misinterpreta-
tion of the word
"medieval"

359

institutions of the sixth century, for example, were the same as those of the thirteenth. Nothing could be farther from the truth. The medieval period, in western Europe, really encompassed two civilizations, as different from each other as Greece from Rome or the Renaissance from the nineteenth and twentieth centuries. The first of these civilizations, beginning about 400 A.D., when the process of Roman decay was nearly complete, and extending until 1000, was that of the early Middle Ages. It was this period alone which was really distinguished by most of those attributes commonly referred to as "medieval." The culture of the early Middle Ages undoubtedly represented in certain respects a reversion to barbarism. Intellect did not merely stagnate but sank to very low depths of ignorance and credulity. Economic activity declined to primitive levels of barter and ruralism, while morbid asceticism and contempt for this world superseded more normal social attitudes. With the Carolingian Renaissance of the ninth century, however, a brief intellectual revival occurred in Europe. In the eleventh, twelfth, and thirteenth centuries the human spirit soared to much greater heights. The result was another of the world's great cultures, distinguished alike by intellectual progress and a high degree of prosperity and freedom. Indeed, this later medieval civilization, which endured until the end of the thirteenth century, was more nearly similar to the modern age than most people realize.

I. THE CHRISTIAN FOUNDATION OF EARLY MEDIEVAL CULTURE

Three main factors combined to produce the civilization of early medieval Europe: the Christian religion, the influence of the Germanic barbarians, and the heritage from the classical cultures. The effect of the third was probably less than that of the others. Outside the realm of philosophy the influence of the Greek and Hellenistic civilizations was comparatively slight. While the Roman heritage was still powerful, the men of the early Middle Ages rejected some portions of it as inconsistent with Christianity and barbarized much of the remainder.

The most important foundation of the new culture was the Chrisian religion, whose founder, Jesus of Nazareth, was born in a small town of Judea some time near the beginning of the Christian era. Judea was then under Roman rule, though the Jews themselves recognized only their own king, Herod I, as their rightful sovereign. The atmosphere of the country was charged with religious emotionalism and political discontent. Some of the people, notably the Pharisees, looked forward to the coming of a political messiah, a son of David, who would rescue the country from foreign rule. Others, for example, the Essenes, thought in terms of spiritual deliverance through asceticism, repentance, and mystical union with God. It was this latter sect, together with others of a similar character, which prepared the way for the ministry of Jesus. When he was about twenty-eight years old, he was acclaimed by an ascetic evangelist, John the Baptist, as one "mightier than I, whose shoes I am not worthy to bear." [1] Thenceforth for about three years the career of Jesus, according to the New Testament accounts, was a continuous course of preaching and teaching and of healing the sick, "casting out devils," restoring sight to the blind, and raising the dead. He not only denounced shame, greed, and licentious living but set the example himself by a life of humility and self-denial. Though the conception he held of himself is somewhat obscure, he apparently believed that he had a divine mission to save mankind from error and sin. His preaching and other activities eventually aroused the antagonism of some of the chief priests and conservative rabbis. They disliked his caustic references to the legalism of the Pharisees, his contempt for form and ceremony, and his scorn for pomp and luxury. They feared also that his claims to being the Messiah would cause trouble with the Romans. Accordingly, they brought him into the highest court in Jerusalem, where he was solemnly condemned for blasphemy and for setting himself up as "King of the Jews" and

[1] Matthew 3:11.

Nazareth. A modern view of the small town in Judea where Jesus spent his early life, where he worked for a time as a carpenter and began his career of preaching.

turned over to Pontius Pilate, the Roman governor, for execution of the sentence. After hours-of agony he died on the cross between two thieves on the hill of Golgotha outside Jerusalem.

The crucifixion

The crucifixion of Jesus marked a great climax in Christian history. At first his death was viewed by his followers as the end of their hopes. Their despair soon vanished, however, for rumors began to spread that the Master was alive, and that he had been seen by certain of his faithful disciples. The remainder of his followers were quickly convinced that he had risen from the dead, and that he was truly a divine being. With their courage restored, they organized their little band and began preaching and testifying in the name of their martyred leader. Thus another of the world's great religions was launched on a career that would ultimately shake the foundations of no less an empire than mighty Rome.

The teachings of Jesus

There has never been perfect agreement among Christians as to the precise teachings of Jesus of Nazareth. The only dependable records are the four Gospels, but the oldest of these was not written until at least a generation after Jesus' death. According to the beliefs of his orthodox followers, the founder of Christianity revealed himself as the Christ, the divine Son of God, who was sent on this earth to suffer and die for the sins of mankind. They were convinced that after three days in the tomb, he had risen from the dead and ascended into heaven, whence he would come again to judge the world. The Gospels at least make it clear that he included the following among his basic teachings: (1) the fatherhood of God and the brotherhood of man; (2) the Golden Rule; (3) forgiveness and love of one's enemies; (4) repayment of evil with good; (5) self-denial; (6) condemnation of hypocrisy and greed; (7) opposition to ceremonialism as the essence of religion; (8) the imminent approach of the end of the world; and (9) the resurrection of the dead and the establishment of the kingdom of Heaven.

The influence of Paul

Christianity was broadened and invested with a more elaborate theology by some of the successors of Jesus. Chief among them was the Apostle Paul, originally known as Saul of Tarsus. Although of Jewish nationality, Paul was not a native of Palestine but a Jew of the Diaspora,[2] born in the city of Tarsus in southeastern Asia Minor. Here he came into contact with the Stoic philosophy, but he was possibly more deeply influenced by Gnosticism. Eventually converted to Christianity, he devoted his limitless energy to propagating that faith throughout the Near East. It would be almost impossible to overestimate the significance of his work. Denying that Jesus was sent merely as the redeemer of the Jews, he proclaimed Christianity to be a universal religion. But this was not all. He gave major emphasis to the idea of Jesus as the Christ, as the God-man who existed from the foundation of the world and whose death on the cross was a propitiation for the sins of mankind. Not

[2] See pp. 102–03.

only did he reject the works of the Law (i.e., Jewish ritualism) as of primary importance in religion, but he declared them to be utterly worthless in procuring salvation. Man is a sinner by nature, and he can therefore be saved only by faith and by the grace of God "through the redemption that is in Christ Jesus." It follows, according to Paul, that man's fate in the life to come is almost entirely dependent upon the will of God; for "Hath not the potter power over the clay, of the same lump to make one vessel unto honour, and another unto dishonour?" [3] He has mercy "on whom he will have mercy, and whom he will he hardeneth." [4]

By the beginning of the Middle Ages the triumph of Christianity over all its rivals was almost complete. The Emperor Galerius' edict of toleration in 311 was already an admission that the religion was too strong to be stamped out by persecution. By a series of decrees between 380 and 392 Christianity was recognized as the only lawful faith of the Roman Empire. How is this triumph to be explained? Perhaps as much as anything else it was a result of the composite character of Christianity. Here was a religion which ultimately came to embody elements from a wide variety of sources. A large number of them were taken from Judaism: the name of the deity, the cosmogony, the world history, the Ten Commandments, and such doctrines as original sin and the providence of God. In addition, several of the ethical doctrines were really of Jewish origin. Although many of these elements were modified by Jesus and his followers, there can be no doubt that the Hebrew contributions to Christianity were of great importance.

But obviously Christianity derived much from other than Jewish sources. Some idea of the debt it owed to the various religions of Persian origin has been indicated in a preceding chapter. [5] Zoroastrianism had already made the ancient world familiar with such concepts as otherworldliness and an eternal conflict between good and evil. Gnosticism had developed the belief in secret revelation and had taught the notion of a primal man or God-man becoming incarnate in human form. Mithraism had fixed men's attention upon forms of ritual, such as baptism and the use of holy water, and upon the celebration of Sunday and the twenty-fifth of December as sacred days. Supplementing these influences was that of the philosophy of Stoicism, which had familiarized the educated classes with ideals of cosmopolitanism and the brotherhood of man. In short, mystery religions and Hellenistic philosophy had already brought into existence a large deposit of doctrines and practices upon which Christianity could draw, at the same time preserving its distinctive character. The early Church was an organism that fed upon the whole pagan world, selecting and incorporating a wide variety of

[3] Romans 9:21.
[4] Romans 9:18.
[5] See the chapter on The Civilization of Ancient Persia.

ideas and practices which were not inconsistent with its own nature. The appeal of Christianity was therefore more nearly universal than that of any other of the ancient religions.

The other main reasons for the triumph of Christianity can be summarized briefly. It admitted women to full rights of participation in worship, whereas Mithraism, the strongest of its early competitors, excluded them. It enjoyed the advantage for about fifty years of systematic persecution by the Roman government, a factor which enormously strengthened the cohesiveness of the movement, since those who remained in the faith had to be ready to die for their convictions. While most of the other religions revolved around imaginary figures, the creatures of grotesque legends, Christianity possessed as its founder a historic individual of clearly defined personality. Lastly, the triumph of Christianity is partly explained by the fact that it made a stronger appeal to the poor and oppressed than did any of the other mystery religions. Although it included the ideal of the equality of all men in the sight of God, its founder and some of his followers had condemned the rich and exalted the lowly. It propagated a new and exceedingly democratic morality, with meekness, self-effacement, and love of one's enemies as primary virtues. Perhaps these were the qualities most likely to find ready acceptance among the helpless masses who had long since abandoned hope of bettering their material condition.

Hardly had Christianity emerged victorious over its rivals than disaffection developed within its own ranks. This was due partly to the heterogeneous elements out of which the religion had been formed, and partly also to the compromising attitudes displayed by the leaders as the success of the movement increased. A more fundamental reason seems to have been the conflict between the intellectual and emotional tendencies within the religion. Representing the former were the two most important sects of *subordinationist* Christians [6]—the Arians and the Nestorians. Both of them agreed in their refusal to accept what has since become the orthodox doctrine of the Trinity. Under the influence of Greek philosophy they rejected the idea that the Christ could be the equal of God. The Arians maintained that the Son was created by the Father and therefore was not co-eternal with him or formed of the same substance. Their chief opponents were the Athanasians, who held that Father, Son, and Holy Ghost were all absolutely equal and composed of identical substance. The Nestorians broke away from the rest of the Church with the contention that Mary should be called the mother of Christ but not the mother of God, implying of course that they considered the Christ something less than divine.

The most important of the sects that emphasized the emotional character of Christianity were the Gnostics and the Manicheans.

Other reasons for the Christian triumph

The division of Christians into rival sects: Arians, Athanasians, and Nestorians

[6] Called "subordinationist" because they insisted upon subordinating Christ to God the Father.

Both were extreme ascetics and mystics. Believing that genuine religious truth was a product of revelation exclusively, they were inclined to be strongly suspicious of any attempt to rationalize the Christian faith. They were opposed also to the tendency toward worldliness which was making itself evident among many of the clergy. The Gnostics and the Manicheans were not originally sects of Christianity at all, but eventually many of them went over to that faith. Those who became Christians retained their old doctrines of exaggerated spiritualism and contempt for matter as evil. Naturally, along with these went an abiding distrust of every variety of human knowledge. The doctrines of all these sects, with the exception of the Athanasian, were eventually condemned by Church councils as heresies.

Notwithstanding the condemnation of many beliefs as heresies, the body of Christian doctrine was never very firmly fixed during the early Middle Ages. Of course, all Christians believed in a God who was the creator and governor of the universe, in salvation from sin, and in rewards and punishments after death. But as regards many other questions of dogma there was confusion and uncertainty. Even the concept of the Trinity continued to be an issue of debate for several centuries. Many of the Eastern Christians never accepted the extreme Athanasian view of the relation of the Father and the Son adopted by the Council of Nicaea (325). Furthermore, there was no clearly formulated theory at this time of the number and the precise nature of the sacraments, nor was the doctrine of the powers of the priesthood definitely established. The theory of the Mass was not formally defined until 1215. In general, there were two main points of disagreement affecting all of these issues. Some very devout believers clung to an ideal of Christianity similar to that of the Apostolic age, when the Church was a community of mystics, each of them guided by the Inner Light in matters of faith and conduct. Others envisaged the Christian Church as an organized society prescribing its own rules for the government of its members in accordance with the practical requirements of the time.

The growth of Christian organization was one of the outstanding developments of the whole medieval era. Even during the first few centuries of that period the Church and its related institutions evolved into an elaborate structure which ultimately became the principal framework of society itself. As the Roman Empire in the West decayed, the Church took over many of its functions and helped to preserve order amid the deepening chaos. That anything at all was saved out of the wreckage was due in large part to the stabilizing influence of the organized Church. It aided in civilizing the barbarians, in promoting ideals of social justice, and in preserving and transmitting the antique learning.

The organization of the Church was at first quite simple. The early Christian congregations met in the homes of their members

Gnostics and Manicheans

The persistence of doctrinal disputes

The importance of Christian organization

365

and listened to the spiritual testimony of various of the brethren
who were believed to have been in direct communication with the
Holy Ghost. No distinction between laymen and clergy was recognized. Each independent church had a number of officers, generally
known as bishops and elders, whose functions were to preside at the
services, discipline members, and dispense charity. Gradually, under
the influence of the pagan mystery religions, the ritual of Christianity increased to such a stage of complexity that a professional priesthood seemed to become necessary. The need for defense against
persecution and the desire to attain uniformity of belief also favored
the development of ecclesiastical organization. The consequence
was that about the beginning of the second century one bishop in
each important city came to be recognized as supreme over all the
clergy in that vicinity. The sphere of his jurisdiction corresponded
to the *civitas*, the smallest administrative unit of the Roman state. As
the number of congregations multiplied, and as the influence of the
Church increased due to the adoption of Christianity as the official
religion of Rome, distinctions of rank among the bishops themselves
began to appear. Those who had their headquarters in the larger
cities came to be called metropolitans, with authority over the
clergy of an entire province. In the fourth century the still higher
dignity of patriarch was established to designate those bishops who
ruled over the oldest and largest of Christian communities—such
cities as Rome, Constantinople, Antioch, and Alexandria, with their
surrounding districts. Thus the Christian clergy by 400 A.D. had
come to embrace a definite hierarchy of patriarchs, metropolitans,
bishops, and priests.

The climax of all this development was the growth of the
primacy of the bishop of Rome, or in other words the rise of the
papacy. For several reasons the bishop of Rome enjoyed a preeminence over the other patriarchs of the Church. The city in which he
ruled was venerated by the faithful as a scene of the missionary
activities of the Apostles Peter and Paul. The tradition was widely
accepted that Peter had founded the bishopric of Rome, and that
therefore all of his successors were heirs of his authority and prestige. This tradition was supplemented by the theory that Peter had
been commissioned by the Christ as his vicar on earth and had been
given the keys of the Kingdom of Heaven with power to punish
men for their sins and even to absolve them from guilt.[7] This theory, known as the doctrine of the Petrine Succession, has been used
by Popes ever since as a basis for their claims to authority over the
Church. The bishops of Rome had an advantage also in the fact that
after the transfer of the imperial capital to Constantinople there was
seldom any emperor with effective sovereignty in the West. Finally,
in 455 the Emperor Valentinian III issued a decree commanding all
Western bishops to submit to the jurisdiction of the Pope. It must

[7] See Matthew 16:18–19.

not be supposed, however, that the Church was yet under a monarchical form of government. The patriarchs in the East regarded the extreme assertions of the papal claims as a brazen effrontery, and even many bishops in the West continued to ignore them for some time.

The organization of the Church was by no means confined to an ecclesiastical hierarchy. In any study of Christian institutions a prominent place must be given to monasticism. Since monasticism was originally an outgrowth of asceticism, it becomes necessary, first of all, to examine the relationship between that ideal and the Christian religion. Original Christianity was only mildly ascetic. Neither Jesus nor his immediate followers practiced any extremes of self-torture. To be sure, Jesus did not marry; he declared that he had no place to lay his head; and he was supposed to have fasted for forty days in the wilderness; but these examples could scarcely have encouraged the pathological excesses of mortification of the flesh indulged in by the hermits of the third and fourth centuries. We must therefore look for additional causes of the growth of this later asceticism. Perhaps the following may be considered fundamental:

(1) The desire of many pious Christians to protest against the increasing worldliness of the Church. The farther they might go to the opposite extreme of the luxurious lives of some of the clergy, for example, the more effective that protest would become.

(2) The choice of morbid self-torture as a substitute for martyrdom. With the abandonment of persecution by the Romans all chances of winning a crown of glory in heaven by undergoing death for the faith were eliminated. But the desire to give evidence of one's religious ardor by self-abasement and suffering was still present and demanded an outlet.

(3) The desire of some Christians who were sincerely devoted to the faith to set an example of exalted piety and unselfishness as an inspiration to their weaker brethren. Even though most men should fail to attain the ideal, the general level of morality and piety would be raised.

(4) The influence of other Oriental religions, especially Gnosticism and Manicheism, with their exaggerated spiritualism, contempt for this world, and degradation of the body.

The earliest Christian ascetics were hermits, who withdrew from the world to live in seclusion in some wilderness or desert. This form of asceticism seems to have originated in Egypt in the third century. From there it spread into other provinces of the eastern section of the Empire and continued to be popular for more than 100 years. It developed into a kind of religious mania characterized by morbid excesses. We read of hermits or anchorites grazing in the fields after the manner of animals, rolling naked in thorn bushes, or living in swamps infested with snakes. The famous St. Simeon Stylites passed a whole summer "as a rooted vegetable in a garden"

A Monastery of the Basilian Order on Mt. Athos. The asceticism of the Basilian monks caused them to build their monasteries in almost inaccessible places on lofty crags or on the steep sides of rugged mountains.

and then began the construction of his celebrated pillar. He built it to a height of sixty feet and spent the remaining thirty years of his life on the top. Such absurdities as these, while certainly not typical of the attitude of the majority of Christians at this time, were probably the natural fruit of too strong an emphasis upon the spiritual way of life.

In time the force of the anchorite hysteria subsided. Certain of the more practical Christian ascetics came to the conclusion that the solitary life of the hermit was not good for the soul, since it sometimes drove men insane. The result of this conclusion was the origin of monasticism. The most prominent early leader of monasticism was St. Basil, a bishop of Cappadocia, who was the first to issue a set of rules for the government of a monastic order. Disapproving of extreme self-torture, St. Basil required his monks to discipline themselves by useful labor. They were not to engage in prolonged fasting or in degrading laceration of the flesh, but they were compelled to submit to obligations of poverty and humility and to spend many hours of the day in silent religious meditation. The Basilian type of monasticism came to be adopted universally in the eastern areas of Christendom. Many of its units are still to be seen perched on lofty crags to which access can be gained only by climbing long rope ladders or being hauled up in a basket. There was no important

The rise of monasticism

368

monasticism in the West until the sixth century, when St. Benedict drafted his famous rule which ultimately became the guide for nearly all the monks of Latin Christendom. The Benedictine rule imposed obligations similar to those of the rule of St. Basil— poverty, obedience, labor, and religious devotion. Yet there was an absence of severe austerities. The monks were allowed a sufficiency of simple food, good clothing, and enough sleep. They were permitted to have wine but no meat. They were allowed no recreation and few baths, unless they were sick. They were subject to the absolute authority of the abbot, who could flog them for disobedience. The original Benedictine monastery was established at Monte Cassino, halfway between Rome and Naples. Eventually it came to possess one of the finest libraries in medieval Europe. It was destroyed by Allied bombing during World War II, but has since been rebuilt.

The influence of monasticism upon the society of the early Middle Ages would be difficult to exaggerate. The monks were generally the best farmers in Europe; they reclaimed waste lands, drained swamps, and made numerous discoveries relating to the improvement of the soil. They preserved some of the building skill of the Romans and achieved noteworthy progress in many of the industrial arts, especially in wood carving, metal-working, weaving, glass-making, and brewing. It was monks, furthermore, who wrote most of the books, copied the ancient manuscripts, and maintained the majority of the schools and libraries and nearly all of the hospitals that existed during the early Middle Ages. The growth of monasticism also profoundly affected the history of the Church. It led to a division in the ranks of the clergy. Living according to a definite rule or *regula*, the monks came to be called the *regular* clergy; while the priests, bishops, and archbishops, who carried on their activities in the midst of the affairs of the world (*saeculum*), were henceforth known as the *secular* clergy. Between the two groups intense rivalry developed, with the monks sometimes organizing reform movements against the worldliness of the priests. The Benedictine monks enjoyed the special favor of the Popes, and it was partly on account of an alliance between the papacy and monasticism that the former was able to extend its power over the Church.

The results of monasticism

2. THE GERMANIC FOUNDATIONS OF THE NEW CULTURE

The second most important of the factors which combined to produce the civilization of early medieval Europe was the influence of the Germanic barbarians. They were not the only northern peoples who helped to mold the pattern of early medieval society; the contributions of the Celts in Brittany and Ireland and of the Slavs in

The ancient Germans

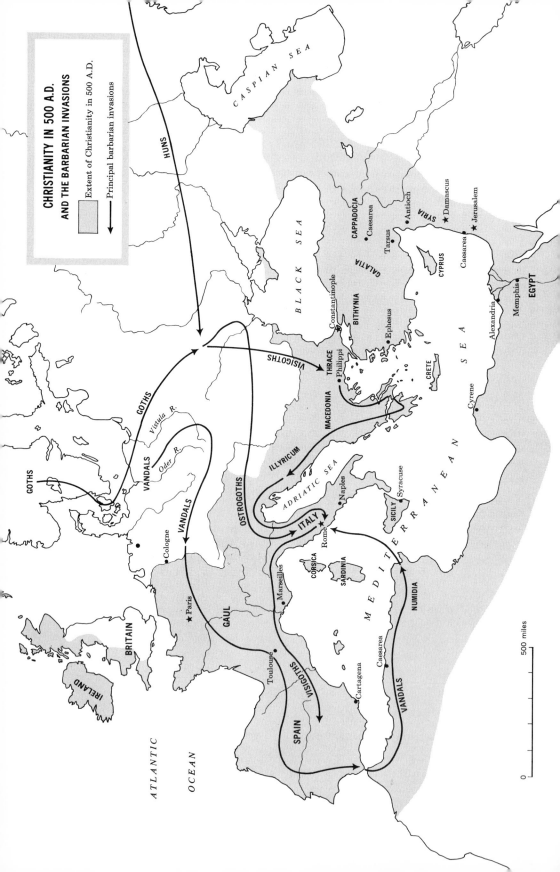

CHRISTIANITY IN 500 A.D.
AND THE BARBARIAN INVASIONS

▨ Extent of Christianity in 500 A.D.

→ Principal barbarian invasions

CASPIAN SEA

HUNS

GOTHS

Vistula R.

Oder R.

VANDALS

GOTHS

VANDALS

BLACK SEA

VISIGOTHS

CAPPADOCIA

Caesarea

Antioch

Damascus

SYRIA

Jerusalem

Tarsus

GALATIA

CYPRUS

Caesarea

Constantinople

BITHYNIA

Ephesus

THRACE

Philippi

CRETE

Memphis

EGYPT

Alexandria

MACEDONIA

ILLYRICUM

ADRIATIC SEA

Naples

Syracuse

SICILY

Cyrene

MEDITERRANEAN SEA

OSTROGOTHS

ITALY

Rome

CORSICA

SARDINIA

NUMIDIA

Cologne

VANDALS

Paris

GAUL

Marseilles

BRITAIN

IRELAND

Toulouse

VISIGOTHS

SPAIN

Caesarea

Cartagena

VANDALS

ATLANTIC OCEAN

500 miles

0

central and eastern Europe were by no means insignificant. Nevertheless, the Germanic influence appears to have been the most extensive. Where the Germans came from originally is a problem upon which scholars disagree, but they seem to have migrated into northern Europe from western Asia. By the beginning of the Christian era they had come to be divided into several peoples: Scandinavians, Vandals, Goths, Franks, Alemanni, Burgundians, Frisians, Anglo-Saxons, Dutch, and so on. Both in language and in physical characteristics they bore some affinity to the Greeks and the Romans.

For centuries different nations of Germanic barbarians had been making incursions into Roman territory. At times they came as invading armies, but generally they filtered in slowly, bringing their families and belongings with them and occupying depopulated or abandoned areas. Many were brought in by Roman commanders and rulers. Julius Caesar was impressed by their value as warriors and enrolled thousands of them in his armies. They were to be found in the bodyguard of nearly every Princeps and Emperor. Finally, by the time of Constantine, they formed the bulk of the soldiers in the entire Roman army. Many were also drawn into the civil service and thousands were settled by the government as *coloni* or serfs on the great estates. In view of these conditions it is not surprising that Rome should eventually have been taken over by the Germans. As more and more of them gained a foothold in Italy, others were bound to be tempted by the opportunities for plunder. It must be emphasized that many of the supposed invasions were mere "folk wanderings," and not necessarily motivated by a desire for conquest. Although armed invasions of Italy began as early as the second century B.C., and were repeated several times thereafter, there were no really disastrous incursions until the fourth and fifth centuries A.D. In 378 the Visigoths, angered by the oppression of imperial governors, raised the standard of revolt. They overwhelmed a Roman army at Adrianople and then marched westward into Italy. In 410 under Alaric they captured and plundered Rome, later moving on into southern Gaul. In 455 Rome was sacked by the Vandals, who had migrated from their original home between the Oder and Vistula rivers and established a kingdom in the province of Carthage. Other Germanic peoples also made their way into Italy, and before the end of the fifth century the Roman Empire in the West had passed completely under the domination of the barbarians.

For our knowledge of ancient Germanic society we are dependent primarily upon the *Germania* of Tacitus, written in 98 A.D. The literature and the laws of the Germans themselves also contain much information, but these were not put into written form until after Roman and Christian influences had begun to exert their effect. When Tacitus wrote, the Germanic barbarians had attained a cultural level about equal to that of the early Greeks. They were illiterate and ignorant of any knowledge of the arts. Their houses were

The Germanic invasions of the Roman Empire

Ancient German society

built of rough timber plastered over with mud. While they had achieved some development of agriculture, they preferred the risks of plundering expeditions to the prosaic labor of tilling the soil. Nearly all of the work was done by the women and old men and other dependents. When not fighting or hunting, the warriors spent most of their time sleeping and carousing. Gambling and drunkenness were glaring vices, but, if we can believe the testimony of Tacitus, sex morality was singularly pure. Monogamous marriage prevailed, except in those cases where a chief might be permitted to take more than one wife for political reasons. Adultery was rare and was severely punished; divorce was almost unknown. In some tribes even widows were forbidden to remarry.

The economic and political institutions of the Germans were such as befitted a people who were just emerging into a settled existence. The tiny proportion of trade carried on rested solely upon a basis of barter, while cattle were still the main article of wealth. Whether the agricultural land was individually or collectively owned is still a debated question, but there seems little doubt that the forests and pastures were held and used in common. Possibly the community controlled the distribution of new lands as they were acquired, allotting the arable portions as individual farms. There is evidence that a class of wealthy proprietors had grown up as an aristocracy in certain of the tribes. Although Tacitus states that the Germans had slaves, it seems probable that most of their dependents were serfs, since they had houses of their own and paid their masters only a portion of what they produced. Their servitude in some cases was a result of capture in war but in others of indebtedness and especially reckless gambling, in which men staked their own liberty when everything else had been lost. The state scarcely existed at all. Law was a product of custom, and the administration of justice remained largely in private hands. While the Germans had their tribal courts, the function of these bodies was chiefly to mediate between plaintiff and defendant. It was left to the former to bring the accused to trial and to carry out the penalty prescribed by the customary law. The court merely decided what proofs should be required of each litigant to determine the validity of his plea. Usually these consisted of oaths and ordeals, both of which were considered as appeals to the judgment of the gods. The most important of the remaining political institutions was the primary assembly of the warriors. But this body had no lawmaking powers beyond those involved in the interpretation of custom. Its main function was to decide questions of war and peace and whether the tribe should migrate to some new locality. Originally the German tribes had no kings. They had chiefs elected by the freemen, but these were little more than ceremonial officials. In time of war a military leader was elected and endowed with considerable power, but as soon as the campaign was over his authority lapsed. Nevertheless, as wars increased in frequency and duration, some of the military leaders actually became kings. The formality of election, however, was generally retained.

The influence of the Germans upon medieval history, while not so important as is sometimes imagined, was extensive enough to deserve consideration. Above all, they were largely responsible for several of the elements of feudalism: (1) the conception of law as an outgrowth of custom and not as the expression of the will of a sovereign; (2) the idea of law as a personal possession of the individual which he could take with him wherever he went, in contrast to the Roman conception of law as limited to a definite territory; (3) the notion of a contractual relationship between rulers and subjects, involving reciprocal obligations of protection and obedience; (4) the theory of an honorable relationship between lord and vassal, growing out of the Germanic institution of the *comitatus* or military band, in which the warriors were bound by pledges of honor and loyalty to fight for and serve their leader; (5) trial by ordeal as a prevailing mode of procedure in the feudal courts; and (6) the idea of elective kingship.

3. POLITICAL AND ECONOMIC DEVELOPMENTS IN EARLY MEDIEVAL EUROPE

Between 500 and 700 A.D. most of western Europe languished in a kind of Dark Age. The barbarian kings who usurped the authority of the Roman Emperors proved themselves wholly incapable of maintaining the administrative organization that passed into their hands. They appeared to have no conception of efficient government for the public welfare and regarded their kingdoms as private estates to be exploited for their own benefit. They allowed the Roman tax system to break down and delegated much of their political authority to the nobility and the Church. Although many of the old Roman towns survived, they declined in importance, and the ancient urban culture largely disappeared. The characteristic institutions were now the monastery, the peasant village, and the great villa or semifeudal estate cultivated by tenant farmers. No longer was the economy international as it had been in the heyday of Rome. Except for the exchange of a few luxury items, it sank rapidly into localism or rural self-sufficiency.

The only barbarian ruler who did anything in Italy to check the progress of deterioration was Theodoric the Ostrogoth, who conquered the peninsula in 493. Until nearly the end of his reign of thirty-three years, he gave Italy a more enlightened rule than it had known under many of the Caesars. He fostered agriculture and commerce, repaired public buildings and roads, patronized learning, and enforced religious toleration. But in his last years he became querulous and suspicious, accusing some of his faithful subordinates of plotting with the Roman aristocracy to overthrow him. Several were put to death, including the philosopher Boethius. After the death of Theodoric decay set in once more, hastened this time by new wars of conquest. When Justinian became Emperor at Constantinople in 527 he determined to reconquer Italy and the provinces in the West. Not until 552 was the project completed. The devastation of the long war was so great that Italy was opened for invasion by the Lombards in 568. The Lombards succeeded in holding most of the peninsula under the rule of semi-independent dukes until the conquest of Charlemagne in the late eighth century.

Deterioration continued apace in Spain. The Spanish Church was corrupt, and the barbarian (Visigothic) kings were ignorant and predatory. By allowing their power to slip into the hands of an oppressive nobility they made their country an easy prey for Moslem conquest in the eighth century. Deterioration was also evident in France. In 481 a youth by the name of Clovis became king of an important tribe of the Salian Franks, who dwelt on the left bank of the Rhine. In less than twenty years Clovis conquered nearly all of what is now France and a portion of Germany besides. His adoption of orthodox Christianity won for him the support of the clergy and made possible the subsequent alliance between the Frankish kings and the Popes. The Merovingian dynasty,[8] which he really founded, occupied the throne of the Frankish state until 751. For more than a century the successors of Clovis continued his policy of savage despotism, annexing the territory of their enemies, dominating the Church, and exploiting the lands of the kingdom as if they were their private possessions. By 639, however, the royal line had begun to degenerate. A series of short-lived weaklings, the so-called do-nothing kings, inherited the crown of their lusty forebears. Absorbed in the pursuit of pleasure, these worthless youths delegated most of their authority to their chief subordinates, the mayors of the palace. Nothing more natural could have happened than the eventual displacement of the Merovingian kings by these very officials to whom they had entrusted their powers. The most capable and aggressive of the mayors of the palace was Charles Martel ("the Hammer"), who may be considered a second founder of the Frankish state. He won fame in 732 by defeating the Moors at Tours, a town only a little more than 100 miles from Paris. Although his opponents were merely a marauding band, the Battle of Tours is nevertheless important as the high-water mark of Moorish invasion of France. Yet, even after his victory, Charles was content with the substance of power and did not bother to assume the royal title. It was left for his son, Pepin the Short, to have himself elected king of the Franks in 751 and thereby to put an end to Merovingian rule. The new dynasty became known as the Carolingian from the name of its most famous member, Carolus Magnus or Charlemagne (742–814).

[8] So called from Merovech, the half-mythical founder of the family to which Clovis belonged.

In the minds of most students of history Charlemagne stands out as one of the two or three most important individuals in the whole medieval period. By some of his contemporaries he was acclaimed as a new Augustus who would bring peace and prosperity to western Europe. There can be no question that he established more efficient government, and that he did much to combat the centrifugal tendencies which had gathered momentum during the reigns of the later Merovingians. Not only did he abolish the office of mayor of the palace, but he eliminated the tribal dukes and bestowed all the powers of local government upon his own appointees, the counts.

karolus imparat   magnus Annus.t+.

The Emperor Charlemagne. From a painting by Albrecht Dürer.

To prevent abuses of authority by the latter he appointed *missi dominici,* or royal messengers, to visit the counties and to report to the king any acts of official injustice. He authorized the *missi* to hold their own courts for the purpose of hearing complaints of oppression and even in extreme cases to remove local officers. He modified the old system of private administration of justice by authorizing the counts to summon accused persons to court and by vesting the magistrates with more control over judicial procedure. He revived the Roman institution of the sworn inquest, in which a number of persons were summoned by agents of the king and bound by oath to tell what they knew of any crimes committed in their locality. This institution survived the downfall of the Carolingian state and was carried by the Normans to England, where it eventually became an important factor in the origin of the grand-jury **375** system. Although much of the remainder of the political structure Charlemagne established perished with the end of his dynasty, the precedent that he set for strong government undoubtedly influenced many of the French kings in the later Middle Ages and the German emperors as well. It should be noted, however, that the glory of Charlemagne's empire rested in large part upon a foundation of slaughter. During the forty-six years of his reign from 768 to 814, he conducted no fewer than fifty-four wars. There was scarcely a people of western Europe against whom he did not fight, except the English. Since most of his campaigns were successful, he annexed to the Frankish domain the greater part of central Europe and northern and central Italy. But some of these conquests were made possible only by a fearful sacrifice of blood and a resort to measures of the harshest cruelty. The campaign against the Saxons met with such stubborn opposition that Charlemagne finally ordered the beheading of 4500 of them. It is typical of the spirit of the times that all of this was done under the pretext of inducing the pagans to adopt Christianity.

Charlemagne becomes emperor

In fact, it was Charlemagne's constant intervention in religious affairs which led to the climax of his whole career—his coronation as Roman Emperor by Pope Leo III. Leo had been in trouble for some time. Accused of being a tyrant and a rake, he so aroused the indignation of the people of Rome that in 799 they gave him a severe beating and forced him to flee from the city. Struggling over the mountains to Germany, he implored the aid of Charlemagne. The great king sent him back to Italy and was instrumental in restoring him to the papal throne. On Christmas Day, 800, as Charles knelt in prayer in St. Peter's Church, the grateful Pope placed a crown on his head while the assembled multitude hailed him as "Augustus, crowned of God, great and pacific Emperor of the Romans." The significance of this event is rather hard to appraise. It seems doubtful that Charles was under any illusions as to the nature of the act. For all practical purposes it was merely the recognition of an accomplished fact. By his conquests Charles had made himself ruler of nearly all of western and central Europe. In 794 he established a permanent capital at Aachen that was called "New Rome." He never acknowledged any sovereignty of the Pope over him. In his view ecclesiastical affairs were as much a part of his domain as were secular matters. Though he did not attempt to prescribe Church doctrine, he displayed an interest in maintaining uniformity of both discipline and theology. He summoned a number of Church synods during his reign and presided over one of them. In the eyes of the Pope the coronation had a quite different significance. He regarded all kings as his stewards exercising their authority for the benefit of the Church. True, Charles was now an emperor, but it was the Pope who had given him this dignity; and what the Pope could grant he could also take away. This conflict of views foreshadowed the great struggle of the eleventh, twelfth, and thirteenth centuries—a struggle over who should be supreme in western Europe, the Emperor or the Pope.

At the beginning of the early Middle Ages a large part of what is now England was still under Roman rule. But in the fifth century the Romans were forced to withdraw on account of increasing trouble with Germanic invasions into Italy. Soon afterward England was overrun by hordes of Saxons, Angles, and Jutes from the Continent. They brought with them the customs and institutions of their homeland, which were similar to those of the other Germanic barbarians. Driving the original Celtic natives into the mountains of Wales and Cornwall, they quickly established their own kingdoms. At one time there were seven—Northumbria, East Anglia, Kent, Essex, Sussex, Wessex, and Mercia—mutually suspicious and hostile. In the ninth century tribes of Danes took advantage of the strife among the Saxon kingdoms and attempted their conquest. Efforts to defeat the new enemy brought the seven kingdoms into a strong confederation under the leadership of Wessex and its celebrated ruler, Alfred the Great (849–899). King Alfred reorganized the army, infused new vigor into local government, and revised and broadened the laws. In addition, he founded schools and fostered an interest in literature and other elements of a national culture.

King Alfred's successors were men of weaker fiber. One of them, Ethelred the Unready, surrendered his kingdom to the powerful Danish King Canute. For eighteen years England was ruled as part of a North Sea empire which also included Norway and Denmark. But in 1035 Canute died, and the Saxon dynasty regained control of England. It was not for long. Ethelred's son, Edward the Confessor, was more interested in cultivating a reputation for piety than he was in statecraft, and allowed affairs of his country to be regulated by the Duchy of Normandy, across the Channel. Upon Edward's death the Duke of Normandy, subsequently known as William the Conqueror (1027–1087), laid claim to the crown of England. Landing an army in Sussex in 1066, he caught the English monarch, Harold, unprepared and defeated him in the Battle of Hastings. Harold fell mortally wounded, and his forces disintegrated. Apparently regarding discretion as the better part of valor, the surviving magnates offered the crown to Duke William. The Battle of Hastings is considered a turning point in English history, for it ended the period of Anglo-Saxon supremacy and prepared the way for the ultimate establishment of a nation state under William the Norman's successors.

Most of the records of economic life in the early Middle Ages present a mournful picture of return to primitive conditions and, in some cases, actual misery. The decline of Italy in the second half of the fifth century was especially swift. The forces that were set in motion by the economic revolution of the preceding 200 years had

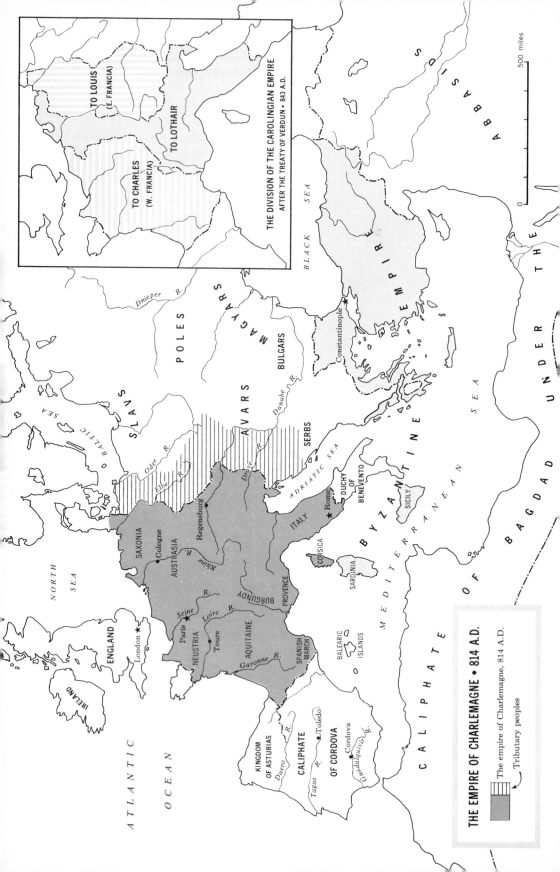

THE DIVISION OF THE CAROLINGIAN EMPIRE
AFTER THE TREATY OF VERDUN • 843 A.D.

TO LOUIS
(E. FRANCIA)

TO LOTHAIR

TO CHARLES
(W. FRANCIA)

500 miles

ABBASIDS

BLACK SEA

Constantinople

DNIEPER R.

POLES

MAGYARS

BULGARS

EMPIRE

UNDER THE

SLAVS

AVARS

SERBS

BYZANTINE

CALIPHATE OF BAGDAD

Oder R.

Elbe R.

Danube R.

Drave R.

ADRIATIC SEA

DUCHY
OF
BENEVENTO

SICILY

MEDITERRANEAN SEA

BALTIC SEA

Regensburg

ITALY

Rome

CORSICA

SARDINIA

SAXONIA

Cologne

AUSTRASIA

Rhine R.

BURGUNDY

PROVENCE

NORTH
SEA

R.

Seine

Paris

NEUSTRIA

Loire R.

Tours

AQUITAINE

SPANISH
MARCH

BALEARIC
ISLANDS

ENGLAND

London

IRELAND

ATLANTIC

OCEAN

Garonne R.

KINGDOM
OF ASTURIAS

Duero R.

CALIPHATE

Tagus R.

Toledo

OF CORDOVA

Cordova

Guadalquivir R.

THE EMPIRE OF CHARLEMAGNE • 814 A.D.

The empire of Charlemagne, 814 A.D.
Tributary peoples

now attained their full momentum. Commerce and industry were rapidly becoming extinct, lands that were formerly productive were growing up in briars and brambles, and the population was declining so noticeably that a law was enacted forbidding any woman under forty years of age to enter a convent. While the proprietors of the great landed estates extended their control over agriculture and over many of the functions of government as well, larger and larger numbers of the masses of the people became serfs. During the reign of Theodoric this process of economic decline was arrested in some measure as a result of the benefits he extended to agriculture and

Duke William of Normandy Crossing the Channel to Conquer England, from the Bayeux Tapestry. The Bayeux Tapestry depicts, in needlework on linen, 72 scenes of the Norman Conquest. It was probably completed under the direction of Bishop Odo of Bayeux, the Conqueror's half-brother.

commerce and his reduction of taxes. But Theodoric was unable to eliminate serfdom or to reverse the concentration of landed wealth, for he felt that he needed the support of the aristocracy. After his death the forces of decay again became operative; yet if it had not been for Justinian's war of reconquest, Italy might still have preserved a degree of the prosperity she had gained under the Ostrogothic king. The long military conflict brought the country to the verge of stark barbarism. Pestilence and famine completed the havoc wrought by the contending armies. Fields were left untilled, and most of the activities in the towns were suspended. Wolves penetrated into the heart of the country and fattened on the corpses that remained unburied. So great was the widespread hunger that cannibalism appeared in some areas. Only in the larger cities were the normal functions of civilization continued to any appreciable extent.

Economic change in what is now France followed a pattern very similar to that in Italy, but it proceeded at a slower rate. In Roman times southern Gaul had had a flourishing commerce and considerable industry. By the end of the ninth century, however, stagnation was almost complete. The streets of the city of Marseilles were grown over with grass and weeds, and the port itself was deserted for over 200 years. In some other Mediterranean towns and in the interior of the country, trade on a petty scale continued to be carried on, mostly by Jews and Syrians and later by Lombards; but even the activities of these men became steadily more difficult as brigandage increased, the roads deteriorated, and money disappeared from general circulation. The economic history of France was also characterized by the growth of an irregular feudalism similar to that which had sprung up in Italy. Several of the causes were closely related to the policies of the Merovingian and Carolingian kings. Nearly all of these rulers compensated their officials by grants of land. Both Pepin the Short and Charlemagne adhered to the example of Charles Martel in expropriating lands of the Church and turning them over to their chief followers as rewards for military services. More serious was the practice of granting *immunities*, or exemptions from the jurisdiction of the king's agents. Originally immunities were given only as favors to bishops and abbots to protect them from unscrupulous officials, but later they were granted to secular nobles as well. Their legal effect was to make the holder subject to the exclusive jurisdiction of the king; but as the king was far away and generally preoccupied with other matters, the nobles took advantage of the opportunity to increase their own independence. Wars, brigandage, and oppression also contributed to the growth of a largely feudal structure of society by forcing the weaker citizens to seek the protection of their more powerful neighbors. The result was a tendency toward a division of the population into two distinct classes: a landed aristocracy and serfs.

4. INTELLECTUAL ATTAINMENTS OF EARLY MEDIEVAL EUROPE

Generally speaking, the intellectual culture of early medieval Europe was not of a high order. Superstition and credulity frequently characterized the work even of many of the outstanding writers. A fondness for compilation rather than for original achievement was also a distinguishing feature of much of the intellectual endeavor. Few men any longer had much interest in philosophy or science, except insofar as these subjects could be made to serve religious purposes. Such an attitude often led to mystical interpretations of knowledge and to the acceptance of fables as fact when they appeared to be freighted with symbolical significance for the sphere of religion. In spite of all this, the mind of the times was not hopelessly submerged in darkness. The light of antique learning was never entirely extinguished; even some of the most pious of Church Fathers recognized the value of classical literature. Moreover, there were a few men in the period who, if not creative geniuses, at least had abilities of scholarship which would not have been rated inferior in the best days of Greece.

Nearly all of the philosophers of the early Middle Ages may be classified as either Christians or pagans, although a few seem to have been nominal adherents of the Church who wrote in the spirit of pagan thought. The Christian philosophers tended to divide into two different schools: (1) those who emphasized the primacy of authority; and (2) those who believed that the doctrines of the faith should be illumined by the light of reason and brought into harmony with the finest products of pagan thinking. The authoritarian tradition in Christian philosophy stemmed originally from Tertullian, a priest of Carthage who lived about the beginning of the third century. For him, Christianity was a system of sacred law to be accepted entirely upon faith. God was an absolute sovereign, whose decrees no mortal had any right to question. Human knowledge was of no value for religion; indeed, now that the Christ had come, and men had the Gospels, there was no need for any further curiosity. As Tertullian would have it, the wisdom of men was mere foolishness with God, and the more a tenet of the faith contradicted reason the greater was the merit in accepting it. Even today theologians can be found who insist upon this absolute supremacy of authority over intellect, of faith over the powers of reason.

The authoritarian Christian philosophers: Tertullian

While few of the Christian Fathers went as far as Tertullian in despising intellectual effort, there were several who adhered to his general principle that the dogmas of the faith were not to be tested by reason. The most influential was Pope Gregory I (540–604), known in Church history as Gregory the Great. The scion of a rich senatorial family, Gregory scorned the seductions of wealth and power in order that he might dedicate his life to the Church. He turned his father's palace into a convent and gave all of the remainder of the wealth he had inherited to the poor. In his work as a theologian he laid great stress upon the idea of penance as essential to the remission of sins and strengthened the notion of purgatory as a place where even the righteous must suffer for minor offenses in order to be purified for admission to heaven. Perhaps more than anyone else he was responsible for developing the doctrine that the priest in celebrating the Mass cooperates with God in performing a miracle which has the effect of repeating and renewing the sacrifice of Christ on the cross. He believed fervently that the Pope, as the successor of the Apostle Peter, was the divinely authorized ruler of

Gregory the Great

the Church.

The most eminent of the Christian philosophers who may be described as representatives of a rationalist tradition were Clement of Alexandria and Origen. Both lived in the third century and were deeply influenced by Neo-Platonism and Gnosticism. Far from despising all human knowledge, they taught that the best of the Greek thinkers had really anticipated the teachings of Jesus, and that Christianity is improved by being brought into harmony with pagan learning. While Clement and Origen would not qualify as rationalists in the modern sense, inasmuch as they took a great many of their beliefs on faith, they nevertheless recognized the importance of reason as a fundamental basis of knowledge, whether religious or secular. They denied the omnipotence of God and taught that God's power is limited by His goodness and wisdom. They rejected the fatalism of many of their opponents and insisted that man by his own free will molds his course of action while on earth. Neither the universe nor anything in it, they declared, was ever created in time; instead, the process of creation is eternal, new things supplanting the old in unending succession. Both Clement and Origen condemned the extreme asceticism of some of their more zealous brethren; in particular, they deplored the tendency of such men as Tertullian to speak of marriage as simply a legalized form of carnality. They avowed, on the contrary, that wedlock and the begetting of children are necessary not only for the good of society but for the perfection of man himself. Finally, they maintained that the purpose of all future punishment is purification and not revenge. Consequently, punishment in hell cannot be eternal, for even the blackest of sinners must eventually be redeemed. If it were not so, God would not be a God of goodness and mercy.

The most erudite and perhaps the most original of all the early Christian philosophers was St. Augustine. Insofar as it is possible to classify him at all, he occupied an intermediate position between Clement and Origen, on the one hand, and Tertullian and Gregory on the other. Though contending that truths of revelation were above natural reason, he perceived the need for an intellectual understanding of what he believed. Born in 354, the son of a pagan father and a Christian mother, Augustine was torn by conflicting impulses throughout the greater part of his life. As a young man he was addicted to sensual pleasures, from which he tried vainly to escape, though he admits in his *Confessions* that his efforts were not wholly sincere. Even after his engagement to marry he could not resist the temptation to take a new mistress. Meanwhile, when he was about eighteen years old, he was attracted to philosophy by reading Cicero's *Hortensius*. He passed from one system of thought to another, unable to find spiritual satisfaction in any. For a brief period he considered the possibilities of Christianity, but it impressed him as too crude and superstitious. Then for nine years he was a Manichean, but ultimately he became convinced that that faith was decadent. Next he was attracted to Neo-Platonism, and then finally returned to Christianity. Though already in his thirty-third year when he was baptized, Augustine advanced rapidly in ecclesiastical positions. In 395 he became Bishop of Hippo in northern Africa, an office he held until his death in 430.

As a philosopher Augustine derived a great many of his theories from the Neo-Platonists. He believed in absolute and eternal truth and in instinctive knowledge which God implants in the minds of men. The supremely important knowledge, however, is knowledge of God and His plan of redemption for mankind. Though most of this knowledge must be derived from the revelation contained in the Scriptures, it is nevertheless the duty of man to understand as much of it as possible in order to strengthen his belief. On the basis of this conclusion St. Augustine developed his conception of human history as the unfoldment of the will of God. Everything that has happened or ever will happen represents but an episode in the fulfillment of the divine plan. The whole race of human beings comprises two great divisions: those whom God has predestined to eternal salvation constitute the City of God; all others belong to the Earthly City. The end of the drama of history will come with the Day of Judgment, when the blessed few who compose the City of God will put on the garment of immortality, while the vast multitude in the earthly kingdom will be cast into the fires of hell. This, according to St. Augustine, is the whole meaning of human existence.

St. Augustine's theology was an integral part of his philosophy. Believing as he did in a deity who controls the operation of the universe down to the smallest detail, he naturally emphasized the omnipotence of God and set limits to the freedom of the will. Since man is sinful by nature, the will has to struggle against an inclination to commit evil. Although man has the power to choose between good and bad, it is God who provides the motive or "inspiration" for the choice. Therefore the virtuous man must thank God for having been able to choose the path of virtue. God created the world in the knowledge that some men would respond to the divine "invitation" to lead holy lives, and that others would resist or refuse to cooperate. In this way God *predestined* a portion of the human race to be saved and left the remainder to perish; in other words, He fixed for all time the number of inhabitants of the heavenly city. It was not that He elected some for salvation and denied to all others the opportunity to be saved. Rather, He knew infallibly from all eternity that some would not *wish* to be saved. The influence of St. Augustine was enormous. In spite of the fact that his teachings were modified slightly by the Council of Orange in 529, and still more by the theologians of the later Middle Ages, he is revered to this day as one of the most important Fathers of the Roman Catholic religion.

Lutheran and other Protestant Reformers also held him in the high-est esteem, although the interpretations they gave to his teachings frequently differed from those of the Catholics.

Practically the only pagan school of philosophy in early medieval Europe was that of the Neo-Platonists, whose doctrines were dis-cussed in a preceding chapter. There was one other individual thinker, however, who cannot be positively classified as either a pagan or a Christian. It is quite probable that he was a Christian, though he makes no reference to the Church or to the name of Christ in his chief work. The name of this man was Boethius. Born about 480 of aristocratic parentage, Boethius eventually became principal adviser to Theodoric, the Ostrogothic king. Later he fell out with that monarch, was accused of treason, and thrown into prison. In 524 he was put to death. The chief philosophical work of Boethius, which he wrote while languishing in prison, is entitled *The Consolation of Philosophy*. Its dominant theme is the relation of man to the universe. The author considers such problems as fate, the divine government of the world, and individual suffering. After carefully weighing the various conceptions of fortune, he comes to the conclusion that true happiness is synonymous with philosophic understanding that the universe is really good, and that evil is only apparent. Although he seems to assume the immortality of the soul, he refers to no definitely Christian belief as a source of conso-lation. His attitude is essentially that of the Stoics, colored by a trace of Neo-Platonist mysticism. Few treatises on philosophy were more popular in medieval Europe than Boethius' *Consolation of Philosophy*. Not only was it ultimately translated into nearly every vernacular language, but numerous imitations of it also were written.

The history of literature in the early Middle Ages was marked, first of all, by a decline of interest in the classical writings and later by the growth of a crude originality that ultimately paved the way for the development of new literary traditions. By the fifth century the taste for good Latin literature had already begun to decay. Some of the Christian Fathers who had been educated in pagan schools were inclined to apologize for their attachment to the ancient writings; others expressly denounced them; but the attitude that generally prevailed was that of St. Augustine. The great bishop of Hippo declared that men should continue to study the pagan classics, not for their aesthetic value or their human appeal, but "with a view to making the wit more keen and better suited to penetrate the mys-tery of the Divine Word." [9] The Latin language also suffered from the effects of the gradual barbarization of culture. Many theologians appeared to feel that it was almost impious for a Christian to write too well. In composing his commentaries on the Scriptures, Pope Gregory I avowed that he considered it exceedingly inappropriate

[9] Quoted by Thompson and Johnson, *An Introduction to Medieval Europe*, p. 221.

to "fetter the Heavenly Oracle" to the rules of grammar. Toward the close of the period, however, the vernacular languages, which had been slowly evolving from a fusion of barbarian dialects, with some admixture of Latin elements, began to be employed for crude poetic expression. The consequence was a new and vigorous literary growth which attained its full momentum about the thirteenth century.

INTELLECTUAL ATTAINMENTS

The best-known example of this literature in the vernacular is the Anglo-Saxon epic poem *Beowulf*. First put into written form about the eighth century, this poem incorporates ancient legends of the Germanic peoples of northwestern Europe. It is a story of fighting and seafaring and of heroic adventure against deadly dragons and the forces of nature. The background of the epic is heathen, but the author of the work introduced into it some qualities of Christian idealism. *Beowulf* is important, not only as one of the earliest specimens of Anglo-Saxon or Old English poetry, but also for the picture it gives of the society of the English and their ancestors in the early Middle Ages. No account of the vernacular literature of this time would be complete without some mention of the achievements of the Irish. Ireland in the late sixth and early seventh centuries experienced a brilliant renaissance which made that country one of the brightest spots in the so-called Dark Ages. Irish monks and bards wrote stories of fantastic adventure on land and sea and hundreds of poems of remarkable sensitivity to natural beauty. The Irish monasteries of this time were renowned centers of learning and art. Their inmates excelled in illuminating manuscripts and in composing both religious and secular verse. As missionaries, under the leadership of St. Columban, they conveyed their influence to Scotland and to many parts of the Continent.

Beowulf and other examples of vernacular literature

Aside from theological works, the leading productions of authors who wrote in Latin during the early Middle Ages were the histories of Orosius, Gregory of Tours, and Bede. At the request of St. Augustine, a Spanish priest by the name of Orosius wrote his *Seven Books against the Pagans*. Distinguished neither by accuracy nor by literary charm, this work was intended to be a history of the world, showing that the calamities which had befallen ancient nations were the result of wickedness. Bishop Gregory of Tours, a near-contemporary of Clovis, also wrote with a view to defense of the faith. In his *History of the Franks* he condoned the murders of Clovis on the ground that they were committed in the service of the Church. Although his work contains interesting information about the events of his time, he tended to give a supernatural interpretation to every occurrence. By far the best of the historical writings of the early medieval period was the Venerable Bede's *Ecclesiastical History of the English Nation*. Bede, an English monk, lived between 673 and 735. Apparently more interested in scholarship than in pious meditation, he pursued his studies so assiduously that he

The historians

gained a reputation as one of the most learned men of his time. In collecting material for his history he devoted careful attention to sources. He did not hesitate to reject the statements of some of the most respectable authorities when he found them to be in error; and when the evidence was a matter of mere oral tradition, he was honest enough to say so.

Developments in education; the Seven Liberal Arts

No account of intellectual attainments in the early Middle Ages would be complete without some reference to developments in education. After the reign of Theodoric, the old Roman system of state schools rapidly disappeared. Throughout the remainder of western Europe the monasteries had a practical monopoly of education. The man who did most to establish the monasteries as institutions of learning was Cassiodorus, formerly chief secretary to Theodoric. Following his retirement from official service, Cassiodorus founded a monastery on his ancestral estate in Apulia and set the monks to work copying manuscripts. The precedent he established was gradually adopted in nearly all the Benedictine institutions. Cassiodorus also insisted that his monks should be trained as scholars, and for this purpose he prepared a curriculum based upon seven subjects, which came to be called the Seven Liberal Arts. These subjects were divided, apparently by Boethius, into the *trivium* and the *quadrivium*. The former included grammar, rhetoric, and logic, which were supposed to be the keys to knowledge; the *quadrivium* embraced subjects of more definite content—arithmetic, geometry, astronomy, and music.

The value of monastic education

The textbooks used in the monastic schools were for the most part elementary. In some of the best schools, however, translations of Aristotle's logical works were studied. But nowhere was attention given to laboratory science, and history was largely neglected. Learning was mostly memorization, with little opportunity for criticism or discussion. No professional training of any kind was provided, except for careers in the Church. Learning was, of course, a privilege for the few; the masses as a rule received no education, save what they acquired incidentally, and even most members of the secular aristocracy were illiterate. Yet, with all of its shortcomings, this system of education did help to save European culture from complete eclipse. And it is worth remembering that the best of the monastic and cathedral schools—notably those at Yarrow and York in England—provided the main impetus for the first of the revivals of learning which occurred in the later Middle Ages.

SELECTED READINGS

· *Items so designated are available in paperbound editions.*

Artz, F. B., *The Mind of the Middle Ages,* New York, 1954.

· Bark, W. C., *Origins of the Medieval World,* Stanford, 1958 (Doubleday).

- Bury, J. B., *The Invasion of Europe by the Barbarians*, London, 1928 (Norton Library).

 Case, S. J., *The Social Origins of Christianity*, Chicago, 1923.

- Chambers, Mortimer, *The Fall of Rome: Can It Be Explained?* New York, 1963 (European Problem Series, Holt, Rinehart & Winston).

 Coulton, G. G., *Five Centuries of Religion*, New York, 1926.

- Dawson, C. H., *The Making of Europe*, New York, 1932 (Meridian).

 Deanesley, Margaret, *A History of Early Medieval Europe*, New York, 1960.

- Dill, Samuel, *Roman Society in the Last Century of the Western Empire*, London, 1921 (Meridian). Valuable for excerpts from the writers of the fifth century.

- Duckett, E. S., *The Gateway to the Middle Ages*, New York, 1938 (Ann Arbor).

- ———, *The Wandering Saints of the Middle Ages*, New York, 1959 (Norton Library).

 Fisher, G. P., *The History of Christian Doctrine*, New York, 1923. One of the best, but it must be studied and not merely read.

 Hearnshaw, F. J. C., *The Social and Political Ideas of Some Great Medieval Thinkers*, New York, 1923.

 Laistner, M. L. W., *Thought and Letters in Western Europe, A.D. 500–900*, rev. ed., New York, 1957.

 Latouche, Robert, *The Birth of Western Economy*, New York, 1960.

 Latourette, K. S., *A History of Christianity*, New York, 1953.

- Lot, Ferdinand, *The End of the Ancient World and the Beginning of the Middle Ages*, New York, 1931 (Torchbook). An excellent account of the decline of Rome and the transition to the Middle Ages.

- McGiffert, A. C., *History of Christian Thought*, New York, 1932, 2 vols. (Scribner Library).

- Moss, H. St. L. B., *The Birth of the Middle Ages, 395–814*, New York, 1935 (Galaxy). Clear and concise.

 Patch, R. R., *The Tradition of Boethius*, New York, 1935.

- Rand, E. K., *Founders of the Middle Ages*, Cambridge, Mass., 1928 (Dover). A very good presentation of the contributions of individuals.

- Rops, Daniel, *Jesus and His Times*, New York, 1954 (Doubleday).

- Taylor, H. O., *The Classical Heritage of the Middle Ages*, New York, 1925 (Torchbook).

- ———, *The Medieval Mind*, New York, 1927, 2 vols.

- Wallace-Hadrill, J. M., *The Barbarian West*, New York, 1962 (Torchbook).

SOURCE MATERIALS

- Boethius, *The Consolation of Philosophy*, New York, 1962 (Library of Liberal Arts, Ungar).

- Brentano, Robert, *The Early Middle Ages, 500–1000*, 1964, Glencoe, Ill. (Free Press).

COLUMBIA RECORDS OF CIVILIZATIONS

 Gregory of Tours, *History of the Franks*, New York, 1965.

 King, J. E., ed., *The Historical Works of Bede*, 2 vols., Harvard.

 St. Augustine, *The City of God*, especially Books IV, VII, X, XII, XIV, XV, XVII.

 ———, *Confessions*.

 ———, *Enchiridion*, especially Chs. XXVI, XXVII, XXX–XXXIII, XLI, L, LI, XCVIII, XCIX.

 Shotwell, J. T., and Loomis, L. R., eds., *The See of Peter*, New York, 1927.

CHAPTER 14

The Byzantine and Saracenic
Civilizations

What is there greater, what more sacred than imperial majesty?
Who so arrogant as to scorn the judgment of the Prince, when
lawgivers themselves have precisely and clearly laid down that
imperial decisions have the force of law?

—Justinian

Muhammad is the messenger of Allah. And those with him are
hard against the disbelievers and merciful among themselves.
Allah hath promised, unto such of them as believe and do good
works, forgiveness and immense reward.

—*The Koran,* Sûrah XLVIII

The so-called medieval period of history does not concern Europe
alone. In addition to the cultures of the European Middle Ages,
medieval history includes two other civilizations, the Byzantine and
the Saracenic. Although each occupied territory on the European
continent, the larger portions of their empires were located in
Africa and in Asia. Of greater significance is the fact that the features of both civilizations were largely those of the Near Orient.
While the Saracens were Moslems and the Byzantine people Christians, religion was a dominant factor in the lives of both. The two
states were so closely linked with the religious organizations that
their governments appeared more theocratic than many of those in
the West. Moreover, both civilizations were characterized by attitudes of pessimism and fatalism and by a tendency for the mystical
point of view to gain supremacy over the rational. It should be noted,
however, that the Saracens, especially, made distinctive contributions to philosophy and science, while the Byzantine Empire was
exceedingly important for its art and for its work in preserving
innumerable achievements of the Greeks and Romans.

The semi-Ori-
ental character
of the Byzan-
tine and Sara-
cenic civilizations

389

I.   THE BYZANTINE EMPIRE AND ITS CULTURE

In the fourth century the Emperor Constantine established a new capital for the Roman Empire on the site of the old Greek colony of Byzantium. When the western division of the Empire collapsed, Byzantium (or Constantinople, as the city was now more commonly called) survived as the capital of a powerful state which included the Near Eastern provinces of the Caesars. Gradually this state came to be known as the Byzantine Empire, although the existence of a Byzantine civilization was not clearly recognized before the sixth century. Even after that there were many who believed that Rome had merely shifted its center of gravity to the East.

Although Byzantine history covered a period similar to that of the Middle Ages, the cultural pattern was far different from the one which prevailed in western Europe. Byzantine civilization had a more pronounced Near Eastern character. Indeed, most of the territories of the Empire actually lay outside of Europe. The most important among them were Syria, Asia Minor, Palestine, and Egypt. Furthermore, Greek and Hellenistic elements entered into the formation of Byzantine culture to a greater extent than was ever true in western Europe. The language of the eastern state was predominantly Greek, while the traditions in literature, art, and science were largely Hellenistic. Lastly, the Christianity of the Byzantine Empire differed from that of Latin Europe in being more mystical, abstract, and pessimistic, and more completely subject to political control. Notwithstanding all these differences, Byzantine civilization was distinctly superior to that of western Europe.

The population of the territories under Byzantine rule comprised a great number of nationalities. The majority of the inhabitants were Greeks and Hellenized Orientals—Syrians, Jews, Armenians, Egyptians, and Persians. In addition, the European sections of the Empire included numerous barbarians, especially Slavs and Mongols. There were some Germans also, but the emperors at Constantinople were generally able to divert the German invasions to the west. The encroachments of the Slavs and the Mongols, on the other hand, proved to be much more difficult to deal with. The original home of the Slavs, a round-headed people of Alpine stock, was apparently the region northeast of the Carpathian Mountains, principally in what is now southwestern Russia. A peaceful agricultural folk, they seldom resorted to armed invasion but gradually expanded into thinly settled territories whenever the opportunity arose. Not only did they move into the vast empty spaces of central Russia, but they occupied many of the regions vacated by the Germans and then slowly filtered through the frontiers of the Eastern Empire. By the seventh century they were the most numerous people in the entire Balkan peninsula, as well as in the whole region of Europe east of the Germans. The Mongolian inhabitants of the Empire came into Europe from the steppes of what is now Asiatic Russia. They were herdsmen, with the furious energy and warlike habits characteristic of that mode of existence. After entering the valley of the Danube, many of them forced their way into Byzantine territory. It was a fusion of some of these Mongolian peoples with Slavs which gave rise to such modern nations as the Bulgarians and the Serbs.

The details of Byzantine political development have little significance for the modern age. The early history of the Empire was marked by struggles to repel the Germanic barbarians. The confidence inspired by the success of these struggles encouraged the Emperor Justinian to begin the reconquest of Italy and North Africa, but most of Italy was soon afterward abandoned to the Lombards, and Norh Africa to the Moslems. In the early seventh century Byzantium became involved in a great war with Persia, which eventually exhausted both empires and laid their territories open to Saracenic conquest. By 750 the Byzantine state had lost all of its possessions outside of Europe with the exception of Asia Minor. After the tide of Saracenic advance had spent its force, Byzantium enjoyed a brief recovery and even regained the province of Syria, the island of Crete, and some portions of the Italian coast, as well as certain territories on the Balkan peninsula which had been lost to the barbarians. In the eleventh century, however, the Empire was attacked by the Seljuk Turks, who rapidly overran the eastern provinces and in 1071 annihilated a Byzantine army of 100,000 men at Manzikert. The Emperor Romanus Diogenes was taken prisoner and held for a ransom of one million pieces of gold. Soon afterward the government sent an appeal for aid to the West. The result was the Crusades, launched originally against the Moslems but eventually turned into plundering attacks upon Byzantine territory. In 1204 the Crusaders captured Constantinople and treated that city "with more barbarity than the barbarian Alaric had treated Rome eight hundred years before." [1] But even these disasters did not prove fatal. During the late thirteenth and early fourteenth centuries the Empire once again recovered some measure of its former strength and prosperity. Its history was finally brought to an end with the capture of Constantinople by the Ottoman Turks in 1453.

During this long period of approximately 1000 years the stability of Byzantine rule was frequently menaced not only by foreign aggression but also by palace intrigues, mutinies in the army, and violent struggles between political factions. How then can it be explained that the Empire survived so long, especially in view of the rapid decay of the West during the early centuries of this period? Geographic and economic factors were probably the major causes. The location of Constantinople made it almost impregnable. Sur-

[1] J. B. Bury, *History of the Later Roman Empire* (1931 ed.), I, 3.

rounded on three sides by water and on the fourth by a thick, high wall, the city was able to resist capture practically as long as any will to defend it remained. Furthermore, the Near East suffered no decay of industry and commerce like that which had occurred in Italy during the last centuries of the empire in the West. Last of all, the Byzantine government had a well-filled treasury which could be drawn upon for purposes of defense. The annual revenues of the state have been estimated as high as $117 million (1966 dollars).

The government
of the Byzantine
Empire

The government of the Byzantine Empire was similar to that of Rome after the time of Diocletian, except that it was even more despotic and theocratic. The emperor was an absolute sovereign with unlimited power over every department of national life. His subjects not only fell prostrate before him, but in petitioning his grace they customarily referred to themselves as his slaves. Moreover, the spiritual dignity of the emperor was in no sense inferior to his temporal power. He was the vicar of God with a religious authority supposed to be equal to that of the Apostles. Although some of the emperors were able and hard-working officials, most of the actual functions of the government were performed by an extensive bureaucracy, many of whose members were highly trained. A great army of clerks, inspectors, and spies maintained the closest scrutiny over the life and possessions of every inhabitant.

State control of
the economic
system

The economic system was as strictly regulated as in Hellenistic Egypt. In fact, the Byzantine Empire has been described as a "paradise of monopoly, of privilege, and of paternalism." [2] The state exercised a thorough control over virtually every activity. The wage of every workman and the price of every product were fixed by government decree. In many cases it was not even possible for the individual to choose his own occupation, since the system of guilds which had been established in the late Roman Empire was still maintained. Each worker inherited his status as a member of one guild or another, and the walls which surrounded these organizations were hermetically sealed. Nor did the manufacturer enjoy much greater freedom. He could not choose for himself what quantity or quality of raw materials he would purchase, nor was he permitted to buy them directly. He could not determine how much he would produce or under what conditions he would sell his product. All of these matters were regulated by the trade association to which he belonged, and it in turn, was subject to supervision by the government. A number of large industrial enterprises were owned and operated by the state. Chief among them were the murex or purple fisheries, the mines, the armament factories, and the establishments for the weaving of cloth. An attempt was made at one time to extend monopolistic control over the silk industry, but the government factories were unable to supply the demand, and permission had to be given to private manufacturers to resume production.

392   [2] J. W. Thompson, *Economic and Social History of the Middle Ages*, p. 336.

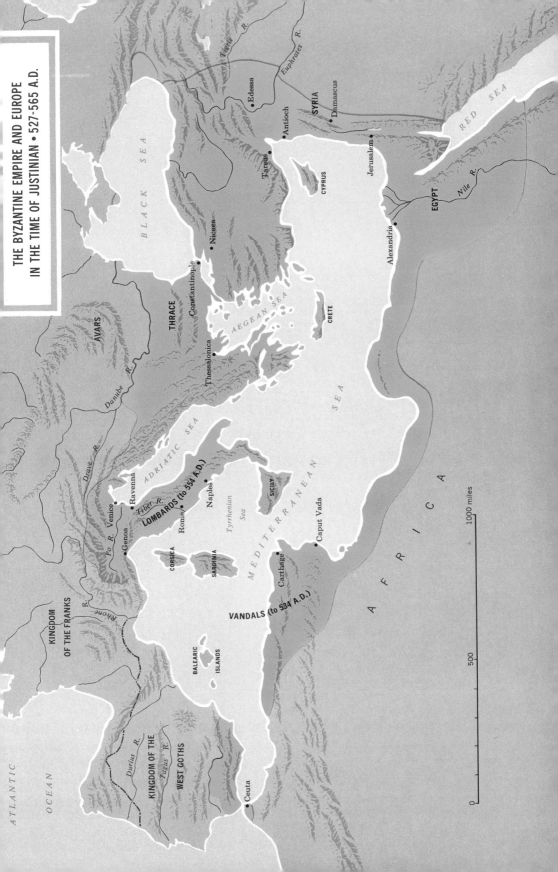

THE BYZANTINE EMPIRE AND EUROPE
IN THE TIME OF JUSTINIAN • 527-565 A.D.

ATLANTIC
OCEAN

KINGDOM
OF THE FRANKS

KINGDOM OF THE
WEST GOTHS

Durius R.
Tagus R.
Rhone R.
Ebro R.

Ceuta

BALEARIC
ISLANDS

Po R.
Venice
Genoa
Ravenna
Tiber R.
LOMBARDS (to 554 A.D.)
Rome
Naples
CORSICA
SARDINIA

Drave R.
Danube R.

AVARS

THRACE
Constantinople
Thessalonica
Nicaea

ADRIATIC SEA

SICILY
Tyrrhenian
Sea
MEDITERRANEAN

Caput Vada
Carthage

VANDALS (to 534 A.D.)

AFRICA

BLACK SEA

AEGEAN SEA

CRETE

Tigris R.
Euphrates R.
Edessa
SYRIA
Damascus
Antioch
Tarsus

CYPRUS

Jerusalem

Alexandria
Nile R.
EGYPT

RED SEA

SEA

0   500   1000 miles

Gold Cup, Byzantine, VI–IX c
The figure is a personification of C
stantinople, a queen or goddess h
ing the scepter and orb of imp
rule. (MMA)

Saint John Writing His Gospel. Fr
an Anglo-Frankish illuminated man
script, *ca.* 850, produced in a Ca
lingian monastery. The unknown art
knew nothing of perspective, but c
celled in coloring and conveying
sense of vitality and energy. (Morg
Library)

Merovingian Fibula or Brooch, VII cent.
A fabulous gold-plated animal set with
garnets and colored paste reveals the lively
imagination of the early Middle Ages.
(MMA)

Enthroned Madonna and Child, Byzantine
School, XIII cent. The painters of Siena
followed the opulent and brilliant style of
Byzantine art. Their madonnas were not
earthly mothers, but celestial queens reigning in dignified splendor. (National Gallery)

The agricultural regime developed under the late Roman Empire was also perpetuated and extended in the Byzantine territories. Most of the land was divided into great estates comparable to the *latifundia* in Italy. Except in the hilly and mountainous regions, there were few independent farmers left. In the richest areas the agricultural population was made up almost entirely of tenant farmers and serfs. The number of the latter was increased in the fifth century, when the Emperor Anastasius issued a decree forbidding all peasants who had lived on a particular farm for thirty years ever to remove therefrom. The purpose of the decree was to ensure a minimum of agricultural production, but its natural effect was to bind the peasants to the soil and make them actual serfs of their landlords. Another of the significant agricultural developments in the Byzantine Empire was the concentration of landed wealth in the hands of the Church. The monasteries, especially, came to be included among the richest proprietors in the country. With the increasing difficulty of making a living from the soil and the growing popularity of asceticism, more and more farmers sought refuge in the cloister and made gifts of their lands to the institutions which admitted them. The estates acquired by the Church were cultivated, not by the monks or the priests, but by serfs. During the seventh and eighth centuries an economic transformation occurred. Many of the serfs gained their freedom and became owners of the lands they cultivated. But by the eleventh century the great estates had reappeared, and the independent peasantry virtually ceased to exist.

No subject appears to have absorbed the interest of the Byzantine people more completely than religion. They fought over religious questions as vehemently as citizens of the modern world quarrel over issues of government control versus private ownership or democracy versus totalitarianism. They took great delight in theological subtleties which would impress most people in our time as barren and trivial. Gregory of Nyssa, one of their own Church Fathers, thus described Constantinople in the fourth century: "Everything is full of those who are speaking of unintelligible things—streets, markets, squares, crossroads. I ask how many oboli I have to pay; in answer they are philosophizing on the born or unborn; I wish to know the price of bread; one answers: 'The Father is greater than the Son'; I inquire whether my bath is ready; one says, 'The Son has been made out of nothing.' " [3]

The most crucial of the religious issues, however, were those which grew out of the Monophysite and Iconoclastic movements, although neither of these movements was exclusively religious in character. The Monophysites derived their name from their contention that the Christ was composed of only one nature, and that that nature was divine. This doctrine, which was probably a reflection of the Neo-Platonist contempt for everything physical or material,

THE BYZANTINE EMPIRE

The agricultural regime

The absorbing interest in religion

Religious controversies; the Monophysite movement

[3] A. A. Vasiliev, *History of the Byzantine Empire*, I, 99 f.

393

flatly contradicted the official theology of Christianity. Having begun as early as the fifth century, the Monophysite movement reached its height during the reign of Justinian (527–565). Its strength lay chiefly in Syria and in Egypt, where it served as an expression of nationalist resentment against subjection to Constantinople. In dealing with the sect Justinian was caught between two fires. Not only was he ambitious to unite his subjects in allegiance to a single faith, but he was anxious to win the support of Rome. On the other hand, he was reluctant to take any steps for the suppression of the Monophysites, partly because of their strength and also because his wife, the popular actress Theodora, was a member of the sect. It was her will that finally prevailed. During the seventh century the Monophysites broke away from the Eastern Church. The sect survives to this day as an important branch of Christendom in Egypt, Syria, and Armenia. They are now commonly called Coptic Christians.

The Iconoclastic movement was launched about 725 by a decree of the Emperor Leo III forbidding the use of images in the Church. In the Eastern Church any image of God, the Christ, or a saint was called an icon. Those who condemned the use of icons in worship were known as Iconoclasts, or image-breakers. The Iconoclastic movement was a product of several factors. First of all, it had a certain affinity with the Monophysite movement in its opposition to anything sensuous or material in religion. Secondly, it was a protest against paganism and worldliness in the Church. But perhaps more than anything else it represented a revolt of certain of the emperors against the increasing power of the ecclesiastical system. The monasteries in particular were absorbing so large a proportion of the national wealth and enticing so many men away from service in the army and from useful occupations that they were undermining the economic vitality of the Empire. Since the monks derived a large part of their income from the manufacture and sale of icons, it was logical that the reforming emperors should center their attacks upon the use of images in the Church. Naturally they had the support of many of their pious subjects, who resented what they considered a corruption of their religion by idolatrous practices.

The Iconoclasts

Although the struggle against the worship of images was continued until well into the ninth century, it really accomplished no more than the elimination of sculptured representations; the flat or painted icons were eventually restored. Nevertheless, the Iconoclastic controversy had more than a trivial significance. It may be said to have represented an important stage in the irrepressible conflict between Roman and Near Eastern traditions, which occupied so large a place in Byzantine history. Those who upheld the use of images generally believed in an ecclesiastical religion in which symbols and ceremony were regarded as indispensable aids to worship. Most of their opponents were mystics and ascetics who condemned any

Significance of the Iconoclastic controversy

form of institutionalism or veneration of material objects and advocated a return to the spiritualism of primitive Christianity. Many of the ideals of the Iconoclasts were similar to those of the Protestant Reformers of the sixteenth century, and the movement itself may be said to have foreshadowed the great revolt of Luther and Calvin against what were considered pagan elements in the Roman Catholic religion. Finally, the Iconoclastic controversy was a potent cause of the separation of the Greek and Roman branches of the Church in 1054. Even though the attack upon the use of images was not en-

Silver Plate Portraying David and Goliath, and Plaque, in Gold and Enamel, Portraying the Christ. Such objects were among the most appealing examples of Byzantine minor arts.

tirely successful, it went far enough to arouse much antagonism between Eastern and Western Christians. The Pope excommunicated the Iconoclasts and turned from the Byzantine emperors to the Frankish kings for support. From this point on the East and the West drew farther apart.

Social conditions in the Byzantine Empire presented a marked contrast with western Europe during the early Middle Ages. Whereas large sections of Italy and France sank to almost primitive levels in the ninth and tenth centuries, Byzantine society continued to maintain its essentially urban and luxurious character. Approximately a million people lived in the city of Constantinople alone, to say nothing of the thousands who dwelt in Tarsus, Nicaea, Edessa, Thessalonica, and other great urban centers. Merchants, bankers, **395**

Social conditions in the Byzantine Empire

and manufacturers ranked with the great landlords as members of the aristocracy, for there was no tendency in Byzantium as there had been in Rome to despise the man who derived his income from industry or trade. The rich lived in elegance and ease, cultivating the indulgence of opulent tastes as a fine art. A large part of the industrial activity of the nation was absorbed in the production of articles of luxury to meet the demand of the wealthier classes. Magnificent garments of wool and silk interwoven with gold and silver thread, gorgeously colored tapestries of brocaded or damasked stuffs, exquisite glass and porcelain ware, illuminated gospels, and rare and costly jeweled ornaments composed only a small part of the sumptuous output of factories and shops, both public and private.

The life of the lower classes was poor and mean by comparison. And yet the common man in the Byzantine Empire was probably better off than the average citizen in most other parts of the Christian world at that time. The extensive industrial and commercial development and the high degree of economic stability provided opportunities for employment for thousands of urban workers, except during the period of Moslem invasions, when Constantinople was filled with refugees who could not be absorbed into the economic system. Even the lot of the serf who was attached to the estate of some one of the great secular proprietors was probably superior to that of the peasants in western Europe, since the landlord's powers of exploitation were at least regulated by law. Nevertheless, the serf's condition was bad enough, for he was doomed to a life of ignorance and dull routine within the narrow horizon of the village in which he was born. His status was unalterably fixed by the mere occident of his having been born of parents who were serfs. The Byzantine population also included a considerable percentage of slaves, but most of them were employed in domestic service and doubtless enjoyed a fairly comfortable existence.

The tone of morality in the Empire exhibited sharp contrasts. The Byzantine people, in spite of their Greek antecedents, apparently had no aptitude for the typical Hellenic virtues of balance and restraint. In place of the golden mean they seemed always to prefer the extremes. Consequently, the most extravagant self-indulgence was frequently to be found side by side with the humblest self-denial or laceration of the flesh. The contradictory qualities of sensuality and piety, charity and heartless cruelty, were commonly evident in the same stratum of society or even in the same individuals. For example, the great reform Emperor, Leo III, tried to improve the lot of the peasants, but he also introduced mutilation as a punishment for crime. Life at the imperial court and among some members of the higher clergy appears to have been characterized by indolence, luxurious vice, effeminacy, and intrigue. As a consequence, the very word "Byzantine" has come to be suggestive of

elegant sensuality and refinements of cruelty.

In the intellectual realm the Byzantine people won little distinction for originality. Comparatively few discoveries or contributions in any of the fields of knowledge can actually be credited to them. Probably their most noteworthy achievement was the revision and codification of the ancient Roman law. After the time of the great jurists (second and third centuries A.D.) the creative genius of the Roman lawyers decayed, and nothing new was added to the philosophy or the science of law. The volume of statutory enactments, however, continued to grow. By the sixth century Roman law had come to contain numerous contradictory and obsolete provisions. Moreover, conditions had changed so radically that many of the old legal principles could no longer be applied, particularly on account of the establishment of an Oriental despotism and the adoption of Christianity as the official religion. When Justinian came to the throne in 527, he immediately decided upon a revision and codification of the existing law to bring it into harmony with the new conditions and to establish it as an authoritative basis of his rule. To carry out the actual work he appointed a commission of lawyers under the supervision of his minister, Tribonian. Within two years the commission published the first result of its labors. This was the Code, a systematic revision of all of the statutory laws which had been issued from the reign of Hadrian to the reign of Justinian. The Code was later supplemented by the Novels, which contained the legislation of Justinian and his immediate successors. By 532 the commission had completed the Digest, representing a summary of all of the writings of the great jurists. The final product of the work of revision was the Institutes, a textbook of the legal principles which were reflected in both the Digest and the Code. The combination of all four of these results of the program of revision constitutes the *Corpus Juris Civilis*, or the body of the civil law.

From the historical standpoint the two most important sections of the *Corpus Juris* were unquestionably the Institutes and the Digest. It was these which contained the philosophy of law and of government which had come to prevail in Justinian's time. There is a popular but somewhat inaccurate belief that this philosophy was the same as that of Ulpian, Papinian, and the other great jurists of 300 years before. While it is true that most of the old theory was preserved, a few fundamental changes were introduced. First, the *jus civile* was more completely denationalized than it had ever been during Roman times and was now made applicable to citizens of a great many divergent nationalities. The *jus naturale* was now declared to be divine and consequently superior to all of the enactments of men—a conception which was destined to become exceedingly popular in later medieval philosophy. There was a tendency also for Justinian's jurists to speak of the emperor as the sole legislator, on the assumption that the people had surrendered all of their power to him. In other words, the classical Roman law was being revised to make it

397

fit the needs of an Oriental monarch whose sovereignty was limited only by the law of God.

As to the remainder of Byzantine intellectual achievements, a brief summation will suffice. The nation produced no philosophers of more than secondary rank. But several made important contributions to the development of Scholasticism, which emerged as the most popular philosophy of the later Middle Ages. They emphasized the value of reason and attempted to reconcile the teachings of Aristole with those of the Scriptures and the Christian Fathers. Byzantine literature consisted for the most part of compilations and religious writings, especially encyclopedias, commentaries, hymns, and biographies of saints. Some epic and lyric poetry was also written, as well as numerous histories. By far the most famous of the historians was Procopius, a contemporary of Justinian. Despite his penchant for scandal-mongering in his celebrated *Secret History,* others of his works contain valuable information about the events of his time.

The Byzantine record in science was possibly somewhat better than in most other branches of learning. Most of the progress was made in the early years of the Empire, perhaps on account of the survival of Hellenistic influence. This first golden age was followed by a long period of stagnation until the middle of the tenth century, when a revival began due in large part to Moslem influence and to the patronage of the Emperor Constantine VII. But neither of these eras of progress lasted for more than two centuries. The leading scientists of the early period were John the Grammarian and Aetius, both of whom lived in the sixth century. John the Grammarian is far more deserving of credit for his work in physics than for any contributions to grammar. He is especially worthy of attention for having been the first to challenge the traditional theories of motion and gravity. Not only did he anticipate the concept of inertia, but he rejected the notion that the speed of falling bodies is directly proportional to their weight, and he denied the impossibility of creating a vacuum. Aetius was primarily an encyclopedist of medicine. He wrote not only the first description of diphtheria but also the best account of diseases of the eye which had been published thus far. The only outstanding scientist of the later period was Symeon Seth, who was also a physician. His chief work was a medical dictionary defining the curative properties of numerous drugs lately discovered by the Hindus and the Saracens.

The tastes of the Byzantine people, with their fondness for luxury and splendor, were signally expressed in their art. However, it was not a mere emblem of sensuous delight. It was profoundly conditioned by the peculiar ideals of the civilization itself. For one thing, the strong undercurrent of asceticism prohibited the glorification of man; as a consequence, sculpture was not permitted to develop very far. The preeminent art form was architecture, and it had to be

SANTA SOPHIA CROWNING ACHIEVEMENT OF BYZANTINE ARCHITECTURE

Church of Santa Sophia, in Constantinople. Built by Justinian in the sixth century A.D., this church is an outstanding example of Byzantine architectural design. As the accompanying diagram shows, the central dome rests upon four massive arches. The tremendous downward thrust of the dome necessitates the buttressing seen in the photograph in the two enormous masonry piles and half domes. The minarets were added later by the Moslems.

mystical and otherworldly. Furthermore, since the Byzantine civilization was a compound of elements both Roman and Oriental, it was inevitable that its art should combine the love of grandeur and the engineering talent of Rome with the gorgeous coloring and richness of detail characteristic of the Orient.

The Church of
Santa Sophia

The supreme artistic achievement of the Byzantine civilization was the Church of Santa Sophia (Holy Wisdom), built at enormous cost by the Emperor Justinian. Although designed by architects of Hellenic descent, it was vastly different from any Greek temple. Its purpose was not to express man's pride in himself or his satisfaction with this life, but to symbolize the inward and spiritual character of the Christian religion. It was for this reason that the architects gave little attention to the external appearance of the building. Nothing but plain brick covered with plaster was used for the exterior walls; there were no marble facings, graceful columns, or sculptured entablatures. The interior, however, was decorated with richly colored mosaics, gold leaf, colored marble columns, and bits of tinted glass set on edge to refract the rays of sunlight after the fashion of sparkling gems. It was for this reason also that the building was constructed in such a way that no light appeared to come from the outside at all but to be manufactured within.

Innovation in
structural design

The structural design of Santa Sophia was something altogether new in the history of architecture. Its central feature was the application of the principle of the dome to a building of square shape. The church was designed, first of all, in the form of a cross, and then over the central square was to be erected a magnificent dome, which would dominate the entire structure. The main problem was how to fit the round circumference of the dome to the square area it was supposed to cover. The solution consisted in having four great arches spring from pillars at the four corners of the central square. The rim of the dome was then made to rest on the keystones of the arches, with the curved triangular spaces between the arches filled in with masonry. The result was an architectural framework of marvelous strength, which at the same time made possible a style of imposing grandeur and even some delicacy of treatment. The great dome of Santa Sophia has a diameter of 107 feet and rises to a height of nearly 180 feet from the floor. So many windows are placed around its rim that the dome appears to have no support at all but to be suspended in mid-air.

Other Byzantine
arts

*See color plates
at page 393*

The other arts of Byzantium included ivory-carving, the making of embossed glassware and brocaded textiles, the illumination of manuscripts, the goldsmith's and jeweler's arts, and considerable painting. The last, however, was not so highly developed as some of the others. In place of painting, the Byzantine artist generally preferred mosaics. These were designs produced by fitting together small pieces of colored glass or stone to form a geometric pattern, symbolical figures of plants and animals, or even an elaborate scene

St. Mark's Cathedral, Venice. The most splendid example of Byzantine architecture in Italy.

of theological significance. Representations of saints and of the Christ were commonly distorted to create the impression of extreme piety.

The importance of the Byzantine civilization is usually underestimated. It was undoubtedly the most powerful factor in determining the course of development of eastern Europe. To a large extent the civilization of imperial Russia was founded upon the institutions and achievements of Byzantium. The Russian church was an offshoot of the so-called Greek Orthodox or Eastern church, which broke away from Rome in 1054. The Tsar as the head of the religion as well as the state occupied a position analogous to that of the emperor at Constantinople. The architecture of the Russians, their calendar, and a large part of their alphabet were also of Byzantine origin. Perhaps even the despotism of the Soviet regime can be traced in some measure to the long-standing tradition of absolute rule in Russia, which ultimately goes back to Byzantine influence.

The Byzantine influence in eastern Europe

But the influence of the Byzantine civilization was not limited to eastern Europe. It would be hard to overestimate the debt of the West to scholars in Constantinople and the surrounding territory who copied and preserved manuscripts, prepared anthologies of Greek literature, and wrote encyclopedias embodying the learning

The Byzantine influence in the West

of the ancient world. Moreover, Byzantine scholars exerted a notable influence upon the Italian Renaissance. In spite of the fact that
the Eastern emperors eventually lost control of Italy, many of their
former subjects continued to live there, and some others fled to the
Italian cities after the overthrow of the Iconoclastic movement. The
extensive trade between Venice and Constantinople in the late Middle Ages also fostered cultural relations between East and West.
Consequently, long before the fifteenth century when eminent
Greek scholars arrived in Italy, a foundation for the revival of interest in the Greek classics had already been laid. Likewise, Byzantine
art exerted its effect upon the art of western Europe. Some authorities regard the stained glass windows of the Gothic cathedrals as an
adaptation of the mosaics in Eastern churches. Several of the most
famous churches in Italy, for example St. Mark's in Venice, were
built in close imitation of the Byzantine style. Byzantine painting
also influenced the painting of the Renaissance, especially of the
Venetian school and of El Greco. Finally, it was the *Corpus Juris* of
Justinian which really made possible the transmission of the Roman
law to the late Middle Ages and to the modern world.

2. ISLAM AND THE SARACENIC CIVILIZATION

The history of the Saracenic or Arabian civilization began a little
later than the history of Byzantium and ended a short time earlier.

Importance of
the Saracenic
Civilization

The dates were roughly 630 A.D. to 1300. In many ways the Saracenic civilization was one of the most important in the Western
world—not only because it was the orbit of a new religion, which
has attracted converts by the hundreds of millions, but mainly because its impact upon Christian Europe was responsible for social
and intellectual changes that can only be described as revolutionary. The term "Saracen" originally meant an Arab, but later it came
to be applied to any member of the Islamic faith, regardless of his
nationality. Some of the Saracens were Jews, some were Persians,
some were Syrians. Nevertheless, the founders of the civilization
were Arabs, and it therefore becomes necessary to examine the culture of that people on the eve of their expansion beyond the borders
of their homeland.

Conditions in
Arabia before
Mohammed

Toward the end of the sixth century the people of Arabia had
come to be divided into two main groups: the urban Arabs and the
Bedouins. The former, who dwelt in such cities as Mecca and
Yathrib, were traders and petty craftsmen. Many were literate, and
some were comparatively wealthy. The Bedouins were mostly
nomads, subsisting on dates and the flesh and milk of their animals.
Ignorant and superstitious, they practiced infanticide and occasional
human sacrifice. They were frequently involved in bloody warfare
over possession of wells and oases. Neither Bedouins nor urban

402 Arabs had any organized government. The clan and the tribe took the place of the state. When a member of one clan committed a crime against a member of another, the issue was settled by means of the blood feud, which sometimes raged until scores had been killed on each side. The religion was generally polytheistic, although some of the better educated townsmen had adopted a belief in Allah as the only God. From time immemorial Mecca had been a sacred city. Here was the shrine known as the Kaaba, which was supposed to contain a sacred black stone miraculously sent down from heaven. The men who controlled this shrine formed the tribe of the Kuraish, the nearest approach to an Arabian aristocracy that ever existed before the migrations.

Whether the Saracenic civilization would ever have originated without the development of the Islamic religion is a question almost impossible to answer. It is commonly assumed that a new religion was necessary to unite the people and to imbue them with ardor in a common cause. Yet other nations had expanded before this and had accomplished great things without the influence of any particularly inspiring system of belief. Nevertheless, in the case of the Arabs it was a new religion which undoubtedly provided much of the driving force behind the development of their civilization. The origin and nature of that religion must therefore be given attention.

The Islamic religion as a driving force in the civilization

The founder of the new faith was born in Mecca about the year 570. The child of parents who belonged to one of the poorest clans of the Kuraish tribe, he was given the common Arabic name of Muhammad or Mohammed. Little is known about his early life. He was left an orphan while still very young and was reared by his grandfather and his uncle. Whether he ever learned to read and write is uncertain, but it is probable that as a member of the leading tribe he would be given some education. When he was about twenty-five years old, he entered the employment of a rich widow and accompanied her caravans, perhaps as far north as Syria. Soon afterward

The early life of Mohammed

The Sacred Kaaba, or Black Stone, in the Courtyard of the Great Mosque in Mecca.

he became her husband, thereby acquiring leisure and security to devote all of his time to religious interests.

Exactly what influences led Mohammed to become the founder of a new religion, no one knows. He was apparently of a highly emotional nature. At times he seems to have believed that he heard voices from heaven. Quite early in his life he became acquainted with numerous Jews and Christians who lived in the cities of northern Arabia, and he appears to have been deeply impressed by their religious beliefs. In addition, he seems to have developed the idea that social and moral conditions in his country were badly in need of reform. He began to denounce the plutocrats of Mecca for their greed and to reproach his people for their bloody feuds and their practice of infanticide. Gradually he came to conceive of himself as the appointed instrument of God to rescue the Arabian people from the path of destruction.

Mohammed's preaching was not at first particularly successful. After almost nine years of communicating the revelations of Allah to all who would listen, he had managed to win very few converts outside of his immediate family. The wealthy Kuraish were naturally against him, and even the common people of Mecca were generally indifferent. As yet he had made no attempt to carry his message to the Bedouins. In 619 he decided to seek a more promising field for the propagation of his teachings. He had learned that the city of Yathrib on the caravan route to the north had been torn for some time by factional strife, and that there might be some chance for a neutral leader to step in and assume control. He sent a number of agents to explore the ground very carefully, and finally in September, 622, he and the remainder of his followers decided to abandon the sacred city of Mecca entirely and to risk their future in the new location. This migration to Yathrib is known to Mohammedans as the Hegira, from the Arabic word meaning "flight," and is considered by them so important that they regard it as the beginning of their era and date all their records from it.

Mohammed changed the name of Yathrib to Medina (the "city of the Prophet"), and quickly succeeded in establishing himself as ruler of the city. But to obtain means of support for his followers was a somewhat more difficult matter. Besides, the Jews in Medina rejected his leadership. Under these circumstances Mohammed began to enlist the support of the Bedouins for a holy war against his enemies. In a single year approximately 600 Jews were massacred, and then the followers of the Prophet launched their plundering attacks upon the caravans of the merchants of Mecca. When the latter took up arms to resist, they were badly defeated in battle. In 630 Mohammed entered Mecca in triumph. He murdered a few of his leading opponents and smashed the idols in the temple, but the Kaaba itself was preserved, and Mecca was established as a sacred

city of the Islamic faith. Two years later Mohammed died, but he lived to see the religion he had founded a militant and successful enterprise.

The doctrines of the Islamic religion as developed by the Prophet are really quite simple. They revolve around a belief in one God, who is called by the old Arabic name Allah, and in Mohammed as His Prophet. This God desires that men shall be kind to their neighbors, lenient toward debtors, honest, and forgiving; and that they shall refrain from infanticide, eating swine's flesh, drinking intoxicating beverages, and waging the blood feud. The religion also enjoins the faithful observance of certain obligations. Chief among these are the giving of alms to the poor, fasting during the day throughout the sacred month of Ramadan, praying five times a day, and making a pilgrimage, if possible, at least once in a lifetime to Mecca. But contrary to a general belief, the religion of the Prophet is far from rigidly formal or mechanical. Almost as much emphasis is placed upon purity of heart and practical benevolence as in Christianity or Judaism. Several passages in the Koran, which constitutes the Islamic Scriptures, provide ample warrant for such a conclusion. One of them declares that "There is no piety in turning your faces toward the east or the west, but he is pious who believeth in God, and the last day, and the angels, and the Scriptures, and the prophets; who for the love of God disburseth his wealth to his kindred, and to the orphans, and the needy, and the wayfarer and those who ask, and for ransoming." [4] Another affirms that the highest merit is "to free the captive; or to feed, in a day of famine, the orphan who is of kin, or the poor man who lieth on the ground." [5] Furthermore, there are no sacraments in the system of worship taught by Mohammed, and there are no priests in the religion. The religion itself is officially known as "Islam," a word meaning "to submit, or to surrender oneself absolutely to God." The official designation of a believer is a "Moslem," which is the participle of the same verb of which "Islam" is the infinitive.

The sources of the religion of Islam are somewhat in doubt. Judaism was unquestionably one of them. Mohammed taught that the Arabs were descendants of Ishmael, Abraham's oldest son. Moreover, a good many of the teachings of the Koran are quite similar to doctrines in the Old Testament: strict monotheism, the sanction of polygamy, and the prohibition of usury, the worship of images, and the eating of pork. Christianity was also an exceedingly important source. Mohammed considered the New Testament as well as the Old to be a divinely inspired book, and he regarded Jesus as one of the greatest of a long line of prophets. Besides, the Islamic doctrines of the resurrection of the body, the last judgment, rewards and punishments after death, and the belief in angels were more probably derived from Christianity than from any other sys-

[4] Sura 2:v. 172.
[5] Sura 90:v. 12.

tem of belief. On the other hand, it is necessary to remember that the Christianity with which Mohammed was acquainted was far from the orthodox variety. Nearly all of the Christians who lived in Syria as well as those in Arabia itself were Ebionites or Nestorians. It is perhaps for this reason that Mohammed always thought of Jesus as human, the son of Joseph and Mary, and not as a god.

It was not long after the origin of Islam that its followers split into a number of sects not entirely dissimilar to some of the off-

shoots of Christianity. The three most important of the Islamic sects were the Sunnites, the Shiites, and the Sufis. The first two had a political as well as a religious character. The Sunnites maintained that the head of the Islamic state and successor to the Prophet should be elected by representatives of the whole body of believers, in accordance with the ancient Arabian custom of election of tribal chiefs. In matters of religion they contended that the *sunna*, or traditions which had grown up outside of the Koran, should be accepted as a valid source of belief. The Shiites were opposed to the elevation of anyone to the highest political and religious office who was not related to the Prophet himself, either by blood or by marriage. In general, they represented the absolutist ideal in Islam as distinct from the democratic ideal of the Sunnites. What is more, the Shiites were against the acceptance of anything but the Koran as a source of religious belief. The Sufis adhered to a mystical and ascetic ideal. Denying absolutely the validity of rational judgment, they maintained that the only truth of any worth is that which proceeds from divine revelation. They believed that it is possible for man to partake of this divine revelation through torturing his body and thereby releasing the soul for a mystic union with God. Many of the fakirs and dervishes in India, Pakistan, and Iran today are members of the Sufi sect.

The political history of the Saracenic civilization is closely interwoven with the growth of the religion. As we have already seen,

Political history
of the Islamic
state: the caliphs

Mohammed became the founder not merely of a religion but also of an Arabic state with its capital at Medina. Following his death in 632 his companions chose as his successor Abu-Bekr, one of the earliest converts to the faith and the father-in-law of Mohammed. The new ruler was given the title of *caliph*, that is, successor to the Prophet. After Abu-Bekr's death two other caliphs were chosen in succession from among the earlier disciples of Mohammed. In 656, however, a long struggle began for possession of the supreme power in Islam. First the Shiites succeeded in deposing a member of the Ommiad family and in electing Ali, the husband of Mohammed's daughter Fatima, as caliph. Five years later Ali was murdered, and the Ommiads came back into power. Soon afterward they transferred the capital to Damascus and established their family as a reigning dynasty with a luxurious court in imitation of the Byzantine model.

In 750 the Shiites revolted again, this time under the leadership of a

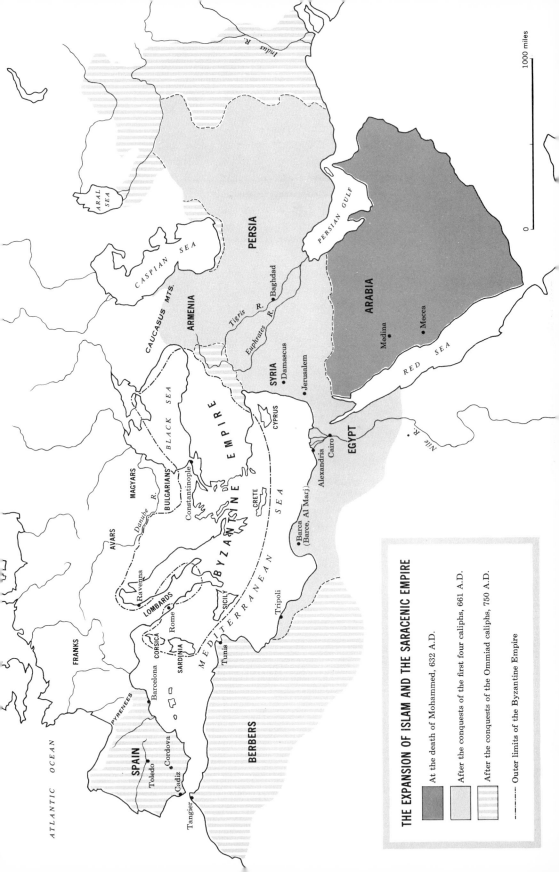

1000 miles

ARAL SEA

CASPIAN SEA

PERSIA

Baghdad
Tigris R.
Euphrates R.
ARMENIA
CAUCASUS MTS.

PERSIAN GULF

ARABIA

Medina
Mecca

RED SEA

SYRIA
Damascus
Jerusalem

BLACK SEA

MAGYARS

BULGARIANS
Constantinople
Danube R.

AVARS

B
Y
Z
A
N
T
I
N
E

E
M
P
I
R
E

CRETE

CYPRUS

EGYPT
Cairo
Alexandria

Nile R.

MEDITERRANEAN SEA

Barca
(Barce, Al Marj)

Ravenna
LOMBARDS
Rome
SICILY
Tripoli
CORSICA
SARDINIA
Tunis

FRANKS

ATLANTIC OCEAN

PYRENEES
Barcelona

SPAIN
Toledo
Cordova
Cadiz
Tangier

BERBERS

THE EXPANSION OF ISLAM AND THE SARACENIC EMPIRE

At the death of Mohammed, 632 A.D.

After the conquests of the first four caliphs, 661 A.D.

After the conquests of the Ommiad caliphs, 750 A.D.

Outer limits of the Byzantine Empire

member of the Abbasid family, who was a distant relative of the Prophet. The Abbasids seized the throne and moved the capital to the city of Baghdad on the Tigris River, where they ruled as Oriental despots for more than three centuries. A few of them were enlightened patrons of learning, especially Harun-al-Raschid (786–809) and Al-Mamun (813–33).

The Saracenic
conquests

In the meantime, a great wave of Saracenic expansion had swept over Asia, Africa, and Europe. When Mohammed died in 632, the authority of his little state probably did not extend over more than one-third of the Arabian peninsula. A hundred years later nearly half of the civilized world was under Moslem domination. The Saracenic empire extended from the borders of India to the Strait of Gibraltar and the Pyrenees Mountains. One after another, with startling rapidity, Persia, Syria, Egypt, North Africa, and Spain had been conquered. How can this prodigious expansion be explained? Contrary to common belief, it was not the result primarily of religious ardor. The Saracens were not engaged in a great crusade to impose their beliefs upon the rest of the world. Naturally there were outbreaks of fanaticism from time to time, but as a rule the Moslems of this period did not really care very much whether the nations they conquered accepted their religion or not. Subject peoples were usually quite leniently treated. As long as they refrained from the possession of arms and paid the tribute levied upon them, they were permitted to retain their own beliefs and customs. Jews and Christians lived unmolested in the Saracenic empire for centuries, and some rose to positions of prominence in political and intellectual circles.

Reasons for the
Saracenic ex-
pansion

In truth, economic and political factors were much more important than religion in causing the Saracenic expansion. First of all, it must be borne in mind that the majority of the Arabs were a prolific race of nomads. Since the men were polygamists, the occasional practice of infanticide was far from sufficient to prevent a rapid increase in population. Arabia, moreover, was suffering from a serious drought, which extended over a number of years shortly after the beginning of the seventh century. Oases that had formerly provided good crops of dates and good pasturage for flocks and herds were gradually being absorbed by the surrounding desert. Discontent among the famished tribes increased to such a point that they would probably have seized upon almost any excuse to plunder neighboring countries. The initial attacks upon Byzantine territory appear to have grown out of a revolt of Arab mercenaries in Syria. The leaders of the rebellion appealed to the followers of the Prophet in Medina, who already had some reputation for military prowess as a result of their conquest of Mecca. The outcome of this appeal was a great wave of military invasion which soon made the Arabs masters not merely of Syria, but also of Persia, Palestine, and Egypt. Finally, it should be noted that the conquests of the Moslems were facilitated by the fact that the Byzantine and Persian empires had fought each other to the point of exhaustion in the previous century, and their governments were now attempting to replenish their treasuries by heavier taxation. As a consequence, many of the inhabitants of these empires were disposed to welcome the Arabs as deliverers.

The decline of the Saracenic empire was almost as swift as its rise. The Arabs themselves lacked political experience; besides, the empire they conquered was too vast in extent and too heterogeneous in population ever to be welded into a strong and cohesive political unit. But a more decisive reason for its downfall was sectarian and factional strife. Sunnites and Shiites were never able to reconcile their differences, and widening cleavages between the mystics and rationalists also helped weaken the religion, which was the basis of the state. In 929 members of the Ommiad family succeeded in establishing an independent caliphate at Cordova in Spain. Soon afterward descendants of Ali and Fatima proclaimed themselves independent rulers of Morocco and Egypt. Meanwhile, the caliphs at Baghdad were gradually succumbing to the debilitating effects of Oriental customs. Aping the practices of Eastern monarchs, they retired more and more into the seclusion of the palace and soon became the puppets of their Persian viziers and later of their Turkish mercenary troops. In 1057 they surrendered all of their temporal power to the Sultan of the Seljuk Turks, who two years before had taken possession of Baghdad. For all practical purposes this marked the extinction of the Saracenic empire, although much of the territory continued to be ruled by peoples who had adopted the Islamic faith—the Seljuk Turks until the middle of the twelfth century and the Ottoman Turks from the fifteenth century to 1918.

The intellectual achievements of the Saracens were far superior to any in Christian Europe before the twelfth century. The explanation can be found partly in the energy and confidence of the Saracens themselves, but it is related also to the fact that in conquering Persia and Syria they came into possession of a brilliant intellectual heritage. In both of these countries traditions of Greek learning had survived. Numerous physicians of Greek nationality had been attracted to the court of the Persian kings, while in Syria there were excellent schools of philosophy and rhetoric and several libraries filled with copies of writings of the Hellenic philosophers, scientists, and poets. Of course, it would be foolish to suppose that very many of the Arabs themselves were able to appreciate this cultural heritage; their function was rather to provide the encouragement and the facilities for others to make use of it.

Saracenic philosophy was essentially a compound of Aristotelianism and Neo-Platonism. Its basic teachings may be set forth as follows: Reason is superior to faith as a source of knowledge; the doctrines of religion are not to be discarded entirely, but should be interpreted by the enlightened mind in a figurative or allegorical sense; when thus interpreted they can be made to yield a pure philosophical knowledge which is not in conflict with reason but supplementary to it. The universe never had a beginning in time but is created eternally; it is a series of emanations from God. Everything that happens is predetermined by God; every event is a link in an unbroken chain of cause and effect; both miracles and divine providence are therefore impossible. Although God is the First Cause of all things, He is not omnipotent; His power is limited by justice and goodness. There is no immortality for the individual soul, for no spiritual substance can exist apart from its material embodiment; only the soul of the universe goes on forever, since its primal substance is eternal.

Periods of
development

The development of Saracenic philosophy was limited to two brief periods of brilliance: the ninth and tenth centuries in the Baghdad caliphate and the twelfth century in Spain. Among the philosophers in the East three great names stand out—Al Kindi, Al Farabi, and Avicenna. The first of them died about 870, and the last was born in 980. All seem to have been of Turkish or Persian nationality. In the eleventh century, under the leadership of Algazel (1058–1111), Saracenic philosophy in the East degenerated into religious fundamentalism and mysticism. Like the Sufis, from whom he derived a great many of his doctrines, Algazel denied the competence of reason and urged a reliance upon faith and revelation. After his time philosophy died out in the Baghdad caliphate. The most renowned of the philosophers in the West, and probably the greatest of all the Saracenic thinkers, was Averroës of Cordova (1126–98). His influence upon the Christian Scholastics of the thirteenth century was especially profound.

Astronomy,
mathematics,
physics, and
chemistry

In no subject were the Saracens farther advanced than in science. In fact, their achievements in this field were the best the world had seen since the end of the Hellenistic civilization. The Saracens were brilliant astronomers, mathematicians, physicists, chemists, and physicians. Despite their reverence for Aristotle, they did not hesitate to criticize his notion of a universe of concentric spheres with the earth at the center, and they admitted the possibility that the earth rotates on its axis and revolves around the sun. Their celebrated poet, Omar Khayyàm, developed one of the most accurate calendars ever devised by the mind of man. The Saracens were also capable mathematicians and developed algebra and trigonometry considerably beyond the stage these had reached in Hellenistic times. Although they did not invent the celebrated "Arabic" system of numerals, they were nevertheless responsible for adapting it from the Indian system and making it available to the West. Saracenic physicists founded the science of optics and drew a number of significant conclusions regarding the theory of magnifying lenses and the velocity, transmission, and refraction of light. As is commonly known, the chemistry of the Moslems was an outgrowth of alchemy, the famous pseudoscience that was based upon the principle that all metals were the same in essence, and that baser metals could therefore be transmuted into gold if only the right instrument, the philosopher's stone, could be found. But the efforts of scientists in this field were by no means confined to this fruitless quest. Some even denied the whole theory of transmutation of metals. As a result of innumerable experiments by chemists and alchemists alike, various new substances and compounds were discovered; among them carbonate of soda, alum, borax, bichloride of mercury, nitrate of silver, saltpeter, and nitric and sulphuric acids. In addition, Saracenic scientists were the first to describe the chemical processes of distillation, filtration, and sublimation.

The accomplishments in medicine were just as remarkable. Saracenic physicians appropriated the knowledge contained in the medical writings of the Hellenistic Age, but some of them were not content with that. Avicenna (980–1037) discovered the contagious nature of tuberculosis, described pleurisy and several varieties of nervous ailments, and pointed out that disease can be spread through contamination of water and soil. His chief medical writing, the *Canon*, was venerated in Europe as an authoritative work until late in the seventeenth century. Avicenna's older contemporary, Rhazes (850–923), was the greatest clinical physician of the medieval world. His supreme achievement was the discovery of the true nature of smallpox. Other Saracenic physicians discovered the value of cauterization and of styptic agents, diagnosed cancer of the stomach, prescribed antidotes for cases of poisoning, and made notable progress in treatment of diseases of the eyes. In addition, they recognized the highly infectious character of the plague, pointing out that it could be transmitted by garments, by eating utensils and drinking cups, as well as by personal contact. Finally, the Saracens excelled all other medieval peoples in the organization of hospitals and in the control of medical practice. Authentic records indicate that there were at least thirty-four great hospitals located in the principal cities of Persia, Syria, and Egypt. They appear to have been organized in a strikingly modern fashion. Each had its wards for particular cases, its dispensary, and its library. The chief physicians and surgeons lectured to the students and graduates, examined them, and issued diplomas or licenses to practice. Even the owners of leeches, who in most cases were also barbers, had to submit them for inspection at regular intervals.

So far as literature was concerned, the Saracens derived their inspiration almost entirely from Persia. If they knew anything about the classic poetry of the Greeks, they evidently found it of little interest. As a result, their own writings are colorful, imaginative, sensuous, and romantic; but with a few exceptions they make no very strong appeal to the intellect. The best-known examples of their poetry are the *Book of Kings* by Al-Firdausi (935–1020) and

Saracenic contributions to medicine

Saracenic literature

411

the *Rubáiyát* by Omar Khayyàm (*ca.* 1048–*ca.* 1124). The *Book of Kings* is not a work dealing with any theme of Saracenic civilization, but is an epic celebrating the glories of the medieval Persian empire. Nevertheless, its 60,000 verses were written under the patronage of Saracenic rulers. The *Rubáiyát*, as it is preserved for us in the translation by Edward Fitzgerald, also appears to reflect the qualities of an effete Persian culture much more than the ideals of the Arabs themselves. Its philosophy of mechanism, skepticism, and hedonism is quite similar to that of the Book of Ecclesiastes in the Old Testament. The most notable example of Saracenic literature in prose is the so-called Arabian Nights, or *Book of the 1001 Nights*, written mainly during the eighth and ninth centuries. The material of the collection includes fables, anecdotes, household tales, and stories of erotic adventures derived from the literatures of various nations from China to Egypt. The chief significance of the collection of tales is to be found in the picture they present of the sophisticated life of the Moslems in the best days of the Baghdad caliphate.

Since the Arabs themselves had scarcely any more of an artistic background than the Hebrews, it was necessary that the art of the Saracenic civilization should be an eclectic product. Its primary sources were Byzantium and Persia. From the former came many of the structural features of the architecture, especially the dome, the column, and the arch. Persian influence was probably responsible for the intricate, nonnaturalistic designs which were used as decorative motifs in practically all of the arts. From both Persia and Byzantium came the tendency to subordinate form to rich and sensuous color. Architecture is generally considered the most important of the Saracenic arts; the development of both painting and sculpture was inhibited by religious prejudice against representation of the human form. By no means all of the examples of this architecture were mosques or churches; many were palaces, schools, libraries, private mansions, and hospitals. Indeed, Saracenic architecture had a much more decidedly secular character than any in medieval Europe. Among its principal elements were bulbous domes, minarets, horseshoe arches, and twisted columns, together with the use of tracery in stone, alternating stripes of black and white, mosaics, and Arabic script as decorative devices. As in the Byzantine style, comparatively little attention was given to exterior ornamentation. The so-called minor arts of the Saracens included the weaving of gorgeous pile carpets and rugs, magnificent leather tooling, and the making of brocaded silks and tapestries, inlaid metal work, enameled glassware, and painted pottery. Most of the products of these arts were embellished with complicated patterns of interlacing geometric designs, plants and fruits and flowers, Arabic script, and fantastic animal figures. The richness and variety of these works of art, produced in defiance of a religion which often displayed a puritanical trend, afford most convincing proof of the vitality of

The eclectic art of the Saracens

412

Saracenic civilization.

The economic development of the Saracenic civilization remains to this day one of the marvels of history. In areas which had produced practically nothing for centuries, the Saracens literally made the desert to blossom as the rose. Where only squalid villages encumbered the landscape, they built magnificent cities. The products of their industries were known from China to France and from the interior of Africa to the shores of the Baltic. As the builders of a vast commercial empire, they excelled the Carthaginians. The reasons for this astounding economic development do not lend themselves to easy explanation. Perhaps it was the result in some measure of the long experience with trade which many of the Arabs had had in their homeland. When a wider field opened up, they made the most of their skill. The diffusion of the Arabic language over a vast expanse of territory also helped to extend the avenues of trade. In addition, the great variety of resources in the various sections of the empire served to stimulate exchange of the products of one region for those of another. The principal reason, however, was probably the advantageous location of the Saracenic empire at the crossroads of the world. It lay athwart the major trade routes between Africa, Europe, India, and China.

Commerce and manufacturing were the main foundations of the national wealth. Both were developed in extraordinary degree. The Saracens made use of a great many of the instruments of commerce familiar to the modern world: checks, receipts, bills of lading, letters of credit, trade associations, joint-stock companies, and various others. Saracenic merchants penetrated into southern Russia and even into the equatorial regions of Africa. Caravans of thousands of

The Court of the Lions in the Alhambra, Granada, Spain. The palace-fortress of the Alhambra is one of the finest monuments to Saracenic architectural style. Notable are the graceful columns, the horseshoe arches, and the delicate tracery in stone that surmounts the arches.

camels traveled overland to the gates of India and China. Saracenic ships furrowed new paths across the Indian Ocean, the Persian Gulf, and the Caspian Sea. Except for the Aegean Sea and the route from Venice to Constantinople, the Saracens dominated the Mediterranean almost as if it were a private lake. But so vast an expansion of commerce would scarcely have been possible without a corresponding development of industry. It was the ability of the people of one region to turn their natural resources into finished products for sale to other regions which provided a basis for a large part of the trade. Nearly every one of the great cities specialized in some particular variety of manufactures. Mosul was a center of the manufacture of cotton cloth; Baghdad specialized in glassware, jewelry, pottery, and silks; Damascus was famous for its fine steel and for its "damask," or woven-figure silk; Morocco was noted for the manufacture of leather; and Toledo for its excellent swords. The products of these cities, of course, did not exhaust the list of Saracenic manufactures. Drugs, perfumes, carpets, tapestries, brocades, woolens, satins, metal products and a host of others were turned out by the craftsmen of many cities. From the Chinese the Saracens learned the art of paper-making, and the products of that industry were in great demand, not only within the empire itself but in Europe as well. The men engaged in the various industries were organized into guilds, over which the government exercised only a general supervision for the prevention of fraudulent practices. For the most part, the guilds themselves regulated the conduct of business by their own members. Control by the state over economic affairs was much less rigid than in the Byzantine Empire.

Agriculture

From what has been said about commerce and industry, it must not be assumed that agriculture was neglected in the Saracenic empire. On the contrary, the Saracens developed farming to as high a level as did any other people of the medieval world. They repaired and extended the irrigation systems originally built by the Egyptians, the Sumerians, and the Babylonians. They terraced the slopes of the mountains in Spain in order to plant them with vineyards, and here as elsewhere they converted many barren wastes into highly productive lands by means of irrigation. Experts attached to the imperial palaces and the mansions of the rich devoted much attention to ornamental gardening, to the cultivation of shrubs and flowers of rare beauty and delightful fragrance. The variety of products of the Saracenic farms and orchards almost passes belief. Cotton, sugar, flax, rice, wheat, spinach, asparagus, apricots, peaches, lemons, and olives were cultivated as standard crops almost everywhere, while bananas, coffee, and oranges were grown in the warmer regions. Some of the farms were great estates, worked in part by serfs and slaves and in part by free peasants as tenants, but the major portion of the land was divided into small holdings cultivated by the owners themselves.

Interior of the Great Mosque at Córdoba, Spain. This splendid specimen of Moorish architecture gives an excellent view of the cusped arches and alternating stripes of black and white so commonly used by Saracenic architects.

The influence of the Saracenic civilization upon medieval Europe and upon the Renaissance was almost incalculable, and some of that influence has, of course, persisted until the present time. The philosophy of the Saracens was almost as important as Christianity in providing a basis for the Scholastic thought of the thirteenth century; for it was the Saracens who made available to the West most of the works of Aristotle and indicated more thoroughly than ever before the use to which those writings could be put as a support for religious doctrine. The scientific achievements of the Saracens furnished even more enduring contributions. Though the activity of the Saracens in literature was not as extensive as in science, their literary influence has been important. The songs of the troubadours and some other examples of the love poetry of medieval France were partly inspired by Saracenic writings. Some of the stories in the *Book of the 1001 Nights* found their way into Boccaccio's *Decameron* and Chaucer's *Canterbury Tales*. The art of the Saracens has likewise had an influence of deep significance, especially upon Gothic architecture. A considerable number of the elements in

415

the design of Gothic cathedrals were apparently derived from the mosques and palaces of the Saracens. A partial list would include the cusped arches, the traceried windows, the pointed arch, the use of script and arabesques as decorative devices, and possibly ribbed vaulting. The architecture of late medieval castles was even more closely copied from the design of Saracenic buildings, especially the fortresses of Syria.[6]

Finally, the Saracens exerted a profound influence upon the economic development of late medieval and early modern Europe. The revival of trade which took place in western Europe in the eleventh, twelfth, and thirteenth centuries would scarcely have been possible without the development of Saracenic industry and agriculture to stimulate the demand for new products in the West. From the Saracens, western Europeans acquired a knowledge of the compass, the astrolabe, the art of making paper, and possibly the production of silk, although knowledge of the last may have been obtained somewhat earlier from the Byzantine Empire. Furthermore, it seems probable that the development by the Saracens of the joint-stock company, checks, letters of credit, and other aids to business transactions had much to do with the beginning of the Commercial Revolution in Europe about 1300. Perhaps the extent of Saracenic economic influence is most clearly revealed in the enormous number of words now in common usage which were originally of Arabic or Persian origin. Among them are "traffic," "tariff," "risk," "check," "magazine," "alcohol," "cipher," "zero," "algebra," "muslin," and "bazaar."[7]

Economic contributions

The Saracenic civilization has significance also for the modern world from the standpoint of international relations. The Saracenic empire was itself an international state. Though loosely organized, it united peoples as diverse as Persians, Arabs, Turks, and Berbers. Its binding cement was a great religion. The spread of this empire and religion constituted the first threat from the Orient that the Western world had faced since the destruction of Carthage. But this threat was quite different from those that had loomed so dangerous in ancient history, for it was essentially ideological rather than political. The long conflict between East and West, which extended at least from the Battle of Tours to the end of the Crusades, was commonly represented as a struggle of ideals. The rise and expansion of the Saracens anticipated in several respects the dynamism of such twentieth-century movements as Nazism and communism. There was one outstanding difference, however. Despite their fanaticism at times, the Saracens devoted only part of their energies to military

International significance of the Saracenic civilization

[6] For a more complete discussion of the influence of Saracenic literature and art, see Arnold and Guillaume, (eds.), *The Legacy of Islam.*

[7] It must not be supposed, of course, that Saracenic influence upon medieval Europe was entirely one-sided. There was also a reverse influence of substantial proportions.

objectives. They adopted the cultures of the peoples they conquered, built a civilization that surpassed in magnificence any that
then existed, and left a splendid legacy of original discoveries and
achievements.

SELECTED READINGS

· *Items so designated are available in paperbound editions.*

BYZANTINE CIVILIZATION

Baynes, N. H., *The Byzantine Empire*, London, 1925. Compact and interest-
ingly written.
· ———, and Moss, H. St. L. B., eds., *Byzantium*, New York, 1948 (Oxford).
· Dawson, C. H., *The Making of Europe*, New York, 1932 (Meridian).
Diehl, Charles, *History of the Byzantine Empire*, New Brunswick, N. J., 1956.
Perhaps the definitive work.
Ostrogorsky, George, *History of the Byzantine State*, New Brunswick, N. J.,
1957.
· Runciman, Steven, *Byzantine Civilization*, New York, 1933 (Meridian). Com-
plete and thorough; easily readable.
· Vasiliev, A. A., *History of the Byzantine Empire, 324–1453*, Madison, Wisc.,
1928–1929, 2 vols. (University of Wisconsin).

SARACENIC CIVILIZATION

Arnold, Thomas, and Guillaume, Alfred, eds., *The Legacy of Islam*, New
York, 1931. Excellent as a study of Saracenic influence.
De Boer, T. J., *History of Philosophy in Islam*, London, 1903. The best ac-
count; concise and clear.
· Gibb, H. A. R., *Mohammedanism: An Historical Survey*, New York, 1953
(Oxford).
· Hitti, P. K., *The Arabs, A Short History*, Princeton, 1946 (Gateway, new
ed.).
· Lewis, Bernard, *The Arabs in History*, New York, 1960 (Torchbook).
Margoliouth, D. S., *Mohammed and the Rise of Islam*, New York, 1927. Com-
plete and interesting.
· Pirenne, Henri, *Mohammed and Charlemagne*, New York, 1939 (Meridian).
Sarton, George, *An Introduction to the History of Science*, Baltimore, 1927,
Vol. I. Detailed and thorough; a valuable reference.
Saunders, J. J., *A History of Medieval Islam*, New York, 1965.
· von Grunebaum, G. E., *Medieval Islam*, 2d ed., New York, 1961 (Phoenix).

SOURCE MATERIALS

Dewing, H. B., tr., *Procopius: History of the Wars*, Harvard, 1915. 7 vols.
Lane-Poole, Stanley, ed., *Speeches and Table Talk of the Prophet Moham-
med*, London, 1882.
Sanders, T. C., tr., *The Institutes of Justinian*, New York, 1924.
· *The Koran* (Penguin).

PART FOUR

The World in the Later Middle Ages

By no means was all of medieval history characterized by stagnation and barbarism. It cannot be too strongly emphasized that the period which used to be called the Dark Ages did not really extend beyond 1000. Soon after that date there were several movements of intellectual awakening which culminated finally in a brilliant flowering of culture in the twelfth and thirteenth centuries. In fact, so remarkable was the progress in western Europe from the eleventh century to the end of the thirteenth that the achievements of that period can justifiably be called a new civilization. In western Asia and northern Africa the Saracenic civilization maintained a high level of accomplishment from the eighth century to the fourteenth. The Byzantine Empire survived even longer, until its principal center at Constantinople was captured by the Ottoman Turks in 1453. The great nations of southern and eastern Asia continued their cultural evolution along lines already established. Both India and China were invaded, however, by Mongols from the West and North who introduced alien elements originally derived from Moslem sources. Japan adopted political feudalism and more and more aspects of Chinese culture.

A Chronological Table

WESTERN EUROPE	BYZANTINE EMPIRE
Rise of papal monarchy, 850–1000 Cluny movement, 950–1100 Holy Roman Empire, 962– Founding of national monarchy in France, 987 Romanesque architecture, 1000–1150	
Revival of trade with East, 1050–1150 Scholasticism, 1050–1300 Struggle between secular and spiritual powers, 1050–1350 Establishment of College of Cardinals, 1059 Norman Conquest of England, 1066 The Crusades, 1096–1204	Separation of Eastern and Western Churches, 1054 Battle of Manzikert, 1071
Growth of cities, 1100–1300 Rise of merchant and craft guilds, 1100–1300 Romances of chivalry, 1100–1300 Development of the sacramental system of the Church, 1100–1300 First universities, *ca.* 1150 Gothic architecture, 1150–1300	
Holy Roman (Hohenstaufen) Empire, 1152–1254 St. Francis of Assisi, 1182–1226 Orders of friars, 1200– Roger Bacon, 1214?–1294 Fourth Lateran Council, 1215 Magna Carta, 1215 St. Thomas Aquinas, 1225–1274 Origin of English Parliament, 1265–1295 Dante, 1265–1321 Hanseatic League, 1300–1500 Feudalism declines, 1300–1500 Rise of capitalism, 1300–1500 Boccaccio, 1313–1375 Origin of Estates-General in France, 1302 Hundred Years' War, 1337–1453 Black Death, 1347–1349 Christian Renaissance, 1400–1500 Savonarola, 1452–1498 Leonardo da Vinci, 1452–1519 War of the Roses in England, 1455–1485 Erasmus, 1466?–1536 Machiavelli, 1469–1527 Copernicus, 1473–1543 Michelangelo, 1475–1564 Tudor dynasty in England, 1485–1603 Unification of Spain, 1492	Capture of Constantinople by Crusaders of Fourth Crusade, 1204 Capture of Constantinople by Ottoman Turks, 1453

1000

1100

1200

1300

1500

THE SARACENS

INDIA AND THE FAR EAST

Sung Dynasty in China, 960–1279

Hindu-Arabic system of numerals, *ca.* 1000
Saracenic world trade, *ca.* 1000–1500

Moslem invasions of India, 1000–1500

1000

1100

Cultivation of cotton, sugar, oranges, lemons, bananas, coffee, *ca.* 1100

Neo-Confucianism, 1130–1200
Highest development of landscape painting in China, 1141–1279

Transmission of complete works of Aristotle to Europe, *ca.* 1150

Explosive powder used in weapons in China, *ca.* 1150
Genghis Khan, 1162?–1227
Establishment of Shogunate in Japan, 1192
Zen Buddhism in Japan, *ca.* 1200
Inoculation for smallpox in China, *ca.* 1200
Turkish Sultanate at Delhi, 1206–1526
Development of Chinese drama, *ca.* 1235
Marco Polo in China, 1275–1292
Mongol (Yüan) Dynasty in China, 1279–1368
Rise of *daimyo* in Japan, 1300–1500

1200

1300

Transmission of compass and astrolabe to Europe, *ca.* 1400

Ming Dynasty, 1368–1644
Sack of Delhi by Timur, 1398

Founding of Sikh religious sect in India, *ca.* 1500
Introduction of Christianity into Japan, 1549–1551

1500

CHAPTER 15

The Later Middle Ages (1050-1350):
Political and Economic Institutions

> The count asked if he was willing to become completely his man,
> and the other replied "I am willing," and with clasped hands,
> surrounded by the hands of the count, they were bound together
> by a kiss. Secondly, he who had done homage gave his fealty to
> the representative of the count in these words, "I promise on my
> faith that I will in future be faithful to count William and will
> observe my homage to him completely against all persons in good
> faith and without deceit," and thirdly, he took his oath to this
> upon the relics of the saints.
> —Description of Ceremony of Homage and Fealty
> at court of Count of Flanders, Twelfth Century

Long before the famous Renaissance of the fourteenth and succeeding centuries, western Europe began slowly to emerge from the
ignorance and barbarism of the so-called Dark Ages. The start of
this gradual awakening can be dated as far back as 1050 A.D. During
the three centuries that followed, the people of Latin Christendom
cast off at least some of their winter garments of repentance and
otherworldliness and put on the less restrictive attire of the man
who is determined to live in this world and mold his environment to
his own advantage. The causes of this change in attitude were many
and various: among them were the influence of contact with the
Saracenic and Byzantine civilizations, the increase in economic security, and the influence of monastic education. In addition, the revival of trade in the eleventh and twelfth centuries and the growth
of cities led to an increase in prosperity and sophistication which
greatly stimulated the progress of enlightenment. The results of
these several causes were reflected in a brilliant intellectual and artistic civilization which reached the zenith of its development in the
thirteenth century. Probably the most distinctive element in the so-

*The cultural re-
vival of the later
Middle Ages*

423

cial and political structure of this civilization was the feudal regime. We must not overlook the fact, however, that from the twelfth century on the role of the commercial and industrial classes in the cities was an exceedingly important one.

1. THE ORIGINS OF THE FEUDAL REGIME

The meaning of feudalism

Feudalism may be defined as a decentralized structure of society in which the powers of government are exercised by private barons over persons economically dependent upon them. It is a system of overlordship and vassalage in which the right to govern is conceived as a property right belonging to anyone who is the holder of a fief. The relationship between the overlord and his vassals is a contractual relationship involving reciprocal obligations. In return for the protection and economic assistance they receive, the vassals are bound to obey their lord or suzerain, to serve him faithfully, and generally to compensate him by dues or taxes for the services he renders in their interest. Defined in this fashion, feudalism was not limited to the later Middle Ages. Examples of it had existed in several other periods of world history—in many parts of the Roman Empire, for instance, and throughout the early Middle Ages. Late medieval feudalism, however, differed from the earlier specimens in being a legally recognized framework of society. Men did not apologize for it as a crude substitute for centralized government but glorified it as an ideal system, much as we idealize democracy and the national state at the present time.

Roman origins of feudalism

How did late medieval feudalism originate? To some extent it was the outgrowth of ancient Roman institutions. One of these was *clientage*. From very early times Roman citizens who had fallen upon evil days had sought the protection of wealthy patrons, becoming their clients or personal dependents. During the confusion that accompanied the decline of the Empire, clientage was greatly extended. A second of these Roman institutions was the *colonate*. In a desperate attempt to check the decline of agricultural production during the economic revolution of the third and fourth centuries, the government of the Empire bound many of the agricultural laborers and tenants to the soil as *coloni* or serfs, and in effect placed them under the control of the proprietors of large estates. The *colonate* had much to do with the growth of an extralegal feudalism in late Roman history, for it increased the wealth and importance of the great landed proprietors. As time went on, the tendency of these men was to ignore or defy the central government and to arrogate to themselves the powers of sovereign rulers over their estates. They levied taxes upon their dependents, made laws for the regulation of their affairs, and administered what passed for justice.

Late medieval feudalism was also derived in part from significant economic and political developments of the early Middle Ages. One

The Young King, Louis IX, XIII cent. Though Louis was widely revered as a saint, the artist has endowed him with distinctively human features. (Morgan Library)

Aquamanile, German, XII–XIII cent. Aquamaniles were water jugs used for handwashing during church ritual, or at meal times. (MMA)

Ivory Plaque, German, X cent. The plaque shows Otto the Great presenting a church to Christ while St. Peter watches, a reference to Otto's building an empire by cooperating with the Church. (MMA)

Kings in Battle, French, ca. 1250. A scene depicting, with the trappings of knighthood, Joshua's fight against the five kings of Canaan. In the center Joshua raises his hand, commanding the sun and moon to stand still to enable him to complete his victory. (Morgan Library)

Chalice, German, XIII cent. A beautifully embellished wine cup used in the sacrament of the Eucharist. (MMA)

Stained Glass, German, *ca.* 1300. Some stained-glass windows were purely decorative; others told a story. (MMA)

Building Operations. From a French picture Bible, *ca.* 1250. Note the treadmill, with wheel, ropes, and pulley, by means of which a basket of stones is brought to the construction level. (Morgan Library)

Gothic Virgin, French, XIII cent. The Queen of Heaven here is a gentle, understanding mother. (MMA)

Siege of a City. From the *Universal Chronicle* by Jean de Courcy, Flemish, *ca.* 1470. The cannon meant the end of feudal knights and medieval towered fortresses. (Morgan Library)

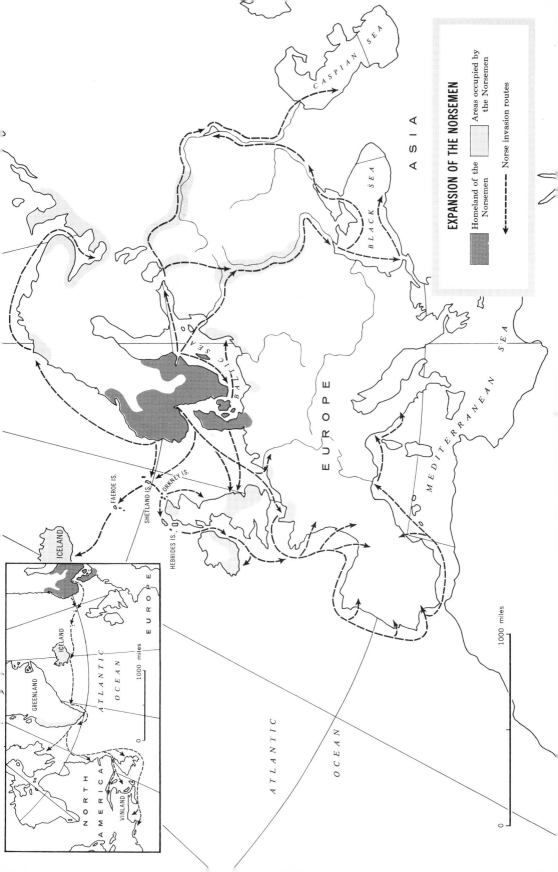

EXPANSION OF THE NORSEMEN

Homeland of the Norsemen

Areas occupied by the Norsemen

Norse invasion routes

CASPIAN SEA

BLACK SEA

ASIA

EUROPE

MEDITERRANEAN SEA

BALTIC SEA

FAEROE IS.

SHETLAND IS.

ORKNEY IS.

HEBRIDES IS.

ICELAND

ATLANTIC OCEAN

1000 miles

GREENLAND

ICELAND

EUROPE

ATLANTIC OCEAN

1000 miles

NORTH AMERICA

VINLAND

of these was the growth of the institution of *beneficium*. *Beneficium* consisted in the grant of a *benefice*, or the right to use land in return for rent or services. In the seventh century the Merovingian kings adopted the practice of rewarding their counts and dukes with benefices, thereby cementing a bond between public office and land-holding. Not long afterward Charles Martel and the Carolingian kings resorted to the granting of benefices to local nobles in return for furnishing mounted troops to fight against the Moors. The result was to increase the dependence of the central government upon the principal landowners throughout the country. The bestowal of *immunities* by the Frankish kings upon some of the holders of bene-fices also accelerated the growth of a feudal regime. Immunities were exemptions of the lands of a secular or ecclesiastical noble from the jurisdiction of the king's agents. The natural outcome was the exercise of public authority by the noble himself as a virtually independent sovereign, subject only to the nominal overlordship of the king. These developments were accentuated by the chaos that accompanied the breakup of Charlemagne's empire following his death in 814. Yet another important development in the early Middle Ages which hastened the growth of a feudal organization of society was the invasions of the Norsemen, the Magyars, and the Moslems. In the eighth and ninth centuries these peoples began making swift incursions into the settled portions of western Europe, plundering the richer areas and occasionally massacring the inhabitants. The attacks of the Norsemen in particular were widely feared. As a consequence, many small farmers who had hitherto maintained their independence now sought the protection of their more powerful neighbors, who frequently had armed retainers and strongholds in which men could take refuge.

But feudalism would never have acquired the special character which it came to possess in the later Middle Ages if it had not been for the Germanic influence. It was the Germans who provided the ideals of honor, loyalty, and freedom which came to occupy a place of considerable importance in the system. The Germanic institution of the *comitatus*, a band of warriors and their chief united by mutual obligations of service and loyalty, was a source of feudal theory and practice. Though the warriors took a personal oath to protect and defend their chief, and he in return agreed to provide them with horses and weapons, the relationship between the two parties was altogether different from that which existed between the Roman clients and their patron. No element of servility was present in it at all; the warriors were practically the equals of their chief, since all were engaged in the same activities of fighting for glory and plunder. This ideal of a relationship of honor and loyalty in the *comitatus* later found its way into feudalism, so far as the relation between lords and vassals was concerned. The feudal practice of **426** *commendation*, by which vassals swore fealty in a ceremony of homage to their suzerain, was also probably an outgrowth of the *comitatus*. Finally, the feudal conception of law as a product of custom instead of authority and as the personal possession of the individual, which he could take with him wherever he went, is likewise traceable to Germanic influence.

2. FEUDALISM AS A POLITICAL AND ECONOMIC STRUCTURE

As a system of government, feudalism embodied a number of basic conceptions. First of all, as we have seen, it included the notion that the right to govern was a privilege belonging to any man who was the holder of a fief; but it was a privilege entailing very definite obligations, the violation of which might be followed by loss of the fief. Secondly, it included the notion that all government rests upon contract. Rulers must agree to govern justly in accordance with the laws, both human and divine. Subjects must pledge themselves to obey so long as their rulers govern justly. If either party violates the contract, the other is absolved from his obligations and has the right to take action for redress. In the third place, feudalism was based upon the ideal of limited sovereignty, upon opposition to absolute authority no matter by whom it might be exercised. Feudal government was supposed to be a government of laws and not of men. No ruler, regardless of his rank, had any right to impose his personal will upon his subjects in accordance with the dictates of his own whims. Indeed, under feudal theory, no ruler had the right to make law at all; law was the product of custom or of the will of God. The authority of the king or the baron was limited to the issuance of what might be called administrative decrees to put the law into effect. Whether the ideals of feudalism were carried out less successfully in practice than the ideals of political systems generally is a very hard question to answer. Doubtless most people, with their prejudices against everything medieval, would answer it in the affirmative. Yet organized revolts against political oppression were not of frequent occurrence in the later Middle Ages, notwithstanding the fact that the existence of the *right* to revolt against a ruler who had made himself a tyrant was commonly taught.

Not only in theory but also in practice the feudal regime was a system of overlordship and vassalage, based upon the granting and holding of fiefs. In the main, a fief was a benefice that had become hereditary. It was not always an area of land, however; it might be an office or position, or the right to collect tolls at a bridge, or even the right to coin money or to establish markets and enjoy the profits therefrom. The man who granted the fief was a lord or suzerain, irrespective of his rank; the man who received the fief to hold and transmit to his descendants was a vassal, whether he was a knight, count, or duke. As a rule, the king was the highest suzerain.

Feudalism as a system of government

Fiefs, vassals, and overlords

427

Immediately below him were the great nobles, who were variously
known as dukes, counts, earls, or margraves. These nobles in turn
had acquired vassals of their own through dividing their fiefs and
granting them to lesser nobles, who were commonly called vis-
counts or barons. At the bottom of the scale were the knights,
whose fiefs could not be divided. Thus, according to the general
pattern, every lord except the king was the vassal of some other
lord, and every vassal except the knight was a lord over other
vassals. But this apparently logical and orderly arrangement was
broken by numerous irregularities. There were vassals who held
fiefs from a number of different lords, not all of them of the same
rank. There were lords some of whose vassals held fiefs from the
same overlord as they themselves did. And in some cases there were
kings who actually held fiefs from certain of their counts or dukes
and were therefore to some extent vassals of their own vassals.

Moreover, the fact must be borne in mind that feudalism was not
the same in all countries of western Europe. Many of its features
commonly assumed to have been universal were found only in
France, where the system was most fully developed, or in one or
two other countries at the most. For example, the rule of primogeniture, under which the fief descended intact to the oldest son, was
not in force in Germany; nor were social distinctions so sharply defined there as in France. Furthermore, not all of the lands and not all
of the inhabitants of any European country were included under
the feudal regime. Most of the farmers in the hilly and mountainous
regions of France, Italy, and Germany did not hold their lands as
fiefs but owned them outright, as their ancestors had for centuries.

Each member of the feudal nobility was involved in an elaborate
network of rights and obligations which varied with his status as a
suzerain or a vassal. The most important rights of the suzerain were
the right to serve as legal guardian in case any of the fiefs he had
granted should be inherited by a minor; the right of escheat, or the
right to take back the fief of a vassal who had died without heirs;
and the right of forfeiture, or the right to confiscate a vassal's fief
for violation of contract. The last of these rights could be exercised,
however, only after the vassal had been condemned by a court composed of his own equals. There were two important obligations that
every suzerain was supposed to perform. First, he was expected to
render military assistance to his vassals in warding off attacks by
their enemies; second, he was required to aid his vassals in righting
their wrongs, which usually meant the summoning of a court to decide their grievances. The suzerain himself merely presided over this
court. The actual decision was rendered by the other vassals, since it
was a cardinal principle of feudal justice that no noble could be
tried except by his peers. Aside from this privilege of being judged
only by his equals, the noble in his capacity as a vassal had only one
other important right. That was the right to repudiate his lord for

Feudal rights
and obligations

acts of injustice or failure to provide adequate protection. The obligations of the vassal were more numerous than his rights. He was required to render military service for a number of days each year, attend the lord's court, ransom his lord if he were captured, and pay a heavy tax if he inherited or sold a fief.

Feudal society was, of course, highly aristocratic. It was a regime of status, not of individual initiative. In almost all cases the members of the various ranks of the nobility owed their positions to heredity, although occasionally noble rank would be conferred upon a commoner for his services to the king. Seldom was it possible for a man to win advancement under the system by his own efforts or intelligence. Nevertheless, an important exception was to be found in the case of the *ministeriales* in Germany and in the Low Counties. The *ministeriales*, as their name implies, formed a class of administrative officials under feudal rule. They had charge of castles, toll gates, bridges, market places, and so on. Some of the most capable rose to be bailiffs or administrators of towns or districts, serving under a great prince or bishop or even under the emperor himself. Their position was of such high advantage that ultimately they invaded the ranks of the lesser nobility and came to form a subordinate class of knights.

A regime of status, with a few exceptions

The life of the feudal nobility was scarcely the idyllic existence frequently described in romantic novels. While there was undoubtedly plenty of excitement, there was also much hardship, and death took its toll at an early age. From a study of medieval skeletons a modern scientist has estimated that the peak of the mortality rate in feudal times came at the age of forty-two,[1] whereas at the present time it occurs at about seventy-five. Moreover, conditions of living even for the richest nobles were comparatively poor. Until almost the end of the eleventh century the feudal castle was nothing but a crude blockhouse of timber. Even the great stone castles of later date were far from being models of comfort and convenience. Rooms were dark and damp, and the bare stone walls were cold and cheerless. Until after the revival of trade with the Orient, which led to the introduction of carpets and rugs, floors were generally covered with rushes or straw, a new layer being put down from time to time as the old became vile from the filth of hunting dogs. The food of the noble and his family, though plentiful and substantial, was neither particularly varied nor appetizing. Meat and fish, cheese, cabbages, turnips, carrots, onions, beans, and peas were the staples of their diet. The only fruits obtainable in abundance were apples and pears. Coffee and tea were unknown, and so were spices until after trade with the Orient had continued for some time. Sugar was eventually introduced, but for a long time it remained so rare and costly that it was often sold as a drug.

The life of the feudal nobles

[1] J. W. Thompson, *An Economic and Social History of the Middle Ages,* p. 718.

Tournament with Lances. Engraving by Lucas Cranach. Tournaments, imitating the conditions of medieval warfare but with blunted spears and lances, were among the principal recreational pursuits of the feudal aristocracy.

Feudal warfare

Although the nobles did not work for a living, their days were not spent in idleness. The conventions of their society dictated an active life of war, high adventure, and sport. Not only did they wage war on flimsy pretexts for the conquest of neighboring fiefs, but they fought for the sheer love of fighting as an exciting adventure. So much violence resulted that the Church intervened with the Peace of God in the tenth century and supplemented this with the Truce of God in the eleventh. The Peace of God pronounced the solemn anathemas of the Church against any who did violence to places of worship, robbed the poor, or injured members of the clergy. Later the same protection was extended to merchants. The Truce of God prohibited fighting entirely from "vespers on Wednesday to sunrise on Monday" and also from Christmas to Epiphany (January 6) and throughout the greater part of the spring, late summer, and early fall. The purpose of the last regulation was obviously to protect the peasants during the seasons of planting and harvesting. The penalty against any noble who violated this truce was excommunication. Perhaps if rules such as these could really have been maintained, human beings would eventually have abandoned war as senseless and unprofitable. But the Church itself, in launching the Crusades, was largely responsible for making the rules a dead letter. The holy wars

430

against the infidel were fought with a great deal more barbarity than had ever resulted from the petty squabbles among feudal nobles.

Early and later feudalism; chivalry

It must be understood that a wide gulf separated the feudalism of the later Middle Ages from that which had existed before. Feudalism flourished throughout the Middle Ages, but until after 1000 it was crude and barbaric. The manners of the lords and their retainers revealed this barbarity. Gluttony was a common vice, and the quantities of wine and beer consumed at a medieval castle brawl would stagger the imagination of a modern toper. At dinner everyone carved his meat with his own dagger and ate it with his fingers. Bones and scraps were thrown on the floor for the omnipresent dogs to fight over. Women were treated with indifference and sometimes with contempt and brutality, for this was a masculine world. During the eleventh century, however, the manners of the aristocratic classes were softened and improved considerably by the growth of what is known as chivalry. Chivalry was the social and moral code of feudalism, the embodiment of its highest ideals and the expression of its virtues. The origins of this code were mainly Germanic and Christian, but Saracenic influence also played some part in its development. Chivalry set forth the ideal of a knight who is not only brave and loyal but generous, truthful, reverent, kind to the poor and defenseless, and disdainful of unfair advantage or sordid gain. Above all, perhaps, the perfect knight must be the perfect lover. The chivalric ideal made the lofty love of ladies a veritable cult with an elaborate ceremonial which the hot-blooded young noble had to be careful to follow. As a result, women in the later Middle Ages were elevated to a much higher status than they had enjoyed in early medieval Europe. Chivalry also imposed upon the knight the obligation of fighting in defense of noble causes. It was especially his duty to serve as the champion of the Church and to further its interest with sword and spear.

The manorial estate; systems of agriculture

The basic economic unit that served as an adjunct to the feudal regime was the manorial estate, although manorialism itself had a political as well as an economic aspect. The manor, or manorial estate, was generally the fief of an individual knight. Lords of higher rank held many manors, the number frequently running into the hundreds or thousands. No one knows even the average size of these economic units, but the smallest appear to have included at least 300 or 400 acres. Each manorial estate comprised one or more villages, the lands cultivated by the peasants, the common forest and pasture lands, the land belonging to the parish church, and the lord's demesne, which included the best farm land on the manor. With minor exceptions, all of the arable land was divided into three main blocks: the spring planting ground, the autumn planting ground, and the fallow. These were rotated from year to year, so that the spring planting ground one year would become the autumn planting ground the next, and so on. Such was the famous *three-field system*, which seems to have originated in western Europe toward the end of the eighth century. Manorial agriculture was also conducted largely under the *open-field system.* The holding allotted to each peasant was not a compact area of the manor, but consisted of a number of strips located in each of the three main blocks of arable land. These strips, averaging about an acre in size, were generally separated only by a narrow band of unplowed turf. The main object of the system was apparently to give to each serf his fair share of the three different kinds of land. In cultivating these strips the peasants worked cooperatively, chiefly because their holdings were scattered, and it was therefore logical for a number of men to combine their efforts in farming all the strips in a particular area. Besides, no one peasant had enough oxen to draw the crude wooden plows through the stubborn soil.

Except for the noble and his family, the parish priest, and possibly a few administrative officials, the entire population of the manor consisted of persons of servile status. These might be embraced in as many as four different classes: villeins; serfs; crofters and cotters; and slaves. Though villeins and serfs eventually came to be almost indistinguishable, there were at one time several important differences between them. Villeins were originally small farmers who had surrendered their lands as individuals to some powerful neighbor. The ancestors of the serfs had frequently been subjected *en masse,* whole villages of them at once. The villeins were perpetual tenants, not bound in person to the soil, whereas the serfs were bought and

The servile
classes; villeins
and serfs

The World of Sports in the Later Middle Ages. Among the activities shown are fishing, bird-netting, archery, and "boar-sticking." From *A Book of Rural Profits* by Petrus Crescentius.

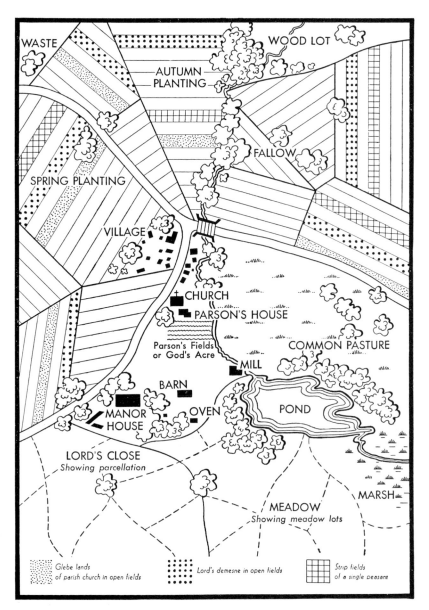

Figure labels: WASTE, WOOD LOT, AUTUMN PLANTING, FALLOW, SPRING PLANTING, VILLAGE, CHURCH, PARSON'S HOUSE, Parson's Fields or God's Acre, COMMON PASTURE, MILL, BARN, OVEN, POND, MANOR HOUSE, LORD'S CLOSE Showing parcellation, MEADOW Showing meadow lots, MARSH

Glebe lands of parish church in open fields — Lord's demesne in open fields — Strip fields of a single peasant

sold with the land to which they were attached. Another difference
was that the villein was liable to obligations only within the definite
terms of his customary contract, while the labor of the serf could be
exploited virtually as his owner saw fit. Finally, the villein could be
taxed only within limits fixed by custom, but the serf was taxable at
the lord's mercy. By the thirteenth century, however, most of these
differences had disappeared. And it is a notable fact that the villeins
were not degraded to the level of serfs; instead, the serfs rose to the
level of villeins. Neither serfs nor villeins were included in the per-   **433**

sonal relations of feudalism. They had numerous obligations of a servile character, but they shared none of the political or social privileges of the lords and vassals.

Although the other dependent classes on the manor were much less numerous than the villeins and serfs, a word or two must be said about them. The crofters and cotters were wretchedly poor men who had no definite status under the feudal regime at all. Unlike even the meanest of the serfs, they had no strips of land which they could cultivate for their living. They occupied small cottages or shanties and hired themselves out to the richer villeins or did odd jobs for the lord of the manor. A few slaves continued to be held throughout the later Middle Ages, but in steadily diminishing numbers. They did not fit in well with the manorial type of economy, for the manor was not a plantation but an aggregate of petty farms cultivated under perpetual lease. The few slaves who were to be found were employed mainly as household servants. After the year 1000 slavery as an institution became practically extinct in western Europe.

Like all other members of the subject classes under feudalism, the villeins and serfs were liable for numerous obligations. Although these appear at first glance to have been exceedingly oppressive, it is necessary to remember that they took the place of both rent and taxes. The most important of these obligations were the following: the *capitatio*, the *cens*, the *taille*, the *banalités*, the *prestations*, and the *corvée*. The *capitatio* was a head tax imposed only upon serfs. The *cens* was a species of rent paid only by villeins and freemen. The *taille* was a percentage of nearly everything produced on the lands of both villeins and serfs. The *banalités* were fees paid to the lord for the use of the village mill, winepress, brewery, bake-oven, and sometimes even for the use of the village well. The *prestations* were a variety of enforced hospitality. The local count or baron, in his travels from one manor to another, had the right to entertainment for the few days he spent in each village. It was consequently the duty of the peasants to provide food and lodging for the great lord and his retinue and even for his horses and dogs. *Prestations* could not be enforced any oftener than three times a year, and in some localities they became entirely obsolete. The final form of peasant obligations, the *corvée* consisted of forced labor which the villeins and serfs were required to perform in cultivating the lord's demesne and in building and repairing roads, bridges, and dams.

By no stretch of the imagination could the lot of the medieval peasant be considered an enviable one. During the planting and harvesting seasons, at least, he toiled from sunrise to sunset, and the rewards of his labor were few. His home was generally a miserable hovel constructed of wattle plastered over with mud. A hole in the thatched roof served as the only outlet for smoke. The floor was the bare earth, which was often cold and damp from the infalling rain

Scene in a Medieval Village. Among the activities shown are plowing, grinding grain, and slaughtering a boar for meat. In the lower right two friars are dispensing bread and soup to the poor.

and snow. For a bed the peasant had a box filled with straw, and his easy chair was a three-legged stool. His food was coarse and monotonous—black or brown bread, a few vegetables from his garden in the summer and fall, cheese and porridge, and salt meats and fish, which were often badly cured and half putrid. When crops were bad, he suffered from famine, and death from starvation was by no means unknown. He was, of course, invariably illiterate and was commonly the victim of superstitious fears and sometimes of the dishonesty of unscrupulous stewards. Perhaps the most lamentable aspect of the peasant's life was the fact that he was a despised and degraded creature. Spokesmen for the nobles and townsmen alike seldom referred to him except in the most scornful and odious terms. It was said that all peasants were shifty, dull-witted, mean, squint-eyed, and ugly; that they were "born of ass's dung," and that "the devil did not want them in hell because they smelled too badly." [2]

Yet the medieval peasant enjoyed some advantages which undoubtedly helped to redress the balance of his miseries. Many of the fears and uncertainties that plague the lowly in modern times meant nothing to him. He was in very little danger of loss of employment or of insecurity in old age. It was an established principle of feudal law that the peasant could not be deprived of his land. If the land was sold, the serf went with it and retained the right to cultivate his holdings as before. When he became too old or too feeble to work,

The medieval peasant and the modern worker

[2] See illustrations from medieval literature in G. G. Coulton, *The Medieval Village.*

it was the duty of the lord to care for him through the remainder of his days. Although he worked hard during the busiest seasons, he had at least as many holidays as are allowed to the laborer today. In some parts of Europe these amounted to about sixty out of the year, not counting Sundays. Moreover, it was customary for the lord of the manor to feast his peasants after the spring planting was completed and after the harvest was gathered, as well as during the principal religious holidays. Last of all, the peasant was under no obligation to render military service. His crops might be trampled and his cattle driven off by the armies of warring nobles, but at least he could not be compelled to sacrifice his life for the benefit of some ruler with questionable motives.

The decline of
feudalism: eco-
nomic causes

No sooner had feudalism reached the height of its development than it began to show signs of decay. The decline was already noticeable in France and Italy by the end of the twelfth century. The system continued longer in Germany and England, but by 1500 it was almost extinct in all countries of western Europe. Many relics of it, of course, survived until much later—some till the middle of the nineteenth century in central and eastern Europe. The causes of the decline of the feudal regime are not far to seek. Many of them were closely associated with the revolutionary economic changes of the eleventh and succeeding centuries. The revival of trade with the Near East and the growth of cities led to an increased demand for products of the farms. Prices rose, and as a consequence some peasants were able to buy their freedom. Moreover, the expansion of commerce and industry created new opportunities for employment and tempted many serfs to flee to the towns. Once they had made good their escape, it was almost impossible to bring them back. Still another economic cause was the opening up of new lands to agricultural production, mainly on account of the higher prices for products of the soil. In order to get peasants to clear forests and drain swamps, it was frequently necessary to promise them their freedom. The Black Death, which swept over Europe in the fourteenth century, while not exactly an economic factor, had results similar to those of the causes already mentioned. It produced a scarcity of labor and thereby enabled the serfs who survived to enforce their demands for freedom. With the peasant a free man, the manorial system was practically impossible to operate and one of the chief props of the feudal regime had been broken.

Political causes

The political causes of the downfall of feudalism were also of major significance. One was the establishment of professional armies and the inducements offered to the peasants to become mercenary soldiers. A second was the increasing complexity of feudal relationships; a single vassal could owe allegiance to several lords, and in some cases lords became vassals to their own vassals. Another was the adoption of new methods of warfare which rendered the knights somewhat less indispensable as a military class. A fourth was the condition of chaos produced by the Hundred Years' War and the peasant insurrections resulting therefrom. A fifth was the influence of the Crusades in eliminating powerful nobles, in promoting the adoption of direct taxation, and in compelling the sale of privileges to communities of serfs as a means of raising money to equip armies. But probably the most important political cause was the rise of strong national monarchies, especially in France and England. By various means the ambitious kings of these countries in the later Middle Ages gradually deprived the nobles of all of their political authority.

3. THE RISE OF NATIONAL MONARCHIES

Soon after the death of Charlemagne in 814 the strong government which he had built up in western Europe collapsed. In 843, by the Treaty of Verdun, his grandsons agreed to divide the Carolingian Empire into three separate parts. The two largest portions became the kingdoms of East Francia and West Francia, corresponding roughly to the modern states of Germany and France. A wide belt of land between the two was formed into a middle kingdom including the territories of modern Belgium, Holland, Alsace, and Lorraine. Such was the beginning of some of the most important political divisions in the map of Europe today.

The division of the Carolingian Empire

[See map of Carolingian Empire, p. 378]

Meanwhile all three of these kingdoms passed rapidly under feudal domination. The real rulers were not the descendants of the great Carolingian king, but a host of petty princes, counts, and dukes. The kings themselves sank to the level of mere feudal overlords, dependent upon the local nobles for their soldiers and their revenues. While as kings their moral preponderance was still very great, their actual authority over the people was practically non-existent. By the end of the eleventh century, however, signs of change in this condition began to appear in France. In 987 the last of the weak Carolingian monarchs was displaced by the Count of Paris, Hugh Capet. The direct descendants of this man were to occupy the throne of France for more than 300 years. Although neither Hugh nor any of his immediate successors exercised the degree of sovereignty commonly associated with the royal office, several of the later Capetians were powerful rulers. A number of factors aided these kings in establishing their dominant position. First of all, they were fortunate enough for hundreds of years to have sons to succeed them, and often an only son. Consequently there were no deadly quarrels over the right of succession, nor was there any necessity of dividing the royal property among disgruntled relatives who might be able to defend a claim to the throne. In the second place, most of these kings lived to an advanced age, with the result that their sons were already mature men when they came to the throne. There were therefore no regencies to haggle the royal

The rise of a national monarchy in France

437

power away during the minority of a prince. Another factor was the growth of trade, which afforded the kings new sources of revenue and enabled them to find powerful allies among the bourgeoisie for their struggle against the nobles. Finally, considerable credit must be given to the shrewdness and vigor of several of the kings themselves.

The first of the Capetian kings who may be considered the founders of a national monarchy in France was Philip Augustus (1180-1223). Although Philip may never have conceived of himself as other than the highest feudal overlord, most of his policies had the effect of seriously weakening the feudal structure. When he granted fiefs to his vassals he required them to agree that their own vassals would owe first allegiance to him. Greedy for revenue, he commuted as many as possible of the feudal reliefs into money payments, sold charters to cities, and levied special taxes on Jews and on all persons who declined to go on a crusade to reconquer the Kingdom of Jerusalem from the Moslems. He appointed bailiffs and seneschals to supervise the administration of justice in the feudal courts and to enforce the king's rights as an overlord. While he continued to depend upon his vassals for contributions of troops, he took steps toward the founding of a national army subject to his own control. He hired mercenary soldiers by the thousands and compelled the towns to furnish recruits from among their own citizens. So aggressively did he crowd the nobles into the background that he actually quadrupled the royal domain and transferred many of the functions of the feudality into his own hands.

When the first Capetian monarch ascended the throne, France consisted of only a small territory surrounding the town of Paris. Most of the remainder of the country was held by such powerful nobles as the Duke of Normandy, the Count of Champagne, the Duke of Brittany, the Duke of Burgundy, and the Duke of Aquitaine. Although all of these rulers were technically vassals of the French king, they had become so domineering or acquired so much power that they seldom made more than a pretense of fulfilling their feudal obligations. For example, William the Conqueror and his immediate successors were still dukes of Normandy and therefore vassals of the king of France, but actually as kings of England they were his powerful rivals and scarcely made even a formal acknowledgment of his overlordship. When Philip Augustus came to the throne of France in 1180 he determined to put an end to such conditions. Taking advantage of the absence of the English kings, he managed by a series of bold strokes to acquire the Duchy of Normandy and a number of adjoining counties, thereby extending the royal domain to the English Channel. By participating in a papal crusade against the Albigenses he also acquired territory in the south. The Albigenses were heretics, and by the standards of the time the lands they inhabited were legitimate plunder. King Philip

ENGLAND AND FRANCE ca. 1000 A.D.

Royal domain

Ecclesiastical seignories

——— Boundary of the Holy Roman Empire

IRELAND

NORTHUMBRIA

•Whitby

NORTH SEA

ENGLAND

WALES

MERCIA

EAST ANGLIA

ESSEX

London•

KENT

WESSEX

SUSSEX

CORNWALL

ENGLISH CHANNEL

HOLY

COUNTY OF FLANDERS

Seine R.

DUCHY OF NORMANDY

Paris•

COUNTY OF CHAMPAGNE

COUNTY OF BRITTANY

COUNTY OF MAINE

COUNTY OF BLOIS

COUNTY OF ANJOU

Loire R.

COUNTY OF NEVERS

DUCHY OF BURGUNDY

ROMAN

ATLANTIC

COUNTY OF BOURBON

DUCHY OF GUIENNE (AQUITAINE)

KINGDOM OF BURGUNDY

OCEAN

EMPIRE

Garonne R.

C. OF GEVAUDAN

C. OF ROUERGUE

DUCHY OF GASCONY

COUNTY OF TOULOUSE

MARQUISATE OF GOTHIA

MEDITERRANEAN SEA

COUNTY OF BARCELONA

SPAIN

0   200 miles

seized as his share of the booty the County of Toulouse.

The second of the kings most active in consolidating monarchical power in France was Louis IX (1226–1270). Probably few rulers in history have had more interesting personalities. Louis was a strange mixture of exaggerated piety, shrewd benevolence, and ambitious practicality. At times he imitated the life of a monk, wearing a hair-cloth shirt next to his skin, fasting punctiliously, and having himself whipped with small chains. He often entertained paupers at his table, considered it his duty to wash the feet of the poor, and sometimes even waited on lepers. Because of his wide reputation for piety and his martyrdom for the faith on a crusade to Tunis, he was canonized only twenty-seven years after his death. But Louis was not merely a saintly ascetic. He found time to establish hospitals, to abolish trial by combat, and to emancipate thousands of serfs on the royal domain, being careful to make each one pay a fee for his freedom. So zealously did he patronize learning and the arts that his reign has been called "the Golden Age of Medieval France." In addition, he labored to increase the power of the monarchy by every shrewd device he could think of. He extended the right of appeal from decisions in the feudal courts to his own court and encouraged his lawyers to draw up a category of cases which would be subject only to the king's jurisdiction. This category was made broad enough to include cases of treason and practically all breaches of the peace. He commanded that his own currency should be accepted in all parts of the kingdom. He made an earnest but not altogether successful attempt to curb the power of the nobles by prohibiting their right of private warfare. Perhaps most significant of all, he assumed for himself the authority to issue ordinances for the entire country without the previous consent of his vassals. Probably nothing could have expressed a more emphatic disavowal of feudal principles than this, since under feudal theory the king could make no departures from customary law without the approval of the chief men of the realm.

The evolution of a national monarchy in medieval France was carried still farther during the reign of Philip IV (1285–1314), or Philip the Fair as he is more commonly called. The policies of this king were determined largely by an increasing need for revenue, but they partially resulted from the growing popularity of Roman law with its basic doctrine of the absolute sovereignty of the state. Philip's ambition to raise money led not only to his expulsion of the Jews and the Italian bankers and the confiscation of their property, but prompted him also to change nearly all of the remaining feudal dues into direct taxes. In addition, he devised new levies upon incomes and upon the goods and property of the merchants. But it was Philip's attempt to tax the possessions of the Church that was fraught with the deepest significance. This precipitated an angry quarrel with the Pope which had two momentous results: (1) the

440

subordination of the French Catholic clergy to the king; and (2) the summoning of what has come to be considered the first parliament in the history of France.

In order to determine the attitude of his subjects toward his quarrel with the Pope, Philip in 1302 convoked an assembly of the clergy, the lay nobles, and representatives of the towns. Since these were the principal estates or classes of all of his subjects, the assembly came to be known as the Estates-General. The idea of such an assembly was not really novel. Representative councils composed of members of the various estates, or classes, were common in several parts of medieval Europe. Few, however, developed into major organs of government. The Estates-General was summoned on two other occasions by Philip to approve new modes of taxation. His successors continued the precedent of convoking it more or less regularly thereafter until 1614. The Estates-General, of course, was not really intended to be an independent legislative assembly but a body of advisers to the king. It was only under the influence of eighteenth-century liberalism that men came to look back upon it as a true parliament. On the other hand, since it included representatives outside the nobility, its establishment may be considered another stage in the transformation of the French government from a feudal to a national character.

Monarchical power in France underwent still further consolidation as a result of the Hundred Years' War (1337–1453). This war grew out of a number of causes. The primary one was probably the long-standing conflict between the French and English kings over territory in France. At the end of the thirteenth century, English monarchs still held part of Guienne and Gascony in southwestern France as vassals of the French crown. The French monarchs resented the presence of a foreign power on their soil. Moreover, they feared that the English interest in the woolen trade of Flanders might lead to an alliance with the Flemish burghers against their sovereign, the King of France. To add fuel to the flames, Edward III, who succeeded to the throne of England in 1327, had a claim to the French crown through his mother, who was a daughter of Philip the Fair. Sensing that war was inevitable, he determined to press this claim in the hope that by so doing he might find a convenient pretext for conquering the Flemish cities.

The Hundred Years' War actually covered more than a century, although the fighting was by no means continuous. Hostilities between the royal armies were interrupted by several truces and were accompanied by a number of bloody uprisings of townsmen and peasants. During the greater part of the conflict the English armies were generally victorious. They were better organized, better disciplined, and better equipped. Besides, England did not suffer from the extremes of internal discord which plagued the French. By 1420 the Duke of Burgundy had deserted the French cause, and all of the

The Estates-General

Causes of the Hundred Years' War

The course and climax of the conflict

441

Statue of Joan of Arc, Orléans. A modern idealization of the French heroine of the 15th century.

northern half of France had been occupied by English soldiers. Soon afterward occurred the most dramatic incident of the war, which infused new confidence into the French armies and paved the way for their ultimate victory. A devout but simple peasant girl, Jeanne d'Arc or Joan of Arc, came forward with the declaration that she had been commissioned by God to "drive the English out of the whole kingdom of France." Though she was completely uneducated, "knowing neither A nor B," her piety and sincerity made such a strong impression upon the French soldiers that they firmly believed they were being led by an angel from heaven. In a few months she had liberated most of central France and had brought the dauphin Charles VII to Reims, where he was crowned King of France. But in May 1430, she was captured by the Burgundians and turned over to the English. The latter regarded her as a witch and set up a special court of the clergy to try her for heresy. Found guilty, she was given over to the secular government on May 30, 1431, and burned in the public square of Rouen.

As is often true of martyrs, Jeanne d'Arc was more powerful dead than alive. Her memory lingers in France to this day as the spiritual embodiment of a patriotic cause. The years that followed her death witnessed a series of uninterrupted triumphs for the French armies. In 1453 the capture of Bordeaux, the last of the English strongholds, brought the war to an end. Only the port of Calais

remained of the once extensive English holdings in France. But the
Hundred Years' War did more than expel the English from French
territory. It added the capstone to the consolidation of royal power
in the kingdom of France. The attempts of both the Estates-General
and the great nobles to control the government had proved abortive.
In spite of the confusion and sufferings of the greater part of the
war, France had emerged with enough of a national consciousness to
enable her kings to centralize their power in accordance with a pattern of absolute monarchy. The completion of this process marked
the final transition from feudalism to something resembling a modern state.

The development of a national monarchy in England goes back to
the reign of William the Conqueror. His conquest of the island in
1066 resulted in the establishment of a stronger monarchy than had
previously existed under the Saxon rulers. The enlargement of
power thus effected was not necessarily deliberate. King William
made few sweeping changes. For the most part he preserved Anglo-
Saxon laws and institutions. He brought over certain elements of
feudalism from the Continent, but he took care to prevent too great
a degree of decentralization. By the Salisbury Oath he required his
vassals to swear allegiance to him directly instead of to their immediate overlords. He prohibited private warfare and retained the
right to coin money as a royal prerogative. When he granted lands
to his followers, he rarely gave any of them large estates composed
of compact territory. He transformed the old *witan*, or advisory
council of the Anglo-Saxon kings, into a *curia regis*, or court of the
king, composed primarily of his own retainers and administrative
subordinates. By the end of his reign the constitution of England
had been markedly changed, but the alterations had been so gradual
that few were aware of their significance.

Foundations of national monarchy in England

William the Conqueror's immediate successors continued their father's policies, but after the death of Henry I in 1135 a violent quarrel broke out between rival claimants for the throne, and the
country was plunged into the depths of anarchy. When Henry II
(1133–1189) became king in 1154, he found the treasury depleted
and the barons entrenched in power. His first objectives, therefore,
were to increase the royal revenues and to reduce the power of the
nobles. In pursuance of the first, he made a regular practice of com-
muting the feudal obligation of military service to a money payment known as *scutage*, and levied the first English taxes on personal
property and on incomes. In his war against the nobles he demolished hundreds of castles that had been built without authorization
and curtailed the jurisdiction of the feudal courts. But he apparently
realized that the power of the barons could not be permanently restricted without thoroughgoing changes in the law and in judicial
procedure. Accordingly, he gathered around him a staff of eminent
lawyers to advise him regarding the laws that ought to be in force.

The reforms of Henry II

443

In addition, he followed a practice already established of appointing itinerant judges to administer justice in the various parts of the realm. These judges, traveling from one region to another, applied a uniform law throughout the kingdom. The precedents laid down by their decisions gradually supplanted local customs and came to be recognized as the Common Law of England. Henry also issued writs commanding the sheriffs to bring before the judges as they went from shire to shire groups of men who were familiar with local conditions. Under oath these men were required to report every case of murder, arson, robbery, or similar crime they knew to have occurred since the judges' last visit. This was the origin of the grand jury. Another of Henry's reforms made it possible for either party to a civil dispute to purchase a writ which would order the sheriff to bring both plaintiff and defendant, together with twelve citizens who knew the facts, before the judge. The twelve were then asked under oath if the plaintiff's statements were true, and the judge rendered his decision in accordance with the answer. Out of this practice grew the institution of the trial jury.

There was one branch of the administration of justice which Henry failed to bring under royal control, though he made strenuous efforts to do so. This was the judging and punishing of members of the clergy. Priests and other members of the ecclesiastical hierarchy were not tried in ordinary courts but in Church courts under the rules of the canon law. Punishment was notoriously lax. A priest, for instance, convicted of murder, was deprived of his clerical status but was rarely given any further penalty. Not only this, but decisions handed down in any English courts on ecclesiastical matters could be appealed to the papal court in Rome. In an effort to eradicate these practices Henry issued the Constitutions of Clarendon in 1164. The Constitutions provided that any clergyman accused of crime must be taken into a royal court first. If the royal court found that a crime had been committed, the defendant would be sent to a Church court for trial. If found guilty he would be sent back to the royal court to be sentenced. From such judgments no appeal could be taken to Rome without the king's consent. In attempting to enforce the constitutions, Henry ran afoul of the Archbishop of Canterbury. The latter, Thomas à Becket, was as devoted to the interests of the Church as Henry was to the strengthening of the monarchy. The quarrel reached a tragic climax when the Archbishop was murdered by a band of Henry's knights after the king, in an outburst of anger, had rebuked his followers for doing nothing to rid him of "a turbulent priest." The crime so shocked the English public that the whole program of bringing the ecclesiastical courts under royal control was largely abandoned. The Archbishop was revered as a martyr and eventually canonized by the Pope.

Henry's quarrel
with Thomas à
Becket

444

During the reigns of Henry's sons, Richard I and John, feudalism enjoyed a partial recovery. For all but six months of his ten-year reign Richard was absent from England waging the Third Crusade or defending his possessions on the Continent. Moreover, the heavy taxation which had to be imposed to defray his military expenses angered many of the barons. The feudal revolt reached its height during the reign of King John, who was perhaps not much worse a tyrant than some of his predecessors. But John had the misfortune to have two powerful enemies in King Philip Augustus of France and Pope Innocent III; and when he lost most of his possessions in France to Philip and suffered a humiliating defeat at the hands of the Pope, it was inevitable that the barons would take advantage of the opportunity to regain their power. In 1215 they compelled John to sign the famous Magna Carta, a document which remains to this day an important part of the British Constitution. The popular interpretation placed upon Magna Carta is really erroneous. It was not intended to be a Bill of Rights or a charter of liberties for the common man. On the contrary, it was a feudal document, a written feudal contract in which the king as an overlord pledged himself to respect the traditional rights of his vassals. It was chiefly important at the time as an expression of the principle of limited government, of the idea that the king is bound by the law. Some of its feudal provisions, however, lent themselves to a boader application later on; for example, the declaration that no man could be imprisoned or otherwise punished "except by the legal judgment of his peers or by the law of the land."

The opposition of the barons continued during the reign of John's son, Henry III (1216–1272). They now drew considerable support from the middle class and found a new leader in Simon de Montfort. Civil war broke out, in which the king was taken prisoner. In 1265 Simon de Montfort, wishing to secure popular support for his plans to limit the powers of the crown, called together an assembly or parliament which included not only the higher nobles and churchmen but also two knights from each shire and two citizens from each of the more important towns. Thirty years later this device of a parliament composed of members of the three great classes became a regular agency of the government when Edward I (1272–1307) convoked the so-called Model Parliament in 1295. Edward's purpose in summoning this parliament was not to inaugurate democratic reform but merely to broaden the political structure and thereby make the king less dependent upon the nobles. Nevertheless, a precedent was established that representatives of the commons should always meet with the two higher classes to advise the king. By the end of the reign of Edward III (1327–1377) Parliament had divided for all practical purposes into two houses, and they had increased their control over taxation and were assum-

Revolt of the barons against King John

Origin of the English Parliament

ing lawmaking authority. The subsequent evolution of the English Parliament into the sovereign power in the country will be discussed in later chapters.

During the fourteenth century England was profoundly affected by economic changes which had begun somewhat earlier on the Continent. The development of commerce and industry, the growth of cities, the greater use of money, the scarcity of labor—all of these seriously weakened the manorial system and consequently undermined feudal power. In addition, the Hundred Years' War increased the military and financial powers of the kings and tended to make them more independent of baronial support. Feudalism in England was finally extinguished in a great struggle among rival factions for control of the crown. This struggle, known as the War of the Roses, lasted from 1455 to 1485. The death of a great many of the nobles in this war and the disgust of the people with continual disorder enabled the new king, Henry Tudor, or Henry VII (1485–1509), to establish a more highly consolidated rule than the country had known up to this time.

The failure of
Germany and
Italy to form
national states

Although the feudal regime became extinct in Germany by the fifteenth century and in Italy somewhat earlier, in neither of these countries was a national monarchy set up until long after the close of the Middle Ages. The power of the dukes in Germany and the power of the Pope always proved too strong to overcome. Some of the German emperors might have succeeded in building up centralized rule if they had been content to remain in their own country, but they persisted in interfering in Italy, thereby antagonizing the Popes and encouraging revolts at home.

When the eastern branch of the Carolingian dynasty died out in 911, the Germans returned to their ancient practice of electing a king. Their first choice was Conrad of Franconia. He, in turn, was succeeded by Henry I, the founder of the Saxon dynasty. The most famous member of this dynasty was Henry's son, Otto the Great, who became king in 936. From the beginning of his reign Otto apparently entertained ambitions of becoming something more than a mere king of Germany. He had himself crowned at Aachen, probably to convey the idea that he was the rightful successor of Charlemagne. Soon afterward he intervened in Italian affairs and assumed the title of King of the Lombards. From this it was only a step to becoming involved with the papacy. In 961 Otto responded to an appeal from Pope John XII for protection against his enemies, and in January of the following year he was rewarded by being crowned Roman Emperor. Although the empire of Otto the Great was confined to Germany and Italy, there was doubtless the belief in the mind of its founder that it would eventually be enlarged, perhaps to embrace all of Latin Christendom. It was, of course, not conceived as a new state at all but as a continuation of

the Carolingian Empire and the Empire of the Caesars.

NORTH SEA

KINGDOM OF ENGLAND

London •

FRIESLAND

DUCHY OF SAXONY

Elbe R.

DUCHY OF POMERANIA

MARCH OF BRANDENBURG

Oder R.

KINGDOM OF POLAND

Cologne •

DUCHY OF LORRAINE

THURINGIA

DUCHY OF FRANCONIA

KINGDOM OF BOHEMIA

MARCH OF MORAVIA

Seine R.

Paris •

Rhine R.

Danube R.

DUCHY OF SWABIA

DUCHY OF AUSTRIA

Vienna

Loire R.

KINGDOM OF FRANCE

COUNTY OF BURGUNDY

DUCHY OF BAVARIA

KINGDOM OF HUNGARY

Rhone R.

KINGDOM OF ARLES

Po R.

LOMBARDY

Venice

Genoa •

• Bologna

ADRIATIC SEA

Marseilles

Florence

PAPAL STATES

CORSICA

Rome

SARDINIA

500 miles

Palermo

KINGDOM

OF THE

TWO SICILIES

MEDITERRANEAN SEA

THE HOLY ROMAN EMPIRE ca. 1200 A.D.

In the twelfth century the crown of Otto the Great came into possession of the Hohenstaufen family, whose most distinguished representatives were Frederick Barbarossa (1152–1190) and Frederick II (1220–1250). Both of these rulers were outspoken in asserting their claims to imperial dignity. Frederick Barbarossa called the empire of Germany and Italy the Holy Roman Empire on the theory that it was a universal empire established directly by God and coordinate in rank with the Church. Frederick II, who was king of Sicily and southern Italy as well as Holy Roman Emperor, was much more interested in his southern kingdom than he was in Germany. Nevertheless, he believed just as firmly as did his grandfather Barbarossa in a universal empire as the highest secular power in western Europe. But he considered that the only possible way to

The Holy Roman Empire of Frederick Barbarossa and Frederick II

447

make the claims of the Emperor a reality was to build a strong state
in Sicily and southern Italy and then extend its power northward.
Accordingly, he proceeded to reorganize his southern kingdom into
a divine-right despotism. He swept away the vestiges of feudalism
almost at a single stroke. Like William the Conqueror, he required
all nobles, regardless of rank, to swear allegiance to him directly. He
established a professional army, introduced direct taxation, and abolished trial by ordeal and by combat. He appointed traveling judges
to promote the development of a uniform law and judicial procedure. He decreed it to be an act of sacrilege even to discuss the

*The Emperor Frederick Bar-
barossa (Frederick I) and His
Two Sons.* A miniature dating
from about 1180.

Emperor's statutes or judgments. He set up rigid control over commerce and industry and founded government monopolies of the
grain trade, the exchange of money, and the manufacture of textiles
and other commodities. He even anticipated modern dictators in a
campaign for racial purity, declaring that "When the men of Sicily
ally themselves with the daughters of foreigners, the purity of the
race becomes besmirched." He seemed to forget the fact that the
blood of most of his people was already mixed with Saracenic,
Greek, Italian, and Norman infusions, and that he himself was half
German and half Norman.

Frederick II was no more successful than any of his predecessors
in increasing the power of the Holy Roman Empire. His great mistake was his failure to enlist the support of the middle class in the
cities, as the Capetian monarchs in France had done. Without this it
was impossibe to break through the wall of papal opposition. After
Frederick died the Popes proceeded to annihilate the remaining
members of the Hohenstaufen line. In 1273 Rudolf of Hapsburg was
elected to the imperial throne, but the Holy Roman Empire over

The succession of
the Hapsburgs to
the throne

which he and his descendants ruled was seldom very powerful.
When finally abolished in 1806 by Napoleon, it was little more than
a political fiction.

4. URBAN LIFE IN THE LATER MIDDLE AGES

By no means all of the inhabitants of western Europe in the later
Middle Ages lived in castles, manor houses, or peasant villages.
Thousands of others dwelt in cities and towns; and from the *Importance of the*
eleventh century on, at least, the activities of the urban classes were *cities*
just as important as the fighting and love-making of nobles or the toil-
ing and roistering of peasants. Indeed, the cities were the real centers of most of the intellectual and artistic progress of the later Middle Ages.

The oldest of the medieval cities in western Europe were undoubtedly those which had survived from Roman times. But outside
of Italy these were few indeed. Others came into being through a *Origins of the*
variety of causes. A great many were towns which had increased in *medieval cities*
size and importance because of the establishment of bishoprics
there. Some had grown out of the expansion of monasteries into
centers of trade and industry. Still others had developed from castles
or strongholds where people congregated because of the need for
protection. But by far the greatest number originated as a result of
the revival of trade which began in the eleventh century. The leaders in this revival were the Italian towns of Venice, Genoa, and Pisa.
Their merchants rapidly built up a flourishing commerce with the
Byzantine Empire and with the great Saracenic cities of Baghdad,
Damascus, and Cairo. The products brought in by these merchants
stimulated a brisk demand not only in Italy but also in Germany,
France, and England. As a result, new markets were opened up,
and many people turned to manufacturing to imitate products imported from the Near East. Cities and towns multiplied so rapidly
that in some regions half the population had been drawn from agriculture into commercial and industrial pursuits by the fourteenth
century.

As one would expect, the largest cities of late medieval Europe
were located in the south. Palermo on the island of Sicily, with possibly 300,000 inhabitants, surpassed all the others in size and proba- *The cities and*
bly in magnificence also. The metropolis of northern Europe was *their governments*
Paris, with a population of about 240,000 in the thirteenth century.
The only other cities with a population of 100,000 or over were
Venice, Florence, and Milan. Although England doubled the number of her inhabitants between the eleventh century and the fourteenth, only about 45,000 of them lived in London in the thirteenth
century. By the end of the Middle Ages nearly all of the cities of
western Europe had gained some degree of exemption from feudal
control. Their citizens had complete freedom to dispose of their **449**

THE MEDIEVAL CITY

Top left: *A Medieval Bridge.* Pont Valentre on the Lot River (tributary of the Garonne in southwest France). The town in the background is Cahors.

Bottom left: *A Section of the Medieval Town of Nordlingen, Germany.* The need for protection against invaders led to congested housing conditions inside the walls.

Right center: *The Palazzo Communale, or City Hall, in Siena (1288–1309).* Built of brick, with a tower 334 feet high, it was a fine example of pointed Gothic. The chapel at the foot of the tower was built as a public thank offering after the plague of 1348.

Upper right: *The Walls of Avila, Central Spain.* Medieval cities were generally surrounded by fortified walls. The apse of the cathedral built into the massive walls is the supposed birthplace of St. Teresa (1515–1582).

Bottom right: *Relic of a Medieval City Gate*. The Eastgate of Chester, England. The Eastgate is the principal entrance to the city of Chester. Its present archway, built in 1769, replaced a narrow medieval gateway. The keepers of the gate had the duty of inspecting weights and measures, and they levied a toll on all merchandise entering the city from the east. The clock tower above the present gateway was erected in 1897 to commemorate Queen Victoria's Jubilee.

property as they saw fit, to marry whom they pleased, and to go and come as they liked. All feudal dues were either abolished or commuted to monetary payments; provision was made for cases involving townsmen to be tried in the municipal courts. Some of the largest and wealthiest towns were almost entirely free, having organized governments with elected officials to administer their affairs. This was especially true in northern Italy, Provence, northern France, and Germany. The great cities of Ghent, Bruges, and Ypres, grown rich from trade and woolen manufactures, virtually dominated all of Flanders. The freedom of the medieval cities was secured in a variety of ways—frequently by purchase, occasionally by violence, and sometimes by taking advantage of the weakness of the nobles or their preoccupation with quarrels of their own. The governments of these cities were generally dominated by an oligarchy of merchants, but in some cases forms of democracy prevailed. Annual elections of magistrates were relatively common; universal suffrage was occasionally employed; in a few towns the rich were disfranchised entirely, and the government was controlled by the masses.

Most of the medieval cities grew so rapidly that it would have been almost impossible to provide optimum standards of healthfulness and comfort for the inhabitants even if there had been sufficient knowledge and inclination to do so. Overcrowding was so bad that sometimes as many as sixteen people lived in three rooms. Part of this congestion was due to the need of the cities for protection against nobles and brigands. To fulfill this need, fortified walls had to be built around each city with gates that could be securely barred to shut out marauders. Naturally, it was too much trouble to tear down these walls and build new ones with every substantial increase in the population, although eventually this had to be done several times in a great many of the principal towns. Land values within these walls rose to fantastic heights and brought into existence a wealthy rent-collecting class, usually composed of the leading members of the merchant guilds. Because of the high cost of land, houses were built with upper stories that projected over the street, and even space on the walls was utilized for cottages and gardens. Streets were narrow and crooked and generally remained unpaved for centuries. The practice of paving began in Italy in the eleventh century and then gradually spread northward, but no thoroughfare in Paris had a hard surface until 1184 when Philip Augustus paved a single roadway in front of the Louvre. With space in the cities so limited, the streets served as the common playgrounds for boys and young men. Many were the protests voiced by their elders and by the clergy against wrestling, bowling, and pitching of quoits in the streets. "Football was constantly denounced, with good reason, as it was not an orderly game with a fixed number of players . . . but a wild struggle between opposing parties to force the ball through the

Social problems in
the cities

streets from one end of the town to the other, frequently resulting in broken legs." [3]

Prominent among the economic institutions in the medieval cities were the guilds. Of the two, the merchant and the craft guilds, the merchant organizations were the older, having developed as far back as the eleventh century. At first these included both traders and artisans, and then as industry became more specialized, the original guilds were split into separate organizations of craftsmen and merchants. The main functions of the merchant guild were to maintain a monopoly of the local market for its own members and to preserve a stable, noncompetitive economic system. To accomplish these ends the guild severely restricted trading by foreign merchants in the city, guaranteed to every member the right to participate in every purchase of goods made by any other member, required all of its members to charge uniform prices for the goods they sold, drastically punished cornering of the market, and prohibited many forms of advertising. It should be borne in mind that the merchant guilds were involved primarily in local trade. They had little or nothing to do with international commerce. This was conducted by large commercial firms, chiefly in Italy and Flanders. Their methods were not dissimilar to those of modern capitalism. Vigorous competition, adjustment of prices to market conditions, and use of the credit facilities of banks were typical examples.

Each of the craft guilds had three different classes of members— the master craftsmen, the journeymen, and the apprentices. Only the first two had any voice in the management of guild affairs, and toward the close of the Middle Ages even the journeymen lost most of their privileges. The master craftsmen were always the aristocrats of medieval industry; they owned their shops, employed other workers, and were responsible for the training of apprentices. The whole craft guild system operated largely for their benefit. The journeymen (from the French *journée* meaning "day" or "day's work") were craftsmen who worked in the masters' shops for wages. In some parts of Germany it was customary for the young journeyman to spend a year wandering about the country picking up casual employment, the so-called *Wanderjahr*, before settling down in any particular place. But in most other sections of Europe he seems to have lived with the master's family. The industrious and intelligent journeyman could eventually become a master craftsman by accumulating enough money to set up his own shop and by passing an examination, which sometimes included the submission of a masterpiece. As in many specialized trades today, entrance into the medieval craft could be accomplished only through serving an apprenticeship, varying in length from two to seven years, the longer period being more common. The apprentice was entirely under the

[3] L. F. Salzman, *English Life in the Middle Ages*, pp. 82–83.

Medieval Craftsmen. The tailor, the shoemaker, the baker, and the weaver.

control of the master craftsman, who was commonly held responsible for the boy's education in elementary subjects and for the development of his character as well as for teaching him his trade. Usually the apprentice received no compensation except his food, lodging, and clothing. When the period of training was over, he became a journeyman. During the waning of the Middle Ages the craft guilds grew more and more exclusive. Terms of apprenticeship were lengthened, and it was made increasingly difficult for journeymen ever to become masters. The guilds themselves came to be dominated by the richer members, who endeavored to restrict their particular crafts to their own families. But dissatisfied journeymen could often evade these restrictions by leaving a particular city and setting themselves up in competitive business in some nearby village or town.

The functions of the craft guilds were similar to those of the related organizations of merchants, except for the additional responsibility of maintaining standards of quality. The craftsmen were just as ambitious as the merchants to preserve monopolies in their particular fields and to prevent any real competition among those producing the same article. Consequently, they required uniformity of prices and wages, prohibited working after hours, and set up

Functions of the craft guilds

454

elaborate regulations governing methods of production and the quality of materials used. They even went to the extreme of discouraging new inventions and discoveries unless they were made available to all and everyone adopted them. As a rule, no one was permitted to practice his trade in a town without first becoming a member of the guild. But in spite of all these regulations there were evidently a good many "chiselers." We read of millers who stole part of their customers' grain, of upholsterers who stuffed their mattresses with thistledown, and of metal-workers who substituted iron for copper and covered it over with gilt.

The medieval craft guilds bore no actual relationship to the labor unions of today, despite a superficial resemblance to those modern unions which are organized on the basis of separate crafts, such as the associations of carpenters, plumbers, and electricians. But the differences are much more fundamental. Unlike the modern labor union, the craft guilds were not strictly confined to the working class; the master craftsmen were capitalists, owners of the means of production, and employers as well as workers. Furthermore, they included not only men who worked with their hands but some who would now be classified as professional men entirely outside the ranks of labor. For example, there were guilds of notaries, physicians, and pharmacists. Finally, the craft guild had a much greater breadth of purpose. It was really a miniature industrial system in itself, combining the functions of the modern corporation, the trade association, and the labor union.

A comparison between the craft guilds and labor unions

Both the craft and merchant guilds performed other functions besides those directly related to production and trade. They served the purposes of religious associations, benevolent societies, and social clubs. Each guild had its patron saint and chapel, and its members celebrated together the chief religious holidays and Church festivals. With the gradual secularization of the drama, the miracle and mystery plays were transferred from the church to the market place, and the guilds assumed charge of presenting them. In addition, each organization ministered to the needs of its members who were sick or in distress of any kind. Money was appropriated to provide for the care of widows and orphans. A member who was no longer able to work or who had been thrown into jail by his enemies could look to his colleagues for assistance. Even an unfortunate brother's debts might be assumed by the guild if his financial plight was serious.

Social functions of the guilds

The economic theory upon which the guild system rested was vastly different from that which prevails in capitalist society. It reflected, first of all, some of the ascetic flavor of Christianity. In the eyes of the Church the vitally important aim in life should be the salvation of one's soul. Everything else should be kept in a subordinate place. It was not proper that men should expend their energies in the pursuit of luxury, or even that they should strive to become too comfortable. Moreover, the religion had been founded upon the

The economic theory of the guild system

idea that riches are a hindrance to the welfare of the soul. St. Ambrose, one of the most influential of the Christian Fathers, had even referred to private property as "a damnable usurpation." However, the economic theory of the later Middle Ages was influenced not only by Christianity but by Aristotle's doctrines of the golden mean and the just price and by his condemnation of usury. This theory included the following basic assumptions:

(1) The purpose of economic activity is to provide goods and services for the community and to enable each member of society to live in security and freedom from want. Its purpose is not to furnish opportunities for the few to get rich at the expense of the many.

(2) Every commodity has its "just price," which is equal to its cost of production, plus expenses and a reasonable profit. The contract price and the true economic value of the product must be equivalent. Generally speaking, the just price was simply the price for which goods could be sold without fraud.

(3) No man is entitled to a larger share of this world's goods than is necessary for his reasonable needs. Any surplus that may come into his possession is not rightfully his but belongs to society. St. Thomas Aquinas, the greatest of all the medieval philosophers, taught that if a rich man refuses to share his wealth with the poor, it is entirely justifiable that his surplus should be taken from him.

(4) No man has a right to financial reward unless he engages in socially useful labor or incurs some actual risk in an economic venture. The taking of interest on loans where no genuine risk is involved constitutes the sin of usury.

It would be foolish, of course, to suppose that these lofty ideals were ever carried out to perfection. As we have seen, manifestations of greed were not lacking among many members of the guilds. But more than this, the noncapitalistic guild system did not extend into every sphere of medieval economic activity. For example, long-distance trade, as we have seen, was carried on by great mercantile establishments in Flanders and in the cities of Italy. In other cases it was in the hands of *associations* of merchants. Characteristic of the latter were the Teutonic Hanse, or associations of German merchants engaged in exchanging the furs, fish, amber, leather, salt, and grain from the Baltic region for the wines, spices, textiles, fruits, and other products of the west and the south. By the fourteenth century these associations had developed into the powerful Hanseatic League with a membership of about eighty towns under the leadership of Lübeck, Hamburg, and Bremen. The Hanse was essentially a profit-making organization, and the activities of its members foreshadowed the growth of a capitalist economy in northern Europe.

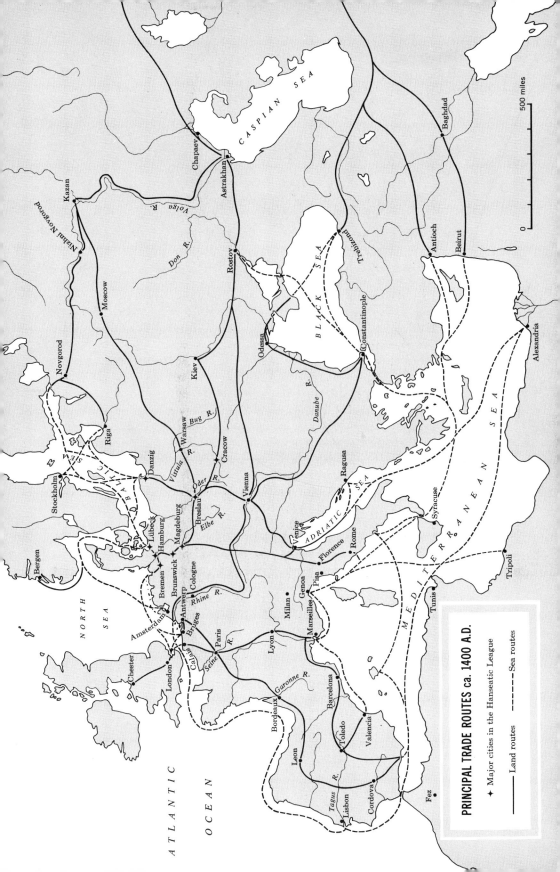

PRINCIPAL TRADE ROUTES ca. 1400 A.D.

✦ Major cities in the Hanseatic League

——— Land routes
------ Sea routes

500 miles

CASPIAN SEA

Chapaev

Astrakhan

Kazan

Nizhni Novgorod

Volga R.

Don R.

Moscow

Rostov

Baghdad

Antioch

Beirut

Trebizond

Novgorod

BLACK SEA

Constantinople

Odessa

Kiev

Bug R.

Warsaw

Vistula R.

Oder R.

Cracow

Vienna

Danube R.

Riga

Danzig

Alexandria

ADRIATIC SEA

Ragusa

BALTIC SEA

Stockholm

Lübeck

Hamburg

Magdeburg

Breslau

Elbe R.

Venice

Florence

Rome

Syracuse

MEDITERRANEAN SEA

Bergen

Bremen

Brunswick

Cologne

Rhine R.

Milan

Genoa

Pisa

Marseilles

Tunis

Tripoli

NORTH SEA

Amsterdam

Antwerp

Bruges

Paris

Seine R.

Lyon

Barcelona

Chester

London

Calais

Bordeaux

Garonne R.

Tagus R.

Leon

Toledo

Valencia

Lisbon

Cordova

Fez

ATLANTIC OCEAN

SELECTED READINGS

· *Items so designated are available in paperbound editions.*

Barraclough, Geoffrey, ed., *Medieval Germany*, New York, 1961, 2 vols.

· ———, *Origins of Modern Germany*, New York, 1946 (Capricorn).

· Bloch, Marc, *Feudal Society*, Chicago, 1961 (Phoenix, 2 vols.).

· Boissonnade, Prosper, *Life and Work in Medieval Europe*, New York, 1927 (Torchbook). Interesting and dependable.

· Brooke, Christopher, *From Alfred to Henry III, 871–1272*, London, 1961 (Norton Library History of England).

· Bryce, James, *The Holy Roman Empire*, New York, 1919 (Schocken).

Buchan, Alice, *Joan of Arc and the Recovery of France*, New York, 1948.

Clough, S. B., and Cole, C. W., *Economic History of Europe*, Boston, 1947. Contains excellent chapters on medieval economy.

Davis, H. W. C., *Medieval Europe*, London, 1948. Brief and interesting.

· Fawtier, Robert, *The Capetian Kings of France*, New York, 1960 (St. Martin's Library).

· Ganshof, F. L., *Feudalism*, New York, 1952 (Torchbook). A high-level and somewhat technical account. Valuable for a clear understanding of feudal theory and institutions.

· Haskins, Charles H., *The Normans in European History*, Boston, 1915 (Norton Library).

· Hollister, C. W., *Medieval Europe: A Short History*, New York, 1964 (Wiley). Concise, authoritative, and delightfully written.

· Holmes, *The Later Middle Ages, 1272–1485*, (Norton Library History of England).

Kantorowicz, Ernst, *Frederick II*, New York, 1957.

· Labarge, M. W., *A Baronial Household of the Thirteenth Century*, New York, 1965 (Barnes & Noble).

Loyn, H. R., *Anglo-Saxon England and the Norman Conquest*, New York, 1963.

Luchaire, A., *Social France in the Time of Philip Augustus*, New York, 1912.

· Maitland, Frederick W., *The Domesday Book and Beyond*, Boston, 1897 (Norton Library).

· Mundy, J. H., and Riesenberg, Peter, *The Medieval Town*, Princeton, 1958 (Anvil). A valuable supplement to Pirenne.

· Myers, A. R., *England in the Late Middle Ages*, London, 1952 (Penguin).

· Painter, Sidney, *The Rise of Feudal Monarchies*, Ithaca, 1951 (Cornell).

· ———, *Medieval Society*, 1951 (Cornell). A brief but scholarly survey.

· Perroy, Edouard, *The Hundred Years War*, New York, 1951 (Capricorn).

· Pirenne, Henri, *Economic and Social History of Medieval Europe*, New York, 1956 (Harvest). Stimulating and authoritative.

· ———, *Medieval Cities*, Princeton, 1925 (Anchor). The most highly regarded book on the subject.

· Power, Eileen, *Medieval People*, London, 1924 (Anchor).

Raftis, J. A., *Tenure and Mobility: Studies in the Social History of the Medieval English Village*, Toronto, 1964.

· Runciman, Steven, *A History of the Crusades, The First Crusade and the Foundation of the Kingdom of Jerusalem*, New York, 1951, Vol. 1 (Torchbook).

Salzman, L. F., *English Life in the Middle Ages*, Oxford, 1926.

· Sayles, G. O., *The Medieval Foundations of England*, London, 1952 (Perpetua).

· Stephenson, Carl, *Medieval Feudalism*, New York, 1935 (Cornell).

· Tawney, R. H., *Religion and the Rise of Capitalism*, New York, 1947 (Men-

tor). Interesting for the light it throws on medieval economic theory under
the influence of the Church.

Tellenbach, Gerd, *Church, State, and Christian Society*, Oxford, 1959.

Tilley, A., *Medieval France*, Cambridge, 1922.

SOURCE MATERIALS

Coulton, G. G., *Life in the Middle Ages*, New York, 1955, 4 vols.

· ——, *The Medieval Village, Manor, and Monastery*, New York, 1960 (Torchbook).

· Dante, *De Monarchia* (*On World Government*), 2d rev. ed., New York, 1957 (Library of Liberal Arts).

John of Salisbury, *Policraticus*, New York, 1909, 2 vols.

· Johnes, Thomas, *Froissart's Chronicles of England, France, Spain and the Adjoining Countries*, Vol. I, 240–41; Vol. II, 94–95, New York, 1961 (Dutton).

· Lopez, Robert S., and Raymond, Irving W., *Medieval Trade in the Mediterranean World*, New York, 1955 (Norton).

McKechnie, W. S., *Magna Carta*, 2d rev. ed., New York, 1914.

Marsiglio of Padua, *Defensor Pacis* (*Defender of the Peace*), especially Book I, Chs. IV, XII, XV.

· Otto of Freising, *The Deeds of Frederick Barbarossa*, New York, 1953 (Norton).

· *Portable Medieval Reader* (Viking).

Riley, H. T., *Memorials of London and London Life*, London, 1868.

Thatcher, O. J., and MacNeal, E. H., *A Source Book for Medieval History*, New York, 1905, pp. 283–306, "The Golden Bull of Charles IV"; also documents of feudalism, pp. 341–87.

Webster, Hutton, *Historical Selections*, pp. 467–500, documents of the Feudal Regime.

CHAPTER 16

The Later Middle Ages (1050-1350): Religious and Intellectual Developments

> Now in those things which we hold about God there is truth in two ways. For certain things that are true about God wholly surpass the capability of human reason, for instance that God is three and one; while there are certain things to which even natural religion can attain, for instance that God is, that God is one, and others like these, which even the philosophers proved demonstratively of God, being guided by the light of natural reason.
> —St. Thomas Aquinas, *Summa Contra Gentiles*, Book I

It has already been mentioned more than once that the civilization of western Europe between 1050 and 1350 was vastly different from that which had existed at the beginning of the medieval period. Nowhere was the contrast more striking than in the spheres of religion and the intellect. The religious and intellectual attitudes of the early Middle Ages were products of a time of transition and of considerable chaos. The Roman political and social structure had disintegrated, and no new regime had yet emerged to take its place. As a consequence, the thinking of this time was directed toward pessimism and otherworldly concerns. In the midst of conditions of barbarism and decadence, there did not seem to be much hope for man's earthly future or much reason for confidence in the powers of ·the mind. But after the tenth century these attitudes gradually gave way to more optimistic sentiments and to an increasing interest in wordly affairs. The original causes were directly related to the progress of monastic education, to the rise of more stable government, and to an increase in economic security. Later such factors as the influence of the Saracenic and Byzantine civilizations and the

The change in religious and intellectual attitudes

461

growth of prosperity in the cities and towns brought the culture of
the later Middle Ages to a magnificent climax of intellectual
achievement in the twelfth and thirteenth centuries. At the same
time religion took on a less otherworldly aspect and evolved into an
institution more deeply concerned with the affairs of this life.

I. THE NEW CHRISTIANITY

Late medieval
Christianity

During the later Middle Ages, Christianity underwent so many
significant developments from its early medieval character that it
seemed in some respects to be almost a new religion. To be sure,
such cardinal features as faith in one God, the belief in the Trinity,
and the hope for salvation in a world to come continued to be accepted in their original form, but other elements in the religion of
St. Augustine and Gregory the Great were modified or eliminated
and different ones substituted for them. The transformation began
about 1050 and reached its zenith in the thirteenth century under
the influence of such leaders as St. Thomas Aquinas, St. Francis, and
Innocent III.

New doctrines
and new attitudes

Perhaps the most important developments were in matters of doctrine and religious attitudes. The religion of the early Middle Ages
had been pessimistic, fatalistic, and, theoretically at least, opposed to
everything worldly as a compromise with the devil. Man was considered to be inherently wicked and incapable of any good works
except as the beneficiary of God's grace. God Himself was omnipotent, selecting for reasons of His own those human beings who
would enter His paradise, and leaving the rest to follow the path to
destruction. By the thirteenth century, however, quite different
religious conceptions had come to prevail. Life in this world was
now held to be exceedingly important, not only as a preparation for
eternity but for its own sake as well. No longer was human nature
regarded as totally evil. Man could therefore cooperate with God in
achieving the salvation of his soul. Instead of emphasizing the omnipotence of God, philosophers and theologians now stressed the divine justice and mercy.

The new theology:
(1) the theory of
the priesthood

The first great summary of late medieval theology was the *Sen-
tences* of Peter Lombard, written during the second half of the
twelfth century. More inclusive statements of doctrine were contained in the *Summa theologica* of St. Thomas Aquinas and in the
pronouncements issued by Church councils, especially the Fourth
Lateran Council of 1215. Probably the most important of the new
elements in this theology were the theory of the priesthood and the
theory of the sacraments. There had, of course, been priests and sacraments in the Church long before the eleventh century, but neither
the exact functions of the priests nor the precise nature of the sacraments had ever been clearly formulated. The theory now came to
be held that the priest, by virtue of his ordination by a bishop and

the latter's confirmation by the Pope, was the inheritor of a portion of the authority conferred by the Christ upon the Apostle Peter. In effect, this meant that the priest had the power to cooperate with God in performing certain miracles and in releasing sinners from the temporal consequences of their wickedness.

It was primarily a result of Peter Lombard's influence that the number of sacraments came to be accepted as seven. The seven were and still are: baptism; confirmation; penance; the Eucharist, or Lord's Supper; marriage; ordination; and extreme unction, or the last rites administered to the dying. The Roman Church defines a sacrament as an instrumentality whereby divine grace is communicated to men. The sacramental theory as it came to be accepted during the last centuries of the Middle Ages included a number of separate doctrines. First, there was the doctrine that the sacraments were indispensable means of procuring God's grace, that no individual could be saved without them. Second, there was the principle that the sacraments were automatic in their effects. In other words, it was held that the efficacy of the sacraments did not depend upon the character of the priest who administered them. The priest might be a very unworthy man, but the sacraments in his hands would remain as unpolluted as if they were administered by a saint. Finally, at the Fourth Lateran Council, the doctrine of transubstantiation was made an integral part of the sacramental theory. This doctrine means that the priest, at a given moment in the Eucharistic ceremony, actually cooperates with God in the performance of a miracle whereby the bread and wine of the sacrament are changed or transubstantiated into the body and blood of Christ. The change, of course, is considered a change in essence only; the "accidents" of taste and appearance remain the same.

The adoption of these two fundamental theories, the theory of the priesthood and the theory of the sacraments, had potent effects in exalting the power of the clergy and in strengthening the formal and mechanical elements in the Latin Church. However, medieval Catholicism was revitalized and made into a civilizing influence by two other developments that marked the later Middle Ages. One was the adoption of a rationalist philosophy by the leading theologians, and the other was the growth of a humanizing attitude. The influence of rationalist philosophy will be discussed farther on in this chapter. The humanizing element in religion expressed itself in a variety of ways—in the revolt against the selfish asceticism of monks and hermits, in the naturalism of St. Francis, and perhaps most of all in the veneration of saints and the Virgin Mary. All through the later medieval period, the veneration or "invocation" of saints was a popular practice, especially among the common people. For the average person God and Christ were remote and sublime beings who could hardly be bothered with the petty problems of men. But the saints were human; one could ask them for favors **463** which one would hesitate to request of God. For example, a woman could implore the aid of St. Agnes in helping her find a husband. Even more popular than the invocation of saints was reverence for the Virgin Mary, which came to be almost a religion in itself during the twelfth and thirteenth centuries. Devotion to Mary as the beautiful and compassionate Mother undoubtedly served as one of the strongest expressions of the humanizing tendency in medieval religion. For she was venerated not only as the ideal woman but also as Our Lady of Sorrows. The grief that she experienced over the tragic death of her Son was believed to endow her with a special sympathy for the sorrows of mankind. Though revered as the Queen of Heaven, she was, above all, the goddess of this life.

Significant developments in ecclesiastical organization and the adoption of new forms of religious discipline also occurred during the later Middle Ages. In 1059 the College of Cardinals was established as a papal electoral college. Originally the members of this body were the deacons, priests, and bishops of certain churches in the city of Rome. Later high ranking clergy from nearly all countries of the Western world were appointed to membership, although the College included a majority of Italians until 1946. At present there are 120 members, and a two-thirds vote is necessary to elect the Pope, who is invariably a cardinal himself. Prior to 1059 Popes were chosen in a variety of ways. In the early days they had been elected by the clergy of the diocese of Rome, but later they were often appointed by powerful nobles and frequently by the German emperors. The vesting of the sole right of election in the College of Cardinals was part of a great reform movement to free the Church from political control. The other main development in religious organization was the growth of the papal monarchy. The first of the Popes to achieve much success in extending his supremacy over the whole ecclesiastical hierarchy was Nicholas I (858–867). Intervening in disputes between bishops and archbishops, he forced all of them to submit to his own direct authority. Nicholas was followed, however, by a series of weak successors, and the papal monarchy was not revived until the reign of Gregory VII (1073–1085). It reached the highest stage of its medieval developments during the pontificate of Innocent III (1198–1216).

Changes in the organization of the church

During the later centuries of the Middle Ages the Church made systematic attempts to extend its moral authority over all of its lay members, whether of high or of low degree. The chief methods adopted were excommunication and the requirement of oral confession. Excommunication was not used to any extent before the eleventh century. Its effect was to expel an individual from the Church and to deprive him of all the privileges of a Christian. His body could not be buried in consecrated ground, and his soul was temporarily consigned to hell. All other Christians were forbidden to associate with him, under penalty of sharing his fate. Sometimes a

New methods of discipline

decree of excommunication against a king or a powerful noble was fortified by placing an *interdict* upon the area over which he ruled. The interdict, by withholding most of the benefits of religion from a ruler's subjects, was intended to kindle their resentment against him and force him to submit to the Church. Both excommunication and the interdict proved to be powerful weapons until about the end of the thirteenth century; after that their effectiveness waned. By a decree of the Fourth Lateran Council in 1215 the Church adopted the requirement that every individual must make an oral confession of his sins to a priest at least once a year, and then undergo the punishment imposed before becoming eligible to partake of the Eucharist. The result of this decree was to give the priest the authority of a moral guardian over every individual in his parish.

As the Church became more successful, it tended to become more worldly. Long before the great Reformation of the sixteenth century, medieval Catholicism went through a series of reformations calculated to restore the institutions of the Church to some earlier state of purity or to make them more useful to society. The first of these reform movements was the Cluny movement or the Cluniac revival, which derived its name from the French monastery of Cluny founded in 910. The original purpose of the Cluny movement was simply to reform monasticism. The Benedictine monasteries, which were practically the only ones in existence by the tenth century in western Europe, had grown corrupt and were rapidly passing under the control of feudal nobles. Consequently the Cluniac leaders took as their objectives the enforcement of the rules of piety and chastity upon the monks and the liberation of the monasteries themselves from feudal domination. But by the eleventh century the movement had gained a much broader significance. In fact, its purposes were now so different from the original ones that it is often referred to as the New Cluny movement. No longer were the reformers content merely to purify monasticism and free it from the clutches of the lay feudality; their primary aims were now to eliminate corruption and worldliness from the entire Church, to abolish feudal control over the secular clergy as well as over monks, and to establish the absolute supremacy of the Pope in ecclesiastical matters. They centered their attacks, first of all, upon *simony*, which was interpreted to include the buying and selling of Church offices, any form of appointment to Church offices contrary to the canon law, and the investing of bishops and abbots with the symbols of their spiritual power by secular authorities. In addition, the reformers demanded celibacy for all grades of the clergy. Nearly all of these elements in their program were directed toward making the Church entirely independent of the great nobles, especially by depriving them of their power to dictate the appointment of bishops, abbots, and priests. The movement aroused bitter opposition, for it struck at the very basis of the feudal relationship which had been established between secular rulers and the clergy. But most of the program was eventually put into effect, due in large part to the fanatical zeal of such leaders as Hildebrand, the "holy Satan" who in 1073 became Pope Gregory VII.

(2) the Carthusian and Cistercian movements

By the middle of the eleventh century the Cluniac monks had begun to sink into the same morass of worldliness as their older Benedictine brothers whom they had set out to reform. The result was the launching of new movements to set an even stronger example of purity and austerity for the regular clergy. In 1084 the Carthusian order was established with a set of rules more rigorous than any hitherto adopted in the West. The Carthusian monks were required to live in cells, to fast three days each week on bread and water, to wear hair shirts, and to spend all their time in prayer, meditation, and manual labor. A few years later the Cistercian order was founded at Citeaux in Burgundy and soon proved to be one of the most popular of them all. By the middle of the twelfth century more than 300 Cistercian monasteries were receiving converts from all over western Europe. Although not so strict in their requirements of individual asceticism as the Carthusians, the founders of the Cistercian order saw to it that the rules would be puritanical enough to constitute an emphatic protest against the luxury and idleness of the Cluniac monks. Only a vegetarian diet was allowed, and manual labor was strictly enforced. Both the Cistercian and Carthusian orders ultimately went down the same road to decline as their predecessors, partly as a result of the accumulation of wealth, and also because monasticism of the old-fashioned type was by the thirteenth century no longer consistent with the ideals of the time.

(3) the rise of the orders of friars: the Franciscan order

Undoubtedly the most significant reform movement of the later Middle Ages was the rise of the friars in the thirteenth century. Though the friars are often regarded as simply another species of monks, they were really quite different. Originally they were not members of the clergy at all but laymen. Instead of shutting themselves up in monasteries, they devoted all of their time to social welfare work and to preaching and teaching. The growth of the new orders was symptomatic of an attempt to bring religion into harmony with the needs of a world which had completely outgrown the so-called Dark Ages. Men were now coming to realize that the main business of religion was not to enable a few selfish monks to save their own souls at the expense of society, but to help make this world a happier place in which to live and to rescue the great mass of mankind from the slough of ignorance and sin.

St. Francis of Assisi

The founder of the original order of friars was St. Francis of Assisi (1182–1226). The son of a rich merchant, the young Francis became dissatisfied with the ambitions and values of his social class and determined to become a servant of the poor. Giving away all of his property and donning the rags of a beggar, he set out on his great mission of preaching salvation in the darkest corners of the

Italian cities and ministering to the needs of poor, diseased, and help-less outcasts. The philosophy of St. Francis was different from that of many other Christian leaders. The major portion of it was founded almost literally upon the gospel of Jesus. St. Francis fol-lowed Jesus in his selflessness, in his devotion to poverty as an ideal, in his indifference to doctrine, and in his contempt for form and ceremony. In addition he had a profound love not merely for man but for every creature around him, and even for the objects of inanimate nature. He found God revealed in the sun, the wind, the flowers, and everything that existed for the use or delight of man. His disciples related how he would never put out a fire, but "treated it reverently," and how "he directed the brother who cut and fetched the fire wood never to cut a whole tree, so that some part of it might remain untouched for the love of Him who was willing to work out our salvation upon the wood of the cross." [1] Finally, it should be made clear that St. Francis was not an ascetic in the accurate meaning of that term. Although he denied himself com-forts and pleasures, he did not despise the body or practice lacera-

[1] Quoted by H. O. Taylor, *The Medieval Mind*, I, 454–55.

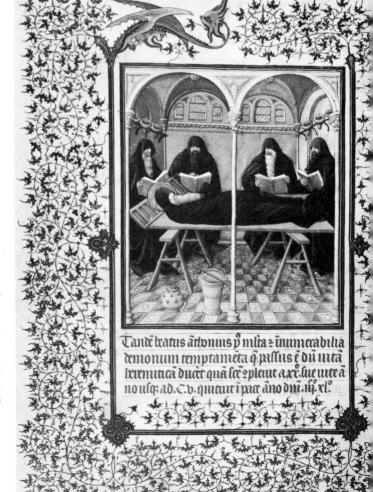

Illuminated Manuscript from *Les Belles Heures de Jean, Duc de Berry,* a book of hours. Monks reading prayers at the bier of their deceased brother, St. Anthony. Illuminated manu-scripts have value not merely as works of art but for their portrayals of medieval life and culture.

tion of the flesh to achieve the salvation of his soul. His abandonment of earthly possessions was done primarily to conquer pride
and bring himself down to the level of the people whom he wished
to help.

The second of the orders of friars was the Dominican order,
founded about 1215 by St. Dominic, a Castilian noble who lived in
southern France. The Dominicans adopted as their principal task
the combating of heresy. Believing that an effective means to this
end was education, they prepared themselves by diligent study to
refute the arguments of pagans and skeptics. Many members of the
order gained teaching positions in the universities and contributed
much to the development of philosophy and theology. Unfortunately, they were carried away at times by a zeal for persecuting;
they were active leaders of the medieval, or Papal Inquisition. By
the fourteenth century both the Dominican and Franciscan orders
had departed widely from the teachings of their founders, but they
continued to exert a strong influence upon late medieval civilization.
The majority of the philosophers and scientists of the thirteenth and
fourteenth centuries were either Dominicans or Franciscans.

2. THE STRUGGLE BETWEEN THE SECULAR AND SPIRITUAL AUTHORITIES

As it happened, the growth of the Church in the later Middle
Ages was accompanied by the rise of ambitious political leaders. A

conflict between secular and spiritual authorities was practically un-
avoidable, since the jurisdictions claimed by each frequently overlapped. The struggle began about 1050 and continued with varying
intensity until well into the fourteenth century. Two separate stages
in the conflict can be distinguished, the first ending in 1122, and the
second beginning about twenty years later.

The two great opponents in the first stage were Pope Gregory
VII and the German emperor, Henry IV. The quarrel between

these powerful rivals was a direct outgrowth of the New Cluny
movement, of which Gregory had been the leader for some time before he became Pope. As noted previously, one of the fundamental
aims of this movement was to free the Church from secular control.
During a period of many years the practice had been established
that a bishop, abbot, or priest who held his position as a fief should
be invested with the symbols of his office by the king or noble who
granted the fief. This practice, known as lay investiture, was a thorn
in the side of such zealous reformers as Gregory; they feared that as
long as the clergy owed allegiance in any degree to secular overlords, papal supremacy would be impossible. But this was not the
only issue involved; there was also the question of the Pope's right

to exercise temporal authority. Just how much temporal jurisdiction

Shrine of the Three Kings, Cologne Cathedral. Richly decorated shrines are one of the principal forms of interior ornamentation in Gothic cathedrals. The cathedral of Cologne (Köln) in western Germany contains the Shrine of the Three Kings, or the Three Wise Men of the East, who are supposed to have brought gifts to the infant Jesus. According to legend, the bones of the Three Kings were brought from Italy in the twelfth century by Frederick Barbarossa and buried in Cologne.

Gregory intended to claim is not clear. Sometimes it appears from his decrees that he regarded himself as the supreme ruler of the world and thought of all princes and kings as his vassals. But leading scholars of medieval political theory have denied that this was the case. They contend that Gregory's conception of his authority was merely that of *pastor of the Christian flock,* and that he never claimed an unlimited right to create and depose secular rulers or annul their decrees. He would intervene only to protect the interests of the Church and the religious rights of Christians.[2] Naturally, this was a rather extensive authority, but it would still fall short of the right to rule as an autocrat over the whole world.

The quarrel between Henry and Gregory was one of the most bitter in the Middle Ages. When Henry refused to obey decrees of the Pope prohibiting lay investiture, Gregory threatened to excommunicate him. The king retaliated by denouncing the Pope as a false monk and ordering him to descend from the throne "to be damned throughout the ages." Whereupon Gregory not only excommunicated Henry but declared his throne vacant and released all his subjects from allegiance to him. Faced with revolt by his vassals, Henry had no alternative but to make peace with the Pope. How he journeyed over the Alps in the depth of winter to Canossa in northern Italy and implored the Pope's forgiveness is a familiar story and need not be recounted here. Later on, Henry had his revenge when he led an army into Italy, set up an anti-pope, and compelled Gregory to flee from Rome. The great apostle of reform died in exile in 1085.

The first stage of the conflict was brought to an end by the Con-

Outcome of the struggle

[2] *Cf.* C. H. McIlwain, *The Growth of Political Thought in the West,* pp. 208 ff.

469

The compromise
of 1122 and the
beginning of the
second stage of
the struggle

cordat of Worms, an agreement ratified by a meeting of German princes and clergy and papal legates in 1122. The settlement was a compromise providing that in the future bishops should be invested with the symbols of their political authority by the king and should take an oath of fealty to him as his vassals, but the archbishop was to have the right to invest them with the symbols of their spiritual functions. It was not long, however, before the struggle was renewed, this time on a much larger scale. Before it ended in the fourteenth century, nearly all of the monarchs of western Europe had been involved. Among them were the Holy Roman Emperors, Frederick Barbarossa and Frederick II; the French kings, Philip Augustus and Philip the Fair; and the English king, John. The leading contenders on the papal side were Innocent III, Innocent IV, and Boniface VIII. The issues in this second stage of the struggle were more numerous than in the first. They included localism versus centralization in Germany, the right of the Holy Roman Emperors to rule over Italy, the freedom of Italian towns from German domination, and the right of kings to tax the property of the Church. Furthermore, the Popes were now extending their claims to temporal authority a degree or two beyond what had been asserted by Gregory VII. Innocent III declared that "it is the business of the pope to look after the interests of the Roman empire, since the empire derives its origin, and its final authority from the papacy." [3] Innocent IV appears to have gone a step further and to have claimed jurisdiction over all temporal affairs and over all human beings, whether Christians or not. Nevertheless, it must be borne in mind that none of these Popes was really demanding absolute power. What they were insisting upon was not legislative but a judicial authority, an authority to judge and punish rulers for their sins. The fundamental issue was whether rulers were directly responsible to God for their official acts or indirectly through the Pope.

The second stage of the conflict had momentous results not only for medieval Europe but for subsequent ages as well. For a time the Popes were almost uniformly successful. With the aid of the Lombard cities and the rebellious dukes in Germany, they checked the ambitions of the Holy Roman Emperors and finally broke the power of the Empire entirely. By means of interdicts Innocent III compelled Philip Augustus to take back the wife he had repudiated and forced King John to recognize England and Ireland as fiefs of the papacy. At the beginning of the fourteenth century, however, Boniface VIII went down to humiliating defeat at the hands of King Philip the Fair of France. As the outcome of a quarrel over Philip's attempt to tax the property of the Church, Boniface was taken prisoner by the king's soldiers, and a month later he died. The Archbishop of Bordeaux was chosen to succeed him, and the papal

[3] O. J. Thatcher and E. H. McNeal, *A Source Book for Medieval History*, p. 220.

470

capital was transferred to Avignon in France, where it remained for seventy years. There were also other results. Many pious Christians now came to believe that the Popes were carrying their ambitions for political power too far and were forgetting their spiritual functions. As a consequence, the papacy lost prestige, and the way was opened for repudiation of its leadership even in religious affairs. In like manner, papal meddling in the internal politics of different countries tended to strengthen the growth of national feeling, particularly in England and France. Finally, the struggle led to a quickening of intellectual activity. As each side attempted to justify its position, interest was awakened in ancient writings, an incentive was provided for the study of Roman law, and many valuable contributions were made to political theory.

3. THE CRUSADES

It is probably not inaccurate to regard the Crusades as the chief expression of medieval expansionism. Unfortunately it appears to be true that nearly every civilization sooner or later develops imperialist tendencies. Certain ones, of course, have been much worse offenders than others, but expansionism in some degree has been characteristic of nearly all of them. It seems to be the natural fruit of the increasing complexity of economic life and of the growth of pride in the real or fancied superiority of a system.

The Crusades an expression of medieval imperialism

Although the Crusades were by no means exclusively a religious movement, there can be no denying the importance of the religious factor in producing them. The century in which they were launched was an age when religion occupied a predominant place in men's thinking. The medieval Christian had a deep conviction of sin. He feared its consequences in the form of eternal damnation and was anxious to avert them by acts of penance. For hundreds of years the most popular type of penance had been the making of pilgrimages to sacred places. A trip to the Holy Land, if at all possible, had been the cherished ambition of every Christian. By the eleventh century the religious revivalism generated by the Cluniac reform movement, combined with the opening up of trade with the Near East, had made pilgrimages to Palestine especially appealing. Hundreds of people now joined the roving bands that trailed across central and eastern Europe on their way to the Levant. In 1065 the Bishop of Bamberg led a horde of 7000 Germans to visit the holy places in and around Jerusalem. Of course, not everyone who joined these mass migrations was inspired by religious ardor. Pilgrimages afforded an opportunity for adventure and sometimes even for profit. Besides, what better chance was there to escape the responsibilities of life for a season and have a good time in the bargain? Every pilgrim who returned brought back stories of the wonderful sights he had seen and thereby aroused the desire of others to follow

Religious causes of the Crusades: (1) mass pilgrimages

471

his example. Without these mass pilgrimages, interest in conquest of the Holy Land would probably never have developed.

Other religious causes must also be mentioned. For a time during the late eleventh century, prospects for papal supremacy did not look bright. Gregory VII had been driven from the throne and had died in exile. His successor was an aged friend who went to his own grave after a year of failure. The cardinals then chose a younger and more vigorous man, who adopted the name of Urban II. Urban had been a French noble who had renounced the world to become a monk at Cluny. Subsequently he became the talented assistant of Gregory VII. Elected Pope himself in 1088, he turned his attention to the glorious dream of uniting all classes of Christians in support of the Church. Perhaps he might even force a reunion of the Eastern and Western branches of Christendom. At any rate, a war against the infidel to rescue the Holy Places from desecration would enable Latin Christians to forget their differences and to rally behind the Pope. The papacy had already inspired or given its blessing to wars on behalf of religion. Predecessors of Urban II had blessed the Norman conquest of England, the campaigns of Robert Guiscard against heretical Greeks in Italy, the wars of Teutons against Slavs on Germany's northern and eastern borders, and the crusades of Christians against Moors in Spain. To merge these efforts in a grand enterprise against the whole unbelieving world must have seemed like a logical climax to what had already occurred.

For more than a century religious leaders in Europe had been disturbed by the prevalence of fighting among the feudal nobles. Despite the Peace of God and the Truce of God, the warfare of barons and knights continued to be a menace to the security of the Church. The rights of clergy, peasants, and other noncombatants were often trampled upon, merchants were robbed, and religious edifices pillaged and burned. Against these depredations the penalty of excommunication was of little avail. Small wonder, therefore, that Popes should have turned to the idea of protecting the Church and its members by diverting the military ardor of the nobles into a holy war against the heathen. Still another religious cause was surplus idealism left over from the New Cluny movement. Movements of this kind, which strike deeply into the emotional nature of man, generally stir up more enthusiasm than is necessary for their immediate objectives. Some of this surplus must then find new outlets, just as in later years the fanaticism engendered by the Crusades themselves burst forth into persecution of the Jews.

To discover some of the most important economic causes of the Crusades, one has only to read the speech of Pope Urban II at the Council of Clermont inviting the nobles of France to take up arms for the conquest of Palestine. He urged them to let nothing detain them, "since this land which you inhabit, shut in on all sides by the sea and surrounded by mountain peaks, is too narrow for your large

(marginal notes)

(2) religious wars as means of promoting unity

(3) other religious causes

Economic causes

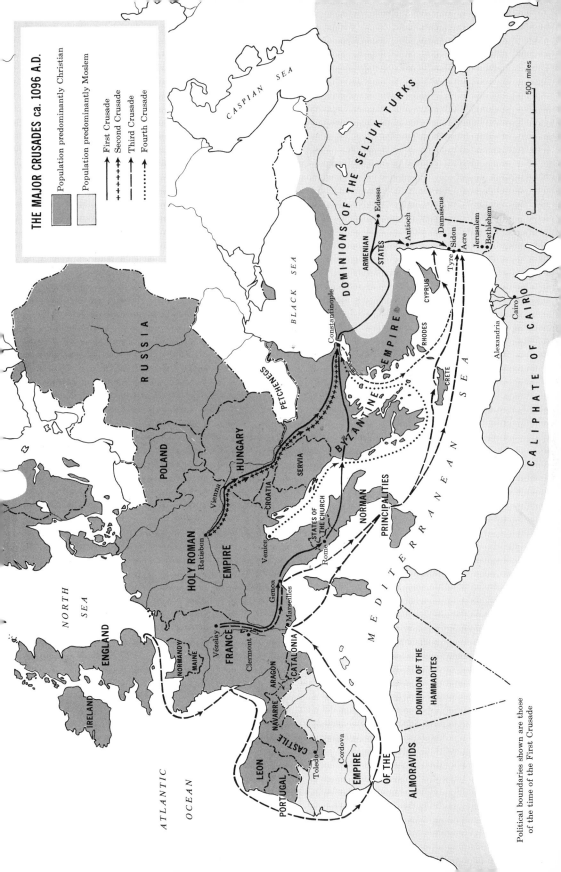

THE MAJOR CRUSADES ca. 1096 A.D.

Population predominantly Christian

Population predominantly Moslem

First Crusade
Second Crusade
Third Crusade
Fourth Crusade

500 miles

CASPIAN SEA

DOMINIONS OF THE SELJUK TURKS

ARMENIAN STATES

• Edessa

• Antioch

Damascus •

Tyre Sidon
Acre

Jerusalem
Bethlehem

CYPRUS

RHODES

CRETE

Alexandria

Cairo •

CALIPHATE OF CAIRO

BLACK SEA

Constantinople

BYZANTINE EMPIRE

RUSSIA

PETCHENEGS

POLAND

HUNGARY

SERVIA

CROATIA

Vienna

Venice

STATES OF THE CHURCH

Rome •

NORMAN PRINCIPALITIES

Genoa

Ratisbon

HOLY ROMAN EMPIRE

Vézelay

FRANCE

Clermont •

Marseilles

MEDITERRANEAN SEA

NORTH SEA

ENGLAND

IRELAND

NORMANDY

MAINE

NAVARRE

ARAGON

CATALONIA

LEON

CASTILE

PORTUGAL

Toledo •

Cordova •

EMPIRE OF THE ALMORAVIDS

DOMINION OF THE HAMMADITES

ATLANTIC OCEAN

Political boundaries shown are those
of the time of the First Crusade

French Knights about to Depart on a Crusade. Their chief weapons are the long bow and the spear.

population; nor does it abound in wealth; and it furnishes scarcely enough food for its cultivators. . . . Enter upon the road to the Holy Sepulchre; wrest that land from the wicked race and subject it to yourselves. That land which, as the Scripture says, 'floweth with milk and honey,' was given by God into the possession of the children of Israel. Jerusalem is the navel of the world; the land is fruitful above others, like another paradise of delights." [4] There is evidence also that a good many nobles, because of extravagance or poor management of their estates had fallen into debt. Furthermore, the rule of primogeniture in France and in England created the problem of what to do with the younger sons. New fiefs were hard to obtain, and positions in the Church were becoming scarce. As a result, these surplus offspring of the nobles tended to form a rebellious and disorderly class, alert for any opportunity to despoil a weak neighbor of his property. Confronted by such problems as these, the nobles of western Europe needed no second invitation to respond to Pope Urban's plea.

The immediate cause of the Crusades was the advance of the Seljuk Turks in the Near East. In about 1050 these people had come down into western Asia and had gained control over the Baghdad caliphate. Soon afterward they conquered Syria, Palestine, and Egypt. In 1071 they slaughtered a Byzantine army at Manzikert and then swept through Asia Minor and captured Nicaea, within a few miles of Constantinople. After the death of the great Sultan, Malik Shah, in 1092 the Seljuk empire began to disintegrate. The time now seemed ripe for the Byzantine Emperor, Alexius Comnenus, to attempt the reconquest of his lost possessions. Realizing the difficulty of this task, since his own government was exhausted from previous struggles, he sent an appeal in 1095 to the Pope, probably for aid in recruiting mercenary soldiers. Urban II, the reigning pontiff, took

The immediate cause of the Crusades

[4] O. J. Thatcher and E. H. McNeal, *A Source Book for Medieval History*, pp. 519–20.

474

full advantage of this opportunity. He summoned a council of French nobles and clergy at Clermont and exhorted them in a fiery speech to make war upon the accursed race of Turks. He employed every artful device of eloquence to arouse the fury and cupidity of his hearers, emphasizing especially the horrible atrocities which he declared the Turks were committing upon Christians. When he had finished, it is reported that all who were present cried out with one accord, "It is the will of God," and rushed forward to take the crusader's oath. The appeal of Urban II was supplemented soon after the Council of Clermont by the impassioned preaching of Peter the Hermit who went among the peasants, rousing them to a frenzied enthusiasm for the holy cause. In the spring of 1096 he led a great mob of them from France and Germany to Constantinople. Most of his followers were ignorant, poorly equipped, and totally untrained for war. When they began looting in the Byzantine capital, the Emperor promptly shipped them across the Bosporus into Asia Minor where the Turks made short work of them.

The first of the organized Crusades was not actually started until late in 1096. The majority of those who participated in it were Frenchmen and Normans, under the leadership of Godfrey of Bouillon, Count Raymond of Toulouse, and Bohemund from the Norman kingdom of Sicily. Altogether, between 1096 and 1244, three other major Crusades and a number of minor ones were launched. Only the first achieved much success in destroying Turkish control over Christian territory. By 1098 most of Syria had been captured, and a year later Jerusalem was taken. But these gains were only temporary. In 1187 Jerusalem was recaptured by the Moslems under Saladin, Sultan of Egypt. Before the end of the thirteenth century every one of the petty states established by the crusaders in the Near East had been wiped out.

The major Crusades

The ultimate failure of the Crusades resulted from several causes. To begin with, the expeditions were frequently badly managed; there was seldom any unified command, and rival leaders quarreled among themselves. In some of the later expeditions the original purpose of conquering the Holy Land from the Turks was lost sight of altogether. The Fourth Crusade, for example, turned out to be a gigantic plundering foray against Constantinople. There was also another cause which cannot be overlooked: the conflicting ambitions of the East and the West. According to the evidence, Alexius Comnenus, in appealing to the Pope for aid, professed a desire to protect the Christian churches of the Orient. But this was not his primary objective. He had come to the conclusion that the time was ripe for a major offensive against the Turks. He was not interested simply or even primarily in driving them out of the Holy Land but in reconquering all of the Asiatic provinces of his empire. By contrast, Pope Urban II had the grandiose dream of a holy war of all of Latin Christendom to expel the infidel from Palestine. His under-

Reasons for the failure of the Crusades

Krak des Chevaliers, Northern Syria. This Castle of the Knights is considered the most magnificent of all the Crusader fortresses and one of the best-preserved relics of the Middle Ages.

lying purpose was not to rescue the Byzantine Empire but to strengthen Latin Christianity, to exalt the papacy, and perhaps to restore the union of the Eastern and Western churches. An additional cause of friction between East and West was the ambition of Italian merchants to extend their commercial empire. They coveted the trade that passed through Constantinople and were ready to capture or destroy the city for their own advantage.

In line with a common tendency to overestimate the importance of wars, the Crusades were at one time considered as the primary cause of nearly all of European progress in the later Middle Ages. It was assumed that they led to the growth of cities, to the overthrow of feudalism, and to the introduction of Saracenic philosophy and science into Latin Europe. For several reasons most historians now regard this assumption as being of limited validity. First, the progress of civilization in the later Middle Ages was already well under way before the Crusades began. Second, the educated classes in Europe did not generally take part in the military expeditions; as a result, the soldiers who actually went were totally devoid of the intellectual background necessary for an appreciation of Saracenic learning. Third, very few of the armies ever reached the real centers of Saracenic civilization, which were not Jerusalem or Antioch, but Baghdad, Damascus, Toledo, and Cordova. European intellectual progress in the twelfth and thirteenth centuries was due far more to the revival of trade with the Near East and to the work of scholars and translators in Spain and Sicily than to any influence of holy wars against the Turks. Nor were the Crusades primarily responsible for the political and economic changes at the end of the Middle Ages. The decline of feudalism, for instance, occurred chiefly because of the Black Death, the growth of an urban economy, and the rise of national monarchies; and these in turn were only in minor degree the results of the Crusades.

What effects, then, is it possible to ascribe to the great holy wars against Islam? To some extent they hastened the emancipation of the common people. Nobles who were hard pressed for money sold privileges to townsmen and to communities of serfs somewhat earlier than they would otherwise have done. Furthermore, many peasants took advantage of the absence of the nobles to break away from bondage to the soil. Among other economic effects were an increased demand for products of the East, the growth of banking, and the elimination of Constantinople as the middleman in the trade between East and West. Venice, Genoa, and Pisa now gained a virtual monopoly of commerce in the Mediterranean area. In addition, the Crusades had some influence in strengthening the monarchies of France and England by eliminating powerful nobles and providing a pretext for direct taxation; but the political consequences were relatively slight. In the domain of religion, where we would normally expect the most profound results, few positive effects can be discovered. It is impossible to prove that the Popes enjoyed any increase in power or repute as a result of having launched the Crusades. On the contrary, as the true character of the expeditions became more and more transparent, the papacy seems rather to have suffered a loss of prestige. There was, however, an increase in religious fanaticism, which expressed itself particularly in savage persecution of the Jews. These unfortunate people suffered nearly everywhere. They were cruelly beaten, sometimes killed in mob attacks, and expelled from several countries. Naturally, the fury against them was partly economic in origin, since they were the chief moneylenders of the time; nevertheless, it is a significant fact that hostility to Jews had one of its chief sources in the holy wars against Islam. Finally, it is doubtless true that the Crusades had some effect in widening geographic knowledge and in encouraging travel and exploration, but these developments were more the result of the gradual expansion of trade.

The actual results of the Crusades

4. THE LATE MEDIEVAL MIND

Intellectual progress in the later Middle Ages received its original stimulus from the so-called Carolingian Renaissance of the ninth century. This was a movement initiated by Charlemagne when he brought to his court at Aachen the most distinguished scholars he could find. In doing this the emperor was prompted partly by his own interest in learning but also by his desire to find uniform standards of orthodoxy which could be imposed upon all of his subjects. Fortunately he seems to have allowed the scholars he imported a generous freedom to pursue their own inclinations. The result was a brilliant though superficial revival of learning which continued for

The revival of learning in western Europe

some years after the death of its sponsor. Among the leaders in the movement were Alcuin, director of the palace school; John Scotus Erigena, the rationalist philosopher; and Walafrid Strabo, the poet. After the Carolingian Renaissance intellectual progress in western Europe was interrupted for some time on account of the Norse and Saracenic invasions. A brief revival under the patronage of the Ottos in Germany in the tenth century was followed by a more virile growth of classical studies in Italy and France after the year 1000. But the climax of intellectual achievement in the later Middle Ages was not reached until the twelfth and thirteenth centuries.

Scholasticism

I. PHILOSOPHY The outstanding philosophic achievement of the late Middle Ages was the famous system of thought known as Scholasticism. This system is usually defined as the attempt to harmonize reason and faith or to make philosophy serve the interest of theology. But no such definition is sufficient to convey an adequate conception of the Scholastic mind. The great thinkers of the Middle Ages did not limit their interests to problems of religion. On the contrary, they were just as anxious as philosophers in any period to answer the great questions of life, whether they pertained to religion, politics, economics, or metaphysics. Perhaps the best way to explain the true nature of Scholasticism is to define it in terms of its characteristics. In the first place, it was rationalistic, not empirical; in other words, it was based primarily upon logic rather than upon science or experience. The Scholastic philosophers, like the Greek thinkers of the Socratic school, did not believe that the highest truth could be derived from sense perception. They admitted that the senses could provide man with a knowledge of the appearances of things, but they maintained that reality or the essential nature of the universe is discoverable mainly by reason. In the second place, Scholastic philosophy was authoritarian. Even reason was not considered a sufficient instrument for the discovery of all knowledge, but the deductions of logic needed to be buttressed by the authority of the Scriptures, of the Church Fathers, and especially of Plato and Aristotle. Third, Scholastic philosophy had a predominantly ethical approach. Its cardinal aim was to discover how man could improve this life and insure salvation in the life to come. Fourth, Scholastic thought, unlike modern philosophy, was not mainly concerned with causes and underlying relationships. Its purpose was rather to discover the attributes of things; the universe was assumed to be static, and therefore it was only necessary to explain the meaning of things and what they were good for, not to account for their origin and evolution.

Peter Abelard

The primary development of the Scholastic philosophy began with the teachings of Peter Abelard (1079-1142), one of the most significant figures in the history of thought. This handsome and talented Frenchman was educated in the best schools of Paris and gained a wide reputation for dialectical skill before he was out of his twenties. For a number of years he taught in Paris, drawing great crowds to his lectures on philosophy and theology. Despite the fact that he was a monk, his habits of life were far from ascetic. He was proud, belligerent, and egotistical—boastful of his intellectual triumphs and even of his prowess in love. He avowed that he possessed such advantages of comeliness and youth that "he feared no repulse from whatever woman he might deign to honor with his love." His tragic affair with Heloïse, which he poignantly describes in his autobiography, *The Story of My Misfortunes*, contributed to his downfall. But he had already incurred the enmity of some powerful theologians who regarded him as a heretic. As a philosopher Abelard had accomplishments to his credit for which he had a right to be proud. He was probably the most critical of all the medieval thinkers. In his most famous philosophical work, *Sic et Non* (*Yes and No*), he exposed many of the shabby arguments based on authority that were commonly accepted in his time. The preface to this work contains a statement which expresses clearly his conviction about the vital importance of critical reasoning: "For the first key to wisdom is called interrogation, diligent and unceasing. . . . By doubting we are led to inquiry; and from inquiry we perceive the truth."

The heyday of Scholasticism came in the thirteenth century, as a result of the labors of numerous intellectuals in various fields of learning. Two of the greatest were Albertus Magnus and his renowned pupil, St. Thomas Aquinas. These men had the advantage of being able to study most of the works of Aristotle, recently translated from copies in the possession of the Saracens. Albertus Magnus, the only scholar ever to be honored with the title of Great, was born in Germany in 1193. During a long and active career he served as a teacher, especially at Cologne and at the University of Paris. A profound admirer of Aristotle, he strove to emulate the example of that ancient master by taking the whole field of knowledge as his province. His writings included more than twenty volumes on subjects ranging from botany and physiology to the soul and the creation of the universe. He was often skeptical of ancient authorities, and he attempted to found his conclusions upon reason and experience. In referring to hoary myths, such as the one about ostriches eating iron, he would frequently say: "but this is not proved by experience." He defined natural science "as not simply receiving what one is told, but the investigation of causes in natural phenomena." [5]

The heyday of Scholasticism; Albertus Magnus

Thomas Aquinas, the most noted of all the Scholastic philosophers, was born in southern Italy in 1225. Following the example of the great Albert, he entered the Dominican order and devoted his life to teaching. He was a professor at the University of Paris by the time he was thirty-one. His most famous work was his *Summa*

St. Thomas Aquinas

[5] Lynn Thorndike, *A History of Magic and Experimental Science*, II, ch. 59.

theologica, but he wrote on many other subjects as well, including politics and economics. The fundamental aims of St. Thomas were, first, to demonstrate the rationality of the universe, and second, to establish the primacy of reason. He believed that the universe is an ordered whole governed by intelligent purpose. All things were created in order to make possible the fulfillment of the great Christian plan for the promotion of justice and peace on earth and the salvation of mankind in a world to come. The philosophy of St. Thomas implied a serene confidence in the ability of man to know and understand his world. He regarded the intellectual faculties of man and also his senses as God-given. The great *Summaries* he wrote were

St. Thomas Aquinas (1225–1274).

attempts to build up out of logic and the wisdom of the past comprehensive systems of knowledge which would leave no mysteries unsolved. Though he leaned heavily upon the authority of Aristotle and the Church Fathers he regarded reason as the primary key to truth. Even his attitude toward religion was essentially intellectual rather than emotional; piety to him was a matter of knowledge much more than of faith. He admitted that a few doctrines of Christianity, such as the belief in the Trinity and the creation of the world in time, could not be proved by the intellect; but he denied that they were contrary to reason, for God Himself is a rational being. As a disciple of Aristotle, St. Thomas taught that the highest good for man is the realization of his true nature; this, he maintained, consists in the knowledge of God, which can be attained in large measure by reason in this life, but will be perfectly realized only in the hereafter. The influence of St. Thomas was not only of

480 cardinal importance in his own time, but it survives to this day. In

the late nineteenth century Pope Leo XIII exhorted the bishops of
the Church "to restore the golden wisdom of St. Thomas and to
spread it far and wide for the defense of the faith, for the good of
society, and for the advantage of all the sciences." He recommended
St. Thomas as a master and guide for everyone interested in scholarly studies.

By the end of the thirteenth century Scholasticism had begun to
decline. Its decay was due partly to the teachings of the last of the
Scholastics, John Duns Scotus. A member of the Franciscan order,
Duns Scotus was inclined to emphasize the emotional and practical
side of religion in place of the intellectual. He conceived of piety as
an act of will rather than an act of intellect. Less confident of the
powers of reason than St. Thomas, he excluded a large number of
the doctrines of religion from the sphere of philosophy altogether.
From this it was only a step to denial that any religious beliefs were
capable of rational demonstration; all would have to be accepted on
faith or rejected entirely. When this step was finally taken by Duns
Scotus' successors, the overthrow of Scholasticism was speedily
accomplished.

The other main reason for the decline of Scholasticism was the
growing popularity of nominalism. Although nominalism is often
considered a branch of Scholasticism, actually the nominalists were
fundamentally opposed to nearly everything the Scholastics taught.
They denied that concepts or class names have any reality, insisting
that they are nothing but abstractions invented by the mind to express the qualities common to a number of objects or organisms.
Only individual things are real. Far from accepting the Scholastic
confidence in reason, the nominalists contended that all knowledge
has its source in experience. Anything beyond the realm of concrete
experience must be taken on faith, if it is to be accepted at all; the
truths of religion cannot be demonstrated by logic. Although some
of the earlier nominalists inclined toward religious skepticism, the
majority became mystics. Nominalism flourished in the fourteenth
century and for some time was the most popular philosophy in
western Europe. Its ablest exponent was the English Franciscan,
William of Occam. Nominalism is especially important for having
laid the foundations for the scientific progress of the Renaissance
and for the mystical religious movements which helped to bring on
the Protestant Revolution.

A good many medieval philosophers devoted earnest attention to
questions of political authority; a few, in fact, were primarily concerned with such questions. The political theorists of the later Middle Ages were in substantial agreement on a large part of their philosophy. Practically all of them had abandoned the idea of the
Church Fathers that the state was established by God as a remedy
for sin, and that men must therefore render faithful obedience even
to the tyrant. It was now commonly held that the state is a product

of man's social nature, and that when justice is the guiding principle of the ruler, government is a positive good, not a necessary evil. In the second place, it was generally agreed by the philosophers of the later Middle Ages that all of western Europe should constitute a single commonwealth under one supreme ruler. There might be many subordinate kings or princes in the different parts of the continent, but one supreme overlord, either the Pope or the Holy Roman Emperor, should have the highest jurisdiction. The most noted of those who defended the supremacy of the Emperor was Dante in his *De Monarchia*. On the papal side were the Englishman John of Salisbury (*ca.* 1115–1180) and Thomas Aquinas. Virtually without exception the political theorists of the later Middle Ages believed in limited government. They had no use for absolutism in any form. John of Salisbury even went so far as to defend the right of the subjects of a tyrant to put him to death. Practically all of late medieval theory was based upon the assumption that the authority of every ruler, whether pope, emperor, or king, was essentially judicial in character. His function was merely to apply the law, not to make or alter it in accordance with his will. Indeed, the medievalists did not conceive of law as the command of a sovereign at all, but as the product of custom or of the divine order of nature. On the other hand, the medieval political theorists were not democrats, for not one of them believed in the doctrine of majority rule. The man who came closest to an exposition of the democratic ideal was Marsiglio of Padua in the fourteenth century. He advocated that the people should have the right to elect the monarch and even to depose him if necessary. He believed also in a representative body with power to make laws. But Marsiglio was no champion of unlimited popular sovereignty. In fact, he defined democracy as a degraded form of government. His idea of representative government was representation of the citizens according to quality rather than mere numbers, and the law-making powers of his representative body would be confined to the enactment of statutes regulating the structure of the government.

II. SCIENCE   The record of scientific achievements in the later Middle Ages can scarcely be considered an imposing one. Yet it was probably about all we should expect in view of the absorption of interest in other fields. The names of only a few individual scientists need to be mentioned. One of the most original was Adelard of Bath, who lived in the early years of the twelfth century. Not only did he condemn reliance upon authority, but he devoted many years of his life to direct investigation of nature. He discovered some important facts about the causes of earthquakes, the functions of different parts of the brain, and the processes of breathing and digestion. He was probably the first scientist since the Hellenistic Age to affirm the indestructibility of matter.

482   The toughest-minded of all the medieval scientists was the notorious Holy Roman Emperor, Frederick II, whose reign occupied the first part of the thirteenth century. Frederick was skeptical of almost everything. He denied the immortality of the soul, and he was accused of having written a brochure entitled *Jesus, Moses and Mohammed: The Three Great Impostors.* But he was not satisfied merely to scoff. He performed various experiments of his own to gratify his boundless curiosity, testing the artificial incubation of eggs, for example, and sealing the eyes of vultures to determine whether they found their food by sight or by smell. His most important scientific contributions were made, however, as a patron of learning. An ardent admirer of Saracenic culture, he brought distinguished scholars to Palermo to translate the writings of the Saracens

Alchemists in Their Laboratory. Note the great variety of instruments used and the spectacles worn by the experimenter.

into Latin. He subsidized leading scientists, especially Leonard of Pisa, the most brilliant mathematician of the thirteenth century. In addition, Frederick instituted measures for the improvement of medical practice. He legalized the practice of dissection, established a system of examining and licensing physicians, and founded the University of Naples with one of the best medical schools in Europe.

By far the best known of medieval scientists was Roger Bacon (*ca.* 1214–1294), possibly because he predicted certain modern inventions such as horseless carriages and flying machines. In reality, Bacon was less critical than Frederick II; he believed that all knowledge must enhance the glory of theology, the queen of the sciences. Moreover, Adelard of Bath preceded him by more than a century in advocating and using the experimental method. Nevertheless, Bacon, by virtue of his strong insistence upon accurate investigation, deserves a high place among medieval scientists. He denied that either **483** reason or authority could furnish valid knowledge unless supported by experimental research. Besides, he himself did some practical work of great value. His writings on optics remained authoritative for several centuries. He discovered much about magnifying lenses, and it seems more than probable that he invented the simple microscope. He demonstrated that light travels faster than sound, and he was apparently the first scientist to perceive the inaccuracy of the Julian calendar and to advocate its revision.

III. EDUCATION   Much of the advancement in philosophy and science in the later Middle Ages would have been quite impossible

The transfer of
education from
the monasteries
to the cathedral
schools

without the educational progress which marked the centuries from the ninth to the fourteenth. The Carolingian Renaissance resulted in the establishment of better schools and libraries in several of the monasteries of western Europe. Many of these institutions, however, were destroyed during the chaos of the ninth century. As a consequence of the religious reform movements of the eleventh century, the monasteries tended to neglect education, with the result that the monastic schools that had survived were gradually overshadowed by the cathedral schools. Some of the latter developed into what would now be considered the equivalent of colleges, providing excellent instruction in the so-called liberal arts. This was notably true of the cathedral schools located at Canterbury, Chartres, and Paris. But by far the most important educational development of the Middle Ages was the rise of the universities.

The term university (from the Latin, *universitas*) originally meant a corporation or guild. In fact, many of the medieval univer-

The rise of the
universities

sities were very much like craft guilds, organized for the purpose of training and licensing teachers. Gradually the word came to have the meaning of an educational institution with a school of liberal arts and one or more faculties in the professional subjects of law, medicine, and theology. No one knows which of the universities

See color map
at page 488

was the oldest. It may have been Salerno, which was a center of medical study as far back as the tenth century. The universities of Bologna and Paris are also very ancient, the former having been established about 1150 and the latter before the end of the twelfth century. The next oldest included such famous institutions as the universities of Oxford, Cambridge, Montpellier, Salamanca, and Naples. There were no universities in Germany until the fourteenth century, when schools of this type were organized at Prague, Vienna, Heidelberg, and Cologne. By the end of the Middle Ages some eighty universities had been established in western Europe.

Practically every university in medieval Europe was patterned after one or the other of two different models. Throughout Italy,

Organization
of the medieval
universities

Spain, and southern France the standard was generally the University of Bologna, in which the students themselves constituted the guild or corporation. They hired the teachers, paid their salaries,

and fined or discharged them for neglect of duty or inefficient in-

A Noted Teacher, Henricus de Alemania, Lecturing in a Medieval University. Some interesting comparisons and contrasts may be observed between his students and those in a modern classroom.

struction. Nearly all of these southern institutions were secular in character, specializing in law or medicine. The universities of northern Europe were modeled after the one at Paris, which was not a guild of students but of teachers. It included the four faculties of arts, theology, law, and medicine, each headed by an elected dean. In the great majority of the northern universities arts and theology were the leading branches of study. Before the end of the thirteenth century separate colleges came to be established within the University of Paris. The original college was nothing more than an endowed home for poor students, but the discovery was soon made that discipline could best be preserved by having all of the students live in colleges. Eventually the colleges became centers of instruction as well as residences. While on the Continent of Europe most of these colleges have ceased to exist, in England the universities of Oxford and Cambridge still retain the pattern of federal organization copied from Paris. The colleges of which they are composed are practically independent educational units.

Though modern universities have borrowed much of their organization from their medieval prototypes, the course of study has been radically changed. No curriculum in the Middle Ages included **485** much history or natural science, nor any great amount of mathematics. The educator of today who believes that mathematics and the sciences should form the backbone of university training can find no support for his argument in the history of the medieval universities. The student in the Middle Ages was required, first of all, to spend four or five years in studying the *trivium*—grammar, rhetoric, and logic, or dialectic. If he passed his examinations he received the preliminary degree of bachelor of arts, which conferred no particular distinction. To assure himself a place in professional life he must devote some additional years to the pursuit of an advanced degree, such as master of arts, doctor of laws, or doctor of medicine. For the master's degree three or four years had to be given to study of the *quadrivium*—arithmetic, geometry, astronomy, and music. These subjects were not quite what their names imply now. Their content was highly philosophical; arithmetic, for example, included primarily a study of the theory of numbers, while music was concerned largely with the properties of sound. The requirements for the doctor's degree were generally more severe and included more specialized training. By the end of the Middle Ages the course for the doctorate of theology at Paris had been extended to fourteen years, and the degree could not be conferred unless the candidate was at least thirty-five years of age. Both the master's and doctor's degrees were teaching degrees; even the title of doctor of medicine meant a teacher of medicine, not a practicing physician.

The life of medieval students differed in many ways from that of their modern descendants. The student body in any one university was not a homogeneous group but was composed of diverse nationalities. The young Frenchman or German who wanted to study law would almost certainly go to Bologna or Padua, just as the young Italian with an interest in theology would probably enroll at Paris. The entire university was usually an independent community, and the students were consequently exempt from the jurisdiction of political authorities. A relic of this ancient autonomy is to be found in the fact that some of the German universities still have their own jails. The learning process consisted primarily in taking down copious notes on wax tablets from the master's lecture and then analyzing and discussing them afterwards. The young man's education was supposed to be acquired through logic and memory rather than from extensive reading or research. In other respects, however, student life in the Middle Ages was not so far different from what it is now. If the medieval student knew nothing of intercollegiate sports, he at least had his violent fights with the hoodlums of the town to absorb his surplus energy. In the medieval universities as in those of today there were the sharply contrasting types of sincere, intelligent scholars and frank and frivolous loafers. We hear much about radicalism and irreverence in modern colleges, but these tendencies were certainly not absent in the universities of the Mid-

The course of study

The university students

dle Ages. Many of these institutions were roundly denounced as breeding places of heresy, paganism, and worldliness. It was said that young men "seek theology at Paris, law at Bologna, and medicine at Montpellier, but nowhere a life that is pleasing to God." The students at Paris even had to be admonished to stop playing dice on the altar of Notre Dame after one of their holiday celebrations.

IV. LITERATURE No one who has more than a casual acquaintance with the literature of the later Middle Ages could ever imagine the whole medieval period to have been an era of darkness and otherworldliness. For much of this literature expresses a zest for living as spontaneous, joyous, and gay as any attitude revealed in the writings of the Renaissance of the fourteenth and succeeding centuries. Indeed, the spirit of late medieval literature was even closer to that of the modern age than most people realize. Probably the actual amount of religious literature in the later Middle Ages did not bear a much larger ratio to the total quantity of writings produced than would be true at the present time.

Late medieval writings can be classified, first of all, as either Latin or vernacular literature. The revival of classical studies in the cathedral schools and in the earliest universities led to the production of some excellent Latin poetry. The best examples of this were the secular lyrics, especially those written by a group of poets known as the Goliards or Goliardi. The Goliards derived their name from the fact that they commonly referred to themselves as disciples of Golias. Who Golias was, no one knows, but one scholar thinks that he was probably the devil.[6] Such a choice of a master would undoubtedly have been appropriate enough, for most of the Goliard poets were regarded by the Church as lewd fellows of the baser sort for whom nothing was too sacred to be ridiculed. They wrote parodies of the creeds, travesties of the mass, and even burlesques of the Gospels. Their lyrics were purely pagan in spirit, celebrating the beauties of the changing seasons, the carefree life of the open road, the pleasures of drinking and gambling, and especially the joys of love. The authors of these rollicking and satirical songs were mostly wandering students, although some appear to have been men more advanced in years. The names of nearly all of them are unknown. Their poetry is particularly significant as the first emphatic protest against the ascetic ideal of Christianity. The following stanzas taken from *The Confession of Golias* may be considered typical of what they wrote:

> Prelate, most discreet of priests,
> Grant me absolution!
> Dear's the death whereof I die,
> Sweet my dissolution;
> For my heart is wounded by

THE LATE MEDIEVAL MIND

The humanistic quality of late medieval literature

Latin literature: the poetry of the Goliards

[6] C. H. Haskins, *The Renaissance of the Twelfth Century*, p. 177.

487

Beauty's soft suffusion;
All the girls I come not nigh
Mine are in illusion.
'Tis most arduous to make

Nature's self-surrender;
Seeing girls, to blush and be
Purity's defender!
We young men our longings ne'er
Shall to stern law render,
Or preserve our fancies from
Bodies smooth and tender.[7]

The growth of vernacular literature

By no means all of medieval literature was written in Latin. As the Middle Ages waned, the vernacular languages of French, German, Spanish, English, and Italian became increasingly popular as media of literary expression. Until the beginning of the twelfth century nearly all of the literature in the vernacular languages assumed the form of the heroic epic. Among the leading examples were the French *Song of Roland*, the German *Song of the Nibelungs*, the eddas and sagas of the Norsemen, and the Spanish *Poem of My Cid*. These epics picture a virile but unpolished feudal society in its earlier stage of evolution, when valorous deeds in battle on behalf of one's suzerain represented the fulfillment of the highest knightly ideal. Heroism, honor, and loyalty were practically the exclusive themes. The tone of the epics was almost entirely masculine. If women were mentioned at all, it was generally in a condescending fashion. The hero must show the utmost devotion to his superior, but it was not considered inappropriate that he should beat his wife.

The literature of chivalry: (1) the songs of the troubadours

During the twelfth and thirteenth centuries feudal society in western Europe attained the full flower of its growth. As a result of the progress of learning and of contact with the higher civilization of the Saracens, the feudal aristocracy adopted new attitudes and interests. Chivalry, with its glorification of woman and its emphasis upon kindness and refinement of manners, tended to displace the older conception of a feudal ideal limited to the virtues of the battlefield. The first literary works to reflect and in part to inspire this change in ideals were the songs of the troubadours. The original home of the troubadours was southern France, especially the region known as Provence. Here was one of the most highly civilized areas of feudal Europe. It received the full impact of Saracenic influence from Spain, and it seems to have preserved an extensive inheritance from ancient Rome. Whatever the reasons, there can be no doubt that the troubadours of Provence initiated a movement of profound importance in late medieval literature. The central theme of their

[7] J. A. Symonds, *Wine, Women and Song*, p. 66.

0   500 miles

NORWAY

SWEDEN

△ Upsala

NORTH
SEA

SCOTLAND
△ Aberdeen
△ St. Andrews
△ Glasgow

DENMARK

△ Copenhagen

BALTIC SEA

ENGLAND

Cambridge ■
△ Oxford

Elbe R.

Rostock ▲
Greifswald ▲

Frankfurt △

Vistula R.

POLAND

Cracow △

Rhine R.

Louvain ●
Cologne ●
Trèves ▲
Mayence ●
HOLY ROMAN

Wittenburg ●
Leipzig △
Erfurt ●

Oder R.

Würzburg △
Heidelberg △

Prague ●

ATLANTIC

OCEAN

Caen △
Seine R.
Paris △

Freiburg △
EMPIRE
Ingolstadt △
Tübingen ▲

Danube R.

Vienna △
AUSTRIA

Pressburg △

Buda ●

HUNGARY

Angers ■
Orléans ■
Nantes ●
Bourges ▲
Poitiers △
Loire R.
FRANCE
Besançon ●
Dole ●
Basel ▲
SWITZ.

Treviso ●

VENETIAN REPUBLIC

Bordeaux △
Cahors ●
Lyons ●
Grenoble ●
Vercelli ■
Turin ●
Pavia ●
Vicenza △
Piacenza ●
Reggio ●
Padua ■
Ferrara ●
Bologna △

ADRIATIC SEA

Montpellier △
Rhone R.
Valence ●
Orange ●
Avignon ●
Aix ●
Toulouse △
Florence ●
Siena ●
Arezzo ●
Perugia ●

Perpignan ●

Ebro R.
Palencia ■
Valladolid ●
Huesca ●
Saragossa ●
Lérida ●
Siguenza △
Barcelona △

CORSICA

PAPAL
STATES
Rome ●

Coimbra ●
Salamanca ■
Avila △
Alcalá de Henares △
Toledo ●
PORTUGAL
Tagus R.
SPAIN

Naples ■
Salerno △

Lisbon ■

Valencia △

BALEARIC
Palma ● MAJORCA
ISLANDS

SARDINIA

THE TWO

Seville ■

MEDITERRANEAN

Palermo ●
SICILIES
Catania △

SEA

THE RISE OF THE MEDIEVAL UNIVERSITY

△ Founded in the 12th century

■ Founded in the 13th century

● Founded in the 14th century   - - - - - Boundaries ca. 1500 A.D.

▲ Founded in the 15th century

Vespers of the Holy Ghost, with a View of Paris, Jean Fouquet. From the *Book of Hours* of Etienne Chevalier, 1461. Demons in the sky are sent flying by the divine light from Heaven. The cathedral is Notre Dame. (Robert Lehman)

A Scholar at Work. From the Flemish manuscript *The Golden Legend*, 1445–1460. This beautiful book came at the end of the era of costly handwritten, hand-decorated manuscripts. (Morgan Library)

songs was romantic love. Woman was idealized now as never before. The virtues of her who had once been condemned by monks and Church Fathers as the very incarnation of evil were extolled to the skies. But the love of the troubadours for the ladies of the feudal courts was not supposed to be sensual; it was a rarefied, almost mystical emotion which could be satisfied by a smile or some trifling memento from the haughty goddesses who were the objects of the singers' affection. The fact must be emphasized also that romantic love was not the only topic in which the troubadours were interested. Many wrote acrid satires against the rapacity and hypocrisy of the clergy, and one even addressed a powerful "poem of blame" to God. The literary tradition originated by the troubadours was continued by the *trouvères* in northern France and by the *minnesingers* in Germany.

The most important of all the writings which expressed the ideals of the feudal aristocracy were the romances of the Arthurian cycle. The material of these romances consisted of legends woven about the career of a Celtic chieftain by the name of Arthur, who had been the hero of the struggle against the Anglo-Saxon invaders of Britain. In the twelfth century certain Norman and French writers, especially Marie de France and Chrétien de Troyes, became interested in these legends as a background for the chivalric ideal. The result was the composition of a number of romances of love and adventure, famous alike for their colorful narrative and their poetic beauty. Later the best known of these romances were adapted and completed by German poets. Wolfram von Eschenbach developed what is usually considered the most perfect version of the Parzival legend, while Gottfried von Strassburg gave to the story of Tristan and Isolde its classic medieval form. Although these romances differed in form and in substance, they may yet be said to have had features in common. All of them glorified adventure for its own sake, and taught that experience of the deepest and most varied kind is the only sure road to wisdom. All of them strove to inculcate gentleness, protection of the weak, and rescue of those in distress as knightly obligations, in addition to honor, truthfulness, and bravery. The redeeming power of love was another universal element, although not all of the authors agreed as to the form which this love should assume. Some maintained that it ought to be the faithful affection between husband and wife, but others insisted that it must be love unsustained by wedlock. In the minds of the latter group true love was possible only between knight and mistress, never between husband and wife. Finally, in the best of these romances an element of tragedy was nearly always present. Indeed, such a work as Gottfried von Strassburg's *Tristan* might almost be regarded as the prototype of modern tragic literature. He was certainly one of the first to develop the idea of individual suffering as a literary theme and to point out the indistinct dividing line which separates

(2) the romances of the Arthurian cycle

pleasure from pain. For him, to love is to yearn, and suffering and death are integral chapters of the book of life.

By the thirteenth century the merchants and craftsmen of the towns had risen to a position of power and influence equal if not superior to that of the feudal nobles. We can therefore logically expect that some literature would be written to appeal to burgher tastes. Among the foremost examples of such writings were the romance of *Aucassin and Nicolette* and the short stories in verse known as the *fabliaux*. The romance of *Aucassin and Nicolette* resembles in some ways the romances of chivalry. The hero Aucassin is a young noble, and the main theme of the romance is the imperious demands of love; but the plot is frequently turned into channels distinctly at variance with the chivalric ideal. Aucassin has fallen desperately in love, not with the high-born wife of some noble, but with Nicolette, a Saracen slave girl. Warned that he will suffer in hell if he does not give up his beloved, the hero replies that he does not mind, for in hell he will enjoy the company of all who have really lived. The story is also quite different from the romances of chivalry in its occasional expression of sympathy for the peasant. But the writings which undoubtedly made the strongest appeal to the urban classes were the *fabliaux*. These were stories written not to edify or instruct but chiefly to amuse. Often richly spiced with indecency, they reveal a contempt for the trappings of chivalry, with its romanticized love and idiotic pursuit of adventure. Most of them are also strongly anti-clerical and indicate no high regard for the religious spirit. Nearly always it is monks and priests who are made the butts of the jokes. The *fabliaux* are significant as expressions of the growing worldliness of the urban classes and as forerunners of the robust realism which was later to appear in the works of such writers as Chaucer and Boccaccio.

The supreme achievements of medieval literary talent were two great masterpieces written in the thirteenth and fourteenth centuries. The first was the *Romance of the Rose* of William of Lorris and John of Meun, and the second was Dante's *Divine Comedy*. Each in its own way is a kind of summary of late medieval civilization. The *Romance of the Rose* consists of two parts: the first 4000 lines were begun by William of Lorris about 1230; the other part, nearly three times as long, was finished by John of Meun about 1265. The two parts are entirely different, the first being an allegory dealing with the cult of chivalric love, while the second is a eulogy of reason. John of Meun was quite skeptical of the value of the feudal aristocracy to medieval society; he hated superstition; and he satirized the monastic orders, the papacy, and many other established institutions of his time. He embodied the mocking, realistic attitude of the bourgeoisie, as his predecessor, William of Lorris, symbolized the romantic, mystical spirit of chivalry. The work of the two men taken together furnishes a kind of guidebook to the later Middle Ages.

Without doubt the most profound of the medieval summaries was the *Divine Comedy* of Dante Alighieri (1265–1321). Not a great deal is known about the life of Dante except that he was the son of a Florentine lawyer and was active during the early part of his career in the political affairs of his city. Despite his absorption in politics he managed to acquire a full mastery of the philosophic and literary knowledge of his time. In 1302 the party to which he belonged was ousted from power in Florence, and he was compelled to live the remainder of his years outside of his native city. Most of his writings were apparently produced during this period of exile. Dante called his chief work simply the *Comedy*, but his admirers during the Italian Renaissance always spoke of it as the *Divine Comedy*, and that is the title which has come down to us. In form the work may be considered a drama of the struggles, temptations, and ultimate redemption of the soul. But of course it is much more than this; for it embraces a complete summation of medieval culture, a magnificent synthesis of the Scholastic philosophy, the science, the religion, and the economic and ethical ideals of the later Middle Ages. Its dominant theme is the salvation of mankind through reason and divine grace, but it includes many other ideas as well. The universe is conceived as a finite world of which the earth is the center and in which everything exists for the benefit of man. All natural phenomena have their meaning in relation to the divine scheme for peace and justice on earth and salvation in the life beyond. Human beings possess free will to choose the good and avoid the evil. The worst of the sins which man can commit is treason or betrayal of trust; the least serious are those which proceed from weakness of the flesh. Dante took earnest pleasure in the classical authors, almost worshiping Aristotle, Seneca, and Vergil. He chose Vergil rather than some Christian theologian to personify philosophy. By reason of his imaginative power and the warmth and vigor of his style, he deserves to be ranked as one of the greatest poets of all time, but he is especially important to the historian because of the well-rounded picture he presents of the late medieval mind.

The Divine Comedy

5. ART AND MUSIC IN THE LATER MIDDLE AGES

The later Middle Ages produced two great styles of architecture, the Romanesque and the Gothic. The Romanesque was mainly a product of the monastic revival and attained its full development in the century and a half following the year 1000. Fundamentally it was an ecclesiastical architecture, symbolizing the pride of the monastic orders at the height of their power. Naturally, since the Cluniac revival affected the entire Church, the Romanesque style

Architecture: the Romanesque style

MEDIEVAL ARCHITECTURE: ROMANESQUE AND GOTHIC

Top left: *Worms Cathedral, Eleventh Century, Romanesque.* It still stands, though most of the city was destroyed in World War II.

Bottom left: *The Cathedral of Chartres, France.* Regarded by some as the purest and most beautiful example of Gothic design, the Cathedral of Chartres is renowned for the grace and perfect proportions of its towers. The one on the right was built in the thirteenth century and reflects the simpler Gothic style of that period. The one on the left was finished in the sixteenth century and reveals some of the influence of flamboyant Gothic.

Top right: *City Hall of Brussels, Belgium*. The main façade shown here was built between 1400 and 1450. The building is an impressive example of secular Gothic.

Bottom right: *The High Chapel of la Sainte-Chapelle, Paris*. High Gothic is here carried to its logical extreme. Slender columns, tracery, and stained glass windows take the place of walls.

was not confined to monasteries. Nevertheless, it is significant that some of the most impressive Romanesque buildings were houses of the Cluniac order. The essential features of this building style were the round arch, massive walls, enormous piers, small windows, gloomy interiors, and the predominance of horizontal lines. The plainness of interiors was sometimes relieved by mosaics or by frescoing in bright colors, but the style of construction was not such as to encourage elaborate ornamentation. Moreover, the strong religious spirit in which this architecture was conceived did not generally foster an appeal to the senses. Some of the architects of

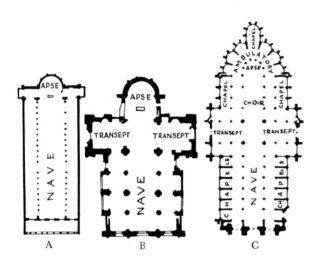

Evolution of the Floor Plan of the Medieval Cathedral. A is the plan of the Early Christian basilica, the Church of Santa Maria Maggiore in Rome, built in the fourth century. It is a simple plan of rectangular building with nave flanked by colonnades and side aisles. *B* is the Church of San Michele at Pavia, twelfth century, Romanesque, with the apse elongated and transepts added, giving the church the form of a Latin cross. *C* is the Cathedral at Amiens, thirteenth-century Gothic. Here the typical Gothic plan shows up—the side aisles continue around the elongated choir and apse, forming the ambulatory, off which radiate the chapels, and the transepts are fully developed with side aisles.

southern Europe, however, succeeded in breaking away from this somber monastic tradition and often decorated their churches with an elaborate symbolic sculpture.

In the late twelfth and thirteenth centuries the Romanesque architecture was superseded in popularity by the Gothic. The increase in wealth, the advancement of learning, the growth of secular interests, and the pride of the cities in their newly acquired freedom and prosperity led to a demand for a more elaborate architectural style to express the ideals of the new age. Besides, the monastic revival had now spent its force. Gothic architecture was almost exclusively urban. Its monuments were not monasteries situated on lonely crags but cathedrals, bishops' churches, located in the largest cities and towns. It must be understood, though, that the medieval cathedral was not simply a church but a center of the community life. It generally housed a school and a library and was sometimes used as a town hall. It was often large enough to accommodate the whole population of the town. The people of the entire community participated in erecting it, and they rightfully regarded it as civic property.

The Romanesque
architecture gives
way to the Gothic

Indeed, many of the Gothic cathedrals were the outcome of town
rivalry. For example, the people of Siena became dissatisfied with
their modest church after the cathedral at Florence was completed
and determined to build a new one on a much more pretentious
scale. Frequently the citizens' ambitions got far out of bounds, with
the result that many of the buildings were left unfinished. The
architects of the Cathedral of Chartres, for instance, planned for
several more lofty towers than were ever completed.

Gothic architecture was one of the most intricate of building
styles. Its basic elements were the pointed arch, groined and ribbed
vaulting, and the flying buttress. These devices made possible a   The Gothic style
much lighter and loftier construction than could ever have been

Cross Sections of Medieval Cathedrals:
A, Romanesque Abbaye-aux-hommes;
B, French Gothic cathedral of Amiens.
Note the round Romanesque arches in
A as well as the method of buttressing
the nave vaulting by the half-barrel
vault over the triforium gallery. In *B*
the pointed Gothic arch makes for a
higher nave vaulting and, in all, the
frame of the structure is lighter. Here
can be seen the typical flying buttress-
es which take the thrust of the nave
vaulting clear of the main structure to
the great masonry buttress piers.

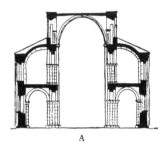
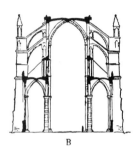

A   B

achieved with the round arch and the engaged pier of the Romanesque. In fact, the Gothic cathedral could be described as a
skeletal framework of stone enclosed by enormous windows. Other
features included lofty spires, rose windows, delicate tracery in
stone, elaborately carved façades, multiple columns, and the use of
gargoyles, or representations of mythical monsters, as decorative devices. Ornamentation in the best of the cathedrals was generally
concentrated on the exterior. Except for the stained glass windows   *See color plates*
and the intricate carving on woodwork and altars, interiors were   *at pages 424, 425,*
kept rather simple and occasionally almost severe. But the inside of   *489*
the Gothic cathedral was never somber or gloomy. The stained glass
windows served not to exclude the light but to glorify it, to catch
the rays of sunlight and suffuse them with a richness and warmth of
color which nature herself could hardly produce even in her gayest
moods.

The significance of Gothic architecture is frequently misunderstood. As a matter of fact, its very name, implying that the art was
of barbarian origin, was originally a term of reproach given to it by
the men of the Renaissance, who wanted to express their contempt
for everything medieval. Many people still think of the Gothic
cathedral as a product of an ascetic and otherworldly civilization. **495**

Nothing could be more inaccurate. Insofar as Gothic architecture was spiritual at all, it was the symbol of a religion which had come to recognize the importance of this life. But as we have already seen, the cathedral was more than a church. It was in large part an expression of the new secular spirit which had grown out of the rise of cities and the progress of enlightenment. Many of the scenes depicted on the stained glass windows—a medieval bakeshop in operation, for instance—had no direct religious significance whatever. The definite appeal to the senses revealed in the sparkling radiance of colored glass and in the naturalistic sculpture of saints and the Virgin gives positive proof that man's interest in his human self and in the world of natural beauty was no longer considered a sin. Last of all, Gothic architecture was an expression of the medieval intellectual genius. The complicated design, the perfect balance of thrust and counterthrust, and the soaring height of the buildings represented not only the triumph of reasoning skill, but also a desire to burst the confines of limited knowledge and push upward into the highest realms of truth. Each cathedral, with its detailed mass of carvings of plant and animal life and symbolic figures, was a kind of encyclopedia of medieval knowledge—a culture epic in stone.

Music in the later Middle Ages was the product of an evolution extending far back into the early history of medieval Europe. The beginning of this evolution was the development of the so-called plain chant, a vast body of melodies that is virtually an anthology of folk, cultic, and composed music of many centuries. Its collection and organization took a long time, though it is ascribed by tradition to Pope Gregory the Great—hence its name: Gregorian chant. The Gregorian chant is a single, unaccompanied line of music of great melodic and rhythmic subtlety, much of which is lost on us, accustomed as we are to a harmonic background. By the tenth century we encounter the first written monuments of music for more than one line, which consisted of another line running parallel with the first at the distance of a fourth or fifth. The next step in evolution was the introduction of the principle of contrary motion; the second part asserted its independence by not running parallel with the first but following its own bent. It is significant, however, that the modern concept of *harmony*, that is, a vertical organization of sounds (melody with accompaniment) was lacking. The new line of music (called "voice" or "part") was set *against* the existing one, dot against dot, *punctus contra punctum* ("dot" standing for "note") —hence the term counterpoint. Thus the development was linear, each melodic line was largely independent. This type of music is called polyphonic in contrast to homophonic, the harmonically ordered style. The twelfth and thirteenth centuries produced great schools of musical composition that demonstrated considerable skill in weaving together two, three, and even four independent voice-parts. A particular manifestation of music in the later Middle Ages

was the art of the troubadours, *trouvères*, and minnesingers. With
them a new and altogether Western conception enters music: individual invention. Troubadour comes from the French verb *trouver*, to find (invent); this kind of musician does not use inherited, traditional tunes but "finds" his own. Among the kings and knights of France of the north and of Provence, there were many fine creative artists. The German minnesingers (from the Middle High German word *minne*, "love") patterned themselves after the composing French aristocracy. Secular music was kept under wraps by the Church, but it was nevertheless well developed and by 1300 we come across reliable descriptions of its nature. Music also formed part of the liberal arts as taught at the university, but its study was purely mathematical and philosophical.

SELECTED READINGS

· *Items so designated are available in paperbound editions.*
· Adams, Henry, *Mont-Saint-Michel and Chartres*, New York, 1913 (Mentor). Stimulating and provocative.
Artz, F. B., *The Mind of the Middle Ages*, New York, 1954. Brief but scholarly and interesting.
· Bainton, R. H., *The Medieval Church*, Princeton, 1964 (Anvil).
· Brundage, J. A., *The Crusades: Motives and Achievements*, New York, 1964 (Heath).
Chaytor, H. J., *The Troubadours*, Cambridge, Mass., 1912.
· Cheyney, E. P., *The Dawn of a New Era, 1250–1453*, New York, 1936 (Torchbook). Written in a clear and interesting style.
· Copleston, F. C., *Medieval Philosophy*, New York, 1961 (Torchbook).
Crombie, A. C., *From Augustine to Galileo*, Cambridge, 1961.
Crump, C. G., and Jacob, E. F., *The Legacy of the Middle Ages*, New York, 1926. Especially good on medieval arts and crafts.
Easton, Stewart C., *Roger Bacon and His Search for a Universal Science*, New York, 1952.
Evans, Joan, *Art in Medieval France*, London, 1948.
Flick, A. C., *The Decline of the Medieval Church*, New York, 1930, 2 vols. A mine of information.
Gardner, Helen, *Art through the Ages*, New York, 1948. Comprehensive and valuable.
Gilson, E. H., *The Philosophy of St. Thomas Aquinas*, Cambridge, Mass., 1924.
· ———, *Dante the Philosopher*, London, 1948 (Torchbook).
Haskins, C. H., *Studies in Medieval Culture*, New York, 1929.
· ———, *The Renaissance of the Twelfth Century*, Cambridge, Mass., 1928 (Meridian). Excellent.
Hearnshaw, F. J. C., *The Social and Political Ideas of Some Great Medieval Thinkers*, New York, 1923.
· Heer, Friedrich, *The Medieval World*, New York, 1964 (Mentor).
· Huizinga, J., *The Waning of the Middle Ages*, New York, 1954 (Anchor). A provocative interpretation.
Jones, Charles W., ed., *Medieval Literature in Translation*, New York, 1950.
497

Lang, Paul, *Music in Western Civilization*, New York, 1941.

Latourette, K. S., *A History of Christianity*, New York, 1953.

• Lieff, Gordon, *Medieval Thought*, Baltimore, 1958 (Penguin).

Mazzeo, J. A., *The Medieval Cultural Tradition in Dante's Comedy*, Ithaca, N.Y., 1960.

• McGiffert, A. C., *History of Christian Thought*, New York, 1932, Vol. II (Scribner Library).

McIlwain, C. H., *The Growth of Political Thought in the West*, New York, 1932. Perhaps the best interpretation.

Morey, C. R., *Medieval Art*, New York, 1942.

Packard, Sidney, *Europe and the Church under Innocent III*, New York, 1927. Contains much excellent material.

• Panofsky, Erwin, *Gothic Architecture and Scholasticism*, Cleveland, 1957 (Meridian).

Rashdall, Hastings, *The Universities of Europe in the Middle Ages*, New York, 1936, 2 vols. The standard work.

Reese, Gustave, *Music in the Middle Ages*, New York, 1940.

• Runciman, Stephen, *A History of the Crusades*, New York, 1951–54, 3 vols. (Torchbook). Complete and authoritative.

Setton, K. M., ed., *A History of the Crusades*, Philadelphia, 1955. Vol. 1.

• Southern, R. W., *The Making of the Middle Ages*, New Haven, 1953 (Yale University Press).

Taylor, H. O., *The Medieval Mind*, New York, 1927, 2 vols. Good for interpretation.

Tout, T. F., *The Empire and the Papacy, 918–1273*, London, 1941. A standard work.

Vossler, Karl, *Medieval Culture: An Introduction to Dante and His Times*, New York, 1929, 2 vols. Profound and very valuable for the student with a good background of medieval knowledge.

• Waddell, Helen, *The Wandering Scholars*, London, 1927 (Anchor). A vivid and sympathetic account.

• ———, *Peter Abelard*, New York, 1933 (Compass). Valuable not only as biography but for its grasp of the spirit of medieval culture.

SOURCE MATERIALS

Abelard, Peter, *The Story of My Misfortunes*.

Baumer, F. L. V., *Main Currents of Western Thought*, New York, 1952.

Coulton, G. G., *A Medieval Garner*, London, 1910.

Jones, C. W., ed., *Medieval Literature in Translation*, New York, 1950.

Krey, A. C., *The First Crusade; The Accounts of Eyewitnesses and Participants*.

• Marzialis, F. T., tr., *Memoirs of the Crusades*, for *Villehardouin's Chronicle of the Fourth Crusade* and *Joinville's Chronicle of the Crusade of St. Louis* (Dutton).

Pegis, A. C., ed., *Basic Writings of St. Thomas Aquinas*, 2 vols.

• Polo, Marco, *Travels* (Dell and others).

• Poole, R. L., *Illustrations of the History of Medieval Thought and Learning* (Dover).

Robinson, Paschal, tr., *The Writings of St. Francis of Assisi*.

Thatcher, O. J., and McNeal, E. H., *A Source Book for Medieval History*, New York, 1905, pp. 513–21, Speech of Urban at Council of Clermont.

CHAPTER 17

India and the Far East in the
Later Middle Ages

Seldom [have] two civilizations, so vast and so strongly developed, yet so radically dissimilar as the Muhammadan and Hindu, [met and mingled] together. The very contrasts which existed between them, the wide divergences in their culture and their religions, make the history of their impact peculiarly instructive and lend an added interest to the art and above all to the architecture which their united genius called into being.
—Sir John Marshall, in *Cambridge History of India*, Vol. III

The centuries which are known in the West as the Middle Ages did not have quite the same importance for the civilizations of the Eastern lands as they did for the evolution of European civilization. The cultures of India and China were already highly advanced, while the Western Europeans were only beginning to develop a stablized society and to utilize their intellectual resources to a significant degree. In contrast to Western Europe, which during the late medieval centuries was relatively free from external disturbances, both India and China experienced fresh invasions more sweeping in character than any they had known since the beginnings of their recorded history. They were able to survive the shock of these invasions with the essential features of their cultures intact, although permanent modifications took place in Indian society. Japan was unique among the principal Asiatic states in the fact that she was not subjected to foreign conquest. The tensions and conflicts within her own society, however, were tremendous, and they gradually produced a type of social and political organization which was remarkably similar to the feudal system of Western Europe.

Contrasts with the European Middle Ages

499

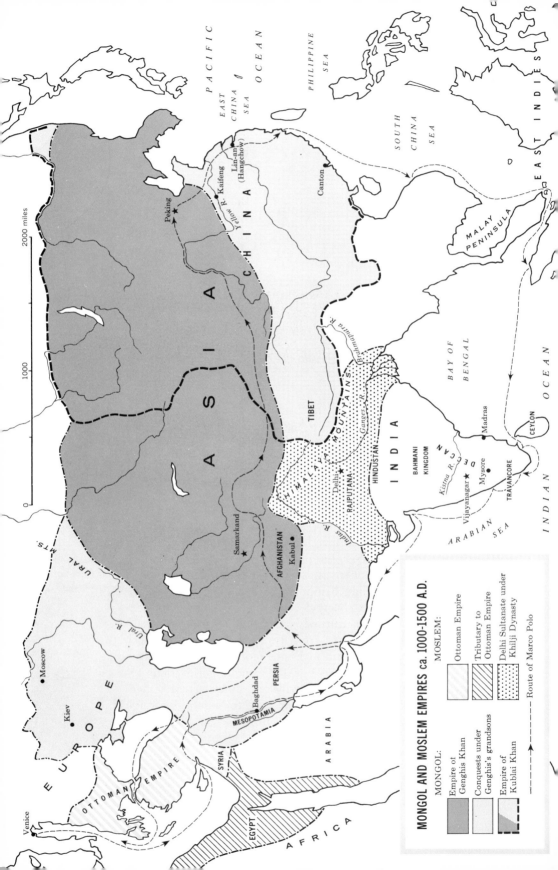

PACIFIC OCEAN

EAST CHINA SEA

PHILIPPINE SEA

SOUTH CHINA SEA

EAST INDIES

MALAY PENINSULA

A S I A

C H I N A

Peking

Yellow R.
Kaifeng
Lin-an (Hangchow)

Canton

TIBET

HIMALAYA MOUNTAINS

Brahmaputra R.
Ganges R.

BAY OF BENGAL

Madras

CEYLON

INDIAN OCEAN

Samarkand

Indus R.

AFGHANISTAN
Kabul

Delhi
RAJPUTANA
HINDUSTAN

INDIA

DECCAN

Kistna R.
BAHMANI KINGDOM

Mysore

Vijayanagar
TRAVANCORE

ARABIAN SEA

URAL MTS.

E U R O P E

Moscow

Kiev

Ural R.

PERSIA

Baghdad
MESOPOTAMIA

SYRIA

ARABIA

Venice

OTTOMAN EMPIRE

EGYPT

A F R I C A

2000 miles

1000

0

MONGOL AND MOSLEM EMPIRES ca. 1000–1500 A.D.

MONGOL:

☐ Empire of Genghis Khan

☐ Conquests under Genghis's grandsons

☐ Empire of Kublai Khan

MOSLEM:

☐ Ottoman Empire

▨ Tributary to Ottoman Empire

⋯ Delhi Sultanate under Khilji Dynasty

– – – Route of Marco Polo

1. THE ESTABLISHMENT OF MOSLEM KINGDOMS IN INDIA (*ca.* 1000–1500)

About the same time that the nations of Western Europe were initiating the economic and intellectual progress which distinguished the later Middle Ages and which made possible the brilliant culture of the Renaissance, the peoples of India were harried by a series of marauding raids that devastated their society and sorely impaired their creative talents. The invaders of this period were devotees of Islam. They implanted the Moslem religion in India so firmly that it has ever since been the faith of a substantial minority of the population. But while the expansion of Islam in Africa, Spain, and the Middle East was associated with the quickening of cultural activities and with the attainment of relatively harmonious relations between the conquerors and their subject peoples, the Moslem conquests in India led to wanton destruction and created a deep and abiding cleavage between the opposing religious groups.

The conquests of
the Turks and
Afghans

The first of the Moslem conquerors of India were Turks from Afghanistan. They did not come in numberless hordes, nor were they unresisted by native troops. The fact that they were able to sweep across the country and work such havoc is a commentary on the fateful political division of India and the lack of solidarity among her people. Ever since the decay of Harsha's empire in the seventh century, Hindustan had been disunited and subject to contention among various states. The strongest of the Hindu states were those inhabited by a group known as Rajputs. The origin of the Rajputs (the word means literally "sons of kings") is not known certainly. It is probable that they were not Indians to begin with but the descendants of Huns and other invaders of the fifth and sixth centuries who had become assimilated to Hindu society. Generally they were regarded as belonging to the *kshatriya* (warrior) caste, and they prided themselves on their military traditions. The rulers and nobility of the Rajput kingdoms had developed a code of chivalrous conduct somewhat like the cult of chivalry of the medieval European knights. They were redoubtable horsemen, proud of their skill with the sword, and hypersensitive to insult. The Rajputs were the fiercest and bravest fighters in India, but they were unable to stem the Moslem advance.

Undoubtedly the helplessness of the Indian people during this time of invasion was intensified by the caste system, which was now exacting a heavy penalty. Each stratum of the population was hedged in by its own prescribed activities and loyalties—military defense was considered to be the function of the *kshatriyas* alone. The lower classes were impoverished and dispirited, and there was little incentive for concerted action in the common interest. By contrast, the Moslem invaders were a fresh and energetic people, excited by the prospect of rich spoils and inspired by an activist creed that promised certain recompense for service in a holy war against idolators. The Hindus were not prepared to cope with such fanatical zeal as their adversaries displayed. Nevertheless, the Rajputs gave a good account of themselves in combat; and some of them, when they saw that opposition was useless, removed with their retainers into the heart of the Indian desert to rebuild their shattered communities in the region which came to be called Rajputana.

Extension of the
Moslem conquests

After its initial impact the Moslem conquest of northern India entered a new phase, characterized by the establishment of governmental centers and permanent residences on Indian soil. The most important kingdom founded by the Turks, with Delhi as its capital, gradually acquired control over all of Hindustan and even penetrated into the Deccan. Between the thirteenth and the sixteenth centuries, five successive dynasties of Turks or Afghans ruled from Delhi. The fortunes of the kingdom and the character of the rulers during these 300 years cannot be detailed here, but they varied tremendously. In one instance the sultan was a woman named Raziya, who demonstrated great energy and ability but was murdered with her husband—an Ethiopian—by jealous nobles (in 1240). Intrigues and assassinations were frequent because of the absence of an established rule of succession to the throne. By comparison with the Hindu caste-bound society, the Islamic community was democratic, and even an upstart who seized the throne by violence might be accepted as a legitimate sovereign if he proved capable. It was not uncommon for a slave who had been trained for administrative work to be entrusted with large responsibilities both civil and military and finally to usurp authority when a favorable opportunity arose. In fact, one line of Delhi rulers is known as the "Slave Kings" (1206–1290) because its founder had been a slave and viceroy of an early sultan.

Characteristics of
Moslem rule

In spite of the fact that high positions were open to men of low birth, the administration was thoroughly autocratic in operation, and it derived its character from the personality, the ambitions, or the whims of the ruler. Cruelty, depravity, enlightened statesmanship, and humanitarian sensibilities were all exemplified in erratic sequence. For example, the founder of the Khilji Dynasty (1290–1318) was a benevolent and mild-tempered old gentleman who hated to shed the blood even of criminals. The nephew who assassinated and succeeded him was a monster of treachery and cruelty, and so extortionate that he reduced his Hindu subjects to poverty. The next sultan, although scholarly and abstinent by habit, was in some ways even worse than his predecessor. He compelled the entire population of Delhi to move to another site 600 miles distant, leaving the great city desolate. He disrupted commerce by debasing the currency, exacted such heavy taxes that whole villages were abandoned, hunted down men like wild beasts for sport, and dreamed of conquering Persia and China. But this dismal tyrant's

502

successor (promoted to the throne by the army chiefs) during a
long and peaceful reign of thirty-seven years adhered to principles
of justice and benevolence considerably above the general standard
of fourteenth-century states the world over. He reduced taxes, provided poor relief, granted loans to the peasants, and promoted
prosperity by reclaiming waste lands and by building extensive irrigation works.

The five-century period of the Turkish invasions and the Delhi
Sultanate witnessed many changes in India but few original or constructive cultural developments. The central fact, of course, was the
introduction of the Moslem religion and its gradual accommodation
to the conditions of the country. At the outset, reconciliation between Islam and Hinduism seemed impossible. Islam was strictly
monotheistic, possessed a clear-cut and simple but dogmatic creed,
regarded graven images as sinful, and emphasized the equality of believers. Hinduism was polytheistic (although tending toward monotheism or pantheism in its philosophy), taught that there are many
equally valid approaches to an understanding of the divine being, delighted in symbols, pictorial forms and architectural profusion, and
carried the concept of human inequality to absurd extremes. The
Hindus were noncredal and disposed to tolerance; the Moslems considered it their sacred duty to spread the one true faith of Allah and
his Prophet. Nevertheless, the two peoples gradually drew closer together. The Moslem sovereigns did not exterminate the Hindus
whom they had subjected. They followed the shrewder policy of
laying discriminatory assessments upon the "unbelievers"—a poll tax
and a tax on Hindu religious festivals and pilgrimages. Naturally, a
good many Hindus became converts to Islam, and those who did so
were accepted on an equal basis by the dominant Moslem faction.
Moreover, intermarriage took place between Hindus and Moslems
in spite of religious scruples on both sides. As already indicated,
some of the sultans and their officials were intelligent and progressive in outlook. The best of them tried to improve economic conditions; some were patrons of literature and the arts, encouraged
scholarship, and erected splendid monuments.

It is apparent, however, that the general effects of the Turkish
conquests were depressing. They were accompanied by orgies of
slaughter and spoliation. They threw a pall over the creative spirit
of the Hindus, bringing a marked decline in a tradition of intellectual and artistic enterprise that had once been vigorous, and they almost completely wiped out the remnants of Buddhism. Mosques of
excellent workmanship were constructed—often from the stones of
demolished Hindu temples—and not all the existing Indian temples
were destroyed; but the building of new Hindu religious edifices
was prohibited under severe penalties. It is doubtful whether the
equalitarian aspects of the teachings of Islam produced any amelio-
rative effects upon the Indian population. The immediate result, at

*Contrasts
between Islam
and Hinduism*

*General effects
of the Turkish
conquests*

The Great Mongol Conqueror Genghis Khan, Grandfather of the Founder of the Mongol (Yüan) Dynasty in China.

least, was to create new divisions in an already too sharply divided society. One social effect of the Moslem impact was the subjection of women to a greater degree than ever before. The custom of *purdah* (the veiling and seclusion of women) dates from this era.

After the Turkish sultans had established themselves as sovereigns in Hindustan, they found their position threatened not only by

Mongol invaders: Genghis Khan

potential Hindu rebellion and by intrigues among their own viceroys but also by new invasions from Central Asia, that inexhaustible reservoir of nomadic peoples. At this time the chief source of disturbance was the expansion of the Mongols, whose force was felt throughout the breadth of Asia and even in Europe. Early in the thirteenth century the famous Mongol chieftain and empire builder Genghis Khan made a brief foray into the Indus valley. His raid was only an incident, but the danger of a Mongol attack upon India persisted. Gradually groups of Mongols settled in northern India and adopted agricultural or industrial pursuits, most of them embracing the Moslem religion. So numerous were they in Delhi in the late thirteenth century that a section of the city was called "Mongoltown." Mongols were employed by the sultan as mercenary troops, in which capacity they were sometimes victimized by his suspicion of their loyalty, and tens of thousands of them were massacred.

Near the end of the fourteenth century northern India was visited by the most devastating raid in all its history, led by Timur the

Timur, the "Earth Shaker"

Lame (Tamerlane). Timur, of Turkish descent, had started his career as the chieftain of a small tribal state in Turkestan. After misfortunes and amazing adventures he had welded together a powerful force of cavalry and embarked on a sensational career of conquest. Although he never assumed the title of Khan, he won recognition as overlord from most of the Mongols who had previously followed Genghis Khan. He overran Afghanistan, Persia, and Mesopotamia; then he invaded India with the avowed intention of converting infidels to Islam and procuring booty. He and his troops spent less than a year in India (1398–1399) but left a ruin behind them. The city of Delhi, sacked in a three-day orgy, was turned into a ghost town, so destitute that—to quote a contemporary—"for two whole months not a bird moved a wing in the city." Any place that offered resistance was destroyed and its inhabitants slaughtered or enslaved. Lord Timur carried off with him inestimable quantities of gold and precious stuffs, slaves for all his soldiers, and thousands of skilled craftsmen, including stonemasons to build a great mosque at his capital city of Samarkand in Turkestan. The Delhi Sultanate never fully recovered from the blow dealt to it and to its helpless Hindu subjects by Timur, the "Earth Shaker."

Throughout this period India embraced a number of states, both Moslem and Hindu, which were not included in the Delhi Sultanate. In the fourteenth century two large kingdoms came into existence in the Deccan. Ruled by Moslems, the Bahmani kingdom at its height included about half the Deccan, stretching from sea to sea, and was divided into four provinces. Some of the Bahmani sultans were well educated and intelligent men, who built lavishly, encouraged trade, and maintained a cosmopolitan atmosphere at their court. In the late fifteenth century the administration deteriorated and the kingdom was broken up into five separate states.

Even more splendid than the Bahmani kingdom was the Hindu empire of Vijayanagar, which at one time dominated the whole southern end of the peninsula as far north as the Kistna River (in- cluding, roughly, Madras, Travancore, and Mysore). The capital city, also named Vijayanagar ("City of Victory"), was strongly fortified, heavily populated, and probably—on the testimony of Italian, Portuguese, and Afghan visitors—one of the greatest cities in the world during the fifteenth century. The commerce of the kingdom was eagerly sought. Several kinds of precious stones, particularly large diamonds, were prominent among its exports. The court was sumptuous and the palaces magnificent. Architecture flourished on a grand scale and with an imaginative boldness reminiscent of the classical Sanskrit age. The foundations which underlay the brilliant culture of this last great Hindu empire, however, were not sound. In spite of an orderly government and in the midst of great wealth, the common people suffered from extreme privation and were fleeced by avaricious officials. Luxurious and profligate courts, the encouragement of prostitution in the temples, and the compulsory burning of widows (requiring the mass immolation of thousands of women on the death of a king) were hardly evidences of a healthy society. Unfortunately, a haughty and embittered rivalry between the Hindu and the Bahmani kingdoms weakened both states. In 1565 the almost impregnable city of Vijayanagar was taken and wantonly destroyed by troops from a league of neighboring Moslem powers, and the southern Hindu empire sank into a permanent decline.

2. CHINA UNDER THE SUNG, MONGOL, AND MING DYNASTIES (960–1644)

For about fifty years following the collapse of the great T'ang Dynasty in the early tenth century, China was a divided country with power in the hands of military dictators. After this chaotic but relatively brief interregnum (known to Chinese tradition as the "Five Dynasties"), unity and a strong central government were re-established by an able general who assumed the imperial title and founded the Sung Dynasty. This dynasty, like its predecessor, the T'ang, endured for about three centuries (960–1279). Although the first Sung had been an army officer, he revived the ancient administrative system and restored the power of the civilian bureaucracy. In contrast to the T'ang, the Sung rulers did not adopt a policy of imperialism, and even relinquished control over portions of the empire. Territories in the north and the northwest were lost to seminomadic peoples who, while founding independent kingdoms, assimilated many aspects of Chinese culture. One of these northern groups, the Khitan, established a kingdom in southern Manchuria, annexed territory south of the Great Wall in the Peking area, and collected tribute from the Sung emperors. Although the Khitan were entirely separate from the Chinese in origin, a corruption of their name—"Cathay"—came to be a Western designation for China, a circumstance which indicates that the Khitan did not long retain their distinctive traits after coming into close contact with China's mature civilization.

Early in the twelfth century the Khitan state (Liao) was overthrown by a people of similar stock, the Juchên, who not only occupied Manchuria and Mongolia but also conquered the greater part of northern China. Thus, beginning about 1141, the Sung actually controlled only the Yangtze valley and regions to the south. They established their capital at Hangchow (then known as Lin-an), a magnificent port but far distant from the traditional centers of imperial administration. The later, or southern, Sung period was characterized by a less vigorous administration and by the familiar but depressing symptoms of dynastic decay. These disadvantages, however, were to some extent counterbalanced by the fact that southern China felt the influence of Chinese culture more fully than it had before. The peoples of the south and southwest not only became more completely incorporated into Chinese society but also began to contribute leadership to the state. The center of population was shifting to the south, and there was evidence also that originality and initiative were abundant in this area. During the Southern Sung period (1141–1279) northern China continued to be ruled by the Juchên from the old Sung capital at Kaifeng on the Yellow River. While the loss of so much territory to alien conquerors was humiliating to the Sung emperors, it produced no appreciable permanent changes in the north. The Juchên adapted themselves to Chinese ways as readily as had the Khitan. Both Buddhism and Confucianism obtained a strong hold upon them, and the rulers, following the established convention, adopted a Chinese dynastic title (*Chin* or *Kin*, meaning "Gold").

Peace, internal stability, and prolific cultural activity were characteristic of the Sung period, especially during the first century and a half. As earlier, a flourishing commerce contributed to an increase in wealth and promoted a knowledge of foreign lands. Overland trade declined, partly because the caravan routes were no longer controlled by the Chinese, but business was brisk in port cities of the southeastern coast. Foreign merchants, among whom the Arabs still predominated, were granted the right of residence in the trading centers, subject to the jurisdiction of an Inspector of Foreign Trade. At the same time the Chinese themselves were beginning to participate more extensively in oceanic commerce. The early Sung emperors undertook ambitious public works, including irrigation projects. Apparently society as a whole attained a fair level of prosperity, as evidenced by an increase in population.

The late eleventh century was significant for a reform movement launched by a scholar-official, Wang An-shih (1021–1086), who held the position of chief minister for a number of years. His proposals were the subject of acrimonious controversy and never were carried out in entirety, but they represented a realistic attempt to improve the administration, and they focused attention upon the plight of the common man. Wang promoted the establishment of public schools endowed with state lands, and he advocated revision of the civil-service examinations to encourage a knowledge of practical problems instead of proficiency in classical literary forms. His most determined efforts were directed toward a program of relief for the poor farmers by direct government assistance, by revision of the inequitable tax system and the abolition of forced labor, and by a redistribution of land. He wanted the government to control commerce, fix prices, buy up farm surpluses, and make loans to farmers at a low rate of interest on the security of their growing crops. Wang An-shih's proposals for agrarian relief anticipated some of the measures inaugurated by governments in recent times, and his over-all program approximated a kind of state socialism. Although he insisted that he was merely adapting genuine Confucian principles to the needs of the time, his opponents branded him as a dangerous innovator. The contest between the Innovators (Wang's disciples) and the Conservatives continued into the next century, with the emperors favoring sometimes one and sometimes the other group; but the conservative faction ultimately prevailed. Wang's radical proposals, however, have been studied with interest by modern reformers in China and elsewhere.

Peace, stability, and prosperity

The reforms of Wang An-shih (1021–1086)

An invasion by the Mongols brought about the final collapse of the Sung Dynasty and subjected all China, for the first time in its history, to the rule of a foreign conqueror. The Mongol Asiatic empire, like so many of its predecessors, was established with almost incredible swiftness in a series of military campaigns, but it was for a brief period one of the largest ever known. In the early thirteenth century the great Mongol conqueror Genghis Khan overthrew the kingdoms adjacent to China on the north and then swept westward across all Asia. After making a brief foray into India he subdued Persia and Mesopotamia and occupied large stretches of Russian territory north and west of the Caspian Sea. Although the invasion of China was probably inevitable, the Sung emperor contributed to his own downfall by playing a double game with the Mongols. So eager was he to get rid of the Juchên rulers in north China that he sent troops to help the Mongols against them; then he rashly attacked the Mongol forces and exposed his own dominions to the fury of the ruthless and swift-riding horsemen. The conquest of southern China was completed by Genghis Khan's grandson, Kublai Khan, after many years of hard fighting, during which the Mongols not only had to occupy the coastal cities but also had to accustom themselves to naval warfare. In 1279 the last Chinese army was defeated (the commanding general is said to have jumped into the sea with the infant Sung prince in his arms), and Kublai became the master of China.

The huge Asiatic empire of the Mongols, which reached from the China Sea to Eastern Europe, was too large to be administered effectively as a unit and did not long remain intact. Religious differences contributed to its dissolution. Before the end of the thirteenth century most of the western princes (khans) had become Moslems and repudiated the authority of Kublai's family, who favored a Tibetan form of Buddhism. Kublai's descendants, however, from their imperial capital of Peking, governed China for the better part of a century (1279–1368).

The accession of the Mongol (or Yüan) Dynasty seemed to threaten a serious interruption in the normal course of Chinese civilization. Fortunately the damage inflicted was only temporary, and there was actually some progress during this period of foreign domination. The Mongols were notoriously cruel conquerors, leaving ruined cities and mutilated corpses as monuments to the folly of those who resisted them. The bitterly contested occupation of southern China was accompanied by a decimation of the native population in some areas. Nevertheless, the Mongol rulers were wise enough to recognize the desirability of preserving such a great state as China and the advantage to be gained from taxing its people instead of exterminating them. The nomad warriors could not resist the influence of Chinese culture, and the traditional Chinese administrative system was not completely uprooted. The civil-service examinations were suspended for a time and Chinese were excluded from most governmental posts, although the Mongol emperors employed foreigners of various nationalities in high positions at court. In the fourteenth century, when the dynasty showed signs of weakening and native unrest became ominous, the emperor reinstituted the examination system and admitted Chinese to office, chiefly at the lower level.

The Mongol rulers were no more intolerant in religious matters than their predecessors. While they patronized Buddhism, they did not seriously interfere with the other native cults and they authorized the construction of Confucian colleges and temples. They also permitted the introduction of Western religions, although Islam was the only one of these to retain a permanent place. Following the precedent of earlier dynasties, the Mongol emperors endowed charitable and educational institutions and maintained public granaries to provide relief in time of famine. They also gave attention to irrigation projects and the improvement of communications. A notable undertaking was the reconstruction of the Grand Canal linking the capital city of Peking to the Yangtze valley by an inland waterway.

Religious and welfare policies

During the Mongol period China was by no means isolated from other regions. The area under the jurisdiction of Peking was considerably larger than the empire of the Sung, and the emperors attempted to increase it still further by schemes of conquest of dubious value. Kublai Khan made two attempts to invade Japan (in 1274 and 1281), employing both Chinese and Korean vessels, but a typhoon wrecked many of his ships and the Japanese annihilated the landing party. Fortunately, peaceful intercourse was continued with other nations, near and far. Overland commerce was facilitated by imperial highways which the Mongols built deep into Central Asia and even to Persia. That travel was comparatively safe is indicated by the large number of foreign visitors in China during this period and also by the fact that Chinese journeyed far from home—to Russia, Persia, the Near East, and occasionally Europe. Russians, Arabs, and Jews entered China for purposes of trade, as did Genoese and Venetians. The renowned Marco Polo was only one of many European visitors. He lived in China for seventeen years (1275–1292), was received at court, and visited various parts of the country. The glowing report with which he astonished his countrymen upon returning home (he described Hangchow, the Southern Sung capital, as "the finest and noblest city in the world") was less a tribute to the Mongol Dynasty than to the maturity of Chinese civilization, and was also an unintentional commentary upon the relatively primitive conditions still prevalent in Western Europe.

Extension of foreign contacts

In the fourteenth century, Mongol power was undermined by the decadence of the ruling house and by the growing discontent of the Chinese people, who never forgot that they had been subjugated by a barbarian conqueror. Rebellion was brought to a successful con-

The overthrow of
the Mongols and
establishment of
the Ming Dynasty

clusion under the leadership of a dynamic, if somewhat grotesque, soldier of fortune, who captured Peking in 1368 and drove the last Mongol emperor into the wastes of Mongolia. This rebel leader was a man of low birth who had been orphaned at an early age and had exchanged the life of a Buddhist monk for that of a bandit. Nevertheless, he was accepted as having won the Mandate of Heaven and became the first emperor of the Ming ("Brilliant" or "Glorious") Dynasty, which lasted from 1368 to 1644. The dynasty proved to be extremely successful and gave renewed proof of the potency of Chinese institutions, although it added little that was new. The government adhered to the Sung patterns, or in some ways more closely to the T'ang, particularly in its emphasis upon the forceful expansion of territorial boundaries. Ming China was a large state, with its authority extending into Manchuria, Mongolia, Indochina, Burma, and the southwestern region facing Tibet. While the great Mongol empire of the thirteenth century had fallen to pieces, it gave promise of being resurrected by Timur (Tamerlane), the master of Turkestan and scourge of India. Although the Ming court regarded Timur's emissaries as tribute bearers, the "Earth Shaker" was actually setting forth on an expedition to conquer China when he died prematurely in 1405. In spite of this stroke of fortune, the Ming emperors made little effort to recover either Turkestan or Sinkiang.

A noteworthy aspect of the early Ming period was the development and rapid expansion of Chinese navigation. The mariner's compass had been in use perhaps since the eleventh century, and some large ships had been constructed; but now maritime enterprise was given tremendous impetus. Chinese sailing vessels, equipped with as many as four decks and comfortable living quarters, undertook voyages to the East Indies, the Malay Peninsula, Ceylon, India, and Arabia, returning with merchandise, tribute, and valuable geographical information. For reasons unknown, these naval expeditions were discontinued about 1424. Henceforth the government restricted Chinese shipping to coastal waters and discouraged foreign travel on the part of its subjects. The result was not only a loss of revenue from commerce but also an unfortunate isolation of China at the very time when the Western peoples were beginning to emerge from their provincialism. Instead of retaining the initiative on the high seas, the later Ming rulers proved inefficient in defending their own coasts against Japanese pirates and other marauding groups.

A decline in the vitality of the administration was apparent long before the Ming Dynasty came to a close. Officials became lazy and corrupt; power passed into the hands of court favorites and eunuchs; and exorbitant taxes oppressed the peasants to the point of ruin. While the costs of government mounted dizzily—in 1639 military expenditures alone were ten times greater than the entire revenue of the first Ming emperor—territories were being lost through incompetence and rebellion. Although the dynasty finally succumbed to another foreign invasion, internal dissension was the real cause of its collapse.

In turning from the political to the cultural developments that took place in China during the Sung, Mongol, and Ming dynasties, we may note that a renewal of interest in philosophical speculation occurred, reaching a climax in the latter half of the twelfth century. This revival represented a return to the fountainhead of Chinese thought—the sages of antiquity, particularly Confucius—but it introduced several new ideas and was not a mere repetition of ancient formulas. The most noted Chinese thinker of this period was Chu Hsi (1130–1200), who held a position at the Sung court and was an opponent of the so-called Innovators (disciples of Wang An-shih). Although Chu Hsi claimed to be interpreting Confucius' teachings in accordance with their original and uncorrupted meaning, he and his associates actually founded a Neo-Confucian school, with a metaphysics which incorporated elements of Taoism and Buddhism. They stressed the concept of the "Supreme Ultimate" or Absolute, a Final Cause which underlies the whole material universe and is antecedent to every rational or moral principle. Nevertheless, Chu Hsi, like his ancient master Confucius, was chiefly interested in human nature and its proper development in an ethical and social order. He reaffirmed Mencius' faith in man's natural capacity for good and upheld the traditional ethical system exemplified by the family and embodied in a paternalistic state administered by a bureaucracy of scholar-officials. The teachings of Chu Hsi, although stoutly contested by rival scholars in his day, eventually came to be regarded as the definitive commentary on the doctrines of the ancient sage. Venerated as orthodoxy, they discouraged creative thought among later scholars and administrators.

A prodigious output of literature has been characteristic of Chinese civilization during almost every period except the most ancient. Printing was very common from Sung times on. Books were printed from wooden blocks, from metal plates, and from movable type made of earthenware, tin, and wood. Poetry seldom equaled the best of the T'ang age in beauty or spontaneity, but lengthy histories, encyclopedias, dictionaries, geographies, and scientific treatises were produced. The most original literary developments were in the fields of the drama and the novel. The Chinese drama attained the level of a major art form during the Mongol Dynasty, partly because the suspension of the civil-service examinations, by cutting off opportunities for official careers, prompted men of talent to turn their attention to a medium of popular entertainment which they had previously considered unworthy of notice. The dramas of the Mongol period, of which more than a hundred have survived, combined lively action with vivid portrayal of character, and they were written in the common idiom of the people rather than in the classical language of scholars. The Chinese theater, like the English theater of Shakespeare's day, was largely devoid of scenery and properties, although the performers made use of elaborate costumes and heavy make-up. Ordinarily all the parts were filled by male actors. The plays were in verse, but, in contrast to the Elizabethan and modern Western drama, the speeches were sung rather than recited and the orchestra (placed directly on the stage) contributed an essential element to the production.

The Chinese novel, originating apparently in the tales of public story-tellers, developed contemporaneously with the drama but matured a little later. Its growth was aided indirectly by the sterility of the academic atmosphere that pervaded the court and the bureaucracy of the Ming Dynasty. In the fifteenth century, veneration for Confucian orthodoxy, especially as embodied in the teachings of Chu Hsi, had become such a fetish among the official coterie of scholars that one of them declared: "The truth has been made manifest. . . . No more writing is needed." [1] Some men of letters sought a creative outlet by composing narratives in the plain language of the people. In their hands the novel became a highly successful literary medium, skillfully contrived but purveying robust adventure, humor, warm feeling, and salty realism. Frequently historical themes were chosen for subject matter, but the tales also provided commentary—sometimes satirical—upon contemporary society and government.

A large proportion of the Chinese works of art still extant was produced during the period which is being reviewed here. Sculpture had declined in quality since T'ang times, but painting reached its highest peak of excellence under the Sung. The most beautiful and

The Chinese novel

Landscape painting

[1] L. C. Goodrich, *A Short History of the Chinese People*, p. 196.

Spring Morning at the Palace of Han. Sung Dynasty. Chinese painting emphasized landscapes rather than people and the representation of poetic or philosophic ideas rather than facts.

Sage under a Pine Tree. Sung Dynasty. The gnarled and twisted tree exemplifies the Chinese interest in nature in both her pleasant and perverse moods.

typical Sung paintings are landscapes, frequently executed in only one color but conveying the impression of an intimate understanding of nature in her various moods. Through economy of line, omission of nonessentials, and painstaking treatment of significant detail, the artists sought to bring to light the reality which lies hidden behind the world of appearances. Their dreamy creations were obviously influenced by the mystical teachings of Buddhism and Taoism. Landscape painting was at its ripest during the Southern Sung period, when the leading artists took full advantage of the natural beauty of the Hangchow region. They sometimes painted panoramic scenes on long strips of silk. These were fastened to rollers and could be viewed leisurely by simply holding the rollers in one's hands and winding the painted scroll from one roller to the other.

Architecture attained particular pre-eminence under the Ming, a dynasty which delighted in glorifying and embellishing the visible aspects of Chinese culture. Ming architecture was by no means new in conception, but it was prolific and has left many impressive monuments. The popularity of elaborate gardens, summer residences, game preserves, and hunting lodges among the aristocracy provided opportunities for the designing of graceful pavilions and arched bridges. Fully developed by this period was the pagoda style of temple, distinguished by curving roofs which were usually of tile and frequently in brilliant colors.

Architecture

China has only rarely been isolated from other parts of the world, and many of her cultural changes were the result of foreign contacts. The Chinese were indebted to the Arabs for contributions in the field of mathematics and probably also in medicine, although the Chinese had themselves accumulated a considerable store of medical **513**

Ten Thousand Li of the Yangtze (1 li = about ⅓ mile), Ming Dynasty. Chinese hand scroll exemplifying the continued supremacy of landscape painting. Landscape was considered the most important of subjects because it includes all life.

Wooden Statue of Kuan-yin, "Goddess of Mercy." This popular deity, usually represented in female form, was actually derived from a legendary Indian bodhisattva. (In Mahayana Buddhism a bodhisattva was one who had attained enlightenment but chose to remain in the world to help others.)

Fantastic Ceramic Figure of a Deity Ming Dynasty.

"War Spirit." A Ming Dynasty painting (1368-1644).

Heavy Porcelaneous vase with simple design. Sung Dynasty (960-1279).

ART OF THE
SUNG AND
MING DYNASTIES

Porcelain Vase. Ming Dynasty. This vase, with dragon figure, bears a glaze of white and the beautiful "cobalt blue" which was a distinctive hallmark of the Ming craftsmen.

Pottery Figure of a Lohan (A Buddhist devotee engaged in the process of seeking his own salvation). (Met. Mus.)

INDIA AND THE
FAR EAST IN
THE LATER
MIDDLE AGES

Achievements
in agriculture
and in the
applied sciences

data. Inoculation against smallpox seems to have been practiced before the end of the Sung Dynasty. Eyeglasses came into use (from Italy) during the Ming period. New crops of Western origin began to be cultivated in China. Sorghum, introduced in the thirteenth century, and maize in the sixteenth have been raised extensively in northern China ever since. Cotton production, which also began in the thirteenth century, was greatly expanded under the Ming. One innovation which may have been of domestic rather than foreign inspiration was in the technique of warfare. The explosive properties of gunpowder had long been known, but not until the eleventh century were they utilized for the manufacture of lethal weapons. The Mongols, in the thirteenth and fourteenth centuries, employed bombs that perhaps were propelled by primitive cannons. Although these early artillery pieces were crude, they foreshadowed the increasingly destructive character of modern warfare.

3. THE RISE OF FEUDALISM AND MILITARY DICTATORS IN JAPAN (*ca.* 900–1600)

Even though Chinese culture had been incorporated into the foundations of Japanese civilization and exerted a lasting influence, social and political trends in Japan during the medieval era were very different from those in the great mainland state. While China was frequently harassed by nomadic invaders and was temporarily subjugated by a foreign dynasty, her society and culture departed little from the ancient pattern. By contrast, Japan, enjoying the natural protection of her insular position, was not seriously affected by disturbances from without; yet her institutions were profoundly altered as the result of conflicts taking place within her own society. A theoretical unity and an arbitrary and artificial scheme of government had been imposed upon Japan by the reform of the mid-seventh century, which attempted to introduce the Chinese imperial system in its entirety. How completely the attempt had failed is illustrated by the events of the next thousand years. Only belatedly, and after indecisive and exhausting strife, was the basis discovered for a stable and unified society. And when stability was achieved, it was through improvised institutions which were inadequate to solve the problems certain to arise in the wake of economic and cultural change.

The political history of Japan during this period is characterized mainly by two factors: (1) the persistence of an indirect method of government, with the actual power shifting from one family to another but exercised in the name of an inviolate emperor, whose effective authority rarely extended beyond the environs of Kyoto; (2) the feudalization of society and the growth of extralegal military units which imposed their will upon territories under their control. To the end of the sixteenth century the technique of government was variable and uncertain, although the trend from civilian to military authority was unmistakable. At the opening of the seventeenth century a centralized administration was finally established which ended a long period of civil wars, enforced a coherent national policy, and endured almost unshaken until the middle of the nineteenth century. Even when it was overthrown, the habits which it had instilled in the Japanese people could not easily be uprooted.

In the ninth century the Fujiwara family, through intermarriage with the imperial family and through possession of the office of regent, had acquired a dominant position in the government, reducing the emperor to a figurehead. The Fujiwara retained their ascendancy until the twelfth century, but their rule over the outlying sections became more and more nominal as new lands were brought into production by reclamation or by conquest of the aborigines, and as aggressive landowners succeeded in withdrawing their estates from the jurisdiction of the imperial tax collectors. The men who possessed estates in these frontier regions were not hampered by the elaborate rules of etiquette or by the mania for classical Chinese studies that absorbed the energies of the courtiers at Kyoto. They formulated their own standards of conduct, largely dictated by the desire to preserve and extend their holdings, and quarreled with one another over conflicting claims. Naturally, many small farmers relinquished their property to powerful neighbors in return for protection and sank to a position of serfdom. Gradually a manorial economy came into existence, showing some points of similarity to the manorial regime in Western Europe during the later Middle Ages.

The beginning of feudalism

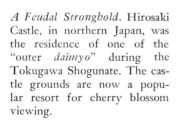

A Feudal Stronghold. Hirosaki Castle, in northern Japan, was the residence of one of the "outer *daimyo*" during the Tokugawa Shogunate. The castle grounds are now a popular resort for cherry blossom viewing.

INDIA AND THE
FAR EAST IN
THE LATER
MIDDLE AGES

Parallels between
Japanese and
European feud-
alism

By a remarkable coincidence of history Japanese society took on the aspects of feudalism at the very time when feudal institutions were evolving in Western Europe. Of course it would be a mistake to assume that Japanese and Western feudalism were identical, but the parallels between them are striking. In Japan and Western Europe alike, leadership was passing to a class of mounted warriors who owned land, dominated the peasantry, and exercised governmental power as a private right. In Japan the rising class of warrior-landlords was derived partly from clan chieftains, partly from adventurers who had established title purely by the sword, and partly from imperial officials who had converted an administrative office into a family possession. The members of the landed class established hereditary claims to their holdings and entered into binding

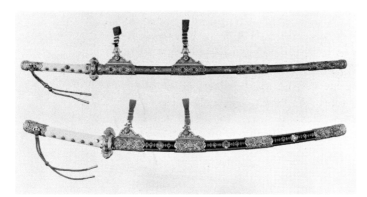

Swords of the Feudal Nobility. This type of curved sword, of fine steel, was worn suspended from the girdle by great *daimyo* or court nobles during Japan's early feudal age (12th to 14th centuries). Note the jeweled hilts, the ornately decorated scabbards, and the loops for hanging the swords.

agreements with one another, creating a series of dependent relationships equivalent to a system of lords and vassals. As in the case of European feudalism, the system was extended partly through commendation—by which a landowner voluntarily transferred his property to a more powerful noble to whom he rendered military service while retaining the actual use of the land—and partly through the granting of benefices or fiefs by great lords to lesser men in order to secure their services as vassals. Another parallel to the growth of European feudalism is seen in the fact that property belonging to religious foundations was frequently converted into fiefs. Buddhist monasteries and temples which had been generously endowed used their lands to enlist the allegiance of fighting men, and some religious establishments became formidable military units.

The Japanese warriors, who corresponded in status and in profession to the medieval knights, were known as *samurai*, or *bushi*. The *samurai* developed a fraternal spirit and a code of conduct to which they jealously clung as their special prerogative and which they called "the way of the horse and the bow." (The term *bushido*, not used before the eighteenth century, denoted a romantic and artificial version of the old feudal code.) Like the European code of chivalry it stressed valor, loyalty, and the necessity of preferring death to dishonor. The *samurai* was bound above all else to protect, defend, or avenge his lord, to this end sacrificing his own life and, if need be, the lives of his family—a remarkable ideal in view of the sacredness of family ties in Japan. So sensitive was the *samurai* to any taint of dishonor that he was expected to commit suicide (by a ritual of falling on one's sword, known as *hara-kiri*) if there was no other way to wipe out the stain on his reputation.

In the twelfth century, feudal warfare culminated in a struggle between two powerful families, the Taira and the Minamoto. With the victory of the Minamoto, their leader reorganized the government on a basis which frankly recognized the paramount role of the landowning warrior-nobility. To avoid appearing as a usurper, the head of the Minamoto family assumed only a military title, becoming known as *Shogun*, and pretended to be acting as the agent of the emperor. In reality, for the next six and one-half centuries (1192–1867) Japan had a dual government: the civil authority at Kyoto headed by the emperor and embracing various ranks of court nobility whose functions were ornamental rather than essential, and the Bakufu ("Tent Government") headed by the Shogun and commanding the services of the powerful military leaders who owned most of the land. The creation of the Shogunate, as this military-feudal government came to be called, indicates how thoroughly feudalism had permeated Japanese society. The real governors of the country now were not the imperial bureaucracy but the vassals of the Shogun.

The rise of the Shoguns

Although the Shogunate proved to be a durable institution, it did not remain perpetually in the hands of any one family. On the death of the first Shogun his widow's relatives seized control, with her connivance. This extremely capable woman became known as the "Nun Shogun," because she wielded political influence even after she had nominally retired into holy orders, and with her help the Hojo family came into power. For more than a century the Hojo appointed puppet Shoguns over whom they maintained a regency. Thus, by the early thirteenth century the government of Japan was a confusing series of subterfuges. The central authority (so far as any existed) was exercised by a regent in the name of a puppet general (the Shogun) who, in turn, was theoretically an underling of an emperor, who was himself controlled by a regent (or, in some cases, by an elder member of the imperial family living in retirement). Because the Hojo family had no inherent claim to superiority over other great feudal houses, its ascendancy created jealous dissatisfaction and led inevitably to further conflict. A remarkable incident occurred in 1333 when the Emperor Daigo II attempted to cut through the sham governmental fabric and assert his right to rule as well as reign. He mustered sufficient military forces to capture and burn the Shogun's headquarters at Kamakura and ended the Hojo regency. The sequel to this bold stroke, however, was simply a half-

The Shogunate under the Hojo family

century of civil war, with two rival emperors, each bidding for support. The schism in the imperial household was healed and order temporarily restored with the triumph of another great military family, the Ashikaga, who again reduced the emperor to a position of impotence.

The Ashikaga Shoguns (1392–1568) made the serious mistake of taking up residence in Kyoto, where they were exposed to the softening influence of court society and, by relaxing their vigilance, lost effective control over the turbulent lords of outlying districts. Feudal rivalry became increasingly unrestrained until, beginning in the late fifteenth century, Japan experienced 100 years of almost continual warfare. Robbery and pillage were rampant; almost all vestiges of a central government disappeared; even the private estates which the emperor had owned in various parts of the country were absorbed into the feudal domains. The imperial family as well as the Kyoto courtiers were subjected to humiliation by swaggering soldiers. Reduced to poverty, one emperor eked out a living by selling his autograph. In 1500 an imperial corpse lay unburied for six weeks because there was no money in the treasury. The Ashikaga Shogun was almost as impotent as the emperor and quite unable to stop the brigandage and slaughter carried on wantonly by feudal retainers and robber monks. Conditions in Japan seemed to be fast approaching anarchy when, at the close of the sixteenth century, the Shogunate was drastically and effectively reorganized by the Tokugawa family.

In spite of all the confusion and turmoil, however, there were constructive forces at work. The character of Japanese feudalism was changing in a significant direction. Large territorial units were taking shape under fairly competent administrative systems. This trend was the result partly of natural evolution and partly of the policy of the Shoguns. At the outset the Shogun had attempted to control the various fiefs by sending out officials responsible to him and appointed from the military capital at Kamakura; but these officials acquired hereditary status and merged into the hierarchy. The Constable in particular—an officer who was given administrative authority over a province—gradually became a great baron or magnate, absorbing into his own dominion the estates within his jurisdiction. The great lords grew in prestige and material resources at the expense of the lesser fiefholders. During the almost constant warfare of the fifteenth and sixteenth centuries, peasants were pressed into military service, and consequently the importance of the knights began to decline. The appearance of mass armies composed of commoners was comparable to the trend in European countries during this same period; but, while the European armies were recruited chiefly by the kings of national states, the Japanese forces were under the control of feudal lords.

The tragic period
of feudal warfare

The ascendancy
of the great lords

The Nativity, Fra Angelico (1387–1455). A Dominican friar, Fra Angelico is noted for his serenely happy religious paintings. (MMA)

The Flight into Egypt, Giotto (1276–1337). Giotto is regarded as the founder of the modern tradition in painting. This is one of the frescoes in the Arena Chapel, Padua, depicting scenes from the life of Christ.

St. Lawrence Enthroned, Fra Lippo Lippi (1406–1469). One of the first of the psychological painters, Fra Lippo Lippi exhibited in this work his gift for portraying pensive melancholy. (MMA)

Spring, Sandro Botticelli (1444–1510). Despite the pagan symbolism, the faces are thoughtful and sober, for Botticelli was a mystic as well as a lover of classical beauty. (Uffizi)

Mona Lisa, Leonardo da Vinci (1452–1519). Unlike most other Renaissance painters who sought to convey an understandable message, Leonardo created questions to which he gave no answer. Nowhere is this more evident than in the enigmatic countenance of Mona Lisa. (Louvre)

The Virgin of the Rocks, Leonardo da Vinci. Th painting reveals not only Leonardo's interest human character, but also his absorption in t phenomena of nature. (Louvre)

The Last Supper, Leonardo da Vinci. This great fresco depicts the varying reactions of Jesus' disciples when he announces that one of them will betray Him. (Santa Maria della Grazie, Milan)

Leadership was passing from the knightly (*samurai*) class as a whole to the great lords, who were known as *daimyo* ("Great Names"). The *daimyo* incorporated many small estates into their own possessions and employed the *samurai* as managers and as subordinate military commanders. The families which attained the status of *daimyo* came to be referred to as clans, but they were actually very different from the clans of early Japanese society. Their territories were feudal provinces, and the people under their rule were bound by vassalage or servitude rather than by blood relationship. The ascendancy of the *daimyo*, while it by no means eliminated feudal dissension, greatly reduced the number of rival units and also ensured a considerable measure of stability within each unit.

Economically and culturally, Japan's feudal age was a period, not of retrogression or stagnation, but of progress. That this was so may seem strange in view of the roughness of the times and the instability of political institutions, but the evidence is undeniable. The Japanese maintained commerical contacts with other Far Eastern countries and continued to receive stimulating influences from China. Foreign trade, increasing steadily from the twelfth century, led to the substitution of money for rice or cloth as a medium of exchange and promoted diversified economic activity. By the fifteenth century the Japanese were exporting not only raw materials, such as lumber, gold, and pearls, but also manufactured goods. Japanese folding fans and screens were in great demand in China, and steel swords were exported by the thousands to a large Far Eastern market. The curved swords forged by Japanese craftsmen in the thirteenth century are said to have been unsurpassed even by the famous blades of Toledo and Damascus. Society during Japan's feudal period was far from being purely agrarian. Commercial and industrial centers came into being, and a few developed into populous cities. Groups of merchants organized guilds for mutual protection and to promote the marketing of their wares. Moreover, in contrast to most of Western Europe, the feudal classes participated in capitalistic enterprises. In addition to professional merchants, monasteries, *samurai*, great nobles, and occasionally even the Shogun invested in trade.

As in earlier times, various schools of Buddhism contributed to cultural development, largely because they continued to serve as channels for intellectual and aesthetic currents from China. One of the most prominent sects, the Zen (from the Chinese *Ch'an*), was introduced at the close of the twelfth century and spread rapidly among the *samurai*. Zen Buddhism taught that Enlightenment would come to the individual not through study or any intellectual process but by a sudden flash of insight experienced when one was in tune with nature. Because it stressed physical discipline, self-control, and the practice of meditation in place of formal scholarship, the sect appealed to the warrior class, who felt that Zen teachings gave supernatural sanction to the attitudes which they had already come to regard as essential to their station. Though its doctrines were fundamentally anti-intellectual, its monks fostered both learning and art and injected several refinements into Japanese upper-class society. Among these were an unrivaled type of landscape architecture, the art of flower arrangement, and a delicate social ritual known as the tea ceremony—all of which were Chinese importations but elaborated with great sensitivity in Japan.

The growth of
religious sects

Religious developments in Japan during the medieval period were in many ways distinctive. New sects sprang up and caught the imagination of the common people. Some of them proposed the elimination of ceremony and the abolition of distinctions between clergy and laity. Others encouraged a fierce intolerance and a worship of national greatness.[2] That the Japanese lower classes were aroused and encouraged by the new teachings is certain. During the tumultuous fifteenth and sixteenth centuries uprisings against the feudal nobles were instigated by religious congregations, and in a few instances the revolts were successful. These manifestations of popular intransigence, though, had little or no permanent effect upon Japanese society, which remained predominantly aristocratic in structure and tone.

Literature and
the arts

Many other cultural changes resulted from the growth of a productive and diversified economy and from the mutual stimulation among competing religious sects. While sacred writings were being collected and translated in the monasteries, and while courtiers continued to write in the polished but lifeless classical manner, literature was enriched by the addition of tales of daring and high adventure conceived for the entertainment and edification of men of arms. These stories of knightly prowess, composed in a flowing poetical prose and sometimes sung to the accompaniment of a lute, are comparable to the heroic epics of medieval European chivalry. No counterpart of the European poems of romantic love, however, arose in feudal Japan, where woman's role (with a few notable exceptions) was definitely subordinate. All the arts were influenced by Chinese models, but the Japanese had long since demonstrated their originality in adapting styles to their own tastes. Particularly impressive were the paintings executed by monks of the Zen sect in the fifteenth and sixteenth centuries. These were chiefly landscapes and similar in style to those of the Chinese artists of the Ming Dynasty, but they possessed an individuality and freshness of their own.

[2] E. O. Reischauer observes that the Japanese religious reformers anticipated to a surprising degree the position of the Protestant Reformers of Europe. *Japan Past and Present*, p. 60.

Costume for the No *Dance-Drama* (*17th century*). Lavish and colorful pictorial decoration was characteristic of the costumes worn by *No* actors.

The exacting aesthetic standards of the aristocratic patrons of the Zen sect are also evident in a specialized form of dramatic art, the *No,* which emerged during this period. The *No* "lyric-drama" or "dance-drama" was not a foreign importation but almost purely a native product. Its origins can be traced to ancient folk dances and also to ritualistic dances associated with both Shintoist and Buddhist modes of worship. In its perfected form, it became a unique vehicle of artistic expression and entertainment, which heightened the appeal of rhythm and graceful postures by relating them to dramatic incidents. The themes of the dance-dramas were traditional narratives, but they were presented with great restraint and by suggestive symbolism rather than by literal re-enactment, somewhat in the manner of a series of tableaus. The performers wore masks as well as rich costumes and chanted their lines to the accompaniment of drums and flutes. The *No* drama achieved great popularity among the *samurai* class and was at its height from the fourteenth to the sixteenth centuries. In spite of its extremely stylized character, it has never entirely disappeared from the artistic heritage of Japan.

The No drama

SELECTED READINGS

· *Items so designated are available in paperbound editions.*
INDIA — *See also Readings for Chapters 7 and 12*

Cambridge History of India, Vol. III.
Phillips, C. H., *India,* London, 1949. A useful survey, although devoting little space to the period before the coming of Europeans.
Sharma, S. R., *The Crescent in India,* Bombay, 1954.

CHINA — *See also Readings for Chapters 8 and 12*

Bruce, J. P., *Chu Hsi and His Masters*, London, 1923.

· Chang, Carsun, *The Development of Neo-Confucian Thought*, New York, 1957 (College and University Press Services).

Eliot, Charles, *Hinduism and Buddhism: An Historical Sketch*, New York, 1954, Vol. III.

Fairbank, J. K., ed., *Chinese Thought and Institutions*, Chicago, 1957.

· Fitzgerald, C. P., *China, a Short Cultural History*, rev. ed., New York, 1954. Takes a harsh view of the Mongols and their influence.

Hucker, C. O., *The Traditional Chinese State in Ming Times (1368–1644)*, Tucson, 1961. Brief but informative on political structure and operation.

· Hudson, G. F., *Europe and China: A Survey of Their Relations from the Earliest Times to 1800*, London, 1930 (Beacon). Interestingly presented.

Kracke, E. A., Jr., *Civil Service in Early Sung China, 960–1067*, Cambridge, Mass., 1959. A careful study.

Lin Yutang, *Imperial Peking: Seven Centuries of China*, New York, 1961. A richly illustrated popular account of the great capital under successive dynasties.

Liu, James T. C., *Reform in Sung China: Wang An-shih (1021–1086) and His New Policies*, Cambridge, Mass., 1959. A good, brief interpretive study.

Nivison, D. S., and Wright, A. F., eds., *Confucianism in Action*, Stanford, 1959. Explores the relationship between Neo-Confucianist thought and Chinese institutions.

· Prawdin, Michael, (E. and C. Paul, trs.), *The Mongol Empire: Its Rise and Legacy*, London, 1940 (Free Press).

Sowerby, A. deC., *Nature in Chinese Art*, New York, 1940.

Waley, Arthur, *An Introduction to the Study of Chinese Painting*, New York, 1958.

Williamson, H. R., *Wang An Shih, a Chinese Statesman and Educationalist of the Sung Dynasty*, 2 vols., London, 1935–1937.

Wright, Arthur F., ed., *Studies in Chinese Thought*, Chicago, 1953.

———, ed., *The Confucian Persuasion*, Stanford, 1960.

JAPAN — *See also Readings for Chapter 12*

Barrett, William, ed., *Zen Buddhism*, Garden City, 1956. Selections from the writings of a modern Japanese authority, D. T. Suzuki.

Sansom, George B., *A History of Japan, 1334–1615*, Stanford, 1961. Clear and insightful; a major contribution to an understanding of the period.

———, *The Western World and Japan*, New York, 1950.

· Waley, Arthur, *No Plays of Japan*, New York, 1922 (Evergreen).

SOURCE MATERIALS

Asakawa, Kanichi, ed., *The Documents of Iriki, Illustrative of the Development of the Feudal Institutions of Japan.*

Boxer, C. R., ed., *South China in the Sixteenth Century* (narratives of Portuguese and Spanish visitors, 1550–1575).

Chinese Novels and Short Stories: Buck, Pearl, tr., *All Men Are Brothers;* Howell, E. B., tr., *Inconstancy of Madam Chuang and Other Stories;* Waley, Arthur, tr., *The Monkey.*

- de Bary, W. T., ed., *Sources of Chinese Tradition*, "The Confucian Revival." (Columbia).
- ———, ed., *Sources of Indian Tradition*, "Islam in Medieval India." (Columbia).
- ———, ed., *Sources of Japanese Tradition*, "Medieval Japan." (Columbia).

Gallagher, L. J., tr., *China in the Sixteenth Century: The Journals of Matthew Ricci. 1583–1610* (a Jesuit missionary).

McCullough, H. C., *The Taiheiki: A Chronicle of Medieval Japan.*

Reischauer, E. O., and Yamagiwa, J. K., *Translations from Early Japanese Literature* (eleventh to thirteenth centuries).

Shinoda, M., *The Founding of the Kamakura Shogunate 1180–1185, with Selected Translations from the Azuma Kagami.* Translation of part of the chief source for the institution and early history of the Shogunate.

Waley, Arthur, tr., *The Travels of an Alchemist, the Journeys of the Taoist Ch'ang Ch'un.*

Yule, Henry, tr., *The Book of Ser Marco Polo.*

PART FIVE

The Transition from Medieval to Modern

By the end of the thirteenth century the world described as medieval had begun to fade. Ideals of chivalry, of a static economy, of a universal Church and empire, and of a collectivist society were gradually giving way to institutions and conceptions more modern in character. The heyday of feudalism, of Gothic architecture, and of the Scholastic philosophy was practically over. Yet other elements of medieval culture lingered for centuries. Such was true of the universities, of the Roman law, of the discoveries in science, and of the classicism and humanism that flowered in the medieval schools. These elements merged with others to form a new civilization in Italy and eventually in other European countries between 1300 and 1650. Known as the Renaissance, this civilization contained such components of individualism, secularism, optimism, and naturalism as to mark an important transition stage to the modern world. After 1517 it was accompanied by religious reform and revolution, which owed at least some of their inspiration to the individualism already rampant. But the religious movement, commonly called the Reformation, also harked back to the Middle Ages. Virtually without exception the Reformers believed that the Scriptures and the writings of the Church Fathers should be the exclusive sources of Christian doctrine. Both the Renaissance and the Reformation had their economic counterpart in the Commercial Revolution, which likewise had medieval roots in the growth of cities and the revival of trade with the East during the eleventh and succeeding centuries.

A Chronological Table

POLITICS AND ECONOMICS	ARTS AND LETTERS
1300 Rise of capitalism, 1300–1500 Growth of banking and development of money economy, 1300–1600	Development of the novel in China, 1300– Boccaccio, 1313–1375
1400 The domestic system, 1400–1750 The enclosure movement, 1400– Voyages of discovery and exploration, 1450–1600 War of the Roses in England, 1455–1485 Tudor Dynasty in England, 1485–1603 Unification of Spain, 1492	Leonardo da Vinci, 1452–1519 Michelangelo, 1475–1564 Rabelais, *ca.* 1490–1553
1500 Revolt of the knights in Germany, 1522–1523 Peasants' Revolt in Germany, 1524–1525 Mogul Dynasty in India, 1526–1857	Montaigne, 1533–1592 Cervantes, 1547–1616
1550 Akbar the Great Mogul, 1556–1605 Revolt of the Netherlands, 1565–1609 Spanish Armada, 1588 Bourbon Dynasty in France, 1589–1792	Shakespeare, 1564–1616 Rubens, 1577–1640 Velásquez, 1599–1660
1600 Cameralism, 1600–1800 Joint stock companies, 1600– Mercantilism, 1600–1789 Tokugawa Shogunate (Japan), 1603–1867 Beginning of isolation policy in Japan, 1637 British trading posts in India, 1641	Baroque architecture, 1600–1750 Rembrandt, 1606–1669 Taj Mahal, 1632–1647 Development of *Kabuki* drama in Japan, 1650

PHILOSOPHY AND SCIENCE

RELIGION

1300

Babylonian Captivity of Papacy, 1309–1379
The Great Schism, 1379–1417

1400

Christian Renaissance, 1400–1500

Savonarola, 1452–1498

Machiavelli, 1469–1527
Erasmus, 1466?–1536
Copernicus, 1473–1543

Martin Luther, 1483–1546

1500

Founding of Sikh religious sect in India, *ca.* 1500
Catholic Reformation, 1500–1563
John Calvin, 1509–1564
Beginning of Protestant Revolution, 1517
Zwinglian movement in Switzerland, 1519–1529
Rise of Anabaptists, *ca.* 1520

Founding of Society of Jesus, 1534
Henry VIII establishes Anglican Church, 1534
Council of Trent, 1545–1563
Introduction of Christianity into Japan, 1549–1551
Jesuit missionaries active in China, 1550
Religious toleration in India, 1556–1632

1550

Sir Francis Bacon, 1561–1626

Galileo, 1564–1642
Sir William Harvey, 1578–1657

Elizabethan compromise, 1570

Edict of Nantes, 1598

1600

Growth of Confucian scholarship in Japan, 1603

Expulsion of Christians from Japan, 1637

CHAPTER 18

The Civilization of the Renaissance:

In Italy

> Wherefore it may be surely said that those who are the possessors
> of such rare and numerous gifts as were seen in Raphael of Ur-
> bino, are not merely men, but, if it not be a sin to say it, mortal
> gods . . .
>
> —Giorgio Vasari, *Lives of the Painters*

Soon after 1300 the majority of the characteristic institutions and ideals of the Middle Ages had begun to decay. Chivalry, feudalism, the Holy Roman Empire, the universal authority of the papacy, the guild system of trade and industry were all gradually being weakened and would eventually disappear. The great age of the Gothic cathedrals was practically over, the Scholastic philosophy was beginning to be ridiculed and despised, and the supremacy of the religious and ethical interpretations of life was being slowly but effectively undermined. In place of all these there gradually emerged new institutions and ways of thinking of sufficient importance to stamp the centuries that followed with the character of a different civilization. The traditional name applied to this civilization, which extended from 1300 to approximately 1650, is the Renaissance.

The transition from the Middle Ages to the Renaissance

The term Renaissance leaves much to be desired from the standpoint of historical accuracy. Literally it means rebirth, and it is commonly taken to imply that in the fourteenth century, or Trecento[1], there was a sudden revival of interest in the classical learning of Greece and Rome. But this implication is far from strictly true. Interest in the classics was by no means rare in the

Meaning of the term Renaissance

[1] So called from the Italian word for three hundred, *trecento*, used to designate the century which followed 1300. Quattrocento, from the word four hundred, is applied to the period of the fifteenth century and Cinquecento to the sixteenth.

later Middle Ages. Such writers as John of Salisbury, Dante, and the Goliard poets were just as enthusiastic admirers of Greek and Latin literature as any who lived in the fourteenth century. Indeed, the so-called Renaissance was in considerable measure simply the culmination of a series of revivals which began as far back as the tenth century. All of these movements were characterized by a reverence for the ancient authors. Even in the cathedral and monastic schools Cicero, Vergil, Seneca, and, later on, Aristotle frequently received as much worshipful adoration as was given to any of the saints.

The Renaissance was a great deal more than a mere revival of pagan learning. It embraced, first of all, an impressive record of new achievements in art, literature, science, philosophy, education, and religion. Although the foundation of many of these was classical, they soon expanded beyond the measure of Greek and Roman influence. Indeed, many of the achievements in painting, science, politics, and religion bore little relation to the classical heritage. Secondly, the Renaissance incorporated a number of dominant ideals and attitudes that gave it the impress of a unique society. Conspicuous among these were optimism, secularism, and individualism; but the most significant of them all was humanism. In its broadest meaning humanism may be defined as emphasis on the human values implicit in the writings of the ancient Greeks and Romans. It was a term derived from Cicero, who used it in the sense of devotion to the liberal arts, or the subjects most compatible with the dignity of man. The humanists rejected the Scholastic philosophy with its preoccupation with theology and logic. They strove for a smooth and elegant style that would appeal more to the aesthetic than to the rational side of man's nature. Though the viewpoint of many of them was pagan, this was not always the case. A large number took Christianity for granted, and some extolled it as the noblest of moral philosophies.

Not only culturally but socially, economically, and politically the Renaissance constituted a new society which differed in many ways from the social pattern of the Middle Ages. To begin with, it was nonecclesiastical. Its great accomplishments were chiefly the work of laymen, not of monks or priests. Such arenas of achievement as the universities, hitherto dominated by the clergy, now went into temporary decline. Gothic and Romanesque architectures, preeminently associated with the medieval church, were superseded by a new style based upon classical models. Latin as a medium of literary expression survived, of course, for it was Roman in origin. But gradually literature in the vernacular acquired a status at least equal to that in Latin. Renaissance society took on an urban rather than a predominantly rural character. The centers of both social and economic life were no longer castles of the feudal nobility or manorial estates but rich cities such as Florence, Milan, Venice, and Rome. Politically, also, the changes were momentous. The decentralized

The Renaissance
more than a
revival of pagan
learning

feudal regime gave way to consolidated government in either large or small units. The rule of dukes and counts was succeeded by that of monarchs, or in some cases by that of oligarchs whose power sprang from their wealth as bankers or merchants. As a noted authority points out, "the fifteenth and sixteenth centuries were the age of kings." [2]

1. THE CAUSES OF THE RENAISSANCE

To determine the causes of a movement as complex as the Renaissance is not an easy task. In large measure it was a result of the disintegration of a medieval society that was no longer in harmony with changed economic and cultural conditions. The growth of commerce and the rise of national monarchies made the decentralized feudal regime obsolete. The self-sufficient manorial system decayed with the development of trade between distant regions and the appearance of new employment opportunities for villeins and serfs. As cities multiplied the nobles suffered a loss of power to the emerging middle class. Culturally, also, there was radical change. Medieval Scholasticism failed to satisfy the growing interest in natural science. Gothic architecture, which had reached its zenith of harmony and restraint in the thirteenth century, became exaggerated and flamboyant. Asceticism as an ideal was losing its appeal as men uncovered a greater variety of worldly satisfactions. Nearly everywhere, especially in southern Europe, there was a demand for a broader expanse of knowledge, a new style of living, and a greater recognition of the status of the individual. One factor, it may be said, was primarily responsible for nearly all these changes. That factor was the growth of cities, with their stimulating influence and the tendency of their populations to be impatient with old ways of living. But the cities themselves were chiefly the product of the revival of commerce. As far back as the eleventh century a flourishing trade had begun with the Saracenic and Byzantine empires. Material commodities were not the only things exchanged. There was a prosperous commerce also in ideas, manuscripts, and artistic influences. By the fourteenth century the Italian cities engaged in this trade had reached such a state of affluence that they were well adapted to becoming the centers of a cultural revival.

The main causes

Soon after the Renaissance got under way, its progress was greatly accelerated by the influence of secular and ecclesiastical patrons of learning. Outstanding among the former were the Medici family in Florence, the Sforza family in Milan, the Este lords of Ferrara, and Alfonso the Magnanimous of Naples. Most of these patrons were wealthy merchants who had become despots of the city republics in which they lived. The ecclesiastical patrons included such Popes as Nicholas V, Pius II, Julius II, and Leo X. The

Influence of patrons of learning

[2] Denys Hay, *The Italian Renaissance in Its Historical Background*, p. 15.

attitude of these men was singularly at variance with what is normally expected of occupants of the fisherman's throne. They displayed no interest in theology or in the conversion of the ungodly. They kept on the payroll of the Church men who openly attacked fundamental Christian doctrines. Nicholas V, for example, employed as a papal secretary the celebrated Lorenzo Valla, who exposed an important document of the Church as a forgery and preached a philosophy of carnal pleasure. Whatever the incongruity of their attitude, the work of these Popes was of inestimable value to cultural progress, for they bestowed their patronage upon some of the most brilliant artists and literary men of the Italian Renaissance.

Before leaving this subject of factors responsible for the Renaissance, it will be desirable to dispose of two alleged causes commonly believed to have been of decisive importance. One of these is the Crusades, and the other is the invention of printing. In a preceding chapter we observed that the intellectual influence of the Crusades was slight. The introduction of Saracenic learning into Europe came about as a result of the work of scholars in the libraries of Toledo and Cordova and as a consequence of the trade revival between the Italian cities and the Near East. Only to the extent that the Crusades weakened feudalism, diminished the prestige of the papacy, and helped to give the Italian cities a monopoly of Mediterranean trade may they be considered as in any way responsible for the beginning of Renaissance civilization. And even these results can be ascribed in large part to other factors.

Although the invention of printing was an achievement of the utmost importance, it was perhaps even less than the Crusades a direct cause of the Renaissance. For one thing, it came too late. So far as the evidence shows, no printing press was in operation much before the middle of the fifteenth century. The earliest work known to have been printed from movable type actually dates from 1454.[3] By this time the Renaissance in Italy was already well under way, having started about a century and a half before. Furthermore, many of the early humanists were decidedly hostile toward the new invention. They regarded it as a barbarous German contraption and refused to allow their works to be printed lest they obtain too wide a circulation and be misunderstood by the common people. It should also be noted that the earliest publishing firms were far more interested in turning out religious books and popular stories than in printing the writings of the new learning. Devotional tracts, service books for the Church, writings of the theologians, and collections of ancient legends were the types of reading matter which really ap-

Alleged causes of the Renaissance: (1) the Crusades

(2) the invention of printing by movable type

---

[3] This was an indulgence issued from the press of Johann Gutenberg at Mainz, who is commonly credited with the invention of printing, though it is somewhat doubtful that he did more than perfect the technique developed by others.

pealed to the public of that day, and were accordingly more profitable to the printers than any of the recondite works of the humanists. The conclusion seems amply justified that the invention of printing served chiefly to accelerate the Renaissance in its later stages, particularly in northern Europe. Most of the great benefits of the invention came after the Renaissance had ended.

2. THE RENAISSANCE IN ITALY

Reference has already been made to the fact that the Renaissance had its beginning in Italy. Why should this have been so? For one reason, Italy had a stronger classical tradition than any other country of western Europe. All through the medieval period the Italians had managed to preserve the belief that they were descendants of the ancient Romans. They looked back upon their ancestry with pride, ignoring of course the infiltrations of Lombard, Byzantine, Saracenic, and Norman blood that had been poured into the people from time to time. In some of the Italian cities traces of the old Roman system of education still survived in the municipal schools. It is likewise true that Italy had a more thoroughly secular culture than most other regions of Latin Christendom. The Italian universities were founded primarily for the study of law or medicine rather than theology, and, with the exception of the University of Rome, few of them had any ecclesiastical connections whatever. In addition to all this, Italy received the full impact of cultural influences from the Byzantine and Saracenic civilizations. Finally, and perhaps most important of all, the Italian cities were the main beneficiaries of the revival of trade with the East. For years the seaport towns of Venice, Naples, Genoa, and Pisa enjoyed a virtual monopoly of the Mediterranean trade, while the merchants of Florence, Bologna, Piacenza, and other cities of the Lombard plain served as the chief middlemen in the commerce between northern and southern Europe. The economic prosperity thus acquired was the principal foundation of the intellectual and artistic progress.

I. THE POLITICAL BACKGROUND It is generally assumed that orderly and efficient government is a necessary condition for the development of a superior culture; but such was not the case with the civilization we are now considering. The Renaissance was born in the midst of political turmoil. Italy was not a unified state when the Renaissance began, and throughout the period the country remained in a turbulent condition. The reasons for this chaos were several. The first was the failure of universal government. In common with the rest of central Europe, Italy was supposed to be part of the Holy Roman Empire. But after the death of Conrad IV in 1254 the imperial throne was vacant for nineteen years. When successors were finally chosen, they proved to be too weak to wield any effective authority beyond their own family domains. The Pope

Why the
Renaissance began in Italy

The political
crisis in Italy

Statue of the condottiere Bartolommeo Colleoni by Verrocchio. In front of the Church of SS. Giovanni e Paolo, Venice.

also lost his power as a political ruler over the Italian peninsula. As a result of a quarrel between Pope Boniface VIII and King Philip IV of France the papacy was transferred to Avignon, France, where it remained under greater or less subjection to the French king for seventy years. By the time a Pope was finally crowned again in Rome in 1378, the political authority of the universal Church had been eroded. The dozen or more petty states into which Italy was divided had grown accustomed to managing their own affairs. Politically, the Pope was little more than another Italian prince with an uncertain authority limited to a belt of land stretching across the peninsula.

The principal
Italian states:
Milan

The remainder of the Italian states rapidly solidified their rule as a means of preserving their power. But stability was not easily accomplished. Interstate rivalries, internal revolts, wars of conquest, and threats of invasion combined to continue the enveloping chaos. At the beginning of the Renaissance most of the Italian states were nominally republics. As conflicts increased and ambitions grew, many of them evolved into tyrannies or oligarchies. As early as 1311 the government of Milan became a dictatorship under the head of the Visconti family. In 1450 the Visconti were succeeded by Francesco Sforza, notorious as a *condottiere*, or leader of a band of mercenary soldiers. The new despotism was no less tyrannical than the old and was tolerated by its subjects chiefly because of its success in maintaining order and prosperity.

Despotism in Venice differed from that in Milan in being collective rather than individual. Although a *doge* was the nominal head of the state, he was hemmed in by so many restrictions that he was little more than a figurehead. The real power rested with the heads of the chief business houses, who constituted a tight little oligarchy. They wielded effective authority through the Council of Ten, which took swift and merciless action against suspected enemies of the government. Politically as well as culturally, the most progressive of the Italian states was Florence. But even the Florentines were by no means entirely free from oligarchic evils. Though a constitution adopted in 1282 vested the government in an elected council whose members served short terms, restrictions on the suffrage ensured control of this body by the dominant business interests. Defeat in war and failure to maintain unbroken prosperity discredited this oligarchy, and in 1434 it was replaced by the rule of Cosimo de' Medici. Although Cosimo held no official title, he was accepted by the people as a virtual dictator, mainly because he ruled with an eye to their welfare. He and his descendants, the most famous of whom was his grandson Lorenzo the Magnificent, controlled the political life of Florence for sixty years. To the heads of the Medici family must be given a large measure of credit for the fact that Florence remained for so long the most brilliant center of the Italian Renaissance.

In the view of a number of historians the origins of the modern state system can be traced to Renaissance Italy. The rulers of such states as Milan, Florence, and Venice repudiated the conception of the state as existing for religious purposes and gave it a secular character. They emphasized civic responsibility, loyalty, and concern for the public welfare. They developed a strong notion of the end of the state as the advancement of its own interests. They invented procedures of diplomacy, including a system of permanent ambassadors in foreign capitals. They fostered alliances and toyed with the idea of a balance of power to keep the peace. The balance never really worked, however. Ambitious politicians in some of the states, notably Milan, disturbed it by soliciting help for their schemes from powerful nations outside the peninsula. A tragic consequence was the invasion of Italy by the French in 1494, followed soon afterward by a Spanish invasion from the Kingdom of Aragon. Henceforth the peninsula was at the mercy of competing armies of major European powers.

Perhaps the most "modern" of the activities of the Italian Renaissance states were their ventures in "imperialism." Before the end of the fourteenth century Milan reached out and annexed nearly the whole of the Lombard plain. Needing an agricultural province as a source of food supply and coveting control of mainland trade routes, Venice conquered nearly all of northeastern Italy, including the cities of Padua and Verona. Nor did the republic of Florence lag behind in the development of expansionist ambitions. Before the end of the fourteenth century practically all of the territory of Tuscany had been taken, and in 1406 the great mercantile city of Pisa suc-

THE STATES OF ITALY DURING THE RENAISSANCE ca. 1494

cumbed to Florentine domination. The papacy also took part in the
general movement of territorial aggrandizement. Under such
worldly and aggressive Popes as Alexander VI (1492–1503) and
Julius II (1503–1513) the dominion of the Papal States was extended over most of central Italy. By the early 1500's nearly the
whole peninsula had been brought under the five most powerful
states: Milan, Venice, Florence, the Kingdom of Naples, and the
538 States of the Church.

II. THE LITERARY AND ARTISTIC CULTURE No wide gulf separated Italian Renaissance literature from the literature of the later Middle Ages. The majority of the literary achievements between 1300 and 1550 were already foreshadowed in one or another of the different trends initiated in the twelfth and thirteenth centuries. The so-called father of Italian Renaissance literature, Francesco Petrarca or Petrarch (1304–1374), was himself very close to the medieval temper. He employed the same Tuscan dialect which Dante had chosen as the basis of an Italian literary language. Moreover, he believed firmly in Christianity as the way of salvation for man, and he was addicted at times to a monkish asceticism. His best-known writings, the sonnets he addressed to his beloved Laura, partook of the same flavor as the chivalrous love poetry of the thirteenth-century troubadours. Although Petrarch has been widely acclaimed as the father of humanism, the humanism he founded differed but slightly from that of many a medieval poet. About all that was new in Petrarch was his intense absorption in his own personality and his passionate devotion to the Greek as well as to the Latin classics.[4] Even here the novelty was primarily a matter of degree. It is not quite accurate to think of Petrarch as "the first modern man."

Petrarch, the father of Italian Renaissance literature

The second of the great figures in the Italian literary Renaissance, Giovanni Boccaccio (1313–1375), was scarcely more of an original genius. Like Petrarch, Boccaccio was a Florentine, the illegitimate son of a prosperous merchant. His father having planned for him a business career, he was sent to Naples to serve an apprenticeship in a branch of the great Florentine banking house of the Bardi. But the young Boccaccio soon displayed more ardor in worshiping in the temple of the Muses than in computing the interest on loans. It was perhaps natural that this should be so, for Naples was a center of gracious living under languorous skies and of strong poetic traditions emanating from the lands of the Saracens and the troubadours. It was an environment especially fitted to stimulate the poetic fancies of youth. Boccaccio was also inspired by a passionate love for the beautiful wife of a Neapolitan citizen. Nearly all of his earlier works were poems and romances dealing with the triumphs and tortures of this love. Gradually his skill in the story-telling art attained perfection, and he eventually found prose a more suitable medium for his purposes. His first work of merit in the new style was *Fiammetta*, a forerunner of the psychological novel. But by far the most notable of Boccaccio's writings was his *Decameron*, which he wrote after his return to Florence about 1348. The *Decameron* con-

The more robust humanism of Boccaccio

The Decameron

[4] Curiously enough, Petrarch could not read Greek. His knowledge of Hellenic culture was acquired entirely from what the Romans said about it. His earnest attempts to learn the language resulted in failure, for he could find no competent tutor. He therefore contented himself to the end of his life with gazing admiringly at the pages of Homer but with no more than a vague understanding of what they contained.

sists of 100 stories which the author puts into the mouths of seven young women and three young men. The stories do not form a novel revolving about a continuous theme but are united by the artificial plot of having been told by a group of people who are concerned merely with passing the time during their sojourn at a villa outside of Florence to escape the ravages of the Black Death. Though some of the tales were probably invented by Boccaccio, most of them were drawn from the *fabliaux*, from the *Book of the 1001 Nights*, and from other medieval sources. In general, they differ from their medieval prototypes in being slightly more ribald, egoistic, and anticlerical and more deeply concerned with a frank justification of the carnal life. Yet the *Decameron* certainly does not represent, as many people think, the first emphatic protest against the ascetic and impersonal ideals of the early Middle Ages. Its real significance lies in the fact that it set the pattern for Italian prose and exerted considerable influence upon Renaissance writers in other countries.

The character of literature in the Quattrocento

The death of Boccaccio in 1375 marks the end of the first period of the Italian Renaissance in literature, the Trecento. The age which followed, known as the Quattrocento, was characterized by a more zealous devotion to the Latin language and a broader conception of humanistic studies. The Italian of Dante and Boccaccio was regarded now by many writers as an inferior language unsuited to the perfection of an elegant style and the expression of noble ideas. No longer were the humanities thought of as synonymous with rhetoric, oratory, grammar, ethics, and poetry, but were held to include history, philosophy, and religion as well. In fine, they embraced every subject considered by the ancients as a proper medium for the study of man. As a third difference, the men of the Quattrocento turned away from the asceticism of Petrarch. They taught that nature had endowed man for action, for usefulness to his family and society, not for religious seclusion. Passion, ambition, and the quest for glory are noble impulses and ought to be encouraged. They refused to condemn the striving for material possessions, for they argued that the history of man's progress is inseparable from his success in gaining mastery over the earth and its resources. A few of the writers of the Quattrocento were completely pagan or atheistic, but most of them were neither religious nor antireligious. They took Christianity for granted and were concerned primarily with worldly interests.

The passion for Greek studies

The Quattrocento was also the period when the passion for Greek studies was at its zenith. Prior to this time the Italian humanists had achieved but indifferent success in their attempts to learn the Greek language and to discover the treasures of Hellenic culture. But in 1393 a famous scholar of Constantinople, Manuel Chrysaloras, arrived in Venice on a mission from the Byzantine emperor to implore the aid of the West in a war against the Turks.

Almost immediately acclaimed by the Italians as an apostle of the glorious Hellenic past, he was eventually persuaded to accept a professorship of the Greek classics at the University of Florence. About the beginning of the fifteenth century several other Byzantine scholars, notably Platonist philosophers, migrated to Italy. The influence of these men in providing information about the achievements of the ancient Greeks seems to have been considerable. At any rate, it was not long until Italian scholars began to make trips to Constantinople and other Byzantine cities in search of manuscripts. Between 1413 and 1423 a certain Giovanni Aurispa, for example, brought back nearly 250 manuscript books, including works of Sophocles, Euripides, and Thucydides. It was in this way that many of the Hellenic classics, particularly the writings of the dramatists, historians, and earlier philosophers, were first made available to the modern world.

The last great age in the development of Italian Renaissance literature was the Cinquecento, the period from 1500 to about 1550. Italian was now raised to a full equality with Greek and Latin, classical and modern influences were more perfectly blended, and a deeper originality of both form and content was achieved. But the literary capital of the Renaissance was no longer Florence. In 1494 that city came under the rule of the fanatical reformer Savonarola; and, while the Medici were restored to power about eighteen years later, the brilliant Tuscan metropolis soon afterward fell a victim of factional disputes and foreign invasion. During the first half of the sixteenth century the city of Rome gradually rose to a position of cultural leadership, mainly because of the patronage of the Church, especially during the reign of Pope Leo X (Giovanni de' Medici), the son of Lorenzo the Magnificent. When he was only fourteen years old, his father's influence had been sufficient to procure his appointment as a cardinal. Elevated to St. Peter's throne in 1513, he is reported to have said, "Let us enjoy the papacy since God has given it to us." There can be little doubt that he did enjoy it, for he was a magnificent spendthrift, lavishing rewards upon artists and writers and financing the construction of beautiful churches.

The chief forms of literature developed in the Cinquecento were epic and pastoral poetry, drama, and history. The most eminent of the writers of epics was Ludovico Ariosto (1474–1533), author of a lengthy poem entitled *Orlando Furioso*. Although woven largely of materials taken from the romances of adventure and the legends of the Arthurian cycle, this work differed radically from any of the medieval epics. It incorporated much that was derived from classical sources; it lacked the impersonal quality of the medieval romances; and it was totally devoid of idealism. Ariosto wrote to make men laugh and to charm them with felicitous descriptions of the quiet splendor of nature and the passionate beauty of love. His work represents the disillusionment of the late Rennaissance, the loss of hope

The Cinque-cento

The epic and the pastoral romance

and faith, and the tendency to seek consolation in the pursuit of aesthetic pleasure. The development of pastoral poetry at this time probably reflects a similar attitude of disenchantment and loss of confidence. As the name implies, the pastoral romance glorifies the simple life amid rustic surroundings and expresses the yearning for a golden age of unspoiled pleasures and freedom from the worries and frustrations of artificial urban society. The chief author of this type of literature in the Italian Renaissance was Jacopo Sannazaro (1458–1530), who gave to his main work the title of *Arcadia*.

In the field of the drama the Italians never achieved more than moderate success. Their failure as writers of tragedy was particularly noticeable, despite the fact that they had considerable knowledge of classical models from which to profit. The Italian was apparently too much of an individualist to be influenced profoundly by the Greek conception of a tragic conflict between man and society and too much of an optimist to brood over personal suffering. His mind was fixed upon the compensations of life rather than upon its grim and terrifying aspects. His real talents lay in naturalistic description, in the development of light and joyous themes, and in the expression of personal egotism. It was natural, therefore, that the best of his dramas should have been comedies, especially satirical comedies, rather than tragedies. The first and the greatest of the Italian comedians was a man who is far better known as a political philosopher—Niccolò Machiavelli (1469–1527). The finest product of his dramatic skill was a work entitled *Mandragola*, which has been called "the ripest and most powerful play in the Italian language." [5] Sparkling with salacious wit and based upon incidents typical of life in the author's native city of Florence, it is a lurid satire of Renaissance society. In this as in his other writings, Machiavelli reveals his cynical views of human nature. He appears to believe that all human beings are knaves and fools at heart, with their meanness and stupidity only partly concealed by a thin veneer of refinement and learning.

The historians of the High Renaissance in Italy displayed a critical spirit and a degree of objectivity which had not been seen since the end of the ancient world. First among them in order of time although not in order of greatness was Machiavelli. In his main historical work, an account of the evolution of the Florentine republic to the death of Lorenzo de' Medici, he rigidly excluded all theological interpretations and sought to discover the natural laws which govern the life of a people. More scientific in his methods of analysis was Machiavelli's younger contemporary, Francesco Guicciardini (1483–1540). Having served many years as an ambassador of Florence and as a governor of papal territories, Guicciardini enjoyed a unique advantage in acquiring familiarity with the cynical

[5] J. A. Symonds, "Machiavelli," *Encyclopedia Britannica* (14th ed.), XIV, 577.

and tortuous political life of his day. His special gifts as a historian were a capacity for minute and realistic analysis and an uncanny ability in disclosing the springs of human action. His masterpiece was his *History of Italy*, a detailed and dispassionate account of the varying fortunes of that country from 1492 to 1534. No study of Renaissance historians would be complete without some mention of Lorenzo Valla (1406–1457), who may properly be regarded as the father of historical criticism. By careful scrutiny of their literary style he challenged the authenticity of a number of accepted documents. He proved the famous "Donation of Constantine" to be a forgery, thereby demolishing one of the principal bases of papal supremacy, since this document purported to have been a grant by the Emperor Constantine of the highest spiritual and temporal power in the West to the Pope. In addition, Valla denied that the so-called Apostles' Creed had ever been written by the Apostles, and he pointed out numerous corruptions in the Vulgate edition of the New Testament as compared with the earlier Greek texts. His critical methods served later on to stimulate a much broader attack by the northern humanists upon the doctrines and practices of the organized Church.

Despite the wealth of brilliant accomplishments in literature, the proudest achievements of the Italian Renaissance were made in the realm of art. Of all the arts, painting was undoubtedly supreme. The evolution of Italian painting followed a course of development which roughly paralleled the history of literature. During the initial period of the Trecento, however, there was only one artist of distinction worthy to be compared to Petrarch and Boccaccio in literature. His name was Giotto (1276–1337). With him, painting definitely took on the status of an independent art, although his master Cimabue had already made some beginnings in this direction. Giotto was preeminently a naturalist. So skillful was he in depicting the semblance of life that, according to the story, one of his drawings of a fly so completely deceived Cimabue that he attempted to brush the creature away with his hand. Giotto also displayed more than ordinary talent in the portrayal of action, especially in such frescoes as *Saint Francis Preaching to the Birds*, *The Massacre of the Innocents*, and his scenes from the life of Christ.

Italian painting in the Trecento: Giotto the naturalist

See color plates at page 520

It was not till the Quattrocento, however, that Italian Renaissance painting really attained its majority. By this time the increase in wealth and the partial triumph of the secular spirit had freed the domain of art to a large extent from the service of religion. The Church was no longer the only patron of artists. While subject matter from Biblical history was still commonly employed, it was frequently infused with nonreligious themes. The painting of portraits for the purpose of revealing the hidden mysteries of the soul now became popular. Paintings intended to appeal primarily to the intellect were paralleled by others whose only purpose was to de-

Painting in the Quattrocento

Masaccio, *The Expulsion of Adam and Eve from the Garden of Eden.* As the first of the realists, Masaccio departed from the tradition of Giotto and introduced emotion and psychological study into his paintings. In the Church of Santa Maria del Carmine, Florence.

light the eye with gorgeous color and beauty of form. The Quattrocento was characterized also by the introduction of painting in oil, probably from Flanders. The use of the new technique doubtless had much to do with the artistic advance of this period. Since oil does not dry so quickly as water, the painter could now work more leisurely, taking his time with the more difficult parts of the picture and making corrections if necessary as he went along.

The majority of the painters of the Quattrocento were Florentines. First among them was a precocious youth known as Masaccio (1401–1428). Although he died at the age of twenty-seven, Masaccio inspired the work of Italian painters for a hundred years. He is commonly considered the first of the realists in Renaissance art. Besides, he introduced a tactile quality into his work which profoundly influenced many of his successors. The greatest of his paintings, *The Expulsion of Adam and Eve from the Garden* and *The Tribute Money*, dealt not with specific themes but with the simple emotions common to mankind in all ages. Masaccio was also the first to achieve any notable success in imparting unity of action to groups of figures and in giving the effect of thickness to objects by the use of light and shade.

The best known of the painters who followed directly the paths

The Florentine painters: Masaccio

marked out by Masaccio was Sandro Botticelli (1444–1510), who specialized in depicting both religious and classical themes. He excelled in representing human emotions, but always with an eye for harmony and rhythm. In spite of his sensitive feeling for nature which led him to paint with such delicate skill the subtle loveliness of youth, the summer sky, and the tender bloom of spring, Botticelli was really more deeply interested in the spiritual beauty of the soul. Like others of his time, he was strongly influenced by Neo-Platonism and dreamed of the reconciliation of pagan and Christian thought. As a consequence many of the countenances he painted reveal a pensive sadness, a mystic yearning for the divine. By no means all of his work had a religious import. His *Allegory of Spring* and *Birth of Venus* are based entirely upon classical mythology and suggest little more than an absorbing pleasure in the unfolding of life and a romantic longing for the glories of ancient Greece and Rome.

See color plates at page 520

Perhaps the greatest of the Florentine painters was Leonardo da Vinci (1452–1519), one of the most talented and versatile geniuses who ever lived. Not only was he a gifted painter but a sculptor, musician, and architect of outstanding ability and a brilliant engineer and philosopher. The son of an illicit union of a prominent lawyer and a woman of humble station, he was placed by his father at an early age under the instruction of Verrocchio, a sculptor and painter of some renown and the most celebrated teacher of art in Florence. By the time he was twenty-five Leonardo was already sufficiently distinguished as a painter to win the favor of Lorenzo the Magnificent. But after five or six years he appears to have become dissatisfied with the intellectual and artistic views of the Medici and gladly accepted an offer of regular employment at the court of the Sforza in Milan. It was under the patronage of the Sforza that he produced some of the finest achievements of his life. His work, which embraces the late years of the fifteenth century and the first two decades of the sixteenth, marks the beginning of the so-called High Renaissance in Italy.

As a painter Leonardo da Vinci was impatient with the established tradition of striving to imitate classical models. He believed that all art should have as its basis a scientific study of nature. But he had no intention of confining his interests to the mere surface appearances of things. He was convinced that the secrets of nature are deeply hidden, and that the artist must examine the structure of a plant or probe into the emotions of a human soul as painstakingly as the anatomist would dissect a body. He appears especially to have been fascinated by the grotesque and unusual in nature. Yawning fissures in the earth, jagged pinnacles of rocks, rare plants and animals, embryos, and fossils—these were the phenomena he loved to ponder, evidently in the belief that this mysterious universe yields more of its secrets in the fantastic and unaccustomed than in the things that are commonplace and obvious. For the same reason he devoted much time to the study of exceptional human types, often wandering the streets for hours in quest of some face that would reveal the beauty or terror, the sincerity or hypocrisy, of the personality behind it. As a result of this deliberate selection of subjects, the paintings of Leonardo have a quality of realism decidedly at variance with the ordinary type. He did not generally portray the aspects of nature as they appear to the casual observer but strove to present them as symbols of his own philosophic reflections. He was one of the most profoundly intellectual of painters.

Leonardo's famous paintings

See color plates
at page 521

It is generally agreed that Leonardo da Vinci's masterpieces are his *Virgin of the Rocks*, his *Last Supper*, and his *Mona Lisa*. The first represents not only his marvelous technical skill but also his passion for science and his belief in the universe as a well-ordered place. The figures are arranged in geometric composition with every rock and plant depicted in accurate detail. The *Last Supper*, painted on the walls of the rectory of Santa Maria delle Grazie in Milan, is a study of psychological reactions. A serene Christ, resigned to his terrible fate, has just announced to his disciples that one of them will betray him. The purpose of the artist is to portray the mingled emotions of surprise, horror, and guilt revealed in the faces of the disciples as they gradually perceive the meaning of their master's statement. The third of Leonardo's major triumphs, the *Mona Lisa*, reflects a similar interest in the varied moods of the human soul. Although it is true that the *Mona Lisa* (or *Monna Lisa*, *i.e.*, "my Lady Lisa") is a portrait of an actual woman, the wife of Francesco del Giocondo, a Neapolitan, it is more than a mere photographic likeness. The distinguished art critic and historian Bernard Berenson has said of it, "Who like Leonardo has depicted . . . the inexhaustible fascination of the woman in her years of mastery? . . . Leonardo is the one artist of whom it may be said with perfect literalness: 'Nothing that he touched but turned into a thing of eternal beauty.' " [6] Also distinguishing the *Mona Lisa* are its "stimulating" and "convincing" tactile values and the fact that it is the supreme embodiment of the artist's skill in depicting the play of light and shade. In place of the old technique of showing a gradual transition from light to dark, Leonardo introduced a new method of punctuating darker areas with little spots of light, and *vice versa*. The effect was to surround the faces in many of his paintings with a gentle haze, accentuating their tender and pensive look. His use of this method had the result of illuminating some of the figures in the background of his paintings and of giving a suggestion of dark mystery to others.

The late Quattrocento, or the beginning of the High Renaissance, was marked by the rise of another celebrated school of Italian paint-

ing, the so-called Venetian school. Its chief representatives included
Giorgione (1478–1510), Titian (*ca.* 1488–1576), and Tintoretto
(1518–1594). Of the three, Titian was perhaps the greatest. The
work of all these men reflected the luxurious life and the pleasure-
loving interests of the thriving commercial city of Venice. The
Venetian painters had none of the preoccupation with philosophical
and psychological themes that had characterized the Florentine
school. Their aim was to appeal to the senses rather than to the
mind. They delighted in painting idyllic landscapes and gorgeous
symphonies of color. For their subject matter they chose not merely
the opulent beauty of Venetian sunsets and the shimmering silver of
lagoons in the moonlight but also the man-made splendor of sparkling jewels, richly colored satins and velvets, and gorgeous palaces.
Their portraits were invariably likenesses of the rich and the powerful. In the subordination of form and meaning to color and elegance
there were mirrored not only the sumptuous tastes of a wealthy
bourgeoisie but also definite traces of Oriental influence which had
filtered through from Byzantium during the late Middle Ages.

The remaining great painters of the High Renaissance all lived
their active careers in the Cinquecento. It was in this period that the
evolution of art reached its peak, and the first signs of decay began
to appear. Rome was now almost the only artistic center of importance on the mainland of the Italian peninsula, although the traditions of the Florentine school still exerted a potent influence.
Among the eminent painters of this period at least two must be
given more than passing attention. One of the most noted was
Raphael (1483–1520), a native of Urbino, and perhaps the most
popular artist of the entire Renaissance. The lasting appeal of his
style is due primarily to his intense humanism. He developed a conception of a spiritualized and ennobled humanity. He portrayed the
members of the human species, not as dubious, tormented creatures,
but as temperate, wise, and dignified beings. Although he was influenced by Leonardo da Vinci and copied many features of his work,
he cultivated to a much greater extent than Leonardo a symbolical
or allegorical approach. His *Disputá* symbolized the dialectical relationship between the church in heaven and the church on earth. In a
worldly setting against a brilliant sky, doctors and theologians vehemently debate the meaning of the Eucharist, while in the clouds
above saints and the Trinity repose in the possession of a holy mystery. The *School of Athens* is an allegorical representation of the
conflict between the Platonist and Aristotelian philosophies. Plato is
shown pointing upward to emphasize the spiritual basis of his world
of Ideas, while Aristotle gestures toward the earth to exemplify his
belief that concepts or ideas are inseparably linked with their material embodiments. Raphael is noted also for his portraits and
Madonnas. To the latter, especially, he gave a softness and warmth
that seemed to endow them with a sweetness and piety quite

The Venetian painters

See color plates at page 584

The painters of the late Renais-sance: Raphael

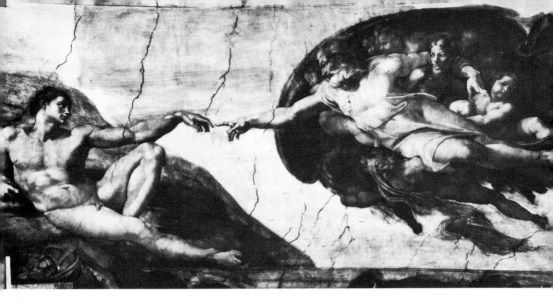

Michelangelo, *The Creation of Adam*. One of a series of frescoes on the ceiling of the Sistine Chapel in Rome. Suggesting philosophical inquiries into the meaning of life and the universe, it represents Renaissance realism at its height.

different from the enigmatic and analytical portraits of Leonardo da Vinci.

Michelangelo

Another towering giant of the Cinquecento in painting was Michelangelo (1475–1564). Beset by the hardships of poverty, harassed by grasping relatives, and torn by the emotional conflicts of his own tempestuous nature, Michelangelo appears as one of the most tragic figures in the history of art. His dark presentiments were often reflected in his work, with the result that some of his paintings are overwrought and almost morbidly pessimistic. Nevertheless, the sense of tragedy he implanted in the scenes he portrayed was not really personal but universal. After the manner of the Greek dramatists he conceived of the tragic fate of mortals as something external to man himself, a product of the cosmic order of things. If there was any one theme that dominated all of his work, it was humanism in its most intense and eloquent form. He considered the pathos and nobility of man as the only legitimate subjects

See color plates at page 585

of art. Rocks and trees and flowers meant nothing to him, not even as background. Michelangelo's grandest achievement as a painter was the series of frescoes he produced on the ceiling of the Sistine Chapel and on the wall above the altar. The sheer physical labor required to complete the task was prodigious. For four and a half years he toiled on a lofty scaffold, most of the time face upward, covering the 6000 square feet of ceiling with nearly 400 figures, many of them as much as ten feet in stature. The series embraces a number of scenes in the mighty epic of the human race according to Christian legend. Among them are *God Dividing the Light from the Darkness, God Creating the Earth, The Creation of Adam, The Fall of Man, The Deluge*, and so on. The culminating scene is *The Last*

Judgment, which Michelangelo finished some thirty years later on the wall back of the altar. Sometimes referred to as the most famous painting in the world, this scene depicts a Herculean Christ damning the great mass of mankind to perdition. Although the subject matter is Christian, the spirit is pagan, as indicated by the naked and muscular figures and the suggestion of a ruthless deity who punishes men beyond their deserts. Nowhere else is Michelangelo's conception of universal tragedy more strongly expressed than in this work of his lonely old age.

Medieval sculpture, as we have already seen, was not an independent art but a mere adjunct of architecture. During the Italian Renaissance a gradual evolution began which ultimately had the effect of freeing sculpture from its bondage to architecture and establishing its status as a separate art frequently devoted to secular purposes. Though the work of a number of earlier artists pointed the way to this evolution, the first great master of Renaissance sculpture was Donatello (1386?–1466). He emancipated his art from Gothic mannerisms and introduced a more vigorous note of individualism than did any of his predecessors. His statue of David standing triumphant over the body of the slain Goliath established a precedent of naturalism and of glorification of the nude which sculptors for many years afterward were destined to follow. Donatello also produced the first

Statue of John the Baptist by Donatello. A fine example of the realistic sculpture of the Italian Renaissance. The forerunner of the Christ is shown as a primitive holy man clad in goatskins and with warts and an impish smile on his face. At the Cathedral of Siena.

Michelangelo,
greatest
of Renaissance
sculptors

monumental equestrian statue in bronze since the time of the Romans, a commanding figure of the *condottiere*, Gattamelata.

One of the greatest sculptors of the Italian Renaissance, and probably of all time, was Michelangelo. Sculpture, in fact, was the artistic field of Michelangelo's personal preference. Despite his success as a painter he considered himself unfitted for that work. Whether he was ever particularly happy as a sculptor might be open to debate, for he smashed some of the works upon which he had spent months of labor and invested others with the same quality of pessimism that characterized much of his painting. The dominant purpose which motivated all of his sculpture was the expression of thought in stone. His art was above mere naturalism, for he subordinated nature to the force and sweep of his ideas. Other features of his work included the use of distortion for powerful effect, preoccupation with themes of disillusionment and tragedy, and a tendency to express his philosophical ideas in allegorical form. Most of his great masterpieces were done for the embellishment of tombs, a fact significantly in harmony with his absorbing interest in death, especially in his later career. For the tomb of Pope Julius II, which was never finished, he carved his famous figures of the *Bound Slave* and *Moses*. The first, which is probably in some degree autobiographical, represents tremendous power and talent restrained by the bonds of fate. The statue of Moses is perhaps the leading example of Michelangelo's sculpture showing his use of anatomical distortion to heighten the effect of emotional intensity. Its purpose was evidently to express the towering rage of the prophet on account of the disloyalty of the children of Israel to the faith of their fathers.

Michelangelo's
allegorical
sculpture

Some other examples of Michelangelo's work as a plastic artist create an even more striking impression. On the tombs of the Medici in Florence he produced a number of allegorical figures representing such abstractions as sorrow and despair. Two of them are known by the traditional titles of *Dawn* and *Sunset*. The first is that of a female figure, turning and raising her head like someone called from a dreamless sleep to awake and suffer. *Sunset* is the figure of a powerful man who appears to sink under the load of human misery around him. Whether these allegorical figures were intended to symbolize the disasters that had overtaken the republic of Florence or merely to express the artist's own sense of the repletion of disappointment and defeat in the world is unknown. As Michelangelo's life drew toward its close, he tended to introduce into his sculpture a more exaggerated and spectacular emotional quality. This was especially true of the *Pietà* intended for his own tomb. The *Pietà* is a statue of the Virgin Mary grieving over the body of the dead Christ. The figure standing behind the Virgin is possibly intended to represent Michelangelo himself, contemplating the stark tragedy which seemed to epitomize the reality of life. It is perhaps fitting that this profound but overwrought interpretation of

Pietà by Michelangelo. This portrayal of tragedy was made by the sculptor for his own tomb. Note the distortion for effect exemplified by the elongated body and left arm of the Christ. The figure in the rear is Nicodemus, but was probably intended to stand as a symbol of Michelangelo himself. Original in the Cathedral of Florence.

human existence should have brought the Renaissance epoch in sculpture to a close.

To a much greater extent than either sculpture or painting, Renaissance architecture had its roots in the past. The new building style was eclectic, a compound of elements derived from the Middle Ages and from pagan antiquity. It was not the Hellenic or the Gothic, however, but the Roman and the Romanesque which provided the inspiration for the architecture of the Italian Renaissance. Neither the Greek nor the Gothic had ever found a congenial soil in Italy. The Romanesque, by contrast, was able to flourish there, since it was more in keeping with Italian traditions, while the persistence of a strong admiration for Latin culture made possible a revival of the Roman style. Accordingly, the great architects of the Renaissance generally adopted their building plans from the Romanesque churches and monasteries and copied their decorative devices from the ruins of ancient Rome. The result was an architecture based upon the cruciform floor plan of transept and nave and embodying the decorative features of the column and arch, or the column and lintel, the colonnade, and frequently the dome. Horizontal lines predominated; and, though many of the buildings were churches, the ideals they expressed were the purely secular ones of joy in this life and pride in human achievement. Renaissance architecture emphasized harmony and proportion to a much greater extent than did the Romanesque style. Under the influence of Neo-Platonism, Italian

Renaissance architecture

THE ITALIAN RENAISSANCE IN ARCHITECTURE

The Nave of St. Peter's Church in Rome. The canopy in the center supported by twisted columns covers the papal altar.

The Villa Rotonda of Palladio near Vicenza. A Renaissance building combining the Roman features of a square floor plan and a central dome with the Greek features of Ionic columns and colonnades.

The Cathedral of Florence. Completed by Filippo Brunelleschi in the fifteenth century, the Cathedral of Florence is a prime example of Renaissance architecture. With its majestic dome, massive construction, and horizontal lines, it harks back to the Romans. The bell tower, or campanile, however, begun by Giotto, reflects medieval influence.

architects concluded that perfect proportions in man reflect the harmony of the universe, and that, therefore, the parts of a building should be related to each other and to the whole in the same way as the parts of the human body. A fine example of Renaissance architecture is St. Peter's Church in Rome, built under the patronage of Popes Julius II and Leo X and designed by some of the most celebrated architects of the time, including Donato Bramante and Michelangelo. Profusely decorated with costly paintings and sculpture, it remains to this day the most magnificent church in the world.

III PHILOSOPHY AND SCIENCE The popular impression that the Renaissance represented in every way a marked improvement over the Middle Ages is not strictly true. It was certainly not more than half true in the realm of philosophy. The early humanists scorned logic and even the rationalism of Scholastic philosophy. Such disciplines they regarded as formal and mechanical hindrances to a fine literary style and to the enhancement of the nobility of man. Instead of Aristotle they chose Cicero as their idol and centered their interest almost exclusively upon moral philosophy. During the Quattrocento many became Platonists after the founding of the Platonic Academy by Cosimo de' Medici in Florence. Outstanding among the philosophers of the Academy were Marsilio Ficino (1433–1499) and Pico della Mirandola (1463–1494). Both were deeply pious and sought to reconcile Christianity with philosophy and even to show the basic harmony of all religions and philosophies. They rejected some of the cardinal tenets of humanism—the indissoluble unity of mind and body and the high valuation of material goods—and preached an asceticism that harked back to the Middle Ages. They adulterated their Platonism with some elements taken from Neo-Platonism and even from astrology and other occult pseudosciences.

But not all the Italian humanists were ecstatic worshipers of Plato. In their zeal for a revival of pagan culture some sought to reawaken an interest in Aristotle for his own sake and not as a bulwark of Christianity. Others became Stoics, Epicureans, or Skeptics. The most original philosophers of the Italian Renaissance were Lorenzo Valla, Leonardo da Vinci, and Niccolò Machiavelli. The fearless and sensational ventures of Lorenzo Valla into the field of historical criticism have already been noted. He was equally unconventional as a philosopher. Declaring himself a follower of Epicurus, he avowed the highest good to be tranquil pleasure, condemned asceticism as utterly vain and worthless, and insisted that it is irrational to die for one's country. Although Leonardo da Vinci wrote nothing that could be called a philosophical treatise, he may yet be considered a philosopher in the broad meaning of the word. He was one of the first to condemn unequivocally reliance upon authority as a source of truth, and he urged the use of the inductive method. It may be worthwhile also to take note of his strictures on war, which

Margin notes:
THE RENAISSANCE IN ITALY

Italian Renaissance philosophy: the Platonists

Lorenzo Valla and Leonardo da Vinci

553

he called "that most bestial madness." He wrote that "It is an infinitely atrocious thing to take away the life of a man," and he even refused to divulge the secret of one of his inventions for fear it might be used by unscrupulous rulers to increase the barbarity of war.[7]

Niccolò Machiavelli is by far the most famous—and also the most infamous—political philosopher of the Italian Renaissance. No man did more than he to overturn the basic political conceptions of the Middle Ages, the ideas of universalism, limited government, and the ethical basis of politics. He was the first to conceive of the state in its modern form as a completely sovereign and independent unit. In his *Discourses on Livy* he praised the ancient Roman republic as a model for all time. He lauded constitutionalism, equality, liberty in the sense of freedom from outside interference, and subordination of religion to the interests of the state. But Machiavelli also wrote *The Prince*. More than the *Discourses* it reflects the unhappy condition of Italy in his time. At the end of the fifteenth century Italy had become the cockpit of international struggles. Both France and Spain had invaded the peninsula and were competing with each other for the allegiance of the Italian states. The latter, in many cases, were torn by internal dissension which made them an easy prey for foreign conquerors. In 1498 Machiavelli entered the service of the republic of Florence as Second Chancellor and Secretary. His duties largely involved diplomatic missions to other states. While in Rome he became fascinated with the achievements of Cesare Borgia, son of Pope Alexander VI, in cementing a solidified state out of scattered elements. He noted with approval Cesare's combination of ruthlessness with shrewdness and his complete subordination of morality to political ends. In 1512 the Medici overturned the government of Florence, and Machiavelli was deprived of his position. Disappointed and embittered, he spent the remainder of his life in exile, devoting his time primarily to writing. In his books, especially in *The Prince*, he described the policies and practices of government, not in accordance with some lofty ideal, but as they actually were. The supreme obligation of the ruler, he avowed, was to maintain the power and safety of the country over which he ruled. No consideration of justice or mercy or the sanctity of treaties should be allowed to stand in his way. Cynical in his views of human nature, Machiavelli maintained that all men are prompted exclusively by motives of self-interest, particularly by desires for personal power and material prosperity. The head of the state should therefore take nothing for granted as to the loyalty or affection of his subjects. Machiavelli was the first important realist in political theory since the time of Polybius. The one ideal he kept before him in his later years was the unification of Italy. But this he

[7] Edward MacCurdy (ed.), *The Notebooks of Leonardo da Vinci*, I, 24.

believed had no chance of accomplishment except by the methods of the hard-core realist.

Not only did the narrow attitude of the early humanists in Italy retard the progress of philosophy; it also hindered for some time the advancement of science. The early humanists, as we have seen, were not critical minded. They accepted revered authorities of classical antiquity much too readily. Moreover, their interests were in art and literature, not in science. Part of this emphasis may undoubtedly be attributed to the fact that the leaders of the Renaissance for some time had only a limited knowledge of Greek achievements. The early pagan revival was predominantly a revival of Latin antiquity. And it will be recalled that the contributions of the Romans to science were few and mediocre. But in spite of the unfavorable influence of early humanism, Italy became by the fifteenth century the most important center of scientific discovery in Renaissance Europe. Much of the work was done, however, by non-Italians. Men from all over the Continent came to study in Italy and to profit from the researches of her eminent scholars. They laid the foundations for nearly every major discovery of the fifteenth and sixteenth centuries. Such was notably the case in the fields of astronomy, mathematics, physics, and medicine.

The achievement *par excellence* in astronomy was the revival and demonstration of the heliocentric theory. Contrary to popular opinion, this was the work not of any one man but of several. It will be remembered that the idea of the sun as the center of our universe had originally been set forth by the Hellenistic astronomer Aristarchus in the third century B.C. But then, some 400 years later, the theory of Aristarchus had been superseded by the geocentric explanation of Ptolemy. For more than twelve centuries thereafter the Ptolemaic theory was the universally accepted conclusion as to the nature of the physical universe. The Romans seem never to have questioned it, and it was adopted as a cardinal dogma by the Saracenic and Scholastic philosophers. It was first openly challenged about the middle of the fifteenth century by Nicholas of Cusa, who argued that the earth is not the center of the universe. Soon afterward Leonardo da Vinci taught that the earth rotates on its axis and denied that the apparent revolutions of the sun actually occur. In 1496 the now famous Pole, Nicholas Copernicus (1473–1543), came down into Italy to complete his education in civil and canon law. For ten years he studied in the universities of Bologna, Padua, and Ferrara, adding to his course in the law such subjects as mathematics and medicine. He also acquired an interest in astronomy and studied and worked for some years with the leading professors of that science. But he made no significant discoveries of his own. In the main, he was content to rely upon the observations of others, especially the ancients. His approach was not really scientific. It contained elements of the mystical and such Neo-Platonic assumptions as the notion that the sphere is the perfect shape and the idea that motion is more nearly divine than rest. He accepted most of Ptolemy's premises but denied that they pointed to Ptolemy's conclusion of a geocentric universe. Despite the conservatism of his methods, he feared that his teaching that the planets revolve around the sun would evoke the hostility of the Church. He refrained from publishing his book, *On the Revolutions of the Heavenly Spheres*, until 1543. The proof sheets were brought to him on his deathbed.

The most important astronomical evidence for the heliocentric theory was furnished by the greatest of Italian scientists, Galileo Galilei (1564–1642). With a telescope which he had perfected to a magnifying power of thirty times, he discovered the satellites of Jupiter, the rings of Saturn, and spots on the sun.[8] He was able also to determine that the Milky Way is a collection of celestial bodies independent of our solar system and to form some idea of the enormous distances of the fixed stars. Though there were many who held out against them, these discoveries of Galileo gradually convinced the majority of scientists that the main conclusion of Copernicus was true. The final triumph of this idea is commonly called the Copernican Revolution. Few more significant events have occurred in the intellectual history of the world; for it overturned the medieval world-view and paved the way for modern conceptions of mechanism, skepticism, and the infinity of time and space. Some thinkers believe that it contributed also to the degradation of man, since it swept man out of his majestic position at the center of the universe and reduced him to a mere particle of dust in an endless cosmic machine.

In the front rank among the physicists of the Renaissance were Leonardo da Vinci and Galileo. If Leonardo da Vinci had failed completely as a painter, his contributions to science would entitle him to considerable fame. Not the least of these were his achievements in physics. Though he actually made few complete discoveries, his conclusion that "every weight tends to fall toward the center by the shortest way" contained the kernel of the law of gravitation.[9] In addition, he worked out the principles of an astonishing variety of inventions, including a diving boat, a steam engine, an armored fighting car, and a marble saw. Galileo is especially noted as a physicist for his law of falling bodies. Skeptical of the traditional theory that bodies fall with a speed directly proportional to their weight, he demonstrated by dropping weights from various heights that the distance covered in the fall increases as the square of the time involved. Rejecting the Scholastic notions of absolute gravity and absolute levity, he taught that these are purely relative terms, that

[8] Galileo was not the original inventor of the telescope. That honor is usually accorded to Johannes Lippershey, an obscure optician who lived in the Low Countries about the beginning of the seventeenth century. Galileo learned of Lippershey's invention and improved upon it in a single night.
[9] Edward MacCurdy (ed.), *The Notebooks of Leonardo da Vinci*, I, 18.

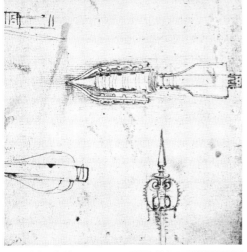

NOTEBOOK SKETCHES BY LEONARDO DA VINCI

Designs for Weapons. Studies of the Shoulder. Cannon Foundry. War Machines.

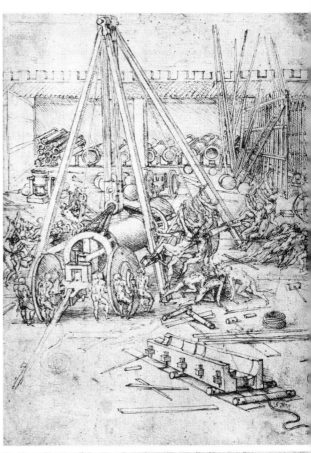

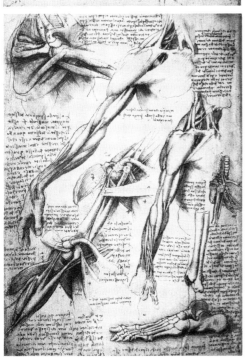

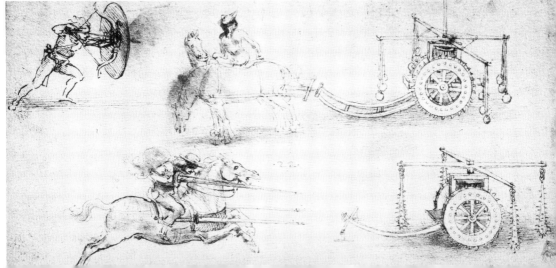

all bodies have weight, even those which like the air are invisible, and that in a vacuum all objects would fall with equal velocity. Galileo seems to have had a broader conception of a universal force of gravitation than Leonardo da Vinci, for he perceived that the power which holds the moon in the vicinity of the earth and causes the satellites of Jupiter to circulate around that planet is essentially the same as the force which enables the earth to draw bodies to its surface. He never formulated this principle as a law, however, nor did he realize all of its implications, as did Newton some fifty years later.

The record of Italian achievements in the various sciences related to medicine is also an impressive one. As early as the fourteenth century a physician by the name of Mundinus introduced the practice of dissection at the University of Bologna as the only proper source of anatomical knowledge. Somewhat later Fallopio (1523–1562) discovered the human oviducts, or Fallopian tubes, and Eustachio (1524?–1574) described the anatomy of the teeth and rediscovered the tube which bears his name, leading from the middle ear to the throat. A number of Italian physicians contributed valuable information pertaining to the circulation of the blood. One of them described the valves of the heart, the pulmonary artery, and the aorta, while another located the valves in the veins. Equally significant was the work of certain foreigners who lived and taught in Italy. Andreas Vesalius (1514–1564), a native of Brussels, issued the first careful description of the human body based upon actual investigation. As a result of his extensive dissections he was able to correct many ancient errors. He is commonly considered the father of the modern science of anatomy. Nevertheless, there is danger in giving him too much credit. He was almost as conservative as Copernicus. Whereas the Polish astronomer could not refrain from worshiping Ptolemy, Vesalius revered Galen and deviated from him with great reluctance. Fortunately, Galen was a better physician than Ptolemy was an astronomer. Two other physicians of foreign nationality who were heavily indebted to Italian progress in medicine were the Spaniard Michael Servetus (1511–1553) and the Englishman William Harvey (1578–1657). Servetus discovered the lesser or pulmonary circulation of the blood. In his work entitled *Errors concerning the Trinity* (his major interest was theology, but he practiced medicine for a living), he described how the blood leaves the right chambers of the heart, is carried to the lungs to be purified, then returns to the heart and is conveyed from that organ to all parts of the body. But he had no idea of the return of the blood to the heart through the veins. It was left for William Harvey, who had studied under Italian physicians at Padua, to complete the discovery. This he did after his return to England about 1610. In his *Dissertation upon the Movement of the Heart* he described how an artery bound by a ligature would fill with blood in the section

Palace of the Doge, Venice. Since Venice was the richest city in the world during the Renaissance, it was fitting that her public buildings should be noted for their opulence. The palace of the Doge, or Duke, was built of creamy white Istrian stone and red Verona marble. The style combined Saracenic, Byzantine, and Gothic elements.

nearer the heart, while the portion away from the heart would empty, and how exactly the opposite results would occur when a ligature was placed on a vein. By such experiments he reached the conclusion that the blood is in constant process of circulation from the heart to all parts of the body and back again.

3. THE WANING OF THE ITALIAN RENAISSANCE

About 1550 the Renaissance in Italy came to an end after two and a half centuries of glorious history. The causes of its sudden demise are by no means perfectly clear. Possibly at the head of the list should be placed the French invasion of 1494 and the chaos that quickly ensued. The French monarch, Charles VIII, ruled over the richest and most powerful kingdom in Europe. Italy, weak and divided, seemed an easy prey for his grandiose ambitions. Accordingly, in 1494, he led an army of 30,000 well-trained troops across the Alps. The Medici of Florence fled before him, leaving their city to immediate capture. Halting only long enough to establish a puppet government, the French resumed their advance and conquered Naples. By so doing they aroused the suspicions of the rulers of Spain, who feared an attack on their own possession of Sicily. An alliance of Spain, the Papal States, the Holy Roman Empire, and Venice finally forced Charles to abandon his project. Upon his death in 1498 his successor, Louis XII, repeated the invasion of Italy.

Invasion and conquest

559

Alliances and counteralliances succeeded one another in bewildering confusion. Louis himself formed a combination with Ferdinand of Spain, Pope Julius II, and the Holy Roman Emperor to despoil Venice of her rich lands in the Po valley, but it foundered on the rocks of distrust and perfidy. In 1511 the Pope, fearful of French domination, organized a new "Holy League" with Venice and Spain, which was joined later by Henry VIII of England and the Emperor Maximilian. The French were defeated on two fronts and left Italy in 1512 to the miseries of her own weakness and internal squabbles. In 1530 the peninsula was conquered by the Emperor Charles V after a series of struggles involving pillage and wholesale destruction.

Other causes
of decline

Charles made a practice of restoring favorite princes to the nominal headship of Italian states in order to win their support in his unending struggle with France. They continued to preside over their courts, to patronize the arts, and to adorn their cities with luxurious buildings. But the great days of Italy were over. To the political disorders was added a waning of prosperity. It apparently brought no severe hardship until after 1600, but the shift of trade routes from the Mediterranean to the Atlantic region, following the discovery of America, was bound ultimately to have its effect. Italian cities gradually lost their supremacy as the centers of world trade. The prosperity they had enjoyed from a monopoly of trade with the Near East had been one of the chief nourishing influences in the development of their brilliant culture. A source of strength and of great expectations for the future was now being drained away. Yet another cause of cultural decline would seem to have been the Catholic Reformation. During the first half of the sixteenth century the Roman Church was engulfed by waves of intolerance, dogmatism, and asceticism. The objects were partly to combat increasing worldliness and sensuality and partly to strengthen the Church in its campaigns against heresy. In 1542 the Inquisition was established in Rome and soon afterward an Index of Prohibited Books was issued. The arts were censored, publication was controlled, and heretics were burned at the stake. Such procedures could hardly be other than inimical to the free spirit of Renaissance culture.

The Savonarola
affair

A glaring symptom of the flimsy foundations of much of Renaissance civilization may be found in the Savonarola affair. Underneath the proud structure of Italian art and learning were smoldering embers of ignorance and superstition ready to be kindled into flame by the first bigot or fanatic who happened along. Girolamo Savonarola was born in Ferrara in 1452, the son of a shiftless and spendthrift father. Though he lived in a gay and worldly city, his early education, directed by his mother and grandfather, seems to have been chiefly religious. At the age of nineteen he fell passionately in love with the daughter of an aristocratic neighbor. The young lady spurned him contemptuously, and soon afterward he

A View of Florence Showing the Burning of Savonarola. The Palazzo Vecchio is in the right center and a portion of the Cathedral at the extreme left. From a painting by an artist of the sixteenth (?) century.

decided to renounce the world and fled to a Dominican monastery in Bologna. In 1482 he was transferred to Florence, where Lorenzo the Magnificent was then at the height of his power. The longer Savonarola remained in Florence, the more he was dismayed by the frivolity and paganism he saw all around him. Within two or three years he began preaching in the cloister garden and in the churches of the city, burning into the hearts of his hearers the terrible wrath that would overtake them if they did not flee from their sins. His fiery eloquence and gaunt and unearthly appearance attracted hordes of frightened people. By 1494 his power over the mob had reached such proportions that he became virtual dictator of Florence. For four long years the gay Tuscan metropolis was then subjected to a puritanical rule surpassing in austerity anything that Italy had witnessed since the days of Gregory the Great. Half the year was devoted to Lenten abstinence, and even marriage was discouraged. Citizens were commanded to surrender their articles of luxury and their books and paintings alleged to be immoral; all of these works of the devil were cast into the flames in the public square in the celebrated "burning of the vanities." Though he **561** claimed the gift of prophecy and the ability to work miracles, he finally ran into trouble when he agreed under pressure to go through an ordeal by fire to prove the truth of his doctrines. In April 1498, an immense throng gathered in the Piazza della Signoria to witness the grisly spectacle. A sudden rainstorm, however, caused the authorities to postpone the ordeal on the ground that God had interposed against it. Deprived of its cruel diversion, the mob turned in rage against Savonarola and forced his arrest and imprisonment. Pope Alexander VI, whose sins he had condemned, took advantage of the opportunity to demand that he be destroyed as a heretic. After a month of excruciating tortures resulting in forced confessions, he was sentenced to death. He was burned in front of the Medici palace and his remains thrown into the Arno River. His career may be regarded not only as a symptom of the weakness of Renaissance society, but as a forerunner of the fanatical zeal of the Reformation.

SELECTED READINGS

GENERAL

· *Items so designated are available in paperbound editions.*

· Allen, J. W., *Political Thought in the Sixteenth Century*, London, 1951 (Barnes & Noble). The standard work on the subject.

· Baron, Hans, *The Crisis of the Early Italian Renaissance*, Princeton, 1955, 2 vols. (Princeton University Press, rev. ed.).

· Berenson, Bernard, *The Italian Painters of the Renaissance*, New York, 1957 (Meridian). Accurate and interesting.

Bishop, Morris, *Petrarch and His World*, Bloomington, Ind., 1963.

· Butterfield, Herbert, *The Origins of Modern Science*, New York, 1951 (Collier).

· Ferguson, W. K., *The Renaissance*, New York, 1940 (Torchbook). A splendid introduction.

Gilbert, Felix, *Machiavelli and Guicciardini: Politics and History in Sixteenth-century Florence*, Princeton, 1965.

· Gilmore, M., *The World of Humanism*, New York, 1952 (Torchbook). An excellent general account.

Gould, Cecil, *An Introduction to Italian Renaissance Painting*, London, 1957. Discerning and authoritative.

· Hall, A. R., *The Scientific Revolution, 1450–1650*, Boston, 1956 (Beacon).

Hay, Denys, *The Italian Renaissance in Its Historical Background*, New York, 1961.

· ———, *The Renaissance Debate*, New York, 1965 (European Problem Series).

· Huizinga, J., *The Waning of the Middle Ages*, London, 1924 (Anchor). A good analysis of the decline of feudalism.

· Kristeller, Paul, *Renaissance Thought*, New York, 1961–65, 2 vols. (Torchbook).

Lang, Paul, *Music in Western Civilization*, New York, 1941. The best survey yet published.

Lucas, Henry S., *The Renaissance and the Reformation*, New York, 1934.

· Mattingly, Garrett, *Renaissance Diplomacy*, Baltimore, 1964 (Penguin).

Owen, John, *The Skeptics of the Italian Renaissance*, London, 1893.

· Pater, Walter, *The Renaissance*, New York (Mentor, 1959, Meridian, 1961). Interesting interpretations.

Ridolfi, R., *The Life of Girolamo Savonarola*, New York, 1959.

———, *The Life of Niccolò Machiavelli*, Chicago, 1963. Presents Machiavelli in a new and more favorable light.

· Roeder, R., *The Man of the Renaissance*, New York, 1933 (Meridian).

Schevill, Ferdinand, *The First Century of Italian Humanism*, New York, 1928. Scholarly and stimulating.

· Smith, Preserved, *A History of Modern Culture*, New York, 1930, Vol. I (Collier). Thorough and scholarly.

Symonds, J. A., *A Short History of the Renaissance in Italy*, New York, 1893. Provocative but contains some doubtful interpretations.

· Taylor, H. O., *Thought and Expression in the Sixteenth Century*, London, 1920. Reliable and suggestive. Also available in paperback under the title, *The Humanism of Italy* (Collier, 2 vols.).

Thorndike, Lynn, *A History of Magic and Experimental Science in the Fourteenth and Fifteenth Centuries*, New York, 1934, 2 vols. Detailed but authoritative.

———, *Science and Thought in the Fifteenth Century*, New York, 1929.

· Vallentin, Antonina, *Leonardo da Vinci*, New York, 1938 (Grosset and Dunlap).

Wilkins, Ernest H., *A History of Italian Literature*, Cambridge, Mass., 1954. One of the best accounts of Italian writing since Dante.

· Woodward, G. W. O., *A Short History of Sixteenth-century England*, New York, 1963 (Mentor).

SOURCE MATERIALS

Baumer, F. L. V., *Main Currents of Western Thought*, New York, 1952.

Galileo Galilei, *The Sidereal Messenger*.

MacCurdy, Edward, ed., *The Notebooks of Leonardo da Vinci*, 2 vols. New York, 1955.

· Machiavelli, Niccolo, *The Prince*, especially Chs. 15–21, 26 (Modern Library College Edition).

· ———, *Discourses on Livy*, especially Book I, Chs. 3, 4, 6, 9, 11, 12, 25, 32, 33, 34, 47, 53, 55, 58, 59; Book II, Chs. 2, 5, 13, 19, 22 (Modern Library College Editions).

Robinson, J. H., and Rolfe, H. W., *Petrarch, the First Modern Scholar and Man of Letters*.

Willis, Robert, tr., *The Works of William Harvey, M. D.*

CHAPTER 19

The Expansion of the Renaissance

Art and sciences are not cast in a mould, but are formed and perfected by degrees, by often handling and polishing, as bears leisurely lick their cubs into form.
> —Michel de Montaigne, *Works* II.xii

If a rock falls on your head, that is clearly painful; but shame, disgrace, and curses hurt only so far as they are felt. What isn't noticed isn't troublesome. So long as you applaud yourself what harm are the hisses of the world? And folly is the only key to this happiness.
> —Erasmus, *The Praise of Folly*, II, The Powers and Pleasures of Folly

That a movement as vigorous as the Italian Renaissance should have spread into other countries was a result no less than inevitable. For years there had been a continuous procession of northern European students coming down into Italy to bask in the genial intellectual climate of Florence, Milan, and Rome. Moreover, the economic and social changes in northern and western Europe had roughly paralleled those of Italy for some time. Everywhere feudalism was being supplanted by a capitalist economy, and a new individualism was superseding the corporate structure of society sanctified by the Church in the Middle Ages. Common economic and social interests fostered the growth of a similar culture. But it must not be supposed that the Renaissance in northern and western Europe was exactly the same as that in the south. The Italian and the Teuton differed markedly in temperament and in historical background. More deeply affected by Saracenic and Byzantine influences, the Italian was disposed to find in art and literature the most suitable media of self-expression. Besides, he was the heir of classical traditions, which also enhanced his aesthetic interests. The northern European, on the other hand, by reason of his harder struggle for existence, was in-

The spread of the Renaissance

565

clined toward more serious and more practical pursuits. He tended to view the problems of life from a moral or religious angle. As a result of these differences the northern European Renaissance was less distinctly an artistic movement than the Renaissance in the south. Though painting flourished in the Low Countries, elsewhere it had no more than a limited scope, and sculpture was largely neglected. The main efforts of the northern peoples were concentrated in literature and philosophy, often with some religious or practical purpose. It may be added that there was less paganism in the northern Renaissance than there was in the Renaissance in Italy. Perhaps this condition reflected the fact that theological studies predominated in the curricula of the northern universities as late as 1550.

The political history of the countries of northern and western Europe during the age of the Renaissance was characterized by developments somewhat similar to those which had occurred in Italy. There was the same transition from a weak and decentralized feudal regime to the concentrated rule of despotic princes. There was also the destruction of the political power of the guilds and the absorption of their prerogatives of sovereignty by the state. The chief difference was to be found in the fact that many of the states outside of Italy were beginning to take on the character of national units. Each of them occupied a territory of considerable size and embraced a population knit together by bonds of language and a vague consciousness of unity as a people. But for the most part these great political organisms were the creations of ambitious monarchs, who broke the power of local nobles and welded their petty princi-

The political
background of
the Renaissance
outside of Italy;
conditions in
England

Portrait of Henry VIII by Hans Holbein the Younger. In the Palazzo Corsini, Rome.

The Tower of London; fortress and prison on the Bank of the Thames. Founded, according to tradition, by Julius Caesar, it was rebuilt and enlarged by the Norman and Tudor sovereigns. It was the scene of many executions by English monarchs. It is also the repository of the crown jewels.

palities into huge dynastic empires. In England this process was abetted by the so-called Wars of the Roses, a series of bloody struggles beginning about 1455 between rival factions of barons. So many were the nobles killed in these wars and so profound was the disgust with the long period of disorder that the Tudor dynasty, founded by Henry VII in 1485, was soon able to crush completely the remnants of feudal power. The most noted members of this dynasty, Henry VIII and Queen Elizabeth I, were the real founders of despotic government in England—with the support of the middle classes, who desired more protection for their commercial interests than the feudal regime could give.

In the case of France it was also a war which led to the establishment of a consolidated state—but an international war rather than an internal squabble. The struggle which enabled the French kings to stamp out feudal sovereignty was the Hundred Years' War (1337–1453), fought primarily to expel the English from France and to break their commercial alliance with the Flemish cities. As a result of this conflict a national consciousness was aroused in the French people, the nobles who had followed their own selfish ambitions were discredited, and the monarchy was extolled for having saved the country from ruin. Within thirty years the shrewd but unscrupulous Louis XI (1461–1483) extended the royal domain over all of France with the exception of Flanders and Brittany. His policies paved the way for the absolute rule of the Bourbons. Still another important country of western Europe began its emergence as a nation-state toward the end of the fifteenth century. This country was Spain, united partly as a result of the marriage of Ferdinand of Aragon and Isabella of Castile in 1469 and partly through the exigencies of the long war against the Moors. Under Philip II (1556–1598) Spain rose to a place in the very front rank of European powers. Aside from Italy, the only major country of western Europe which was not united into a consolidated state during the age of the Renaissance was Germany. Though it is true that political

Conditions in France, Spain, and Germany

authority in some of the individual German kingdoms was solidified, the country as a whole remained a part of the Holy Roman Empire, now headed by the Hapsburg monarchs of Austria. The sovereignty of the Holy Roman Emperors was a mere fiction, mainly because during the Middle Ages they had wasted their energies in a vain attempt to extend their control over Italy, thereby enabling the German dukes to entrench themselves in power.

1. THE INTELLECTUAL AND ARTISTIC RENAISSANCE IN GERMANY

The limited scope of the German Renaissance

One of the first countries to receive the full impact of the Italian humanist movement was Germany. This was a natural development, not only because of the proximity of the two countries, but also because of the large-scale migration of German students to the Italian universities. But the influence of this humanism was short-lived and its fruits rather scanty and mediocre. What the results might have been if Germany had not been hurled so soon into the maelstrom of religious contention cannot be determined. The fact remains, however, that the Protestant Revolution stirred up passions of hate and intolerance which could not be other than inimical to the humanist ideal. A premium was now set upon bigotry and faith, while anything resembling the worship of man or reverence for pagan antiquity was almost certain to be regarded as a work of the devil.

German humanism: the *Letters of Obscure Men*

To fix a date for the beginning of the German Renaissance is practically impossible. In such prosperous cities of the south as Augsburg, Nuremberg, Munich, and Vienna there was a lively humanist movement, imported from Italy, as early as 1450. By the beginning of the sixteenth century it had taken firm root in university circles, particularly in the cities of Heidelberg, Erfurt, and Cologne. Its most notable representatives were Ulrich von Hutten (1488–1523) and Crotus Rubianus (1480–1539). Both were less interested in the literary aspects of humanism than in its possibilities as an expression of religious and political protest. Von Hutten, especially, made use of his gifts as a writer to satirize the worldliness and greed of the clergy and to indite fiery defenses of the German people against their enemies. He was himself an embittered rebel against almost every institution of the established order. The chief title of von Hutten and Rubianus to fame is their authorship of the *Letters of Obscure Men*, one of the wittiest satires in the history of literature. The circumstances under which it was written are so strikingly like those which frequently occur in the evolution of nations that they deserve to be recounted here. A learned humanist at the University of Heidelberg by the name of Johann Reuchlin had developed a passionate enthusiasm for the study of Hebrew writings. Because he criticized some of the theologians' interpretations of the Old Testament, he was savagely attacked by Christian fanatics and was finally haled before the Inquisitor-General for the Catholic Church in Germany. Numerous pamphlets were published on both sides of the controversy, and the issue was soon sharply drawn between freedom and tolerance, on the one hand, and authoritarianism and bigotry on the other. When it became apparent that rational argument was accomplishing nothing, the friends of Reuchlin decided to make use of ridicule. Rubianus and von Hutten published a series of letters purporting to have been written by some of Reuchlin's opponents, with such ridiculous signatures as Ziegenmelker (Goat-milker), Honiglecker (Honey-licker), and Mistlader (Dungloader). Heinrich Shafmaul (Sheep's mouth), the supposed writer of one of the letters, professed to be worried lest he had sinned grievously by eating an egg which contained a chick on Friday. The author of another of the letters boasted of his brilliant "discovery" that Julius Caesar could not have written the *Commentaries on the Gallic Wars* because he was too busy with his military exploits ever to have learned the Latin language. How much effect these letters had in undermining the influence of the Catholic hierarchy in Germany is impossible to say, but it must have been considerable, for they enjoyed a wide circulation.

The German Renaissance in art was limited entirely to painting and engraving, represented chiefly by the work of Albrecht Dürer (1471–1528) and Hans Holbein (1497–1543). Both of these artists were profoundly influenced by Italian traditions, though much of

German painting: Dürer and Holbein

Melancholy. A Famous Engraving from a Series by Albrecht Dürer. In the National Gallery, Washington, D.C.

the Germanic spirit of somber realism is also expressed in their work. Dürer's best-known paintings are his *Adoration of the Magi,* the *Four Apostles,* and *The Crucified Christ.* The last is a study in tragic gloom. It shows the body of the pale Galilean stretched on the cross against a bleak and sinister sky. The glimmer of light on the horizon merely adds to the somber effect of the scene. Some of Dürer's best-known engravings exhibit similar qualities. His *Melancholy* represents a female figure, with wings too small to lift her body, meditating hopelessly on the problems of life, which appear to defy all solution. A compass is in her hand, and various other implements upon which man has relied for the control of his environment lie strewn about the floor. Hans Holbein, the other great artist

*See color plate
at page 617*

of the German Renaissance, derives his renown primarily from his portraits and drawings. His portraits of Erasmus, of Henry VIII, of Jane Seymour, and of Anne of Cleves are among the most famous in the world. An impressive example of his drawings is the one known as *Christ in the Tomb.* It depicts the body of the Son of God, with staring eyes and mouth half open, as neglected in death as the corpse of an ordinary criminal. The artist's purpose was probably to express the utter degradation which the Savior had suffered for the redemption of man. In his later career Holbein also drew many religious pictures satirizing the abuses in the Catholic Church which were believed to be the chief justification for the Protestant Revolution. He was one of the few prominent artists to devote his talents to the Protestant cause.

The only German during the age of the Renaissance to make any significant contribution to science was Johann Kepler (1571-1630).

German science:
Kepler and
Paracelsus

His interest aroused by the work of Copernicus, he improved the theory of the distinguished Pole by proving that the planets move in elliptical, rather than circular, orbits around the sun. Thus he may be said to have destroyed the last important vestige of the Ptolemaic astronomy, which had assumed the planets to be imbedded in perfect crystalline spheres. In addition, the laws of planetary motion which Kepler formulated were of tremendous value in suggesting to Newton his principle of universal gravitation. There was another scientist of German nationality whose work can be appropriately discussed in this connection, though he was actually born in the vicinity of Zürich, about the end of the fifteenth century. The name of this man was Theophrastus von Hohenheim, but he chose to call himself Paracelsus to indicate his own belief in his superiority to Celsus, the great Roman physician. Although Paracelsus is often referred to as a quack and an impostor, there is really comparatively little evidence that this was the case. He was at least sufficiently skillful as a practitioner of healing to be appointed professor of medicine at the University of Basel and town physician in 1527. Moreover, it is his special merit that he went straight to the book of

experience for his knowledge of diseases and their cures. Instead of following the teachings of ancient authorities, he traveled widely, studying cases of illness in different environments and experimenting with innumerable drugs. He denied that the quest for the philosopher's stone should be the function of the chemist and insisted upon the close interrelation of chemistry and medicine. Perhaps his most important specific contribution was his discovery of the relation between cretinism in children and the presence of goiter in their parents.

2.   RENAISSANCE CULTURE IN THE LOW COUNTRIES

Despite the fact that the Low Countries did not win independence of foreign domination until the seventeenth century,[1] they were nevertheless one of the most splendid centers of Renaissance culture on the Continent of Europe outside of Italy. The explanation is to be found primarily in the wealth of the Dutch and Flemish cities and in the important trade connections with southern Europe. As early as 1450 there were significant attainments in art in the Low Countries, including the development of painting in oil. Here also some of the first books were printed. While it is true that the Renaissance in the Low Countries was no broader in scope than in several other areas of northern Europe, its achievements were generally of surpassing brilliance.

The derivation and character of Renaissance culture in the Low Countries

The history of Renaissance literature and philosophy in the Low Countries begins and ends with Desiderius Erasmus, universally acclaimed as the Prince of the Humanists. The son of a priest and a servant girl, Erasmus was born near Rotterdam, probably in the year 1466. For his early education he had the benefit of the excellent training given in the school of the Brethren of the Common Life at Deventer.[2] Later, after his father and mother were both dead, his guardians placed him in an Augustinian monastery. Here the young Erasmus found little religion or formal instruction of any kind but plenty of freedom to read what he liked. He devoured all the classics he could get his hands on and the writings of many of the Church Fathers. When he was about thirty years of age, he obtained permission to leave the monastery and enroll in the University of Paris, where he completed the requirements for the degree of bachelor of divinity. But Erasmus never entered into the active duties of a priest, choosing rather to make his living by teaching and writing. By extensive reading of the classics he achieved a style of Latin expression so remarkable for its wit and urbanity that everything he wrote was widely read. But Erasmus' love of the classics was not born of pedantic interest. He admired the ancient authors because

Erasmus, Prince of the Humanists

---

[1] They were ruled by the Duchy of Burgundy until 1506 when they were inherited by Charles, the young king of Spain, whose grandfather had married the sole heiress of the Burgundian duke.
[2] See The Renaissance in Religion, §7 in this chapter.

they gave voice to the very ideals of naturalism, tolerance, and humanitarianism which held so exalted a place in his own mind. He was wont to believe that such pagans as Cicero and Socrates were far more deserving of the title of Saint than many a Christian canonized by the Pope. In 1536 Erasmus died in Basel at the end of a long and unfaltering career in defense of scholarship, high standards of literary taste, and the life of reason. He has rightfully been called the most civilized man of his age.

The liberal
philosophy of
Erasmus

As a philosopher of humanism Erasmus was the incarnation of the finest ideals of the northern Renaissance. Convinced of the inherent goodness of man, he believed that all misery and injustice would eventually disappear if only the pure sunlight of reason could be allowed to penetrate the noisome caverns of ignorance, superstition, and hate. With nothing of the fanatic about him, he stood for liberality of mind, for reasonableness and conciliation, rather than for fierce intolerance of evil. He shrank from the violence and passion of war, whether between systems, classes, or nations. Much of his teaching and writing was dedicated to the cause of religious reform. The ceremonial, dogmatic, and superstitious extravagances in sixteenth-century Catholic life repelled him. But it was alien to his temper to lead any crusade against them. He sought rather by gentle irony, and occasionally by stinging satire, to expose irrationalism in all of its forms and to propagate a humanist religion of simple piety and noble conduct based upon what he called the "philosophy of Christ." Although his criticism of the Catholic faith had considerable effect in hastening the Protestant Revolution, he recoiled in disgust from the bigotry of the Lutherans. Neither did he have much sympathy for the scientific revival of his time. Like most of the humanists he believed that an emphasis upon science would serve to promote a crude materialism and to detract men's interests from the ennobling influences of literature and philosophy. The

The writings of
Erasmus

chief writings of Erasmus were his *Praise of Folly*, in which he satirized pedantry, the dogmatism of theologians, and the ignorance and credulity of the masses, and his *Familiar Colloquies* and *The Handbook of the Christian Knight*, in which he condemned ecclesiastical Christianity and argued for a return to the simple teachings of Jesus, "who commanded us nothing save love for one another." In a less noted work entitled *The Complaint of Peace*, he expressed his abhorrence of war and his contempt for despotic princes.

The Flemish
school of
painting

The artistic Renaissance in the Low Countries was confined almost entirely to painting; and in this field the outstanding achievements were those of the Flemish school. Flemish painting derived no small measure of its excellence from the fact that it was an indigenous art. Here there were no classical influences, no ancient statues to imitate, and no living traditions from the Byzantine or Saracenic cultures. Until comparatively late, even the Italian influ-

572

ence was of little consequence. The painting of Flanders was rather the spontaneous product of a virile and prosperous urban society dominated by aspiring merchants interested in art as a symbol of luxurious tastes. The work of nearly all the leading painters—the van Eycks, Hans Memling, and Roger van der Weyden—betrayed this flair for depicting the solid and respectable virtues of their patrons. It was distinguished also by powerful realism, by a relentless attention to the details of ordinary life, by brilliant coloring, and by a deep and uncritical piety. Hubert and Jan van Eyck are noted for *See color plates at page 617* their *Adoration of the Lamb,* an altarpiece produced for a church in Ghent soon after the beginning of the fifteenth century. Described by some critics as the noblest achievement of the Flemish school, it portrays a depth of religious feeling and a background of ordinary experience unmatched in Italian art. It was the first great work of the Renaissance to be done by the new method of painting in oil, a process believed to have been invented by the van Eycks. The other two Flemish painters of the fifteenth century, Hans Memling and Roger van der Weyden, are noted, respectively, for naturalism and for the expression of emotional intensity. About 100 years later came the work of Peter Breughel, the most independent and the most socially conscious of the northern artists. Spurning the religious and bourgeois traditions of his predecessors, Breughel chose to depict the life of the common man. He loved to portray the boisterous pleasures of peasant folk at their wedding feasts and village fairs or to illustrate proverbs with scenes from the lives of humble people close to the earth. While he was enough of a realist never to idealize the characters in his paintings, his attitude toward them was definitely sympathetic. He employed his talents for the purpose also of condemning the tyranny of the Spanish regime in the Low Countries. One of his paintings, *The Massacre of the Innocents,* pictures the slaughter of women and children by Spanish soldiers. Seldom has great art been used more effectively as a weapon of political protest.

3. THE FRENCH RENAISSANCE

Despite the strong aesthetic interests of the French people, as evidenced by their perfection of Gothic architecture during the Middle Ages, the achievements of their artists in the age of the Renaissance were of comparatively little importance. There was some minor progress in sculpture and a modest advancement in architecture. It was during this time that the Louvre was built, on the site of an earlier structure bearing the same name, while numerous châteaux erected throughout the country represented a more or less successful attempt to combine the grace and elegance of the Italian style with the solidity of the medieval castle. Nor was science

French achievements in art and science

The Chateau of Chenonceaux, in Central France, as it appears today. Built during the 16th century, it represents a type of architecture transitional between Gothic and Renaissance.

entirely neglected, although the major accomplishments were few. They included the contributions of François Viète (1540–1603) to mathematics and of Ambroise Paré (1517?–1590) to surgery. The former invented modern algebraic symbols and elaborated the theory of equations. Paré improved upon the method of treating gunshot wounds by substituting bandages and unguents for applications of boiling oil. He was also responsible for introducing the ligature of arteries as a means of controlling the flow of blood in major amputations. He has rightfully been called the father of modern surgery.

But the outstanding achievements of the French Renaissance were in literature and philosophy, illustrated especially by the writings of François Rabelais (1490?–1553) and Michel de Montaigne (1533–1592). Like Erasmus, Rabelais was educated as a monk, but soon after taking holy orders he left the monastery to study medicine at the University of Montpellier. He finished the course for the bachelor's degree in the short space of six weeks and obtained his doctorate about five years later, in the meantime having served for a period as public physician in Lyon in addition to lecturing and editing medical writings. He seems from the start to have interspersed

Achievements in literature and philosophy; Rabelais

574

his professional activities with literary endeavors of one sort or another. He wrote almanacs for the common people, satires against quacks and astrologers, and burlesques of popular superstitions. In 1532 Rabelais published his first edition of *Gargantua*, which he later revised and combined with another book bearing the title of *Pantagruel*. Gargantua and Pantagruel were originally the names of legendary medieval giants noted for their prodigious strength and their gross appetites. Rabelais' account of their adventures served as a vehicle for his robust, sprawling wit and for the expression of his philosophy of exuberant naturalism. In language far from delicate he satirized the practices of the Church, ridiculed Scholasticism, scoffed at superstitions, and pilloried every form of bigotry and repression. No man of the Renaissance was a more uncompromising individualist or exhibited more zeal in glorifying the human and the natural. For him every instinct of man was healthy, provided it was not directed toward tyranny over others. In common with Erasmus he believed in the inherent goodness of man, but unlike the great Prince of the Humanists he was a thoroughgoing pagan, rejecting not only Christian dogma but Christian morality as well. Any degree of restraint, intellectual or moral, was repugnant to Rabelais. His celebrated description of the abbey of Theleme, built by Gargantua, was intended to show the contrast between his conception of freedom and the Christian ascetic ideal. At Theleme there were no clocks summoning to duties and no vows of celibacy or perpetual membership. The inmates could leave when they liked; but while they remained they dwelt together "according to their own free will and pleasure. They rose out of their beds when they thought good; they did eat, drink, labour, sleep, when they had a mind to it, and were disposed for it. None did awake them, none did offer to constrain them . . . for so Gargantua had established it. In all their Rule and strictest tie of their order there was but this one clause to be observed, *Do what thou wilt*." [3]

A man of far different temperament and background was Michel de Montaigne (1533–1592). His father was a Catholic, his mother a Jewess who had become a Protestant. Almost from the day of his birth their son was subjected to an elaborate system of training. Every morning he was awakened by soft music, and he was attended throughout the day by servants who were forbidden to speak any language but Latin. When he was six years old he was ready for the College of Guienne at Bordeaux and at the age of thirteen began the study of law. After practicing law for a time and serving in various public offices, he retired at thirty-seven to his ancestral estate to devote the remainder of his life to study, contemplation, and writing. Always in delicate health, he found it necessary now more than ever to conserve his strength. Besides, he was re-

Montaigne

[3] Urquhart and Motteux (trans.), *Works of Rabelais*, First Book, p. 165.

pelled by the bitterness and strife he saw all around him and was for
that reason all the more anxious to find a refuge in a world of intellectual seclusion.

Montaigne's ideas are contained in his famous *Essays*, written during his years of retirement. The essence of his philosophy is skepticism in regard to all dogma and final truth. He knew too much
about the diversity of beliefs among men, the welter of strange
customs revealed by geographic discoveries, and the disturbing
conclusions of the new science ever to accept the idea that any one
sect had exclusive possession of "the Truth delivered once for all to
the saints." It seemed to him that religion and morality were as
much the product of custom as styles of dress or habits of eating.
He taught that God is unknowable, and that it is as foolish to "weep
that we shall not exist a hundred years hence as it would be to weep
that we had not lived a hundred years ago." Man should be encouraged to despise death and to live nobly and delicately in this life
rather than to yearn piously for an afterlife that is doubtful at best.
Montaigne was just as skeptical in regard to assumptions of final
truth in philosophy or science. The conclusions of reason, he
taught, are sometimes fallacious, and the senses often deceive us.
The sooner men come to realize that there is no certainty anywhere
the better chance they will have to escape the tyranny which flows
from superstition and bigotry. The road to salvation lies in doubt,
not in faith.

A second element in Montaigne's philosophy was cynicism. He
could see no real difference between the morals of Christians and
those of infidels. All sects, he pointed out, fight each other with
equal ferocity, except that "there is no hatred so absolute as that
which is Christian." Neither could he see any value in crusades or
revolutions for the purpose of overthrowing one system and establishing another. All human institutions in his judgment were about
equally futile, and he therefore considered it fatuous that man
should take them so seriously as to wade through slaughter in order
to substitute one for its opposite. No ideal, he maintained, is worth
burning your neighbor for. In his attitude toward questions of
ethics Montaigne was not so ribald a champion of carnality as
Rabelais, yet he had no sympathy for asceticism. He believed it
ridiculous that men should attempt to deny their physical natures
and pretend that everything connected with sense is unworthy. "Sit
we upon the highest throne in the world," he declared, "yet we do
but sit upon our own behind." The philosophy of Montaigne, tinc-
tured as it was with escapism and disenchantment, marked a fitting
close of the Renaissance in France. But in spite of his negative attitude he did more good in the world than most of his contemporaries
who founded new faiths or invented new excuses for absolute monarchs to enslave their subjects. Not only did his ridicule help to
quench the flames of the cruel hysteria against witches, but the in-

*Montaigne's
philosophy of
skepticism*

*Montaigne's
cynicism*

576

fluence of his skeptical teachings had no small effect in combating fanaticism generally and in paving the way for a more generous tolerance in the future.

4. THE SPANISH RENAISSANCE

During the sixteenth and early seventeenth centuries Spain was at the height of her glory. Her conquests in the Western Hemisphere brought wealth to her nobles and merchants and gave her a proud position in the front rank of European states. Notwithstanding these facts the Spanish nation was not one of the leaders in Renaissance culture. Apparently her citizens were too deeply absorbed in plundering the conquered territories to devote much attention to intellectual or artistic pursuits. Moreover, the long war with the Moors had engendered a spirit of bigotry, the position of the Church was too strong, and the expulsion of the Jews at the end of the fifteenth century had deprived the country of talent it could ill afford to lose. For these reasons the Spanish Renaissance was limited to a few achievements in painting and literature, albeit some of these rank in brilliance with the best that other countries produced.

Reasons for the
backwardness of
Spain in the
Renaissance

Spanish painting bore the deep impression of the bitter struggle between Christian and Moor. As a result it expressed an intense preoccupation with religion and with themes of anguish and tragedy. Its background was medieval; upon it were engrafted influences from Flanders and from Italy. The first of the eminent Spanish painters was Luis de Morales (1517–1586), frequently called "The Divine." His Madonnas, Crucifixions, and Mater Dolorosas typified that earnest devotion to Catholic orthodoxy regarded by many Spaniards of this time as a duty both religious and patriotic. But the most talented artist of the Spanish Renaissance was not a native of Spain at all, but an immigrant from the island of Crete. His real name was Domenico Theotocopuli, but he is commonly called El Greco (1541?–1614?). After studying for some time under Titian in Venice, El Greco settled in Toledo about 1575, to live there until his death. A stern individualist in temperament, he seems to have imbibed little of the warmth of color and serene joy in satin splendor of the Venetian school. Instead, nearly all of his art is characterized by fevered emotionalism, stark tragedy, or enraptured flights into the supernatural and mystical. His figures are often those of gaunt, half-crazed fanatics; his colors sometimes are cold and severe. His scenes of suffering and death seem deliberately contrived to produce an impression of horror. Among his famous works are *The Burial of the Count of Orgaz, Pentecost,* and *The Apocalyptic Vision.* Better than any other artist, El Greco expresses the fiery religious zeal of the Spanish people during the heyday of the Jesuits and the Inquisition.

The character
of Spanish
painting; El
Greco

Literature in the Spanish Renaissance displayed tendencies not dissimilar to those in painting. This was notably true of drama, which frequently took the form of allegorical plays depicting the mystery of transubstantiation or appealing to some passion of religious fervor. Others of the dramatic productions dwelt upon themes of political pride or sang the praises of the bourgeoisie and expressed contempt for the dying world of feudalism. The colossus among the Spanish dramatists was Lope de Vega (1562–1635), the most prolific author of plays the literary world has seen. He is supposed to have written no fewer than 1500 comedies and more than 400 religious allegories. Of the total about 500 survive to this day. His secular dramas fall mainly into two classes: (1) the "cloak and sword plays," which depict the violent intrigues and exaggerated ideals of honor among the upper classes; and (2) the plays of national greatness, which celebrate the glories of Spain in her prime and represent the king as the protector of the people against a vicious and degenerate nobility.

Few would deny that the most gifted writer of the Spanish Renaissance was Miguel de Cervantes (1547–1616). His great masterpiece, *Don Quixote*, has even been described as "incomparably the best novel ever written." Composed in the best tradition of Spanish satirical prose, it recounts the adventures of a Spanish gentleman (Don Quixote) who has been slightly unbalanced by constant reading of chivalric romances. His mind filled with all kinds of fantastic adventures, he finally sets out at the age of fifty upon the slippery road of knight-errantry. He imagines windmills to be glowering giants and flocks of sheep to be armies of infidels, whom it is his duty to rout with his spear. In his disordered fancy he mistakes inns for castles and the serving-wenches within them for courtly ladies on fire with love of him. The advances they have no intention of making he must graciously repel in order to prove his devotion to his own Dulcinea. Set off in bold contrast to the ridiculous knight-errant is the figure of his faithful squire, Sancho Panza. The latter represents the ideal of the practical man, with his feet on the ground and content with the substantial pleasures of eating, drinking, and sleeping. The book as a whole is a pungent satire on feudalism, especially on the pretensions of the nobles as the champions of honor and right. Its enormous popularity was convincing proof that medieval civilization was approaching extinction even in Spain.

5. THE RENAISSANCE IN ENGLAND

In common with Spain, England also enjoyed a golden age in the sixteenth and early seventeenth centuries. Though her vast colonial empire had not yet been established, she was nevertheless reaping big profits from the production of wool and from her trade with the Continent. Her government, recently consolidated under the rule of the Tudors, was making the prosperity of the middle class the object of its special solicitude. Through the elimination of foreign traders, the granting of favors to English shipping, and the negotiation of reciprocal commercial treaties, the English merchant classes were given exceptional advantages over their rivals in other countries. The growth of a national consciousness, the awakening of pride in the power of the state, and the spread of humanism from Italy, France, and the Low Countries also contributed toward the flowering of a brilliant culture in England. Nevertheless, the English Renaissance was confined primarily to philosophy and literature. The arts did not flourish; perhaps because of the Calvinist influence, which began to make itself felt in Britain by the middle of the sixteenth century.

The earliest philosophers of the English Renaissance may best be described simply as humanists. Although they were not unmindful of the value of classical studies, they were interested chiefly in the more practical aspects of humanism. Most of them desired a simpler and more rational Christianity and looked forward to an educational system freed from the dominance of medieval logic. Others were concerned primarily with individual freedom and the correction of social abuses. The greatest of these early thinkers was Sir Thomas More (1478–1535), esteemed by contemporary humanists as "excellent above all his nation." Following a successful career as a lawyer and as Speaker of the House of Commons, More was appointed in 1529 Lord Chancellor of England. He was not long in this position, however, before he incurred the enmity of his royal master, Henry VIII. More was loyal to Catholic universalism and did not sympathize with the king's design to establish a national church under subjection to the state. When, in 1534, he refused to take the Oath of Supremacy acknowledging the king as the head of the Church of England, he was thrown into the Tower. A year later he was tried before a packed jury, convicted, and beheaded. More's philosophy is contained in his *Utopia*, which he published in 1516. Purporting to describe an ideal society on an imaginary island, the book is really an indictment of the glaring abuses of the time—of poverty undeserved and wealth unearned, of drastic punishments, religious persecution, and the senseless slaughter of war. The inhabitants of Utopia hold all their goods in common, work only six hours a day so that all may have leisure for intellectual pursuits, and practice the natural virtues of wisdom, moderation, fortitude, and justice. Iron is the precious metal "because it is useful," war and monasticism are abolished, and tolerance is granted to all creeds that recognize the existence of God and the immortality of the soul. Despite criticism of the *Utopia* as deficient in wit and originality, the conclusion seems justified that the author's ideals of humanity and tolerance were considerably in advance of those of most other men of his time.

The early English humanists; Thomas More

The thinker who has gone down in history as the greatest of all

English Renaissance philosophers is Sir Francis Bacon. Born in 1561, the son of a high government official, Bacon was nurtured in the lap of luxury until the age of seventeen when the death of his father compelled him to work for a living. Thereafter the dominating ambition of his life was to obtain some profitable position with the government which would enable him to pursue his intellectual interests. Probably it was this mania for security which accounts for the shady morality of his public career. When occasion arose, he did not shrink from concealing his true beliefs, from disloyalty to his friends, or from sharing in graft. In 1618 he was appointed Lord Chancellor, but after a scant three years in this office he was impeached for accepting bribes. Despite his protestations that the taking of money from litigants had never influenced his decisions, he was convicted and sentenced to pay a fine of $200,000 and to undergo imprisonment in the Tower "at the king's pleasure." King James I remitted the fine and limited the term of imprisonment to four days. Bacon devoted the remaining five years of his life to writing, especially to the completion of the third and enlarged edition of his essays. Among his most valuable works are the *Novum Organum* and *The Advancement of Learning*.

Bacon's monumental contribution to philosophy was the glorification of the inductive method. He was by no means the discoverer of that method, but he trumpeted it forth as the indispensable ground of accurate knowledge. He believed that all seekers of truth in the past had stumbled in darkness because they were slaves of preconceived ideas or prisoners in the dungeons of Scholastic logic. He argued that in order to overcome these obstacles the philosopher should turn to the direct observation of nature, to the accumulation of facts about things and the discovery of the laws that govern them. Induction alone, he believed, was the magic key that would unlock the secrets of truth. Authority, tradition, and syllogistic logic should be as sedulously avoided as the plague. Admirable as these teachings are, they were honored by Bacon himself almost as much in the breach as in the observance. He believed in astrology, divination, and witchcraft. Moreover, the distinction he drew between ordinary knowledge and the truths of religion was hardly in keeping with his staunch defense of induction. "The senses," he wrote, "are like the sun, which displays the face of the earth, but shuts up that of the heavens." For our voyage to the realm of celestial truth, we must "quit the small vessel of human reason and put ourselves on board the ship of the Church, which alone possesses the divine needle for justly shaping the course. The stars of philosophy will be of no further service to us. As we are obliged to obey the divine law, though our will murmur against it, so we are obliged to believe in the word of God, though our reason is shocked at it. The more absurd and incredible any divine mystery is, the greater honor we do God in believing it." It was not such a far cry after all from Roger Bacon in the thirteenth century to Francis Bacon in the seventeenth.

In literature, also, the English followed much more closely in the footsteps of their medieval forerunners than did the Renaissance writers in any other country with the exception of Italy. Indeed, it is difficult to say just when the English Renaissance in literature began. Chaucer's great work, the *Canterbury Tales,* written toward the end of the fourteenth century, is commonly considered medieval; yet it breathed a spirit of earthiness and of lusty contempt for the mystical quite as pronounced as anything to be found in the writings of Shakespeare. If there were any essential dfferences between the English literature of the Renaissance and that produced during the late Middle Ages, they would consist in a bolder individualism, a stronger sense of national pride, and a deeper interest in themes of philosophic import. The first great poet in England after the time of Chaucer was Edmund Spenser(1552?–1599). His immortal creation, *The Faërie Queene,* is a colorful epic of England's greatness in the days of Queen Elizabeth. Though written as a moral allegory to express the author's desire for a return to the virtues of chivalry, it celebrates also the joy in conquest and much of the gorgeous sensuousness typical of Renaissance humanism.

But the most splendid achievements of the English in the Elizabethan Age were in the realm of drama. Not since the days of the Greeks had the writing of tragedies and comedies attained such heights as were reached in England during the sixteenth and early seventeenth centuries. Especially after 1580 a galaxy of playwrights appeared whose work outshone that of all their predecessors in 2000 years. Included in this galaxy were such luminaries as Christopher Marlowe (1564–1593), Beaumont and Fletcher (1584–1616; 1579–1625), Ben Jonson (1573?–1637), and Shakespeare (1564–1616), of whom the first and the last are chiefly significant to the historian. Better than anyone else in his time, Christopher Marlowe embodies the insatiable egoism of the Renaissance— the everlasting craving for the fullness of life, for unlimited knowledge and experience. His brief but stormy career was a succession of scandalous escapades and fiery revolts against the restraints of convention until it was terminated by his death in a tavern brawl before he was thirty years old. The best known of his plays, entitled *Doctor Faustus,* is based upon the legend of Faust, in which the hero sells his soul to the devil in return for the power to feel every possible sensation, experience every possible triumph, and know all the mysteries of the universe.

William Shakespeare, the most talented genius in the history of drama since Euripides, was born into the family of a petty tradesman in the provincial market town of Stratford-on-Avon. His life is

MR. WILLIAM
SHAKESPEARES
COMEDIES,
HISTORIES, &
TRAGEDIES.

Published according to the True Originall Copies.

William Shakespeare. Portrait made for the First Folio edition of his works, 1623.

The life and writings of William Shakespeare

enshrouded in more mists of obscurity than the careers of most other great men. It is known that he left his native village when he was about twenty years old, and that ultimately he drifted to London to find employment in the theater. Tradition relates that for a time he earned his living by holding the horses of the more prosperous patrons of the drama. How he eventually became an actor and still later a writer of plays is unknown, but there is evidence that by the time he was twenty-eight he had already acquired a reputation as an author sufficient to excite the jealousy of his rivals. Before he retired to his native Stratford about 1610 to spend the rest of his days in ease, he had written or collaborated in writing nearly forty plays, to say nothing of 150 sonnets and two narrative poems.

In paying homage to the universality of Shakespeare's genius, we must not lose sight of the fact that he was also a child of the Renaissance. His work bore the deep impression of most of the virtues and defects of Renaissance humanism. Almost as much as Boccaccio or Rabelais, he personified that intense love of things human and earthly which had characterized most of the great writers since the close of the Middle Ages. Moreover, like the majority of the humanists, he showed a limited concern with the problems of politics and the values of science. Virtually the only political theory that interested him greatly was whether a nation had a better chance of prospering under a good king who was weak or under a bad king who was strong. Though his knowledge of the sciences of his time was

The character of Shakespeare's work

extensive, he regarded them as consisting primarily of alchemy, astrology, and medicine.[4] But the force and range of Shakespeare's intellect were far from bounded by the narrow horizons of the age in which he lived. While few of the works of his contemporaries are now widely read, the plays of Shakespeare still hold their rank as a kind of secular Bible wherever the English language is spoken. The reason lies not only in the author's unrivaled gift of expression, but especially in his scintillating wit and his profound analysis of human character assailed by the storms of passion and tried by the whims of fate.

Shakespeare's dramas fall rather naturally into three main groups. Those written during his earlier years conformed to the traditions of existing plays and generally reflected his own confidence in personal success. They include such comedies as *A Midsummer Night's Dream* and *The Merchant of Venice*, a number of historical plays, and the lyrical tragedy, *Romeo and Juliet*. Shortly before 1600 Shakespeare seems to have experienced a change of mood. The restrained optimism of his earlier plays was supplanted by some deep disillusion which led him to distrust human nature and to indict the whole scheme of the universe. The result was a group of dramas characterized by bitterness, overwhelming pathos, and a troubled searching into the mysteries of things. The series begins with the tragedy of intellectual idealism represented by *Hamlet*, goes on to the cynicism of *Measure for Measure* and *All's Well That Ends Well*, and culminates in the cosmic tragedies of *Macbeth* and *King Lear*. Perhaps the famous speech of Gloucester in the last of these plays may be taken to illustrate the depths of the author's pessimism at this time:

The main groups of Shakespeare's plays

> As flies to wanton boys are we to the gods;
> They kill us for their sport.[5]

The final group of dramas includes those written during the closing years of Shakespeare's life, probably after his retirement. Among them are *The Winter's Tale* and *The Tempest*. All of them may be described as idyllic romances. Trouble and grief are now assumed to be only the shadows in a beautiful picture. Despite individual tragedy, the divine plan of the universe is somehow benevolent and just.

6. RENAISSANCE DEVELOPMENTS IN MUSIC

Music in western Europe in the fifteenth and sixteenth centuries reached such a high point of development that it constitutes, together with painting and sculpture, one of the most brilliant aspects

The evolution of music as an independent art

[4] In psychology, however, he gives evidence of having been ahead of his time, especially in his treatment of insanity. Perhaps this was natural in view of his profound interest in human emotions, in man's conflict with himself and with the universe of which he is a part.
[5] *King Lear*, Act IV, scene 1.

Musical Instruments in the Sixteenth Century. In the lower left is shown a small pipe organ, with a bellows operated by the man seated opposite the player. The boxlike instrument on the table is a clavichord. The triangular shaped tube in the lower right corner is a *trumsheit*, or German "drum log."

of Renaissance activity. While the visual arts were stimulated by the study of ancient models, music flowed naturally from an independent evolution which had long been in progress in medieval Christendom. As earlier, leadership was supplied by men trained in the service of the Church, but the value of secular music was now appreciated, and its principles were combined with those of sacred music to bring a decided gain in color and emotional appeal. The distinction between sacred and profane became less sharp; most composers did not restrict their activities to either field. Music was no longer regarded merely as a diversion or an adjunct to worship but as an independent art.

Different sections of Europe vied with one another for musical leadership. As with the other arts, advance was related to the increasingly generous patronage made possible by the expansion of commerce, and was centered in the prosperous towns. During the fourteenth century a pre- or early Renaissance musical movement called Ars Nova (new art) flourished in Italy and France. Its outstanding composers were Francesco Landini (*ca.* 1325–1397) and Guillaume de Machaut (1300–1377). The madrigals, ballads, and other songs composed by the Ars Nova musicians testify to a rich secular art, but the greatest achievement of the period was a highly complicated yet delicate contrapuntal style adapted for motet and chanson. With Machaut we reach the first integral polyphonic setting of the Ordinary of the Mass.

Leadership provided by Italy and France

584 The fifteenth century was ushered in by a synthesis of English,

Madonna and Child, Luca della Robbia (1400–1482). This enameled terra cotta plaque is typical of the work of the della Robbia family. (MMA)

Pope Paul III and His Nephews, Titian (1477–1576). This painting, with its rich harmony of color, is unusual in being both a group portrait and a study of action. (National Museum, Naples)

Portrait of a Young Man, Giovanni Bellini (1430–1516). Though noted for opulence and color, artists of the Venetian school also excelled in portrait painting. (MMA)

The Madonna of the Chair, Raphael (1483–1520). Raphael's art was distinguished by warmth and serenity, and by an uncritical acceptance of the traditions and conventions of his time. (Pitti Palace, Florence)

Portrait of a Girl, Domenico Veneziano (1400–1461). Though born and probably trained in Venice, Domenico was strongly influenced by the technical achievements of the Florentines. (MMA)

"Christ and Madonna." From *The Last Judgment*, Michelangelo (1475-1564). This painting above the altar in the Sistine Chapel, Rome, shows Christ as judge condemning sinners to perdition. Even the Madonna at His side seems to shrink from His wrath.

Young Man, Bronzino (1502-1572). The portrait displays the typical Renaissance spirit of the proud young man who glories in his achievement. (MMA)

Rospigliosi Cup. Attributed to Benvenuto Cellini (1500-1571). Cellini was not only an adventurer and writer, but also a talented goldsmith. The cup shown was intended to hold salt. (MMA)

Boy with a Greyhound, Veronese (1528-1588). Veronese personifies consummate artistic skill with little attention to meaning. (MMA)

The Doge Presented to the Redeemer, Tintoretto (1518-1594). This dramatic painting commemorates a pledge by the Doge in 1576 to build a temple to the Redeemer if Venice were saved from the plague. (MMA)

Four Saints, Correggio (1494-1534). Correggio was noted for his skill in composition and technical detail. He painted the *Four Saints* while still in his teens. (MMA)

French, Flemish, and Italian elements that took place in the Duchy
of Burgundy. It produced a remarkable school of music inspired by
the cathedral of Cambrai and the ducal court at Dijon. This music
was gentle, melodious, and euphonious, but in the second half
of the century it hardened a little as the northern Flemish element
gained in importance. The Franco-Flemish school led by Jean *Synthesis of*
d'Ockeghem (*ca.* 1430–1495) carried the art of vocal counterpoint *national*
to a complexity never again equaled. As the sixteenth century *elements*
opened we find these Franco-Flemish composers in every important
court and cathedral choir all over Europe, gradually establishing
regional-national schools, usually in attractive combinations of
Flemish with German, Spanish, and Italian musical cultures. The
various genres thus created show a close affinity with Renaissance
art and poetry. In the second half of the sixteenth century the leaders
of the nationalized Franco-Flemish style were the Italian Palestrina
(*ca.* 1525–1594), who, by virtue of his position as papal composer and
his devotion to a subtle and crystal-clear vocal style, became the venerated symbol of church music; the Flemish Roland de Lassus
(1532–1594), the most versatile composer of the age; and Tomas
Luis de Victoria (*ca.* 1540–1611), the glowing mystic of Spanish
music. Music also flourished in England, for the Tudor monarchs
were not behind the Medici or the Bavarian dukes in patronizing the
arts; several of them were accomplished musicians. It was inevitable
that the reigning Franco-Flemish style should reach England, where
it was superimposed upon an ancient and rich musical culture. The
Italian madrigal, imported toward the end of the sixteenth century,
found a remarkable second flourishing in England, but songs and instrumental music of an original cast anticipated future developments
on the Continent. In William Byrd (1543–1623) English music
produced a master fully the equal of the great Flemish, Roman, and
Spanish composers of the Renaissance. The general level of music
proficiency seems to have been higher in Queen Elizabeth's day
than in ours: the singing of part-songs was a popular pastime in
homes and at informal social gatherings, and the ability to read a
part at sight was expected of well-bred persons.

In conclusion, it may be observed that while counterpoint had
matured, our modern harmonic system had been born, and thus a
way was opened for fresh experimentation. At the same time one *The greatness of*
should realize that the music of the Renaissance constitutes not *the Renaissance*
merely a stage in evolution but a magnificent achievement in itself, *achievement*
with masters who rank among the great of all time. The composers
Palestrina and Lassus are as truly representative of the artistic triumph of the Renaissance as are the painters Raphael and Michelangelo. Their heritage, long neglected except at a few ecclesiastical
centers, has within recent years begun to be appreciated, and is now
gaining in popularity as interested groups of musicians devote themselves to its revival.

7.   THE RENAISSANCE IN RELIGION

No account of the age of the Renaissance would be complete
without some attention to the Renaissance in religion, or the Christian Renaissance as it is commonly called. This was a movement
almost entirely independent of the Protestant Revolution, which
will be discussed in the next chapter. The leaders of the Christian
Renaissance were generally humanists, not Protestants. Few of them
ever deserted the Catholic faith; their aim was to purify that faith
from within, not to overthrow it. Most of them found the bigotry
of early Protestantism as repugnant to their religious ideals as any of
the abuses in the Catholic Church. The original impetus for the
Christian Renaissance appears to have come from the Brethren of
the Common Life, a group of pious laymen who maintained schools
in the Low Countries and in western Germany. Their aim was to
propagate a simple religion of practical piety, as free as possible
from dogmatism and ritual. The most noted of their early followers
was Thomas a Kempis (1380–1471) who wrote or edited about
1425 a book entitled *The Imitation of Christ*. Though profoundly
mystical in tone, the book nevertheless repudiated the extreme
otherworldliness of medieval mystics and urged a life of simple
devotion to the teachings of Jesus. For over a century the *Imitation*
was more widely read in Europe than any other book with the exception of the Bible.

By 1500 the Christian Renaissance had become definitely associated with northern humanism. Writers and philosophers in every
country lent their support to the movement. Prominent among
them were Sebastian Brant in Germany, Sir Thomas More in England, Erasmus in the Low Countries, and figures of lesser renown in
France and Spain. The religious teachings of these men were thoroughly in keeping with the humanist ideal as it was understood in
northern Europe. Believing that religion should function for the
good of man and not for the benefit of an organized church or even
for the glory of an ineffable God, they interpreted Christianity primarily in ethical terms. Many of the theological and supernatural
elements in it they regarded as superfluous, if not positively harmful. They likewise had little use for ceremonies of any kind, and
they ridiculed the superstitions connected with the veneration of
relics and the sale of indulgences. While they recognized the necessity of a limited amount of ecclesiastical organization, they denied
the absolute authority of the Pope and refused to admit that priests
were really essential as intermediaries between man and God. In
fine, what most of these Christian humanists really desired was the
superiority of reason over faith, the primacy of conduct over
dogma, and the supremacy of the individual over the organized system. They believed that this simple and rational religion could best
be achieved, not through violent revolt against the Catholic Church,

Stultifera Nauis,

ia omnium mortalium narratur ſtultitia,admo=
dum vtilis & neceſſaria ab omnibus ad ſuam ſalutem perlegenda,
è Latino ſermone in noſtrum vulgarem verſa,& iam diligenter
impreſſa. An. Do. 1 5 7 0.

Title Page of an English Translation of Sebastian Brant's Allegorical Satire *Das Narren-
schiff* (*Ship of Fools*), 1494.

The Ship of Fooles, wherin is ſhewed the folly
of all States, with diuers other workes adioyned vnto the ſame,
very profitable and fruitfull for all men.

but through the gradual conquest of ignorance and the elimination
of abuses.

The decline of Renaissance culture in the countries of northern
and western Europe came much less abruptly than in Italy. Indeed,
the change in some respects was so gradual that there was simply a
fusion of the old with the new. The achievements in science, for example, were merely extended, although with a definite shift of
emphasis as time went on from the mathematical and physical
branches to the biological. The Renaissance art of northern Europe,
moreover, gradually evolved into the baroque, which dominated the
seventeenth and early eighteenth centuries. On the other hand,
humanism, in its Renaissance meaning of the worship of man and
indifference to everything else, practically died out after the six-

The decline of
the Renaissance
outside of Italy

587

teenth century. In philosophy there has since been a tendency to
exalt the universe and to relegate man to a place of insignificance as
the helpless victim of an all-powerful destiny. When the end of the
northern Renaissance did finally come, it probably resulted chiefly
from the heritage of bitterness and unreason left by the Protestant
Revolution. But that is a subject which can be discussed more appropriately in the chapter that follows.

SELECTED READINGS

· *Items so designated are available in paperbound editions.*

Allen, P. S., *The Age of Erasmus*, New York, 1914.

· Beard, M. R., *A History of the Business Man*, New York, 1938 (Ann Arbor).
Interesting sketches of Renaissance capitalists.

Benesch, Otto, *The Art of the Renaissance in Northern Europe*, Cambridge,
Mass., 1945.

· Bush, D., *The Renaissance and English Humanism*, Toronto, 1939 (University
of Toronto Press). A brief but excellent introduction.

Elton, G. R., *England Under the Tudors*, London, 1955.

· Gilmore, M., *The World of Humanism*, New York, 1952 (Torchbook). An
excellent general account.

· Hay, Denys, *The Renaissance Debate*, New York, 1965 (European Problem
Series).

· Huizinga, Johan, *The Waning of the Middle Ages*, London, 1924 (Anchor).

Hyma, Albert, *The Christian Renaissance*, New York, 1924. The most authoritative work on this subject.

———, *Erasmus and the Humanists*, New York, 1930.

Lang, Paul, *Music in Western Civilization*, New York, 1941. The best survey
yet published.

Lucas, Henry S., *The Renaissance and the Reformation*, New York, 1934.

McGinn, D. F., *Shakespeare and the Drama of His Age*, New Brunswick, N.J.,
1938.

Oxford History of Music, Vols. I–II.

Panofsky, E., *Early Netherlandish Painting; Its Origins and Character*, Cambridge, Mass., 1954. Valuable for an understanding of Flemish painters.

· Pater, Walter, *The Renaissance*, New York (Mentor, 1959, Meridian, 1961).
A thoughtful interpretation.

Reese, Gustave, *Music in the Renaissance*, rev. ed., New York, 1959.

· Smith, Preserved, *A History of Modern Culture*, New York, 1930, Vol. I
(Collier). Thorough and scholarly.

· ———, *Erasmus, A Study of His Life, Ideals and Place in History*, New York,
1923 (Dover).

· Taylor, H. O., *Thought and Expression in the Sixteenth Century*, London,
1920. Also available in paperback under the title *Humanism of Italy* (Collier, 2 vols.). Reliable and suggestive.

Thorndike, Lynn, *A History of Magic and Experimental Science in the Fourteenth and Fifteenth Centuries*, New York, 1934, 2 vols. Detailed and authoritative.

———, *Science and Thought in the Fifteenth Century*, New York, 1929.

· Wolf, A., *A History of Science, Technology and Philosophy in the XVIth
and XVIIth Centuries*, New York, 1935 (Torchbook, 2 vols.).

SOURCE MATERIALS

- Bacon, Sir Francis, *The Great Instauration*, Preface (Washington Square Press and others).

  Erasmus, Desiderius, *The Complaint of Peace*.

  ———, *The Handbook of a Christian Knight*.
- ———, *The Praise of Folly* (Ann Arbor, Bantam).
- Montaigne, Michel de, *Essays* (Penguin).
- More, Sir Thomas, *Utopia*, especially Book II (Penguin and others).
- Rabelais, François, *Gargantua and Pantagruel*, especially Book I (Penguin).

CHAPTER 20

The Age of the Reformation
(1517-ca.1600)

For the word of God cannot be received and honored by any
works, but by faith alone.
—Martin Luther, *On Christian Liberty*

In conformity to the clear doctrine of the Scripture, we assert
that by an eternal and immutable counsel, God has once for all
determined both whom he would admit to salvation and whom
he would condemn to destruction. . . . In the elect, we consider
calling as an evidence of election, and justification as another
token of its manifestation, till they arrive in glory, which constitutes its completion.
—John Calvin, *Institutes* III.xxi

Preceding chapters have described the unfolding of a marvelous culture which marked the transition from the Middle Ages to the modern world. It became apparent that this culture, known as the
Renaissance, was almost as peculiarly an echo of the past as a herald
of the future. Much of its literature, art, and philosophy, and all of
its superstitions, had roots that were deeply buried in classical
antiquity or in the fabulous centuries of the Middle Ages. Even its
humanism breathed veneration for the past. Only in science and
politics and in the vigorous assertion of the right of the individual to
pursue his own quest for freedom and dignity was there much that
was really new. But the Renaissance in its later stages was accompanied by the growth of another movement, the Reformation, which
somewhat more accurately foreshadowed the modern age. This
movement included two principal phases: the Protestant Revolution, which broke out in 1517 and resulted in the secession of most
of northern Europe from the Roman faith; and the Catholic Reformation, which reached its height about 1560. Although the latter is

*The later
stages of the
Renaissance
accompanied by
a religious
revolution*

591

not called a revolution, it really was such in nearly every sense of the term; for it effected a profound alteration of some of the notable features of late medieval Catholicism.

In a number of ways the Renaissance and the Reformation were closely related. Both were products of that powerful current of individualism which wrought such havoc to the established order in the fourteenth and fifteenth centuries. Each had a similar background of economic causes in the growth of capitalism and in the rise of a bourgeois society. Both partook of the character of a return to original sources: in the one case, to the literary and artistic achievements of the Greeks and Romans; in the other, to the Scriptures and the doctrines of the Church Fathers. But in spite of these important resemblances, it is misleading to think of the Reformation as merely the religious aspect of the Renaissance. The guiding principles of the two movements had comparatively little in common. The essence of the Renaissance was devotion to the human and the natural, with religion relegated to a subordinate place. The spirit of the Reformation was otherworldliness and contempt for the things of this life as inferior to the spiritual. In the mind of the humanist, man's nature was generally considered good; in the view of the Reformer it was unspeakably corrupt and depraved. The leaders of the Renaissance believed in urbanity and tolerance; the followers of Luther and Calvin emphasized faith and conformity. While both the Renaissance and the Reformation aimed at a recovery of the past, they were really oriented in different directions. The past the humanists strove to revive was Greek and Roman antiquity, though a few were concerned with the original Gospels as sources of an unspoiled religion. The Reformers, by contrast, were interested chiefly in a return to the teachings of St. Paul and St. Augustine. Here would be found, they maintained, the doctrines of true Christianity.

The Reforma-
tion not really
a part of the
Renaissance

For reasons such as these it seems justifiable to conclude that the Reformation was not really a part of the Renaissance movement. In actual fact, it represented a much sharper break with the civilization of the later Middle Ages than ever did the movement led by the humanists. The radical Reformers would have nothing to do with the basic theories and practices of thirteenth-century Christianity. Even the simple religion of love and selflessness for the betterment of man, as taught by St. Francis of Assisi, appeared to repel them almost as much as the mysteries of the sacramental theory or the bombastic claims of Innocent III to spiritual and temporal power. In the main, the religious results of this clash with medieval Christianity have endured to this day. Moreover, the Reformation was intimately bound up with certain political trends which have persisted throughout the modern era. National consciousness, as we shall see, was one of the principal causes of the Protestant Revolution. While it is true that several of the humanists wrote under the influence of national pride, perhaps the majority were swayed by altogether different considerations. Many were scornful of politics, being interested solely in man as an individual; others, the great Erasmus among them, were thoroughly international in their outlook. But the Protestant Reformers could scarcely have gained much of a hearing if they had not associated their cause with the powerful groundswell of national resentment in northern Europe against an ecclesiastical system that had come to be recognized as largely Italian in character. For this reason as well as for the reasons mentioned previously, it would seem not unwarranted to regard the Reformation as a gateway to the modern world. And when we speak of the Renaissance in religion, we should think, not of the Reformation, but of the so-called Christian Renaissance, initiated by the Brethren of the Common Life and carried to its highest fulfillment in the teachings of Sir Thomas More and Erasmus. The common assumption that Luther hatched the egg which Erasmus had laid is true only in a very limited sense. The bird which Luther hatched belonged to a much tougher and wilder breed than any that could have descended from the Prince of the Humanists.

I. THE PROTESTANT REVOLUTION

The Protestant Revolution sprang from a multiplicity of causes, most of them closely related to the political and economic conditions of the age. Nothing could be more inaccurate than to think of the revolt against Rome as exclusively a religious movement, though doubtless religious ideas occupied a large place in the mind of sixteenth-century man. But without the basic political changes in northern Europe and the growth of new economic interests, Roman Catholicism would probably have undergone no more than a gradual evolution, perhaps in line with the teachings of the Christian Renaissance. Nevertheless, since religious causes were the most obvious ones, it will be appropriate to consider them first.

The multiplicity of causes of the Protestant Revolution

To the majority of Luther's early followers the movement he launched was chiefly a rebellion against abuses in the Catholic Church. That such abuses existed no careful historian would deny, regardless of his religious affiliations. For example, many of the Roman clergy were incredibly ignorant. Some, having obtained their positions through irregular means, were unable to understand the Latin of the Mass they were required to celebrate. Further, a considerable number of the clergy led scandalous lives. While some of the Popes and bishops were living in princely magnificence, the lowly priests occasionally sought to eke out the incomes from their parishes by keeping taverns, gaming houses, or other establishments for profit. Not only did some monks habitually ignore their vows of chastity, but a few indifferent members of the secular clergy surmounted the hardships of the rule of celibacy by keeping mistresses.

Religious causes: abuses in the Catholic Church

Pope Innocent VIII, who reigned about twenty-five years before
the beginning of the Protestant Revolution, was known to have had
eight illegitimate children, several of them born before his election
to the papacy. There were numerous evils also in connection with
the sale of religious offices and dispensations. As in the case of most
civil positions, offices in the Church during the Renaissance period
were commonly sold to the highest bidder. It is estimated that Pope
Leo X enjoyed an income of more than a million dollars a year from
the sale of more than 2000 ecclesiastical offices. This abuse was
rendered more serious by the fact that the men who bought these
positions were under a strong temptation to make up for their investment by levying high fees for their services. The sale of dispensations was a second malodorous form of ecclesiastical graft. A dis-
pensation may be defined as an exemption from a law of the Church
or from some vow previously taken. On the eve of the Reformation
the dispensations most commonly sold were exemptions from fasting and from the marriage laws of the Church. By way of illustration, first cousins would be permitted to marry for the payment of a
fee of one ducat; for closer degrees of relationship—for example
that of uncle and niece—the fee might be as much as thirty times
that amount, depending upon ability to pay.

But the abuses which seemed to arouse the most ardent pressure
for reform were the sale of indulgences and the superstitious ven-

eration of relics. An indulgence is a remission of all or of part of the
temporal punishment due to sin—that is, of the punishment in this
life and in purgatory; it is not supposed to have anything to do with
punishment in hell. The theory upon which the indulgence rests is
the famous doctrine of the Treasure of Merit developed by Scholastic theologians in the thirteenth century. According to this doctrine,
Jesus and the saints, by reason of their "superfluous" virtues on
earth, accumulated an excess of merit in heaven. This excess constitutes a treasure of grace upon which the Pope can draw for the
benefit of ordinary mortals. Originally indulgences were not issued
for payments of money, but only for works of charity, fasting,
going on crusades, and the like. It was the Renaissance Popes, with
their insatiable greed for revenue, who first embarked upon the sale
of indulgences as a profitable business. The methods they employed
were far from scrupulous. The traffic in "pardons" was often turned
over to bankers on a commission basis. As an example, the Fuggers
in Augsburg had charge of the sale of indulgences for Leo X, with
permission to pocket one-third of the proceeds. Naturally, but one
motive dominated the business—to raise as much money as possible.
As a consequence, the agents of the bankers deluded ignorant people
into believing that the indulgences were passports to heaven. By the
sixteenth century the nefarious traffic had assumed the proportions
of a gigantic scandal.

For centuries before the Reformation the veneration of sacred relics had been an important element in Catholic worship. It was believed that objects used by the Christ, the Virgin, or the saints possessed a miraculous healing and protective virtue for anyone who touched them or came into their presence. It was inevitable that this belief should open the way for innumerable frauds. Superstitious peasants could be easily convinced that almost any ancient splinter of wood was a fragment of the true cross. And there was evidently no dearth of relic-mongers quick to take advantage of such credulity. The results were fantastic. According to Erasmus, the churches of Europe contained enough wood of the true cross to build a ship. No fewer than five shinbones of the ass on which Jesus rode to Jerusalem were on exhibition in different places, to say nothing of twelve heads of John the Baptist. Martin Luther declared in a pamphlet lampooning his enemy, the Archbishop of Mainz, that the latter claimed to possess "a whole pound of the wind that blew for Elijah in the cave on Mount Horeb and two feathers and an egg of the Holy Ghost." [1]

Modern historians agree, however, that abuses in the Catholic Church were not the primary religious cause of the Protestant Revolution. It was medieval Catholicism itself, not the abuses therein, to which the Reformers objected. Moreover, just before the revolt broke out, conditions had begun to improve. Many pious Catholics themselves had started an agitation for reform, which in time would probably have eliminated most of the glaring evils in the system. But as so often happens in the case of revolutions, the improvement had come too late. Other forces more irresistible in character had been gradually gathering momentum. Conspicuous among these was the growing reaction against late medieval theology, with its elaborate sacramental theory, its belief in the necessity of good works to supplement faith, and its doctrine of divine authority in the hands of the priests.

From preceding chapters the reader will recall that two different systems of theology had developed within the medieval Church.[2] The first was formulated mainly by followers of St. Augustine in the early Middle Ages, on the basis of teachings in the Pauline Epistles. It was predicated on the assumption of an omnipotent God, who sees the whole drama of the universe in the twinkling of an eye. Not even a sparrow falls to the ground except in accordance with the divine decree. Human nature is hopelessly depraved, and it is therefore as impossible for man to perform good works as for thistles to bring forth figs. Man is absolutely dependent upon God, not only for grace to keep him from sin but also for his fate after death. Only those mortals can be saved whom God for reasons of His own has predestined to inherit eternal life. Such in its barest outlines was the

THE PROTESTANT REVOLUTION

Abuses connected with the veneration of sacred relics

Abuses not the primary causes of the Protestant Revolution

The clash between two different systems of theology: the Augustinian system

---

[1] Preserved Smith, *The Age of the Reformation*, pp. 495-96.
[2] See the chapters on Early Medieval Europe and The Later Middle Ages: Religious and Intellectual Developments.

The late medi-
eval theology of
Peter Lombard
and St. Thomas
Aquinas

system of doctrine commonly known as Augustinianism. It was a theology well suited to the age of chaos which followed the breakup of the classical world. Men in this time were prone to fatalism and otherworldliness, for they seemed to be at the mercy of forces beyond their control. But the system never wholly died out. It was preserved intact for centuries in certain areas, especially in parts of Germany, where the progress of late medieval civilization was comparatively slow. To Luther and many of his followers it seemed the most logical interpretation of Christian belief.

With the growth of a more abundant life in the cities of southern and western Europe, it was natural that the pessimistic philosophy of Augustinianism should have been replaced by a system which would restore to man some measure of pride in his own estate. The change was accelerated also by the growth of a dominant Church organization. The theology of Augustinianism, by placing man's fate entirely in the hands of God, had seemed to imply that the functions of an organized Church were practically unnecessary. Certainly no sinner could rely upon the ministrations of priests to improve his chances of salvation, since those who were to be saved had already been "elected" by God from all eternity. The new system of belief was finally crystallized in the writings of Peter Lombard and St. Thomas Aquinas in the twelfth and thirteenth centuries. Its cardinal premise was the idea that man had been endowed by God with freedom of will, with power to choose the good and avoid the evil. However, man could not make this choice entirely unaided, for without the support of heavenly grace he would be likely to fall into sin. It was therefore necessary for him to receive the sacraments, the indispensable means for communicating the grace of God to man. Of the seven sacraments of the Church, the three most important for the layman were baptism, penance, and the Eucharist. The first wiped out the stain of previous sin; the second absolved the contrite sinner from guilt; the third was especially significant for its effect in renewing the saving grace of Christ's sacrifice on the cross. Aside from baptism, none of the sacraments could ever be administered by anyone outside the ranks of the priesthood. The members of the clergy, having inherited the power of the keys from the Apostle Peter, alone had the authority to cooperate with God in forgiving sins and in performing the miracle of the Eucharist, whereby the bread and wine were transubstantiated into the body and blood of the Savior.

The Protestant Revolution was in large measure a rebellion against the second of these systems of theology. Although the doctrines of Peter Lombard and St. Thomas Aquinas had virtually become part of the theology of the Church, they had never been universally accepted. To Christians who had been brought up under Augustinian influence, they seemed to detract from the sovereignty of God and to contradict the plain teachings of Paul that man's will is in bondage and his nature unspeakably vile. Worse still, in the opinion of these critics, was the fact that the new theology greatly strengthened the authority of the priesthood. In sum, what the Reformers wanted was a return to a more primitive Christianity than that which had prevailed since the thirteenth century. Any doctrine or practice not expressly sanctioned in the Scriptures, especially in the Pauline Epistles, or not recognized by the Fathers of the Church, they were strongly inclined to reject. It was for this reason that they condemned not only the theory of the priesthood and the sacramental system of the Church, but also such medieval additions to the faith as the worship of the Virgin, the belief in purgatory, the invocation of saints, the veneration of relics, and the rule of celibacy for the clergy. Motives of rationalism or skepticism had comparatively little to do with it. While it is true that Luther ridiculed the worship of relics as a form of superstition, in the main the early Protestants were even more suspicious of reason than the Catholics. Their religious ideal rested upon the Augustinian dogmas of original sin, the total depravity of man, predestination, and the bondage of the will—which were certainly more difficult to justify on a rational basis than the liberalized teachings of St. Thomas.

A few remaining religious causes deserve at least passing mention. One was the decline of respect for the papacy in consequence of the so-called "Babylonian Captivity" and the Great Schism. The "Babylonian Captivity" grew out of a quarrel between King Philip IV of France and Pope Boniface VIII at the beginning of the fourteenth century. The soldiers of the king arrested the Pope, and soon afterward Boniface died from the effects of the humiliation. A short time later King Philip's own candidate was elected to St. Peter's throne, and the papal capital was transferred to Avignon in the Rhone valley, where it remained for nearly seventy years. Surrounded by French influences, the Popes who reigned at Avignon were unable to escape the charge of subservience to French interests. In the minds of many Christians the papacy had ceased to be an international institution and had been degraded into the mere plaything of a secular power. In 1378 the head of the Church suffered an even greater loss of prestige. An effort to restore the papacy to its original capital led to the election of two Popes, one at Avignon and one at Rome, each loudly proclaiming himself the rightful successor of the Apostle Peter. The resulting division of the Church into two factions, supporting respectively the claims of the French and Italian Popes, is known as the Great Schism. Though finally healed by the Council of Constance in 1417, its effect in weakening the position of the papacy could hardly be overestimated.

Still another factor of some importance in hastening the Protestant Revolution was the influence of the mystics and early reformers. For more than two centuries before the time of Luther, mysticism had become one of the most popular forms of religious

The Protestant Revolution a rebellion against the late medieval system of theology

Influence of the "Babylonian Captivity" of the papacy and the Great Schism

St. John Lateran, the Pope's Cathedral in Rome. The "Mother Church" of Catholic Christendom, it derives its name from Plautius Lateranus, a rich nobleman whose property in this area was confiscated by Nero.

Influence of
the mystics and
early reformers

expression in northern Europe. And it is not without significance that the vast majority of the mystics were Germans or natives of the Low Countries. Preeminent among them was Meister Eckhart, who lived in the fourteenth century. Though none of the mystics preached open rebellion against the Catholic system, they were vehemently opposed to the ritualistic route to salvation sponsored by the medieval Church. Their version of religion was one in which the individual would attain the highest heaven through extinction of selfish desires and absolute surrender of the soul to God. No sacraments or priestly miracles would be necessary. Faith and a deep emotional piety would accomplish more wonders in reconciling sinful man to God than all the Masses in the calendar of the Church. Along with the mystics a number of pre-Reformation reformers exerted considerable influence in preparing the ground for the Protestant Revolt. At the end of the fourteenth century an Oxford professor by the name of John Wyclif launched an attack upon the Catholic system which anticipated much of the thunder of Luther and Calvin. He denounced the immorality of the clergy, condemned indulgences and the temporal power of the Church, recommended marriage of the clergy, insisted upon the supreme authority of the Scriptures as the source of belief, and denied transubstantiation, though admitting as Luther did later that Christ is actually present in the bread and wine. Most of Wyclif's teachings were ultimately carried to central Europe by Czech students from Oxford. They were actively propagated in Bohemia by John Huss, who was burned at the stake in 1415. Luther acknowledged his deep indebtedness to the Bohemian martyr.

598   As a political movement the Protestant Revolt was mainly the re-

sult of two developments: first, the growth of a national consciousness in northern Europe; and second, the rise of absolute monarchs.
Ever since the late Middle Ages there had been a growing spirit of
independence among many of the peoples outside of Italy. They
had come to regard their own national life as unique and to resent
interference from any external source. Although they were not
nationalists in the modern sense, they tended to view the Pope as a
foreigner who had no right to meddle with local affairs in England,
France, or Germany. This feeling was manifested in England as
early as the middle of the fourteenth century, when the famous
Statutes of Provisors and Praemunire were passed. The first prohibited appointments by the Pope to Church offices in England; the
second forbade the appeal of cases from the English courts to Rome.
A law more extreme than either of these was issued by the king of
France in 1438. The French law, known as the Pragmatic Sanction
of Bourges, practically abolished all papal authority in the country,
including the appointive authority and the right to raise revenue.
To the civil magistrates was given the power to regulate religious
affairs within their own districts. A subsequent decree provided the
death penalty for any agent of the Pope who should bring a bull
into the country contradicting the Pragmatic Sanction. In Germany, despite the fact that there was no solid political unity, national feeling was by no means absent. It expressed itself in violent
attacks upon the clergy by the Imperial Diet and in numerous decrees by the rulers of separate states prohibiting ecclesiastical appointments and the sale of indulgences without their consent.

The growth of a national consciousness in all of these countries
went hand in hand with the rise of absolute monarchs. Indeed, it
would be difficult to say how much of the sense of nationality was
spontaneous and how much of it was stimulated by ambitious
princes intent upon increasing their power. At any rate it is certain
that the claims of rulers to absolute authority were bound to result
in defiance of Rome. No despot could be expected to tolerate long
the exclusion of religion from his sphere of control. He could not be
a despot so long as there was a double jurisdiction within his realm.
The appetite of princes for control over the Church was whetted
originally by the revival of the Roman law, with its doctrine that
the people had delegated *all* of their power to the secular ruler. To
this must be added the effect of the teaching of Wyclif in England
and Pierre Dubois in France that the temporal power of the Pope
should be transferred to the king. From this doctrine it was a comparatively easy step to the idea that all of the Pope's authority could
be properly assumed by the head of the state. But whatever the reasons for its growth, there can be no doubt that the ambition of secular princes to establish churches under their own control was a
primary cause of the mounting antagonism against Rome.

Historians disagree as to the importance of economic causation of

Economic causes:
the desire to
confiscate the
wealth of the
Catholic Church

the Protestant Revolution. Those who conceive of the movement as primarily a religious one think of the sixteenth century as a period of profound and agonized concern over spiritual problems. Such a condition may well have characterized the mass of the people. But it does not alter the fact that in the sixteenth century, as in all ages, there were ruling groups greedy for wealth and quite willing to use and even to cultivate mass ideologies for their own advantage. Prominent among the economic objectives of such groups were acquisition of the wealth of the Church and elimination of papal taxation. In the course of its history from the beginning of the Middle Ages, the Church had grown into a vast economic empire. It was by far the largest landowner in western Europe, to say nothing of its enormous movable wealth in the form of rich furnishings, jewels, precious metals, and the like. Estimates of the amount of land held by bishoprics and monasteries in the sixteenth century range as high as one-third of the total amount of land in Germany and one-fifth of the land in France. Some of these possessions had been acquired by the Church through grants by kings and nobles, but most of them came from the gifts and bequests of pious citizens. Religious restrictions on taxation were also a galling grievance to secular rulers. Kings, panting for big armies and navies, had an urgent need for more revenue. But Catholic law prohibited the taxing of Church property. The exemption of episcopal and monastic property from taxation meant a heavier burden on the possessions of individual owners, especially on the property of merchants and bankers. Moreover, the lesser nobles in Germany were being threatened with extinction on account of the collapse of the manorial economy. Many of them looked with covetous eyes upon the lands of the Church. If only some excuse could be found for expropriating these, their difficult situation might be relieved.

Papal taxation, by the eve of the Protestant Revolution, had assumed a baffling variety of irritating forms. The most nearly universal, if not the most burdensome, was the so-called *Peter's pence*, an annual levy on every household in Christendom.[3] It must be understood that this tax was in addition to the *tithe*, which was supposed to be one-tenth of every Christian's income paid for the support of the parish church. Then there were the innumerable fees paid into the papal treasury for indulgences, dispensations, appeals of judicial decisions, and so on. In a very real sense the moneys collected for the sale of Church offices and the *annates*, or commissions levied on the first year's income of every bishop and priest, were also forms of papal taxation, since the officials who paid them eventually reimbursed themselves through increased collections from the

[3] Peter's pence derived its name from the fact that it was a tax of one penny. But the English penny at the end of the Middle Ages was the equivalent in purchasing power of slightly more than one dollar of our money. H. E. Barnes, *An Economic History of the Western World*, p. 121.

people. But the main objection to these taxes was not that they were so numerous and burdensome. The famous accusation of some modern Catholic writers that the Protestants simply wanted a cheaper religion has no good foundation in fact. The real basis of grievance against the papal levies was their effect in draining the northern countries of so much of their wealth for the enrichment of Italy. Economically the situation was almost exactly the same as if the nations of northern Europe had been conquered by a foreign prince and tribute imposed upon them. Some Germans and Englishmen were scandalized also by the fact that most of the money collected was not being spent for religious purposes, but was being squandered by worldly Popes to maintain luxurious courts. The reason for the resentment, however, was probably as much financial as moral.

A third important economic cause of the Protestant Revolution was the conflict between the ambitions of the new middle class and the ascetic ideals of medieval Christianity. It was shown in a preceding chapter that the Catholic philosophers of the later Middle Ages had developed an elaborate theory designed for the guidance of the Christian in matters of production and trade.[4] This theory was founded upon the assumption that business for the sake of profit is essentially immoral. No one has a right to any more than a reasonable wage for the service he renders to society. All wealth acquired in excess of this amount should be given to the Church to be distributed for the benefit of the needy. The merchant or craftsman who strives to get rich at the expense of the people is really no better than a common thief. To gain an advantage over a rival in business by cornering the market or beating down wages is contrary to all law and morality. Equally sinful is the damnable practice of usury—the charging of interest on loans where no actual risk is involved. This is sheer robbery, for it deprives the person who uses the money of earnings that are justly his; it is contrary to nature, for it enables the man who lends the money to live without labor.

While it is far from true that these doctrines were universally honored even by the Church itself, they nevertheless remained an integral part of the Catholic ideal, at least to the end of the Middle Ages. Even to this day they have not been entirely abandoned, as our study of liberal Catholicism in the nineteenth and twentieth centuries will show.[5] However, the age of the Renaissance was accompanied by the growth of an economic pattern distinctly incompatible with most of these doctrines. A ruthless, dynamic capitalism, based upon the principle of "dog eat dog," was beginning to supplant the old static economy of the medieval guilds. No longer

---

[4] See the chapter on The Later Middle Ages: Political and Economic institutions.
[5] See the paragraphs on Christian Socialism at the end of the chapter on the First Industrial Revolution.

were merchants and manufacturers content with a mere "wage" for the services they rendered to society. They demanded profits, and they could not see that it was any business of the Church to decide what a man's earnings should be. Wages were fit only for hirelings, who had neither the wit nor the industry to go after the big rewards. In addition to all this, the growth of banking meant an even more violent conflict with the ascetic ideal of the Church. As long as the business of moneylending was in the hands of Jews and Moslems, it mattered little that usury should be branded as a sin. But now that Christians were piling up riches by financing the exploits of kings and merchants, the shoe was on another foot. The new crop of bankers resented being told that their lucrative trade in cash was contrary to the laws of God. This seemed to them an attempt of spokesmen for an outmoded past to dictate the standards for a new age of progress. But how was it that Italy did not break with the Catholic Church in view of the extensive development of banking and commerce in such cities as Florence, Genoa, Milan, and Venice? Perhaps one explanation is to be found in the fact that such business activities had taken earlier and deeper roots in Italy than in most parts of Germany. They had been established for so long a time that any possible conflict between them and religious ideals had been largely ignored. Besides, the religion of many Italians, especially during the Renaissance period, tended to approximate that of the ancient Romans; it was external and mechanical rather than profoundly spiritual. To many northern Europeans, by contrast, religion had a deeper significance. It was a system of dogmas and commandments to be observed literally under pain of the awful judgment of a wrathful God. They were, therefore, more likely to be disturbed by inconsistencies between worldly practices and the doctrines of the faith.

The full story of why the Protestant Revolution began in Germany is so complex that only a few of the possible reasons can be suggested as topics for the student to ponder. Was Germany relatively more backward than most other areas of western Europe? Had the Renaissance touched her so lightly that medieval religiosity remained quite pervasive? Or did economic factors operate more strongly in Germany than elsewhere? The Church in Germany held an enormous proportion of the best agricultural lands, and evidence exists that the country was seething with discontent on account of a too rapid transition from a feudal society to an economy of profits and wages. It seems to be true, finally, that Germany was the victim of Catholic abuses to a greater extent than most other countries. How crucial was the shock resulting from these is impossible to say, but at least they provided the immediate impetus for the outbreak of the Lutheran revolt. Unlike England and France, Germany had no powerful king to defend her interests against the papacy. The country was weak and divided. At least partly for this reason, Pope Leo

Portrait of Martin Luther. By
Melchior Lorch, 1548.

X selected German territory as the most likely field for the sale of
indulgences.

I. THE LUTHERAN REVOLT IN GERMANY By the dawn of the sixteenth century Germany was ripe for religious revolution. All
that was necessary was to find a leader who could unite the dissatisfied elements and give a suitable theological gloss to their grievances. Such a leader was not long in appearing. His name was Martin
Luther, and he was born in Thuringia in 1483. His parents were
originally peasants, but his father had left the soil soon after his marriage to work in the mines of Mansfeld. Here he managed to become moderately prosperous and served in the village council.
Nevertheless, young Martin's early environment was far from ideal.
He was whipped at home for trivial offenses until he bled, and his
mind was filled with hideous terrors of demons and witches. Some of
these superstitions clung to him until the end of his life. His parents
intended that he should become a lawyer, and with this end in view
they placed him at the age of eighteen in the University of Erfurt.
During his first four years at the university, Luther worked hard,
gaining more than an ordinary reputation as a scholar. But in 1505,
while returning from a visit to his home, he was overtaken by a violent storm and felled to the ground by a bolt of lightning. In terror
lest an angry God strike him dead, he vowed to St. Anne to become
a monk. Soon afterward he entered the Augustinian monastery at
Erfurt.

Here he gave himself up to earnest reflection on the state of his
soul. Obsessed with the idea that his sins were innumerable, he **603**

strove desperately to attain a goal of spiritual peace. He engaged in long vigils and went for days on end without a morsel of food. But the more he fasted and tortured himself, the more his anguish and depression increased. Told that the way of salvation lies in love of God, he was ready to give up in despair. How could he love a Being who is not even just, who saves only those whom it pleases Him to save? "Love Him?" he said to himself, "I do not love Him. I hate Him." But in time, as he pondered the Scriptures, especially the story of the Crucifixion, he gained a new insight into the mysteries of the Christian theology. He was profoundly impressed by the humiliation of the Savior's death on the cross. For the benefit of sinful humanity, the Christ, the God-man, had shared the fate of common criminals. Why had He done so except out of love for His creatures? The God of the storm whose chief attribute appeared to be anger had revealed Himself as a Father who pities His children.

The doctrine of justification by faith alone

Here was a miracle which no human reason could understand. It must be taken on faith; and by faith alone, Luther concluded, can man be justified in the sight of God. This doctrine of justification by faith alone, as opposed to salvation by "good works," quickly became the central doctrine of the Lutheran theology.

But long before Luther had completed his theological system, he was called to lecture on Aristotle and the Bible at the University of Wittenberg, which had recently been founded by Frederick the Wise of Saxony. While serving in this capacity, he was confronted by an event which furnished the spark for the Protestant Revolution. In 1517 an unprincipled Dominican friar by the name of Tetzel appeared in Germany as a hawker of indulgences. Determined to

Luther's revolt against the sale of indulgences

raise as much money as possible for Pope Leo X and the Archbishop of Mainz who had employed him, Tetzel deliberately represented the indulgences as tickets of admission to heaven. Though forbidden to enter Saxony, he came to the borders of that state, and many natives of Wittenberg rushed out to buy salvation at so attractive a price. Luther was appalled by such brazen deception of ignorant people. Accordingly, he drew up a set of ninety-five theses or statements attacking the sale of indulgences, and posted them, after the manner of the time, on the door of the castle church on October 31, 1517. Later he had them printed and sent to his friends in a number of cities. Soon it became evident that the Ninety-five Theses had voiced the sentiments of a nation. All over Germany, Luther was hailed as a leader whom God had raised to break the power of an arrogant and hypocritical clergy. A violent reaction against the sale of indulgences was soon in full swing. Tetzel was mobbed and driven from the country. The revolt against Rome had begun.

With the revenue from indulgences cut off, it was inevitable that the Pope should take action. Early in 1518 he commanded the general of the Augustinian order to make the rebellious friar recant. Luther not only refused but published a sermon stating his views

Luther Preaching. With one hand he points to popes, monks, and cardinals going down hell's mouth. Hell is a beast with snout, tusk, and eye. With the other hand Luther points to the crucifix. The Lord's Supper is being administered, both the bread and the wine, to the laity. The chalice on the table emphasizes the evangelical practice of giving the cup to the laity.

more strongly than ever. That no more stringent measures were taken against him at this time was a result of the fact that Leo X was absorbed in the coming imperial election. For more than two years the impetuous friar enjoyed an immunity from persecution, protected by his friend, the Elector Frederick of Saxony. He made use of this time in writing pamphlets to expand his doctrines and to keep the enthusiasm of his supporters from flagging. Forced by his critics to answer questions on many points other than indulgences, he gradually came to realize that his own religion was utterly irreconcilable with that of the Roman Church. There was no alternative except to break with the Catholic faith entirely. In 1520 his teachings were formally condemned in a bull promulgated by Leo X, and he was ordered to recant within sixty days or be dealt with as a heretic. Luther replied by publicly burning the Pope's proclamation. For this he was excommunicated and ordered to be turned over to the secular arm for punishment. Germany at this time was still under the technical rule of the Holy Roman Empire. Charles V, who had recently been elevated to the throne of this ramshackle state, was anxious to be rid of the insolent rebel at once, but he dared not act without the approval of the Imperial Diet. Accordingly, in 1521, Luther was summoned to appear before a meeting of this body at Worms. Since many of the princes and electors who composed the Diet were themselves hostile toward the Church, nothing in particular was done, despite Luther's stubborn refusal to retract any of the things he had said. Finally, after a number of the members had gone home, the Emperor forced through an edict branding the obstreperous friar as an outlaw. But Luther had already been hidden away in the castle of his friend, the Elector of Saxony. Here he remained until all danger of arrest by the Emperor's soldiers had passed. Charles soon afterward withdrew to conduct his war with France, and the Edict of Worms was never enforced.

Thenceforth until his death in 1546 Luther was occupied with his work of building an independent German church. Despite the fundamental conflict between his own beliefs and Catholic theology, he nevertheless retained a good many of the elements of the Roman system. With the passing of the years he became more conservative than many of his own followers and compared some of them to Judas betraying his Master. Though he had originally denounced transubstantiation, he eventually came around to adopting a doctrine which bore at least a superficial resemblance to the Catholic theory. Theologians call this doctrine "consubstantiation," meaning that the body and blood of Christ are really present *along with* the bread and wine. He maintained that the words imputed to the Christ in the New Testament, "This is my body," were literally true, even if contrary to reason. He denied, however, that any change in the substance of the bread and wine occurred as the result of a priestly miracle. The function of the clergyman is simply to *reveal* the presence of God in the bread and wine. In like manner, Luther retained the Catholic practice of elevating the "host," or consecrated wafer of the Eucharist, for the adoration of the faithful. Still, the changes he made were drastic enough to preserve the revolutionary character of the new religion. He substituted German for Latin in the services of the church. He rejected the entire ecclesiastical system of Pope, archbishops, bishops, and priests as custodians of the keys to the kingdom of heaven. By abolishing monasticism and insisting upon the right of priests to marry, he went far toward destroying the barrier which had separated clergy from laity and given the former their special status as representatives of God on earth. He eliminated all of the sacraments with the exception of baptism and the Eucharist, and he denied that even these had any supernatural effect in bringing down grace from heaven. Since he continued to emphasize faith rather than good works as the road to salvation, he naturally discarded such formalized practices as fasts, pilgrimages, the veneration of relics, and the invocation of saints. On the other hand, the doctrines of predestination and the supreme authority of the Scriptures were given in the new religion a higher place than they had ever enjoyed in the old. Last of all, Luther abandoned the Catholic idea that the Church should be supreme over the state. Instead of having bishops subject to the Pope as the Vicar of Christ, he organized his church under superintendents who were essentially agents of the government.

Of course, Luther was not alone responsible for the success of the Protestant Revolution. In molding the tenets of the new faith he was ably assisted by Philip Melanchthon (1497–1560), a teacher of Greek and originally a humanist at the University of Wittenberg. It was Melanchthon who drafted the Augsburg Confession (1530), which is still accepted as the creed of the Lutheran church. The overthrow of Catholicism in Germany was also abetted by the outbreak of social revolt. In 1522–1523 there occurred a ferocious rebellion of the knights. These petty nobles were being impoverished by competition from the great estates and by the change to a capitalist economy. They saw as the chief cause of their misery the concentration of landed wealth in the hands of the great princes of the Church. Obsessed with national sentiments, they dreamed of a united Germany free from the domination of powerful landlords and grasping priests. The leaders of the movement were Ulrich von Hutten, who had turned from a humanist into a fierce partisan of Luther, and Franz von Sickingen, a notorious robber baron and soldier of fortune. To these men the gospel of Luther seemed to provide an excellent program for a war on behalf of German liberty. Although their rebellion was speedily crushed by the armies of the archbishops and richer nobles, it apparently had considerable effect in persuading the pillars of the old regime that too much resistance to the Lutheran movement would scarcely be wise.

The revolt of the knights was followed by a much more violent uprising of the lower classes in 1524–1525. Though most who took part were peasants, a great many poor workmen from the cities were attracted to the movement also. The causes of this second rebellion were somewhat similar to those of the first: the rising cost of living, the concentration of holdings of land, and the religious radicalism inspired by Luther's teachings. But the peasants and urban workers were stirred to action by many other factors as well. The decay of the feudal regime had eliminated the paternal relationship between noble and serf. In its place had grown up a mere cash nexus between employer and worker. The sole obligation now of the upper classes was to pay a wage. When sickness or unemployment struck, the laborer had to make shift with his slender resources as best he could. Furthermore, most of the old privileges which the serf had enjoyed on the manorial estate, of pasturing his flocks on the common lands and gathering wood in the forest, were being rapidly abolished. To make matters worse, landlords were attempting to meet advancing prices by exacting higher rents from the peasants. Finally, the lower classes were angered by the fact that the revival of the Roman law had the effect of bolstering property rights and of strengthening the power of the state to protect the interests of the rich.

Many of the downtrodden folk who participated in the so-called Peasants' Revolt belonged to a religious sect known as the Anabaptists. The name means re-baptizers, and was derived from the fact that the members of the sect held infant baptism to be ineffectual and insisted that the rite should be administered only when the indi-

The outbreak of social revolution; the revolt of the knights

The uprising of the lower classes

Der Prophet
Jona.

XXXV.

I.

ES geschach das wort des HER-REN zu Jona dem son Amithai/vnd sprach/Mache dich auff/vnd gehe jnn die grosse Stad Ninene/vnd predige drinnen/Denn jre bosheit ist erauff komen fur mich. Aber Jona machte sich auff vnd flohe fur dem HERRN/vnd wolt auffs Meer/vnd kam hinab gen Japho/vnd da er ein schiff fand/das auffs meer wolt faren/gab er fehrgeld vnd trat drein/das er mit jnen auffs meer füre/fur dem HERRN.

Da lies der HERR einen grossen wind auffs meer komen/vnd hub sich ein gros vngewitter auff dem meer/das man meinet/das schiff würde zubrechen. Vnd die schiffleute furchten sich/vnd schrien/ein jglicher zu seinem Gott. Vnd worffen das gerete / das im schiff war/jns meer/das es leichter würde. Aber Jona war hinunter jnn das schiff gestiegen/lag vnd schlieff. Da trat zu jm der Schiffherr/vnd sprach zu jm/Was schleffestu? Stehe auff/ruffe deinen Gott an/ob villeicht Gott an vns gedencken wolte/das wir nicht verdurben.

Vnd einer

A Page from the Bible Translated by Luther into German. The engraving shows several episodes of the story of Jonah in a single composite picture.

The Anabaptists

vidual had reached the age of reason. But a belief in adult baptism was not really their principal doctrine. The Anabaptists were extreme individualists in religion. Luther's teaching that every man has a right to follow the dictates of his own conscience they took exactly as it stood. Not only did they reject the Catholic theory of the priesthood, but they denied the necessity of any clergy at all, maintaining that every individual should follow the guidance of the "inner light." They refused to admit that God's revelation to man had ceased with the writing of the last book of the New Testament, but they insisted that He continues to speak directly to certain of His chosen followers. They attached much importance to literal interpretation of the Bible, even of its most occult portions. They believed that the church should be a community of saints and required of their followers abstention from lying, profanity, gluttony, lewdness, and drinking intoxicating liquors. Many of the members looked forward to the early destruction of this world and the establishment of Christ's kingdom of justice and peace, in which they would have a prominent place. But the Anabaptists were not merely a group of religious extremists; they represented as well the most radical social tendencies of their time. Though it is certainly an ex-

608

aggeration to call them communists, they did denounce the accumulation of wealth and taught that it was the duty of Christians to share their goods with one another. In addition, they declined to recognize any distinctions of rank or class, declaring all men equal in the sight of God. Many of them also abominated the taking of oaths, condemned military service, and refused to pay taxes to governments that engaged in war. They abstained in general from political life and demanded the complete separation of church and state. Their doctrines represented the extreme manifestation of the revolutionary fervor generated by the Protestant movement.

The Peasants' Revolt of 1524–1525 began in southern Germany and spread rapidly to the north and west until most of the country was involved. At first it had more of the character of a strike than a revolution. The rebels contented themselves with drafting petitions and attempting peaceably to persuade their masters to grant them relief from oppression. But before many months had passed, the movement came under the control of such fanatics as Thomas Münzer, who urged the use of fire and sword against the wicked nobles and clergy. In the spring of 1525 the misguided rustics began plundering and burning cloisters and castles and even murdering some of their more hated opponents. The nobles now turned against them with fiendish fury, slaughtering indiscriminately both those who resisted and those who were helpless. Strange as it may seem, the lords were encouraged in this savagery by several of the Reformers, including the great Luther himself. In a pamphlet *Against the Thievish, Murderous Hordes of Peasants* he urged everyone who could to hunt the rebels down like mad dogs, to "strike, strangle, stab secretly or in public, and let him remember that nothing can be more poisonous, harmful, or devilish than a man in rebellion." [6] To Luther's credit, it should perhaps be added that he feared anarchy more than he did the particular doctrines of the Anabaptists. He believed that the use of force by anyone except the lawful authorities would result in the destruction of the social order.

The Peasants' Revolt of 1524-1525

Suppression of the Peasants' Revolt

But the brutal suppression of the Peasants' Revolt did not mark the end of revolutionary activities on the part of the submerged classes. In 1534 a group of Anabaptists gained control of the episcopal city of Münster in Westphalia. Thousands of their fellow believers from the surrounding country came pouring in, and Münster became a New Jerusalem where all of the accumulated vagaries of the lunatic fringe of the movement were put into practice. The property of unbelievers was confiscated, and polygamy was introduced. A certain John of Leyden assumed the title of king, proclaiming himself the successor of David with a mission to conquer the world and destroy the heathen. But after a little more than a year of this, Münster was recaptured by its bishop, and the leaders of Zion were put to death by horrible tortures. This second disaster

[6] Quoted by H. S. Lucas, *The Renaissance and the Reformation*, p. 457.

Portrait of Ulrich Zwingli. Sixteenth century woodcut by an unknown master.

proved to be the turning point in the revolt of the have-nots of the sixteenth century. Convinced of the futility of violence, they now abandoned the fanatical dogmas of their fallen leaders and returned to the religious quietism of earlier years. Most of the radical economic teachings were also dropped. Some of the survivors of the persecutions now joined the sect of Mennonites, so called from Menno Simons (1492–1559), whose teachings were partly derived from those of the original Anabaptists. Others fled to England to become the spiritual ancestors of the Quakers.

II. THE ZWINGLIAN AND CALVINIST REVOLTS IN SWITZERLAND The special form of Protestantism developed by Luther did not prove to be particularly popular beyond its native environment. Outside of Germany, Lutheranism became the official religion only in Denmark, Norway, and Sweden. But the force of the Lutheran revolt made itself felt in a number of other lands. Such was especially the case in Switzerland, where national consciousness had been gathering strength for centuries. At the close of the Middle Ages the gallant herdsmen and peasants of the Swiss cantons had challenged the right of the Austrians to rule over them, and finally in 1499 had compelled the Emperor Maximilian to recognize their independence, not only of the house of Hapsburg but of the Holy Roman Empire as well. Having thrown off the yoke of a foreign Emperor, the Swiss were not likely to submit indefinitely to an alien Pope. Moreover, the cities of Zürich, Basel, Berne, and Geneva had grown into flourishing centers of trade. Their populations were dominated by solid burghers who were becoming increasingly contemptuous of the Catholic ideal of glorified poverty. Here also northern humanism had found welcome lodgment in cultivated minds, with the effect of creating a healthy distrust of priestly superstitions. Erasmus had lived for a number of years in Basel. Lastly, Switzerland had been plucked by the indulgence peddlers to an extent only less grievous than that in Germany, while the city of

Berne had been the scene of some particularly flagrant monkish frauds.

The father of the Protestant Revolution in Switzerland was Ulrich Zwingli (1484–1531). Only a few weeks younger than Luther, he was the son of a well-to-do magistrate, who was able to provide him with an excellent education. He attended the Universities of Vienna and Basel, completing the course for the master's degree at the latter. As a student he devoted nearly all of his time to philosophy and literature, with no interest in religion save in the practical reforms of the Christian humanists. Although he took holy orders at the age of twenty-two, his purpose in entering the priesthood was mainly the opportunity it would give him to cultivate his literary tastes. For some eight years thereafter he continued to accept the patronage of the Pope and to take his vows of celibacy exceedingly lightly. In 1519, however, he experienced one of those sudden conversions so typical of the careers of religious reformers. For this change of heart there seem to have been two main causes: a serious attack of the plague and the influence of Luther. Which of these causes came first is unknown, but both had a powerful effect. From this time on Zwingli became a fervid crusader, not merely for a purer religion but for a break with the Catholic Church. He accepted nearly all of the teachings of Luther with the exception of consubstantiation. Zwingli maintained that the bread and wine are mere symbols of the body and blood, and he reduced the sacrament of Holy Communion to a simple memorial service. So ably did he marshal the anti-Catholic forces that by 1528 nearly all of northern Switzerland had deserted the ancient faith. But when he attempted to extend his crusade into the conservative forest cantons, he encountered stiff opposition. In 1529 civil war broke out, resulting after two years in the defeat of the Zwinglian forces and in the death of their leader. By the Peace of Kappel (1531) the Protestants agreed that the choice of a religion for the several areas of Switzerland should be made by the cantonal governments.

Ulrich Zwingli

From the northern cantons the Protestant Revolution in Switzerland spread to Geneva. This beautiful city, located on a lake of the same name near the French border, had the doubtful advantage of a double government. The people owed allegiance to two feudal suzerains, the local bishop and the Count of Savoy. When these highborn chieftains conspired to make their power more absolute, the citizens rebelled against them. The result was their expulsion from the town about 1530 and the establishment of a free republic. But the movement could hardly have been successful without some aid from the northern cantons. Thus it was not long until Protestant preachers from Zürich and Berne began arriving in Geneva. Moreover, since the leaders of the political revolution were excommunicated for defying their bishop, it was natural that they should be favorably disposed toward a new religion for their city.

The spread of
the Protestant
Revolution to
Geneva

It was under this constellation of events that John Calvin (1509–1564) arrived in Geneva. Although destined to play so prominent a role in the history of Switzerland, he was not a native of that country but of France. He was born at Noyon in Picardy. His mother died when he was very young, and his father, who did not like children, turned him over to the care of an aristocratic friend. For his higher education he was sent to the University of Paris, where, because of his bilious disposition and fault-finding manner, he was dubbed "the accusative case." Later he shifted at his father's wish to study of law at Orléans. Here he came under the influence of disciples of Luther, evidently to a sufficient extent to cause him to be suspected of heresy. Consequently, in 1534, when the government began an attack on the wavering ones, Calvin fled to Switzerland. He settled for a time in Basel and then moved on to Geneva, which was still in the throes of political revolution. He began preaching and organizing at once, and by 1541 both government and religion had fallen completely under his sway. Until his death from asthma and dyspepsia in 1564 he ruled the city with a rod of iron. History contains few examples of men more dour in temperament and more stubbornly convinced of the rightness of their own ideas.

Under Calvin's rule Geneva was transformed into a religious oligarchy. The supreme authority was vested in the Congregation of the Clergy, who prepared all legislation and submitted it to the Consistory to be ratified. The latter body, composed, in addition to the clergy, of twelve elders representing the people, had as its principal function the supervision of public and private morals. This function was carried out, not merely by the punishment of antisocial conduct

Portrait of John Calvin after Susterman. Original in Boymans Museum, Rotterdam.

but by a persistent snooping into the private life of every individual. The city was divided into districts, and a committee of the Consistory visited each household without warning to conduct an inquisition into the habits of its members. Even the mildest forms of human folly were strictly prohibited. Dancing, card-playing, attending the theater, working or playing on the Sabbath—all were outlawed as major crimes. Innkeepers were forbidden to allow anyone to consume food or drink without first saying grace, or to permit any patron to sit up after nine o'clock unless he was spying on the conduct of others. Needless to say, penalties were severe. Not only murder and treason were classified as capital crimes, but also adultery, witchcraft, blasphemy, and heresy; and the last of these especially was susceptible to a broad interpretation. During the first four years after Calvin became ruler of Geneva, there were no fewer than fifty-eight executions out of a total population of only 16,000.[7] The good accomplished by all of this harshness seems to have been small indeed. There were more cases of vice in Geneva after the Reformation than before.[8]

The essentials of Calvin's theology are contained in his *Institutes of the Christian Religion,* which was published originally in 1536 and revised and enlarged several times thereafter. His ideas resemble those of St. Augustine more than any other theologian. He conceived of the universe as utterly dependent upon the will of an Almighty God, who created all things for His greater glory. Because of Adam's transgression all men are sinners by nature, bound hand and foot to an evil inheritance they cannot escape. Nevertheless, God for reasons of His own has predestined some for eternal salvation and damned all the rest to the torments of hell. Nothing that human beings may do can alter their fate; their souls are stamped with God's blessing or curse before they are born. But this did not mean, in Calvin's opinion, that the Christian could be indifferent to his conduct on earth. If he were among the elect, God would have implanted in him the desire to live right. Abstemious conduct is a sign, though not an infallible one, that he who practices it has been chosen to sit at the throne of glory. Public profession of faith and participation in the sacraments are also presumptive evidences of election to be saved. But most of all, the Calvinists required an active life of piety and good morality as a solemn obligation resting upon members of the Christian Commonwealth. Like the ancient Hebrews, they conceived of themselves as chosen instruments of God with a mission to help in the fulfillment of His purposes on earth. Their duty was not to strive for their soul's salvation but for the glory of God. Thus it will be seen that the Calvinist system did not encourage its followers to sit with folded hands serene in the knowledge that their fate was sealed. No religion has fostered a

Calvin's theology

[7] Preserved Smith, *The Age of the Reformation,* p. 171.
[8] *Ibid.,* p. 174.

The Fury of the Reformation Brandishing Its Three Main Villains, Calvin, Luther, and Beza. Contemporary antireform woodcut.

more abundant zeal in the conquest of nature, in missionary activity, or in the struggle against political tyranny. Doubtless the reason lies in the Calvinist's belief that as the chosen instrument of God he must play a part in the drama of the universe worthy of his exalted status. And with the Lord on his side he was not easily frightened by whatever lions lurked in his path.

The religion of Calvin compared with that of Luther

The religion of Calvin differed from that of Luther in a number of ways. First, it was more legalistic. Whereas the Wittenberg Reformer had emphasized the guidance of individual conscience, the dictator of Geneva stressed the sovereignty of law. He thought of God as a mighty legislator who had handed down a body of rules in the Scriptures which must be followed to the letter. Secondly, the religion of Calvin was more nearly an Old Testament faith than that of Luther. This can be illustrated in the attitude of the two men toward Sabbath observance. Luther's conception of Sunday was similar to that which prevails in modern Continental Europe. He insisted, of course, that his followers should attend church, but he did not demand that during the remainder of the day they should refrain from all pleasure or work. Calvin, on the other hand, revived the old Jewish Sabbath with its strict taboos against anything faintly resembling worldliness. In the third place, the religion of Geneva was more closely associated with the ideals of the new capitalism. Luther's sympathies lay with the nobles, and on at least one occasion he sharply censured the tycoons of finance for their greed. Calvin sanctified the ventures of the trader and the moneylender and gave an exalted place in his ethical system to the business virtues of thrift and diligence. Finally, Calvinism as compared to Lutheranism represented a more radical phase of the Protestant Revolution. As we have seen, the Wittenberg friar retained a good many features of Roman worship and even some Catholic dogmas. Calvin rejected everything he could think of that smacked of "popery." The organ-

614

ization of his church was constructed in such a way as to exclude all traces of the episcopal system. Congregations were to choose their own elders and preachers, while an association of ministers at the top would govern the entire church. Ritual, instrumental music, stained glass windows, pictures, and images were ruthlessly eliminated, with the consequence that the religion was reduced to "four bare walls and a sermon." Even the observance of Christmas and Easter was sternly prohibited.

The spread of
Calvinism

The popularity of Calvinism was not limited to Switzerland. It spread into most countries of western Europe where trade and finance had become leading pursuits. The Huguenots of France, the Puritans of England, the Presbyterians of Scotland, and the members of the Reformed church in Holland were all Calvinists. It was preeminently the religion of the bourgeoisie; though, of course, it drew converts from other strata as well. Its influence in molding the ethics of modern times and in bolstering the revolutionary courage of the middle class was enormous. Members of this faith had much to do with the initial revolts against despotism in England and France, to say nothing of their part in overthrowing Spanish tyranny in the Netherlands.

See color map
at page 616

III. THE PROTESTANT REVOLUTION IN ENGLAND The original blow against the Roman Church in England was not struck by a religious enthusiast like Luther or Calvin but by the head of the government. This does not mean, however, that the English Reformation was exclusively a political movement. Henry VIII could not have succeeded in establishing an independent English church if such action had not had the endorsement of large numbers of his subjects. And there were plenty of reasons why this endorsement was readily given. Though the English had freed themselves in some measure from papal domination, national pride had reached such a point that any degree of subordination to Rome was resented. Besides, England had been the scene for some time of lively agitation for religious reform. The memory of Wyclif's scathing attacks upon the avarice of the priests, the temporal power of Popes and bishops, and the sacramental system of the Church had lingered since the fourteenth century. The influence of the Christian humanists, notably Sir Thomas More, in condemning the superstitions in Catholic worship, had also been a factor of considerable importance. Finally, soon after the outbreak of the Protestant Revolution in Germany, Lutheran ideas were brought into England by wandering preachers and through the circulation of printed tracts. As a result, the English monarch, in severing the ties with Rome, had no lack of sympathy from some of the most influential of his subjects.

Underlying
causes of
the Protestant
Revolution in
England

The clash with the Pope was precipitated by Henry VIII's domestic difficulties. For eighteen years he had been married to Catherine of Aragon and had only a sickly daughter to succeed him. **615**

The death of all the sons of this marriage in infancy was a grievous disappointment to the king, who desired a male heir to perpetuate the Tudor dynasty. But this was not all, for Henry later became deeply infatuated with the dark-eyed lady-in-waiting, Anne Boleyn, and determined to make her his queen. He therefore appealed in 1527 to Pope Clement VII for an annulment of the marriage to Catherine. The law of the Church did not sanction divorce, but it did provide that a marriage could be annulled if proof could be presented that conditions existing at the time of the marriage made it unlawful. Queen Catherine had previously been married to Henry's older brother, Arthur, who had died a few months after the ceremony was performed. Recalling this fact, Henry's lawyers found a passage in the Book of Leviticus which pronounced a curse of childlessness upon the man who should marry his deceased brother's wife. The Pope was now in a difficult position. If he rejected the king's appeal, England would probably be lost to the Catholic faith, for Henry was apparently firmly convinced that the Scriptural curse had blighted his chances of perpetuating his dynasty. On the other hand, if the Pope granted the annulment he would provoke the wrath of the Emperor Charles V, who was a nephew of Catherine. Charles had already invaded Italy and was threatening the Pope with a loss of his temporal power. There seemed nothing for Clement to do but to procrastinate. At first he made a pretense of having the question settled in England, and empowered his own legate and Cardinal Wolsey to hold a court of inquiry to determine whether the marriage to Catherine had been legal. After long delay the case was suddenly transferred to Rome. Henry lost patience and resolved to take matters into his own hands. In 1531 he convoked an assembly of the clergy and, by threatening to punish them for violating the Statute of Praemunire in submitting to the papal legate, he induced them to recognize himself as the head of the English church, "as far as the law of Christ allows." Next he persuaded Parliament to enact a series of laws abolishing all payments of revenue to the Pope and proclaiming the Anglican church an independent, national unit, subject to the exclusive authority of the king. By 1534 the last of the bonds uniting the English church to Rome had been cut.

But the enactments put through by Henry VIII did not really make England a Protestant country. Though the abolition of papal authority was followed by the gradual dissolution of the monasteries and confiscation of their wealth, the church remained Catholic in doctrine. The Six Articles, adopted by Parliament at the king's behest in 1539, left no room for doubt as to official orthodoxy. Auricular confession, Masses for the dead, and clerical celibacy were all confirmed; death by burning was made the penalty for denying the Catholic dogma of the Eucharist. Yet the influence of a minority of Protestants at this time cannot be ignored. Their num-

THE RELIGIOUS SITUATION IN EUROPE
AT THE HEIGHT OF THE REFORMATION

PRINCIPAL CHRISTIAN CHURCHES IN 1560:

- Lutherans
- Anglicans
- Calvinists and Zwinglians
- Roman Catholics

MINORITIES:
- L Lutherans
- RC Roman Catholics
- CZ Calvinists, Zwinglians
- WM Waldensians, Moravians
- ASA Anabaptists, Socinians, Antitrinitarians
- – – – Approximate extent of the revolt from the Roman Church
- · · · · · APPROXIMATE LIMIT OF THE EASTERN ORTHODOX CHURCH

BLACK SEA

OTTOMAN MOSLEMS EMPIRE

AEGEAN SEA

BALTIC SEA

Stockholm
Oslo
Copenhagen
DENMARK
Danzig   RC
Vistula R.
Berlin
Elbe R.
POLAND
Warsaw
CZ CZ CZ
CZ R CZ
WM
ASA
CZ ASA
ASA
CZ
GERMANY
Wittenberg
Frankfort
Worms
HOLY ROMAN EMPIRE
RC
Prague
BOHEMIA
Augsburg
Munich
Salzburg
AUSTRIA
Vienna
HUNGARY
CZ
L L
L
CZ
Danube R.
L
WM
Basel
Luxembourg
SWITZ.
Zurich
Berne
Geneva
CZ
Trent
L
Rhine R.
Milan
Venice
Genoa
Florence
Pisa
Rome
ITALY
ADRIATIC SEA
Naples
Palermo
SICILY
MEDITERRANEAN SEA
CORSICA
SARDINIA
OTTOMAN EMPIRE

NETHERLANDS
Utrecht
Amsterdam   RC
Brussels

NORTH SEA

SCOTLAND
Edinburgh   RC
York   CZ
ENGLAND
Cambridge   CZ
Oxford London
Canterbury
RC

IRELAND
Dublin   RC

English Channel

Rouen
Reims
Paris
Tours
Nantes
Bourges
FRANCE
Avignon
Toulouse
Bordeaux
CZ CZ
CZ Loire R.
CZ
CZ
CZ
CZ

ATLANTIC OCEAN

Madrid
Toledo
Granada
SPAIN
Seville
Tagus R.
PORTUGAL
Lisbon

500 miles
0

The Harvesters, Pieter Breughel the Elder (1520–1569). Spurning the religious and bourgeois traditions of most of the other Flemish painters, Breughel chose to depict the life of humble people close to the earth. (MMA)

The Virgin and Chancellor Rolin, Jan van Eyck (1390–1444). The early Flemish painters loved to present scenes of piety in the sumptuous surroundings of wealthy burghers. (Louvre)

The Betrothal of St. Catherine, Hans Memling (1430–1494). The infant Jesus in the lap of the Virgin is shown placing on the finger of St. Catherine the ring of betrothal to Christ and His Church. (MMA)

Erasmus, Hans Holbein the Younger (1497–1543). This portrait by the German Holbein is generally regarded as the best representation of the character and personality of the Prince of the Humanists. (Louvre)

bers were steadily increasing, and during the reign of Henry's successor, Edward VI (1547–1553), they actually gained the ascendancy. Since the new king was only nine years old when he inherited the crown, it was inevitable that the policies of the government should be dictated by powers behind the throne. The men most active in this work were Thomas Cranmer, Archbishop of Canterbury, and the Dukes of Somerset and Northumberland, who successively dominated the council of regency. All three of these officials had strong Protestant leanings. As a result, the creeds and ceremonies of the Church of England were given some drastic revision. Priests were permitted to marry; English was substituted for Latin in the services; the use of images was abolished; and new articles of belief were drawn up repudiating all sacraments except baptism and the Lord's Supper and affirming the Lutheran dogma of justification by faith. When the youthful Edward died in 1553, it looked as if England had definitely entered the Protestant camp.

Surface appearances, however, are frequently deceiving. They were never more so than in England at the end of Edward's reign. The majority of the people had refused to be weaned away from the usages of their ancient faith, and a reaction had set in against the high-handed methods of the radical Protestants. Moreover, the English during the time of the Tudors had grown accustomed to obeying the will of their sovereign. It was an attitude fostered by national pride and the desire for order and prosperity. The successor of Edward VI was Mary (1553–1558), the forlorn and graceless daughter of Henry VIII and Catherine. It was inevitable that Mary should have been a Catholic, and that she should have abhorred the revolt against Rome, for the origin of the movement was painfully associated with her mother's sufferings. Consequently, it is not strange that upon coming to the throne she should have attempted to turn the clock back. Not only did she restore the celebration of the Mass and the rule of clerical celibacy, but she prevailed upon Parliament to vote the unconditional return of England to papal allegiance. But her policies ended in lamentable failure for several reasons. First of all, she fell into the same error as her predecessors in forcing through changes that were too radical for the temper of the times. The people of England were not ready for a Lutheran or Calvinist revolution, but neither were they in a mood to accept immediate subjection to Rome. Probably a more serious cause of her failure was her marriage to Philip, the ambitious heir to the Spanish throne. Her subjects feared that this union might lead to foreign complications, if not actual domination by Spain. When the queen allowed herself to be drawn into a war with France, in which England was compelled to surrender Calais, her last foothold on the Continent of Europe, the nation was almost ready for rebellion. Death ended Mary's inglorious reign in 1558.

The Catholic reaction under Mary

The question whether England was to be Catholic or Protestant **617** was left to be settled by Mary's successor, her half-sister Elizabeth (1558–1603), daughter of the vivacious Anne Boleyn. Though reared as a Protestant, Elizabeth had no deep religious convictions. Her primary interest was statecraft, and she did not intend that her kingdom should be rent in twain by sectarian strife. Therefore she decided upon a policy of moderation, refusing to ally herself with either the extreme Catholics or the fanatical Protestants. So carefully did she hew to this line that for some years she deceived the Pope into thinking that she might turn Catholic. Nevertheless, she was enough of a nationalist to refuse even to consider a revival of allegiance to Rome. One of the first things she did after becoming queen was to order the passage of a new Act of Supremacy declaring the English sovereign to be the "supreme governor" of the independent Anglican church. The final settlement, completed about 1570, was a typical English compromise. The church was made Protestant, but certain articles of the creed were left vague enough so that a moderate Catholic might accept them without too great a shock to his conscience. Moreover, the episcopal form of organization was retained and much of the Catholic ritual. Long after Elizabeth's death this settlement remained in effect. Indeed, most elements in it have survived to this day. And it is a significant fact that the modern Church of England is broad enough to include within its ranks such diverse factions as the Anglo-Catholics, who differ from their Roman brethren only in rejecting papal supremacy, and the "low-church" Anglicans, who are as radical in their Protestantism as the Lutherans.

While England was engaged in the process of mediating between the extremes of Catholicism and Protestantism, her northern neighbor Scotland was embroiled in a more violent break with the past. The Scottish branch of the Catholic Church at the turn of the sixteenth century was one of the most corrupt in Europe. Enjoying the fruits of their vast possessions, the clergy divided their time between luxurious idleness and political intrigue. But this state of affairs could not long continue. Scotland had a greedy and untamed nobility eager to pounce upon the lands of the Church at the first convenient opportunity. Besides, the political situation was far from satisfactory to the patriotic elements of the nation. The queen, Mary Stuart (1542–1567), was only six days old when she succeeded to the throne, and a regency had been assumed by her mother, who belonged to the French family of Guise. Since the Guises were determined Catholics, Catholicism came to be associated in the minds of many people with the Guises and thus with French domination. In 1557 a revolt broke out, and two years later the whole kingdom was ablaze. Leadership of the movement soon fell to a vigorous and stiff-necked preacher by the name of John Knox (1505–1572), who had sat at the feet of Calvin in Geneva. Knox uprooted every vestige of Catholicism in Scotland and established a Presbyterian church on a radical Calvinist basis.[9] So ripe was the country for a change that upon the death of the regent in 1560 Presbyterianism was proclaimed the official religion of the Scottish nation.

2. THE CATHOLIC REFORMATION

As noted at the beginning of this chapter, the Protestant Revolution was only one of the phases of the great movement known as the Reformation. The other was the Catholic Reformation, or the Counter Reformation as it used to be called, on the assumption that the primary purpose of its leaders was to cleanse the Catholic Church in order to check the growth of Protestantism. Modern historians have shown, however, that the beginings of the movement for Catholic reform were entirely independent of the Protestant Revolt. In Spain, during the closing years of the fifteenth century, a religious revival inaugurated by Cardinal Ximenes, with the approval of the monarchy, stirred that country to the depths. Schools were established, abuses were eliminated from the monasteries, and priests were goaded into accepting their responsibilities as shepherds of their flocks. Though the movement was launched primarily for the purpose of strengthening the Church in the war against heretics and infidels, it nevertheless had considerable effect in regenerating the spiritual life of the nation. In Italy also, since the beginning of the sixteenth century, a number of earnest clerics had been laboring to make the priests of their Church more worthy of their Christian calling. The task was a difficult one on account of the paganism of the Renaissance and the example of profligacy set by the papal court. In spite of these obstacles the movement did lead to the founding of several religious orders dedicated to high ideals of piety and social service. Outstanding among them were the Theatine Order and the Capuchin Order. The first was an organization of priests who took monastic vows of poverty, chastity, and obedience, while the second was an order of friars pledged to follow in the footsteps of St. Francis.

But the fires of Catholic reform burned rather low until after the Protestant Revolution began to make serious inroads upon the ancient faith. Not until it appeared that the whole German nation was likely to be swept into the Lutheran orbit did any of the Popes become seriously concerned about the need for reform. The first of the Holy Fathers to attempt a purification of the Church was Adrian VI of Utrecht, the only non-Italian to be elected to the papal throne in nearly a century and a half, and the last in history. But his reign of only twenty months was too short to enable him to accomplish much, and in 1523 he was succeeded by a Medici (Clement VII),

The beginnings of Catholic reform

The climax of the Catholic Reformation; the reform Popes

[9] The name Presbyterian comes from "presbytery," the assembly of ministers and lay elders which Knox set up to govern the churches of a particular area in place of a bishop.

who ruled for eleven years. The campaign against abuses in the Church was not renewed until the reign of Paul III (1534–1549). He and three of his successors, Paul IV (1555–1559), Pius V (1566–1572), and Sixtus V (1585–1590), were the most zealous crusaders for reform who had presided over the See of Peter since the days of Gregory VII. They reorganized the papal finances, filled the Church offices with priests renowned for austerity, and dealt drastically with those clerics who persisted in idleness and vice. It was under these Popes that the Catholic Reformation reached its height. Unfortunately, they were also responsible for reviving the Inquisition, which had fallen into disuse during the Italian Renaissance.

The Council of Trent

These direct activities of the Popes were supplemented by the decrees of a great Church council convoked in 1545 by Paul III, which met in the city of Trent (modern Trento), at intervals between 1545 and 1563. This council was one of the most important in the history of the Church. The main purpose for which it had been summoned was to redefine the doctrines of the Catholic faith, and several of the steps in this direction were highly significant. Without exception the dogmas challenged by the Protestant Reformers were reaffirmed. Good works were held to be as necessary for salvation as faith. The theory of the sacraments as indispensable means of grace was upheld. Likewise, transubstantiation, the apostolic succession of the priesthood, the belief in purgatory, the invocation of saints, and the rule of celibacy for the clergy were all confirmed as essential elements in the Catholic system. On the much-debated question as to the proper source of Christian belief, the Bible and the traditions of apostolic teaching were held to be of equal authority. Not only was papal supremacy over every bishop and priest expressly maintained, but there was more than a faint suggestion that the authority of the Pope transcended that of the Church council itself. By this admission the government of the Church was reconstituted as monarchical in form. The great movement of the fourteenth and fifteenth centuries which had attempted to establish the superior authority of the general council was ignored entirely.

Reforms of
the Council of
Trent

The Council of Trent did not confine its attention to matters of dogma. It passed important legislation also for the elimination of abuses and for reinforcing the discipline of the Church over its members. The sale of indulgences was flatly prohibited, and even their issuance for considerations other than money was restricted temporarily. Bishops and priests were forbidden to hold more than one benefice, so that none could grow rich from a plurality of incomes. To eliminate the evil of an ignorant priesthood it was provided that a theological seminary must be established in every diocese. Toward the end of its deliberations the Council decided upon a censorship of books to prevent heretical ideas from corrupting the minds of those who still remained in the faith. A commission was appointed to draw up an index or list of writings which ought not to be read. The publication of this list by the Pope in 1564 resulted in the formal establishment of the Index of Prohibited Books as a part of the machinery of the Church. Later a permanent agency known as the Congregation of the Index was set up to revise the list from time to time. Altogether more than forty such revisions have been made. The majority of the books condemned have been theological treatises, and probably the effect in retarding the progress of learning has been slight. Nonetheless, the establishment of the Index must be taken as a symptom of the intolerance which had come to infect both Catholics and Protestants.

The founding of
the Society of
Jesus by Loyola

The Catholic Reformation would never have been as thorough or as successful as it was if it had not been for the activities of the Jesuits, or members of the Society of Jesus. They did most of the rough political work in the Council of Trent, which enabled the Popes to dominate that body in its later and more important sessions. The Jesuits also were largely responsible for winning Poland and southern Germany back into the Catholic fold. The founder of the Society of Jesus was Ignatius of Loyola (1491–1556), a Spanish nobleman from the Basque country. His early career seems not to have been particularly different from that of other Spaniards of his class—a life of philandering and marauding as a soldier of the king. But about the time the Protestant Revolution was getting well under way in Germany, he was painfully wounded in a battle with the French. While waiting for his injuries to heal, he read a pious biography of Jesus and some legends of the saints which profoundly changed his emotional nature. Overwhelmed by a consciousness of his wasted life, he determined to become a soldier of Christ. After a period of morbid self-tortures, in which he saw visions of Satan, Jesus, and the Trinity, he went to the University of Paris to learn more about the faith he intended to serve. Here he gathered around him a small group of devoted disciples, with whose aid in 1534 he founded the Society of Jesus. The members took monastic vows and pledged themselves to go on a pilgrimage to Jerusalem. With this aim in view they set out for Italy, intending to embark from Venice. Finding their pilgrimage blocked by a war with the Turks, they enlisted in the crusade for Catholic reform which was just then begining in Italy. In 1540 their organization was approved by Pope Paul III. From then on it grew rapidly. When Loyola died it could boast of no fewer than 1500 members.

Organization of
the Society of
Jesus

The Society of Jesus was by far the most militant of the religious orders fostered by the spiritual zeal of the sixteenth century. It was not merely a monastic society but a company of soldiers sworn to defend the faith. Their weapons were not to be bullets and spears but eloquence, persuasion, instruction in the right doctrines, and if necessary more worldly methods of exerting influence. The organization was patterned after that of a military company, with a gen-

Portrait of Ignatius Loyola.
Engraving by Lucas Vorster-
man, 1621.

eral as commander-in-chief and an iron discipline enforced on the
members. All individuality was suppressed, and a soldierlike obedience to the general was exacted of the rank and file. Only the
highest of the four classes of members had any share in the government of the order. This little group, known as the Professed of the
Four Vows, elected the general for life and consulted with him on
important matters. They were also bound to implicit obedience.

As suggested already, the activities of the Jesuits were numerous
and varied. First and foremost, they conceived of themselves as the

Activities of the
Jesuits

defenders of true religion. For this object they obtained authority
from the Pope to hear confessions and grant absolution. Many of
them became priests in order to gain access to the pulpit and expound the truth as the oracles of God. Still others served as agents
of the Inquisition in the relentless war against heresy. In all of this
work they followed the leadership of Mother Church as their infallible guide. They raised no questions and attempted to solve no
mysteries. Loyola taught that if the Church ruled that white was
black, it would be the duty of her sons to believe it. But the Jesuits
were not satisfied merely to hold the field against the attacks of
Protestants and heretics; they were anxious to propagate the faith in
the farthest corners of the earth—to make Catholics out of Buddhists, Moslems, the Parsees of India, and even the untutored savages
of the newly discovered continents. Long before the Reformation
had ended, there were Jesuit missionaries in Africa, in Japan and
China, and in North and South America. Yet another important
activity of Loyola's soldiers of Christ was education. They founded
colleges and seminaries by the hundreds in Europe and America and
obtained positions in older institutions as well. Until the Society ran
into conflict with several monarchs and was finally suppressed by

the Pope in 1773, it had a monopoly of education in Spain and a near-monopoly in France. That the Catholic Church recovered so much of its strength in spite of the Protestant secession was due in large measure to the manifold and aggressive activities of the Jesuits.

3. THE REFORMATION HERITAGE

The most obvious result of the Reformation was the division of western Christendom into a multitude of hostile sects. No longer was there one fold and one shepherd for the whole of Latin and Teutonic Europe as had been true in the Middle Ages. Instead, northern Germany and the Scandinavian countries had become Lutheran; England had adopted a compromise Protestantism of her own; Calvinism had triumphed in Scotland, Holland, and French Switzerland. In the vast domain once owing allegiance to the Vicar of Christ only Italy, Austria, France, Spain and Portugal, southern Germany, Poland, and Ireland were left; and even in several of these countries aggressive Protestant minorities were a thorn in the side of the Catholic majority. Strange as it may seem, this splintering of Christianity into rival factions was ultimately a source of some good to man. It worked in the long run to curb ecclesiastical tyranny and thereby to promote religious freedom. As the sects multiplied in various countries, it gradually became evident that no one of them could ever become strong enough to enforce its will upon the rest. Mutual toleration was made necessary in order for any of them to survive. To be sure, this was an incidental and long-delayed result, but its importance cannot be denied.

Results of the Reformation: the effect in promoting religious toleration

See color map at page 616

The Reformation also gave an added momentum to individualism and to the expansion of popular education. By asserting the right of private judgment and by simplifying ritual and organization, the leaders of the Protestant Revolution liberated man from some of the constraints of medieval ecclesiasticism. It would be a mistake, however, to assume that Lutherans, Calvinists, and Anglicans really believed at this time in genuine religious freedom. They had no interest whatever in tolerating anyone who disagreed with their own respective orthodoxies. About all they did was to set a new and stronger precedent for challenging the authority and beliefs of a universal church. By so doing they promoted self-assertion in the religious sphere in somewhat the same degree as it already existed in the political and economic spheres. In addition, the Reformation had some effect in promoting the education of the masses. The Renaissance, with its absorbing interest in the classics, had had the unfortunate result of distorting the curricula of the schools into an exaggerated emphasis upon Greek and Latin and of restricting education to the aristocracy. The Lutherans, Calvinists, and Jesuits changed all of this. Ambitious to propagate their respective doctrines, they established schools for the masses, where even the son of the cobbler or peasant might learn to read the Bible and theological

Effects in promoting individualism and mass education

tracts in the vernacular. Practical subjects were often introduced in
place of Greek and Latin, and it is a significant fact that some of
these schools eventually opened their doors to the new science.

A good case can be made for the theory that the Reformation
furthered democracy, in the form, at least, of limited government.
Every one of the sects, whether Protestant or Catholic, raised arguments against the absolute state. Even the Lutherans, despite their
adoption of St. Paul's doctrine that "the powers that be are ordained
of God," nevertheless recognized the right of the German princes
to rebel against the Holy Roman Empire. Luther wrote that disobedience was a greater sin than murder, unchastity, dishonesty, or
theft; but what he meant was the disobedience of the common man.
He generally held that the authority of kings and princes was absolute and never to be questioned by their subjects. Some observers
see in Luther's influence a powerful stimulus to the growth of
authoritarian government in Germany. A more critical attitude toward secular rulers was taken by the Calvinists. In France, England,
and the Low Countries they not only asserted the right of revolution but actively practiced it. Jesuit philosophers taught that the
authority of the secular ruler is derived from the people, and some
even affirmed the right of the ordinary citizen to kill a tyrant.
Among the leaders of many sects, efforts were made to revive the
medieval idea of a higher law of nature, embodying principles of
right and justice, which should be recognized as an automatic limitation upon the power of rulers.

The Reformation resulted in a series of religious wars which kept
Europe in turmoil for two score years. The first to break out was the
Schmalkaldic War (1546–1547), waged by Charles V in an effort
to restore the unity of the Holy Roman Empire under the Catholic
faith. In a few months he succeeded in cowing the Protestant
princes of Germany into submission, but he was unable to force
their subjects back into the Roman religion. The strife was ultimately settled by a compromise treaty, the Religious Peace of Augsburg (1555), under which each German prince was to be free to
choose either Lutheranism or Catholicism as the faith of his people.
The religion of each state was thus made to depend upon the religion of its ruler. A much more sanguinary struggle took place in
France between 1562 and 1593. Here the Protestants, or Huguenots
as they were called, were decidedly in the minority, but they included some of the ablest and most influential members of the commercial and financial classes. Besides, they composed a political
party involved in machinations against the Catholics for control of
the government. In 1562 a faction of ultra-Catholics under the leadership of the Duke of Guise forced their way into power and, by
their threats of persecution of the Huguenots, plunged the country
into civil war. The struggle culminated ten years later in the frightful massacre of St. Bartholomew's Day. The regent, Catherine de'
Medici, in a desperate effort to put an end to the strife, plotted with

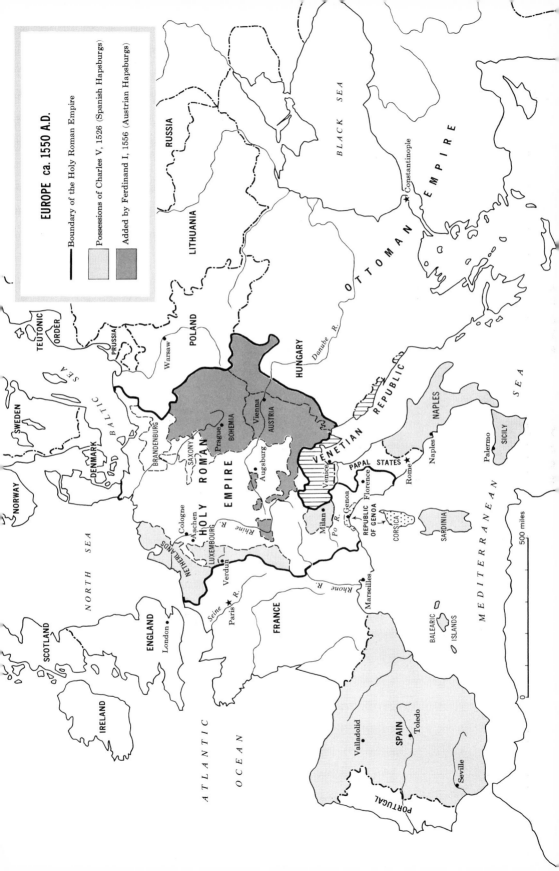

EUROPE ca. 1550 A.D.

—— Boundary of the Holy Roman Empire

Possessions of Charles V, 1526 (Spanish Hapsburgs)

Added by Ferdinand I, 1556 (Austrian Hapsburgs)

NORWAY

SWEDEN

DENMARK

RUSSIA

LITHUANIA

TEUTONIC ORDER

PRUSSIA

POLAND

Warsaw

BALTIC SEA

BRANDENBURG

SAXONY

BOHEMIA

Prague

Vienna

AUSTRIA

HUNGARY

Danube R.

OTTOMAN EMPIRE

BLACK SEA

Constantinople

VENETIAN REPUBLIC

Venice

MEDITERRANEAN SEA

Palermo

SICILY

NAPLES

Naples

SARDINIA

CORSICA

PAPAL STATES

Rome

Florence

REPUBLIC OF GENOA

Genoa

Milan

Po R.

Augsburg

HOLY ROMAN EMPIRE

Rhine R.

Cologne

Aachen

NETHERLANDS

LUXEMBOURG

Verdun

Rhone R.

Marseilles

Seine R.

Paris

FRANCE

BALEARIC ISLANDS

SPAIN

Valladolid

Toledo

Seville

PORTUGAL

ATLANTIC OCEAN

NORTH SEA

ENGLAND

London

SCOTLAND

IRELAND

500 miles

The Cities of the Schmalkaldic League Surrendering to Charles V. Engraving by Hieronymus Cock, 1560.

the Guises to murder the Protestant chiefs. The conspiracy un-loosed the ugly passions of the Paris mob, with the result that in a single night 2000 Huguenots were slain. The war dragged on until 1593 when Henry IV became a Catholic in order to please the majority of his subjects, but the religious issue did not approach a settlement until 1598 when Henry issued the Edict of Nantes guaranteeing freedom of conscience to Protestants.

To a large extent the Revolt of the Netherlands was also an epi-sode in the religious strife stirred up by the Reformation. Long after The Revolt of the Netherlands the Protestant Revolution began in Germany, the countries now known as Belgium and Holland were still being governed as domin-ions of the Spanish crown. Though Lutheranism and Calvinism had gained a foothold in the cities, the Protestants of the Netherlands were yet but a fraction of the total population. With the passage of time, however, the numbers of Calvinists increased until they in-cluded a majority of the townsmen, at least, in the Dutch provinces of the north. Interference by the Spanish government with their freedom of religion led to a desperate revolt in 1565. Religious causes were, of course, not the only ones. Nationalist feeling was a leading factor also, particularly since the Spanish king, Philip II, persisted in treating the Netherlands as mere subject provinces. In **626** addition, there were serious economic grievances—high taxation and

the restriction of commerce for the benefit of Spanish merchants.
On the other hand, it was religious hatred that was largely responsible for the bitterness of the struggle. Philip II regarded all Protestants as traitors, and he was determined to root them out of every
territory over which he ruled. In 1567 he sent the bigoted Duke of
Alva with 10,000 soldiers to quell the revolt in the Netherlands. For
six years Alva terrorized the land, putting hundreds of the rebels to
death and torturing or imprisoning thousands of others. The Protestants retaliated with almost equal savagery, and the war continued
its barbarous course until 1609. It ended in victory for the Protestants, largely through the bravery and self-sacrifice of their
original leader, William the Silent. The chief result of the war was
the establishment of an independent Dutch Republic comprising the
territories now included in Holland. The southern or Belgian provinces, where the majority of the people were Catholics, returned to
Spanish rule.

Actual warfare between nations and sects was not the only type
of barbarity which the Reformation directly encouraged. For other
examples we need only recall the atrocities perpetrated by the Catholic Inquisition, the savage persecution of Anabaptists in Germany,
and the fierce intolerance of Calvinists against Catholics. The horrible witchcraft persecution, which will be discussed in the next
chapter, was also in some measure the product of the seeds of fanaticism sown by the Reformation. On the whole, the amount of
intolerance was now much greater than at any other time in the
history of Christianity, not excepting the age of the Crusades. In
more than one instance the victims of persecution were distinguished philosophers or scientists, whose talents the world of that
day could ill afford to lose. The most eminent of the martyrs to the
new learning put to death by the Catholics was Giordano Bruno.
Despite his philosophy of mystical pantheism, Bruno set forth in
startling fashion a number of the cardinal axioms of modern science.
He taught the eternity of the universe, revived the atomic theory of
matter, and denied that the heavenly bodies contain any superior
element not found in the earth. Partly for these teachings and partly
also for his pantheism and for his rejection of miracles, he was haled
before the Inquisition and burned at the stake in 1600. One of the
victims of Calvinist persecution at Geneva was Michael Servetus,
the discoverer of the lesser circulation of the blood. Servetus was
convicted of rejecting the doctrines of the Trinity and predestination and of teaching that Palestine is a barren country in defiance of
the Old Testament description of it as a land flowing with milk and
honey. In 1553 he was condemned to be burned at the stake by slow
fire. Some admirers of Calvin have argued that the Genevan Reformer opposed the burning of Servetus: he wanted him beheaded!
But even the evidence for this rather doubtful display of mercy is
not conclusive.

SELECTED READINGS

· *Items so designated are available in paperbound editions.*

· Bainton, R. H., *The Age of the Reformation*, New York, 1956 (Anvil). The best short treatise. Half of it consists of documents.

· ——, *Here I Stand: A Life of Martin Luther*, Nashville, 1950 (Apex).

Bax, E. B., *The Peasants' War in Germany*, New York, 1899. The best account in English but not especially scholarly.

· Beard, C., *The Reformation of the Sixteenth Century in Its Relation to Modern Thought and Knowledge*, New York, 1927 (Ann Arbor).

· Burns, E. M., *The Counter Reformation*, Princeton, 1964 (Anvil).

Bury, J. B., *History of the Freedom of Thought*, New York, 1913.

· Erikson, E. H., *Young Man Luther*, New York, 1961 (Norton Library).

· Harkness, G. E., *John Calvin: the Man and His Ethics*, New York, 1931 (Apex).

· Huizinga, Johan, *Erasmus and the Age of Reformation*, New York, 1957 (Torchbook).

Janelle, Pierre, *The Catholic Reformation*, Milwaukee, 1949.

Jenkins, B. A., *The World's Debt to Protestantism*, Boston, 1930.

· Jones, R. M., *The Spiritual Reformers of the Sixteenth and Seventeenth Centuries*, New York, 1914 (Beacon).

Kidd, B. J., *The Counter-Reformation, 1550–1600*, New York, 1933. A complete account of the Jesuits, the Inquisition, and the Council of Trent.

Latourette, K. S., *A History of Christianity*, New York, 1953.

Lindsay, T. M., *History of the Reformation*, New York, 1928, 2 vols. Complete and scholarly.

Lucas, H. S., *The Renaissance and the Reformation*, New York, 1934.

· McGiffert, A. C., *Protestant Thought before Kant*, New York, 1911 (Torchbook).

McNeill, J. T., *The History and Character of Calvinism*, New York, 1954.

Marti, O. A., *The Economic Causes of the Reformation in England*, New York, 1930.

Nelson, E. N., *The Idea of Usury*, Princeton, 1949.

Randall, J. H., Jr., *The Making of the Modern Mind*, New York, 1926. Ch. VII.

Schwiebert, E. G., *Luther and His Times*, St. Louis, 1952.

· Smith, Preserved, *The Age of the Reformation*, New York, 1920 (Collier, 2 vols.). The best general survey.

——, *The Life and Letters of Martin Luther*, New York, 1914.

Smithson, Robert, *The Anabaptists*, London, 1935.

· Tawney, R. H., *Religion and the Rise of Capitalism*, New York, 1926 (Mentor). Thoughtful and provocative.

Van Dyke, P., *Ignatius Loyola, The Founder of the Jesuits*, New York, 1926.

· Weber, Max, *The Protestant Ethic and the Spirit of Capitalism*, New York, 1948 (Scribner Library). A stimulating sociological interpretation.

SOURCE MATERIALS

· Calvin, John, *Institutes of the Christian Religion*, especially Book II, Chs. 1–3; Book III, Chs. 19, 21–25; Book IV, Chs. 3, 14, 17, 20 (Wm. B. Eerdmans Publishing Co., 2 vols.).

Catechism of the Council of Trent.

Luther, Martin, *Works* (Jacobs, tr.), "On Trade and Usury," Vol. IV.

· ——, *On Christian Liberty* (Fortress, 1940).

——, *Address to the Christian Nobility of the German Nation.*

CHAPTER 21

The Commercial Revolution
and the New Society (*ca.* 1300-1700)

> Although a Kingdom may be enriched by gifts received, or by
> purchases taken from some other Nations, yet these are things
> uncertain and of small consideration when they happen. The ordi-
> nary means therefore to encrease our wealth and treasure is by
> *Forraign Trade*, wherein wee must ever observe this rule: to sell
> more to strangers yearly than wee consume of theirs in value.
> —Thomas Mun, *England's Treasure by Forraign Trade*

The last three chapters described in considerable detail the intellectual and religious transition from the medieval to the modern world.
It was observed that the Renaissance, despite its kinship in many
ways with the Middle Ages, spelled the doom of Scholastic philosophy, undermined the supremacy of Gothic architecture, and overthrew medieval conceptions of politics and the universe. Likewise, it
was noted that, before the Renaissance had completed its work, a
mighty torrent of religious revolution had swept Christianity from
it medieval foundations and cleared the way for spiritual and moral
attitudes in keeping with the trends of the new age. That both the
Renaissance and the Reformation should have been accompanied by
fundamental economic changes goes without saying. Indeed, the intellectual and religious upheavals would scarcely have been possible
if it had not been for drastic alterations in the medieval economic
pattern. This series of changes, marking the transition from the
semistatic, localized, nonprofit economy of the late Middle Ages to
the dynamic, worldwide, capitalistic regime of the fourteenth and
succeeding centuries, is what is known as the Commercial Revolution.

The meaning of the Commercial Revolution

I. THE CAUSES AND INCIDENTS OF THE COMMERCIAL REVOLUTION

The causes which led to the beginning of the Commercial Revolution about 1300 are none too clear. This arises from the fact that the initial stage of the movement was more gradual than is commonly supposed. In so far as it is possible to isolate particular causes, the following may be said to have been basic: (1) the capture of a monopoly of Mediterranean trade by the Italian cities; (2) the development of a profitable commerce between the Italian cities and the merchants of the Hanseatic League in northern Europe; (3) the introduction of coins of general circulation, such as the ducat of Venice and the florin of Florence; (4) the accumulation of surplus capital in trading, shipping, and mining ventures; (5) the demand for war materials and the encouragement given by the new monarchs to the development of commerce in order to create more taxable wealth; and (6) the desire for the products of the Far East stimulated by the reports of travelers, especially the fascinating account of the wealth of China published by Marco Polo upon his return from a trip to that country toward the end of the thirteenth century. This combination of factors gave to the men of the early Renaissance new visions of riches and power and furnished them with some of the equipment necessary for an expansion of business. Henceforth they were bound to be dissatisfied with the restricted ideal of the medieval guilds with its ban upon trading for unlimited profit.

About two centuries after it began, the Commercial Revolution received a powerful stimulus from the voyages of overseas discovery. The reasons why these voyages were undertaken are not hard to perceive. They were due primarily to Spanish and Portuguese ambitions for a share in the trade with the Orient. For some time this trade had been monopolized by the Italian cities, with the consequence that the people of the Iberian peninsula were compelled to pay high prices for the silks, perfumes, spices, and tapestries imported from the East. It was therefore quite natural that attempts should be made by Spanish and Portuguese merchants to discover a new route to the Orient independent of Italian control. A second cause of the voyages of discovery was the missionary fervor of the Spaniards. Their successful crusade against the Moors had generated a surplus of religious zeal, which spilled over into a desire to convert the heathen. To these causes should be added the fact that advances in geographical knowledge and the introduction of the compass and the astrolabe [1] gave mariners more courage to venture into the open

---

[1] The astrolabe is a device for measuring the altitude or position of heavenly bodies. It was invented by Hellenistic astronomers and perfected by the Saracens. Especially useful in determining locations at sea, it has since been replaced by the sextant.

Santa María. A representation of Columbus's flagship, exhibited at the Columbian Exposition of 1893 in Chicago.

A Moslem Astrolabe, Thirteenth Century. Invented by Hellenistic astronomers, the astrolabe was perfected by the Saracens. It became available to European navigators by the beginning of the Commercial Revolution.

sea. But the effect of these things must not be exaggerated. The popular idea that all Europeans before Columbus believed that the earth was flat is simply not true. From the twelfth century on it would be almost impossible to find an educated man who did not accept the fact that the earth is a sphere. Furthermore, the compass and the astrolabe were known in Europe long before any mariners ever dreamed of sailing the Atlantic, with the exception of the Norsemen. The compass was brought in by the Saracens in the twelfth century, probably from China. The astrolabe was introduced even earlier.

If we except the Norsemen, who discovered America about 1000 A.D., the pioneers in oceanic navigation were the Portuguese. By the middle of the fifteenth century they had discovered and settled the islands of Madeira and the Azores and had explored the African coast as far south as Guinea. In 1497 their most successful navigator, Vasco da Gama, rounded the tip of Africa and sailed on the next year to India. In the meantime, the Genoese mariner, Christopher Columbus, became convinced of the feasibility of reaching India by sailing west. Rebuffed by the Portuguese, he turned to the Spanish sovereigns, Ferdinand and Isabella, and enlisted their support of his plan. The story of his epochal voyage and its result is a familiar one

The Spaniards and Portuguese

and need not be recounted here. Though he died ignorant of his real achievement, his discoveries laid the foundations for the Spanish claim to nearly all of the New World. Other discoverers representing the Spanish crown followed Columbus, and soon afterward the conquerors, Cortes and Pizarro. The result was the establishment of a vast colonial empire including what is now the southwestern portion of the United States, Florida, Mexico, and the West Indies, Central America, and all of South America with the exception of Brazil.

The English and the French were not slow in following the Spanish example. The voyages of John Cabot and his son Sebastian in 1497–1498 provided the basis for the English claim to North America, though there was nothing that could be called a British empire in the New World until after the settlement of Virginia in 1607. Early in the sixteenth century the French explorer Cartier sailed up the St. Lawrence, thereby furnishing his native land with some shadow of a title to eastern Canada. More than a hundred years later the explorations of Joliet, La Salle, and Father Marquette gave the French a foothold in the Mississippi valley and in the region of the Great Lakes. Following their victory in their war for independence the Dutch also took a hand in the struggle for colonial empire. The voyage of Henry Hudson up the river which bears his name enabled them to found New Netherland in 1623, which they were forced to surrender to the English some forty years later. But the most valuable possessions of the Dutch were Malacca, the Spice Islands, and the ports of India and Africa taken from Portugal in the early seventeenth century.

The results of these voyages of discovery and the founding of colonial empires were almost incalculable. To begin with, they expanded commerce from its narrow limits of Mediterranean trade into a world enterprise. For the first time in history the ships of the great maritime powers now sailed the seven seas. The tight little monopoly of Oriental trade maintained by the Italian cities was thoroughly punctured. Genoa, Pisa, and Venice sank henceforth into relative obscurity, while the harbors of Lisbon, Bordeaux, Liverpool, Bristol, and Amsterdam were crowded with vessels and the shelves of their merchants piled high with goods. A second result was a tremendous increase in the volume of commerce and in the variety of articles of consumption. To the spices and textiles from the Orient were now added potatoes, tobacco, and maize from North America; molasses and rum from the West Indies; cocoa, chocolate, quinine, and the cochineal dye from South America; and ivory, slaves, and ostrich feathers from Africa. In addition to these commodities hitherto unknown or obtainable only in limited quantities, the supply of certain older products was greatly increased. This was especially true of sugar, coffee, rice, and cotton, which were brought in in such amounts from the Western Hemisphere that

The expansion
of commerce in-
to a world en-
terprise

they ceased to be articles of luxury.

Another significant result of the discovery and conquest of lands overseas was an expansion of the supply of precious metals. When Columbus discovered America, the quantities of gold and silver in Europe were scarcely sufficient to support a dynamic economy. Indeed, it was nearly fifty years before the full impact of wealth from America made itself felt. For some time gold was the more abundant metal and was relatively cheap in relation to silver. The white metal, which came chiefly from the mines of Germany, was more highly prized than gold. About 1540 this relation was reversed. Massive imports of silver from the mines of Mexico, Bolivia, and Peru produced such a depreciation in the value of silver that quantities of gold had to hoarded for critical transactions. Henceforth, for about eighty years, the European economy ran on silver. The result was a tremendous inflation. Prices and wages rose to fantastic heights in what may be considered an artificial prosperity. It did not affect all parts of Europe alike. The German mines were ruined by the flood of silver from the Americas. As a consequence, the position of Germany declined, while England and the Netherlands rose to preeminence. For a brief period Spain shared this preeminence, but she was ill-fitted to continue it. Her industrial development was too feeble to supply the demand for manufactured products from the European settlers in the Western Hemisphere. Accordingly, they turned to the north of Europe for the textiles, cutlery, and similar products they urgently needed. About 1535 Spain suffered a severe crisis which gradually spread to other countries.

The incidents or features of the Commercial Revolution have been partly suggested by the foregoing discussion of causes. The outstanding one was the rise of capitalism. Reduced to its simplest terms, capitalism may be defined as a system of production, distribution, and exchange in which accumulated wealth is invested by private owners for the sake of gain. Its essential features are private enterprise, competition for markets, and business for profit. Generally it involves also the wage system as a method of payment of workers; that is, a mode of payment based not upon the amount of wealth they create, but rather upon their ability to compete with one another for jobs. Further, it is a dynamic system, founded upon the assumption that every producer or merchant has the right to expand his business by stimulating demand for his wares. As indicated already, capitalism is the direct antithesis of the semistatic economy of the medieval guilds, in which production and trade were supposed to be conducted for the benefit of society with only a reasonable charge for the service rendered, instead of unlimited profits. Although capitalism did not come to its full maturity until the nineteenth century, nearly all of its cardinal features were developed during the Commercial Revolution.

A second important incident of the Commercial Revolution was

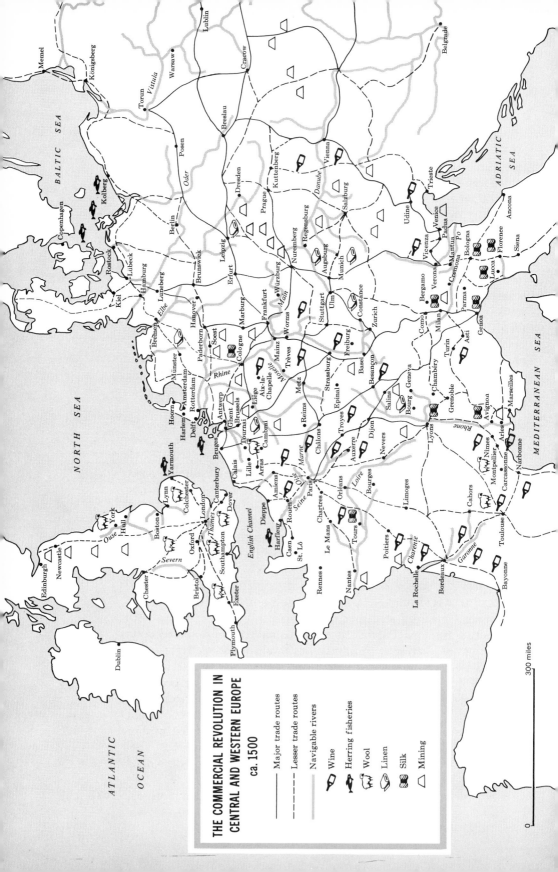

THE COMMERCIAL REVOLUTION IN
CENTRAL AND WESTERN EUROPE
ca. 1500

— Major trade routes
--- Lesser trade routes
— Navigable rivers
Wine
Herring fisheries
Wool
Linen
Silk
Mining

300 miles

the growth of banking. Because of the strong disapproval of usury, banking had scarcely been a respectable business during the Middle Ages. For centuries the little that was carried on was virtually monopolized by Moslems and Jews. Nevertheless, exceptions did exist. Descendants of the Lombards ignored the prohibitions of the Church. The rise of national monarchies toward the end of the Middle Ages led to borrowing on contract to pay for wars or for the operations of government. Lending money for interest on such contracts was not considered sinful if the king took the guilt upon himself in a special clause of the contract. By the fourteenth century the business of lending money for profit was an established business. The rate on loans to governments was often 15 per cent, and in times of crisis much higher. The real founders of banking were certain of the great commercial houses of the Italian cities. Most of them combined money lending with the management of manufacturing enterprises in their localities. Notable among them was the Medici firm, with its headquarters in Florence, but with branches throughout Italy and as far north as Bruges. By the fifteenth century the banking business had spread to southern Germany and France. The leading firm in the north was that of the Fuggers of Augsburg, with a capital of $40,000,000. The Fuggers lent money to kings and bishops, served as brokers for the Pope in the sale of indulgences, and provided the funds that enabled Charles V to buy his election to the throne of the Holy Roman Empire. So shrewdly did they manage their business, and so relentlessly did they pursue their debtors— even browbeating the Emperor himself as if he were a petty trader—that the firm earned an annual profit of 54 per cent for a decade and a half in the sixteenth century. The rise of these private financial houses was followed by the establishment of government banks, intended to serve the monetary needs of the national states. The first in order of time was the Bank of Sweden (1657), but the one which was destined for the role of greatest importance in economic history was the Bank of England, founded in 1694. Although not technically under government control until 1946, it was the bank of issue for the government and the depositary of public funds.

The growth of banking was necessarily accompanied by the adoption of various aids to financial transactions on a large scale. Credit facilities were extended in such a way that a merchant in Amsterdam could purchase goods from a merchant in Venice by means of a bill of exchange issued by an Amsterdam bank. The Venetian merchant would obtain his money by depositing the bill of exchange in his local bank. Later the two banks would settle their accounts by comparing balances. Ultimately a fairly complete system of international clearance was set up making possible the settlement of large numbers of accounts with very little interchange of coin. Among the other facilities for the expansion of credit were the adoption of a system of payment by check in local transactions and the issuance of bank notes as a substitute for gold and silver. Both of these devices were introduced by the Italians and were gradually adopted in northern Europe. The system of payment by check was particularly important in increasing the volume of trade, since the credit resources of the banks could now be expanded far beyond the actual amounts of cash in their vaults.

A Printing Shop in the Seventeenth Century. Engraving by Abraham von Werdt.

(4) the decline
of the craft
guilds and the
rise of new in-
dustries

The Commercial Revolution was not confined, of course, to the growth of trade and banking. Included in it also were fundamental changes in methods of production. The system of manufacture developed by the craft guilds in the later Middle Ages was rapidly becoming defunct. The guilds themselves, dominated by the master craftsmen, had grown selfish and exclusive. Membership in them was commonly restricted to a few privileged families. Besides, they were so completely choked by tradition that they were unable to make adjustments to changing conditions. Moreover, new industries had sprung up entirely outside the guild system. Characteristic examples were mining and smelting and the woolen industry. The rapid development of these enterprises was stimulated by technical advances, such as the invention of the spinning wheel and the stocking frame and the discovery of a new method of making brass, which saved about half of the fuel previously used. In the mining and smelting industries a form of organization was adopted similar to that which has prevailed ever since. The tools and plant facilities belonged to capitalists, while the workers were mere wage laborers subject to hazards of accident, unemployment, and occupational disease.

636   But the most typical form of industrial production in the Commercial Revolution was the domestic system, developed first of all in the woolen industry. The domestic system derives its name from the fact that the work was done in the homes of individual artisans instead of in the shop of a master craftsman. Since the various jobs in the manufacture of a product were given out on contract, the system is also known as the putting-out system. Notwithstanding the petty scale of production, the organization was basically capitalistic. The raw material was purchased by an entrepreneur (known as a clothier in the woolen industry) and assigned to individual workers, each of whom would complete his allotted task for a stipulated payment. In the case of the woolen industry the yarn would be given out first of all to the spinners, then to the weavers, fullers, and dyers in succession. When the cloth was finally finished, it would be taken by the clothier and sold in the open market for the highest price it would bring. The domestic system was, of course, not restricted to the manufacture of woolen cloth. As time went on, it was extended into many other fields of production. It tied in well with the new glorification of riches and with the conception of a dynamic economy. The capitalist could now thumb his nose at the old restrictions on profits. No association of his rivals could judge the quality of his product or the wages he paid to his workers. Perhaps best of all he could expand his business as he saw fit and introduce new techniques that would reduce costs or increase the volume of production.

Undoubtedly the domestic system had advantages for the workers themselves, especially as compared to its successor, the factory system. Though wages were low, there was no regular schedule of hours, and it was generally possible for the laborer to supplement his family income by cultivating a small plot of land and raising a few vegetables, at least. Furthermore, conditions of work in the homes

Merchants' Houses in Amsterdam, 17th Century. Several of the principal streets of Amsterdam are canals.

were more healthful than in factories, and the artisan had his family to assist him with the simpler tasks. Freedom from the supervision of a foreman and from the fear of discharge for petty reasons must also be accounted definite advantages. On the other hand, it must not be forgotten that the workers were too widely scattered to organize effectively for common action. As a consequence they had no means of protecting themselves from dishonest employers, who cheated them out of part of their wages or forced them to accept payment in goods. It is also true that toward the end of the Commercial Revolution the workers became more and more dependent upon the capitalists, who now furnished not only the raw materials but the tools and equipment as well. In some cases the laborers were herded into large central shops and compelled to work under a fixed routine. The difference between this and the high-pressure methods of the factory system was only a matter of degree.

That the Commercial Revolution would involve extensive changes in business organization was practically assured from the start. The prevailing unit of production and trade in the Middle Ages was the shop or store owned by an individual or a family. The partnership was also quite common, in spite of its grave disadvantage of unlimited liability of each of its members for the debts of the entire firm. Obviously no one of these units was well adapted to business involving heavy risks and a huge investment of capital. The first result of the attempt to devise a more suitable business organization was the formation of *regulated companies*. The regulated company was an association of merchants banded together for a common venture. The members did not pool their resources but agreed merely to cooperate for their mutual advantage and to abide by certain definite regulations. Usually the purpose of the combination was to maintain a monopoly of trade in some part of the world. Assessments were often paid by the members for the upkeep of docks and warehouses and especially for protection against "interlopers," as those traders were called who attempted to break into the monopoly. A leading example of this type of organization was an English company known as the Merchant Adventurers, established for the purpose of trade with the Netherlands and Germany.

In the seventeenth century the regulated company was largely superseded by a new type of organization at once more compact and broader in scope. This was the *joint-stock company*, formed through the issuance of shares of capital to a considerable number of investors. Those who purchased the shares might or might not take part in the work of the company, but whether they did or not they were joint owners of the business and therefore entitled to share in its profits in accordance with the amount they had invested. The joint-stock company had numerous advantages over the partnership and the regulated company. First, it was a permanent unit, not subject to reorganization every time one of its members died or with-

(6) changes in business organization; the growth of regulated companies

(7) the joint-stock company

638

Coining Money in the Sixteenth Century. These coins were not "milled," and therefore were easily "clipped."

The Spanish Milled Dollar, or "Piece of Eight." It was one of the first coins to have its circumference scored, or "milled." It was cut into halves and quarters to make change.

drew. Second, it was eventually established on the basis of limited liability; that is, each member was liable for the debts of the company only in proportion to his own investment. And third, it made possible a much larger accumulation of capital, through a wide distribution of shares. In short, it possessed nearly every advantage of the modern corporation except that it was not a person in the eyes of the law with the rights and privileges guaranteed to individuals. While most of the early joint-stock companies were founded for commercial ventures, some were organized later in industry. A number of the outstanding trading combinations were also *chartered companies.* This means that they held charters from the government granting a monopoly of the trade in a certain locality and conferring extensive authority over the inhabitants. Through a charter of this kind the British East India Company ruled over India as if it were a private estate until 1784, and even in a sense until 1858. Other famous chartered companies were the Dutch East India Company, the Hudson's Bay Company, the Plymouth Company, and the London Company. The last of these founded the colony of Virginia and governed it for a time as company property. **639**

The remaining feature of the Commercial Revolution which needs to be considered was the growth of a more efficient money economy. Money, of course, had been in use ever since the revival of trade in the eleventh century. Nevertheless, there were few coins with a value that was recognized other than locally. By 1300 the ducat of Venice and the florin of Florence, each with a value of about $4.00, had come to be accepted in Italy and also in the international markets of northern Europe. But no country could be said to have had a uniform monetary system. Nearly everywhere there was great confusion. Coins issued by kings circulated side by side with the money of local nobles and even with Saracenic currency. Moreover, the types of currency were modified frequently, and the coins themselves were often debased. A common method by which kings expanded their own personal revenues was to increase the proportion of cheaper metals in the coins they minted. But the growth of trade and industry in the Commercial Revolution accentuated the need for more stable and uniform monetary systems. The problem was solved by the adoption of a standard system of money by every important state to be used for all transactions within its borders. Much time elapsed, however, before the reform was complete. England began the construction of a uniform coinage during the reign of Queen Elizabeth, but the task was not finished until late in the seventeenth century. The French did not succeed in reducing their money to its modern standard of simplicity and convenience until the time of Napoleon. In spite of these long delays it appears safe to conclude that national currencies were really an achievement of the Commercial Revolution.

2. MERCANTILISM IN THEORY AND PRACTICE

The Commercial Revolution in its later stages was accompanied by the adoption of a new set of doctrines and practices known as mercantilism. In its broadest meaning, mercantilism may be defined as a system of government intervention to promote national prosperity and increase the power of the state. Though frequently considered as a program of economic policy exclusively, its objectives were quite largely political. The purpose of the intervention in economic affairs was not merely to expand the volume of manufacturing and trade, but also to bring more money into the treasury of the king, which would enable him to build fleets, equip armies, and make his government feared and respected throughout the world. Because of this close association with the ambitions of princes to increase their own power and the power of the states over which they ruled, mercantilism has sometimes been called *statism*. Certainly the system would never have come into existence had it not been for the growth of absolute monarchy in place of the weak, decentralized structure of feudalism. But kings alone did not create it. Naturally the new magnates of business lent support, since they would obviously derive great advantages from active encouragement of trade by the state. The heyday of mercantilism was the period between 1600 and 1700, but many of its features survived until the end of the eighteenth century.

If there was any one principle which held the central place in mercantilist theory, it was the doctrine of bullionism. This doctrine means that the prosperity of a nation is determined by the quantity of precious metals within its borders. The greater the amount of gold and silver a country contains, the more money the government can collect in taxes, and the richer and more powerful the state will become. The growth of such an idea was fostered by knowledge of the prosperity and power of Spain, which seemed to be the direct results of the flood of precious metals pouring in from her American colonies. But what of those countries that owned no bullion-producing colonies? How were *they* to achieve riches and power? For these questions the mercantilists had a ready answer. A nation without access to gold and silver directly should attempt to increase its trade with the rest of the world. If its government took steps to ensure that the value of exports would always exceed the value of imports, more gold and silver would come into the country than would have to be shipped out. This was called maintaining a "favorable balance of trade." To preserve this balance, three main devices would be necessary: first, high tariffs to reduce the general level of imports and to shut out some products entirely; second, bounties on exports; and third, extensive encouragement of manufactures in order that the nation might have as many goods to sell abroad as possible.

Bullionism and the favorable balance of trade

The theory of mercantilism also included certain elements of economic nationalism, paternalism, and imperialism. By the first is meant the ideal of a self-sufficient nation. The policy of fostering new industries was not intended merely as a device for increasing exports, but also as a means of making the nation independent of foreign supplies. In similar fashion, the mercantilists argued that the government should exercise the functions of a watchful guardian over the lives of its citizens. Marriage should be encouraged and regulated, to the end that the population might steadily increase. Wages, hours of labor, prices, quality of products should be carefully controlled by the government. Generous relief should be provided for the poor, including free medical attention if they were unable to pay for it. These things were to be done, however, not with any view to charity or justice, but mainly in order that the state might rest upon a secure economic foundation and have the support of a numerous and healthy citizenry in case of war. Finally, the mercantilists advocated the acquisition of colonies. Again, the primary purpose was not to benefit individual citizens of the mother country, but to make the nation strong and independent. The types

Other elements of mercantilism: economic nationalism, paternalism, and imperialism

of possessions most ardently desired were those that would enlarge the nation's hoard of bullion. If these could not be obtained, then colonies providing tropical products, naval stores, or any other commodities which the mother country could not produce would be acceptable. The theory which underlay this imperialism was the notion that colonies existed for the benefit of the state that owned them. For this reason they were not allowed to engage in manufacturing or shipping. Their function was to produce raw materials and to consume as large a proportion of manufactured products as possible. In this way they would infuse lifeblood into the industries of the mother country and thus give her an advantage in the struggle for world trade.

The majority of those who wrote on mercantilist theory were not professional economists but men of action in the world of business.

**The defenders
of mercantilism**

The best exposition of the subject appears to have been that of Thomas Mun, a leading merchant and for many years a director of the British East India Company. His principal work was published posthumously in 1664 under the title of *England's Treasure by Forraign Trade, or The Balance of Our Forraign Trade Is the Rule of Our Treasure*. In addition to a host of other champions from the ranks of business, mercantilism had its defenders also in certain of the political philosophers. Included among them were such advocates of absolute monarchy as the Frenchman Jean Bodin (1530–1596) and the Englishman Thomas Hobbes (1588–1679), who were naturally disposed to favor any policy that would increase the wealth and power of the ruler. While most of the apologists for mercantilism were interested in it mainly as a device for promoting a favorable balance of trade, others conceived it as a species of paternalism for increasing prosperity within the country. For example, the Englishman Edward Chamberlayne advocated a policy somewhat similar to contemporary ideas of government spending. He recommended that the state should appropriate a huge fund for the relief of the poor and for the construction of public works as a means of stimulating business.

Attempts to put various mercantilist doctrines into practice characterized the history of many of the nations of western Europe in

**Mercantilism in
practice: in
Spain and in
England**

the sixteenth and seventeenth centuries. The theories, however, were not universally applied. Spain, of course, had the initial advantage by reason of the flow of bullion from her American empire. And while the Spaniards did not need to resort to artificial devices in order to bring money into their country, their government nevertheless maintained a rigid control over commerce and industry. The policies of other nations were designed to make up for the lack of bullion-producing colonies by capturing a larger share of export trade. This naturally involved a program of bounties, tariffs, and extensive regulation of manufacturing and shipping. Mercantilist policies were largely adopted in England during the reign of

Queen Elizabeth I and were continued by the Stuart monarchs and by Oliver Cromwell. Most of these rulers engaged in a furious scramble for colonies, bestowed monopolistic privileges upon trading companies, and sought in a wide variety of ways to control the economic activities of the citizens. The most interesting examples of mercantilist legislation in England were, first, the Elizabethan laws designed to eliminate idleness and stimulate production and, second, the Navigation Acts. By a series of laws enacted toward the end of the sixteenth century, Queen Elizabeth gave to the justices of the peace the authority to fix prices, regulate hours of labor, and compel every able-bodied citizen to work at some useful trade. The first of the Navigation Acts was passed in 1651 under Oliver Cromwell. With the aim of destroying Dutch predominance in the carrying trade, it required that all colonial exports to the mother country should be carried in English ships. A second Navigation Act was passed in 1660, which provided not merely that colonial exports should be shipped in British vessels but prohibited the sending of certain "enumerated articles," especially tobacco and sugar, directly to Continental European ports. They were to be sent first of all to England, whence, after the payment of customs duties, they could be reshipped elsewhere. Both of these laws were based upon the principle that colonies should serve for the enrichment of the mother country.

The Germanic states during the Commercial Revolution were too completely occupied with internal problems to take a very active part in the struggle for colonies and overseas trade. As a consequence, German mercantilism was concerned primarily with increasing the strength of the state from within. It partook of the dual character of economic nationalism and a program for a planned society. But, of course, the planning was done chiefly for the benefit of the government and only incidentally for that of the people as a whole. Because of their dominant purpose of increasing the revenues of the state, the German mercantilists are known as cameralists (from *Kammer*, a name given to the royal treasury). Most of them were lawyers and professors of finance. Cameralist ideas were put into practice by the Hohenzollern kings of Prussia, notably by Frederick William I (1713–1740) and Frederick the Great (1740–1786). The policies of these monarchs embraced a many-sided scheme of intervention and control in the economic sphere for the purpose of increasing taxable wealth and bolstering the power of the state. Marshes were drained, canals dug, new industries established with the aid of the government, and farmers instructed as to what crops they should plant. In order that the nation might become self-sufficient as soon as possible, exports of raw materials and imports of manufactured products were prohibited. The bulk of the revenues gained from these various policies went for military purposes. The standing army of Prussia was increased by Frederick the Great to

Mercantilism in Germany: the cameralists

THE COMMERCIAL
REVOLUTION,
ca. 1300–1700

The application
of mercantilism
in France; the
work of Col-
bert

160,000 men.

The most thorough, if not the most deliberate, application of mercantilism was probably to be found in France during the reign of Louis XIV (1643–1715). This was due partly to the fact that the French state was the complete incarnation of absolutism and partly to the policies of Jean Baptiste Colbert (1619–1683), chief minister under *le grand monarque* from 1661 until his death. Colbert was no theorist but a practical politician, ambitious for personal power and intent upon magnifying the opportunities for wealth of the middle class, to which he belonged. He accepted mercantilism, not as an end in itself, but simply as a convenient means for increasing the wealth and power of the state and thereby gaining the approval of his sovereign. He firmly believed that France must acquire as large an amount of the precious metals as possible. To this end he prohibited the export of money, levied high tariffs on foreign manufactures, and gave liberal bounties to encourage French shipping. It was largely for this purpose also that he fostered imperialism, hoping to increase the favorable balance of trade through the sale of manufactured goods to the colonies. Accordingly, he purchased the islands of Martinique and Guadeloupe in the West Indies, encouraged settlements in Santo Domingo, Canada, and Louisiana, and established trading posts in India and in Africa. Furthermore, he was as devoted to the ideal of self-sufficiency as any of the cameralists in Prussia. He gave subsidies to new enterprises, established a number of state-owned industries, and even had the government purchase goods which were not really needed in order to keep struggling companies on their feet. But he was determined to keep the manufacturing industry under strict control, so as to make sure that companies would buy their raw materials only from French or colonial sources and produce the commodities necessary for national greatness. Consequently he clamped upon industry an elaborate set of regulations prescribing nearly every detail of the manufacturing process. Finally, it should be mentioned that Colbert took a number of steps to augment the political strength of the nation directly. He provided France with a navy of nearly 300 ships, drafting citizens from the maritime provinces and even criminals to man them. He sought to promote a rapid growth of population by discouraging young people from becoming monks or nuns and by exempting families with ten or more children from taxation.

3. THE RESULTS OF THE COMMERCIAL REVOLUTION

It goes without saying that the Commercial Revolution was one of the most significant developments in the history of the Western world. The whole pattern of modern economic life would have been impossible without it, for it changed the basis of commerce

644

from the local and regional plane of the Middle Ages to the world-wide scale it has occupied ever since. Moreover, it exalted the power of money, inaugurated business for profit, sanctified the accumulation of wealth, and established competitive enterprise as the foundation of production and trade. In a word, the Commercial Revolution was responsible for a large number of the elements that go to make up the capitalist regime.

But these were not the only results. The Commercial Revolution brought into being wide fluctuations of economic activity. What we now call booms and recessions alternated with startling rapidity. The inflow of precious metals, combined with a "population explosion" which doubled the inhabitants of Europe between 1450 and 1650, led to rising prices and an unprecedented demand for goods. Businessmen were tempted to expand their enterprises too rapidly; bankers extended credit so liberally that their principal borrowers, especially nobles, often defaulted on loans. Spain and Italy were among the first to suffer setbacks. In both, failure of wages to keep pace with rising prices brought incredible hardships to the lower classes. Impoverishment was rife in the cities, and banditry flourished in the rural areas. In Spain some ruined aristocrats were not too proud to join the throngs of vagrants who wandered from city to city. At the end of the fifteenth century the great Florentine bank of the Medici, with its branches in Venice, Rome, and Naples, closed its doors. The middle of the century that followed saw numerous bankruptcies in Spain and the decline of the Fuggers in Germany. Meanwhile, England, Holland, and to some extent France, waxed prosperous. This prosperity was especially characteristic of the "age of silver," which lasted from about 1540 to 1620. In the seventeenth century decline set in once more after inflation had spent its force, and as a consequence of religious and international wars and civil strife.

The alternation of booms and recessions was followed by orgies of speculation. These reached their climax early in the eighteenth century. The most notorious were the South Sea Bubble and the Mississippi Bubble. The former was the result of inflation of the stock of the South Sea Company in England. The promoters of this company agreed to take over a large part of the national debt and in return received from the English government an exclusive right to trade with South America and the Pacific islands. The prospects for profit seemed almost unlimited. The stock of the company rose rapidly in value until it was selling for more than ten times its original price. The higher it rose, the more gullible the public became. But gradually suspicion developed that the possibilities of the enterprise had been overrated. Buoyant hopes gave way to fears, and investors made frantic attempts to dispose of their shares for whatever they would bring. A crash was the inevitable result.

During the very same years when the South Sea Bubble was being inflated in England, the French were going through a similar wave of speculative madness. In 1715 a Scotsman by the name of John Law, who had been compelled to flee from British soil for killing his rival in a love intrigue, settled in Paris, after various successful gambling adventures in other cities. He persuaded the regent of France to adopt his scheme for paying off the national debt through the issuance of paper money and to grant him the privilege of organizing the Mississippi Company for the colonization and exploitation of Louisiana. As the government loans were redeemed, the persons who received the money were encouraged to buy stock in the company. Soon the shares began to soar, ultimately reaching a price forty times their original value. Nearly everyone who could scrape together a few livres of surplus cash rushed forward to participate in the scramble for riches. Stories were told of butchers and tailors who were supposed to have become millionaires by buying a few shares and holding them for a rise in price. But as the realization grew that the company would never be able to pay more than a nominal dividend on the stock at its inflated value, the more cautious investors began selling their holdings. The alarm spread, and soon everyone was as anxious to sell as he had been to buy. In 1720 the Mississippi Bubble burst in a wild panic. Thousands of people who had sold good property to buy the shares at fantastic prices were utterly ruined. The collapse of the South Sea and Mississippi companies gave a temporary chill to the public ardor for gambling. It was not long, however, until the greed for speculative profits revived, and the stock-jobbing orgies that followed in the wake of the Commercial Revolution were repeated many times over during the nineteenth and twentieth centuries.

Europeaniza-
tion of the
world and
the revival of
slavery

Among other results of the Commercial Revolution were the rise of the bourgeoisie to economic power, the beginning of Europeanization of the world, and the revival of slavery. Each of these requires brief comment. By the end of the seventeenth century the bourgeoisie had become an influential class in nearly every country of western Europe. Its ranks included the merchants, the bankers, the shipowners, the principal investors, and the industrial entrepreneurs. Their rise to power was mainly the result of increasing wealth and their tendency to ally themselves with the king against the remnants of the feudal aristocracy. But as yet their power was purely economic. Not until the nineteenth century did middle-class supremacy in politics become a reality. By the Europeanization of the world is meant the transplanting of European manners and culture in other continents. As a result of the work of traders, missionaries, and colonists, North and South America were rapidly stamped with the character of appendages of Europe. No more than a beginning was made in the transformation of Asia, but enough was done to foreshadow the trend of later times when even Japanese and Chinese would adopt Western locomotives and shell-rimmed spectacles.

The most regrettable result of the Commercial Revolution was the revival of slavery. As we learned in our study of the Middle Ages, slavery practically disappeared from European civilization about the year 1000. But the development of mining and plantation farming in the English, Spanish, and Portuguese colonies led to a tremendous demand for unskilled labor. At first an attempt was made to enslave the American Indians, but they usually proved too hard to manage. The problem was solved in the sixteenth century by the importation of African Negroes. For the next 200 years and more, Negro slavery was an integral part of the European colonial system, especially in those regions producing tropical products.

Finally, the Commercial Revolution was exceedingly important in preparing the way for the Industrial Revolution. This was true for a number of reasons. First, the Commercial Revolution created a class of capitalists who were constantly seeking new opportunities to invest their surplus profits. Second, the mercantilist policy, with its emphasis upon protection for infant industries and production of goods for export, gave a powerful stimulus to the growth of manufactures. Third, the founding of colonial empires flooded Europe with new raw materials and greatly increased the supply of certain products which had hitherto been luxuries. Most of these required fabrication before they were available for consumption. As a consequence, new industries sprang up wholly independent of any guild regulations that still survived. The outstanding example was the manufacture of cotton textiles, which, significantly enough, was one of the first of the industries to become mechanized. Last of all, the Commercial Revolution was marked by a trend toward the adoption of factory methods in certain lines of production, together with technological improvements, such as the invention of the spinning wheel and the stocking frame, and the discovery of more efficient processes of refining ores. The connection between these developments and the mechanical progress of the Industrial Revolution is not hard to perceive.

Effects of the Commercial Revolution in preparing the way for the Industrial Revolution

4. REVOLUTIONARY DEVELOPMENTS IN AGRICULTURE

To a large extent the sweeping changes that occurred in agriculture between the fourteenth century and the eighteenth may be regarded as effects of the Commercial Revolution. For example, the rise in prices and the increase in urban population eventually made agriculture a profitable business and thus tended to promote its absorption into the capitalist system. In addition, the development of the woolen industry in England caused many landowners of that country to substitute the pasturing of flocks for ordinary farming as their principal source of income. But there were also other causes not directly connected with the Commercial Revolution at all. One

The transformation of agriculture

Interior of a French Peasant's Cottage, 17th Century.

the soil, but this superstition was eventually abandoned. The other most important mechanical improvement of this period was the drill for planting grain. The adoption of this invention eliminated the old wasteful method of sowing grain broadcast by hand, most of it remaining on top of the ground to be eaten by crows. Significant as these inventions were, however, the real mechanization of agriculture did not come until well along in the nineteenth century.

5. THE NEW SOCIETY

Profound changes in the texture of society inevitably accompany economic or intellectual revolutions. The society which was brought into being by the Renaissance, the Reformation, and the Commercial Revolution, though retaining characteristics of the Middle Ages, was really quite different in its underlying features from that which had gone before. For one thing, the population of Europe was now considerably larger. The number of inhabitants of both Italy and England increased by approximately one-third during the single century from 1500 to 1600. In the same period the estimated population of Germany grew from 12,000,000 to 20,000,000. In 1378 London had a population of about 46,000; by 1605 the total had grown to about 225,000.[3] The reasons for these increases are closely related to the religious and economic developments of the

[3] J. W. Thompson, *Economic and Social History of Europe in the Later Middle Ages*, p. 461; Preserved Smith, *The Age of the Reformation*, pp. 453-458.

...cant so-
...anges:
...ore
growth
...ulation

was the influence of the Crusades and the Hundred Years' War in weakening the power of the nobles and in undermining the structure of the old society. Another was the reduction of the supply of agricultural labor on account of the Black Death and the influx of peasants into the cities and towns to take advantage of the new opportunities for a living resulting from the revival of trade with the Near East. A third was the opening up of new farms to cultivation under a system of free labor and individual enterprise. The combined effect of these factors was the destruction of the manorial system and the establishment of agriculture on something like its modern foundations. The transformation was most complete in England, but there were similar developments in other countries also.

The abandonment of demesne farming and the compacting of holdings

The first of the main incidents of the agricultural revolution was the abandonment of the old system of demesne farming. Under the medieval pattern of agriculture the demesne was that part of the manor reserved for the exclusive benefit of the lord himself. The labor of cultivating it had to be done by the serfs as one of the obligations owed to their master. But as more and more serfs ran away or were killed off by the Black Death, this particular obligation, like many of the others, could no longer be enforced. The lords then resorted to the expedient of leasing their demesne lands to the peasants for rent, either in produce or in money. Gradually the system of leasing was extended to the remaining arable portions of the manors, with the result that the erstwhile feudal proprietors became landlords of the modern type. Concurrently with these developments there occurred the gradual elimination of the open-field system. This, it will be recalled, was the system under which the peasants' lands were divided into strips scattered over the different sections of the manor and farmed on a communal basis.[2] The main purpose seems to have been to make sure that the best and the poorer areas of cultivation would be evenly divided. The system began to break down with the advancing prices for agricultural products at the end of the Middle Ages. The shrewder and more ambitious peasants became increasingly dissatisfied with co-operative farming. Impelled by the belief that they could make more money as individual farmers, they traded strips with each other, rented portions of the lord's demesne, and slowly gathered all of their lands into compact blocks. When finally completed, this process, known as the compacting of holdings, went a long way toward the destruction of manorial agriculture.

The enclosure movement

The third important development of the agricultural revolution was the enclosure movement, which was of notable importance in England. This movement had two main aspects: first, the enclosing of the common wood and pasture lands of the manor, thereby abolishing the communal rights which the peasants had enjoyed of

pasturing their flocks and gathering wood on the untilled portions of the lord's estate; and second, the eviction of large numbers of peasants from their leaseholds or other rights of tenantry on the arable lands. Both of these forms of enclosure resulted in much hardship for the rural population. For centuries the peasant's rights in the common pasture and woodlot had formed an essential element in his scheme of subsistence, and it was difficult for him to get along without them. But the fate of those peasants who were dispossessed entirely of their rights of tenantry was much more serious. In most cases they were forced to become landless wage earners or to make their way in the world as helpless beggars. The chief reason for the enclosures was the desire of the former feudal proprietors to convert as large an area of their estates as possible into pasturage for sheep, on account of the high price which could now be obtained for wool. Usually they began by fencing in the common lands as their own property. This was frequently followed by the conversion of many of the grain fields into pastures also, resulting in the eviction especially of those peasants whose leaseholds were none too secure. Enclosures began in the fifteenth century and were continued beyond the period of the Commercial Revolution. Even as late as 1819 hundreds of acts were still being passed by the British Parliament authorizing the eviction of tenants and the closing in of great estates. In the eighteenth and nineteenth centuries the process was accelerated by the ambition of capitalists to push their way into the aristocracy by becoming gentleman farmers. The enclosure movement completed the transformation of English agriculture into a capitalistic enterprise.

The final stage in the agricultural upheaval which accompanied or followed the Commercial Revolution was the introduction of new crops and improvements in mechanical equipment. Neither of these developments was conspicuous until the beginning of the eighteenth century. It was about this time that Lord Townshend in England discovered the value of raising clover as a means of preventing exhaustion of the soil. Not only is the effect of clover in reducing fertility much less than that of the cereal grains, but it actually helps to improve the quality of the soil by gathering nitrogen and making the ground more porous. The planting of this crop from time to time made unnecessary the old system of allowing one-third of the land to lie fallow each year. Furthermore, the clover itself provided an excellent winter feed for animals, thereby aiding the production of more and better livestock. Only a small number of mechanical improvements were introduced into farming at this time, but they were of more than trivial significance. First came the adoption of the metal plowshare, which made possible a deeper and wider furrow than could ever be accomplished with the primitive wooden plows handed down from the Middle Ages. For a time farmers were reluctant to use the new device in the belief that iron would poison

[2] See the paragraphs on the manorial estate in the chapter on The Later Middle Ages: Political and Economic Institutions.

Signifi
cial ch
(1) a
rapid
of po

time. Undoubtedly in northern countries the overthrow of clerical celibacy and the encouragement of marriage were factors partly responsible. But far more important was the increase in means of subsistence brought about by the Commercial Revolution. Not only were new products, such as potatoes, maize, and chocolate, added to the food supply, but older commodities, especially sugar and rice, were now made available to Europeans in much larger quantities. In addition, the growth of new opportunities for making a living in industry and commerce enabled most countries to support a larger population than would ever have been possible under the predominantly agrarian economy of the Middle Ages. It is significant that the bulk of the increases occurred in the cities and towns.

A development of even greater consequence than the growth in population was the increasing equality and fluidity of classes. The Renaissance, the Reformation, and the accompanying Commercial Revolution were all, in some degree, leveling movements. It is an impressive fact that the majority of the men who rose to positions of leadership in Renaissance culture were not scions of the nobility. Some, like Michelangelo and Shakespeare, sprang from humble families. At least three were of illegitimate birth—Boccaccio, Leonardo da Vinci, and Erasmus. The influence of the Renaissance in promoting social equality is illustrated also by the rise of the professions to a higher dignity than they had ever enjoyed in the Middle Ages. The artist, the writer, the lawyer, the university professor, and the physician emerged into a position of importance roughly comparable to that which they hold in modern society. This is confirmed by the incomes which many are known to have received. Michelangelo enjoyed a pension of thousands of dollars a year from the Pope. Raphael left an estate which even by modern standards would be considered princely.[4] Erasmus was able to live in luxury from the gifts and favors received from his patrons. Although few historians would now subscribe to Nietzsche's dictum that the Reformation was simply a revolt of the ignorant masses against their betters, the influence of that movement in weakening the old aristocracy cannot be ignored. By sanctifying the accumulation of wealth it did much to enthrone the middle class. As for the third of the great leveling movements, the Commercial Revolution, we need only recall its effects in providing the opportunities for any lucky or ambitious burgher to pile up a fortune and thereby to climb some of the higher rungs of the social ladder.

The condition of the lower classes did not improve at a rate commensurate with that of the bourgeoisie. Some historians deny that there was any improvement at all, but this view is open to debate. It is true that real wages remained very low: English masons and carpenters were paid the modern equivalent of not more than a dollar a day about 1550. Attempts were even made to prohibit by law any

(2) an increasing equality and fluidity of classes

(3) the modest gains of the lower classes

[4] Preserved Smith, *The Age of the Reformation*, p. 472.

rise in the level of wages, as in the English Statute of Laborers of
1351. It is also true that there were numerous strikes and insurrections of the lower classes. The most serious were the Great Revolt
in England in 1381 and the so-called Peasants' Revolt in Germany in
1524–1525. In both, large numbers of workers from the towns took
part along with the peasants. But there were also uprisings of the
urban proletariat alone. An example is furnished by the revolt of the
workers of Florence between 1379 and 1382 against the denial of
their right to form unions and to participate in the government of
the city. This revolt, like the others, was put down with merciless
severity. Desperate though these uprisings were, we cannot be sure
that they indicate a condition of absolute wretchedness among the
lower classes. It must be understood that in a time of transition the
spirit of revolution is in the air. There are always many individuals
who are unable to adjust themselves to a changing world and consequently become preachers of discontent. Furthermore, if we can
judge from what happened in later movements of this kind, the fact
that revolts occurred may perhaps be taken as a sign that the lot of
the workers was not always deplorable. Men do not generally rebel
unless their economic condition has improved sufficiently to give
them some confidence of success. Finally, it is almost impossible to
believe that none of the working classes would share in the increasing prosperity of the age. It is probably never strictly true that all of
the poor grow poorer while the rich grow richer.

Notwithstanding the cultural and economic progress of the period under review, social and moral conditions do not appear to
have sustained much improvement. For one thing, the new egoism
that characterized the middle and upper classes stood as a barrier to
more generous treatment of the least fortunate human beings. Hearing a disturbance outside his quarters, the Emperor Charles V, in
1552, was reported to have asked who were causing the commotion.
When told that they were poor soldiers, he said, "Let them die,"
and compared them to caterpillars, locusts, and June bugs that eat
the sprouts and other good things of the earth. As a rule, the most
pitiable fate was reserved for slaves and demented persons. For the
sake of big profits Negroes were hunted like beasts on the coast of
Africa and shipped to the American colonies. It may be of interest
to note that the Englishman who originated this body-snatching
business, Captain John Hawkins, called the ship in which he transported the victims the *Jesus*. In view of the fact that insanity was
regarded as a form of demonic possession, it is not strange that the
sufferers from this disease should have been cruelly treated. They
were generally confined in filthy barracks and flogged unmercifully
to drive the demons out of their bodies. A favorite diversion of
some of our ancestors was to organize parties to visit the madhouses
and tease the insane.

The immediate effect of the Reformation in improving conditions

Albrecht Dürer, *Dancing Peasants*. Though the condition of the peasants had improved since the Middle Ages, this engraving made in 1514 indicates that there was still room for advancement.

of morality appears to have been almost negligible. Perhaps this is explainable in part by the return to the legalism of the Old Testament. But probably the chief cause was the fierce antagonism between sects. A condition of war is never favorable to the growth of a high morality. Whatever the reasons, the licentiousness and brutality continued unchecked. Even some of the clergy who were closely identified with the work of religious reform could scarcely be said to have been armored with the breastplate of righteousness. An acquaintance of Luther's seems to have experienced no difficulty in getting a new pastorate after he had been dismissed from an earlier one on charges of seduction. Several of the Protestant Reformers considered polygamy less sinful than divorce, on the ground that the former was recognized in the Old Testament while the latter was prohibited in the New. So doubtful was the quality of moral standards among the Catholic clergy that the Reformers of that faith found it necessary to introduce the closed confessional box for the protection of female penitents. Formerly women as well as men had been required to kneel at the knees of the priest while confessing their sins. The effects of the Reformation upon the virtues of truthfulness and tolerance were woeful indeed. Catholic and Protestant Reformers alike were so obsessed with the righteousness of their own particular cause that they did not hesitate to make use of almost any extreme of falsehood, slander, or repression that seemed

The effect of the Reformation upon moral standards

653

to guarantee victory for their side. For example, Luther expressly justified lying in the interests of religion, and the Jesuits achieved a reputation for tortuous reasoning and devious plotting for the advantage of the Church. No one seemed to have the slightest doubt that in the sphere of religion the end justified the means.

Manners and customs were generally about as coarse and brutish as the standards of morality. Life had few of the amenities now taken for granted. Not only were the contemporaries of Erasmus and Shakespeare subject to annoying discomforts, but they lacked even many of the common facilities for privacy. Bathhouses, frequented by both sexes, were the usual equipment for bathing. The solitary traveler who stopped at an inn was almost certain to be asked to share his bed with a stranger. Many of the most popular amusements were distinguished by similar features of indelicacy. The dances of the common people were little more than rowdyish romps accompanied by kissing and embracing. A favorite sport for men of all classes was bear-baiting—a pastime in which savage dogs were turned loose upon a chained bear. Naturally there were other amusements less boisterous and cruel. Tennis, played with wooden balls, enjoyed such popularity that there were 250 courts in Paris alone. Card games also had a strong appeal. One of them known as "triumph" or "trump," invented in England in the sixteenth century, was the forerunner of modern whist and bridge.

The widespread adoption of the tobacco and coffee habits in the seventeenth century ultimately had some effect in softening manners, especially insofar as these milder substances diminished the appetite for intoxicating liquors. Although the tobacco plant was brought into Europe by the Spaniards about fifty years after the discovery of America, another half century passed before many Europeans adopted the practice of smoking. At first the plant was believed to possess miraculous healing powers and was referred to as "divine tobacco" and "our holy herb nicotian." [5] The habit of smoking was popularized by English explorers, especially by Sir Walter Raleigh, who had learned it from the Indians of Virginia. It spread rapidly through all classes of European society despite the condemnation of the clergy and the "counterblaste" of King James I against it. The enormous popularity of coffee drinking in the seventeenth century had even more important social effects. Coffee houses or "cafes" sprang up all over Europe and rapidly evolved into leading institutions. They provided not merely an escape for the majority of men from a cribbed and monotonous home life, but they took others away from the sordid excesses of the tavern and the gambling-hell. In addition, they fostered a sharpening of wits and promoted more polished manners, especially inasmuch as they became favorite rendezvous for the literary lions of the time. If we

[5] The word "nicotian" or "nicotine" is derived from Jean Nicot, the French
ambassador to Portugal who introduced the tobacco plant into France.

can believe the testimony of English historians, there was scarcely a social or political enterprise which did not have its intimate connections with the establishments where coffee was sold. Some, indeed, were the rallying places of rival factions, which may in time have evolved into political parties. In London, according to Macaulay,

> There were coffee houses where the first medical men might be consulted. . . . There were Puritan coffee houses where no oath was heard and where lank-haired men discussed election and reprobation through their noses; Jew coffee houses where dark-eyed money-changers from Venice and Amsterdam greeted each other; and Popish coffee houses where, as good Protestants believed, Jesuits planned, over their cups, another great fire, and cast silver bullets to shoot the king.[6]

Despite its remarkable attainments in intellect and the arts, the period was by no means free from crass superstitions. Even at the peak of the Renaissance numerous quaint and pernicious delusions continued to be accepted as valid truths. The illiterate masses clung to their beliefs in goblins, satyrs, and wizards and to their fear of the devil, whose malevolence was assumed to be the cause of diseases, famine, storms, and insanity. But superstition was not harbored in the minds of the ignorant alone. The famous astronomer, Johann Kepler, believed in astrology and depended upon the writing of almanacs, with predictions of the future according to signs and wonders in the heavens, as his chief source of income. Not only did Sir Francis Bacon accept the current superstition of astrology, but he also contributed his endorsement of the witchcraft delusion. Eventually the enlightenment of the Renaissance might have eliminated most of the harmful superstitions if a reaction had not set in during the Reformation. The emphasis of the Reformers upon faith, their contempt for reason and science, and their incessant harping on the wiles of the devil fostered an attitude of mind decidedly favorable to prejudice and error. Besides, the furor of hate stirred up by religious controversy made it almost impossible for the average man to view his social and individual problems in a calm and intelligent spirit.

The persistence of superstitions

The worst of all the superstitions that flourished in this period was unquestionably the witchcraft delusion. Belief in witchcraft was by no means unknown in the Middle Ages or even in the early Renaissance, but it never reached the proportions of a dangerous madness until after the beginning of the Protestant Revolution. And it is a significant fact that the persecutions attained their most virulent form in the very countries where religious conflict raged the fiercest, that is, in Germany and France. The witchcraft super-

The witch-craft delusion

stition was a direct outgrowth of the belief in Satan which obsessed the minds of so many of the Reformers. Luther maintained that he often talked with the Evil One and sometimes put him to rout after a session of argument by calling him unprintable names.[7] Calvin insisted that the Pope never acted except on the advice of his patron the devil. In general, the tendency of each camp of theologians was to ascribe all the victories of their opponents to the uncanny powers of the Prince of Darkness. With such superstitions prevailing among religious leaders, it is not strange that the mass of their followers should have harbored bizarre and hideous notions. The belief grew that the devil was really more powerful than God, and that no man's life or soul was safe from destruction. It was assumed that Satan not only tempted mortals to sin, but actually forced them to sin by sending his minions in human form to seduce men and women in their sleep. This was the height of his malevolence, for it jeopardized chances of salvation.

According to the definition of the theologians, witchcraft consisted in selling one's soul to the devil in return for supernatural powers. It was believed that a woman who had concluded such a bargain was thereby enabled to work all manner of spiteful magic against her neighbors—to cause their cattle to sicken and die, their crops to fail, or their children to fall into the fire. But the most valuable gifts bestowed by Satan were the power to blind husbands to their wives' misconduct or to cause women to give birth to idiots or deformed infants. It is commonly assumed that the so-called witches were toothless old hags whose cranky habits and venomous tongues had made them objects of suspicion and dread to all who knew them. Undoubtedly a great many of the victims of the Salem trials in Massachusetts in 1692 did belong to this class. However, the writers on the Continent of Europe generally imagined the witch to be a "fair and wicked young woman," and a large percentage of those put to death in Germany and France were adolescent girls and matrons not yet thirty.[8]

The earliest persecutions for witchcraft were those resulting from the crusades launched against heretics by the Papal Inquisition in the thirteenth century. With the growth of intolerance of heresy it was probably inevitable that members of sects like the Albigenses should be accused of trafficking with the devil. But the amount of persecution in this period was comparatively small. A second campaign against witches was initiated by Pope Innocent VIII in 1484, who instructed his inquisitors to use torture in procuring convictions. But, as we have already seen, it was not until after the beginning of the Protestant Revolution that witchcraft persecution became a mad hysteria. Luther himself provided some of the impetus by recommending that witches should be put to death with fewer considera-

[7] Preserved Smith, *The Age of the Reformation*, p. 653.
[8] Preserved Smith, *A History of Modern Culture*, I, 436–37.

tions of mercy than were shown to ordinary criminals. Other Reformers quickly followed Luther's example. Under Calvin's administration in Geneva thirty-four women were burned or quartered for the alleged crime in 1545.[9] From this time on the persecutions spread like a pestilence. Women, young girls, and even mere children were tortured by driving needles under their nails, roasting their feet in the fire, or crushing their legs under heavy weights until the marrow spurted from their bones, in order to force them to confess filthy orgies with demons. To what extent the persecutions were due to sheer sadism or to the greed of magistrates, who were sometimes permitted to confiscate the property of those convicted, is impossible to say. Certainly there were few people who did not believe that the burning of witches was justifiable. One of the most zealous defenders of the trials was the political philosopher, Jean Bodin. As late as the eighteenth century John Wesley declared that to give up the belief in witchcraft was to give up the Bible.

The witchcraft persecutions reached their peak during the later years of the sixteenth century. The number of victims will never be known, but it was certainly not fewer than 30,000. We read of cities in Germany in which as many as 900 were put to death in a single year, and of whole villages in which practically no women were left alive.

The peak of the witchcraft persecutions

After 1600 the mania gradually subsided on the Continent of Europe, though it continued for some years longer in England. The reasons for the decline are not far to seek. In some measure it was the consequence of a recovery of sanity by the people themselves, particularly as the fogs of suspicion and hate produced by religious warfare gradually lifted. But the principal causes were the revival of reason and the influence of scientists and skeptical philosophers. At the very zenith of the witch-burning frenzy certain lawyers began to have doubts as to the value of the evidence admitted at the trials. In 1584 an English jurist by the name of Reginald Scott published a book condemning the belief in witchcraft as irrational and asserting that most of the lurid crimes confessed by accused women were mere figments of disordered minds. Such eminent scientists as Pierre Gassendi (1592–1655) and William Harvey also denounced the persecutions. But the most effective protest of all came from the pen of Montaigne. This distinguished French skeptic directed the shafts of his most powerful ridicule against the preposterous nonsense of the sorcery trials and the cruelty of men like Bodin who would have witches killed on mere suspicion.

The end of the witchcraft persecutions

From what has been said in preceding paragraphs the conclusion must not be drawn that the period of the Renaissance, the Reformation, and the Commercial Revolution was an age of universal depravity. Of course, there were numerous individuals as urbane and

The age not one of universal depravity

[9] Preserved Smith, *The Age of the Reformation*, p. 656.

tolerant as any who lived in less boisterous times. Such a one was Sir Philip Sidney, who, mortally wounded and tortured with thirst on the battlefield, handed his cup of water to a humble soldier with the simple words, "Thy need is greater than mine." It must be remembered also that this was the age of Sir Thomas More and Erasmus, who were at least as civilized as the majority of men historians have chosen to honor. The enormous popularity of Castiglione's *Book of the Courtier* may likewise be taken to indicate that the period was not hopelessly barbarous. This treatise, which ran through more than 100 editions, set forth the ideal of a knight who was not merely brave in battle and accomplished in the social graces, but courteous, unaffected, and just. In spite of all this, the dolorous fact remains that for large numbers of men ethics had lost their true meaning. The cardinal aims were now gratification of self and victory in the struggle to make the whole world conform to one's own set of dogmas. Perhaps these were inevitable accompaniments of the chaotic transition from the impersonal society of the Middle Ages.

SELECTED READINGS

· *Items so designated are available in paperbound editions.*

Abbott, Wilbur, *The Expansion of Europe, 1415–1815*, New York, 1938.

Brebner, John, *The Explorers of North America*, New York, 1933. A standard account.

· Burckhardt, Jacob, *The Civilization of the Renaissance in Italy*, London, 1890 (Mentor, Torchbook, 2 vols.) No longer considered authoritative.

· de Roover, Raymond, *The Rise and Decline of the Medici Bank, 1397–1494*, Cambridge, 1964 (Norton Library).

· Ford, Franklin, *Robe and Sword*, Cambridge, 1953 (Torchbook).

· Haring, C. H., *The Spanish Empire in America*, New York, 1947 (Harbinger). One of the best studies of the subject.

Heaton, Herbert, *Economic History of Europe*, New York, 1936.

Heckscher, E. E., *Mercantilism*, New York, 1935, 2 vols.

Kimble, G. H. T., *Geography in the Middle Ages*, London, 1938. A graphic account of geographic notions before the time of Columbus.

Morison, S. E., *Admiral of the Ocean Sea; A Life of Christopher Columbus*, Boston, 1942, 2 vols.

· Nowell, C. E., *The Great Discoveries and the First Colonial Empires*, Ithaca, N.Y., 1954 (Cornell). Brief but good.

Ogg, F. A., and Sharp, W. R., *Economic Development of Modern Europe*, New York, 1929.

Packard, L. B., *The Commercial Revolution*, New York, 1927.

Parr, C. M., *So Noble a Captain: The Life and Times of Ferdinand Magellan*, New York, 1953. Scholarly.

· Penrose, Boies, *Travel and Discovery in the Renaissance (1420–1620)*, Cambridge, Mass., 1952 (Atheneum).

Randall, J. H., Jr., *The Making of the Modern Mind*, New York, 1926, Chs. VI–X.

Sée, Henri, *Modern Capitalism: Its Origin and Evolution*, London, 1928.

· Smith, Preserved, *The Age of the Reformation*, New York, 1920 (Collier,
   2 vols.).

· ———, *A History of Modern Culture*, New York, 1930, Vol. I (Collier).

  Sombart, Werner, *The Quintessence of Capitalism*, London, 1915. A suggestive interpretation.

· Sykes, P., *A History of Exploration from the Earliest Times to the Present*, London, 1934 (Torchbook). Comprehensive.

· Tawney, R. H., *Religion and the Rise of Capitalism*, New York, 1926 (Mentor).

  Wrong, G. M., *The Rise and Fall of New France*, New York, 1928, 2 vols. A thorough account.

SOURCE MATERIALS

· More, Sir Thomas, *Utopia*, Part I, pp. 175–78, the Enclosure Movement (Penguin and others).

  Mun, Thomas, *England's Treasure by Foreign Trade*, Chs. I–IV, XX, XXI.

  Richter, J. P., *The Literary Works of Leonardo da Vinci*, Vol. II, pp. 304–5, Leonardo da Vinci on Witchcraft, New York, 1939, 2 vols.

Rulers of Principal States, to 1600 A.D.

The Carolingian Dynasty

Pepin, Mayor of the Palace, 714
Charles Martel, Mayor of the Palace, 715–741
Pepin I, Mayor of the Palace, 741; King, 751–768
Charlemagne, King, 768–814; Emperor, 800–814
Louis the Pious, Emperor, 814–840

WEST FRANCIA

Charles the Bald, King, 840–877; Emperor, 875
Louis II, King, 877–879

Louis III, King, 879–882
Carloman, King, 879–884

MIDDLE KINGDOMS

Lothair, Emperor, 840–855
Louis (Italy), Emperor, 855–875
Charles (Provence), King, 855–863
Lothair II (Lorraine), King, 855–869

EAST FRANCIA

Ludwig, King, 840–876
Carloman, King, 876–880
Ludwig, King, 876–882
Charles the Fat, Emperor, 876–887

Holy Roman Emperors

SAXON DYNASTY

Otto I, 962–973
Otto II, 973–983
Otto III, 983–1002
Henry II, 1002–1024

FRANCONIAN DYNASTY

Conrad II, 1024–1039
Henry III, 1039–1056
Henry IV, 1056–1106

Henry V, 1106–1125
Lothair II (of Saxony), King, 1125–1133; Emperor, 1133–1137

HOHENSTAUFEN DYNASTY

Conrad III, 1138–1152
Frederick I (Barbarossa), 1152–1190
Henry VI, 1190–1197
Philip of Swabia, 1198–1208 } Rivals
Otto IV (Welf), 1198–1215 }

Frederick II, 1220–1250
Conrad IV, 1250–1254

EMPERORS FROM VARIOUS DYNASTIES

Rudolf I (Hapsburg), 1273–1291
Adolf (Nassau), 1292–1298
Albert I (Hapsburg), 1298–1308
Henry VII (Luxemburg), 1308–1313
Ludwig IV (Wittelsbach), 1314–1347
Charles IV (Luxemburg), 1347–1378

Wenceslas (Luxemburg), 1378–1400
Rupert (Wittelsbach), 1400–1410
Sigismund (Luxemburg), 1410–1437

HAPSBURG DYNASTY

Albert II, 1438–1439
Frederick III, 1440–1493
Maximilian I, 1493–1519
Charles V, 1519–1556
Ferdinand I, 1556–1564
Maximilian II, 1564–1576
Rudolf II, 1576–1612

Kings of France from Hugh Capet

CAPETIAN KINGS

Hugh Capet, 987–996
Robert II, 996–1031
Henry I, 1031–1060
Philip I, 1060–1108
Louis VI, 1108–1137
Louis VII, 1137–1180
Philip II (Augustus), 1180–1223
Louis VIII, 1223–1226
Louis IX, 1226–1270
Philip III, 1270–1285
Philip IV, 1285–1314
Louis X, 1314–1316
Philip V, 1316–1322
Charles IV, 1322–1328

HOUSE OF VALOIS

Philip VI, 1328–1350
John, 1350–1364
Charles V, 1364–1380
Charles VI, 1380–1422
Charles VII, 1422–1461
Louis XI, 1461–1483
Charles VIII, 1483–1498
Louis XII, 1498–1515
Francis I, 1515–1547
Henry II, 1547–1559
Francis II, 1559–1560
Charles IX, 1560–1574
Henry III, 1574–1589

BOURBON DYNASTY

Henry IV, 1589–1610

Rulers of England

ANGLO-SAXON KINGS

Egbert, 802–839
Ethelwulf, 839–858
Ethelbald, 858–860
Ethelbert, 860–866
Ethelred, 866–871
Alfred the Great, 871–900
Edward the Elder, 900–924
Ethelstan, 924–940
Edmund I, 940–946
Edred, 946–955
Edwy, 955–959
Edgar, 959–975

Edward the Martyr, 975–978
Ethelred the Unready, 978–1016
Canute, 1016–1035 (Danish Nationality)
Harold I, 1035–1040
Hardicanute, 1040–1042
Edward the Confessor, 1042–1066
Harold II, 1066

ANGLO-NORMAN KINGS

William I (the Conqueror), 1066–1087
William II, 1087–1100
Henry I, 1100–1135
Stephen, 1135–1154

Rulers of England (Continued)

ANGEVIN KINGS

Henry II, 1154–1189
Richard I, 1189–1199
John, 1199–1216
Henry III, 1216–1272
Edward I, 1272–1307
Edward II, 1307–1327
Edward III, 1327–1377
Richard II, 1377–1399

HOUSE OF LANCASTER

Henry IV, 1399–1413
Henry V, 1413–1422
Henry VI, 1422–1461

HOUSE OF YORK

Edward IV, 1461–1483
Edward V, 1483
Richard III, 1483–1485

TUDOR SOVEREIGNS

Henry VII, 1485–1509
Henry VIII, 1509–1547
Edward VI, 1547–1553
Mary, 1553–1558
Elizabeth I, 1558–1603

Prominent Popes

Silvester I, 314–335
Leo I, 440–461
Gelasius I, 492–496
Gregory I, 590–604
Nicholas I, 858–867
Silvester II, 999–1003
Leo IX, 1049–1054
Nicholas II, 1058–1061
Gregory VII, 1073–1085
Urban II, 1088–1099
Paschal II, 1099–1118
Alexander III, 1159–1181
Innocent III, 1198–1216

Gregory IX, 1227–1241
Boniface VIII, 1294–1303
John XXII, 1316–1334
Nicholas V, 1447–1455
Pius II, 1458–1464
Alexander VI, 1492–1503
Julius II, 1503–1513
Leo X, 1513–1521
Adrian VI, 1522–1523
Clement VII, 1523–1534
Paul III, 1534–1549
Paul IV, 1555–1559
Gregory XIII, 1572–1585

Rulers of Austria and Austria-Hungary

(Also bore title of Holy Roman Emperor)

Maximilian I (Archduke), 1493–1519
Charles I (Charles V in the Holy Roman Empire), 1519–1556
Ferdinand I, 1556–1564
Maximilian II, 1564–1576
Rudolf II, 1576–1612

Rulers of Russia

Ivan III, 1462–1505
Basil III, 1505–1533
Ivan IV, 1533–1584

Theodore I, 1584–1598
Boris Godunov, 1598–1605

Rulers of Spain

Ferdinand {and Isabella, 1479–1504
and Philip I, 1504–1506
and Charles I, 1506–1516
Charles I (Holy Roman Emperor Charles V), 1516–1556
Philip II, 1556–1598
Philip III, 1598–1621

Principal Rulers of India

Chandragupta (Maurya Dynasty), *ca.* 322–298 B.C.
Asoka (Maurya Dynasty), *ca.* 273–232 B.C.
Vikramaditya (Gupta Dynasty), 375–413 A.D..
Harsha (Vardhana Dynasty), 606–648

Dynasties of China

Hsia, *ca.* 2205–1766 B.C. (?)
Shang (Yin), *ca.* 1766 (?)–1027 B.C. (or *ca.* 1523–1027 B.C.)
Chou, *ca.* 1027–249 B.C.
Ch'in, 221–207 B.C.
Han (Former), 206 B.C.–8 A.D.

Interregnum (Wang Mang, usurper), 8–23 A.D.

Han (Later), 25–220
Wei, 220–265
Tsin (Chin), 265–420

Southern Dynasties: Sung (Liu Sung), Ch'i, Liang, Ch'ên, 420–589
Northern Dynasties: Northern Wei, Western Wei, Eastern Wei, Northern Ch'i, Northern Chou, 386–581
Sui, 589–618
T'ang, 618–907
Five Dynasties: Later Liang, Later T'ang, Later Tsin, Later Han, Later Chou, 907–960
Sung, 960–1279
Yüan (Mongol), 1279–1368
Ming, 1368–1644

Periods of Japanese Rule

Legendary Period, *ca.* 660 B.C.–530 A.D.
Foundation Period, 530–709 A.D.
Taika (Great Reform) Period, 645–654
Nara Period, 710–793
Heian Period, 794–1192
Kamakura Period, 1192–1333

Namboku-cho ("Northern and Southern Dynasties") Period, 1336–1392
Muromachi (Ashikaga) Period, 1392–1568
Sengoku ("Country at War") Period, *ca.* 1500–1600

Index

Guide to Pronunciation

The sounds represented by the diacritical marks used in this Index are illustrated by the following common words:

āle	ēve	īce	ōld	ūse	bōōt
ăt	ĕnd	ĭll	ŏf	ŭs	fŏŏt
fâtality	ĕvent		ôbey	ûnite	
câre	makĕr		fôrm	ûrn	
ärm					
àsk					

Vowels that have no diacritical marks are to be pronounced "neutral," for example: Aegean = ê-jê'an, Basel = bäz'el, Basil = bă'zil, common = kŏm'on, Alcaeus = ăl-sē'us. The combinations ou and oi are pronounced as in "out" and "oil."

ARCTIC OCEAN

80°

GREENLAND

60°

Hudson
Bay

HUDSON BAY
COMPANY

NEWFOUNDLAND

NORTH

NEW FRANCE

NEW ENGLAND

40°

NEW NETHERLAND

AMERICA

VIRGINIA

LOUISIANA

EN

PORTUGAL

AZORES
ISLANDS

MADEIRA

CANARY
ISLANDS

NEW SPAIN
(MEXICO)

CUBA

HISPANIOLA

BELIZE

PUERTO RICO

20°

ANGUILA

JAMAICA

GUADELOUPE

MARTINIQUE

ST. LUCIA

CAPE VERDE
ISLANDS

ST. LOUIS

GAMBIA

GUINEA

SIERRA LEONE

CA

ELMINA

PACIFIC

IVORY COAST

GUIANAS

0   2000 miles at the equator

0°

140°   120°   90°   40°   20°   0°

OCEAN

SOUTH

AMERICA

PERU

ATLANTIC

OCEAN

20°

BRAZIL

CHILE

40°

60°

CAPE HORN